American Map®

Business Road Atlas

United States • Canada • Mexico

Contents

Business Road Atlas

TRANSPORTATION

CONTROLLED ACCESS HIGHWAYS

Freeway

Tollway; Toll Booth

Under Construction

Interchange and Exit Number

Ramps
Downtown maps only

Rest Area; Service Area
Yellow with facilities; city maps only

OTHER HIGHWAYS

Primary Highway

Secondary Highway

Multilane Divided Highway
Primary and secondary highways only; city maps only

Multilane Divided Highway
State and province maps only

Other Paved Road
State and province maps only

Other Paved Road
City maps only

Unpaved Road
State and province maps only; check conditions locally

Unpaved Road
City maps only; check conditions locally

HIGHWAY MARKERS

Interstate Route

U.S. Route

State or Provincial Route

County or Other Route

Business Route

Trans-Canada Highway

Canadian Provincial Autoroute

Mexican Federal Route

OTHER SYMBOLS

Distances along Major Highways
Miles in U.S.; kilometers in Canada and Mexico

Tunnel; Pass

Wayside Stop
City maps only

One-way Street
City maps only

Port of Entry
City maps only

Airport
City maps only

Railroad
Downtown maps only

Auto Ferry; Passenger Ferry

RECREATION AND FEATURES OF INTEREST

National Park

National Forest; National Grassland

Other Large Park or Recreation Area

Military Lands

Indian Reservation

Small State Park with and without Camping
City maps only

Public Campsite
City maps only

Trail

Point of Interest

Visitor Information Center
City maps only

Public Golf Course; Private Golf Course
Professional tournament location; city maps only

Hospital
City maps only

Ski Area
City maps only

CITIES AND TOWNS

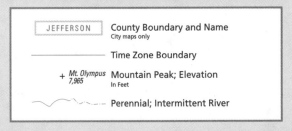

National Capital; State or Provincial Capital

Cities, Towns, and Populated Places
Type size indicates relative importance

Urban Area
State and province maps only

Large Incorporated Cities
City maps only

OTHER MAP FEATURES

JEFFERSON   County Boundary and Name
City maps only

Time Zone Boundary

Mt. Olympus 7,965   Mountain Peak; Elevation
In Feet

Perennial; Intermittent River

1 inch represents 195 miles
or 314 kilometers
(1:12,350,000)

© MapQuest, Inc.

BORDER CROSSING

CANADA

U.S. citizens entering Canada from the U.S. are required to present passports or proof of U.S. citizenship accompanied by photo identification. U.S. citizens entering from a third country must have a valid passport. Visas are not required for U.S. citizens entering from the U.S. for stays of up to 180 days. Naturalized citizens should travel with their naturalization certificates. Alien permanent residents of the U.S. must present their Alien Registration Cards. Individuals under the age of 18 and travelling alone should carry a letter from a parent or legal guardian authorizing their travel in Canada.

U.S. driver's licenses are valid in Canada, and U.S. citizens do not need to obtain an international driver's license. Proof of auto insurance, however, is required.

For additional information, consult http://travel.state.gov/tips_canada.html before you travel.

UNITED STATES (FROM CANADA)

Canadian citizens entering the U.S. are required to demonstrate proof of their citizenship, normally with a photo identification accompanied by a valid birth certificate or citizenship card. Passports or visas are not required for visits lasting less than six months; for visits exceeding six months, they are mandatory. Individuals under the age of 18 and travelling alone should carry notarized documentation, signed by both parents, authorizing their travel.

Canadian driver's licenses are valid in the U.S. for one year, and automobiles may enter free of payment or duty fees. Drivers need only provide customs officials with proof of vehicle registration, ownership, and insurance.

Distances in chart are in miles. To convert miles to kilometers, multiply the distance in miles by 1.609. Example: New York, NY to Boston, MA = 215 miles or 346 kilometers (215 x 1.609)	ALBANY, NY	ALBUQUERQUE, NM	AMARILLO, TX	ATLANTA, GA	BALTIMORE, MD	BILLINGS, MT	BIRMINGHAM, AL	BISMARCK, ND	BOISE, ID	BOSTON, MA	BUFFALO, NY	CHARLESTON, SC	CHARLESTON, WV	CHARLOTTE, NC	CHEYENNE, WY	CHICAGO, IL	CINCINNATI, OH	CLEVELAND, OH	COLUMBUS, OH	DALLAS, TX	DENVER, CO	DES MOINES, IA	DETROIT, MI	EL PASO, TX	HARTFORD, CT	HOUSTON, TX	INDIANAPOLIS, IN	JACKSON, MS	JACKSONVILLE, FL	KANSAS CITY, MO	LAS VEGAS, NV
ALBANY, NY		2095	1811	1010	333	2083	1093	1675	2526	172	292	913	634	771	1789	832	730	484	621	1680	1833	1155	571	2326	111	1768	795	1331	1094	1282	2586
ALBUQUERQUE, NM	2095		286	1490	1902	991	1274	1333	966	2240	1808	1793	1568	1649	538	1352	1409	1619	1476	754	438	1091	1608	263	2139	994	1298	1157	1837	894	578
AMARILLO, TX	1811	286		1206	1618	988	991	1398	1266	1957	1524	1510	1285	1365	534	1069	1126	1335	1192	470	434	808	1324	438	1855	711	1014	874	1517	610	864
ATLANTA, GA	1010	1490	1206		679	1889	150	1559	2218	1100	910	317	503	238	1482	717	476	726	577	792	1403	967	735	1437	998	800	531	386	344	801	2067
BALTIMORE, MD	333	1902	1618	679		1959	795	1551	2401	422	370	583	352	441	1665	708	521	377	420	1399	1690	1031	532	2045	321	1470	600	1032	763	1087	2445
BILLINGS, MT	2083	991	988	1889	1959		1839	413	626	2254	1796	2157	1755	2012	455	1246	1552	1597	1608	1433	554	1007	1534	1255	2153	1673	1432	1836	2237	1088	965
BIRMINGHAM, AL	1093	1274	991	150	795	1839		1509	2170	1215	909	466	578	389	1434	667	475	725	576	647	1356	919	734	1292	1114	678	481	241	494	753	1852
BISMARCK, ND	1675	1333	1398	1559	1551	413	1509		1039	1846	1388	1749	1347	1604	594	838	1144	1189	1200	1342	693	675	1126	1597	1745	1582	1024	1548	1906	801	1378
BOISE, ID	2526	966	1266	2218	2401	626	2170	1039		2697	2239	2520	2182	2375	737	1708	1969	2040	2036	1711	833	1369	1977	1206	2595	1952	1852	2115	2566	1376	760
BOSTON, MA	172	2240	1957	1100	422	2254	1215	1846	2697		462	1003	741	861	1961	1003	862	654	760	1819	2004	1326	741	2465	102	1890	940	1453	1184	1427	2757
BUFFALO, NY	292	1808	1524	910	370	1796	909	1388	2239	462		899	431	695	1502	545	442	197	333	1393	1546	868	277	2039	401	1513	508	1134	1080	995	2299
CHARLESTON, SC	913	1793	1510	317	583	2157	466	1749	2520	1003	899		468	204	1783	907	622	724	637	1109	1705	1204	879	1754	901	1110	721	703	238	1102	2371
CHARLESTON, WV	634	1568	1285	503	352	1755	578	1347	2182	741	431	468		265	1445	506	209	255	168	1072	1367	802	410	1718	639	1192	320	816	649	764	2122
CHARLOTTE, NC	771	1649	1365	238	441	2012	389	1604	2375	861	695	204	265		1637	761	476	520	433	1031	1559	1057	675	1677	760	1041	575	625	385	956	2225
CHEYENNE, WY	1789	538	534	1482	1665	455	1434	594	737	1961	1502	1783	1445	1637		972	1233	1304	1300	979	100	633	1241	801	1859	1220	1115	1382	1829	640	843
CHICAGO, IL	832	1352	1069	717	708	1246	667	838	1708	1003	545	907	506	761	972		302	346	359	936	1015	337	283	1543	901	1108	184	750	1065	532	1768
CINCINNATI, OH	730	1409	1126	476	521	1552	475	1144	1969	862	442	622	209	476	1233	302		253	105	958	1200	599	261	1605	760	1079	116	700	803	597	1955
CLEVELAND, OH	484	1619	1335	726	377	1597	725	1189	2040	654	197	724	255	520	1304	346	253		144	1208	1347	669	171	1854	570	1328	319	950	904	806	2100
COLUMBUS, OH	621	1476	1192	577	420	1608	576	1200	2036	760	333	637	168	433	1300	359	105	144		1059	1266	665	192	1706	659	1179	176	801	818	663	2021
DALLAS, TX	1680	754	470	792	1399	1433	647	1342	1711	1819	1393	1109	1072	1031	979	936	958	1208	1059		887	752	1218	647	1717	241	913	406	1049	554	1331
DENVER, CO	1833	438	434	1403	1690	554	1356	693	833	2004	1546	1705	1367	1559	100	1015	1200	1347	1266	887		676	1284	701	1903	1127	1088	1290	1751	603	756
DES MOINES, IA	1155	1091	808	967	1031	1007	919	675	1369	1326	868	1204	802	1057	633	337	599	669	665	752	676		606	1283	1225	992	481	931	1315	194	1429
DETROIT, MI	571	1608	1324	735	532	1534	734	1126	1977	741	277	879	410	675	1241	283	261	171	192	1218	1284	606		1799	679	1338	318	960	1060	795	2037
EL PASO, TX	2326	263	438	1437	2045	1255	1292	1597	1206	2465	2039	1754	1718	1677	801	1543	1605	1854	1706	647	701	1283	1799		2364	758	1489	1051	1642	1085	717
HARTFORD, CT	111	2139	1855	998	321	2153	1114	1745	2595	102	401	901	639	760	1859	901	760	570	659	1717	1903	1225	679	2364		1788	839	1351	1082	1326	2655
HOUSTON, TX	1768	994	711	800	1470	1673	678	1582	1952	1890	1513	1110	1192	1041	1220	1108	1079	1328	1179	241	1127	992	1338	758	1788		1033	445	884	795	1474
INDIANAPOLIS, IN	795	1298	1014	531	600	1432	481	1024	1852	940	508	721	320	575	1115	184	116	319	176	913	1088	481	318	1489	839	1033		675	879	485	1843
JACKSON, MS	1331	1157	874	386	1032	1836	241	1548	2115	1453	1134	703	816	625	1382	750	700	950	801	406	1290	931	960	1051	1351	445	675		598	747	1735
JACKSONVILLE, FL	1094	1837	1517	344	763	2237	494	1906	2566	1184	1080	238	649	385	1829	1065	803	904	818	1049	1751	1315	1060	1642	1082	884	879	598		1148	2415
KANSAS CITY, MO	1282	894	610	801	1087	1088	753	801	1376	1427	995	1102	764	956	640	532	597	806	663	554	603	194	795	1085	1326	795	485	747	1148		1358
LAS VEGAS, NV	2586	578	864	2067	2445	965	1852	1378	760	2757	2299	2371	2122	2225	843	1768	1955	2100	2021	1331	756	1429	2037	717	2655	1474	1843	1735	2415	1358	
LITTLE ROCK, AR	1354	900	617	528	1072	1530	381	1183	1808	1493	1066	900	745	754	1076	662	632	882	733	327	984	567	891	974	1391	447	587	269	873	382	1478
LOS ANGELES, CA	2859	806	1092	2237	2705	1239	2092	1702	1033	3046	2572	2554	2374	2453	1116	2042	2215	2374	2281	1446	1029	1703	2310	801	2944	1558	2104	1851	2441	1632	274
LOUISVILLE, KY	832	1320	1036	419	602	1547	369	1139	1933	964	545	610	251	464	1197	299	106	356	207	852	1118	595	366	1499	862	972	112	594	766	516	1874
MEMPHIS, TN	1214	1033	750	389	933	1625	241	1337	1954	1353	927	760	606	614	1217	539	493	742	594	466	1116	720	752	1112	1251	586	464	211	733	536	1611
MIAMI, FL	1439	2155	1834	661	1109	2554	812	2224	2883	1529	1425	583	994	730	2147	1382	1141	1250	1163	1367	2069	1632	1401	1959	1427	1201	1196	915	345	1466	2733
MILWAUKEE, WI	929	1426	1142	813	805	1175	763	767	1748	1100	642	1003	601	857	1012	89	398	443	454	1010	1055	378	380	1617	999	1193	279	835	1160	573	1808
MINNEAPOLIS, MN	1245	1339	1055	1129	1121	839	1079	431	1465	1417	958	1319	918	1173	881	409	714	760	771	999	924	246	697	1530	1315	1240	596	1151	1477	441	1677
MOBILE, AL	1344	1344	1106	332	1013	2019	258	1765	2302	1433	1165	642	837	572	1570	923	731	981	832	639	1478	1115	991	1231	1332	473	737	187	410	930	1922
MONTPELIER, VT	167	2226	1943	1193	516	2219	1308	1811	2661	178	423	1096	834	954	1925	967	861	615	752	1811	1969	1291	690	2458	195	1983	927	1546	1277	1413	2722
MONTREAL, QC	230	2172	1888	1241	564	2093	1289	1685	2535	313	397	1145	822	1003	1799	841	815	588	725	1772	1843	1165	564	2363	338	1892	872	1514	1325	1359	2596
NASHVILLE, TN	1003	1248	965	242	716	1648	194	1315	1976	1136	716	543	395	397	1240	474	281	531	382	681	1162	725	541	1328	1034	801	287	423	589	559	1826
NEW ORLEANS, LA	1440	1276	993	473	1142	1955	351	1734	2234	1563	1254	783	926	713	1502	935	820	1070	921	525	1409	1117	1079	1118	1461	360	826	185	556	932	1854
NEW YORK, NY	151	2015	1731	869	192	2049	985	1641	2491	215	400	773	515	631	1755	797	636	466	535	1589	1799	1121	622	2235	115	1660	715	1223	953	1202	2552
NORFOLK, VA	570	1970	1686	558	239	2141	708	1733	2584	660	573	437	415	319	1847	890	624	559	604	1350	1782	1213	714	1996	558	1360	735	944	617	1179	2537
OKLAHOMA CITY, OK	1549	546	262	944	1354	1227	729	1136	1506	1694	1262	1248	1022	1102	773	807	863	1073	930	209	681	546	1062	737	1593	449	752	612	1291	348	1124
OMAHA, NE	1292	973	726	989	1168	904	941	616	1234	1463	1005	1290	952	1144	497	474	736	806	802	669	541	136	743	1236	1362	910	618	935	1336	188	1294
ORLANDO, FL	1235	1934	1613	440	904	2333	591	2003	2662	1324	1221	379	790	525	1926	1161	920	1045	958	1146	1847	1411	1180	1738	1223	980	975	694	141	1245	2512
PHILADELPHIA, PA	223	1954	1671	782	104	2019	897	1611	2462	321	414	685	454	543	1725	768	576	437	474	1501	1744	1091	592	2147	219	1572	655	1135	866	1141	2500
PHOENIX, AZ	2561	466	753	1868	2366	1199	1723	1662	993	2706	2274	2184	2035	2107	1004	1819	1876	2085	1942	1077	904	1558	2074	432	2605	1188	1764	1482	2072	1360	285
PITTSBURGH, PA	485	1670	1386	676	246	1719	763	1311	2161	592	217	642	217	438	1425	467	292	136	190	1246	1460	791	292	1893	491	1366	370	988	822	857	2215
PORTLAND, ME	270	2338	2054	1197	520	2352	1313	1944	2795	107	560	1101	839	959	2059	1101	960	751	858	1917	2102	1424	838	2563	199	1988	1038	1550	1281	1525	2855
PORTLAND, OR	2954	1395	1695	2647	2830	889	2599	1301	432	3126	2667	2948	2610	2802	1166	2137	2398	2469	2464	2140	1261	1798	2405	1767	3024	2381	2280	2544	2994	1805	1188
RALEIGH, NC	639	1782	1499	396	309	2110	547	1702	2495	729	642	279	313	158	1758	861	522	568	482	1189	1680	1157	724	1834	627	1198	639	783	460	1077	2360
RAPID CITY, SD	1750	841	837	1511	1626	379	1463	320	930	1921	1463	1824	1422	1678	305	913	1219	1264	1275	1077	404	629	1201	1105	1820	1318	1101	1458	1859	710	1035
RENO, NV	2747	1020	1306	2440	2623	960	2392	1372	430	2919	2460	2741	2403	2595	959	1930	2191	2262	2257	1933	1054	1591	2198	1315	2817	2072	2073	2337	2787	1598	442
RICHMOND, VA	482	1876	1593	527	152	2053	678	1645	2496	572	485	428	322	289	1760	802	530	471	517	1309	1688	1126	627	1955	471	1330	641	914	609	1085	2444
ST. LOUIS, MO	1036	1051	767	549	841	1341	501	1053	1628	1181	749	850	512	704	892	294	350	560	417	635	855	436	549	1242	1080	863	239	505	896	252	1610
SALT LAKE CITY, UT	2224	624	964	1916	2100	548	1868	960	342	2395	1936	2218	1880	2072	436	1406	1667	1738	1734	1410	531	1067	1675	864	2293	1650	1549	1813	2264	1074	417
SAN ANTONIO, TX	1953	818	513	1000	1671	1500	878	1599	1761	2092	1665	1310	1344	1241	1046	1270	1231	1481	1332	271	946	1009	1490	556	1990	200	1186	644	1084	812	1272
SAN DIEGO, CA	2919	825	1111	2166	2724	1302	2021	1765	1096	3065	2632	2483	2393	2405	1179	2105	2234	2437	2300	1375	1092	1766	2373	730	2963	1487	2122	1780	2370	1695	337
SAN FRANCISCO, CA	2964	1111	1397	2618	2840	1176	2472	1749	646	3135	2677	2934	2620	2759	1176	2146	2407	2478	2474	1827	1271	1807	2415	1181	3034	1938	2290	2232	2822	1814	575
SEATTLE, WA	2899	1463	1763	2705	2775	816	2657	1229	500	3070	2612	2973	2571	2827	1234	2062	2368	2413	2424	2208	1329	1822	2350	1944	2969	2449	2249	2612	3052	1872	1256
TAMPA, FL	1290	1949	1628	455	960	2348	606	2018	2677	1380	1276	434	845	581	1941	1176	935	1101	1036	1161	1862	1426	1194	1753	1278	995	990	709	196	1259	2526
TORONTO, ON	400	1841	1557	958	565	1762	958	1354	2204	570	106	1006	537	802	1468	510	484	303	440	1441	1512	834	233	2032	509	1561	541	1183	1187	1028	2265
VANCOUVER, BC	3032	1597	1897	2838	2908	949	2791	1362	633	3204	2745	3106	2705	2960	1368	2196	2501	2547	2558	2342	1463	1956	2483	2087	3102	2583	2383	2746	3186	2007	1390
WASHINGTON, DC	369	1896	1612	636	38	1953	758	1545	2395	458	384	539	346	397	1659	701	517	370	416	1362	1686	1025	526	2008	357	1433	596	996	720	1083	2441
WICHITA, KS	1471	707	423	989	1276	1067	838	934	1346	1616	1184	1291	953	1145	613	728	7856	995	852	367	521	390	984	898	1515	608	674	771	1337	192	1276

LITTLE ROCK, AR	LOS ANGELES, CA	LOUISVILLE, KY	MEMPHIS, TN	MIAMI, FL	MILWAUKEE, WI	MINNEAPOLIS, MN	MOBILE, AL	MONTPELIER, VT	MONTREAL, QC	NASHVILLE, TN	NEW ORLEANS, LA	NEW YORK, NY	NORFOLK, VA	OKLAHOMA CITY, OK	OMAHA, NE	ORLANDO, FL	PHILADELPHIA, PA	PHOENIX, AZ	PITTSBURGH, PA	PORTLAND, ME	PORTLAND, OR	RALEIGH, NC	RAPID CITY, SD	RENO, NV	RICHMOND, VA	ST. LOUIS, MO	SALT LAKE CITY, UT	SAN ANTONIO, TX	SAN DIEGO, CA	SAN FRANCISCO, CA	SEATTLE, WA	TAMPA, FL	TORONTO, ON	VANCOUVER, BC	WASHINGTON, DC	WICHITA, KS
1354	2859	832	1214	1439	929	1245	1344	167	230	1003	1440	151	151	1549	1292	1235	223	2561	485	270	2954	639	1750	2747	482	1036	2224	1953	2919	2964	2899	1290	400	3032	369	1471
900	806	1320	1033	2155	1426	1339	1344	2226	2172	1248	1276	2015	2015	546	973	1934	1954	466	1670	2338	1395	1782	841	1020	1876	1051	624	818	825	1111	1463	1949	1841	1597	1896	707
617	1092	1036	750	1834	1142	1055	1106	1943	1888	965	993	1731	1731	262	726	1613	1671	753	1386	2054	1695	1499	837	1306	1593	767	964	513	1111	1397	1763	1628	1557	1897	1612	423
528	2237	419	389	661	813	1129	332	1193	1241	242	473	869	869	944	989	440	782	1868	676	1197	2647	396	1511	2440	527	549	1916	1000	2166	2618	2705	455	958	2838	636	989
1072	2705	602	933	1109	805	1121	1013	516	564	716	1142	192	192	1354	1168	904	104	2366	246	520	2830	309	1626	2623	152	841	2100	1671	2724	2840	2775	960	565	2908	38	1276
1530	1239	1547	1625	2554	1175	839	2019	2219	2093	1648	1955	2049	2049	1227	904	2333	2019	1199	1719	2352	889	2110	379	960	2053	1341	548	1500	1302	1176	816	2348	1762	949	1953	1067
381	2092	369	241	812	763	1079	258	1308	1289	194	351	985	985	729	941	591	897	1723	763	1313	2599	547	1463	2392	678	501	1868	878	2021	2472	2657	606	958	2791	758	838
1183	1702	1139	1337	2224	767	431	1765	1811	1685	1315	1734	1641	1641	1136	616	2003	1611	1662	1311	1944	1301	1702	320	1372	1645	1053	960	1599	1765	1749	1229	2018	1354	1362	1545	934
1808	1033	1933	1954	2883	1748	1465	2302	2661	2535	1976	2234	2491	2491	1506	1234	2662	2462	993	2161	2795	432	2495	930	430	2496	1628	342	1761	1096	646	500	2677	2204	633	2395	1346
1493	3046	964	1353	1529	1100	1417	1433	178	313	1136	1563	215	215	1694	1463	1324	321	2706	592	107	3126	729	1921	2919	572	1181	2395	2092	3065	3135	3070	1380	570	3204	458	1616
1066	2572	545	927	1425	642	958	1165	423	397	716	1254	400	400	1262	1005	1221	414	2274	217	560	2667	642	1463	2460	485	749	1936	1665	2632	2677	2612	1276	106	2745	384	1184
900	2554	610	760	583	1003	1319	642	1096	1145	543	783	773	773	1248	1290	379	685	2184	642	1101	2948	279	1824	2741	428	850	2218	1310	2483	2934	2973	434	1006	3106	539	1291
745	2374	251	606	994	601	918	837	834	822	395	926	515	515	1022	952	790	454	2035	217	839	2610	313	1422	2403	322	512	1880	1344	2393	2620	2571	845	537	2705	346	953
754	2453	464	614	730	857	1173	572	954	1003	397	713	631	631	1102	1144	525	543	2107	438	959	2802	158	1678	2595	289	704	2072	1241	2405	2759	2827	581	802	2960	397	1145
1076	1116	1197	1217	2147	1012	881	1570	1925	1799	1240	1502	1755	1755	773	497	1926	1725	1004	1425	2059	1166	1758	305	959	1760	892	436	1046	1179	1176	1234	1941	1468	1368	1659	613
662	2042	299	539	1382	89	409	923	967	841	474	935	797	797	807	474	1161	768	1819	467	1101	2137	861	913	1930	802	294	1406	1270	2105	2146	2062	1176	510	2196	701	728
632	2215	106	493	1141	398	714	731	861	815	281	820	636	636	863	736	920	576	1876	292	960	2398	522	1219	2191	530	350	1667	1231	2234	2407	2368	935	484	2501	517	785
882	2374	356	742	1250	443	760	981	615	588	531	1070	466	466	1073	806	1045	437	2085	136	751	2469	568	1264	2262	471	560	1738	1481	2437	2478	2413	1101	303	2547	370	995
733	2281	207	594	1163	454	771	832	752	725	382	921	535	535	930	802	958	474	1942	190	858	2464	482	1275	2257	517	417	1734	1332	2300	2474	2424	1036	440	2558	416	852
327	1446	852	466	1367	1010	999	639	1811	1772	681	525	1589	1589	209	669	1146	1501	1077	1246	1917	2140	1189	1077	1933	1309	635	1410	271	1375	1827	2208	1161	1441	2342	1362	367
984	1029	1118	1116	2069	1055	924	1478	1969	1843	1162	1409	1799	1799	681	541	1847	1744	904	1460	2102	1261	1680	404	1054	1688	855	531	946	1092	1271	1329	1862	1512	1463	1686	521
567	1703	595	720	1632	378	246	1115	1291	1165	725	1117	1121	1121	546	136	1411	1091	1558	791	1424	1798	1157	629	1591	1126	436	1067	1009	1766	1807	1822	1426	834	1956	1025	390
891	2310	366	752	1401	380	697	991	690	564	541	1079	622	622	1062	743	1180	592	2074	292	838	2405	724	1201	2198	627	549	1675	1490	2373	2415	2350	1194	233	2483	526	984
974	801	1499	1112	1959	1617	1530	1231	2458	2363	1328	1118	2235	2235	737	1236	1738	2147	432	1893	2563	1767	1834	1105	1315	1955	1242	864	556	730	1181	1944	1753	2032	2087	2008	898
1391	2944	862	1251	1427	999	1315	1332	195	338	1034	1461	115	115	1593	1362	1223	219	2605	491	199	3024	627	1820	2817	471	1080	2293	1990	2963	3034	2969	1278	509	3102	357	1515
447	1558	972	586	1201	1193	1240	473	1983	1892	801	360	1660	1660	449	910	980	1572	1188	1366	1988	2381	1198	1318	2072	1330	863	1650	200	1487	1938	2449	995	1561	2583	1433	608
587	2104	112	464	1196	279	596	737	927	872	287	826	715	715	752	618	975	655	1764	370	1038	2280	639	1101	2073	641	239	1549	1186	2122	2290	2249	990	541	2383	596	674
269	1851	594	211	915	835	1151	187	1546	1514	423	185	1223	1223	612	935	694	1135	1482	988	1550	2544	783	1458	2337	914	505	1813	644	1780	2232	2612	709	1183	2746	996	771
873	2441	766	733	345	1160	1477	410	1277	1325	589	556	953	953	1291	1336	141	866	2072	822	1281	2994	460	1859	2787	609	896	2264	1084	2370	2822	3052	196	1187	3186	720	1337
382	1632	516	536	1466	573	441	930	1413	1359	559	932	1202	1202	348	188	1245	1141	1360	857	1525	1805	1077	710	1598	1085	252	1074	812	1695	1814	1872	1259	1028	2007	1083	192
1478	274	1874	1611	2733	1808	1677	1922	2722	2596	1826	1854	2552	2552	1124	1294	2512	2500	285	2215	2855	1188	2360	1035	442	2444	1610	417	1272	337	575	1256	2526	2265	1390	2441	1276
	1706	526	140	1190	747	814	457	1485	1446	355	455	1262	1262	355	570	969	1175	1367	920	1590	2237	889	1093	2030	983	416	1507	600	1703	2012	2305	984	1115	2439	1036	464
1706		2126	1839	2759	2082	1951	2031	2995	2869	2054	1917	2820	2820	1352	1567	2538	2760	369	2476	3144	971	2588	1309	519	2682	1856	691	1356	124	385	1148	2553	2538	1291	2702	1513
526	2126		386	1084	394	711	625	963	920	175	714	739	739	774	704	863	678	1786	394	1062	2362	564	1215	2155	572	264	1631	1125	2144	2372	2364	878	589	2497	596	705
140	1839	386		1051	624	940	395	1345	1306	215	396	1123	1123	487	724	830	1035	1500	780	1451	2382	749	1247	2175	843	294	1652	739	1841	2144	2440	845	975	2574	896	597
1190	2759	1084	1051		1478	1794	727	1622	1671	907	874	1299	1299	1609	1654	232	1211	2390	1167	1627	3312	805	2176	3105	954	1214	2581	1401	2688	3140	3370	274	1532	3504	1065	1655
747	2082	394	624	1478		337	1019	1064	939	569	1020	894	894	880	514	1257	865	1892	564	1198	2063	956	842	1970	899	367	1446	1343	2145	2186	1991	1272	607	2124	799	769
814	1951	711	940	1794	337		1335	1381	1255	886	1337	1211	1211	793	383	1573	1181	1805	881	1515	1727	1273	606	1839	1216	621	1315	1257	2014	2055	1654	1588	924	1788	1115	637
457	2031	625	395	727	1019	1335		1526	1575	450	146	1203	1203	799	1119	506	1115	1662	1019	1531	2731	730	1641	2545	861	688	2000	673	1960	2411	2799	521	1214	2933	970	958
1485	2995	963	1345	1622	1064	1381	1526		138	1134	1656	310	310	1680	1428	1417	414	2693	685	196	3090	822	1886	2883	665	1167	2359	2084	3051	3099	3034	1473	457	3168	551	1602
1446	2869	920	1306	1671	939	1255	1575	138		1094	1632	383	383	1625	1300	1466	454	2637	607	282	2963	871	1758	2756	714	1112	2232	2043	2931	2972	2907	1522	330	3041	600	1547
355	2054	175	215	907	569	886	450	1134	1094		539	906	906	703	747	686	818	1715	569	1234	2405	532	1269	2198	626	307	1675	954	2056	2360	2463	701	764	2597	679	748
455	1917	714	396	874	1020	1337	146	1656	1632	539		1332	1332	731	1121	653	1245	1548	1108	1660	2663	871	1643	2431	1002	690	1932	560	1846	2298	2731	668	1302	2865	1106	890
1262	2820	739	1123	1299	894	1211	1203	310	383	906	1332		430	1469	1258	1094	91	2481	367	313	2920	499	1716	2713	342	956	2189	1861	2839	2929	2864	1150	507	2998	228	1391
1076	2776	666	937	962	987	1303	891	753	801	720	1032	430		1424	1350	758	342	2436	428	757	3012	179	1808	2805	91	927	2282	1560	2725	3022	2957	814	747	3090	196	1368
355	1352	774	487	1609	880	793	799	1680	1625	703	731	1469	1424		463	1388	1408	1012	1124	1792	1934	1237	871	1727	1331	505	1204	466	1370	1657	2002	1403	1295	2136	1350	161
570	1567	704	724	1654	514	383	1119	1428	1300	747	1121	1258	1350	463		1433	1228	1440	928	1561	1662	1265	525	1455	1263	440	932	927	1630	1672	1719	1448	971	1853	1162	307
969	2538	863	830	232	1257	1573	506	1417	1466	686	653	1094	758	1388	1433		1006	2169	963	1422	3091	601	1955	2884	750	993	2360	1180	2467	2918	3149	82	1327	3283	860	1434
1175	2760	678	1035	1211	865	1181	1115	414	454	818	1245	91	342	1408	1228	1006		2420	306	419	2890	411	1686	2683	254	895	2160	1774	2779	2900	2835	1062	522	2968	140	1330
1367	369	1786	1500	2390	1892	1805	1662	2693	2637	1715	1548	2481	2436	1012	1440	2169	2420		2136	2804	1335	2249	1308	883	2343	1517	651	987	358	750	1513	2184	2307	1655	2362	1173
920	2476	394	780	1167	564	881	1019	685	607	569	1108	367	428	1124	928	963	306	2136		690	2590	497	1386	2383	341	611	1859	1519	2494	2599	2534	1019	321	2668	240	1046
1590	3144	1062	1451	1627	1198	1515	1531	196	282	1234	1660	313	757	1792	1561	1422	419	2804	690		3223	827	2019	3016	670	1279	2493	2189	3162	3233	3168	1478	668	3301	556	1714
2237	971	2362	2382	3312	2063	1727	2731	3090	2963	2405	2663	2920	3012	1934	1662	3091	2890	1335	2590	3223		2923	1268	578	2925	2057	771	2322	1093	638	170	3106	2633	313	2824	1775
889	2588	564	749	805	956	1273	730	822	871	532	871	499	179	1237	1265	601	411	2249	497	827	2923		1777	2716	157	825	2193	1398	2563	2894	2926	656	820	3060	265	1266
1093	1309	1215	1247	2176	842	606	1641	1886	1758	1269	1643	1716	1808	871	525	1955	1686	1308	1386	2019	1268	1777		1151	1720	963	628	1335	1372	1368	1195	1970	1429	1328	1620	712
2030	519	2155	2175	3105	1970	1839	2545	2883	2756	2198	2431	2713	2805	1727	1455	2884	2683	883	2383	3016	578	2716	1151		2718	1850	524	1870	642	217	755	2899	2426	898	2617	1568
983	2682	572	843	954	899	1216	861	665	714	626	1002	342	91	1331	1263	750	254	2343	341	670	2925	157	1720	2718		834	2194	1530	2684	2934	2869	805	660	3003	108	1274
416	1856	264	294	1214	367	621	688	1167	1112	307	690	956	927	505	440	993	895	1517	611	1279	2057	825	963	1850	834		1326	968	1875	2066	2125	1008	782	2259	837	441
1507	691	1631	1652	2581	1446	1315	2000	2359	2232	1675	1932	2189	2282	1204	932	2360	2160	651	1859	2493	771	2193	628	524	2194	1326		1419	754	740	839	2375	1902	973	2094	1044
600	1356	1125	739	1401	1343	1257	673	2084	2043	954	560	1861	1560	466	927	1180	1774	987	1519	2189	2322	1398	1335	1870	1530	968	1419		1285	1737	2275	1195	1714	2410	1635	624
1703	124	2144	1841	2688	2145	2014	1960	3051	2931	2056	1846	2839	2725	1370	1630	2467	2779	358	2494	3162	1093	2563	1372	642	2684	1875	754	1285		508	1271	2481	2601	1414	2720	1531
2012	385	2372	2144	3140	2186	2055	2411	3099	2972	2360	2298	2929	3022	1657	1672	2918	2900	750	2599	3233	638	2894	1368	217	2934	2066	740	1737	508		816	2933	2643	958	2834	1784
2305	1148	2364	2440	3370	1991	1654	2799	3034	2907	2463	2731	2864	2957	2002	1719	3149	2835	1513	2534	3168	170	2926	1195	755	2869	2125	839	2275	1271	816		3164	2577	140	2769	1843
984	2553	878	845	274	1272	1588	521	1473	1522	701	668	1150	814	1403	1448	82	1062	2184	1019	1478	3106	656	1970	2899	805	1008	2375	1195	2481	2933	3164		1383	3297	916	1448
1115	2538	589	975	1532	607	924	1214	457	330	764	1302	507	747	1295	971	1327	522	2307	321	668	2633	820	1429	2426	660	782	1902	1714	2601	2643	2577	1383		2711	563	1217
2439	1291	2497	2574	3504	2124	1788	2933	3168	3041	2597	2865	2998	3090	2136	1853	3283	2968	1655	2668	3301	313	3060	1328	898	3003	2259	973	2410	1414	958	140	3297	2711		2902	1977
1036	2702	596	896	1065	799	1115	970	551	600	679	1106	228	196	1350	1162	860	140	2362	240	556	2824	265	1620	2617	108	837	2094	1635	2720	2834	2769	916	563	2902		1272
464	1513	705	597	1655	769	637	958	1602	1547	748	890	1391	1368	161	307	1434	1330	1173	1046	1714	1775	1266	712	1568	1274	441	1044	624	1531	1784	1843	1448	1217	1977	1272	

BORDER CROSSING

MEXICO

U.S. citizens entering Mexico are required to present passports or proof of U.S. citizenship accompanied by photo identification. Visas are not required for stays of up to 180 days. Naturalized citizens should travel with their naturalization certificates, and alien permanent residents must present their Alien Registration Cards. Individuals under the age of 18 traveling alone, with one parent, or with other adults must carry notarized parental authorization or valid custodial documents.

In addition, all U.S. citizens visiting for up to 180 days must procure a tourist card, obtainable from Mexican consulates, tourism offices, and border crossing points, which must be surrendered upon departure. However, tourist cards are not needed for visits shorter than 72 hours to cities along the Mexico/U.S. border.

U.S. driver's licenses are valid in Mexico.

Visitors who wish to drive beyond the Baja California Peninsula or the Border Zone (extending approximately 25 km into Mexico) must obtain a temporary import permit for their vehicles. Permits may be obtained from a Mexican Customs Office at border crossing points as long as the original and two copies of the following documents bearing the driver's name are provided: passport/proof of U.S. citizenship, tourist card, vehicle registration, driver's license, and a major international credit card for use in paying the prevailing fee. Permits are valid for 180 days, and they must be surrendered upon final departure from Mexico.

All visitors driving in Mexico should be aware that U.S. auto insurance policies are not valid and that buying short-term tourist insurance is virtually mandatory. Many U.S. insurance companies sell Mexican auto insurance. American Automobile Association (for members only) and Sanborn's Mexico Insurance (800.638.9423) are popular companies with offices at most U.S. border crossings.

PARTIAL INDEX TO CITIES AND TOWNS

1 inch represents 40 miles
or 64 kilometers
(1:2,530,000)

MI 20 40 60
20 40 60 KM

© MapQuest, Inc.

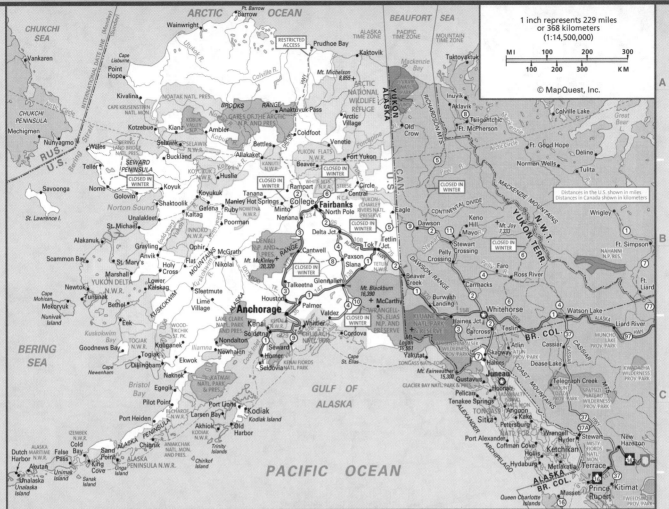

P 58

British Columbia

**1 inch represents 229 miles
or 368 kilometers
(1:14,500,000)**

MI   100   200   300
100   200   300   KM

© MapQuest, Inc.

Distances in the U.S. shown in miles
Distances in Canada shown in kilometers

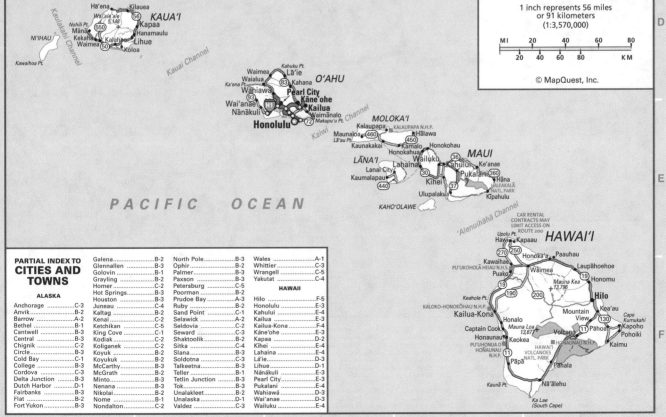

**1 inch represents 56 miles
or 91 kilometers
(1:3,570,000)**

MI   20   40   60   80
20 40 60 80 KM

© MapQuest, Inc.

P 92

Honolulu

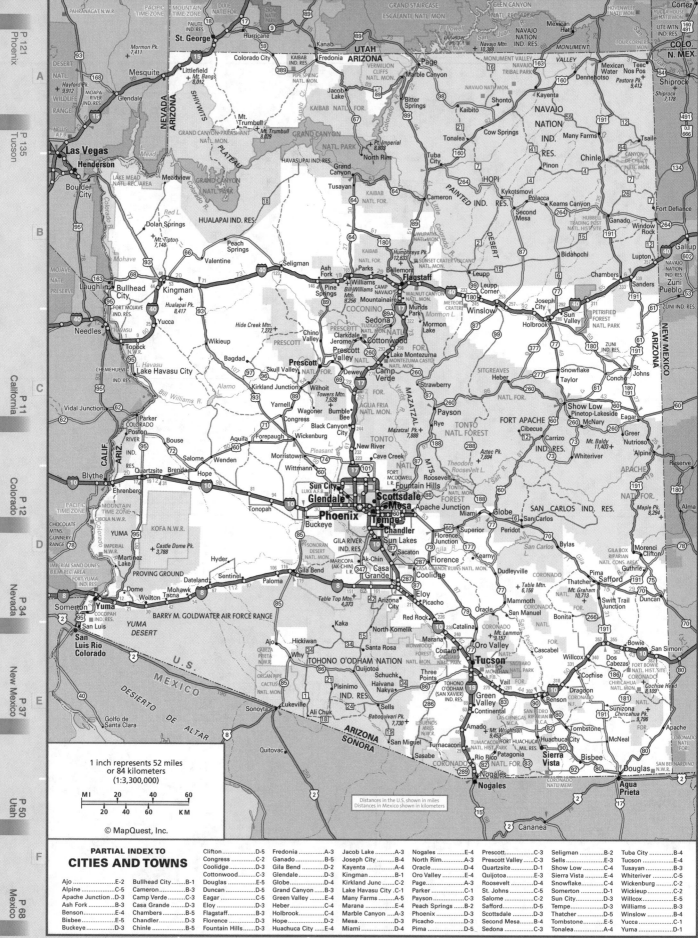

© MapQuest, Inc.

1 inch represents 52 miles
or 84 kilometers
(1:3,300,000)

MI   20   40   60
20   40   60   KM

PARTIAL INDEX TO
CITIES AND TOWNS

P 121 Phoenix
P 135 Tucson
P 11 California
P 12 Colorado
P 34 Nevada
P 37 New Mexico
P 50 Utah
P 68 Mexico

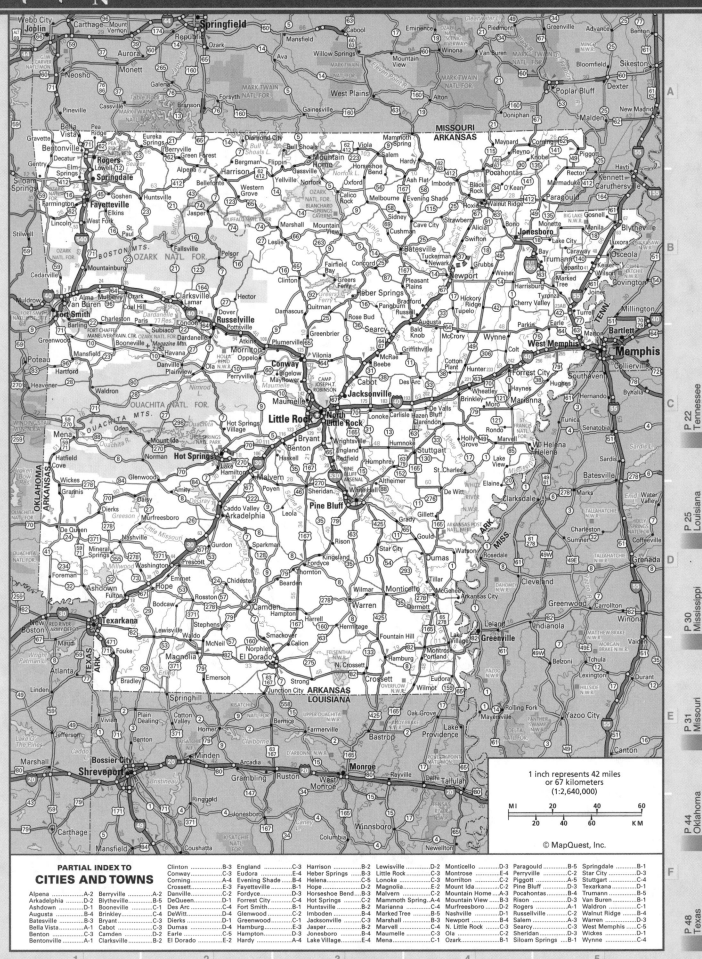

PARTIAL INDEX TO
CITIES AND TOWNS

Alpena A-2	Clinton B-3	England C-3
Arkadelphia D-2	Conway C-3	Eudora E-4
Ashdown D-1	Corning A-4	Evening Shade B-4
Augusta B-4	Crossett E-3	Fayetteville B-1
Batesville B-3	Danville C-2	Fordyce D-3
Bella Vista A-1	DeQueen D-1	Forrest City C-4
Benton C-3	Des Arc C-4	Fort Smith B-1
Bentonville A-1	DeWitt D-4	Glenwood C-2
Berryville A-2	Dierks D-1	Greenwood C-1
Blytheville B-5	Dumas D-4	Hamburg E-4
Booneville C-1	Earle C-5	Hampton D-3
Brinkley C-4	El Dorado E-2	Hardy A-4
Bryant C-3		
Cabot C-3		
Camden D-2		
Clarksville B-2		

Harrison B-2	Lewisville D-2	Monticello D-3	Paragould B-5	Springdale B-1
Heber Springs B-3	Little Rock C-3	Montrose E-4	Perryville C-2	Star City D-3
Helena C-5	Lonoke C-3	Morrilton C-2	Piggott A-5	Stuttgart C-4
Hope D-2	Magnolia E-2	Mount Ida C-2	Pine Bluff D-3	Texarkana D-1
Horseshoe Bend ..B-3	Malvern C-2	Mountain Home A-3	Pocahontas A-4	Trumann B-5
Hot Springs C-2	Mammoth Spring ...A-4	Mountain View B-3	Rison D-3	Van Buren B-1
Imboden B-4	Marianna C-4	Murfreesboro D-2	Rogers A-1	Waldron C-1
Jacksonville C-3	Marked Tree B-5	Nashville D-1	Russellville C-2	Walnut Ridge B-4
Jasper B-2	Marvell C-4	N. Little Rock C-3	Salem A-4	Warren D-3
Jonesboro B-5	Marshall B-3	Newport B-4	Searcy C-3	West Memphis C-5
Lake Village E-4	Maumelle C-3	Ola C-2	Sheridan C-3	Wickes D-1
Hardy A-4	Mena C-1	Ozark B-1	Siloam Springs B-1	Wynne C-4

1 inch represents 42 miles
or 67 kilometers
(1:2,640,000)

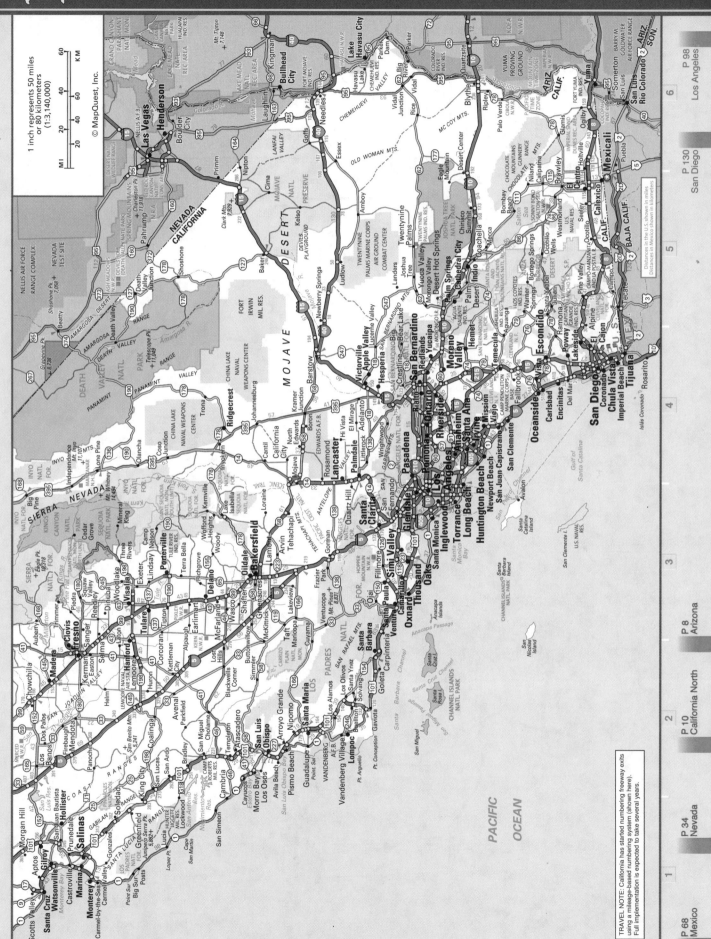

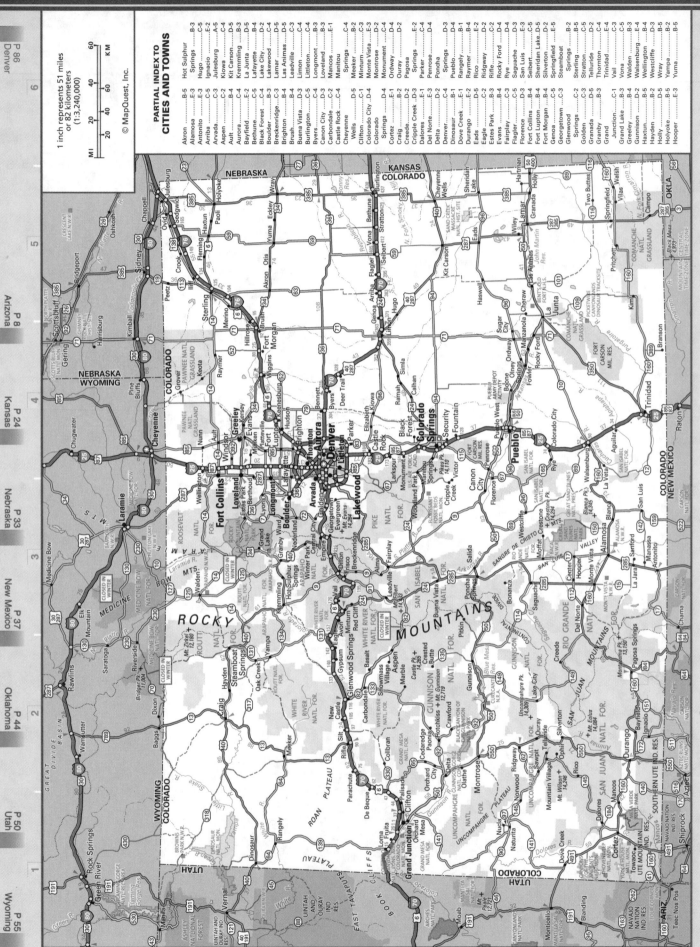

1 inch represents 51 miles
or 82 kilometers
(1:3,240,000)

© MapQuest, Inc.

N

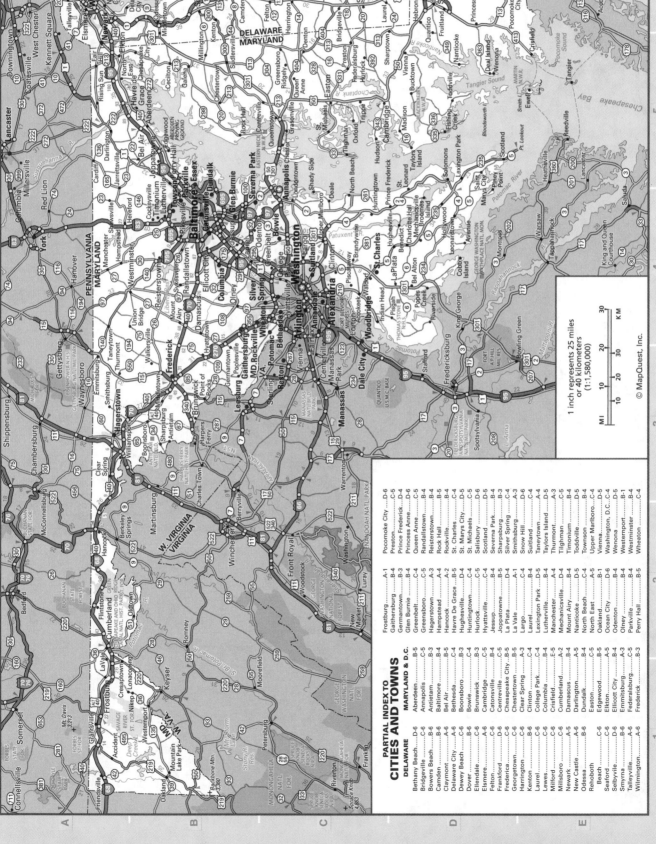

ATLANTIC OCEAN

DELAWARE
MARYLAND

PENNSYLVANIA
MARYLAND

W. VIRGINIA

MD.
VA.

P 72 Baltimore

P 137 Washington, D.C.

P 36 New Jersey

P 46 Pennsylvania

P 52 Virginia

P 52 West Virginia

1 inch represents 25 miles
or 40 kilometers
(1:1,580,000)

© MapQuest, Inc.

PARTIAL INDEX TO CITIES AND TOWNS

DELAWARE

Bethany Beach	D-6
Bridgeville	C-6
Bowers Beach	B-6
Camden	B-6
Claymont	A-6
Delaware City	A-6
Dewey Beach	C-6
Dover	B-6
Ellendale	C-6
Elsmere	A-6
Felton	B-6
Frankford	D-6
Frederica	B-6
Georgetown	C-6
Harrington	B-6
Kenton	B-6
Laurel	C-6
Lewes	C-6
Millsboro	C-6
Milford	C-6
Newark	A-5
New Castle	A-6
Odessa	B-6
Rehoboth Beach	C-6
Seaford	C-6
Selbyville	D-6
Smyrna	B-6
Talleyville	A-6
Wilmington	A-6

MARYLAND & D.C.

Aberdeen	B-5
Annapolis	C-5
Antietam	B-3
Baltimore	B-4
Bel Air	B-5
Bethesda	C-4
Boonsboro	B-3
Bowie	C-4
Brunswick	B-4
Cambridge	D-6
Catonsville	B-4
Centreville	C-5
Chesapeake City	B-5
Chestertown	C-5
Clear Spring	A-3
Clinton	C-4
College Park	C-4
Columbia	B-4
Cumberland	A-2
Damascus	B-4
Darlington	B-5
Dundalk	B-4
Easton	C-5
Edgewood	B-5
Elkton	B-5
Ellicott City	B-4
Emmitsburg	A-3
Federalsburg	C-5
Frederick	B-4

Frostburg	A-1
Gaithersburg	B-4
Germantown	B-4
Glen Burnie	B-4
Greenbelt	C-4
Greensboro	C-5
Hagerstown	A-3
Hampstead	A-4
Hancock	A-2
Havre De Grace	B-5
Hughesville	C-4
Huntingtown	C-4
Hurlock	C-5
Hyattsville	C-4
Jessup	B-4
Joppatowne	B-5
La Plata	C-4
La Vale	A-1
Largo	C-4
Laurel	B-4
Lexington Park	D-5
Lutherville	B-4
Manchester	A-4
Mechanicsville	D-4
Mount Airy	B-4
Nanticoke	D-5
North Beach	C-4
North East	A-5
Oakland	D-1
Ocean City	D-6
Odenton	B-4
Olney	B-4
Parkville	B-4
Perry Hall	B-5

Pocomoke City	D-6
Preston	C-5
Prince Frederick	D-4
Princess Anne	D-6
Queen Anne	C-5
Randallstown	B-4
Reisterstown	B-4
Rock Hall	C-5
Rockville	B-4
St. Charles	C-4
St. Marys City	D-5
St. Michaels	C-5
Salisbury	D-6
Scotland	D-5
Severna Park	B-4
Sharpsburg	B-3
Silver Spring	C-4
Smithsburg	A-3
Snow Hill	D-6
Suitland	C-4
Taneytown	A-4
Thurmont	A-3
Tilghman	C-5
Timonium	B-4
Toddville	D-5
Townson	B-4
Upper Marlboro	C-4
Vienna	B-1
Washington, D.C.	C-4
Wenona	D-5
Westernport	B-1
Westminster	B-4
Wheaton	B-5

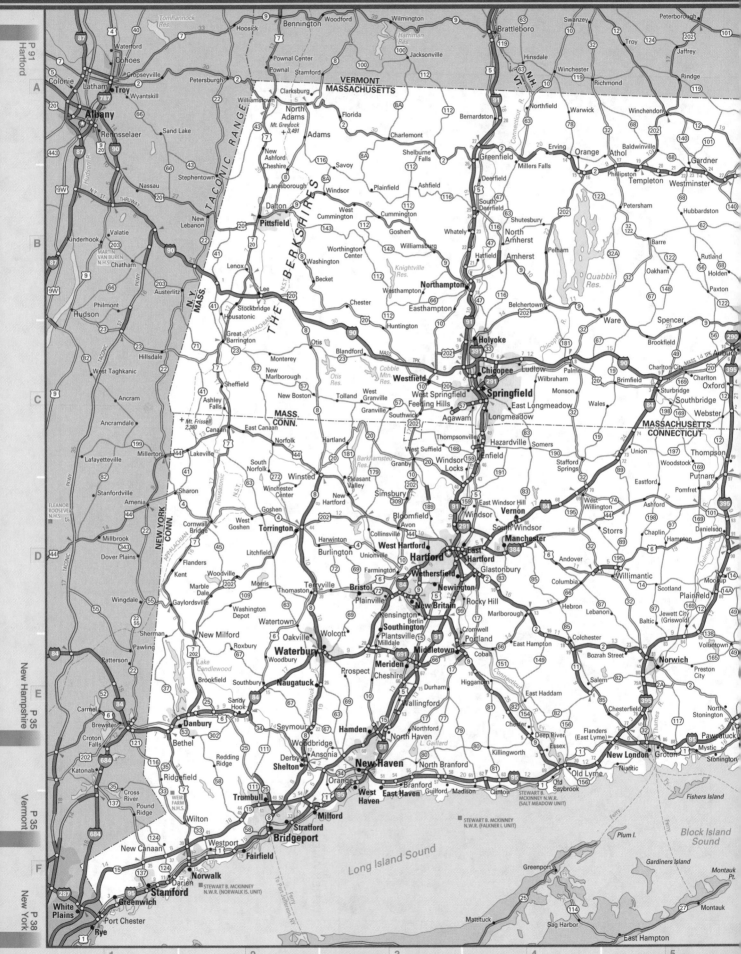

P 35
New Hampshire

P 35
Vermont

P 38
New York

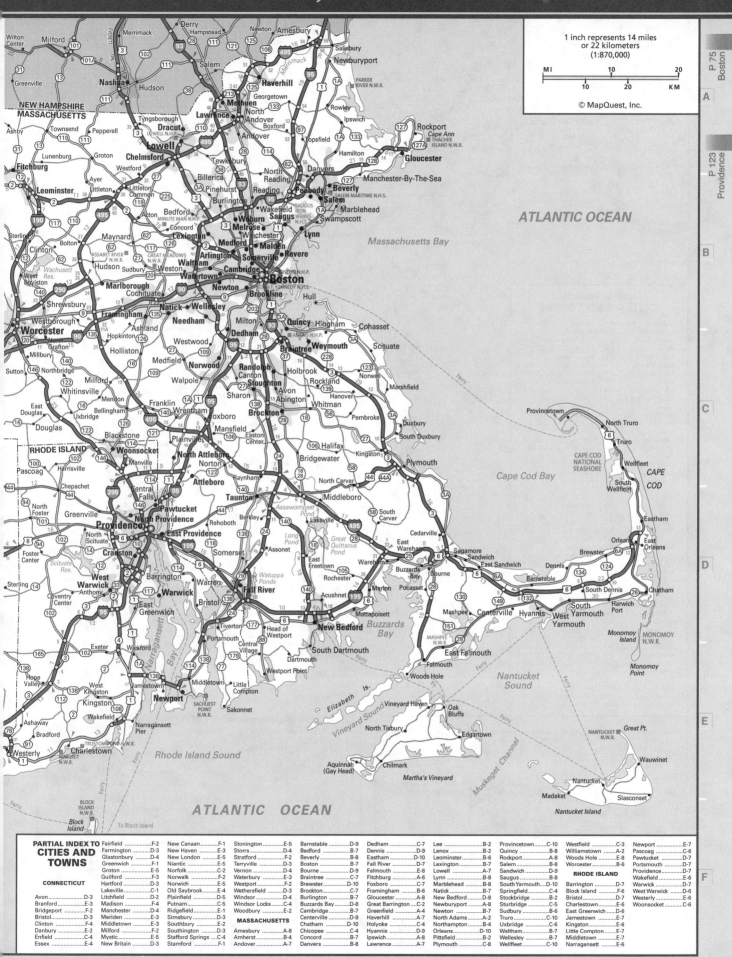

1 inch represents 14 miles or 22 kilometers (1:870,000)

© MapQuest, Inc.

P 95 Jacksonville

P 108 Miami

P 119 Orlando

P 133 Tampa/ St. Petersburg

P 6 Alabama

P 17 Georgia

1 inch represents 48 miles
or 77 kilometers
(1:3,020,000)

© MapQuest, Inc.

ATLANTIC OCEAN

GULF OF MEXICO

PARTIAL INDEX TO CITIES AND TOWNS

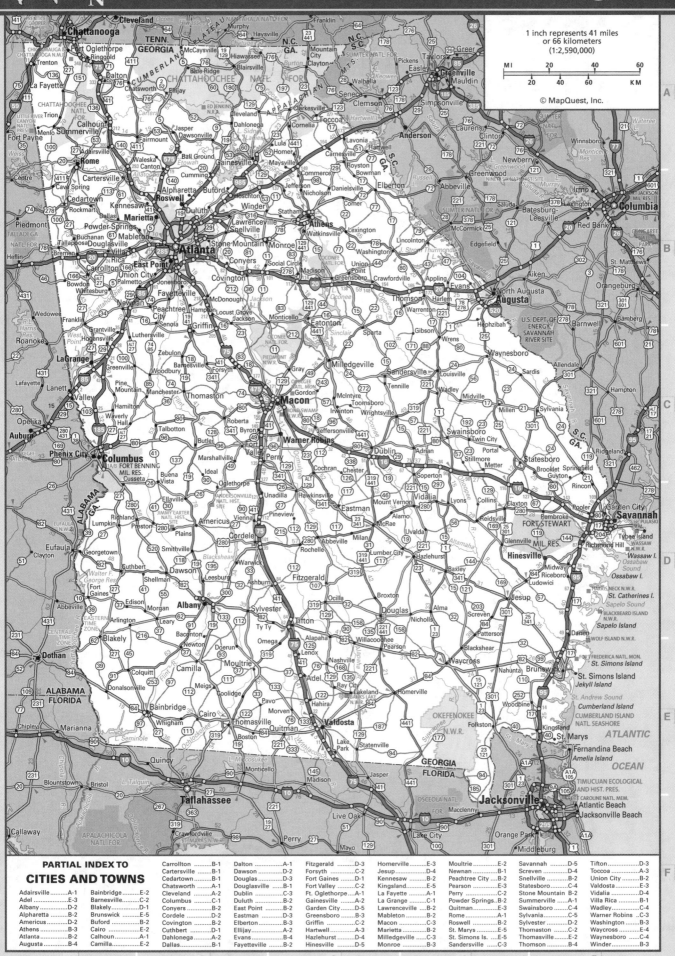

N

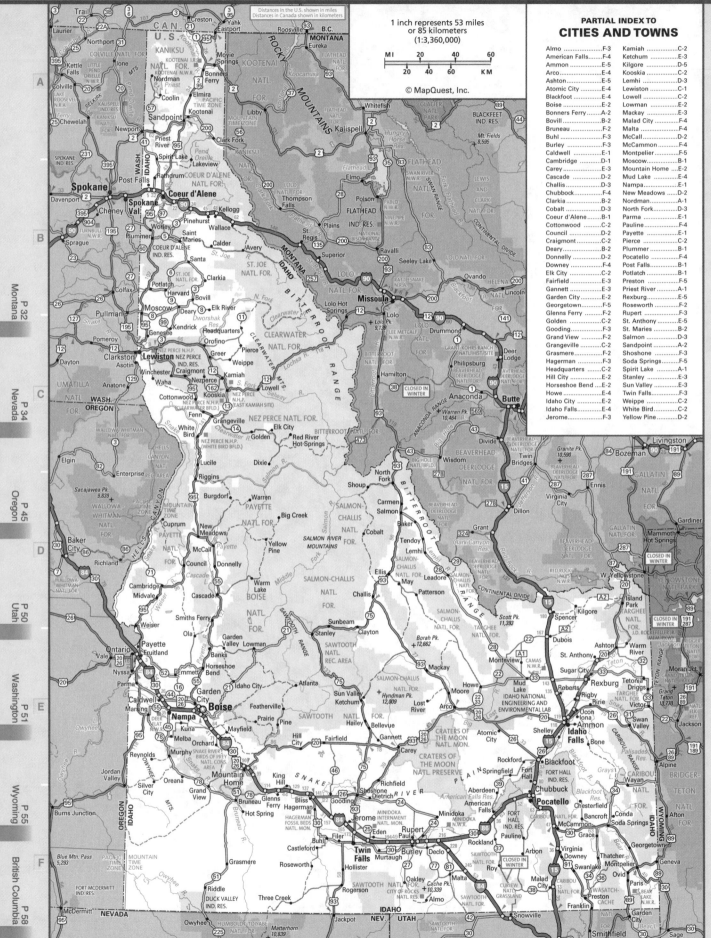

1 inch represents 53 miles
or 85 kilometers
(1:3,360,000)

© MapQuest, Inc.

PARTIAL INDEX TO
CITIES AND TOWNS

P 78 · N. Chicago
P 80 · S. Chicago
P 20 · Indiana
P 21 · Iowa
P 22 · Kentucky
P 31 · Missouri
P 54 · Wisconsin

1 inch represents 42 miles
or 68 kilometers
(1:2,670,000)

MI 20 40 60

KM 20 40 60

© MapQuest, Inc.

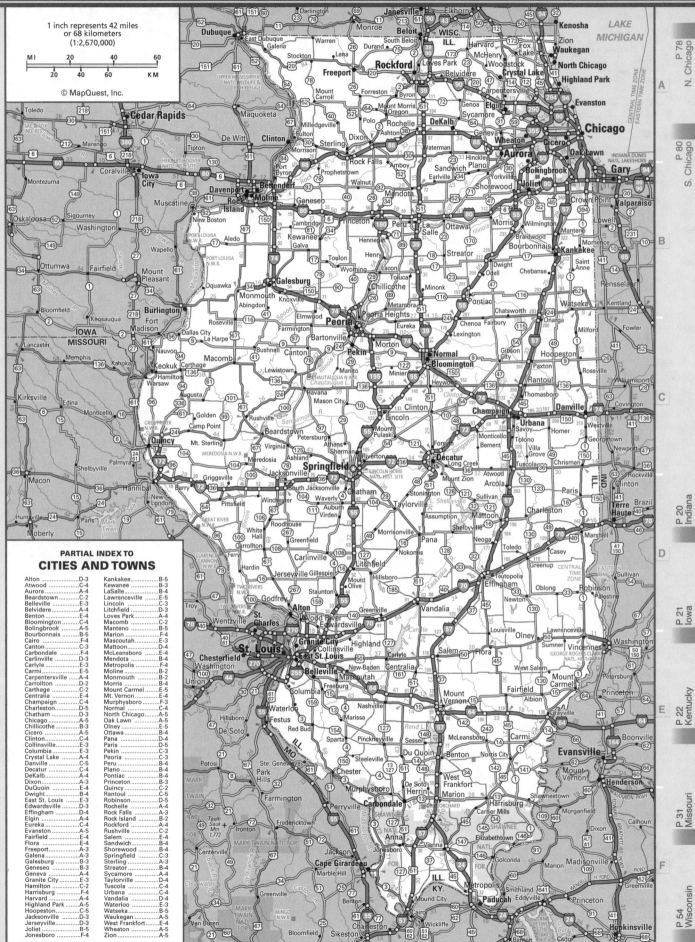

PARTIAL INDEX TO
CITIES AND TOWNS

P 79 Gary

P 94 Indianapolis

P 19 Illinois

P 22 Kentucky

P 28 Michigan

P 43 Ohio

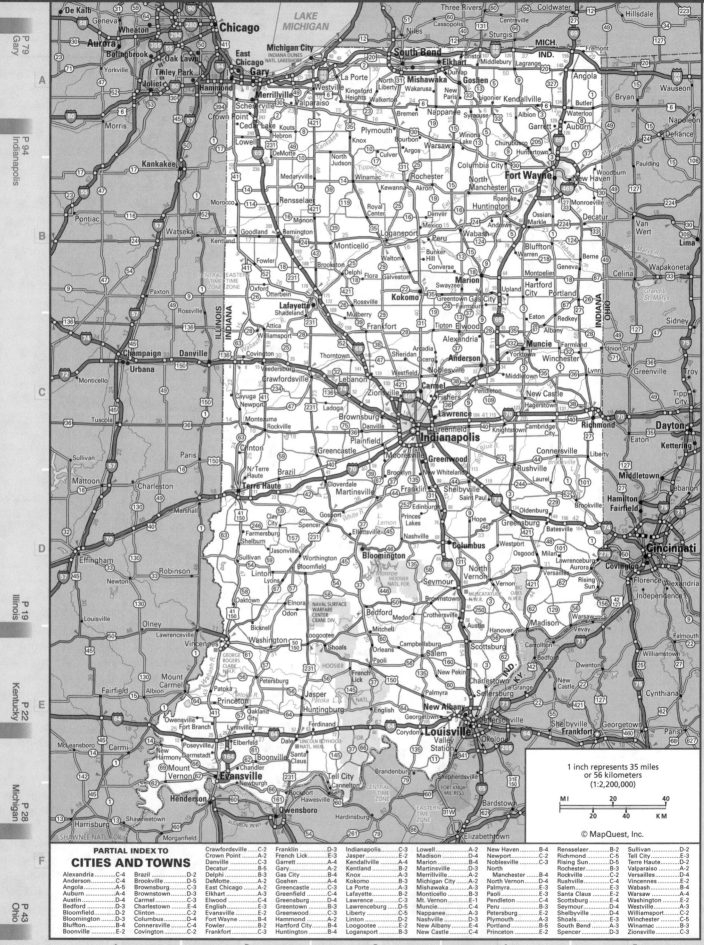

1 inch represents 35 miles
or 56 kilometers
(1:2,200,000)

© MapQuest, Inc.

PARTIAL INDEX TO
CITIES AND TOWNS

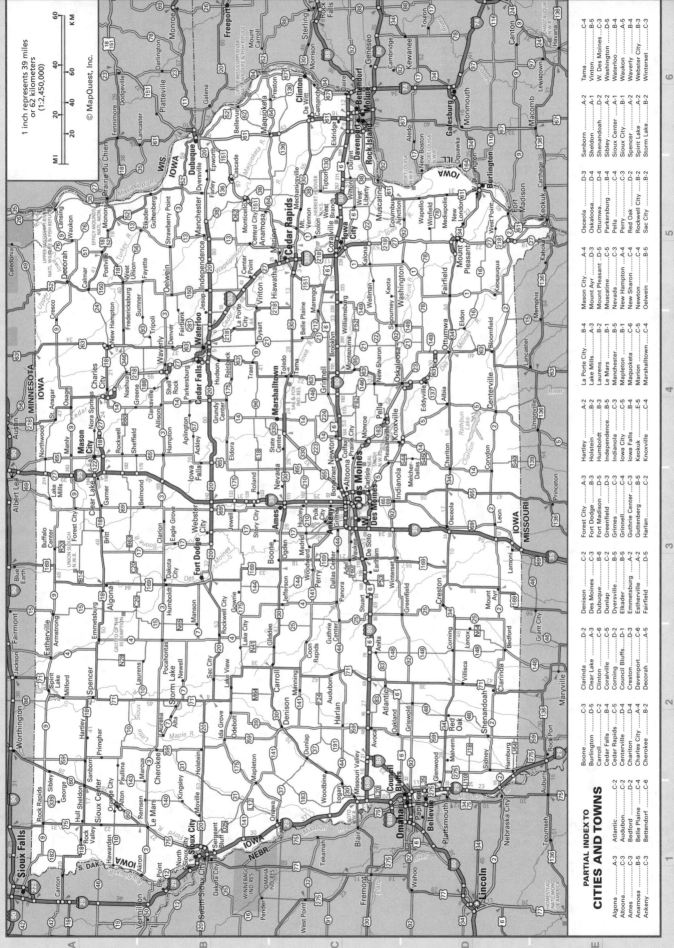

© MapQuest, Inc.

1 inch represents 39 miles
or 62 kilometers
(1:2,450,000)

P 54 Wisconsin
P 47 South Dakota
P 33 Nebraska
P 31 Missouri
P 27 Minnesota
P 19 Illinois
P 87 Des Moines

PARTIAL INDEX TO
CITIES AND TOWNS
KENTUCKY

Albany D-6	Glasgow D-6	Mt. Sterling B-8
Alexandria A-7	Greenville C-4	Mt. Vernon C-7
Ashland B-9	Hardin D-3	Mt. Washington B-6
Barbourville D-8	Hardinsburg C-5	Munfordville C-6
Bardstown C-6	Harlan C-8	Murray D-3
Beattyville C-8	Harrodsburg C-7	New Castle B-6
Booneville C-8	Hazard C-8	Nicholasville C-7
Bowling Green D-5	Henderson C-4	Owensboro C-4
Brandenburg B-6	Hickman D-2	Owenton B-7
Brooksville B-7	Hindman C-8	Paducah D-3
Brownsville C-5	Hopkinsville D-4	Paintsville C-9
Burkesville D-6	Hyden C-8	Paris B-7
Cadiz D-4	Independence ...A-7	Pikeville C-9
Calhoun C-4	Inez C-9	Pineville D-8
Campbellsville ..C-6	Jackson C-8	Prestonburg C-9
Carrollton B-6	Jamestown D-6	Providence C-4
Catlettsburg B-9	Lawrenceburg ...B-7	Princeton C-4
Cave City D-6	Lebanon C-6	Radcliff C-6
Clinton D-3	Leitchfield C-5	Richmond C-7
Columbia D-6	Lexington B-7	Russellville D-5
Corbin D-7	Liberty C-7	Salyersville C-8
Covington A-7	London C-7	Scottsville D-5
Cynthiana B-7	Louisa B-9	Shelbyville B-6
Danville C-7	Louisville B-6	Somerset D-7
Dixon C-4	Madisonville C-3	Stanford C-7
Eddyville C-3	Marion C-3	Taylorsville B-6
Edmonton D-6	Mayfield D-3	Tompkinsville D-6
Elizabethtown ...C-6	Maysville B-8	Vanceburg B-8
Elkhorn City C-9	McKee C-8	Versailles B-7
Falmouth B-7	Middlesboro D-8	Whitesburg C-9
Flemingsburg B-8	Monticello D-7	Whitley City D-7
Frankfort B-7	Morehead B-8	Wickliffe D-2
Franklin D-5	Morganfield C-4	Williamsburg D-7
Fulton D-3	Morgantown C-5	Williamstown B-7
Georgetown B-7	Mt. Olivet B-7	Winchester B-7

TENNESSEE

Adamsville F-2	Franklin E-5
Allardt D-7	Gatlinburg E-8
Ashland City D-4	Germantown F-2
Athens F-7	Greeneville E-9
Baileyton D-9	Harriman E-7
Bartlett F-2	Harrogate D-8
Benton F-7	Henderson E-2
Big Sandy E-3	Hendersonville ...E-5
Blaine E-8	Hohenwald E-4
Brentwood E-5	Hornsby F-3
Brownsville E-2	Huntingdon E-3
Bulls Gap D-8	Jackson E-3
Calhoun F-7	Jamestown D-7
Camden E-3	Jefferson City E-8
Centerville E-4	Johnson City D-9
Chattanooga F-6	Jonesborough D-9
Clarksville D-4	Kingsport D-9
Cleveland F-7	Knoxville E-8
Collegedale F-7	La Follette D-7
Collinwood F-4	Lake City E-7
Columbia E-4	Lawrenceburg F-4
Cookeville E-6	Lebanon E-5
Covington E-2	Lenoir City E-7
Crab Orchard E-7	Lexington E-3
Crossville E-7	Linden E-3
Dandridge E-8	Livingston D-6
Dayton E-7	Madisonville E-7
Dickson E-4	Manchester F-5
Dover D-4	Maryville E-8
Dresden D-3	McKenzie E-3
Ducktown F-7	McMinnville E-6
Dunlap F-6	Memphis F-1
Dyersburg E-2	Milan E-3
Elizabethton D-9	Milledgeville F-3
Elkton F-5	Millington F-2
Erin D-4	Monteagle F-6
Fayetteville F-5	Monterey E-6
	Morristown E-8
	Murfreesboro E-5
	Nashville E-5

New	
Johnsonville E-4	
New Market E-8	
Newport E-8	
Oak Ridge E-7	
Paris D-3	
Parsons E-3	
Pigeon Forge E-8	
Pikeville E-6	
Portland D-5	
Pulaski F-4	
Ripley E-2	
Rockwood E-7	
Rogersville D-9	
Rutledge E-8	
Savannah F-3	
Selmer F-3	
Sevierville E-8	
Shelbyville F-5	
Signal	
Mountain F-6	
Smyrna E-5	
Soddy-Daisy F-6	
Somerville F-2	
Sparta E-6	
Spencer E-6	
Springfield D-5	
Sweetwater E-7	
Tazewell D-8	
Trenton E-3	
Tullahoma F-5	
Union City D-2	
Wartburg E-7	
Waverly E-4	
Waynesboro F-4	
Westmoreland D-5	
Whiteville F-2	
Whitewell F-6	
Winchester F-5	
Winfield D-7	

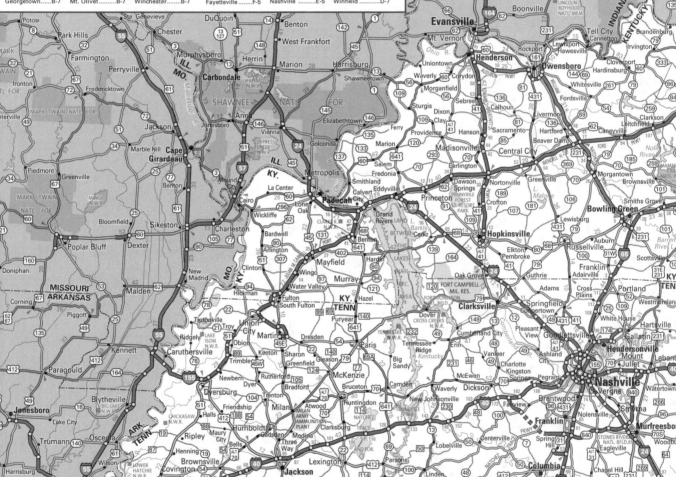

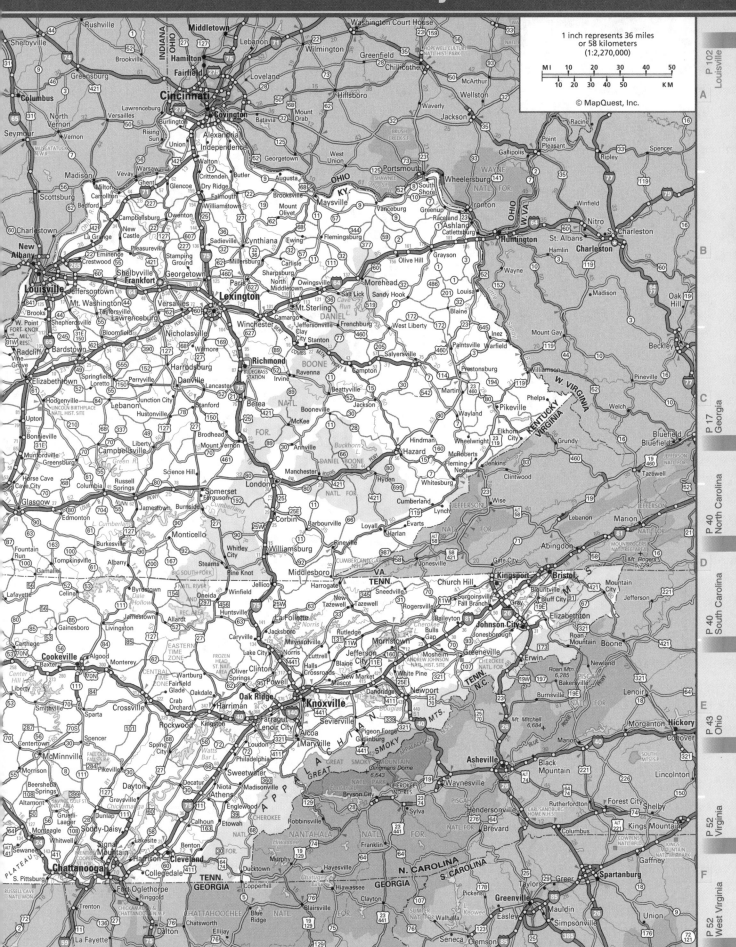

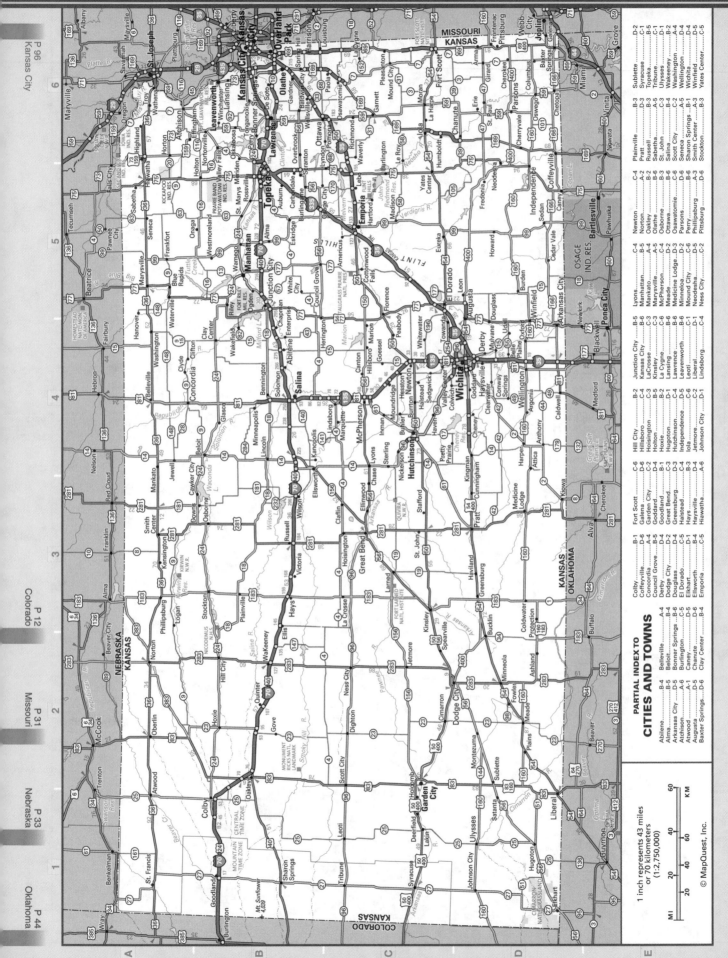

PARTIAL INDEX TO
CITIES AND TOWNS

1 inch represents 43 miles
or 70 kilometers
(1:2,750,000)

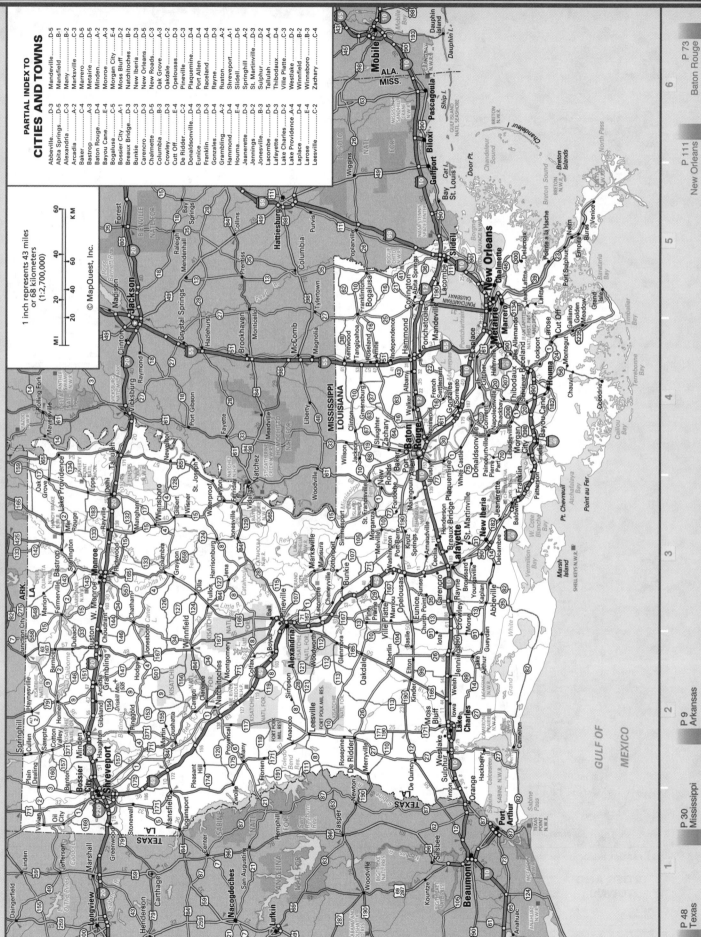

1 inch represents 43 miles or 68 kilometers (1:2,700,000)

© MapQuest, Inc.

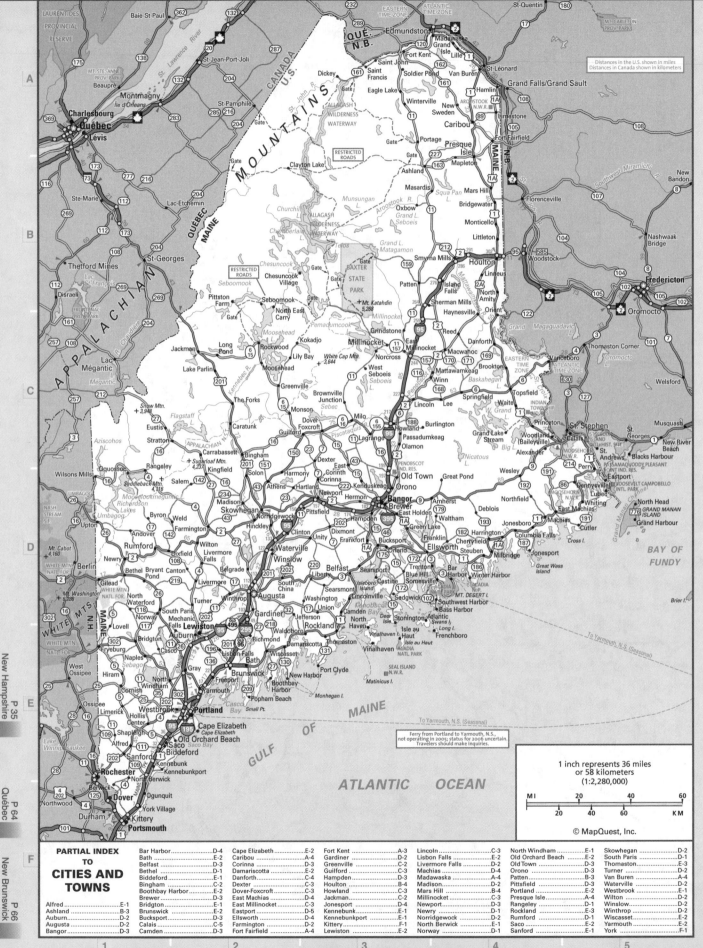

Distances in the U.S. shown in miles
Distances in Canada shown in kilometers

1 inch represents 36 miles
or 58 kilometers
(1:2,280,000)

Ferry from Portland to Yarmouth, N.S.,
not operating in 2005; status for 2006 uncertain.
Travelers should make inquiries.

© MapQuest, Inc.

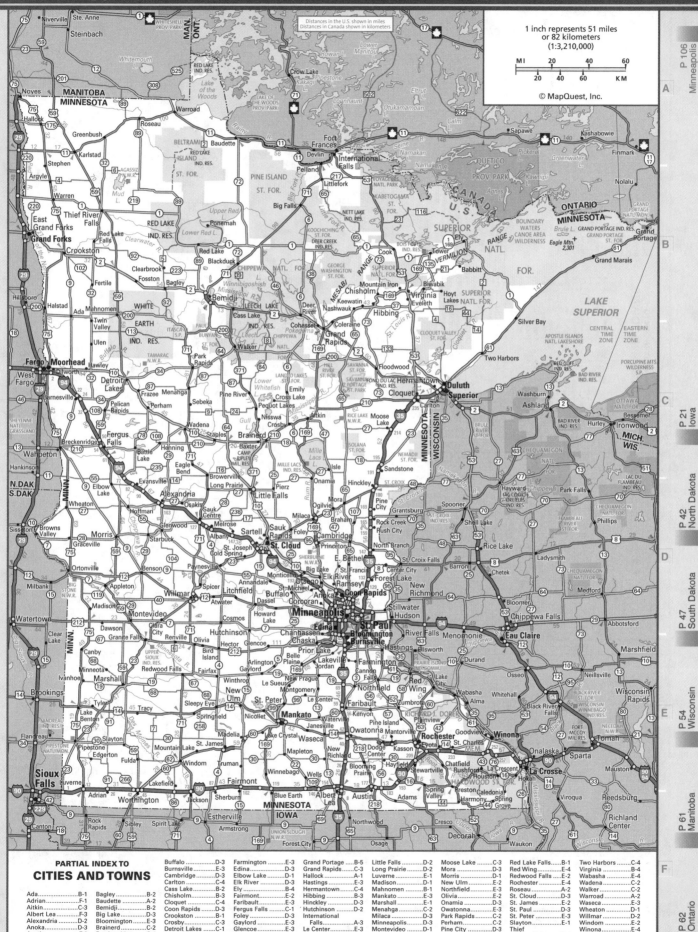

1 inch represents 51 miles
or 82 kilometers
(1:3,210,000)

© MapQuest, Inc.

Distances in the U.S. shown in miles
Distances in Canada shown in kilometers

PARTIAL INDEX TO CITIES AND TOWNS

P 106 Minneapolis
P 21 Iowa
P 42 North Dakota
P 47 South Dakota
P 54 Wisconsin
P 61 Manitoba
P 62 Ontario

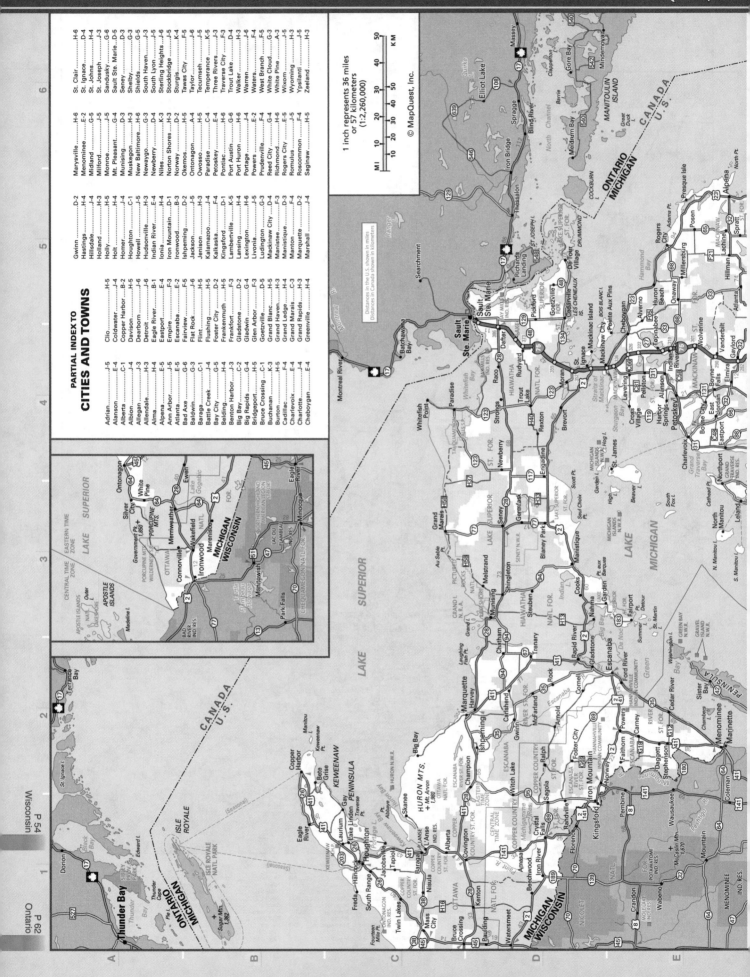

PARTIAL INDEX TO CITIES AND TOWNS

Adrian	J-5	Clio	H-5	Gwinn	D-2	Marysville	H-6	St. Clair	H-6
Alanson	E-4	Coldwater	J-4	Hastings	H-4	Menominee	E-2	St. Ignace	D-4
Alberta	C-1	Copper Harbor	B-2	Hillsdale	J-4	Midland	G-5	St. Johns	G-5
Albion	J-4	Davison	H-5	Holland	H-3	Milford	J-5	St. Joseph	J-5
Allegan	H-5	Dearborn	J-6	Holly	H-5	Monroe	J-5	Sault Ste. Marie	D-5
Allendale	H-3	Detroit	J-6	Holt	H-5	Mt. Pleasant	G-4	Seney	G-3
Alma	H-4	Eagle River	B-1	Homer	J-4	Munising	H-3	Shelby	G-3
Alpena	F-3	Eastport	F-3	Houghton	C-1	Muskegon	H-3	Shields	H-3
Atlanta	E-2	Empire	E-5	Howell	H-5	New Baltimore	H-6	South Haven	J-3
Bad Axe	G-6	Escanaba	E-2	Hudsonville	H-3	Newaygo	G-3	South Lyon	J-5
Baldwin	C-1	Fairview	F-5	Indian River	E-4	Newberry	D-4	Sterling Heights	J-6
Baraga	C-1	Flat Rock	J-5	Ionia	H-4	Niles	K-3	Stockbridge	J-5
Battle Creek	J-4	Flint	H-5	Ironwood	D-1	Norton Shores	H-3	Sturgis	K-4
Bay City	G-5	Flushing	H-5	Ishpeming	D-2	Norway	D-2	Tawas City	F-5
Belding	H-4	Foster City	G-5	Jackson	H-5	Okemos	H-5	Taylor	J-5
Benton Harbor	J-3	Frankenmuth	H-5	Jenison	H-3	Ontonagon	A-4	Tecumseh	J-5
Big Bay	C-2	Frankfort	F-3	Kalamazoo	J-4	Owosso	H-5	Temperance	K-5
Big Rapids	H-5	Gladstone	D-2	Kalkaska	F-4	Paradise	C-4	Three Rivers	J-3
Bridgeport	H-5	Gladwin	D-2	Kingsford	D-1	Petoskey	E-4	Traverse City	F-4
Bruce Crossing	C-1	Glen Arbor	F-3	Lambertville	K-5	Pontiac	H-6	Trout Lake	D-4
Burton	H-5	Goetzville	K-3	Lansing	H-4	Port Austin	G-6	Walker	H-3
Cadillac	F-4	Grand Blanc	H-5	Lexington	H-6	Port Huron	H-6	Warren	F-4
Charlevoix	E-4	Grand Haven	H-5	Livonia	J-5	Portage	J-4	Waters	E-2
Charlotte	J-4	Grand Ledge	H-4	Ludington	G-3	Powers	E-2	West Branch	F-4
Cheboygan	E-4	Grand Marais	C-3	Mackinaw City	D-4	Prudenville	F-4	White Cloud	G-3
		Grand Rapids	H-3	Manistee	G-4	Reed City	G-4	White Pine	A-3
		Greenville	H-4	Manistique	D-3	Richmond	H-6	Wixom	J-5
				Manton	F-4	Rogers City	E-5	Wyoming	J-5
				Marquette	H-3	Romulus	D-3	Ypsilanti	F-4
				Marshall	J-4	Roscommon	F-4	Zeeland	H-3
						Saginaw	J-4		

1 inch represents 36 miles or 57 kilometers (1:2,260,000)

© MapQuest, Inc.

Distances in the U.S. shown in miles
Distances in Canada shown in kilometers

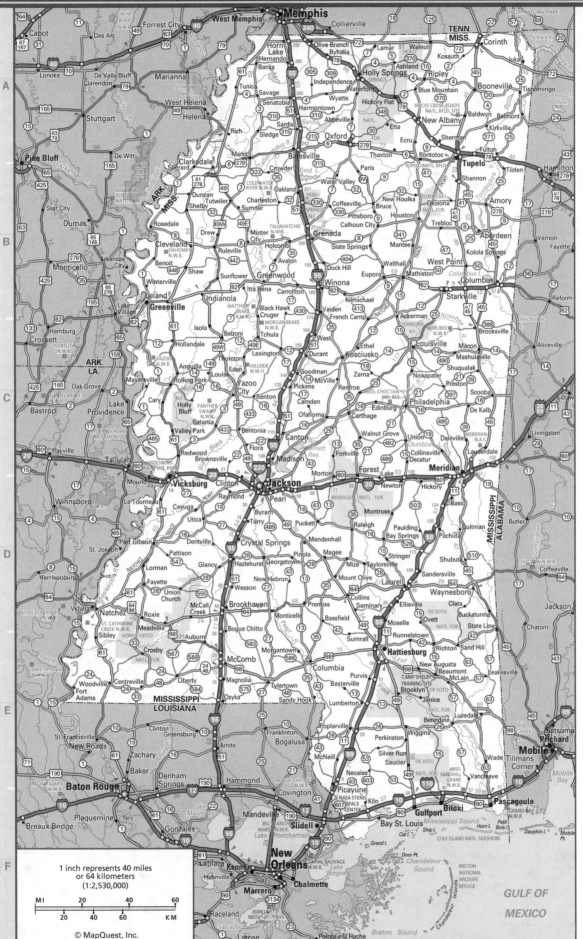

1 inch represents 40 miles
or 64 kilometers
(1:2,530,000)

© MapQuest, Inc.

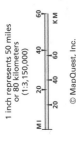
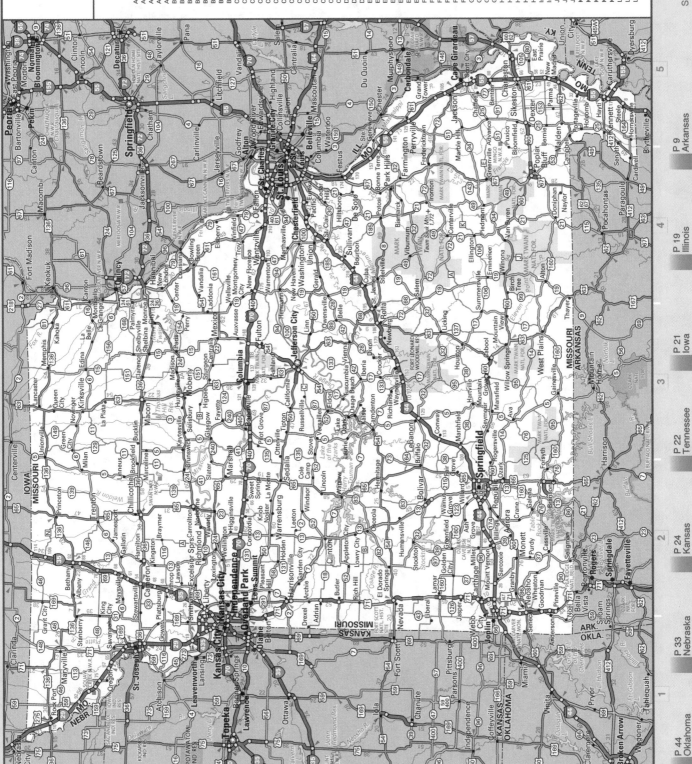

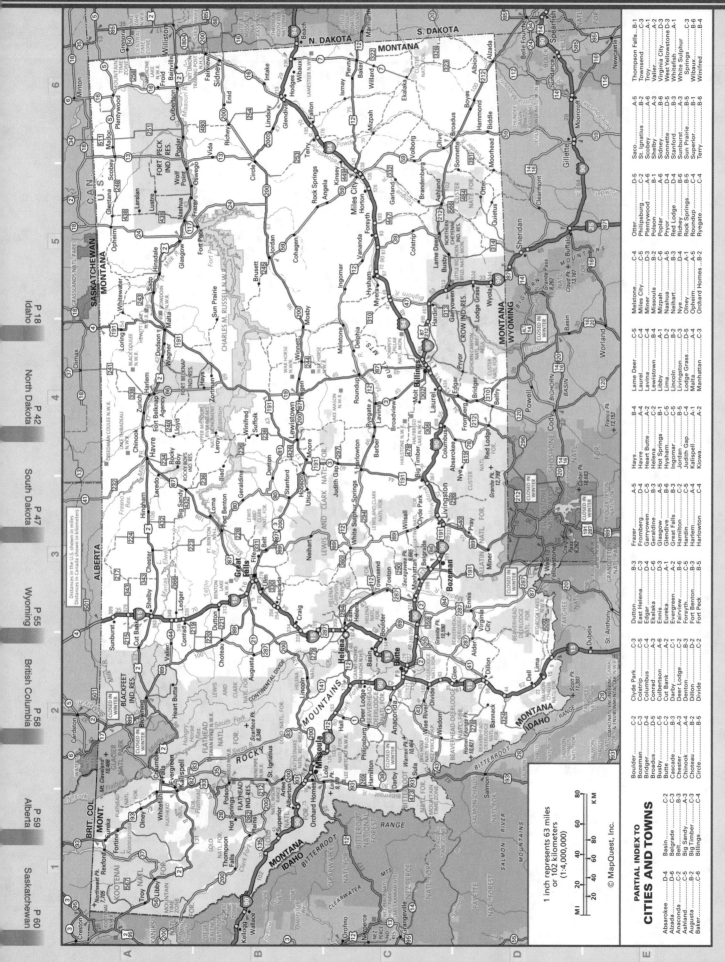

P 18 Idaho
P 42 North Dakota
P 47 South Dakota
P 55 Wyoming
P 58 British Columbia
P 59 Alberta
P 60 Saskatchewan

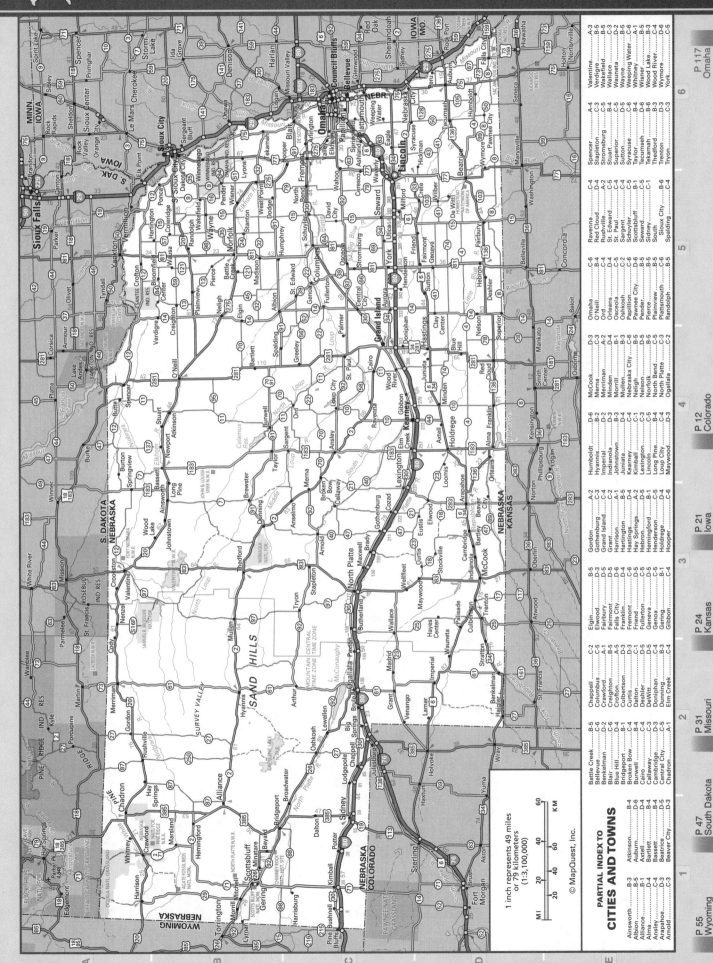

1 inch represents 49 miles
or 79 kilometers
(1:3,100,000)

© MapQuest, Inc.

P 117 Omaha

P 12 Colorado

P 21 Iowa

P 24 Kansas

P 31 Missouri

P 47 South Dakota

P 55 Wyoming

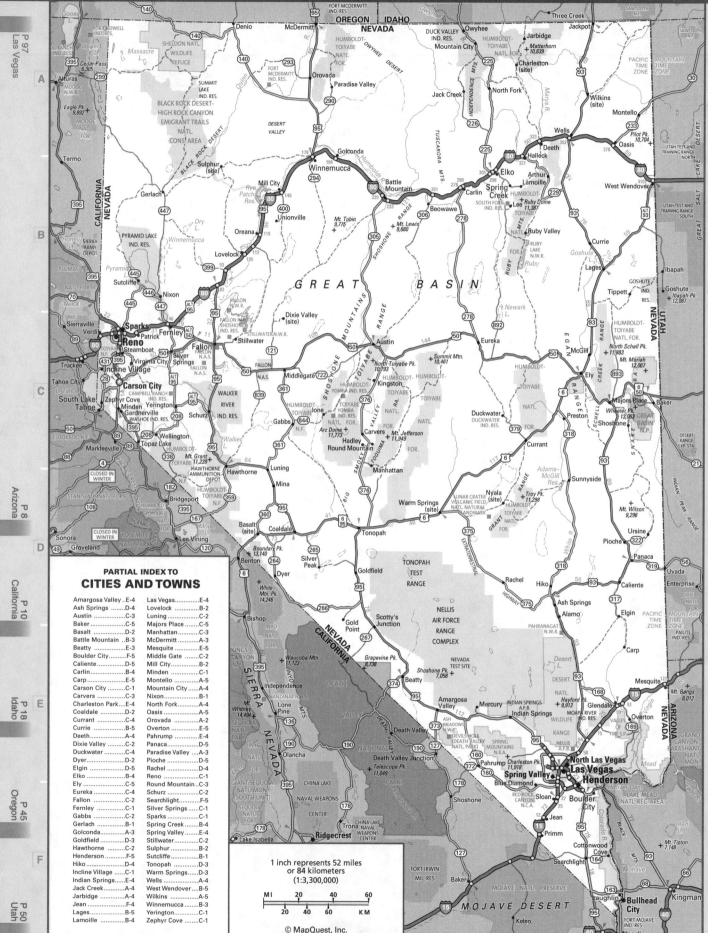

1 inch represents 52 miles
or 84 kilometers
(1:3,300,000)

MI   20   40   60

20   40   60
KM

© MapQuest, Inc.

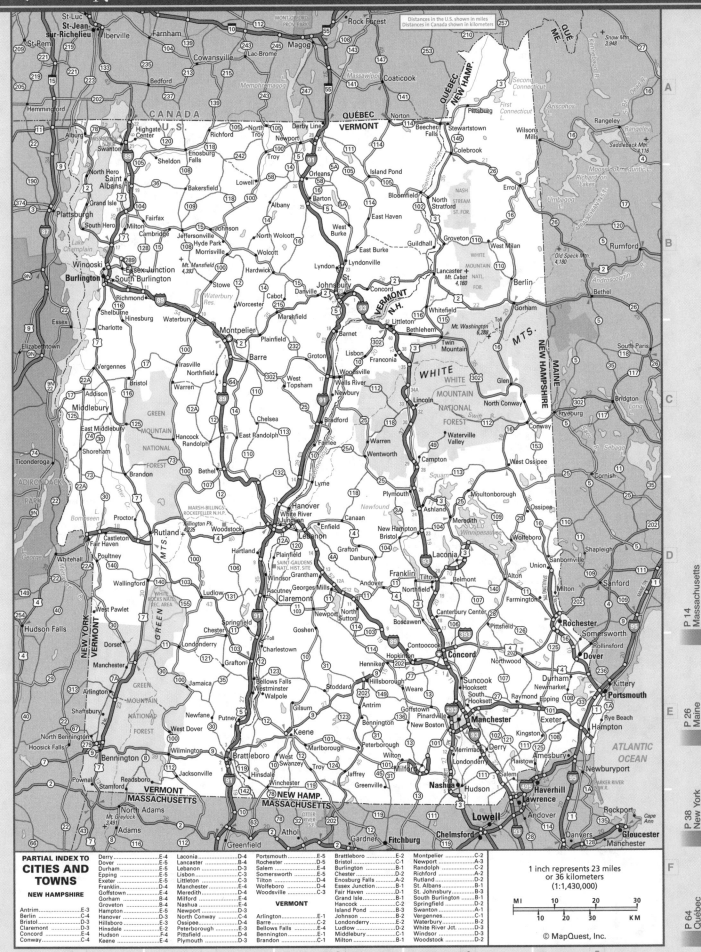

1 inch represents 23 miles or 36 kilometers (1:1,430,000)

N

PARTIAL INDEX TO CITIES AND TOWNS

1 inch represents 18 miles
or 29 kilometers
(1:1,160,000)

MI 0 · 10 · 20
KM 0 · 10 · 20

© MapQuest, Inc.

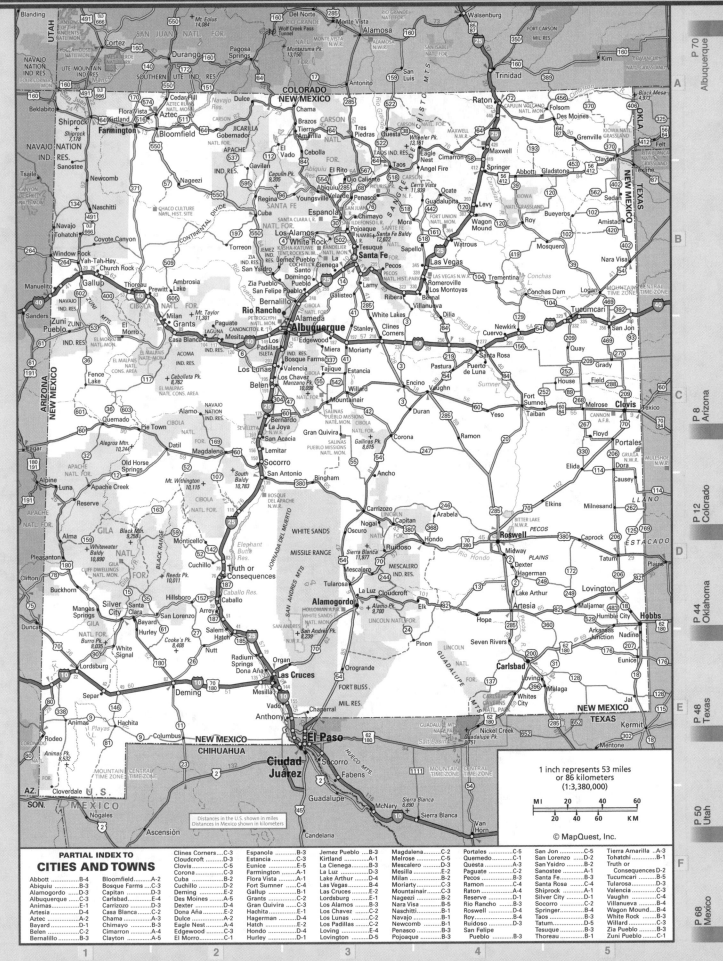

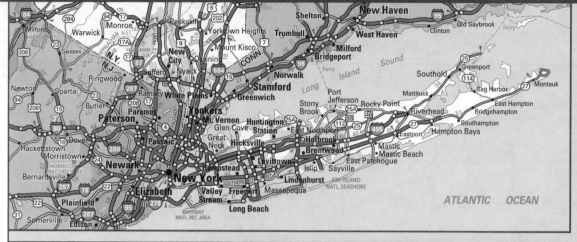

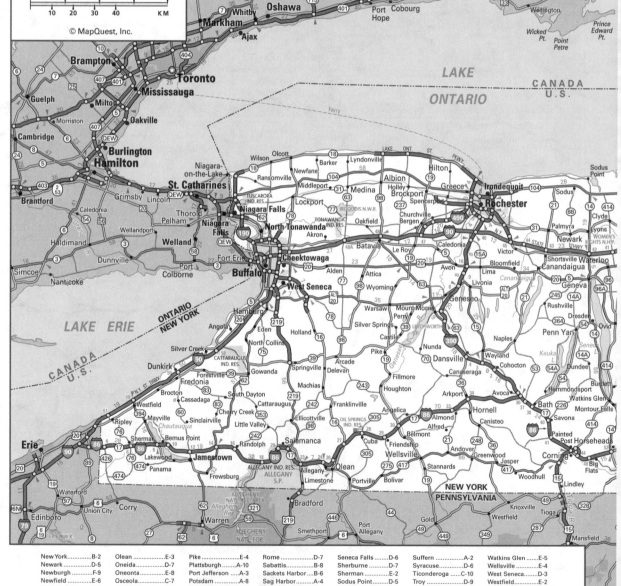

PARTIAL INDEX TO CITIES AND TOWNS

1 inch represents 27 miles
or 43 kilometers
(1:1,700,000)

© MapQuest, Inc.

P 76 Buffalo
P 112 New York City
P 125 Rochester
P 36 New Jersey
P 46 Pennsylvania
P 62 Ontario

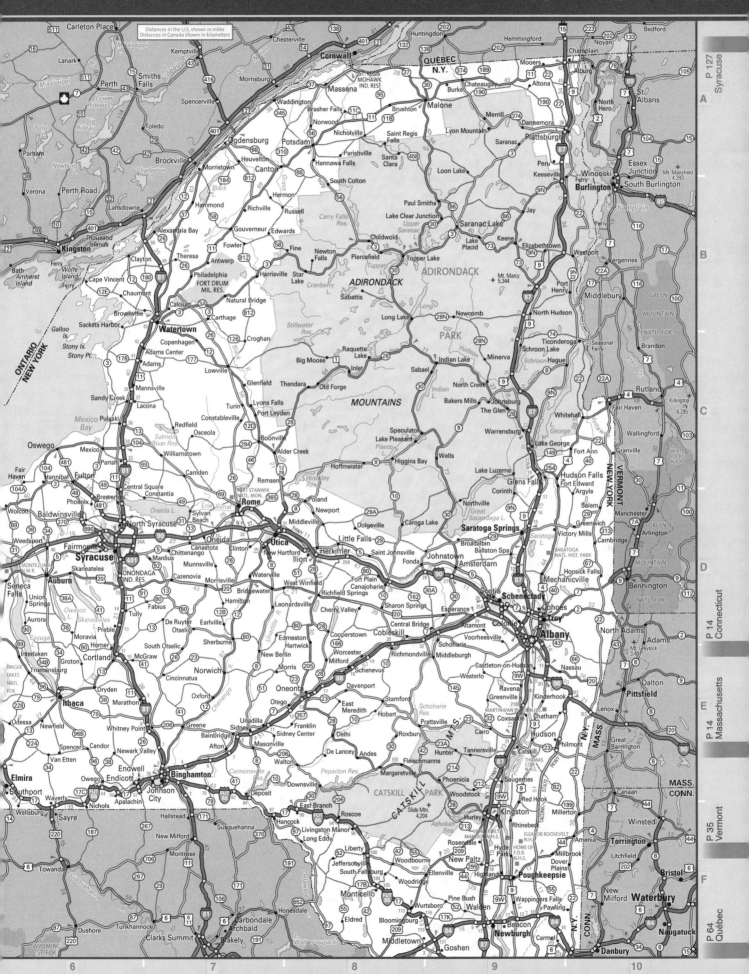

P 73 Charleston
P 77 Charlotte
P 138 Winston-Salem
P 17 Georgia
P 22 Tennessee
P 52 Virginia

1 inch represents 36 miles
or 58 kilometers
(1:2,270,000)

© MapQuest, Inc.

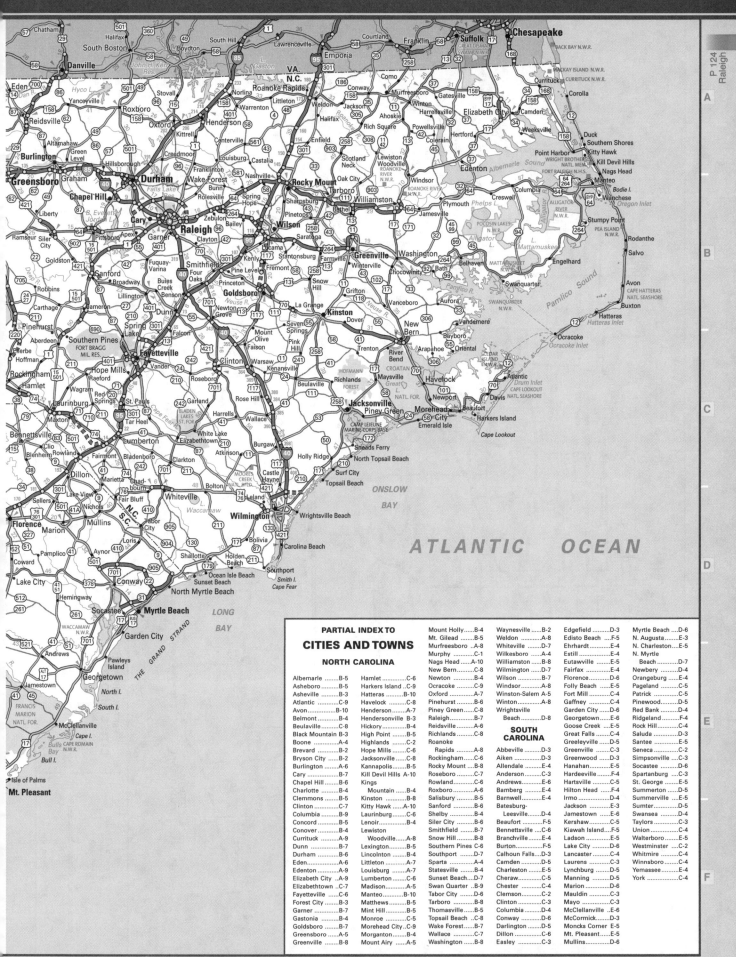

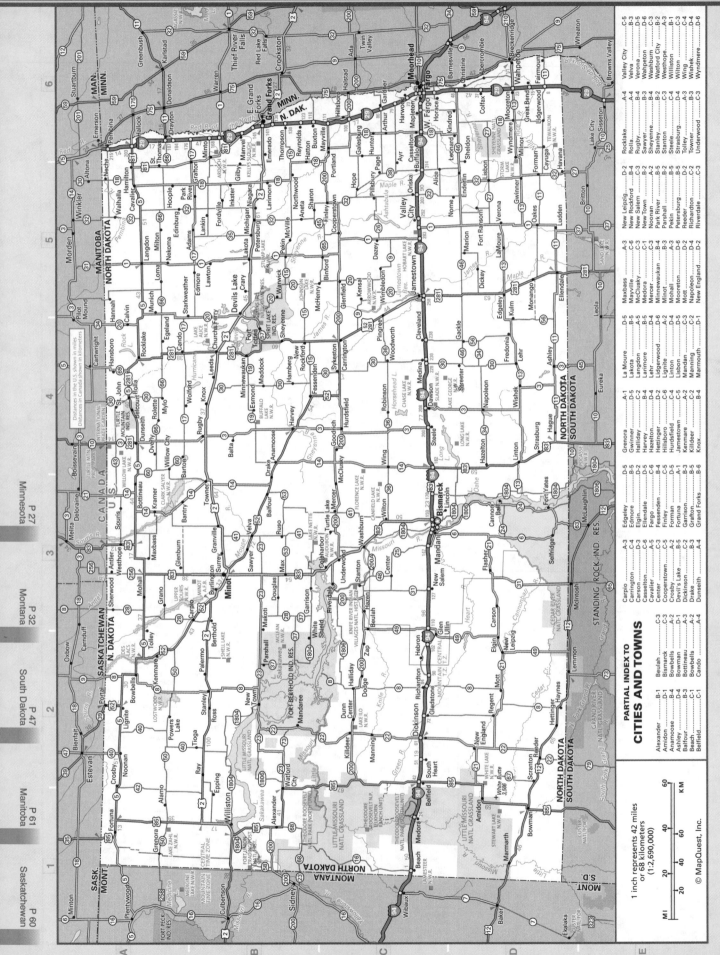

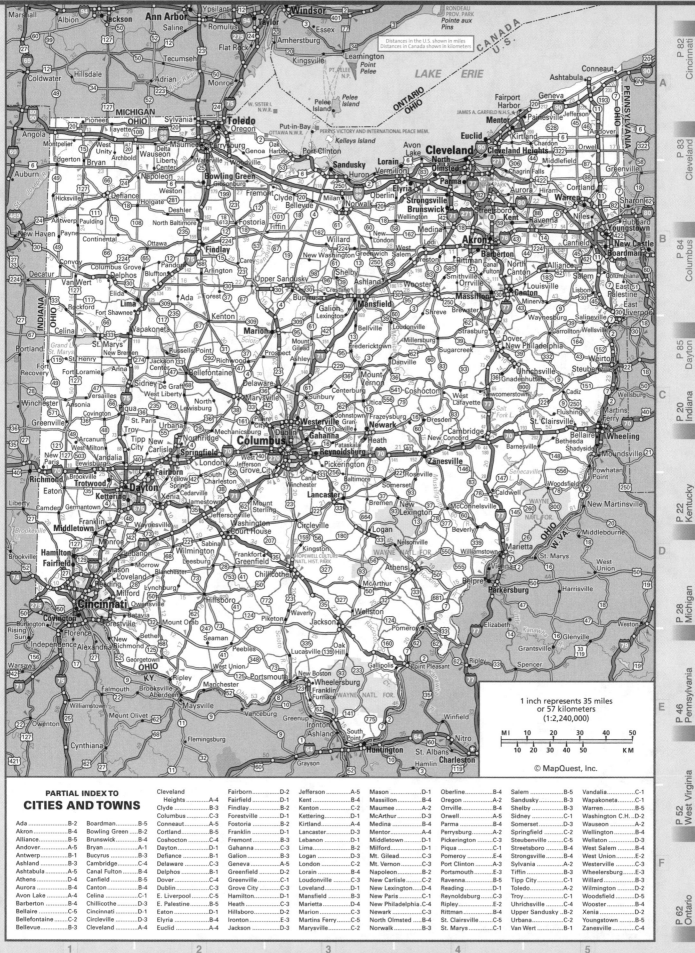

Distances in the U.S. shown in miles
Distances in Canada shown in kilometers

LAKE ERIE

1 inch represents 35 miles
or 57 kilometers
(1:2,240,000)

MI 10 20 30 40 50

10 20 30 40 50 KM

© MapQuest, Inc.

P 82 Cincinnati
P 83 Cleveland
P 84 Columbus
P 20 Indiana
P 22 Kentucky
P 28 Michigan
P 46 Pennsylvania
P 52 West Virginia
P 62 Ontario

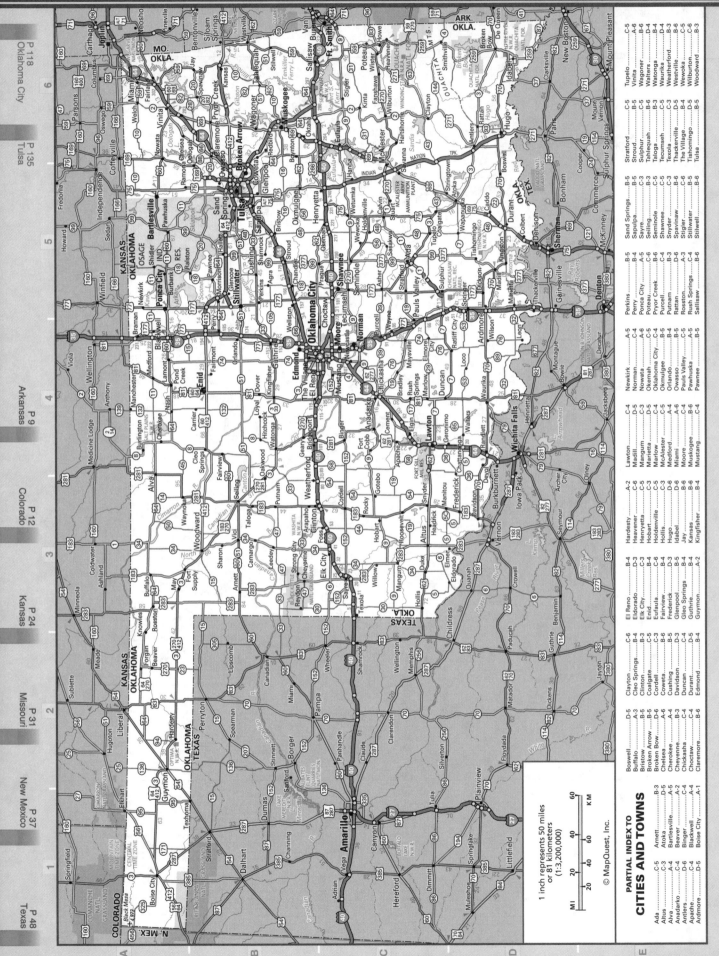

P 118 Oklahoma City

P 135 Tulsa

P 9 Arkansas

P 12 Colorado

P 24 Kansas

P 31 Missouri

P 37 New Mexico

P 48 Texas

© MapQuest, Inc.

1 inch represents 50 miles
or 81 kilometers
(1:3,200,000)

PARTIAL INDEX TO

CITIES AND TOWNS

Ada	C-5
Altus	C-3
Alva	A-4
Anadarko	C-4
Antlers	C-6
Apache	C-4
Ardmore	D-5
Arnett	B-3
Atoka	C-5
Bartlesville	A-5
Beaver	A-2
Binger	C-4
Blackwell	A-4
Boise City	A-1
Boswell	D-5
Buffalo	A-3
Bristow	B-5
Broken Arrow	B-5
Broken Bow	D-6
Chelsea	A-6
Cherokee	A-4
Cheyenne	B-3
Chickasha	C-4
Choctaw	C-4
Claremore	B-6
Clayton	D-5
Cleo Springs	B-4
Clinton	B-3
Coalgate	C-5
Cordell	C-4
Coweta	B-6
Cushing	B-5
Davidson	D-3
Duncan	C-4
Durant	D-5
Edmond	B-6
El Reno	C-4
Eldorado	D-3
Elk City	B-3
Enid	B-4
Eufaula	C-6
Fairview	B-4
Frederick	D-3
Glenpool	B-5
Gleo Springs	C-4
Guthrie	C-5
Guymon	A-2
Hardesty	A-2
Heavener	D-6
Henryetta	C-5
Hobart	C-3
Holdenville	C-5
Hollis	D-3
Hugo	D-6
Idabel	D-6
Jay	B-6
Kansas	B-6
Kingfisher	B-4
Lawton	C-4
Madill	D-5
Mangum	C-3
Marietta	D-5
Marlow	C-4
McAlester	C-5
Medford	A-4
Miami	A-6
Moore	C-4
Mustang	C-4
Newkirk	A-5
Norman	C-4
Nowata	A-6
Okemah	C-5
Oklahoma City	C-4
Okmulgee	C-5
Orlando	B-4
Owasso	B-5
Pauls Valley	C-5
Pawhuska	A-5
Pawnee	B-5
Perkins	B-4
Perry	B-4
Ponca City	A-5
Poteau	C-6
Purcell	C-4
Putnam	B-3
Rattan	D-6
Rosston	A-3
Rush Springs	C-4
Sallisaw	B-6
Sand Springs	B-5
Sapulpa	B-5
Sayre	C-3
Seiling	B-3
Seminole	C-5
Shawnee	C-5
Snyder	C-3
Spavinaw	B-6
Stigler	C-6
Stillwater	B-5
Stilwell	B-6
Stratford	C-5
Stroud	B-5
Sulphur	C-5
Tahlequah	B-6
Taloga	B-3
Tecumseh	C-5
Texola	C-3
Thackerville	D-5
The Village	B-4
Tishomingo	C-5
Tulsa	B-5
Tupelo	C-5
Vinita	A-6
Wagoner	B-6
Walters	D-4
Watonga	B-4
Waurika	D-4
Weatherford	B-3
Westville	B-6
Wewoka	C-5
Wilburton	C-6
Woodward	B-3

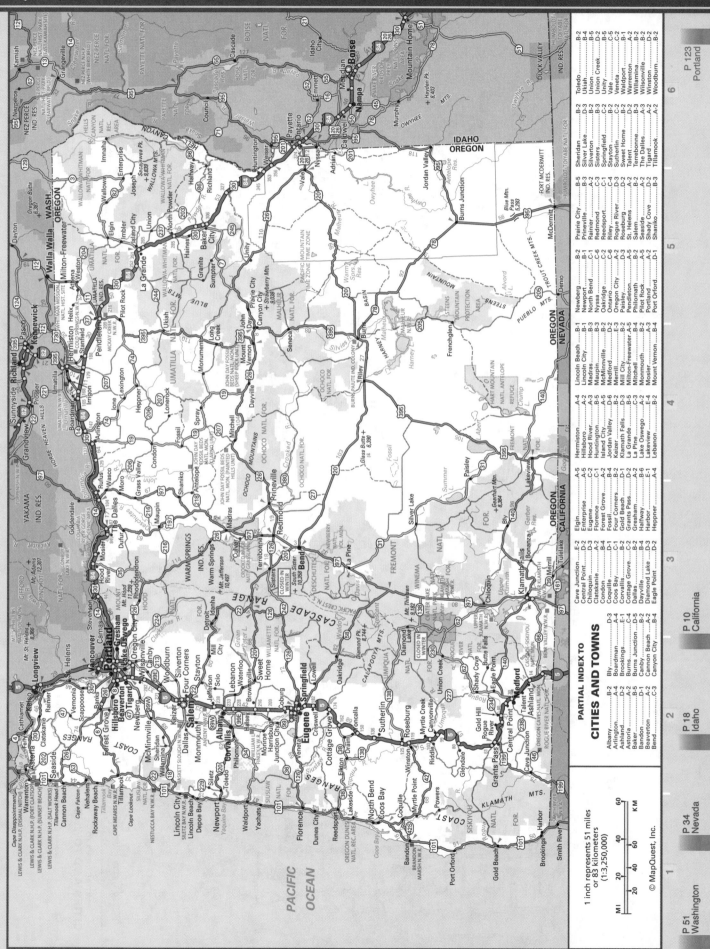

1 inch represents 51 miles
or 83 kilometers
(1:3,250,000)

© MapQuest, Inc.

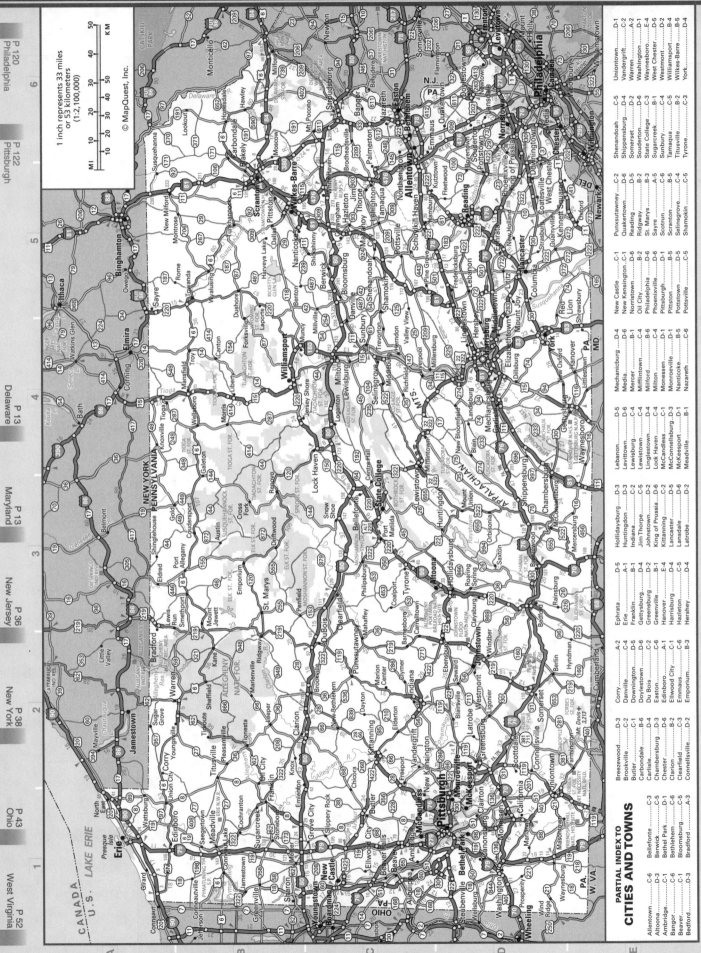

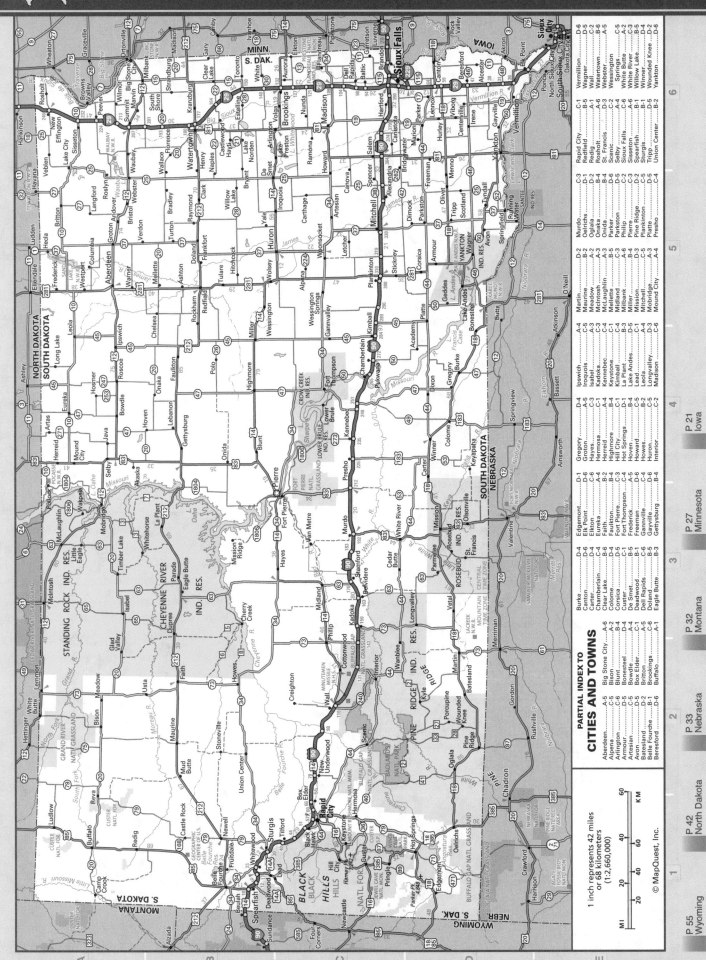

1 inch represents 42 miles
or 68 kilometers
(1:2,660,000)

© MapQuest, Inc.

P 55 Wyoming

P 42 North Dakota

P 33 Nebraska

P 32 Montana

P 27 Minnesota

P 21 Iowa

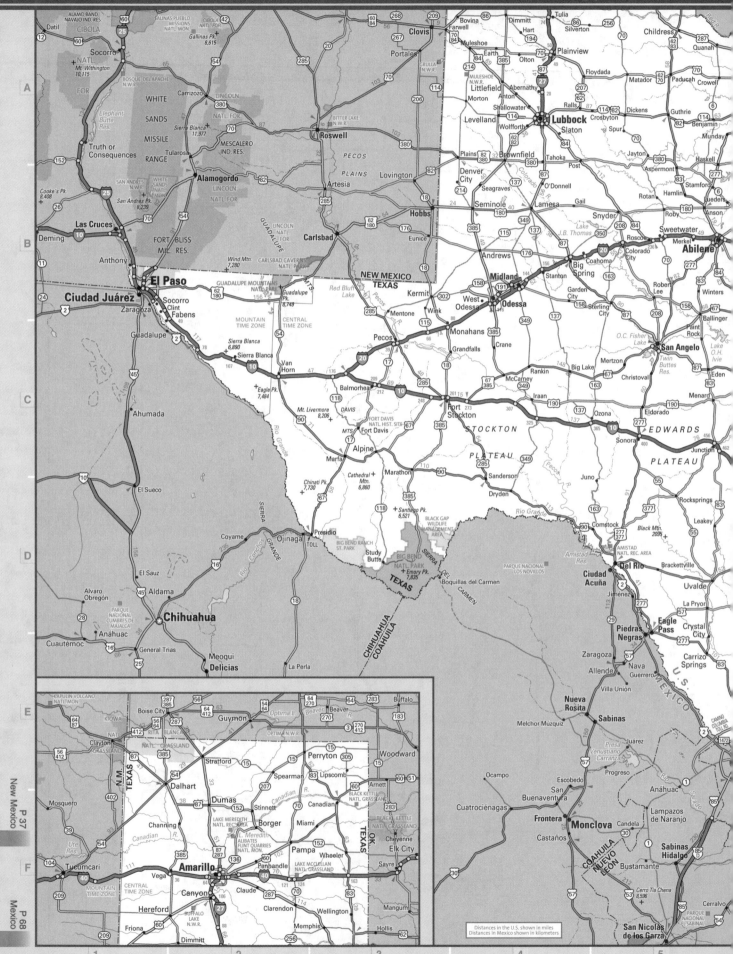

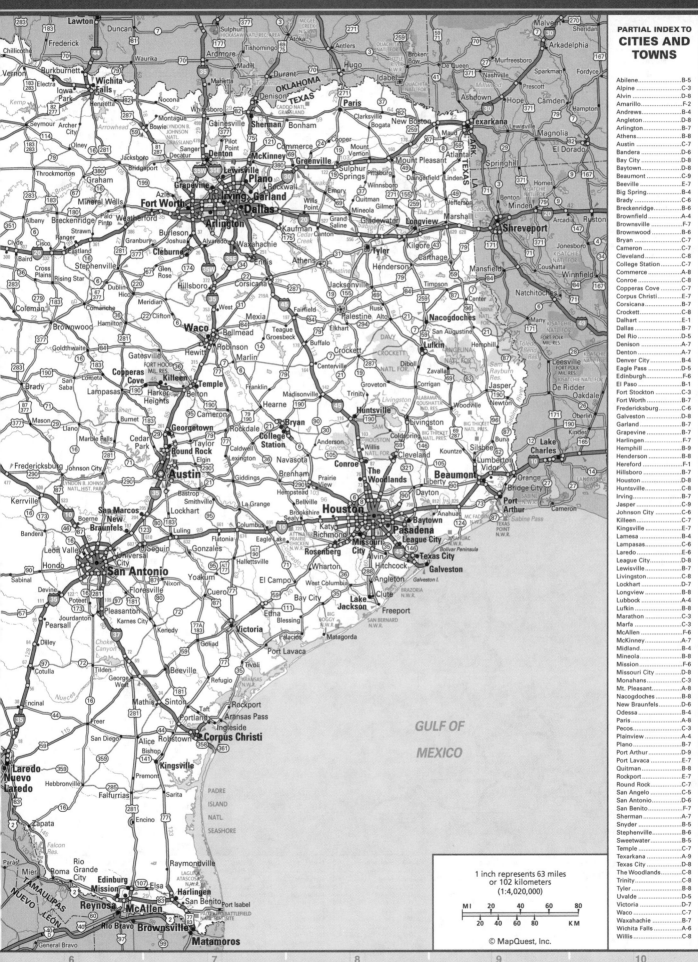

1 inch represents 63 miles
or 102 kilometers
(1:4,020,000)

© MapQuest, Inc.

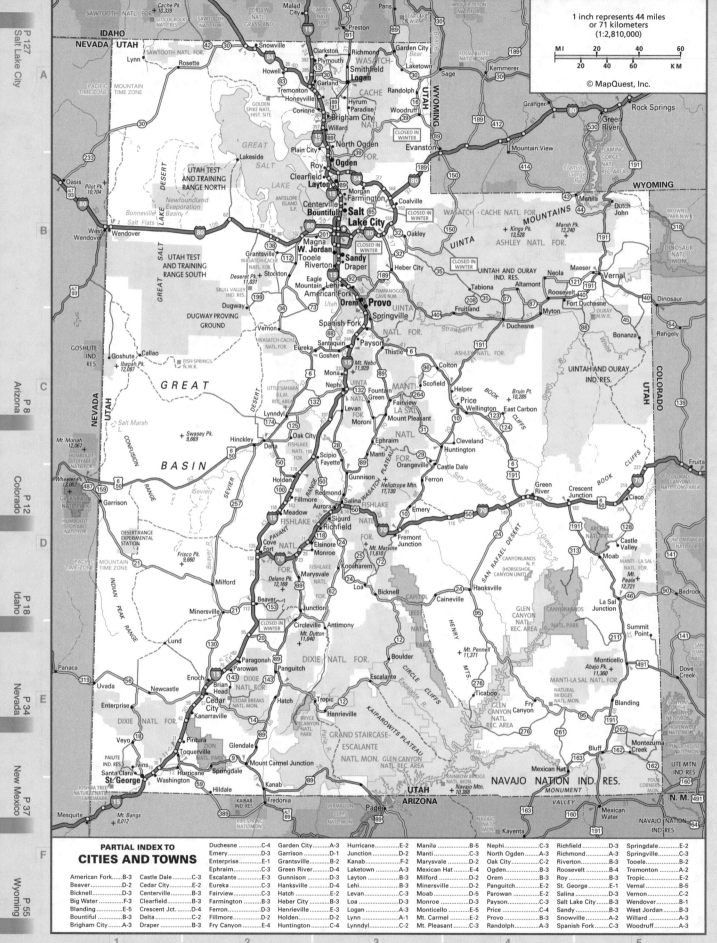

1 inch represents 44 miles
or 71 kilometers
(1:2,810,000)

© MapQuest, Inc.

P 127
Salt Lake City

P 8
Arizona

P 12
Colorado

P 18
Idaho

P 34
Nevada

P 37
New Mexico

P 55
Wyoming

PARTIAL INDEX TO CITIES AND TOWNS

N

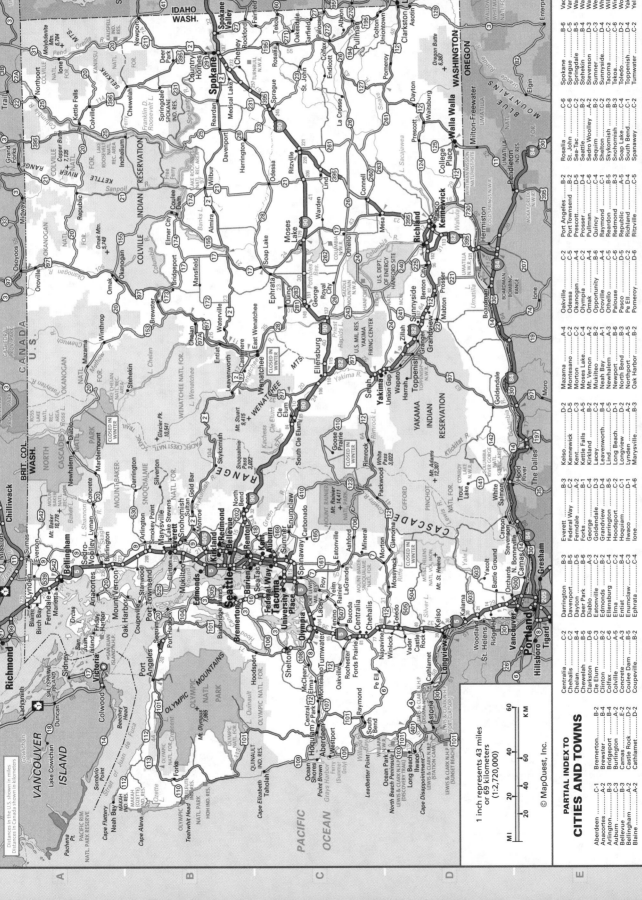

© MapQuest, Inc.

Distances in the U.S. shown in miles
Distances in Canada shown in kilometers

1 inch represents 43 miles
or 69 kilometers
(1:2,720,000)

| MI | 20 | 40 | 60 |
| KM | 20 | 40 | 60 |

PARTIAL INDEX TO
CITIES AND TOWNS

P 127 Spokane

P 132 Seattle

P 18 Idaho

P 45 Oregon

P 58 British Columbia

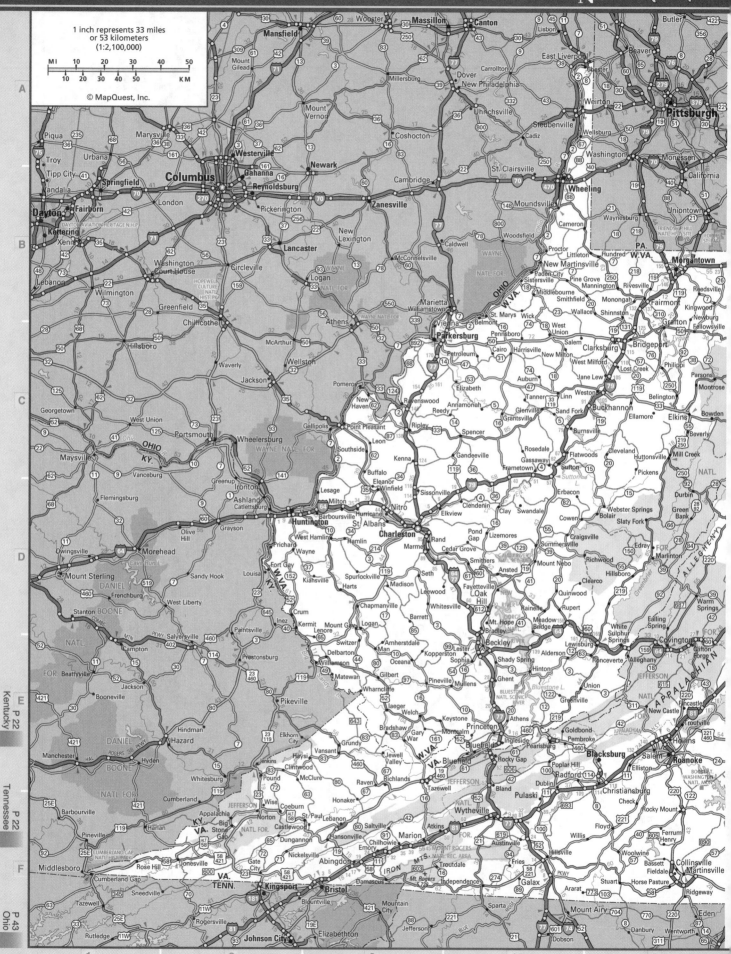

1 inch represents 33 miles
or 53 kilometers
(1:2,100,000)

MI   10   20   30   40   50
10 20 30 40 50   KM

© MapQuest, Inc.

A

B

C

D

E

F

1   2   3   4   5

Columbus
Dayton
Pittsburgh
Wheeling
Morgantown
Parkersburg
Clarksburg
Charleston
Huntington
Beckley
Bluefield
Roanoke
Johnson City
Kingsport
Bristol

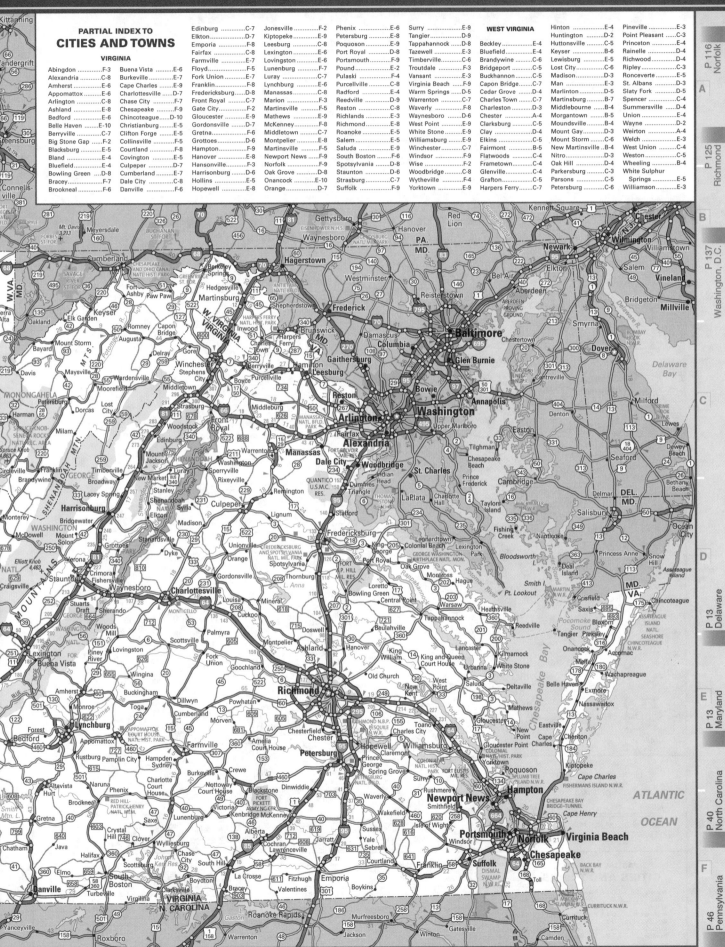

N

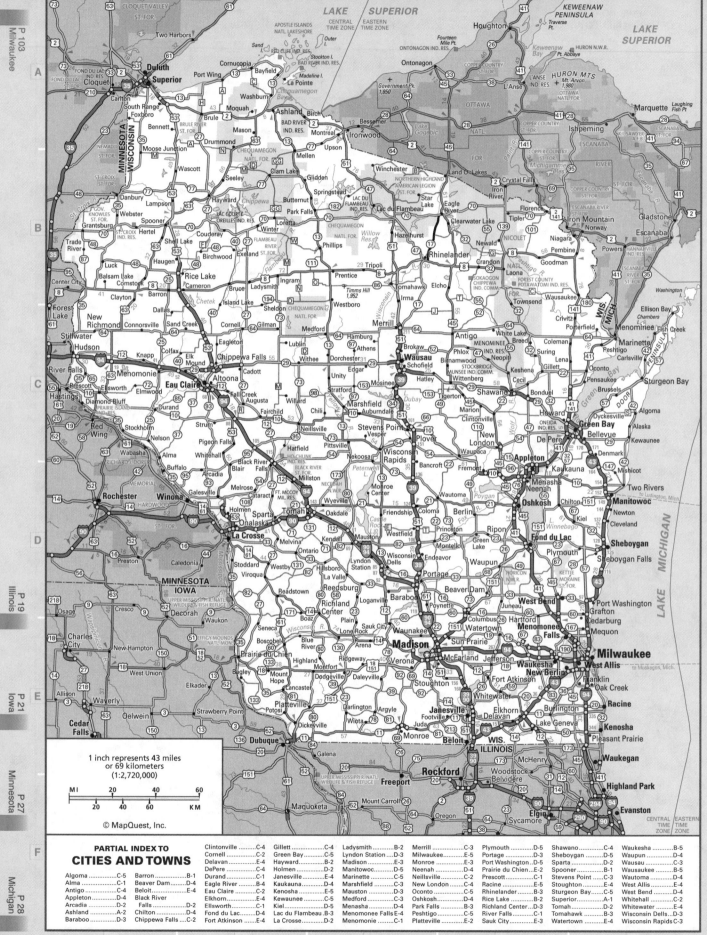

LAKE SUPERIOR

KEWEENAW PENINSULA

MINNESOTA / WISCONSIN

MINNESOTA / IOWA

WIS. MICH.

LAKE MICHIGAN

WIS. ILLINOIS

1 inch represents 43 miles
or 69 kilometers
(1:2,720,000)

MI 20 40 60
KM 20 40 60

© MapQuest, Inc.

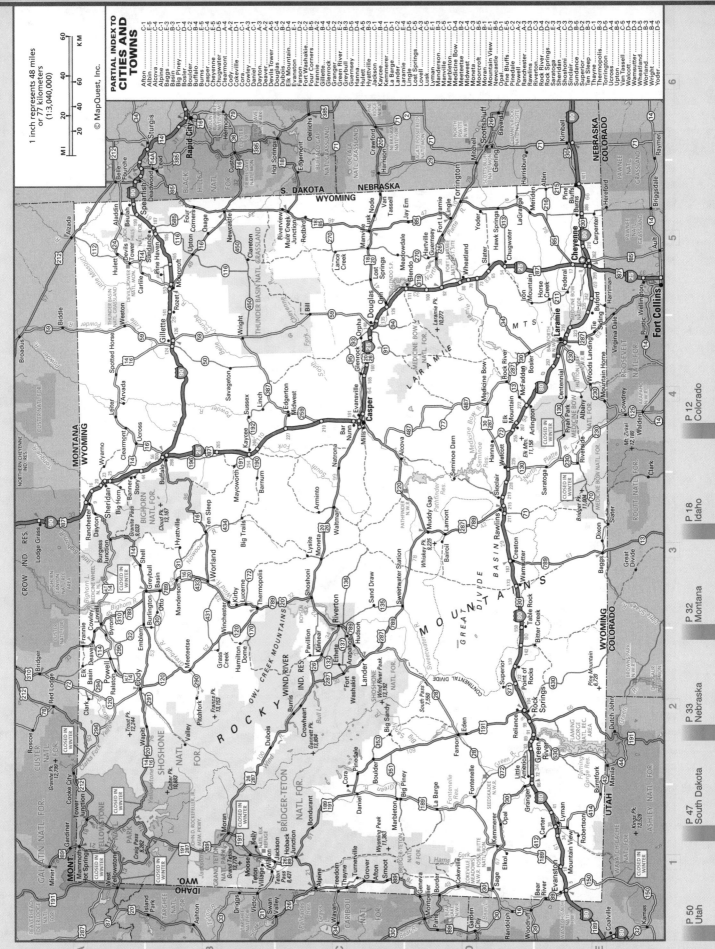

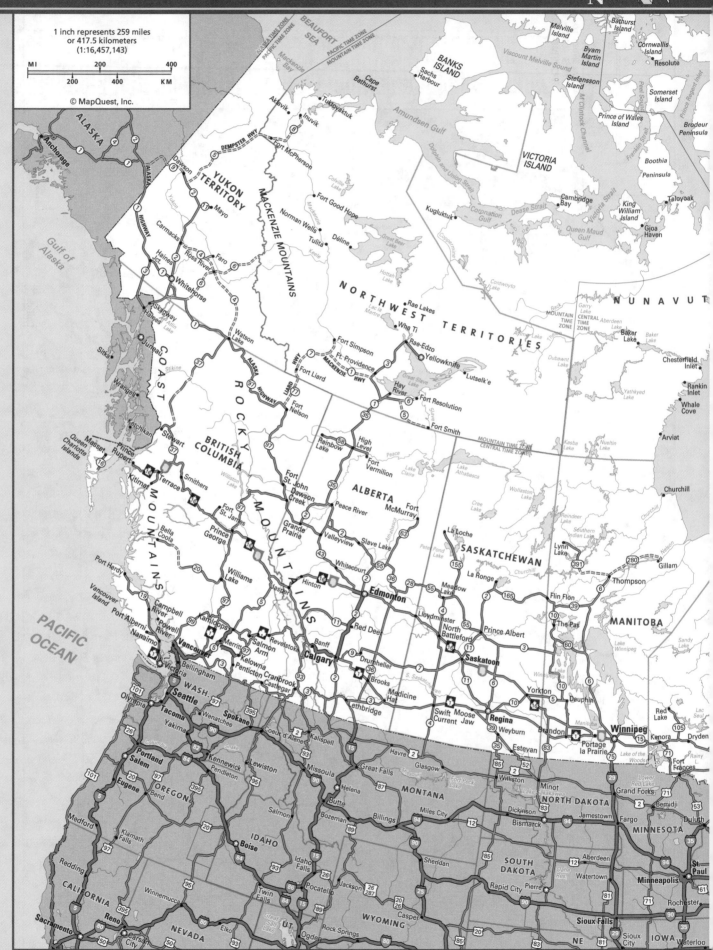

1 inch represents 259 miles
or 417.5 kilometers
(1:16,457,143)

© MapQuest, Inc.

N

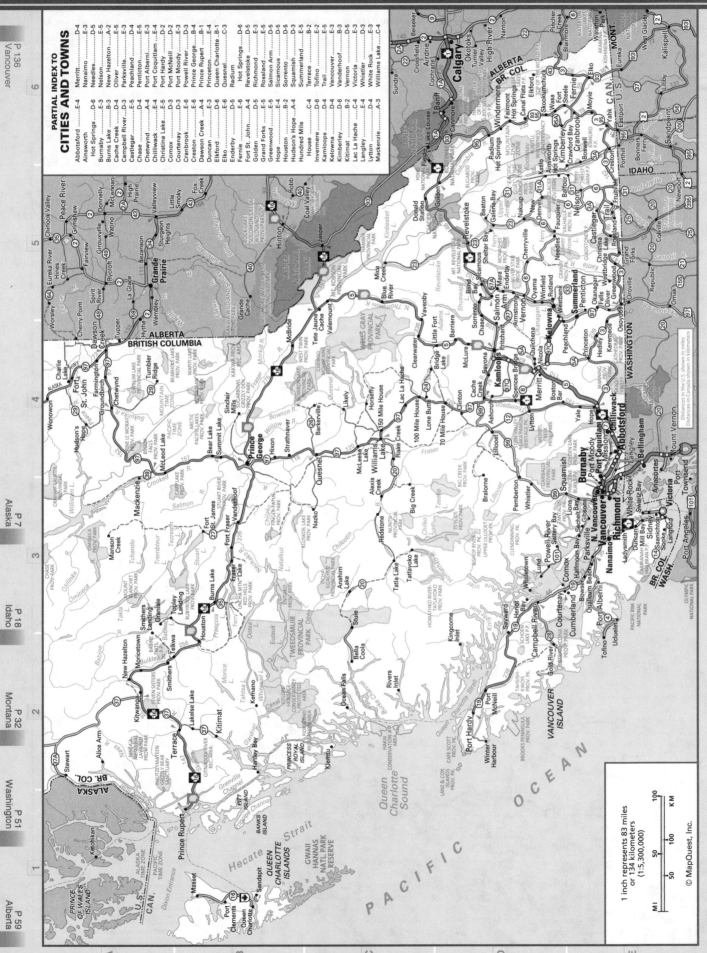

Scale: 1 inch represents 83 miles or 134 kilometers (1:5,300,000)

© MapQuest, Inc.

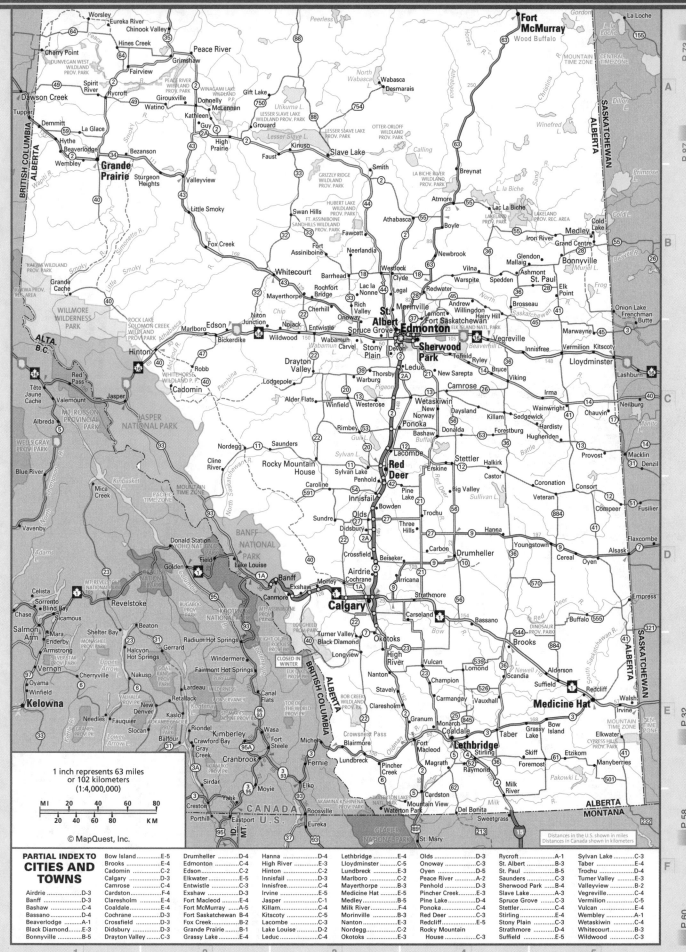

P 73 Calgary
P 87 Edmonton
P 32 Montana
P 58 British Columbia
P 60 Saskatchewan

1 inch represents 63 miles
or 102 kilometers
(1:4,000,000)

MI 20   40   60   80
KM 20   40   60   80

© MapQuest, Inc.

Distances in the U.S. shown in miles
Distances in Canada shown in kilometers

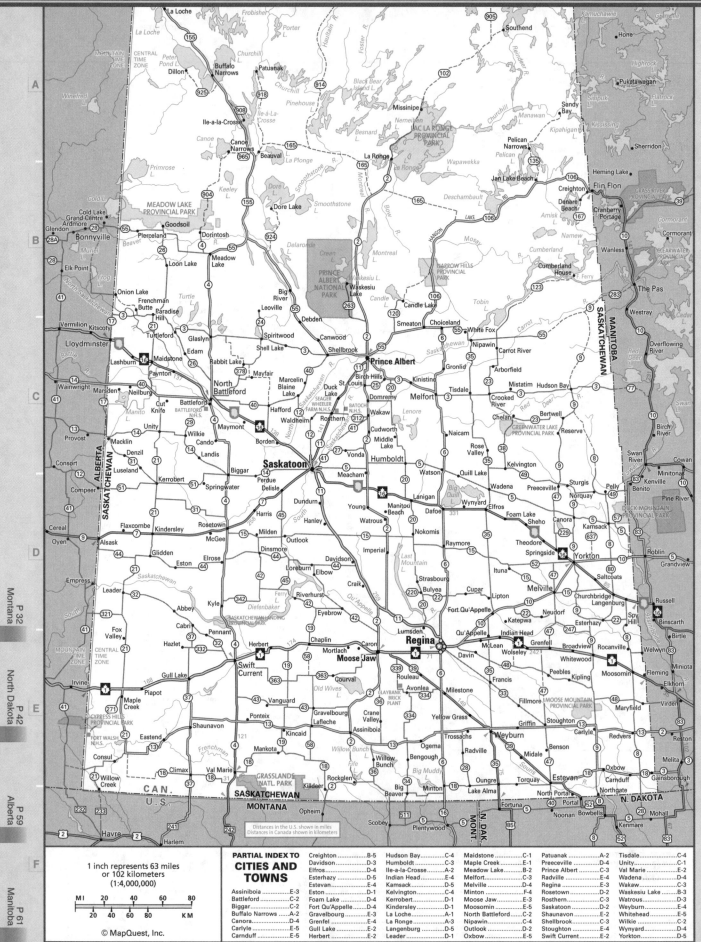

La Loche, Frobisher L., Kamuchawie L., Hone

Porter L., Haultain R., Southend, Pukatawagan

155, Peter Pond L., Dillon, Buffalo Narrows, Patuanak, 914, Black Bear Island L., 102, Missinipe, Reindeer R., Sandy Bay, Sisipuk L., Highrock L., Flatrock L.

MOUNTAIN TIME ZONE, CENTRAL TIME ZONE, 925, 908, 918, Pinehouse, Nemeiben L., Churchill, Manawan L., Kipahigan L., Kississing L., Sherridon

Winefred L., Ile-a-la-Crosse, 965, Beauval, Smoothstone R., La Ronge, LAC LA RONGE PROVINCIAL PARK, Pelican Narrows, 135, Heming Lake, Flin Flon, GRASS RIVER PROVINCIAL PARK

Cold L., Primrose L., Canoe Narrows, Canoe L., La Plonge, 165, 165, Wapawekka L., Pelican L., 106, Jan Lake Beach, Creighton, Denare Beach, 167, Cranberry Portage, Cormorant L.

Cold Lake, Grand Centre, Ardmore, Goodsoil, Pierceland, 904, Dore Lake, 155, Smoothstone, Deschambault Lake, 106, Amisk L., Namew L., Cumberland L., Cormorant

Glendon, 28A, Bonnyville, Beaver R., 26, Meadow Lake, MEADOW LAKE PROVINCIAL PARK, Dorintosh, 924, Delaronde L., PRINCE ALBERT NATIONAL PARK, Waskesiu L., Hanson L., Mossy R., Cumberland House, F Ferry, 283, Wanless, CLEARWATER PROVINCIAL PARK, The Pas

Elk Point, 28, Loon Lake, Big River, Montreal L., NARROW HILLS PROVINCIAL PARK, 123, Tobin L., Red Deer R., Westray, Overflowing River

Vermilion, 41, Frenchman Butte, Paradise Hill, 3, Leoville, 55, Debden, 263, Waskesiu Lake, Candle L., Candle L., Smeaton, Choiceland, 55, White Fox, Nipawin, 35, Carrot River, 9, SASKATCHEWAN, MANITOBA

Kitscoty, 17, Onion Lake, Turtleford, Glaslyn, Shell Lake, Spiritwood, Canwood, Shellbrook, 55, Prince Albert, Birch Hills, Kinistino, Arborfield, Mistatim, Hudson Bay, 77, Swan R.

Lloydminster, 16, Maidstone, Edam, 378, Mayfair, Marcelin, Blaine Lake, St. Louis, Domremy, Melfort, 23, Tisdale, Crooked River, Bertwell, Chelan, Reserve, Birch River

Wainwright, Marsden, Neilburg, Paynton, 131, Rabbit Lake, North Battleford, Hafford, Waldheim, Rosthern, Wakaw, Cudworth, Naicam, Rose Valley, 38, Kelvington, 49, Sturgis, Norquay, Pelly, Swan River, Minitonas, Cowan

Provost, 13, Macklin, Denzil, Unity, Cut Knife, BATTLEFORD N.H.S., 40, Maymont, Borden, 141, Middle Lake, Watson, Quill Lake, Wadena, Preeceville, 47, Kamsack, 637, Benito, Pine River, DUCK MOUNTAIN PROVINCIAL PARK

Consort, 12, Luseland, Kerrobert, Biggar, Perdue, Delisle, Saskatoon, Vonda, Humboldt, Lanigan, 20, Big Quill L., Wynyard, Elfros, Foam Lake, Sheho, Canora, Roblin, Grandview

Compeer, 51, Flaxcombe, Kindersley, Rosetown, Harris, Dundurn, Young, Manitou Beach, Dafoe, 331, Theodore, Springside, 16, Yorkton, 80, Saltcoats, Russell, Binscarth

Cereal, 9, Oyen, Alsask, Glidden, Eston, Elrose, Dinsmore, Milden, Outlook, 15, Imperial, Last Mountain L., Raymore, 15, Ituna, Melville, 15, Churchbridge, Langenburg, 16, Spy Hill, Birtle

Empress, Leader, 32, Abbey, Kyle, Loreburn, Elbow, Davidson, 44, Strasbourg, 220, Bulyea, Cupar, Lipton, 10, Neudorf, Esterhazy, 22, Welwyn, 83

Fox Valley, Cabri, Pennant, Riverhurst, SASKATCHEWAN LANDING PROVINCIAL PARK, Craik, 259, Fort Qu'Appelle, Katepwa, Indian Head, 247, Whitewood, 1, Moosomin, Fleming, Miniota

Hazlet, 332, Herbert, Chaplin, Caron, Regina, McLean, Grenfell, Broadview, Rocanville, Welwyn, 83

Piapot, Maple Creek, CYPRESS HILLS PROVINCIAL PARK, FORT WALSH N.H.S., Gull Lake, Swift Current, 363, Mortlach, Moose Jaw, 71, Davin, Wolseley, 242, Peebles, Kipling, MOOSE MOUNTAIN PROVINCIAL PARK, Maryfield, Virden, Elkhorn

Irvine, 271, Vanguard, Ponteix, Courval, Old Wives L., 339, Rouleau, Avonlea, 334, Francis, Fillmore, 48, Reston

Shaunavon, Lafleche, Gravelbourg, Crane Valley, 334, Yellow Grass, Griffin, Stoughton, 13, Carlyle, Redvers, Melita

Eastend, Kincaid, Mankota, Assiniboia, Ogema, Radville, Midale, Benson, Carnduff, Gainsborough

Consul, Val Marie, Fife, Willow Bunch, Bengough, Big Muddy L., 34, Oungre, Weyburn, Estevan, Oxbow, Northgate

Willow Creek, Climax, GRASSLANDS NATL PARK, Killdeer, Rockglen, Big Beaver, Minton, Lake Alma, Torquay, 52, N. DAKOTA

CAN., U.S., SASKATCHEWAN, MONTANA, Opheim, Scobey, Plentywood, N. DAK., MONT., Noonan, Bowbells, Mohall, Kenmare

232, 233, Havre, Harlem, 2, 241, 242, 511, 16, 85, Fortuna, 40, Portal

© MapQuest, Inc.

1 inch represents 63 miles or 102 kilometers (1:4,000,000)

MI 20 40 60 80
20 40 60 80 KM

PARTIAL INDEX TO CITIES AND TOWNS

Assiniboia	E-3
Battleford	C-2
Biggar	C-2
Buffalo Narrows	A-2
Canora	D-4
Carlyle	E-5
Carnduff	E-5
Creighton	B-5
Davidson	D-3
Elfros	D-4
Esterhazy	D-5
Estevan	E-4
Eston	D-1
Foam Lake	D-4
Fort Qu'Appelle	E-4
Gravelbourg	E-3
Grenfel	E-4
Gull Lake	E-2
Herbert	E-2
Hudson Bay	C-4
Humboldt	C-3
Ile-a-la-Crosse	A-2
Indian Head	E-4
Kamsack	D-5
Kelvington	C-4
Kerrobert	D-1
Kindersley	D-1
La Loche	A-1
La Ronge	A-3
Langenburg	D-5
Leader	D-1
Maidstone	C-1
Maple Creek	E-1
Meadow Lake	B-2
Melfort	C-3
Melville	D-4
Minton	F-4
Moose Jaw	E-3
Moosomin	E-5
North Battleford	C-2
Nipawin	C-4
Outlook	D-2
Oxbow	E-5
Patuanak	A-2
Preeceville	D-4
Prince Albert	C-3
Radville	E-4
Regina	E-3
Rosetown	D-2
Rosthern	C-3
Saskatoon	C-2
Shaunavon	E-2
Shellbrook	C-3
Stoughton	E-4
Swift Current	E-2
Tisdale	C-4
Unity	C-1
Val Marie	E-2
Wadena	D-4
Wakaw	C-3
Waskesiu Lake	B-3
Watrous	D-3
Weyburn	E-4
Whitehead	E-5
Wilkie	C-2
Wynyard	D-4
Yorkton	D-5

Distances in the U.S. shown in miles
Distances in Canada shown in kilometers

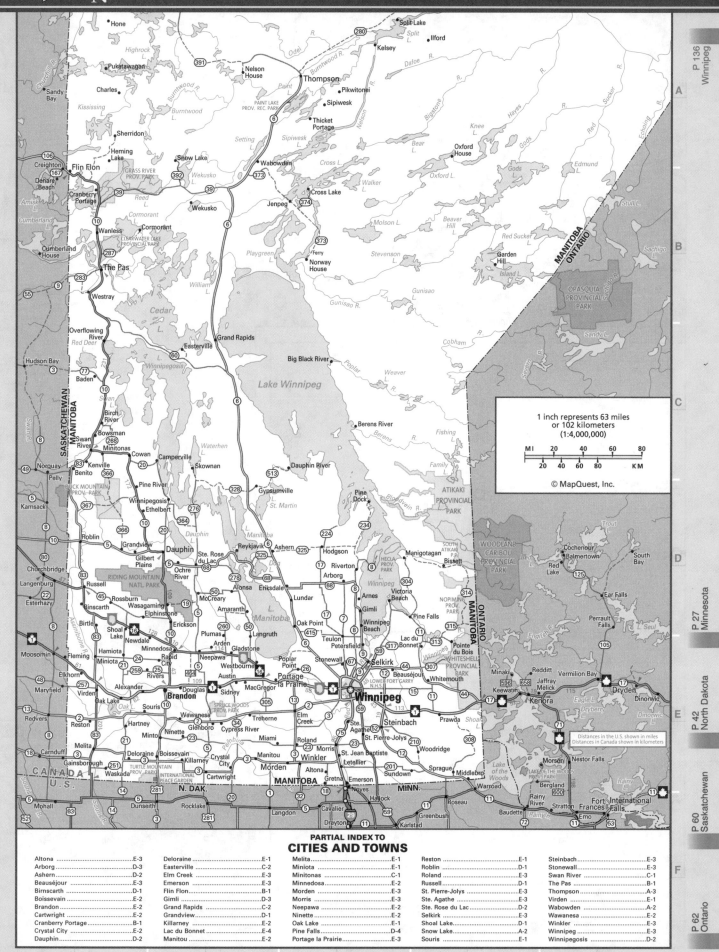

PARTIAL INDEX TO
CITIES AND TOWNS

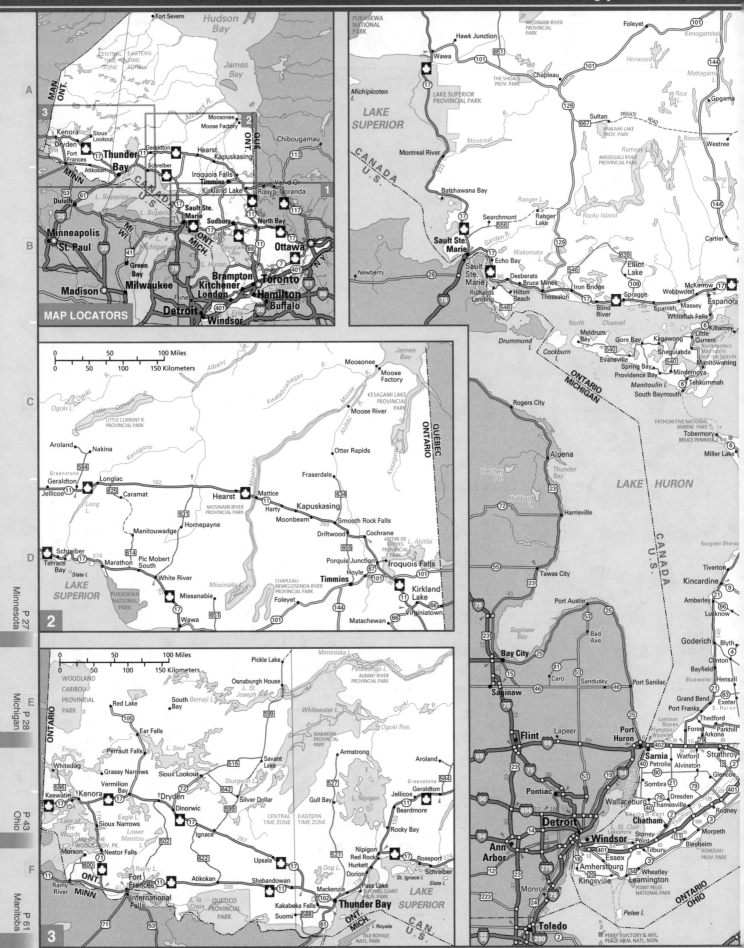

MAP LOCATORS

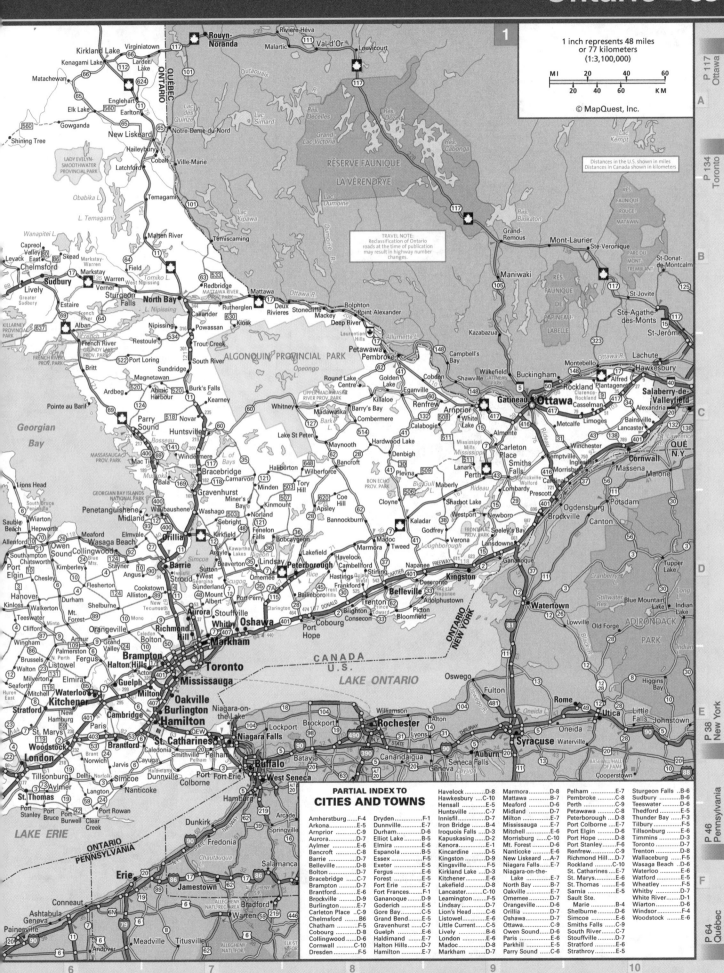

1 inch represents 48 miles
or 77 kilometers
(1:3,100,000)

MI 20 40 60
KM 20 40 60

© MapQuest, Inc.

Distances in the U.S. shown in miles
Distances in Canada shown in kilometers

TRAVEL NOTE:
Reclassification of Ontario
roads at the time of publication
may result in highway number
changes.

PARTIAL INDEX TO
CITIES AND TOWNS

Amherstburg.........F-4	Havelock.............D-8
Arkona...............E-5	Hawkesbury ...C-10
Arnprior.............C-9	Hensall..............E-5
Aurora...............D-7	Huntsville...........C-7
Aylmer E-6	Innisfil..............D-7
Bancroft.............C-8	Iron Bridge B-4
Barrie...............D-7	Iroquois Falls.......D-3
Belleville...........D-8	Kapuskasing.........E-1
Bolton...............D-7	Kenora...............E-1
Bracebridge C-7	Kincardine..........D-5
Brampton............D-7	Kingston.............D-9
Brantford............E-6	Kingsville...........F-5
Brockville...........C-9	Kirkland Lake.......D-3
Burlington E-7	Kitchener............E-6
Carleton Place.......C-9	Lakefield............D-8
Chelmsford..........B6	Lancaster............C-10
Chatham.............F-5	Leamington..........F-5
Cobourg.............D-8	Lindsay..............D-7
Collingwood.........D-6	Lion's Head C-6
Cornwall.............C-10	Listowel.............E-6
Dresden F-5	Little Current........C-5
Dryden...............F-1	Lively...............B-6
Dunnville............E-7	London...............E-6
Durham..............D-6	Madoc...............D-8
Elliot Lake..........B-5	Markham.............D-7
Elmira...............E-6	Marmora............D-8
Espanola.............B-5	Mattawa.............B-7
Essex...............F-5	Meaford.............D-6
Exeter...............E-5	Midland.............D-7
Fergus...............E-6	Milton...............E-7
Forest................E-5	Mississauga.........E-7
Fort Erie............E-7	Mitchell.............E-6
Fort Frances.........F-1	Morrisburg..........C-10
Gananoque...........D-9	Mt. Forest...........D-6
Goderich.............E-5	Nanticoke...........E-7
Gore Bay.............C-5	New Liskeard........A-7
Guelph...............E-6	Niagara Falls.......E-7
Haldimand...........E-7	Niagara-on-the-
Halton Hills.........D-7	Lake................E-7
Hamilton.............E-7	North Bay...........B-7
	Oakville.............E-7
	Omemee.............D-7
	Orangeville..........D-7
	Orillia...............D-7
	Oshawa..............D-7
	Ottawa..............C-9
	Owen Sound.........D-6
	Paris................E-6
	Parkhill.............E-5
	Parry Sound C-6

Marmora..........D-8	Pelham..............E-7
Mattawa..........B-7	Pembroke............C-8
Meaford...........D-6	Perth................C-9
Midland...........D-7	Petawawa...........C-8
Milton.............E-7	Peterborough........D-8
Mississauga........E-7	Port Colborne.......E-7
Mitchell...........E-6	Port Elgin...........D-6
Morrisburg.........C-10	Port Hope...........D-8
Mt. Forest.........D-6	Port Stanley.........F-6
Nanticoke..........E-7	Renfrew..............C-9
New Liskeard.......A-7	Richmond Hill.......D-7
Niagara Falls......E-7	Rockland............C-10
Niagara-on-the-	St. Catharines.......E-7
Lake...............E-7	St. Marys............E-6
North Bay..........B-7	St. Thomas..........E-6
Oakville............E-7	Sarnia...............E-5
Omemee............D-7	Sault Ste.
Orangeville.........D-7	Marie................B-4
Orillia..............D-7	Shelburne...........D-6
Oshawa.............E-6	Simcoe..............E-6
Ottawa.............C-9	Smiths Falls.........C-9
Owen Sound........D-6	South River..........C-7
Paris...............E-6	Stouffville..........D-7
Parkhill............E-5	Stratford............E-6
Parry Sound C-6	Strathroy............E-5

Sturgeon Falls B-6
Sudbury.............B-6
Teeswater...........D-6
Thedford............E-5
Thunder Bay........F-3
Tilbury..............F-5
Tillsonburg..........E-6
Timmins.............D-3
Toronto..............D-7
Trenton..............D-8
Wallaceburg.........F-5
Wasaga Beach D-6
Waterloo.............E-6
Watford..............E-5
Wheatley............F-5
Whitby...............D-7
White River..........D-1
Wiarton..............D-6
Windsor..............F-4
Woodstock...........E-6

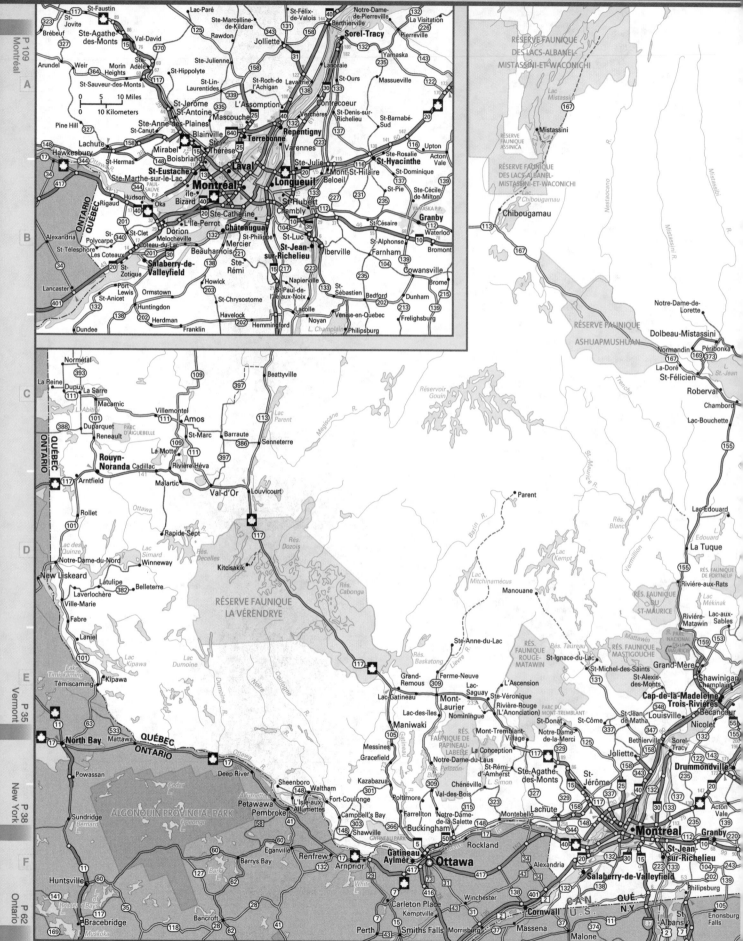

P 109
Montréal

P 35
Vermont

P 38
New York

P 62
Ontario

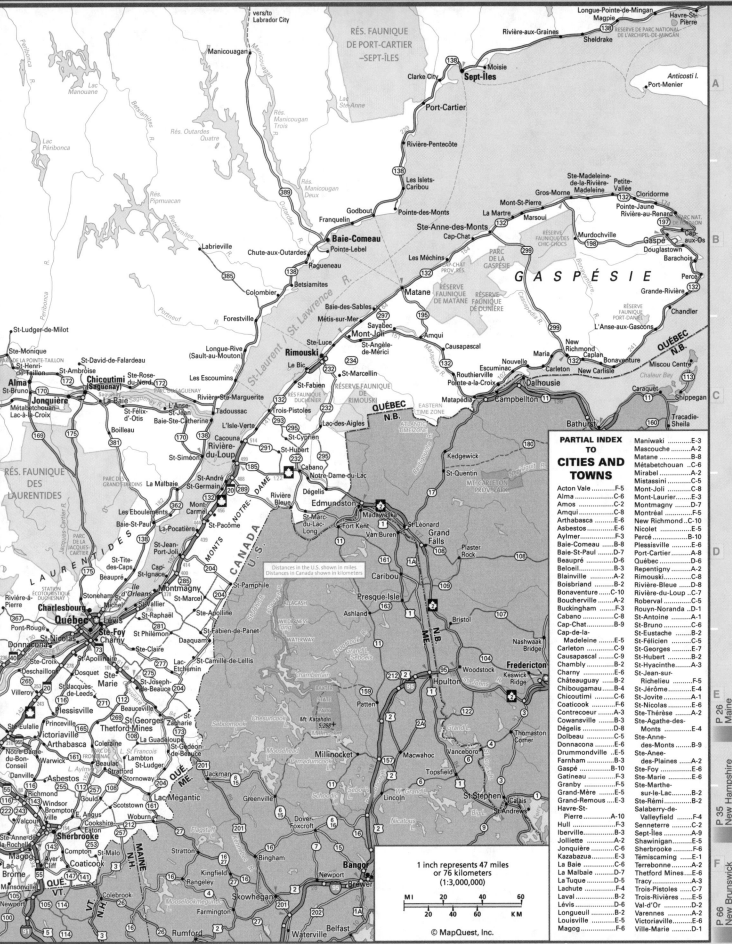

1 inch represents 47 miles
or 76 kilometers
(1:3,000,000)

© MapQuest, Inc.

P 26 Maine

P 35 New Hampshire

P 66 New Brunswick

© MapQuest, Inc.

1 inch represents 51 miles
or 83 kilometers
(1:3,250,000)

MI 20 40 60
20 40 60 KM

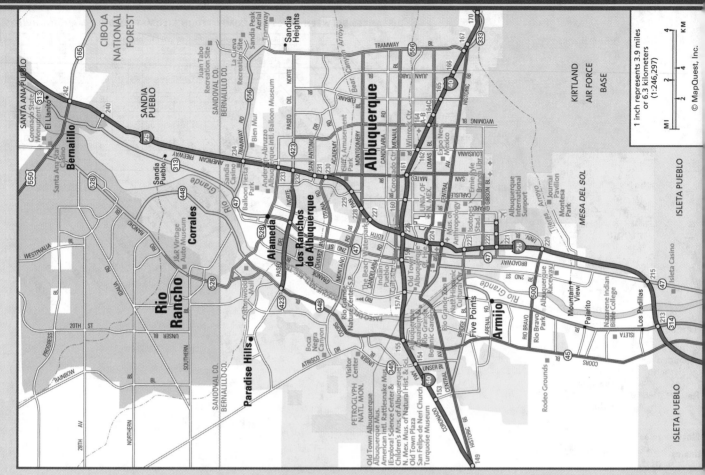

1 inch represents 3.9 miles
or 6.3 kilometers
(1:246,297)

© MapQuest, Inc.

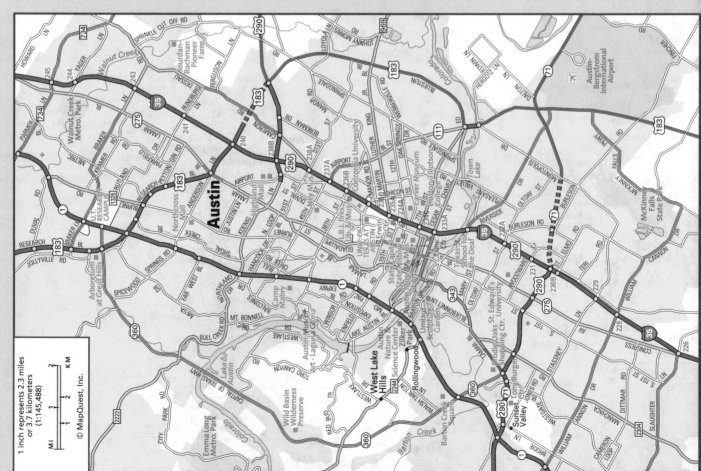

1 inch represents 2.3 miles
or 3.7 kilometers
(1:145,488)

© MapQuest, Inc.

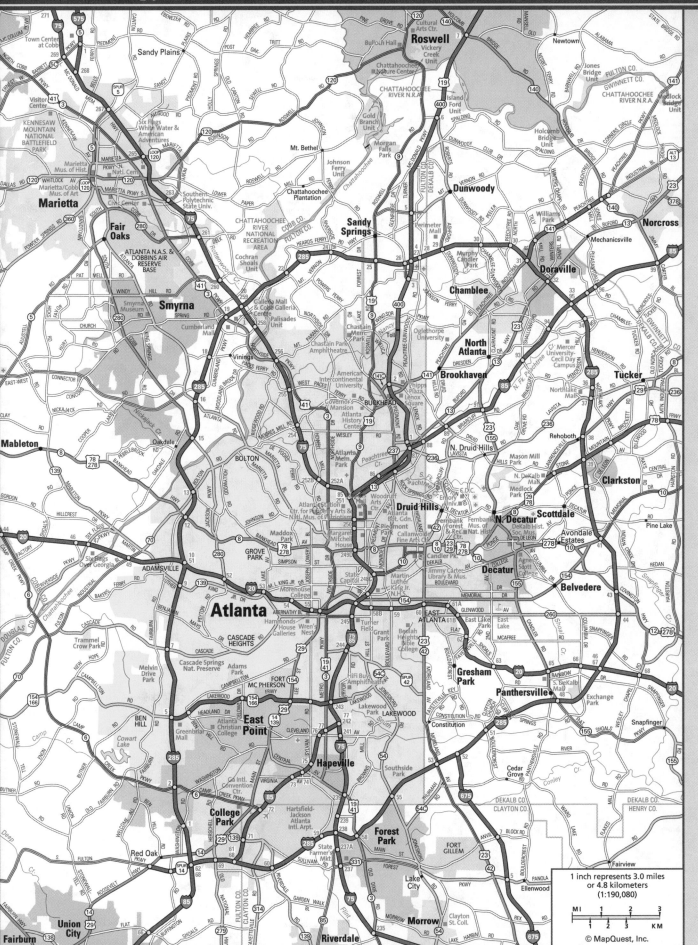

1 inch represents 3.0 miles
or 4.8 kilometers
(1:190,080)

© MapQuest, Inc.

1 inch represents 3.0 miles
or 4.8 kilometers
(1:190,080)

© MapQuest, Inc.

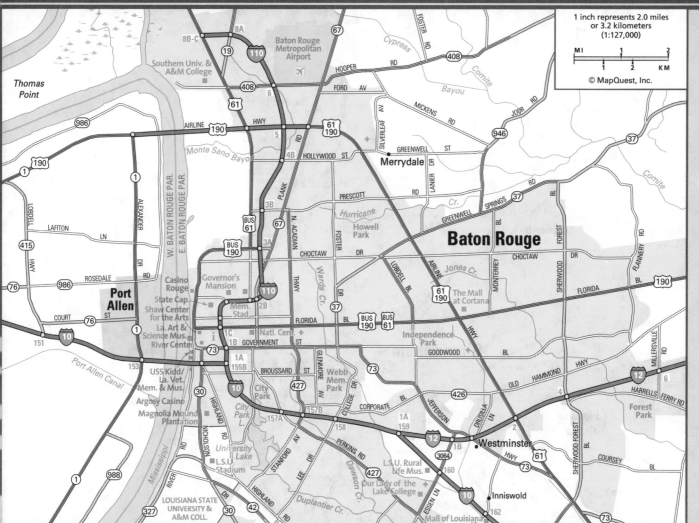

1 inch represents 2.0 miles
or 3.2 kilometers
(1:127,000)
© MapQuest, Inc.

Thomas
Point

Southern Univ. &
A&M College

Baton Rouge
Metropolitan
Airport

Merrydale

Baton Rouge

Port
Allen

Casino
Rouge
State Cap.
Shaw Center
for the Arts
La. Art &
Science Mus.
River Center

Governor's
Mansion

Mem.
Stad.

Natl. Cen.

The Mall
at Cortana

Independence
Park

Goodwood

USS Kidd/
La. Vet.
Mem. & Mus.

Argosy Casino

Magnolia Mound
Plantation

City Park

City
Park
L.

Webb
Mem.
Park

Westminster

University
Lake

L.S.U.
Stadium

L.S.U. Rural
Life Mus.

Our Lady of
the Lake College

Inniswold

LOUISIANA STATE
UNIVERSITY &
A&M COLL.

Mall of Louisiana

Forest
Park

Calgary

Nose
Hill Park

Calgary
Intl. Airport

Deerfoot
Mall

Aero Space
Mus.

Market
Mall

Univ. of
Calgary

McMahon
Stadium

Canada
Olympic
Park

OLD BANFF

COACH RD

Edworthy
Park

Naval Mus.
of Alta.

S.A.I.T.
TELUS
Convention
Centre
Glenbow
Mus.
Zoo
Calgary
Tower
Stampede Park
& Saddledome

Sunridge Mall

Bow Habitat Station

River
Park

Mus. of the
Regiments

Chinook
Ctr.

Heritage
Park

Glenmore Park

Sarcee Military Reserve

Glenmore
Res.

SARCEE INDIAN
RESERVE NO. 145

1 inch represents 4.5 miles
or 7.3 kilometers
(1:285,405)

© MapQuest, Inc.

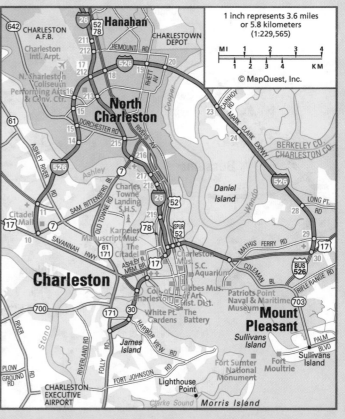

CHARLESTON
A.F.B.

Charleston
Intl. Arpt.

Hanahan

CHARLESTOWN
DEPOT

N. Charleston
Coliseum
Performing Arts
& Conv. Ctr.

**North
Charleston**

Daniel
Island

BERKELEY CO.
CHARLESTON CO.

Charles
Towne
Landing
S.H.S.

Citadel
Mall

Karpeles
Manuscript Mus.

The
Citadel

Charleston

Charleston
Mus.

S.C.
Aquarium

Col. of
Charleston
Hist. Dist.

Gibbes Mus.
of Art

White Pt.
Gardens
The
Battery

Patriots Point
Naval & Maritime
Museum

**Mount
Pleasant**

Sullivans
Island

James
Island

Fort Johnson

Fort
Moultrie

CHARLESTON
EXECUTIVE
AIRPORT

Lighthouse
Point

Fort Sumter
National
Monument

Morris Island

Clarke Sound

1 inch represents 3.6 miles
or 5.8 kilometers
(1:229,565)

© MapQuest, Inc.

P 25 Louisiana
P 40 South Carolina
P 59 Alberta

N

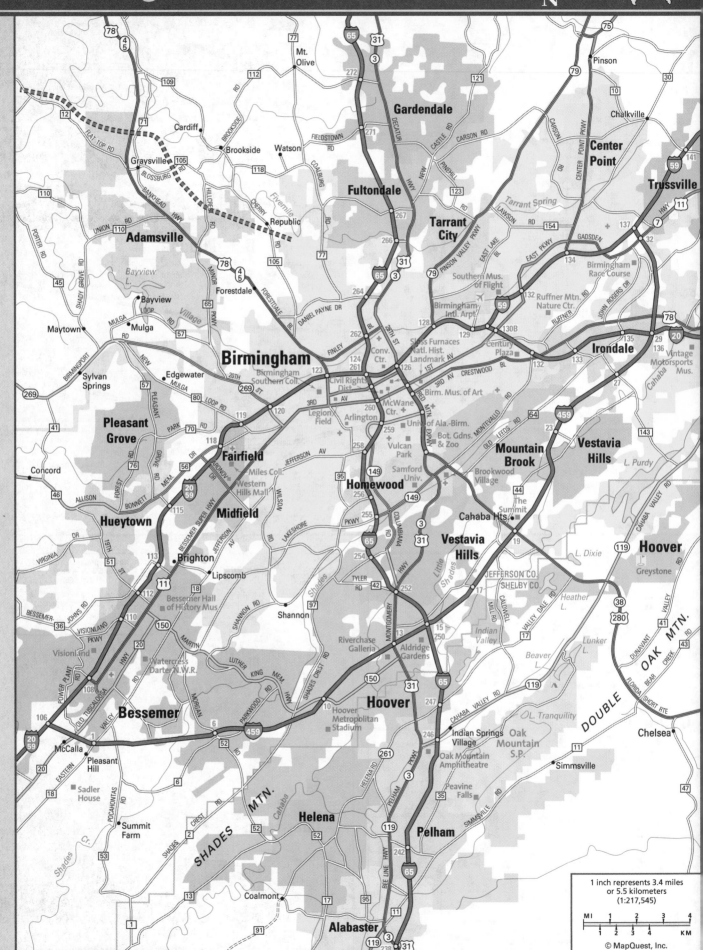

1 inch represents 3.4 miles
or 5.5 kilometers
(1:217,545)

MI 1   2   3   4
KM 1 2 3 4

© MapQuest, Inc.

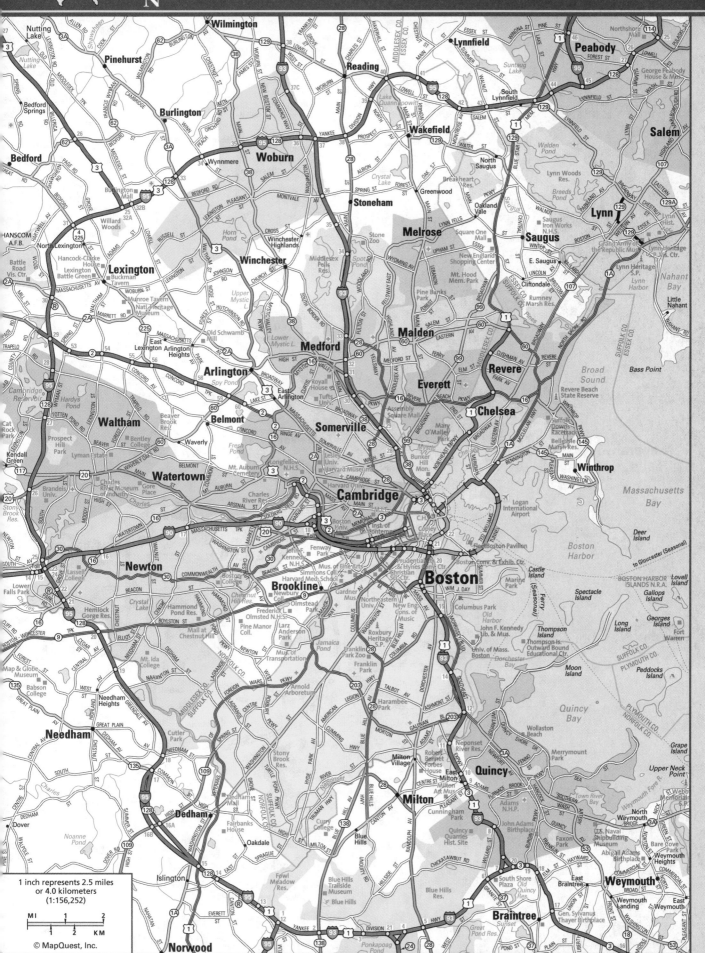

1 inch represents 2.5 miles
or 4.0 kilometers
(1:156,252)

© MapQuest, Inc.

P 14
Massachusetts

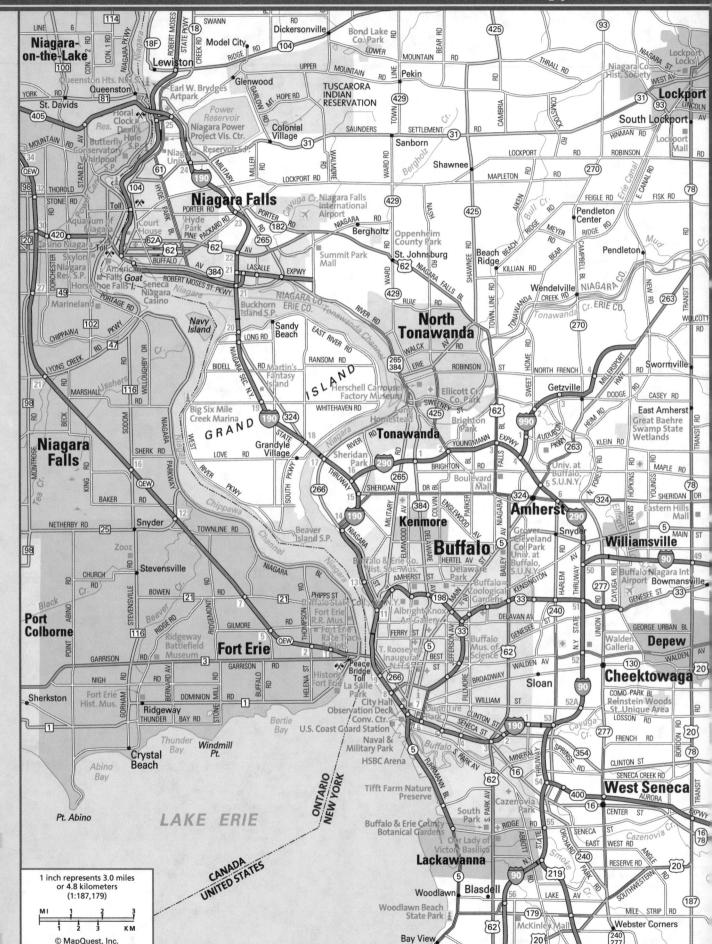

Niagara-on-the-Lake

Lewiston

Queenston

St. Davids

Niagara Falls

Niagara Falls

Port Colborne

Fort Erie

Crystal Beach

Pt. Abino

LAKE ERIE

TUSCARORA INDIAN RESERVATION

Sanborn

Shawnee

North Tonawanda

Tonawanda

Kenmore

Buffalo

Lackawanna

Blasdell

Amherst

Williamsville

Depew

Cheektowaga

West Seneca

Lockport

South Lockport

Pendleton Center

Pendleton

Wendelville

Getzville

East Amherst

1 inch represents 3.0 miles
or 4.8 kilometers
(1:187,179)

© MapQuest, Inc.

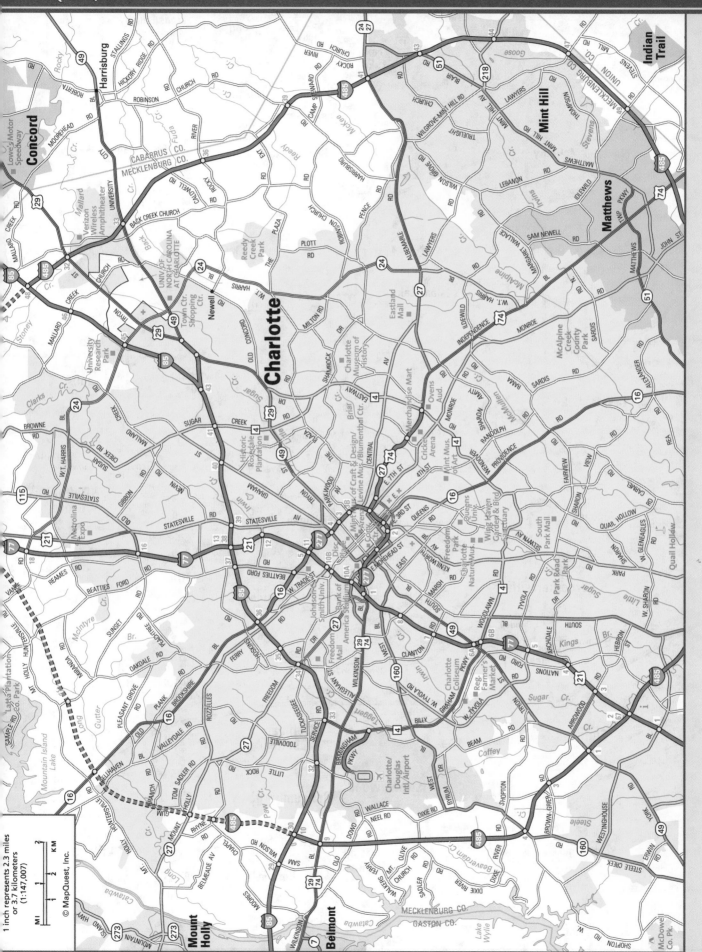

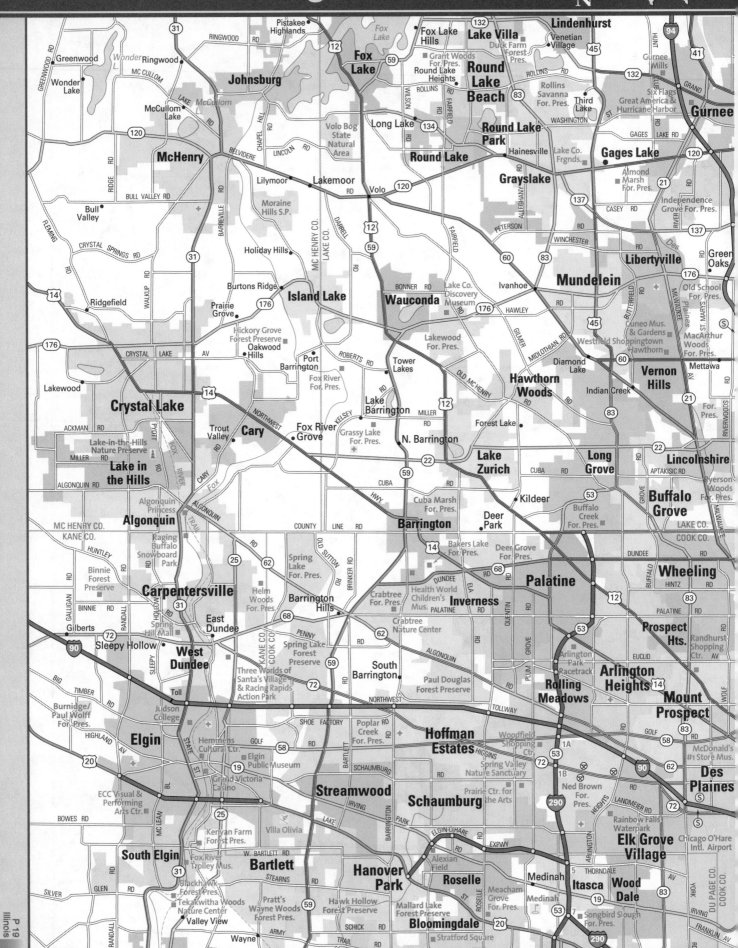

N

1 inch represents 3.3 miles
or 5.3 kilometers
(1:209,801)

MI   4

2   2   4

KM

© MapQuest, Inc.

LAKE

MICHIGAN

Chicago

Franklin
Park
River
Grove
Elmwood
Park
BELMONT
Northlake
The
Brickyard
De Paul
Univ.
Peggy Notebaert Nature Center
Lincoln Park Zoo
Facets Multimedia
Maywood Park
Race Track
Concordia Univ.
Stone
Park
Melrose Park
Oak Park
Frank Lloyd
Wright Home
Polish Mus.
of America
International Mus. of Surgical Science
Chicago Historical Society
Bellwood
River
Forest
Forest Park
Garfield
Park
Ukrainian
Natl. Mus.
Mus. of
Holography
Sears
Tower
Hillside
Maywood
United Center
Broadview
Berwyn
Eisenhower
Mexican
Fine Arts
Ctr. Mus.
Westchester
North Riverside
Mall
Roosevelt
Cermak
La
Grange
Park
Brookfield
Zoo
North Riverside
Cicero
Riverside
Lyons
Brookfield
Illinois Institute
of Technology
Western
Sprs.
La
Grange
McCook
Hawthorne
Race Course
Stickney
Forest
View
U.S. Cellular
Field
Douglas Tomb
State Historic Site
DuSable Museum of
African-American History
Chicago Portage
N.H.S.
Chicago Motor
Speedway at
Sportsman's Park
University
of Chicago
Museum of
Science & Industry
Countryside
Summit
Chicago
Midway
Intl. Airport
Washington
Park
Jackson
Park
Indian
Head
Park
Hodgkins
Bedford
Park
Balzekas Museum of
Lithuanian
Culture
Marquette
Justice
Chicago
Fire MLS
Stadium (u.c.)
Marquette
Park
Ford City
Shopping
Center
Willow
Sprs.
Burbank
Little Red
School-Hse.
Nature Ctr.
Hickory
Hills
Bridgeview
Westfield
Shoppingtown
Chicago Ridge
Hometown
Evergreen
Park
Palos Hills
Chicago
Ridge
Oak Lawn
St. Xavier
University
Beverly Hills/
Morgan Park
Historic Dist.
Beverly Arts Ctr.
Chicago State
Univ.
The Plaza
Palos
Forest
Pres.
Worth
Merrionette
Park
Pullman Hist.
District
William W.
Powers
Cons. Area
Horseshoe
Casino
Palos
Park
Alsip
Blue
Island
Calumet
Park
Whiting
The Center
Childrens Farm
Palos
Heights
L.
Calumet
Wolf
Lake
Harrah's
East Chicago
Majestic
Star
Casino &
Trump
Casino
McGinnis
Slough
For.
Pres.
Crestwood
Forest
Pres.
Hawkinson Ford Field
Robbins
Posen
Riverdale
Burnham
East
Chicago
Orland
Square
Midlothian
Chicago
Gaelic Park
Dixmoor
Dolton
Calumet
City
Gary
Regional
Airport
Orland Park
Oak
Forest
Harvey
Phoenix
Sand Ridge
Nature Ctr.
Gibson Woods
Nature Pres.
For.
Pres.
Markham
Hazel
Crest
S. Holland
River Oaks
Center
Hammond
Purdue Univ.
Calumet
Orland
Hills
Tinley
Park
Midwest
Carver's Mus.
Thornton
E. Hazel
Crest
Lansing
Highland
Munster
Griffith
Mokena
Arbury
Hills
Tweeter
Center
Chicago
South Green
Belt
Country
Club
Hills
Homewood
Flossmoor
Glenwood
For.
Pres.
Odyssey
Fun World
Forest Pres.
Flossmoor
Commons
Dyer
Hoosier
Prairie State
Nature Pres.
Hickory
Creek
For. Pres.
Olympia
Fields
Chicago Heights
Lynwood
Matteson
Olympia
Fields
Park
Forest
S. Chicago
Heights
Ford Heights
Frankfort
Lincoln
Mall
Freedom
Hall
S. Chicago
Heights
Sauk
Village
Schererville
Richton Park
Sauk Trail
Forest Preserve
Sauk Trail
Woods
For. Pres.
Steger
Plum
Creek
For.
Pres.
Crete

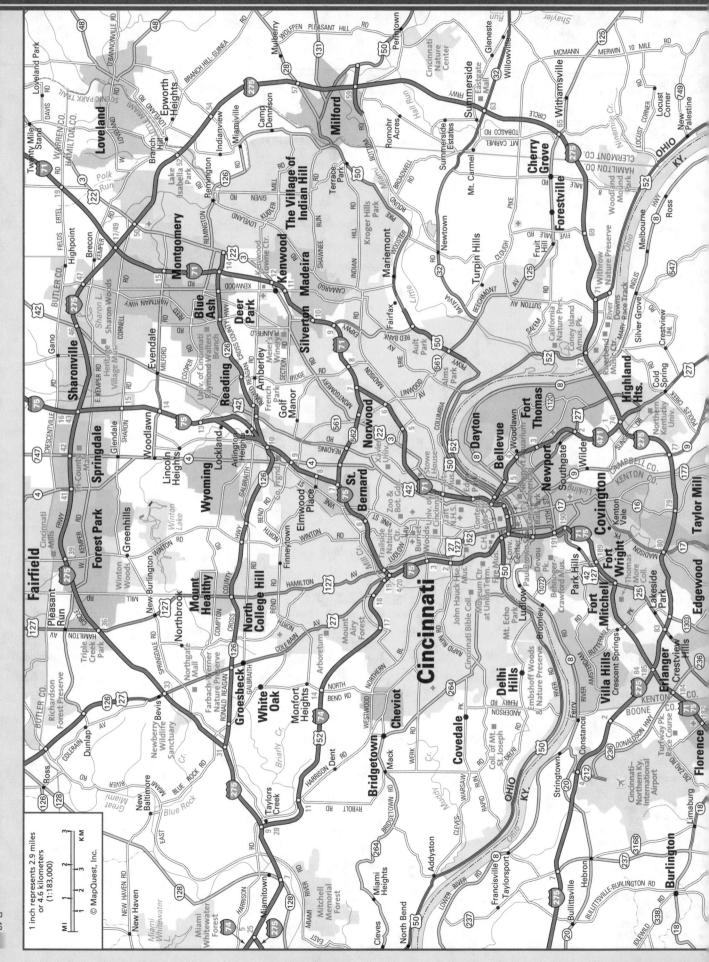

1 inch represents 2.9 miles
or 4.6 kilometers
(1:183,000)

© MapQuest, Inc.

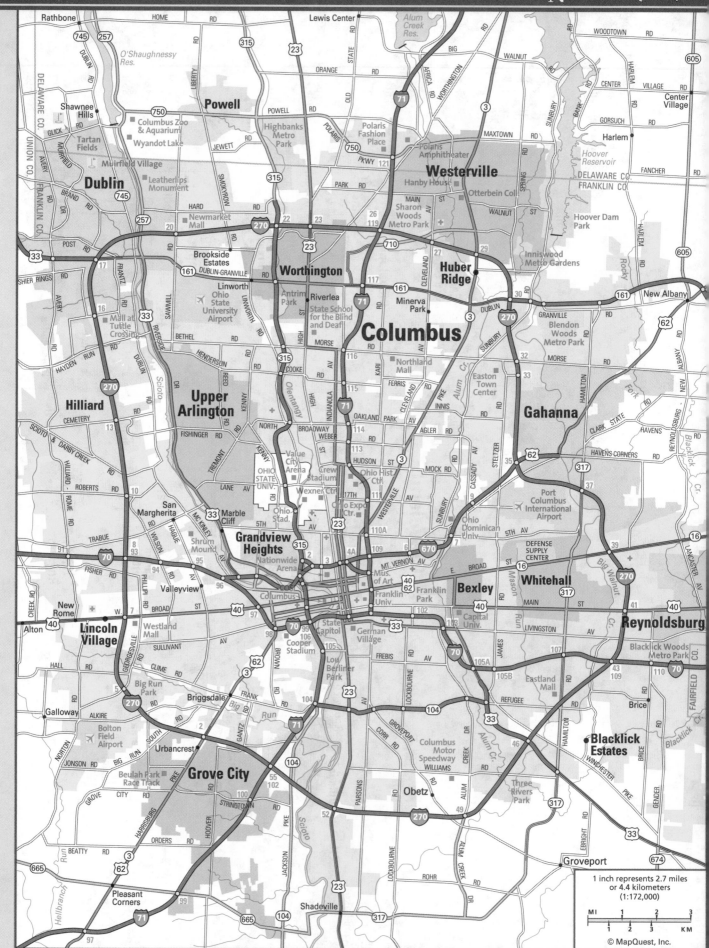

Rathbone

745 257

HOME RD

Lewis Center

Alum
Creek
Res.

WOODTOWN RD

605

O'Shaughnessy
Res.

315

23

STATE RD

BIG

WALNUT

HARLEM RD

AFRICA RD

WORTHINGTON RD

CENTER

VILLAGE RD

Center
Village

Powell

750

Columbus Zoo
& Aquarium

Wyandot Lake

Highbanks
Metro
Park

POLARIS

ORANGE RD

POWELL RD

LIBERTY RD

OLD STATE RD

MAXTOWN RD

Polaris
Fashion
Place

Polaris
Amphitheater

SUNBURY RD

SPRING RD

GORSUCH RD

FANCHER RD

Harlem

Hoover
Reservoir

**Shawnee
Hills**

DELAWARE CO.

UNION CO.

FRANKLIN CO.

MUIRFIELD DR

GLICK RD

AVERY RD

BRAND RD

Dublin

Tartan
Fields

745

Muirfield Village

Leatherlips
Monument

257

315

JEWETT RD

HARD RD

750 PKWY 121

PARK RD

Westerville

Hanby House

Otterbein Coll.

MAIN ST

Sharon
Woods
Metro Park

WALNUT ST

DELAWARE CO.
FRANKLIN CO.

Hoover Dam
Park

HARLEM RD

605

33

POST RD

Newmarket
Mall

270 20

22 23

26
119

710

27

29

Inniswood
Metro Gardens

ROCKY FORK

SHIER RINGS RD

17

FRANTZ RD

Brookside
Estates

161

DUBLIN-GRANVILLE RD

Worthington

117

161

CLEVELAND AV

30

**Huber
Ridge**

DUBLIN RD

270

GRANVILLE RD

Blendon
Woods
Metro Park

161

New Albany

NEW ALBANY RD

62

33 AVERY RD

16

33

SAWMILL RD

Linworth

Ohio State
University
Airport

LINWORTH RD

Antrim
Park

Riverlea

HIGH ST

Ohio
State School
for the Blind
and Deaf

Minerva
Park

3

Columbus

SUNBURY RD

32

MORSE RD

HAMILTON RD

Mall at
Tuttle
Crossing

BETHEL RD

RD

315

COOKE RD

116

KARL RD

Northland
Mall

33

Easton
Town
Center

Hilliard

HAYDEN RUN RD

DUBLIN RD

RIVERSIDE DR

Scioto

CEMETERY RD

13

KENNY RD

**Upper
Arlington**

HENDERSON RD

REED RD

OLENTANGY

FISHINGER RD

NORTH BROADWAY

WEBER RD

INDIANOLA AV

115

71

FERRIS RD

CLEVELAND AV

PIKE

Alum Cr.

INNIS RD

Gahanna

35

STELZER RD

CASSADY AV

CLARK STATE RD

HAVENS RD

HAVENS CORNERS RD

317

37

SCIOTO & DARBY CREEK RD

HILLIARD -
ROBERTS RD

10

WILSON RD

MCKINLEY RD

HAGUE AV

33

Marble
Cliff

Value
City
Arena

OHIO
STATE
UNIV.

Crew
Stadium

Wexner Ctr.

Ohio
Stad.

114

113

HUDSON ST

Ohio Hist.
Ctr.

MOCK RD

AGLER RD

WESTERVILLE RD

SUNBURY RD

Port
Columbus
International
Airport

Ohio
Dominican
Univ.

5TH AV

DEFENSE
SUPPLY
CENTER

39

16

TRABUE RD

91 70

8
93

94

95

96

San
Margherita

Shrum
Mound

5TH

315

2

4A

109

6

670

7

E. BROAD ST

16

Whitehall

Big Walnut

270

FISHER RD

Valleyview

PHILLIPI RD

Grandview
Heights

Nationwide
Arena

COLS.

Columbus

MT. VERNON AV

Mus.
of Art

40
62

Franklin
Park

Bexley

317

40

Reynoldsburg

**New
Rome**

Alton

40 W. 7

**Lincoln
Village**

GEORGESVILLE RD

BROAD ST

Westland
Mall

SULLIVANT AV

CLIME RD

97

40

62

3

99

98

State
Capitol

70

106

105

Cooper
Stadium

German
Village

105A

Lou
Berliner
Park

FREBIS AV

33

Franklin
Univ.

102

Capital
Univ.

MAIN ST

LIVINGSTON AV

JAMES RD

103

40

107

41

40

Blacklick Woods
Metro Park

43
109

110 70

Eastland
Mall

Brice

**Blacklick
Estates**

BRICE RD

FAIRFIELD CO.

HALL RD

270

Big
Run
Park

ALKIRE RD

FRANK RD

Big Run

104

71

GROVEPORT RD

LOCKBOURNE RD

REFUGEE RD

46

Galloway

NORTON RD

JONSON RD

Bolton
Field
Airport

2

Urbancrest

GANTZ RD

104

Columbus
Motor
Speedway

WILLIAMS RD

WINCHESTER PIKE

Three
Rivers
Park

270

BRICE RD

Grove City

Beulah Park
Race Track

GROVE
CITY RD

HARRISBURG PIKE

ORDERS RD

HOOVER RD

STRINGTOWN RD

55
102

100

52

PARSONS AV

Scioto

JACKSON RD

Obetz

ALUM CREEK DR

49

ALUM CREEK

EBRIGHT RD

317

GENDER RD

33

665

BEATTY RD

62

3

PLEASANT
CORNERS RD

71

99

104

665

23

317

Shadeville

ROHR RD

Groveport

674

Hellbranch Run

97

1 inch represents 2.7 miles
or 4.4 kilometers
(1:172,000)

MI 1 2 3

KM 1 2 3

© MapQuest, Inc.

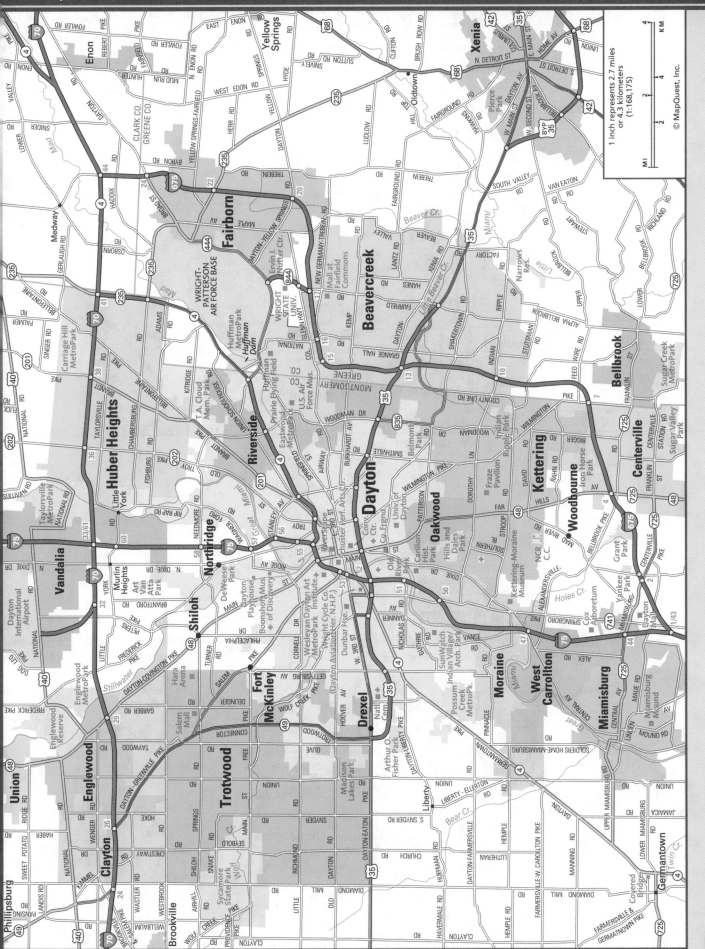

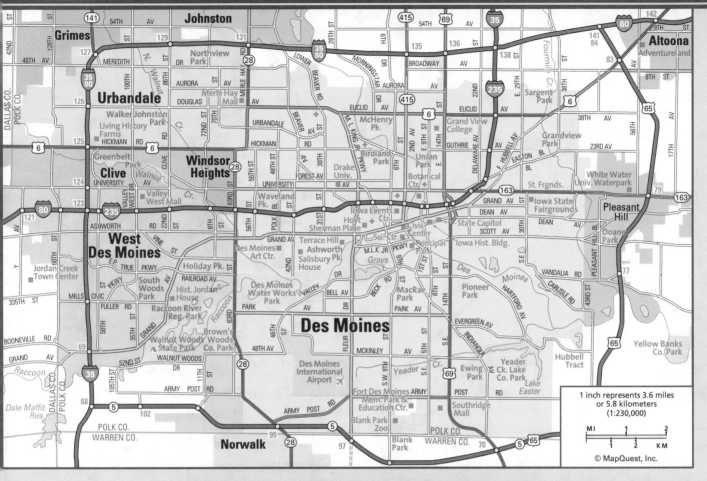

Des Moines

Johnston

Grimes

Altoona
Adventureland

Urbandale

Windsor Heights

Clive

West Des Moines

Pleasant Hill

Norwalk

1 inch represents 3.6 miles
or 5.8 kilometers
(1:230,000)

© MapQuest, Inc.

P 21
Iowa

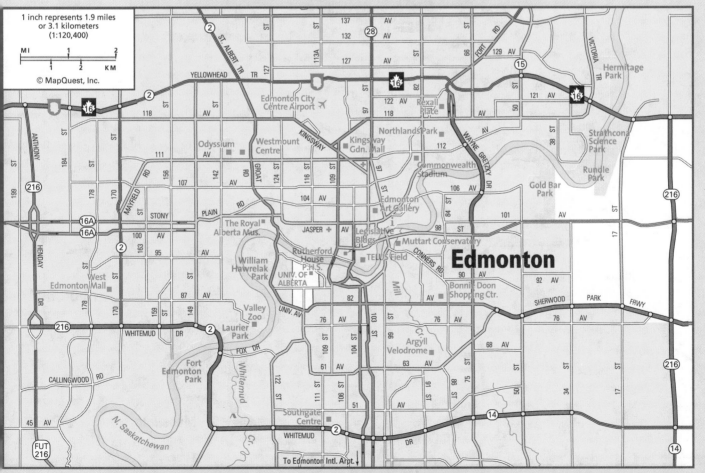

1 inch represents 1.9 miles
or 3.1 kilometers
(1:120,400)

© MapQuest, Inc.

Edmonton

West Edmonton Mall

Fort Edmonton Park

P 59
Alberta

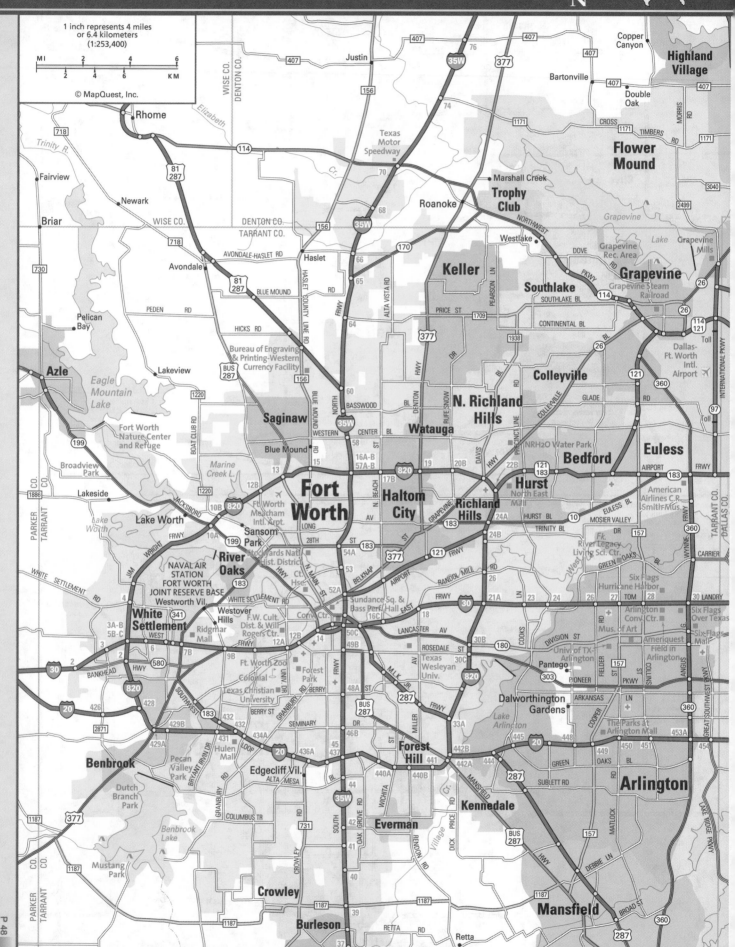

1 inch represents 4 miles
or 6.4 kilometers
(1:253,400)

MI   2   4   6

2   4   6   KM

© MapQuest, Inc.

Rhome

Fairview

Newark

Briar

Azle

Pelican Bay

Lakeview

Avondale

Haslet

WISE CO.
DENTON CO.

DENTON CO.
TARRANT CO.

Eagle Mountain Lake

Broadview Park

Lakeside

Lake Worth

Fort Worth Nature Center and Refuge

Saginaw

Blue Mound

Marine Creek L.

Fort Worth Meacham Intl. Arpt.

Fort Worth

Lake Worth

Sansom Park

River Oaks

NAVAL AIR STATION FORT WORTH JOINT RESERVE BASE Westworth Vil.

Westover Hills

White Settlement

Ridgmar Mall

F.W. Cult. Dist. & Will Rogers Ctr.

Ft. Worth Zoo

Colonial

Texas Christian University

Benbrook

Dutch Branch Park

Pecan Valley Park

Hulen Mall

Edgecliff Vil.

Benbrook Lake

Mustang Park

Crowley

Burleson

Bureau of Engraving & Printing-Western Currency Facility

Haltom City

Richland Hills

Watauga

N. Richland Hills

Keller

Southlake

Colleyville

Westlake

Trophy Club

Roanoke

Marshall Creek

Bedford

Euless

Hurst

NRH2O Water Park

North East Mall

River Legacy Living Sci. Ctr.

Six Flags Hurricane Harbor

Grapevine Rec. Area

Grapevine Lake

Grapevine

Grapevine Steam Railroad

Grapevine Mills

Dallas-Ft. Worth Intl. Airport

American Airlines C.R. Smith Mus.

Mosier Valley

Arlington Conv. Ctr.

Six Flags Over Texas

Ameriquest Field in Arlington

Six Flags Mall

Univ of TX-Arlington

Pantego

Dalworthington Gardens

Lake Arlington

The Parks at Arlington Mall

Arlington

Mus. of Art

Sundance Sq. & Bass Perf. Hall

Conv. Ctr.

Stockyards Natl. Hist. District

Forest Park

Texas Wesleyan Univ.

Forest Hill

Kennedale

Everman

Mansfield

Retta

Justin

Texas Motor Speedway

Bartonville

Double Oak

Copper Canyon

Highland Village

Flower Mound

Rhome

1 inch represents 4.5 miles
or 7.2 kilometers
(1:282,018)

MI 1 2 3 4
1 2 3 4
KM

© MapQuest, Inc.

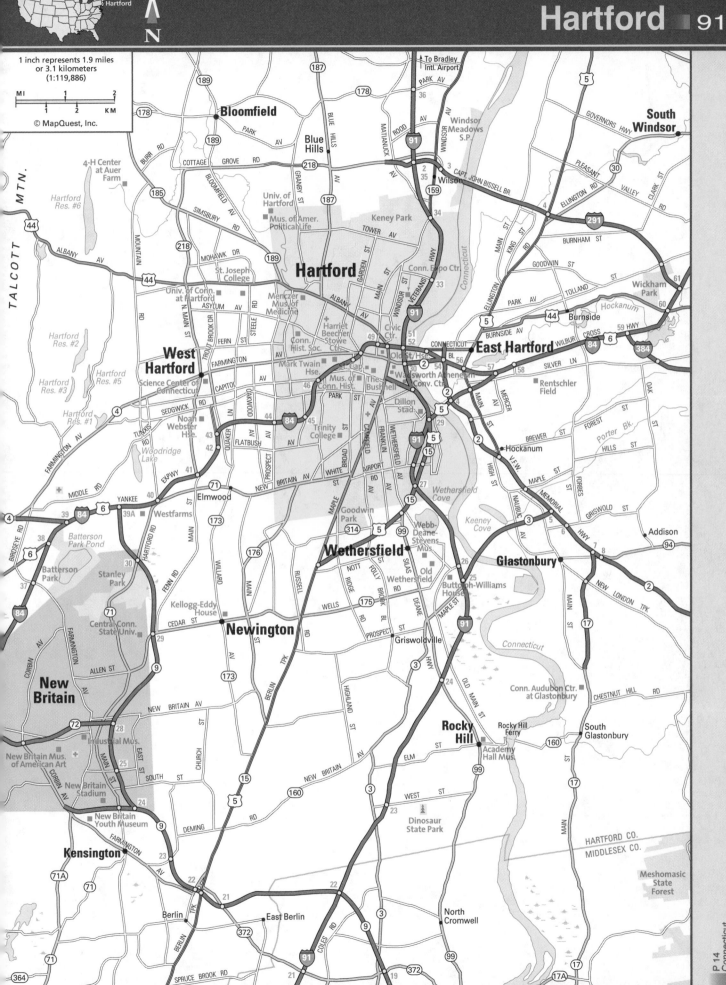

1 inch represents 1.9 miles
or 3.1 kilometers
(1:119,886)

© MapQuest, Inc.

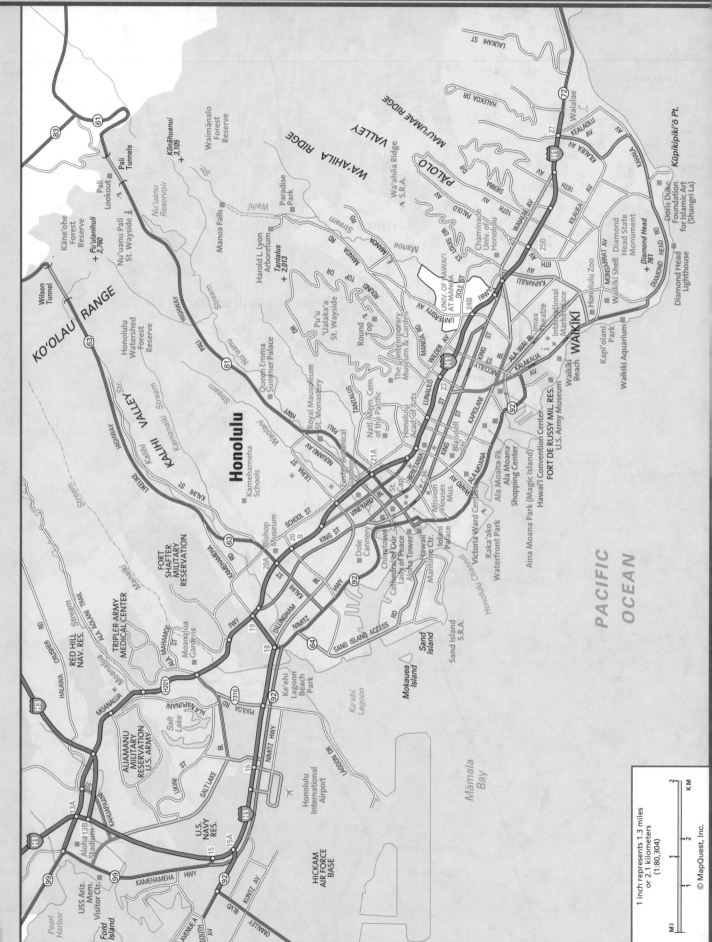

Eagle Village

Zionsville

Carmel

Fishers

334 Patrick Henry Sullivan Mus.

116TH ST

WESTFIELD RD

116TH ST

5

106TH ST

Home Place

ELLER

ALLISONVILLE RD

HAGUE RD

CUMBERLAND RD

69

37

106TH ST

129

865

BOONE CO.

MARION CO.

421

96TH ST

31

431

465

31 421

HAMILTON CO.

MARION CO.

31 421

33

3

Royalton

COOPER RD

25

27

TOWNE RD

35

Castleton Square Mall

1

37

86TH ST

23

ST

86TH ST

COLLEGE AV

Fashion Mall, Keystone at the Crossing

82ND ST

CR.

HENDRICKS CO.

MARION CO.

52

65

LAFAYETTE RD

EAGLE CR

465

79TH ST

MERIDIAN

Williams Creek

79TH ST

79TH

Indian Lake

Mud CREEK

FALL CREEK RD

71ST ST

124

21

ZIONSVILLE RD

GEORGETOWN RD

GRANDVIEW

73RD ST

ST

Marott Park

37

71ST ST

Broad Ripple Park

ALLISONVILLE RD

BINFORD BL

Woollen's Garden

63RD RD

Ft. Harrison State Park

Eagle Creek Park

62ND

ST

Meridian Hills

Holliday Park

North Crows Nest

KESSLER BL

Glendale Shopping Center

KEYSTONE AV

56TH ST

40

20 123

56TH ST

Northwestway Park

BL

Crows Nest

White R.

52ND ST

CR.

56TH ST

19

52

School RD

Eagle Creek Res.

Rocky Ripple

Holcomb Bot. Gdns.

46TH ST

State Fairgrounds

Lawrence

36

74

465

38TH ST

17

HIGH

GEORGETOWN RD

LAFAYETTE CR.

121

65

Spring Hills

Indianapolis Mus. of Art

Butler Univ.

M.L. KING JR. ST

Crown Hill Natl. Cem.

38TH ST

Indianapolis

42

67

38TH ST

136

Clermont

16 73

Wynnedale

119

Pepsi Coliseum

31

30TH ST

Indianapolis Raceway Park

30TH ST

Marian College

116

The Children's Museum

Martin Univ.

Washington Park

30TH ST

SHERMAN DR

87

SHADELAND AV

465

70

Indianapolis Motor Speedway & Hall of Fame Mus.

25TH

134

117

115

Riverside Park

65

MERIDIAN

President Benjamin Harrison Home

85

70

89

44 90

91

21ST ST

16TH ST

113

MASSACHUSETTS

Brookside Park

16TH ST

RURAL ST

EMERSON AV

Warren Park

36 421

Washington Square Mall

Speedway

14

10TH ST

St. Cap.

WASHINGTON ST

46

US 40

ROCKVILLE RD

COUNTRY CLUB RD

GIRLS SCHOOL RD

13

10TH ST

EAGLE

Indiana Conv. Ctr. & RCA Dome

ENGLISH AV

47

BROOKVILLE RD

52

Avon

36

HIGH SCHOOL RD

LYNHURST DR

77

70

78

79A

SOUTHEASTERN AV

48

Plainfield

RACEWAY RD

US 40

12

HOLT RD

TIBBS AV

CR.

RAYMOND ST

80 110

Pleasant

MADISON AV

65

KEYSTONE AV

107

49 94

Marion Co. Fairgrounds

TROY AV

74 421

70

AIRPORT EXPWY

75

11

Indianapolis International Airport

36 52

9 73

40

KENTUCKY AV

Garfield Park

Lick Cr.

TROY AV

Univ. of Indianapolis

37

54 106

Beech Grove

31 36

40 52

SOUTHEASTERN

74 465

96

SIX POINTS RD

8

74 465

7

HARDING ST

BLUFF RD

EAST ST

2

MADISON

31 36

52

THOMPSON RD

DAVIS RD

74

RACEWAY RD

East Fork

White R.

AMERIPLEX BLVD

4

Buck Cr.

EDGEWOOD AV

EMERSON AV

SHELBYVILLE RD

SHELBY ST

POINTS

FRANKLIN RD

HICKORY RD

67

MANN RD

Banta RD

Little

Homecroft

Southport

103

SOUTHPORT RD

MC GREGOR RD

Camby

CAMBY RD

Southport RD

MC FARLAND RD

SHERMAN DR

ARLINGTON AV

FIVE

Mann RD

West Newton

RALSTON RD

MERIDIAN

37

STOP 11

Perry Park

US 31

101

MAZE RD

Friendswood

Southwestway Park

MARION CO.

JOHNSON CO.

COUNTY LINE RD

135

Greenwood Park Mall

MORGAN CO.

Pleasant

65

ARLINGTON

SHERMAN DR

MARION CO.

JOHNSON CO.

EAST ST

525

600

FAIRVIEW RD

Greenwood

MAIN ST

99

Creek

Run

Rocklane

1 inch represents 4.2 miles
or 6.8 kilometers
(1:267,000)

MI 1 2 3 4
KM 1 2 3 4

© MapQuest, Inc.

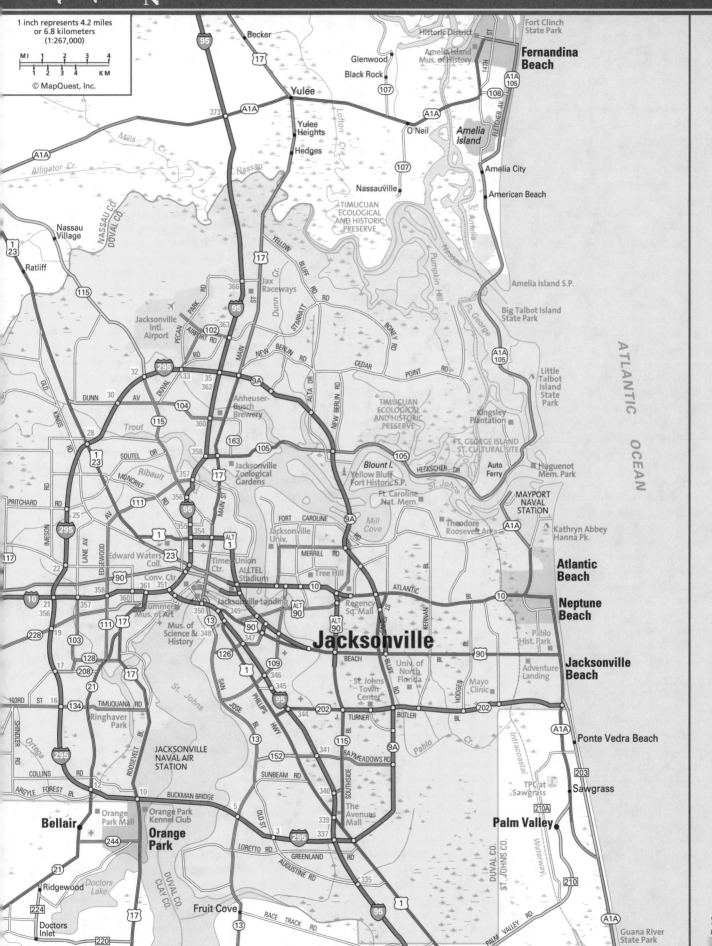

Becker

Glenwood

Black Rock

Yulee

Yulee Heights

Hedges

Nassauville

Nassau Village

Ratliff

Jacksonville Intl. Airport

Anheuser-Busch Brewery

Jacksonville Zoological Gardens

Edward Waters Coll.

Conv. Ctr.

Times Union Ctr.

ALLTEL Stadium

Jacksonville Landing

Cummer Mus. of Art

Mus. of Science & History

Jacksonville

JACKSONVILLE NAVAL AIR STATION

Ringhaver Park

Bellair

Orange Park Mall

Orange Park Kennel Club

Orange Park

Ridgewood

Doctors Lake

Doctors Inlet

Fruit Cove

Historic District

Fort Clinch State Park

Amelia Island Mus. of History

Fernandina Beach

O'Neil

Amelia Island

Amelia City

American Beach

TIMUCUAN ECOLOGICAL AND HISTORIC PRESERVE

Amelia Island S.P.

Big Talbot Island State Park

Little Talbot Island State Park

Kingsley Plantation

FT. GEORGE ISLAND ST. CULTURAL SITE

Auto Ferry

Huguenot Mem. Park

TIMUCUAN ECOLOGICAL AND HISTORIC PRESERVE

Blount I.

Yellow Bluff Fort Historic S.P.

Ft. Caroline Nat. Mem.

Mill Cove

MAYPORT NAVAL STATION

Theodore Roosevelt Area

Kathryn Abbey Hanna Pk.

Atlantic Beach

Neptune Beach

Pablo Hist. Park

Jacksonville Beach

Jacksonville Univ.

Regency Sq. Mall

Tree Hill

Univ. of North Florida

Adventure Landing

St. Johns Town Center

Mayo Clinic

Ponte Vedra Beach

The Avenues Mall

TPC at Sawgrass

Sawgrass

Palm Valley

Guana River State Park

ATLANTIC OCEAN

Jax Raceways

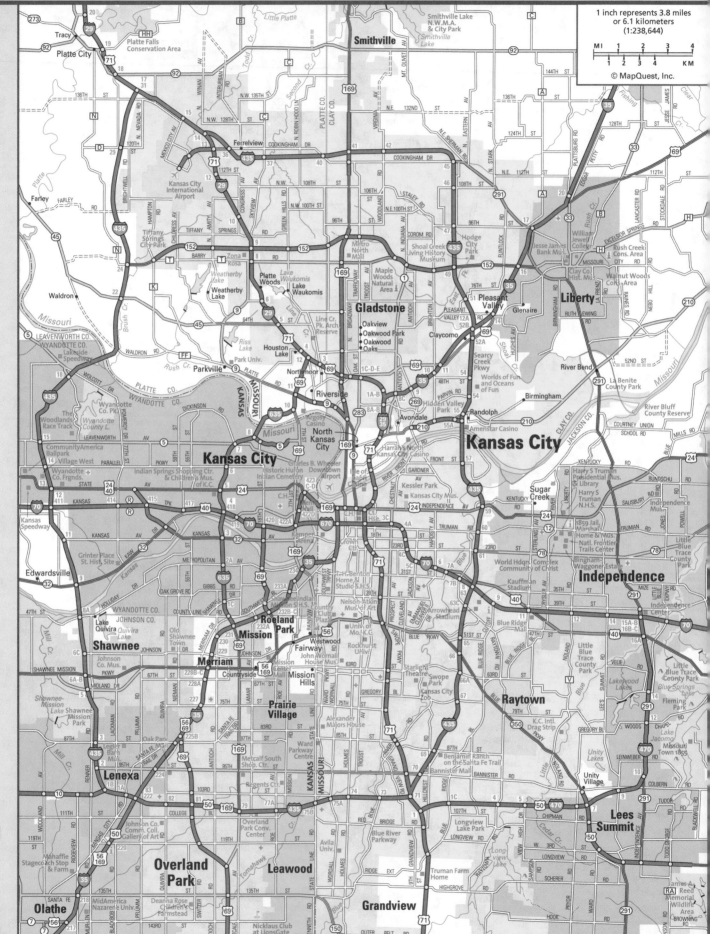

N

1 inch represents 3.8 miles
or 6.1 kilometers
(1:238,644)

MI 1 2 3 4
KM 1 2 3 4

© MapQuest, Inc.

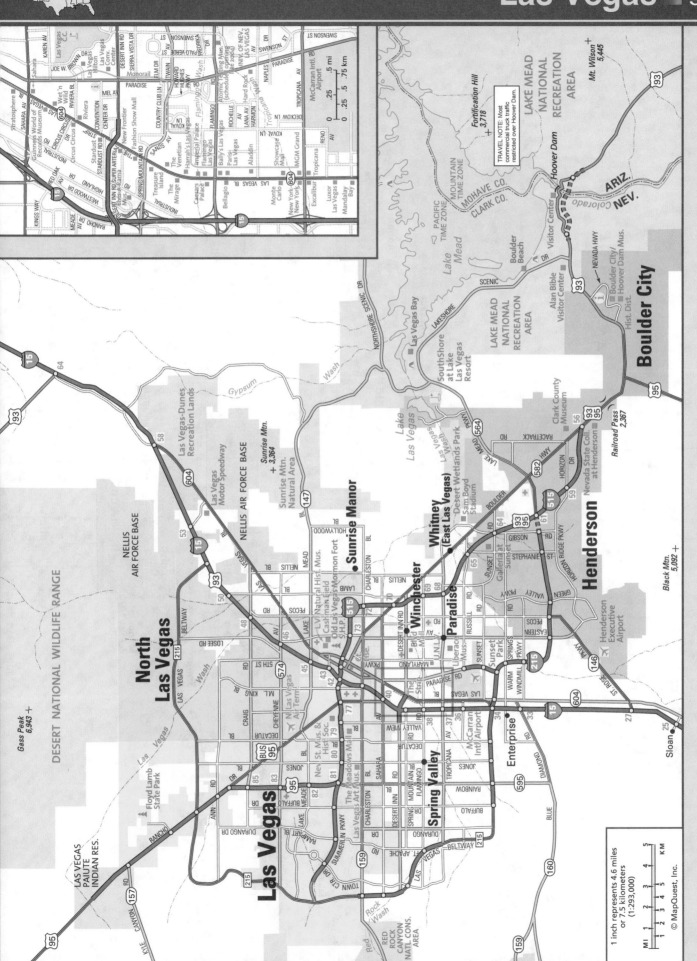

Las Vegas

LAKE MEAD NATIONAL RECREATION AREA

Mt. Wilson + 5,445

Fortification Hill + 3,718

TRAVEL NOTE: Most commercial truck traffic restricted over Hoover Dam.

Hoover Dam

Visitor Center

MOUNTAIN TIME ZONE

PACIFIC TIME ZONE

MOHAVE CO.
CLARK CO.

93

ARIZ.
NEV.

Colorado

Boulder Beach

DR

SCENIC

LAKE MEAD NATIONAL RECREATION AREA

Alan Bible Visitor Center

NEVADA HWY

Boulder City/ Hoover Dam Mus.

Hist. Dist.

93

Boulder City

McCarran Intl. Airport (schedule)

Lake Mead

NORTHSHORE SCENIC DR

Wash

Gypsum

Lake Las Vegas

Southshore at Lake Las Vegas Resort

Las Vegas Bay

LAKESHORE

Clark County Museum

582

56

93 95

95

64

93

58

604

15

Las Vegas-Dunes Recreation Lands

Las Vegas Motor Speedway

Sunrise Mtn. + 3,364

Sunrise Mtn. Natural Area

147

NELLIS AIR FORCE BASE

53

15

NELLIS AIR FORCE BASE

Clark County Museum

RACETRACK

LAKE MEAD

Desert Wetlands Park

564

Sam Boyd Stadium

HORIZON

Railroad Pass 2,367

Nevada State Coll. at Henderson

515

611

DESERT NATIONAL WILDLIFE RANGE

Gass Peak 6,943 +

604

93

NELLIS

MEAD

HOLLYWOOD

BL

LAMB

Sunrise Manor

CHARLESTON

NELLIS

70

Whitney (East Las Vegas)

Las Vegas Wash

BOULDER

93 95

GIBSON

65

SUNSET

STEPHANIE ST

HORIZON RIDGE PKWY

Black Mtn. 5,092 +

Henderson

515

GREEN VALLEY PKWY

North Las Vegas

BELTWAY

215

LOSEE RD

LAKE

50

48

Cashman Field

LV Natural Hist. Mus.

Old Las Vegas Mormon Fort S.H.P.

515

73

Winchester

DESERT INN RD

Boulevard Mall

Paradise

UNLV

Liberace Mus.

RUSSELL

SUNSET

Sunset Park

PECOS

EASTERN

Galleria at Sunset

WARM SPRINGS

Henderson Executive Airport

146

215

PECOS

5TH ST

574

45

46

43

MLK

Las Vegas Blvd

Las Vegas Art Mus.

N Las Vegas Air Term.

PARADISE PKWY

MARYLAND

The Strip

SAHARA

FLAMINGO

TROPICANA

McCarran Intl. Airport

VALLEY VIEW

37

34

33

27

25

Sloan

CRAIG

CHEYENNE

DECATUR

New St. Mus. & Hist Soc.

The Meadows Mall

SUMMERLIN PKWY

SPRING MOUNTAIN RD

CHARLESTON

DESERT INN

SPRING MOUNTAIN

RAINBOW

Spring Valley

JONES

DIAMOND

595

160

ST. ROSE

604

15

Enterprise

BUFFALO

BLUE

Las Vegas

LAS VEGAS PAIUTE INDIAN RES.

Floyd Lamb State Park

RANCHO

DURANGO DR

ANN

BUFFALO

RAMPART BL

TOWN CTR DR

FT APACHE

215

LAS VEGAS BELTWAY

159

95

85

83

82

81

80

79

77

38

40

41

42

KYLE CANYON RD

157

Red Rock Wash

RED ROCK CANYON NATL. CONS. AREA

159

1 inch represents 4.6 miles or 7.5 kilometers (1:293,000)

MI 1 2 3 4 5
KM 1 2 3 4 5

© MapQuest, Inc.

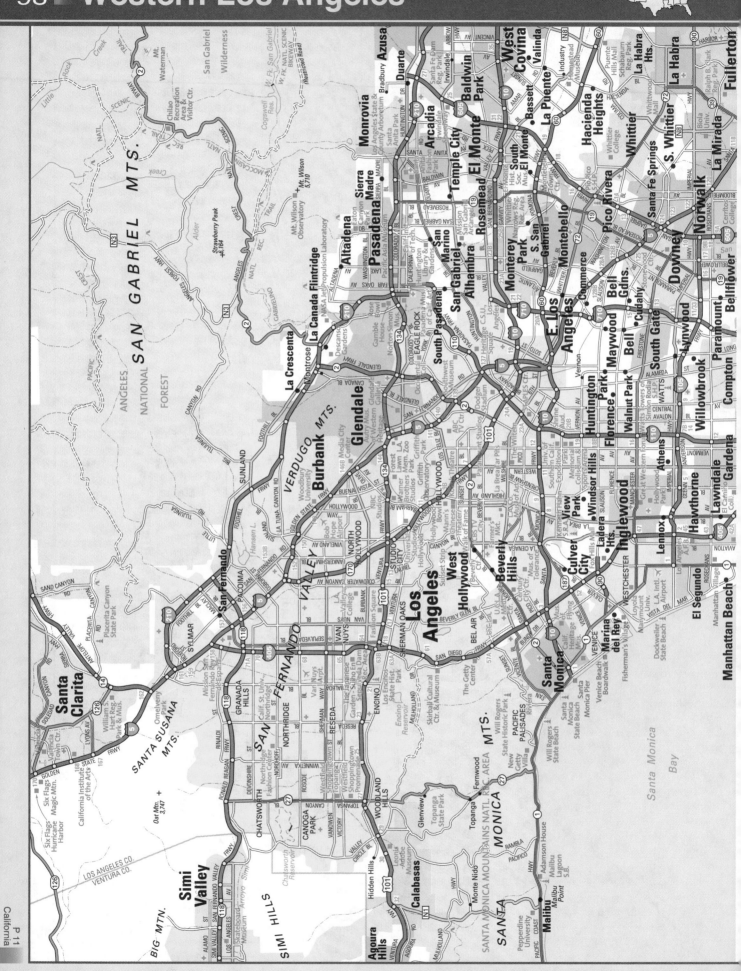

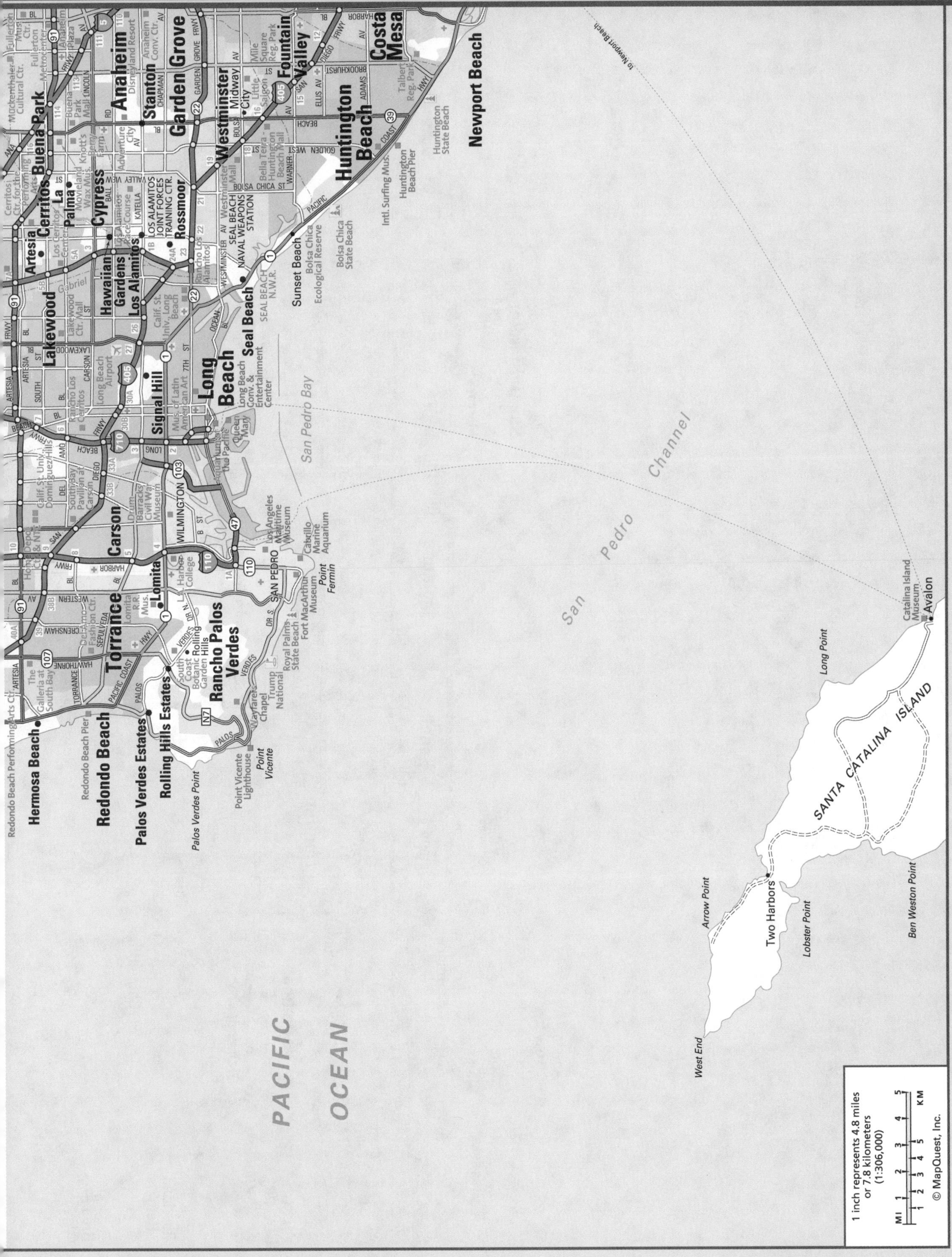

Anaheim
Garden Grove
Westminster
Fountain Valley
Costa Mesa
Huntington Beach
Newport Beach

to Newport Beach

Buena Park
Cerritos
La Palma
Cypress
Stanton
Rossmoor
Los Alamitos
Hawaiian Gardens
Midway City

Artesia
Cerritos
Lakewood

Int'l. Surfing Mus.
Huntington Beach Pier
Huntington State Beach

Seal Beach
Sunset Beach
Bolsa Chica Ecological Reserve
Bolsa Chica State Beach

SEAL BEACH N.W.R.
SEAL BEACH NAVAL WEAPONS STATION
Rancho Los Alamitos

Signal Hill
Long Beach Airport
Long Beach

Mus. of Latin American Art
Long Beach Conv. & Entertainment Center
Queen Mary

San Pedro Bay

San Pedro Channel

Carson
Wilmington
Drum Barracks Civil War Mus.

Los Angeles Maritime Museum
Cabrillo Marine Aquarium
SAN PEDRO
Point Fermin
Fort MacArthur Museum

San Pedro

Torrance
Lomita
Harbor College

Rancho Palos Verdes

Royal Palms State Beach
South Coast Botanic Garden
Rolling Hills
Trump National
Wayfarers Chapel

Hermosa Beach
Redondo Beach
Redondo Beach Pier
Palos Verdes Estates
Rolling Hills Estates

The Galleria at South Bay

Palos Verdes Point
Point Vicente Lighthouse
Point Vicente

PACIFIC OCEAN

Long Point

Catalina Island Museum
Avalon

SANTA CATALINA ISLAND

Arrow Point
West End
Two Harbors
Lobster Point
Ben Weston Point

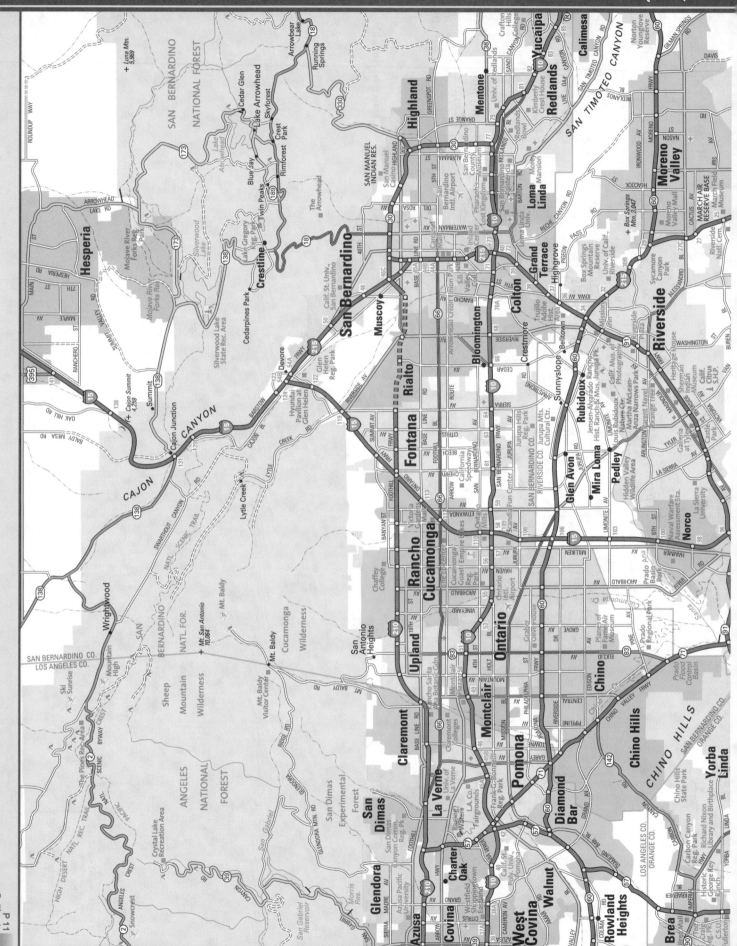

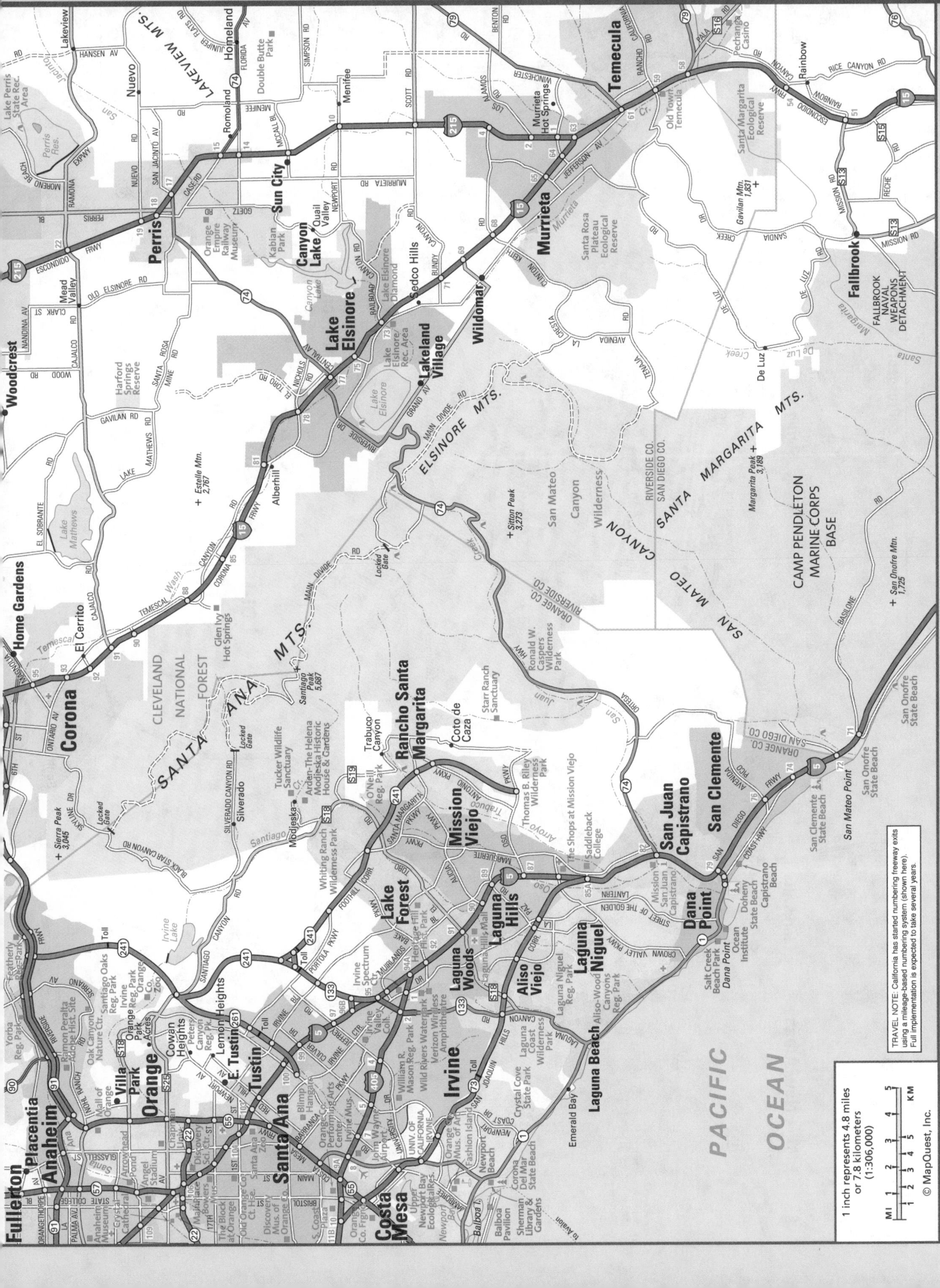

Lakeview

Nuevo
Homeland
Florida
Double Butte Park
Homeland
Lakeview MTS.
HANSEN AV

Menifee
Sun City

Temecula
Murrieta Hot Springs
Old Town Temecula
Pechanga Casino
Rainbow
RICE CANYON RD

Perris
Perris Res.
Lake Perris State Rec. Area

Murrieta
Santa Margarita Ecological Reserve
Gavilan Mtn. 1,831

Mead Valley

Canyon Lake
Quail Valley

Santa Rosa Plateau Ecological Reserve

Fallbrook
FALLBROOK NAVAL WEAPONS DETACHMENT

Woodcrest

Lake Elsinore
Sedco Hills
Wildomar
Lakeland Village
Lake Elsinore Rec. Area
Lake Elsinore

De Luz

Home Gardens
El Cerrito

ELSINORE MTS.

RIVERSIDE CO.
SAN DIEGO CO.

SANTA MARGARITA MTS.
Margarita Peak 3,189

Estelle Mtn. 2,767
Alberhill

Sitton Peak 3,273
San Mateo Canyon

Ronald W. Caspers Wilderness Park

CAMP PENDLETON MARINE CORPS BASE

San Onofre Mtn. 1,725

Corona
Lake Mathews

CLEVELAND NATIONAL FOREST

SANTA ANA MTS.

Santiago Peak 5,687

Rancho Santa Margarita
Coto de Caza
Trabuco Canyon

Starr Ranch Sanctuary

ORANGE CO.
RIVERSIDE CO.

San Clemente State Beach
San Onofre State Beach

Sierra Peak 3,045

Silverado
Modjeska

Arden-The Helena Modjeska Historic House & Gardens
Tucker Wildlife Sanctuary

Thomas F. Riley Wilderness Park

San Juan Capistrano
San Clemente

Mission Viejo
Saddleback College
The Shops at Mission Viejo

Dana Point
Mission San Juan Capistrano
Ocean Institute
Doheny State Beach
Capistrano Beach

Lake Forest
Laguna Hills
Laguna Woods
Aliso Viejo
Laguna Niguel

Irvine

Orange
Villa Park
Anaheim
Placentia
Fullerton

Tustin
E. Tustin
Lemon Heights

Santa Ana
Costa Mesa

Laguna Beach

Emerald Bay
Laguna Coast Wilderness Park

Newport Beach
Balboa

PACIFIC OCEAN

TRAVEL NOTE: California has started numbering freeway exits using a mileage-based numbering system (shown here). Full implementation is expected to take several years.

1 inch represents 4.8 miles or 7.8 kilometers (1:306,000)

MI 1 2 3 4 5
KM 1 2 3 4 5

© MapQuest, Inc.

N

Louisville

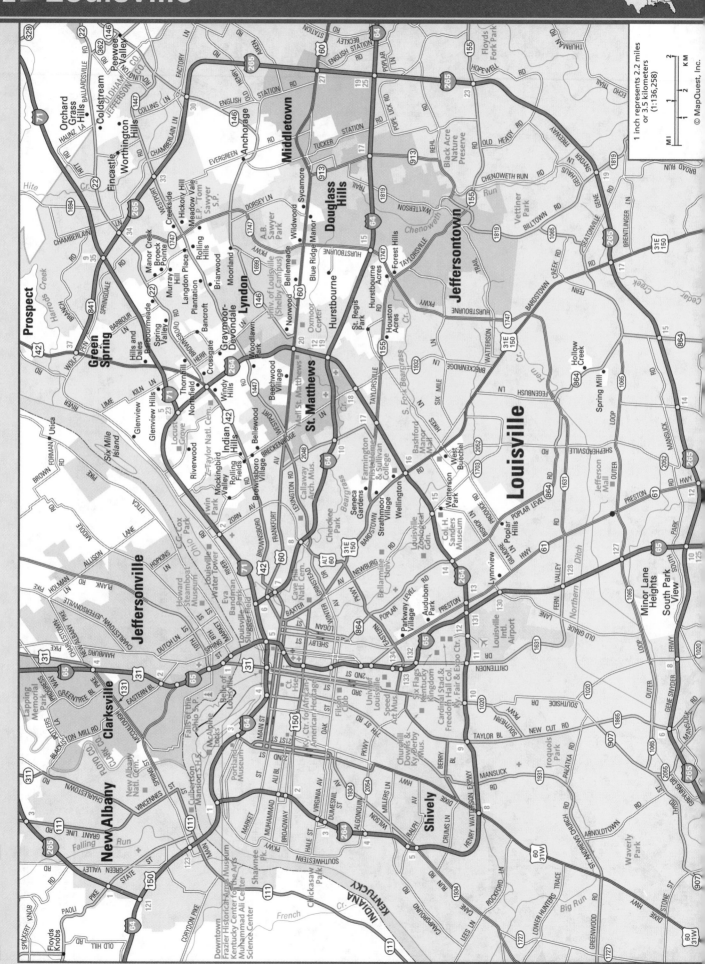

1 inch represents 2.2 miles
or 3.5 kilometers
(1:136,258)

© MapQuest, Inc.

1 inch represents 2.5 miles
or 3.9 kilometers
(1:155,167)

© MapQuest, Inc.

P 54
Wisconsin

1 inch represents 2.4 miles
or 3.9 kilometers
(1:152,920)

MI

KM

© MapQuest, Inc.

TENN.
ARK.

Mississippi

Redman
Point Bar

Loosahatchie

Loosahatchie Bar

SHELBY CO.

CRITTENDEN CO.

West
Memphis

ARKANSAS

TENNESSEE

Presidents
Island

Harbor Channel

Treasure Island

Chucalissa
Museum

T.O.
Fuller S.P.

Lake
McKellar

North
Horn
Lake

Cora L.

Robco L.

Horn
L.

Meeman-
Shelby
Forest
S.P.

Memphis
Motorsports
Park

FITE RD

MILLINGTON RD

Drainage

Canal

SINGLETON PKWY

AUSTIN PEAY HWY

OLD BROWNSVILLE RD

BENJESTOWN RD

N. WATKINS ST

388

51

Loosahatchie

HUSE

BOLEN

204

14

Bartlett

FRAYSER

JAMES

RD

NEW ALLEN RD

BL

YALE

RD

RALEIGH

Raleigh
Springs
Mall

COVINGTON PIKE

PIKE

BL

SYCAMORE VIEW DR

BARTLETT

STAGE RD

64

70
79

300

2A 3

5

6

8

204

14

15

51

Wolf

40

40

Slave Haven
Underground
Railroad Mus.

Univ. of
Tenn.
Health Sci.

CHELSEA

Rhodes
Coll.

JACKSON

Memphis
Natl. Cem.

MACON RD

PLEASANT VIEW RD

12A

12
B-C

12

40

WHITTEN

The Pyramid
Convention Center

14

NORTH PKWY

64

70
79

SUMMER

AV

Shelby
Farms

131

280

281

4

70
79

3

55

40

1

1E

31B

1F

Poplar

Memphis
Zoo Overton
Park

Memphis
College of Art

Memphis

13

Mud Island
Victorian Village
AutoZone Park
Ctr. for Southern Folklore
Beale St. Hist. Dist.
FedExForum/Rock 'n Soul Mus.
Natl. Civil Rights Mus.

Natl.
Ornamental
Metal Mus.

Sun
Studio

Brooks
Mus. of Art

BROAD AV

SAM

COOPER

GRAHAM ST

WALNUT

GROVE

PERKINS

MENDENHALL

23 RD

SHADY GROVE

240

Memphis
Mem.
Park

Germantown

Christian
Bros. Univ.

UNION AV

POPLAR AV

E. PKWY

Liberty
Bowl

CENTRAL

Libertyland

Memphis
Pink Palace
Mus.

HIGHLAND ST

PARK

Oak Court
Mall

GOODLETT ST

The Dixon
Gallery
& Gdns.

Memphis
Bot. Gdn.

QUINCE

72

15

Univ. of
Memphis

MT. MORIAH RD

Lichterman
Nature Ctr.

PARK AV

KIRBY RD

16

385

11

61

STAX Mus.

29

28

78

BARRON AV

RHODES

PRESCOTT

GETWELL RD

Frgnds.

Nonconnah

NONCONNAH PKWY

55

14

240

Frgnds.

S. PRESLEY BL

E. LAMAR

AIRWAYS BL

AV

20

18

17

Cr. EXT

9

DUNN RD

MALLORY AV

7

26

NORRIS RD

23

240

21

176

Mall of
Memphis

MT. MORIAH RD EXT

ARNOLD

MENDENHALL

8

Nonconnah
Cr.

6
25

24

DEMOCRAT RD

KNIGHT-

78

HICKORY

Hickory
Ridge
Mall

KIRBY RD

GERMANTOWN RD EXT

Lake
McKellar

51

5B

BROOKS RD

5A

RD

176

PERKINS RD

MITCHELL RD

WINCHESTER

BL

WINCHESTER

GETWELL

HORN LAKE RD

NEELY RD

Graceland

MILL BRANCH

Memphis
Intl. Airport

Caplevile

LAMAR AV

Johns

175

WEAVER RD

RAINES

ELVIS PRESLEY

AIRWAYS BL

PLOUGH BL

SHELBY DR

61

14

175

SHELBY

DR

TULANE

2

Southland
Mall

176

HOLMES

HOLMES

RD

TENNESSEE

MISSISSIPPI

SHELBY CO.
DESOTO CO.

STATE

LINE

RD

291

61

301

302

LAKE RD

GOODMAN

51

302

289

Southaven
Towne Center

TCHULAHOMA

Southaven

302

305

Horn
Lake

HORN

302

55

Olive
Branch

78

FUT
22

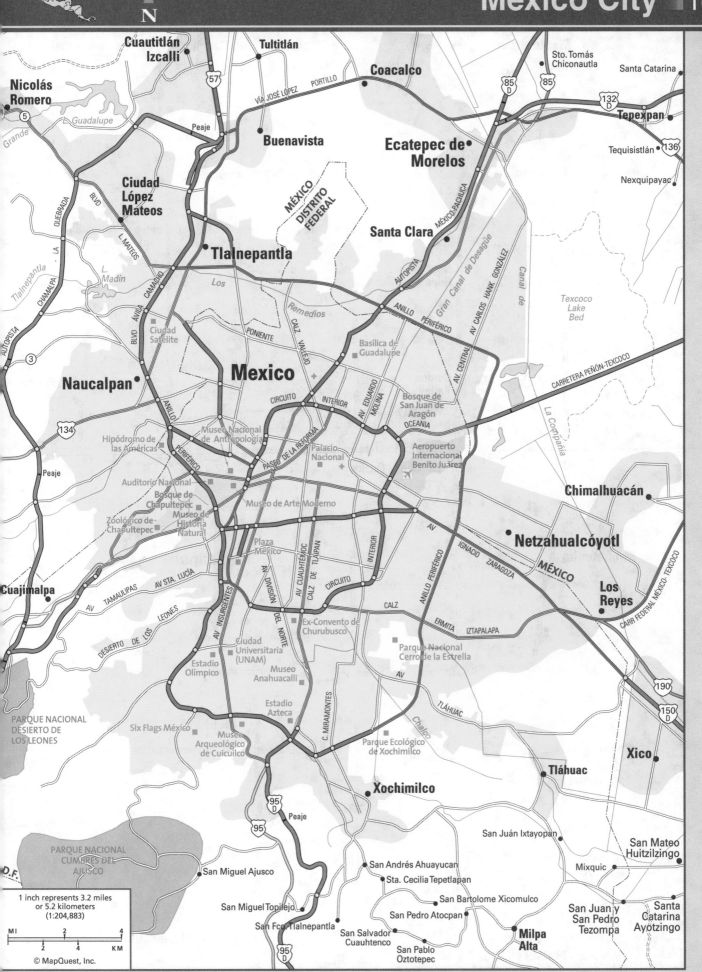

Cuautitlán Izcalli

Tultitlán

Coacalco

Sto. Tomás Chiconautla

Santa Catarina

Nicolás Romero

VIA JOSÉ LÓPEZ

PORTILLO

MÉXICO-PACHUCA

Tepexpan

Guadalupe

Peaje

Buenavista

Ecatepec de Morelos

Tequisistlán

Grande

Ciudad López Mateos

MÉXICO DISTRITO FEDERAL

Santa Clara

Nexquipayac

Tlalnepantla

L. Madín

Los Remedios

AUTOPISTA

ANILLO

Gran Canal de Desagüe

AV CARLOS HANK GONZÁLEZ

Canal de

Texcoco Lake Bed

Ciudad Satélite

CALZ VALLEJO

PONIENTE

PERIFÉRICO

Basílica de Guadalupe

AV CENTRAL

CARRETERA PEÑÓN-TEXCOCO

Naucalpan

ANILLO

Mexico

CIRCUITO

INTERIOR

AV EDUARDO MOLINA

Bosque de San Juan de Aragón

OCEANIA

La Compañía

Museo Nacional de Antropología

PASEO DE LA REFORMA

Palacio Nacional

Aeropuerto Internacional Benito Juárez

Hipódromo de las Américas

PERIFÉRICO

Auditorio Nacional

Bosque de Chapultepec

Museo de Arte Moderno

Chimalhuacán

Zoológico de Chapultepec

Museo de Historia Natural

AV

Netzahualcóyotl

MÉXICO

Plaza México

AV CUAUHTÉMOC

CALZ DE TLALPAN

INTERIOR

IGNACIO ZARAGOZA

Los Reyes

Cuajimalpa

AV TAMAULIPAS

AV STA. LUCÍA

AV DIVISIÓN DEL NORTE

CIRCUITO

ANILLO PERIFÉRICO

CALZ

Ex-Convento de Churubusco

ERMITA

IZTAPALAPA

CARR FEDERAL MÉXICO-TEXCOCO

DESIERTO DE LOS LEONES

AV INSURGENTES

Ciudad Universitaria (UNAM)

Museo Anahuacalli

Parque Nacional Cerro de la Estrella

Estadio Olímpico

Estadio Azteca

C. MIRAMONTES

AV

TLÁHUAC

Chalco

190

PARQUE NACIONAL DESIERTO DE LOS LEONES

Six Flags México

Museo Arqueológico de Cuicuilco

Parque Ecológico de Xochimilco

Xico

150 D

Tláhuac

Xochimilco

San Juán Ixtayopan

San Mateo Huitzilzingo

PARQUE NACIONAL CUMBRES DEL AJUSCO

95 D

Peaje

San Miguel Ajusco

San Andrés Ahuayucan

Sta. Cecilia Tepetlapan

Mixquic

San Juan y San Pedro Tezompa

Santa Catarina Ayotzingo

D.F.

San Miguel Topilejo

San Bartolome Xicomulco

San Pedro Atocpan

San Fco. Tlalnepantla

San Salvador Cuauhtenco

San Pablo Oztotepec

Milpa Alta

1 inch represents 3.6 miles
or 5.8 kilometers
(1:228,943)

© MapQuest, Inc.

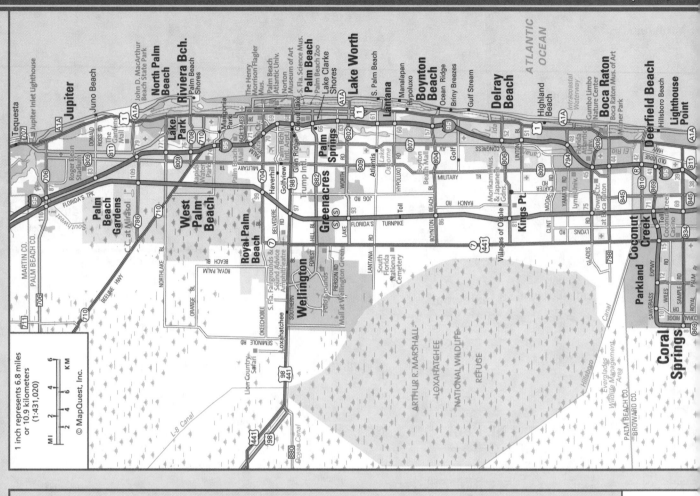

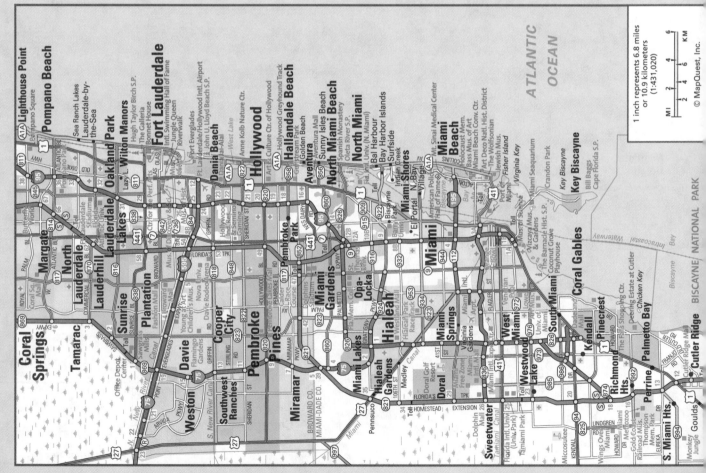

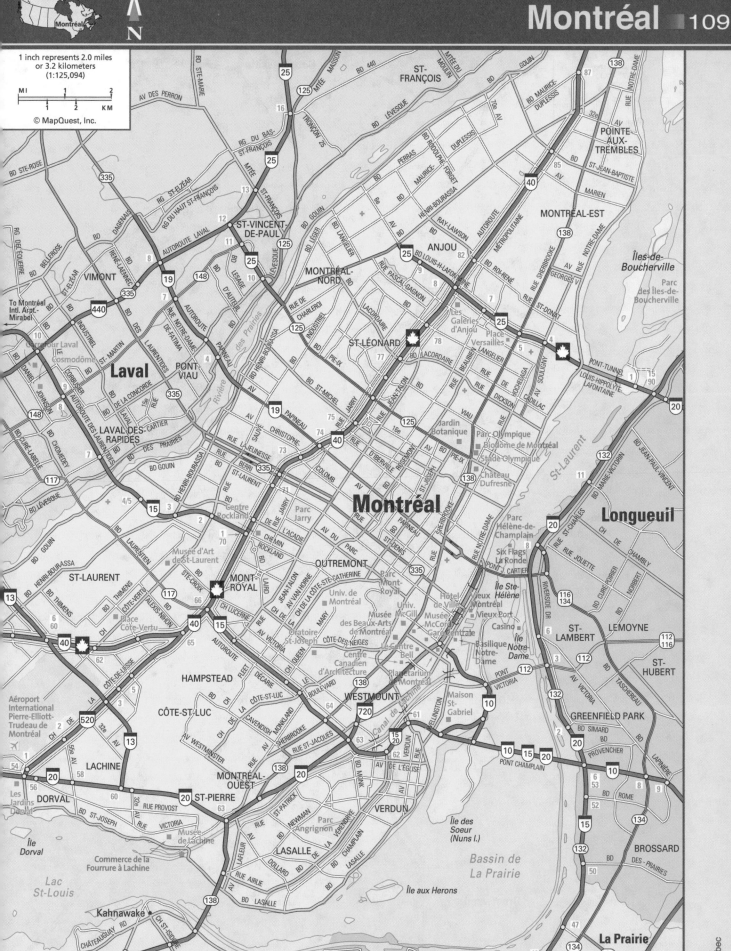

1 inch represents 2.0 miles
or 3.2 kilometers
(1:125,094)

MI 1 2
KM 1 2

© MapQuest, Inc.

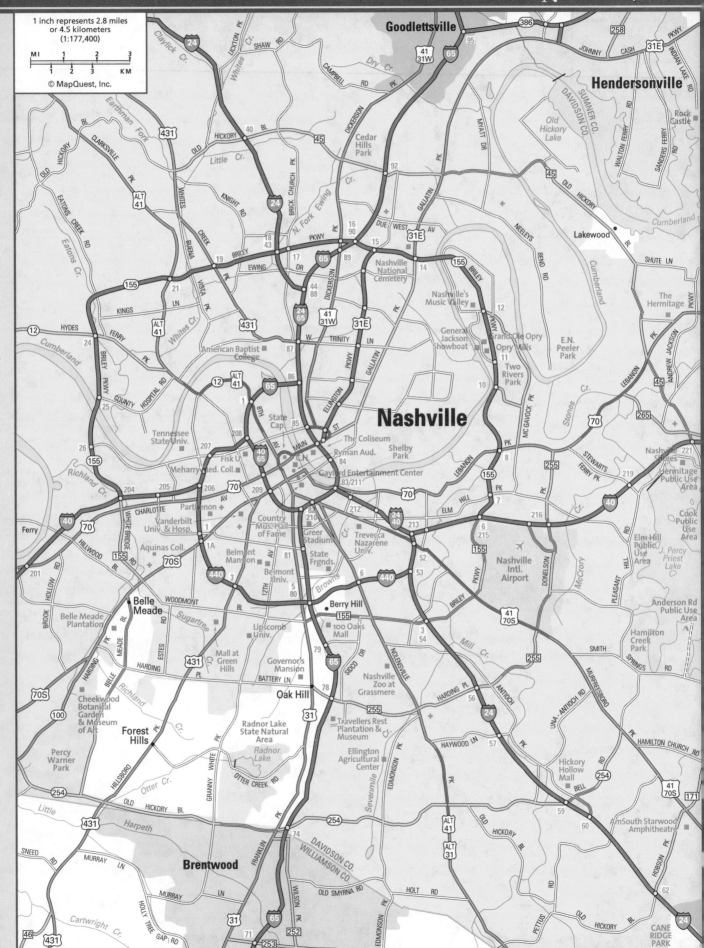

1 inch represents 2.8 miles
or 4.5 kilometers
(1:177,400)

© MapQuest, Inc.

Goodlettsville

Hendersonville

Lakewood

Nashville
National
Cemetery

Nashville's
Music Valley

General
Jackson
Showboat

Grand Ole Opry
Opry Mills

E.N.
Peeler
Park

Two Rivers
Park

The
Hermitage

American Baptist
College

Nashville

The Coliseum

Ryman Aud.
Shelby Park

Gaylord Entertainment Center

Tennessee
State Univ.

Fisk U.

Meharry Med. Coll.

Country
Mus. Hall
of Fame

Greer
Stadium

Trevecca
Nazarene
Univ.

Nashville Shores

Hermitage
Public Use
Area

Cook
Public
Use
Area

Nashville
Intl.
Airport

Elm Hill
Public Use
Area

J. Percy
Priest
Lake

Parthenon

Vanderbilt
Univ. & Hosp.

Aquinas Coll.

Belmont
Mansion

Belmont
Univ.

State
Frgnds.

Berry Hill

100 Oaks
Mall

Anderson Rd
Public Use
Area

Hamilton Creek
Park

**Belle
Meade**

Belle Meade
Plantation

Lipscomb
Univ.

Mall at
Green
Hills

Governor's
Mansion

Nashville
Zoo at
Grassmere

Hickory
Hollow
Mall

Cheekwood
Botanical
Garden
& Museum
of Art

**Forest
Hills**

Percy
Warner
Park

Oak Hill

Radnor Lake
State Natural
Area

Radnor
Lake

Travellers Rest
Plantation &
Museum

Ellington
Agricultural
Center

AmSouth Starwood
Amphitheatre

Brentwood

DAVIDSON CO.
WILLIAMSON CO.

CANE
RIDGE
PARK

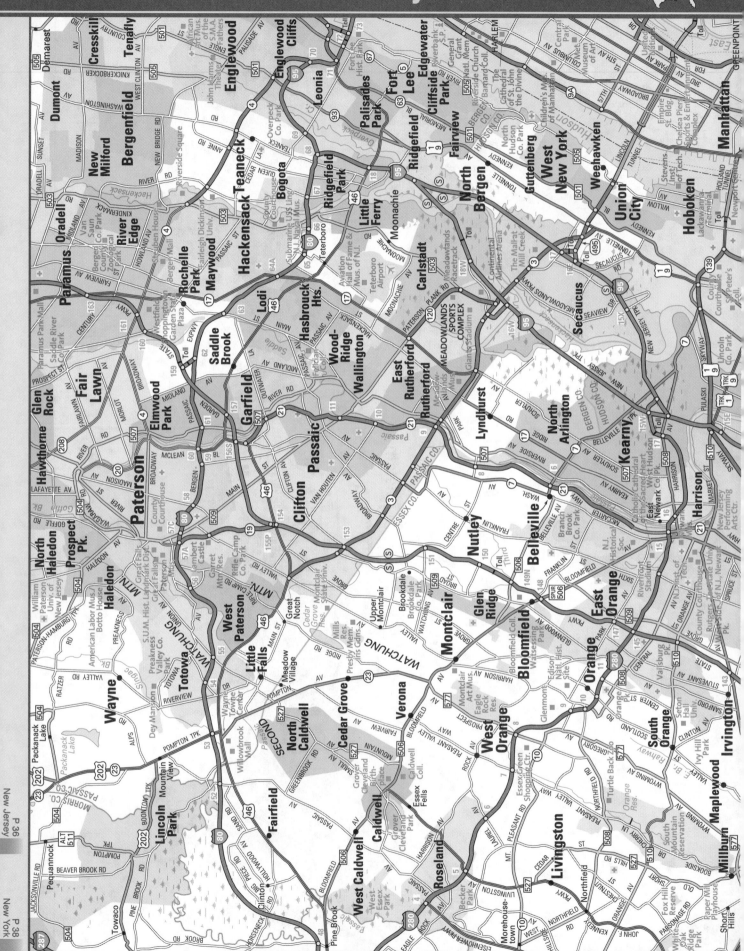

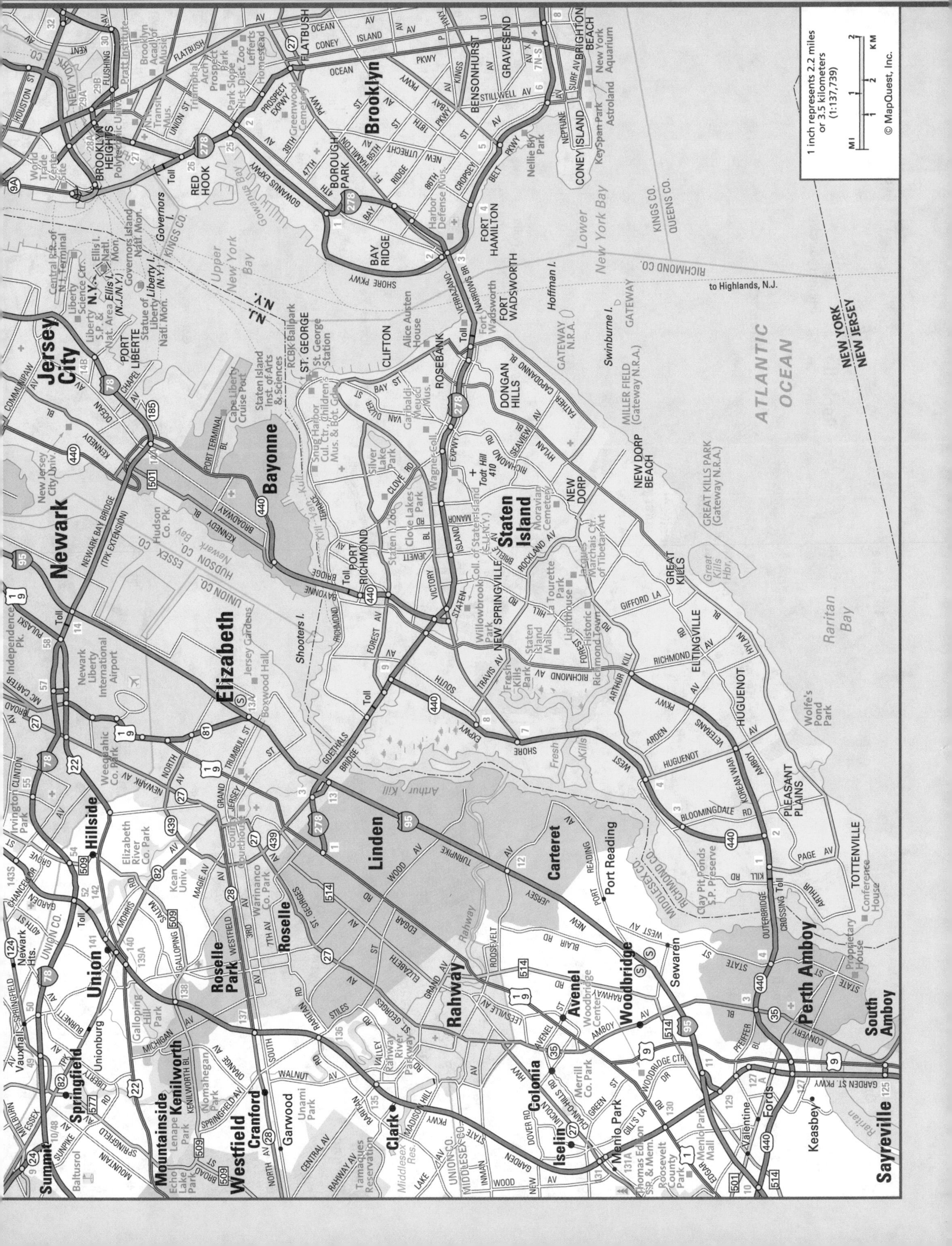

1 inch represents 2.2 miles
or 3.5 kilometers
(1:137,739)

© MapQuest, Inc.

Brooklyn

Jersey City

Newark

Bayonne

Elizabeth

Staten Island

Linden

Carteret

Rahway

Woodbridge

Perth Amboy

South Amboy

Sayreville

Union

Hillside

Roselle

Roselle Park

Westfield

Cranford

Clark

Iselin

Colonia

Avenel

Springfield

Mountainside

Summit

Kenilworth

Garwood

NEW DORP

GREAT KILLS

HUGUENOT

PLEASANT PLAINS

TOTTENVILLE

BLOOMINGDALE

ARDEN

ELTINGVILLE

NEW SPRINGVILLE

DONGAN HILLS

CLIFTON

ROSEBANK

ST. GEORGE

PORT RICHMOND

FORT WADSWORTH

FORT HAMILTON

BAY RIDGE

BOROUGH PARK

BENSONHURST

GRAVESEND

CONEY ISLAND

BRIGHTON BEACH

RED HOOK

BROOKLYN HEIGHTS

ATLANTIC OCEAN

Lower New York Bay

Upper New York Bay

Raritan Bay

Arthur Kill

NEW YORK
NEW JERSEY

RICHMOND CO.
QUEENS CO.

KINGS CO.

Newark Liberty International Airport

to Highlands, N.J.

GATEWAY N.R.A.

GREAT KILLS PARK (Gateway N.R.A.)

MILLER FIELD (Gateway N.R.A.)

Prospect Park

Verrazano Narrows Br.

Goethals Bridge

Bayonne Bridge

Newark Bay Bridge

Outerbridge Crossing

Todt Hill 410

Statue of Liberty Natl. Mon.

Ellis I. Natl. Mon.

Kean Univ.

New Jersey City Univ.

Staten Island Mall

N

New York City

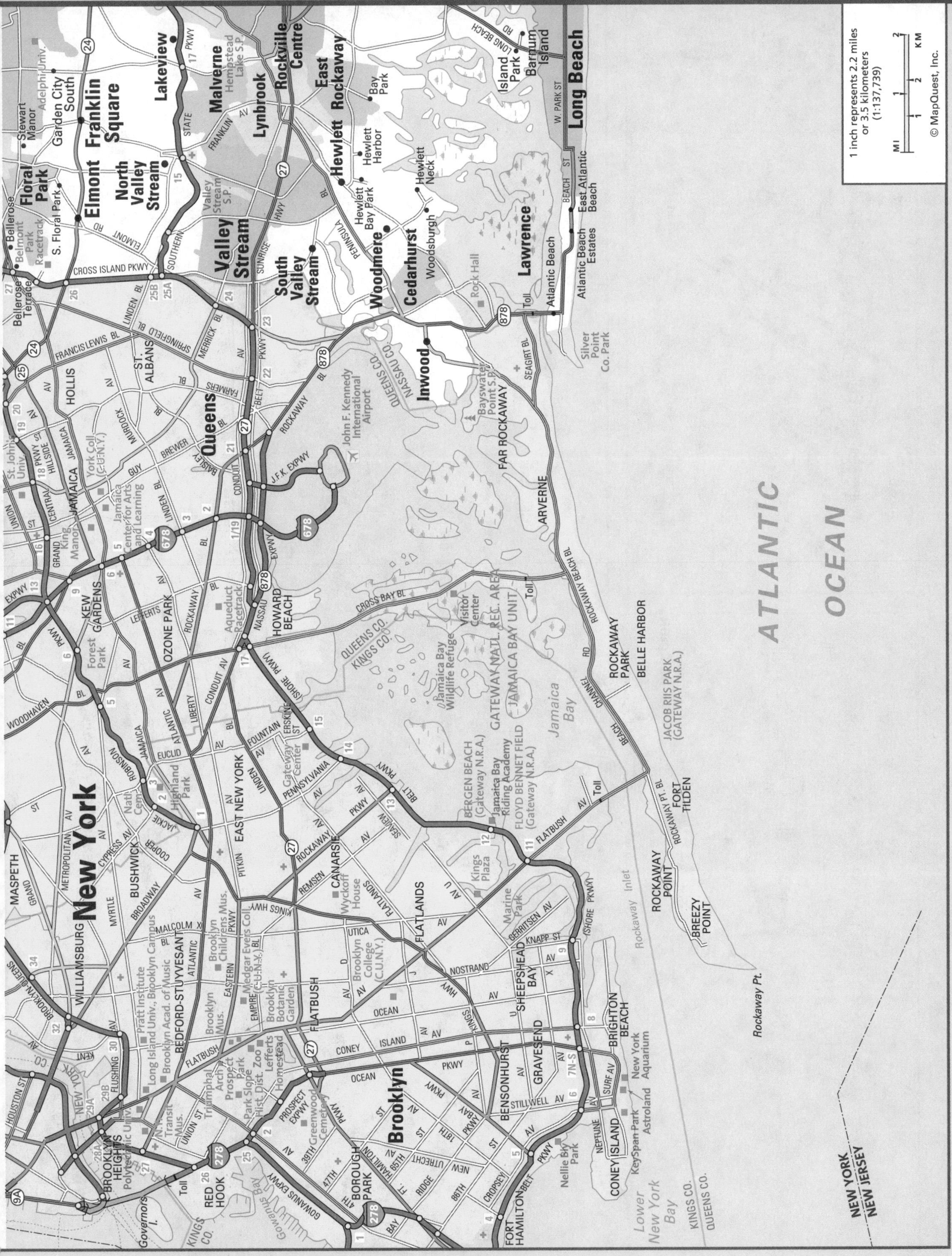

1 inch represents 2.2 miles
or 3.5 kilometers
(1:137,739)

MI
KM

© MapQuest, Inc.

Lakeview

Malverne

Hempstead
Lake S.P.

Rockville Centre

Lynbrook

East Rockaway

Bay Park

Island Park

Barnum Island

Long Beach

Stewart Manor

Garden City South

Adelphi Univ.

Franklin Square

North Valley Stream

Elmont

Floral Park

Valley Stream S.P.

Hewlett Harbor

Hewlett

Hewlett Neck

Hewlett Bay Park

Woodmere

Woodsburgh

Cedarhurst

East Atlantic Beach

Atlantic Beach Estates

Atlantic Beach

Bellerose Terrace

Belmont Park Racetrack

S. Floral Park

Valley Stream

South Valley Stream

CROSS ISLAND PKWY

SOUTHERN

SUNRISE HWY

PENINSULA

Rock Hall

Silver Point Co. Park

Lawrence

Inwood

Bayswater Point S.P.

SEAGIRT BL

HOLLIS

ST. ALBANS

JAMAICA

FRANCIS LEWIS BL

SPRINGFIELD BL

LINDEN BL

MERRICK BL

FARMERS BL

St. John's Univ.

York Coll. (C.U.N.Y.)

Jamaica Center for Arts and Learning

Queens

QUEENS CO.

NASSAU CO.

John F. Kennedy International Airport

J.F.K. EXPWY

Far Rockaway

ROCKAWAY BEACH BL

Arverne

KEW GARDENS

OZONE PARK

Forest Park

Aqueduct Racetrack

HOWARD BEACH

CONDUIT AV

CROSS BAY BL

Rockaway Park

Belle Harbor

Jacob Riis Park (Gateway N.R.A.)

ROCKAWAY PT. BL

FORT TILDEN

ROCKAWAY POINT

GATEWAY NATL. REC. AREA

JAMAICA BAY UNIT

Visitor Center

Jamaica Bay Wildlife Refuge

Jamaica Bay

BELLE HARBOR

New York

MASPETH

WILLIAMSBURG

BROOKLYN HEIGHTS

BUSHWICK

BEDFORD-STUYVESANT

EAST NEW YORK

RED HOOK

BOROUGH PARK

CANARSIE

FLATLANDS

FLATBUSH

Highland Park

Natl. Cem.

Pratt Institute

Long Island Univ., Brooklyn Campus

Brooklyn Childrens Mus.

Medgar Evers Coll. (C.U.N.Y.)

Brooklyn Mus.

Brooklyn Botanic Garden

Prospect Park

Brooklyn Acad. of Music

Brooklyn Transit Mus.

Empire Archl. Hist. Dist.

Park Slope

Greenwood Cemetery

Lefferts Homestead

Prospect Park Zoo

Brooklyn College (C.U.N.Y.)

Wyckoff House

Marine Park

Kings Plaza

Gerritsen Park

SHEEPSHEAD BAY

GRAVESEND

BENSONHURST

BRIGHTON BEACH

CONEY ISLAND

Brooklyn

New York Aquarium

Astroland

KeySpan Park

FORT HAMILTON

Nellie Bay Park

ATLANTIC

OCEAN

Rockaway Inlet

Rockaway Pt.

BREEZY POINT

Lower New York Bay

KINGS CO.

QUEENS CO.

NEW YORK

NEW JERSEY

Governors I.

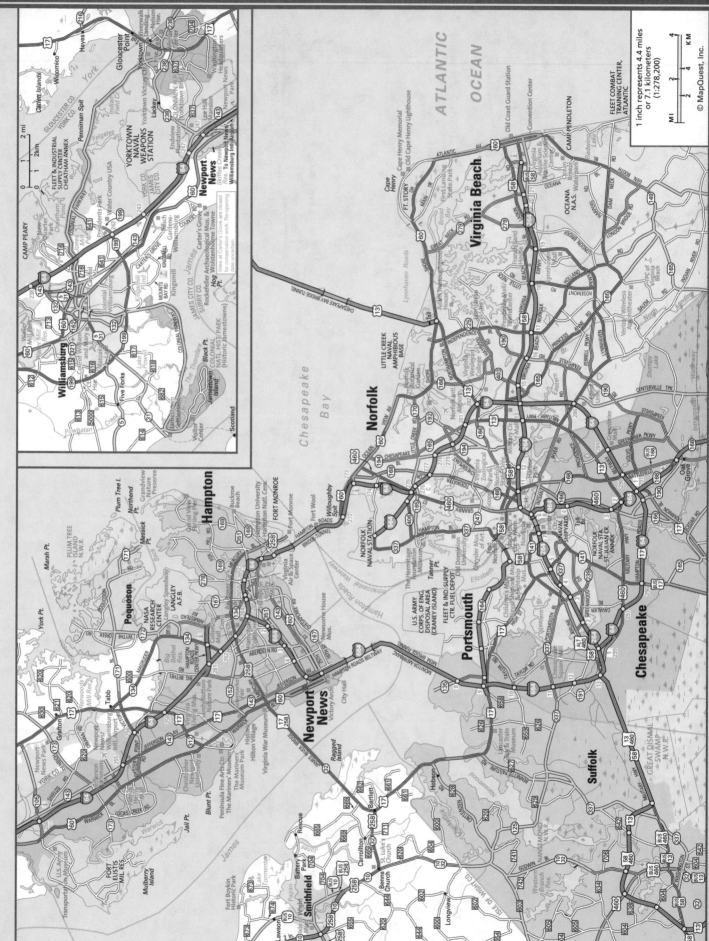

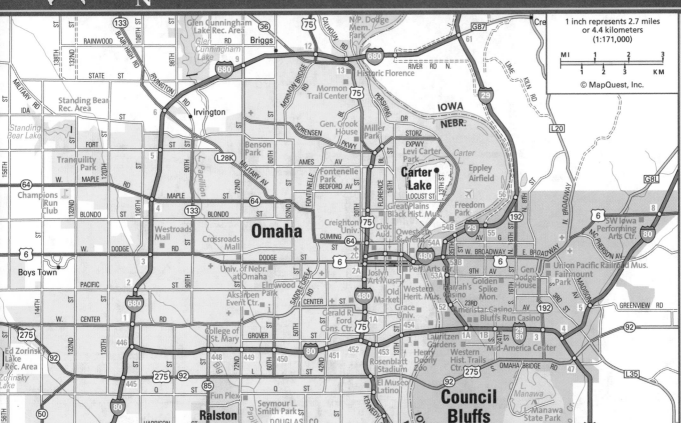

1 inch represents 2.7 miles
or 4.4 kilometers
(1:171,000)

© MapQuest, Inc.

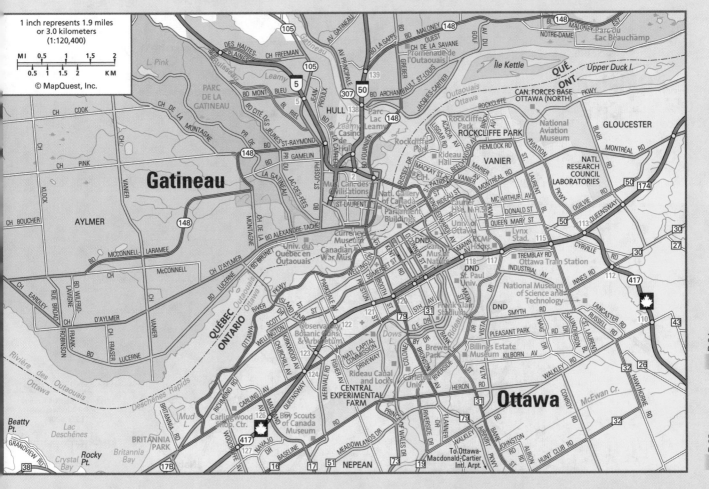

1 inch represents 1.9 miles
or 3.0 kilometers
(1:120,400)

© MapQuest, Inc.

1 inch represents 4.0 miles
or 6.4 kilometers
(1:252,000)

© MapQuest, Inc.

1 inch represents 3.0 miles
or 4.8 kilometers
(1:189,000)

MI 1   2   3   4
KM 1 2 3 4

© MapQuest, Inc.

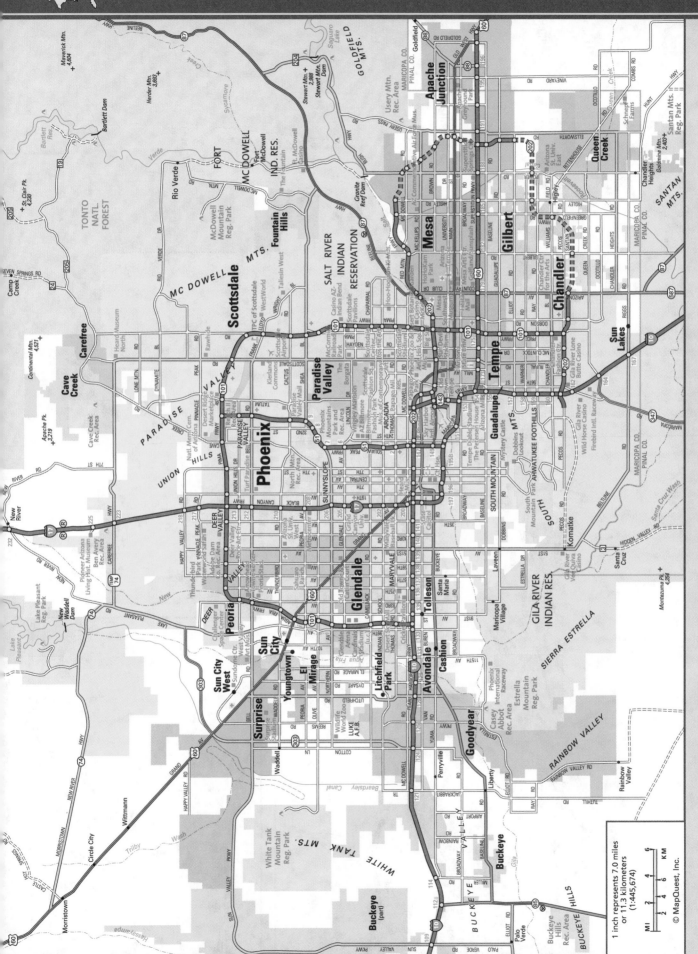

1 inch represents 7.0 miles
or 11.3 kilometers (1:445,674)

© MapQuest, Inc.

P 8
Arizona

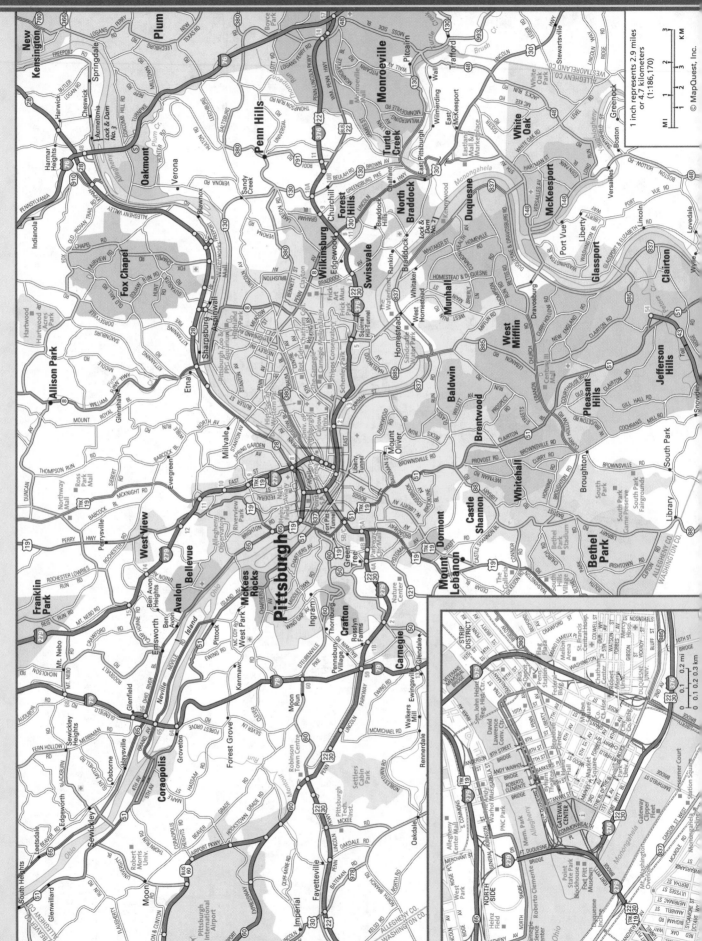

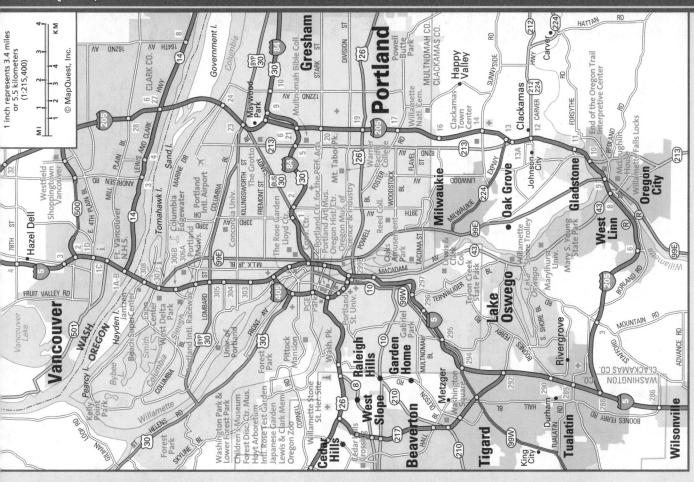

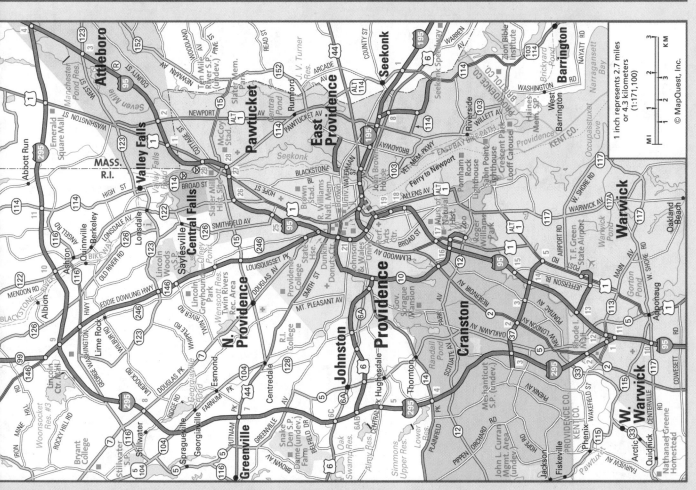

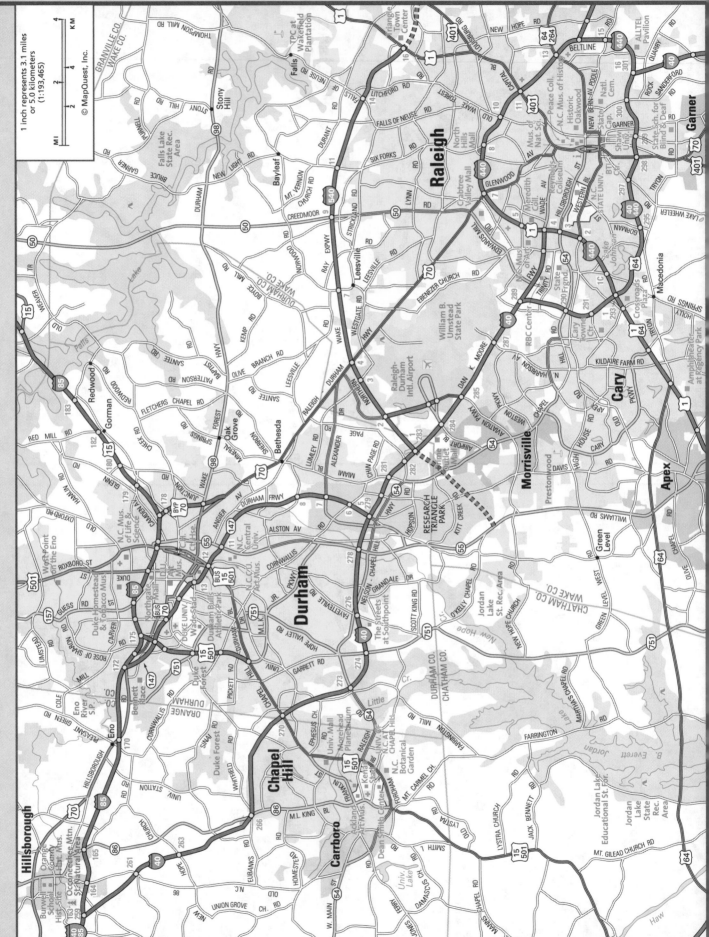

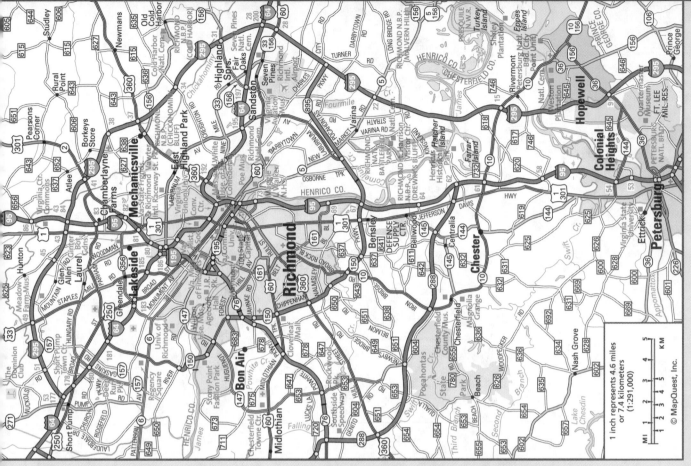

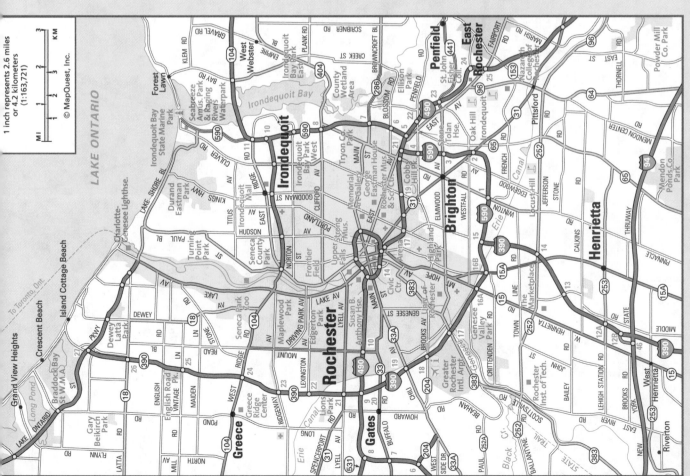

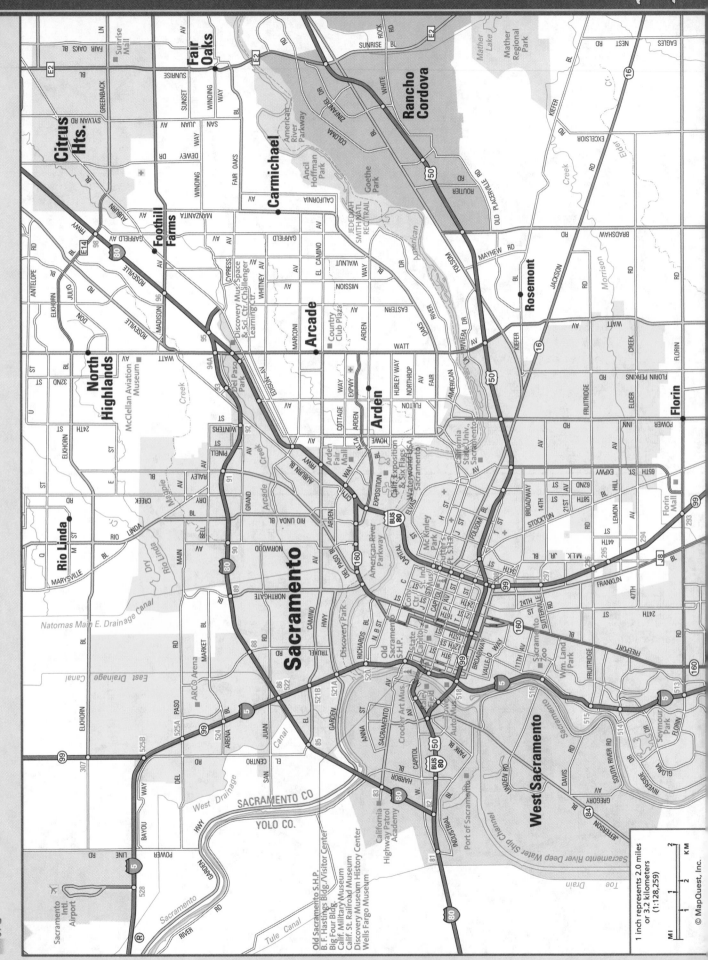

N
Sacramento

Sunrise Mall

Fair Oaks

Citrus Hts.

Foothill Farms

Carmichael

Rancho Cordova

Mather Lake

Mather Regional Park

American River Parkway

Ancil Hoffman Park

Goethe Park

Jedediah Smith Natl. Rec./Trail

Rosemont

North Highlands

McClellan Aviation Museum

Discovery Mus./Space & Sci. Ctr./Challenger Learning Ctr.

Arcade

Country Club Plaza

Arden

Arden Fair Mall

Florin

Florin Mall

California State Univ., Sacramento

Calif. Exposition

Cal Expo

Elvas Waterworld USA

Rio Linda

Rio Linda

Marysville

Sacramento

ARCO Arena

Discovery Park

Sutter's Ft. S.H.P.

McKinley Park

Crocker Art Mus.

Raley Field

Towe Auto Mus.

Old Sacramento S.H.P.

State Capitol

Wm. Land Park

Sacramento Zoo

Fruitridge

Natomas Main E. Drainage Canal

East Drainage Canal

West Sacramento

Sacramento Co
Yolo Co

West Drainage

Sacramento River Deep Water Ship Channel

California Highway Patrol Academy

Port of Sacramento

Toe Drain

Tule Canal

Sacramento Intl. Airport

Old Sacramento S.H.P.
B. F. Hastings Bldg./Visitor Center
Big Four Bldg.
Calif. Military Museum
Calif. St. Railroad Museum
Discovery Museum History Center
Wells Fargo Museum

1 inch represents 2.0 miles or 3.2 kilometers (1:128,259)

© MapQuest, Inc.

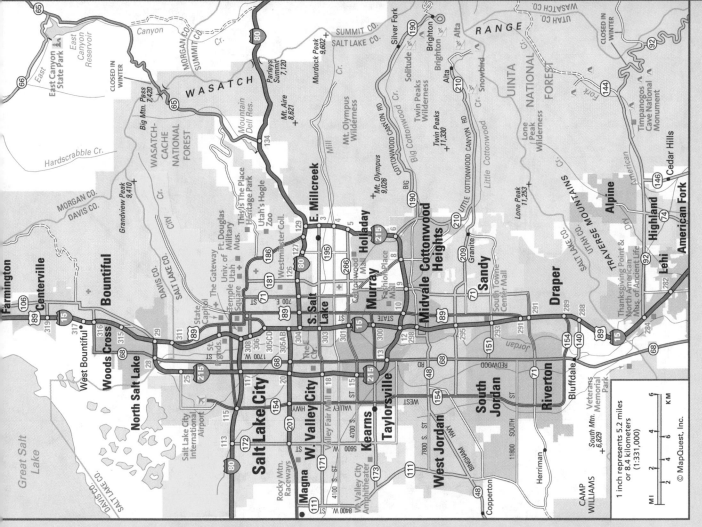

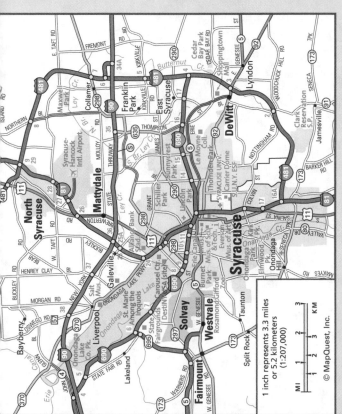

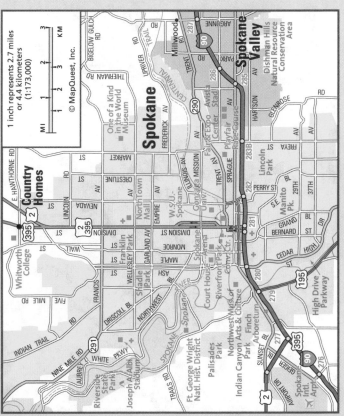

P 50
Utah

P 38
New York

P 51
Washington

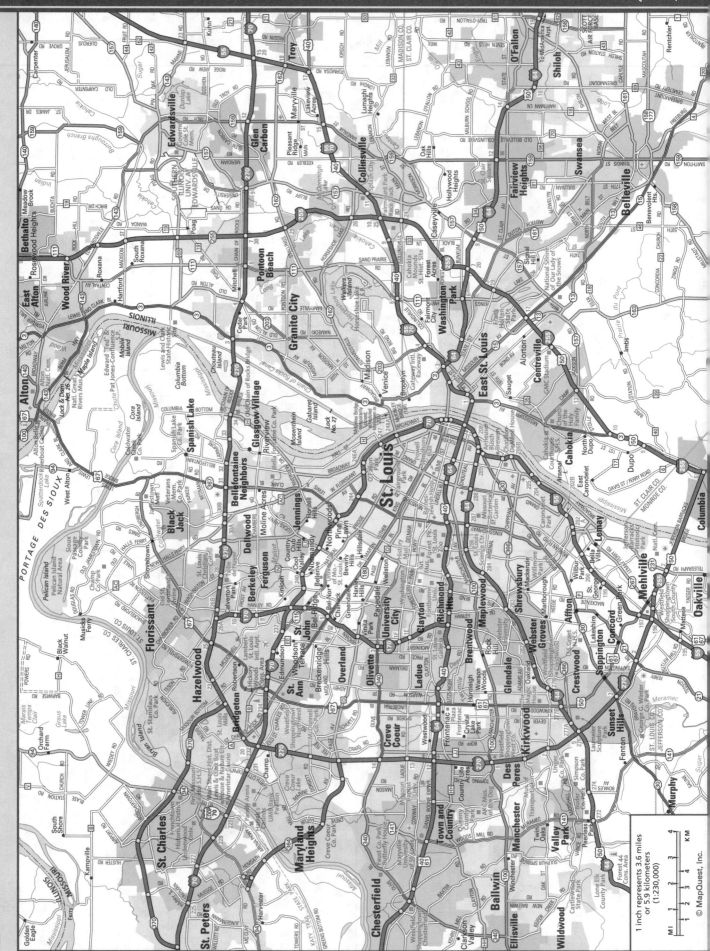

1 inch represents 3.6 miles
or 5.9 kilometers (1:230,000)

© MapQuest, Inc.

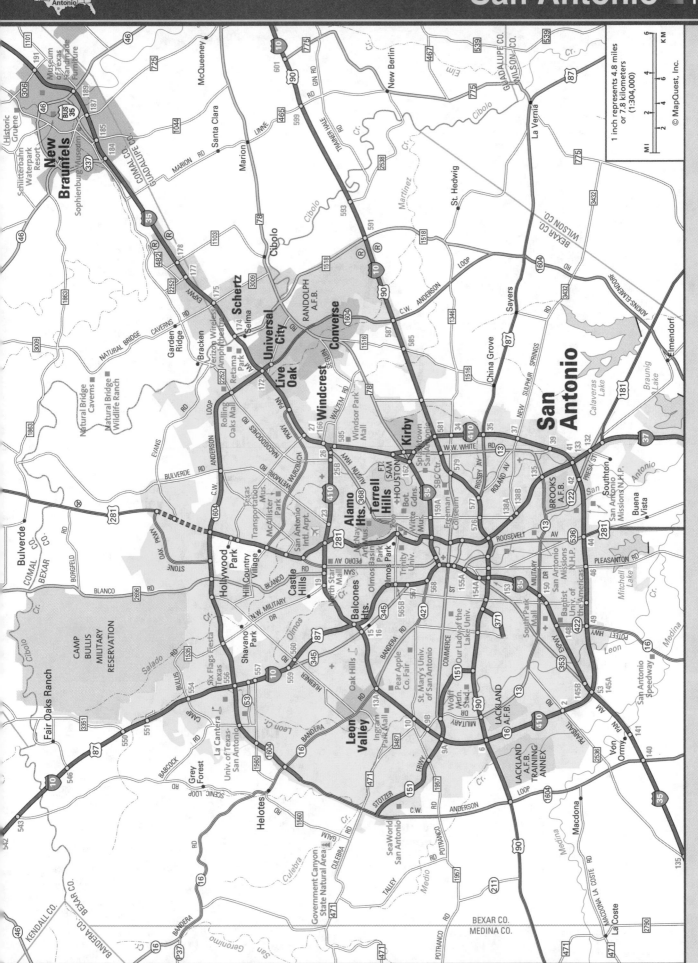

1 inch represents 4.8 miles or 7.8 kilometers (1:304,000)

© MapQuest, Inc.

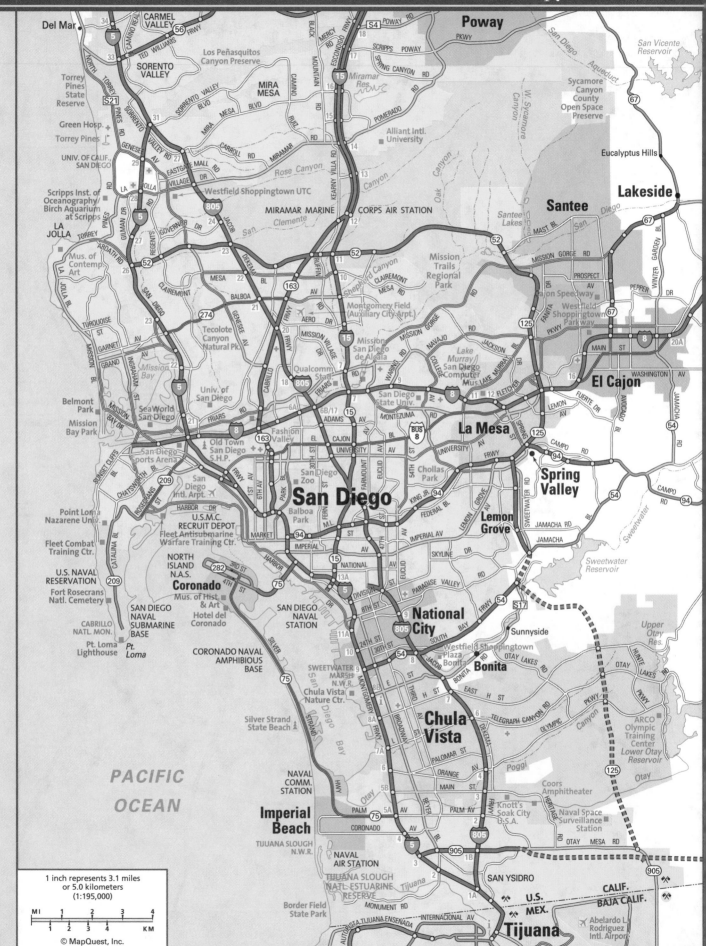

PACIFIC OCEAN

San Diego

1 inch represents 3.1 miles
or 5.0 kilometers
(1:195,000)

© MapQuest, Inc.

San Francisco

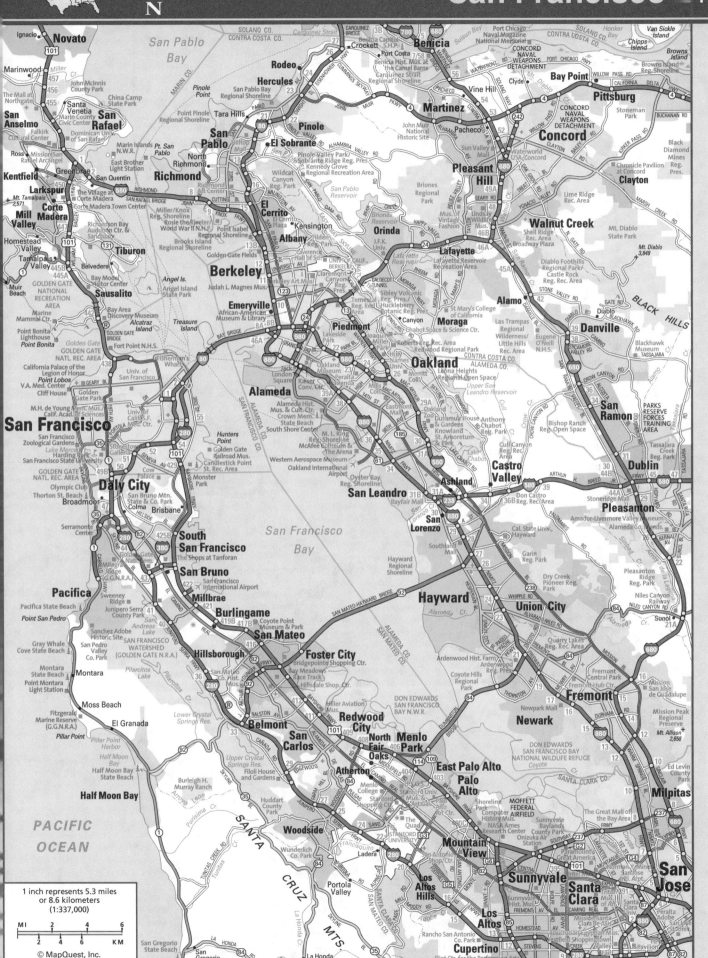

1 inch represents 5.3 miles
or 8.6 kilometers
(1:337,000)

MI 2 4 6
KM 2 4 6

PACIFIC
OCEAN

San Francisco
Bay

San Pablo
Bay

SOLANO CO.
CONTRA COSTA CO.

SANTA
CRUZ
MTS.

P 10
California

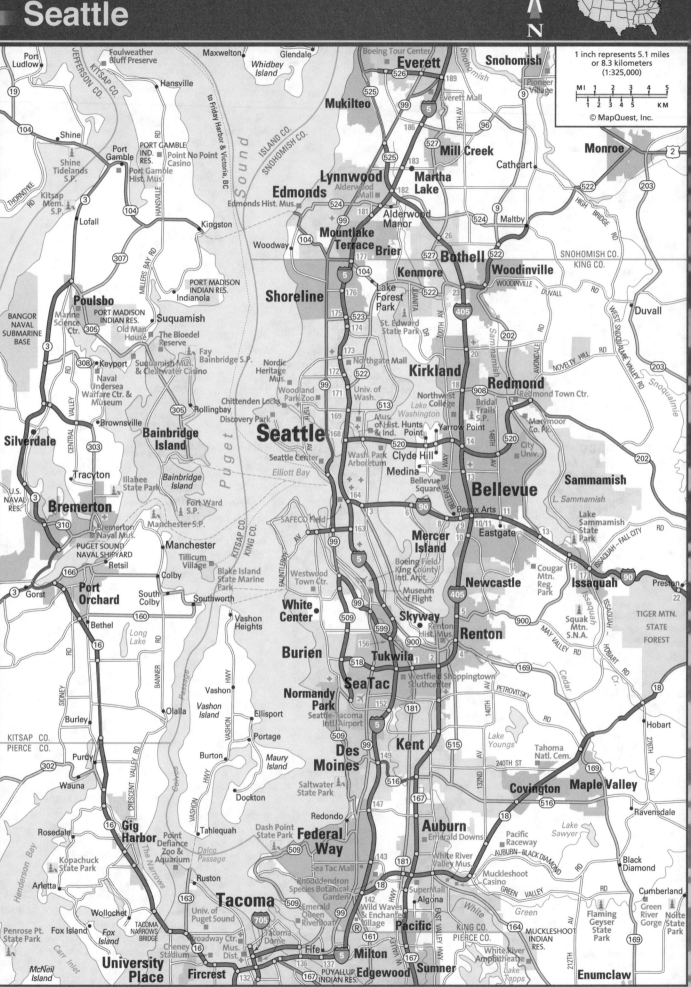

Seattle

1 inch represents 5.1 miles
or 8.3 kilometers
(1:325,000)

MI
KM

© MapQuest, Inc.

Tampa
St. Petersburg

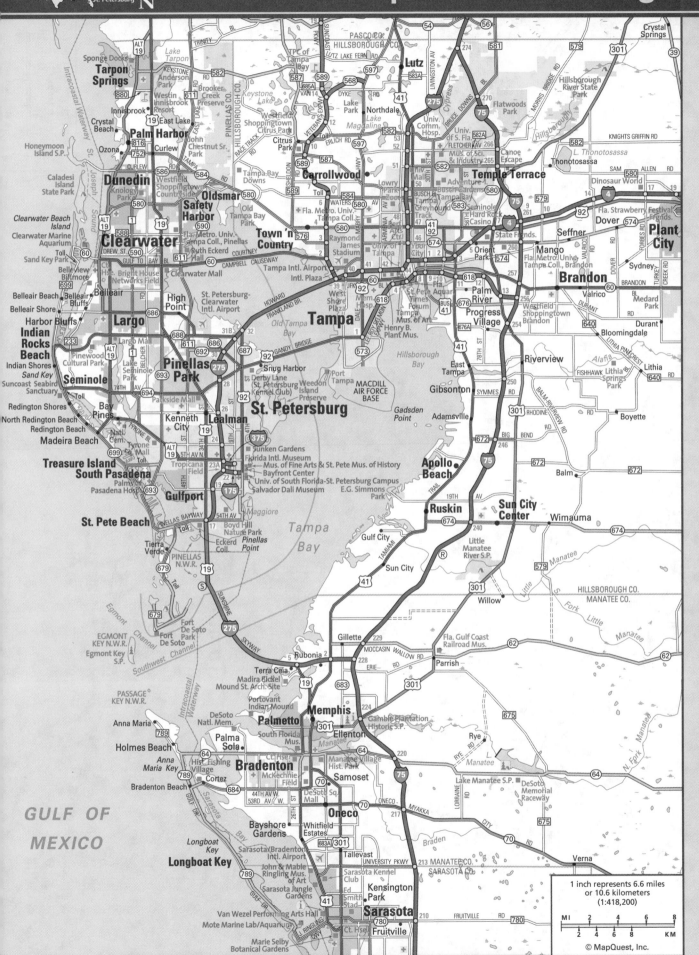

GULF OF MEXICO

1 inch represents 6.6 miles
or 10.6 kilometers
(1:418,200)

© MapQuest, Inc.

P 16
Florida

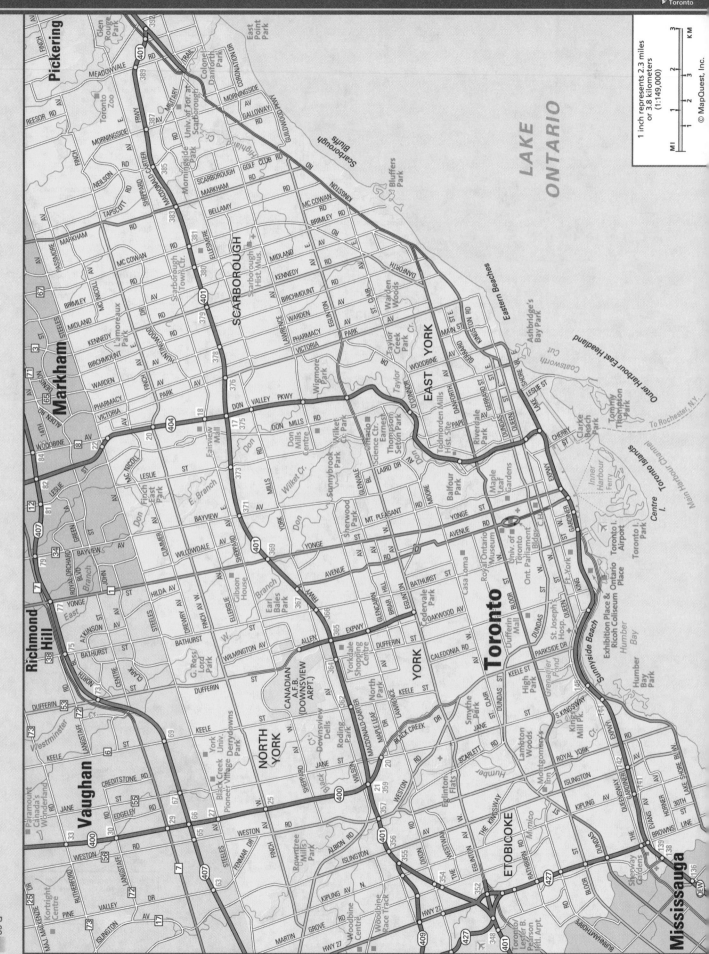

1 inch represents 2.3 miles
or 3.8 kilometers
(1:149,000)

© MapQuest, Inc.

LAKE
ONTARIO

Pickering

Markham

Richmond
Hill

Vaughan

SCARBOROUGH

NORTH
YORK

EAST
YORK

YORK

Toronto

ETOBICOKE

Mississauga

1 inch represents 3.6 miles
or 5.7 kilometers
(1:226,000)

© MapQuest, Inc.

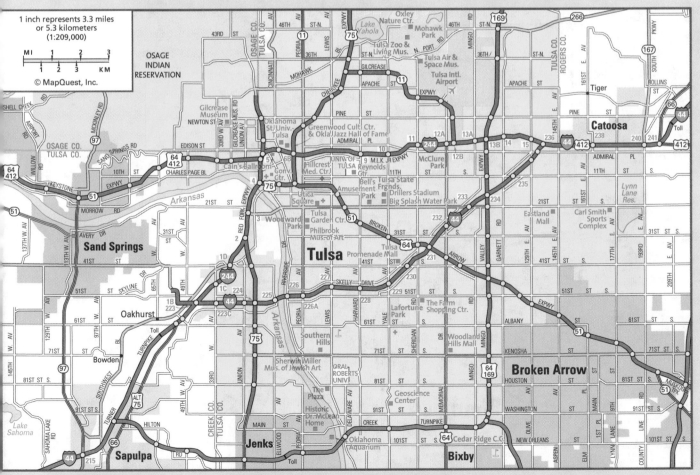

1 inch represents 3.3 miles
or 5.3 kilometers
(1:209,000)

© MapQuest, Inc.

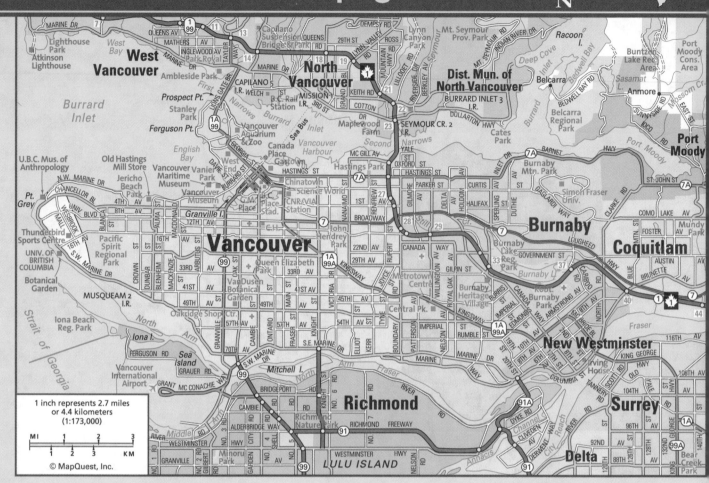

Vancouver

West Vancouver

North Vancouver

Dist. Mun. of North Vancouver

Port Moody

Burnaby

Coquitlam

New Westminster

Surrey

Richmond

Delta

LULU ISLAND

Burrard Inlet

Strait of Georgia

Lighthouse Park
Atkinson Lighthouse
West Bay
Ambleside Park
Prospect Pt.
Stanley Park
Ferguson Pt.
U.B.C. Mus. of Anthropology
Old Hastings Mill Store
Vancouver Maritime Museum
Vanier Park
Vancouver Museum
Jericho Beach Park
Pt. Grey
Thunderbird Sports Centre
Univ. of British Columbia
Botanical Garden
Pacific Spirit Regional Park
MUSQUEAM 2 I.R.
Iona Beach Reg. Park
Iona I.
Sea Island
Vancouver International Airport
Queen Elizabeth Park
VanDusen Botanical Garden
Oakridge Shop. Ctr.
Chinatown
Science World
B.C. Place Stad.
John Hendry Park
Metrotown Centre
Central Pk.
Burnaby Heritage Village
Robt. Burnaby Park
Burnaby Lake Reg. Park
Simon Fraser Univ.
Burnaby Mtn. Park
Capilano Suspension Bridge & Park
Lynn Canyon Park
Mt. Seymour Prov. Park
Deep Cove
Racoon I.
Buntzen Lake Rec. Area
Port Moody Cons. Area
Belcarra
Anmore
Sasamat
Bedwell Bay
Belcarra Regional Park
Maplewood Farm
Cates Park

1 inch represents 2.7 miles
or 4.4 kilometers
(1:173,000)

MI | 1 | 2 | 3
KM | 1 | 2 | 3

© MapQuest, Inc.

Winnipeg

1 inch represents 3.4 miles
or 5.6 kilometers
(1:215,400)

MI | 1 | 2 | 3 | 4
KM | 1 | 2 | 3 | 4

© MapQuest, Inc.

Prairie Dog Central Railway
Middle Church
Birds Hill
Spring Hill Winter Park
Garden City Shop. Ctr.
Seven Oaks House
Kil-cona Park
Winnipeg Intl. Airport
Western Canada Aviation Museum
Living Prairie Mus.
Canad Inns Stadium
Univ. of Winnipeg
Manitoba Museum
Kildonan Place
Transcona Hist. Mus.
Assiniboia Downs
Unicity Fashion Square
Arena
Polo Park
Zoo
Dalhavert
MTS Ctr.
The Forks N.H.S.
St. Boniface Mus.
Royal Canadian Mint
Fun Mountain Waterslide Park
Canadian Mennonite Bible College
Pan-Am Pool
St. Vital Center
Riel House N.H.S.
Ft. Whyte Centre
Univ. of Manitoba
Headingley
Oak Bluff
Prairie Grove
Grande Pointe
St. Norbert Prov. Park
Assiniboine Forest

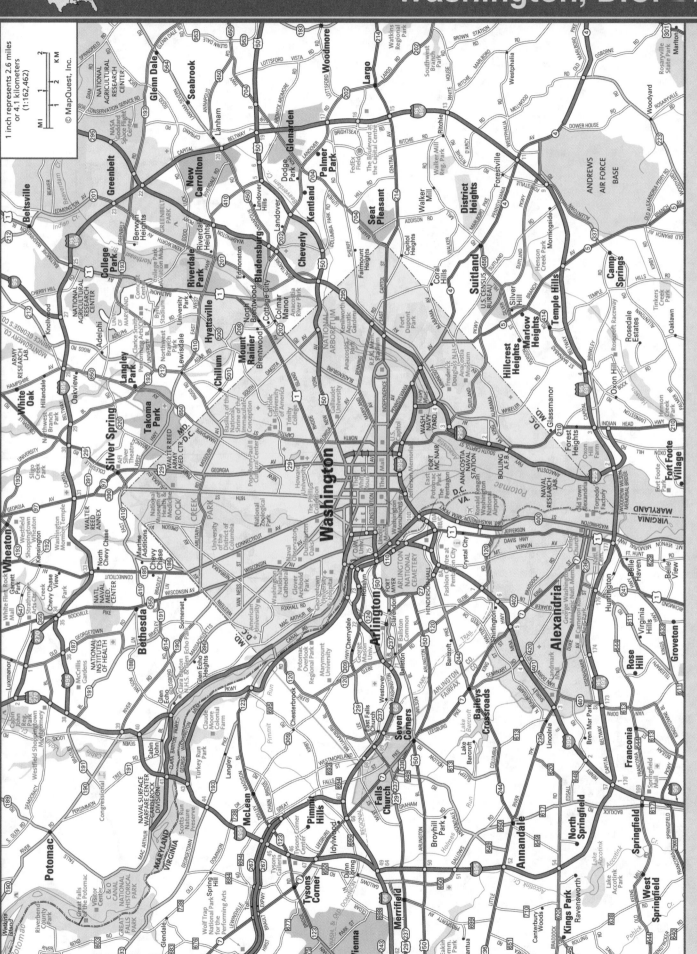

1 inch represents 2.6 miles
or 4.1 kilometers
(1:162,462)

N

Washington, D.C.

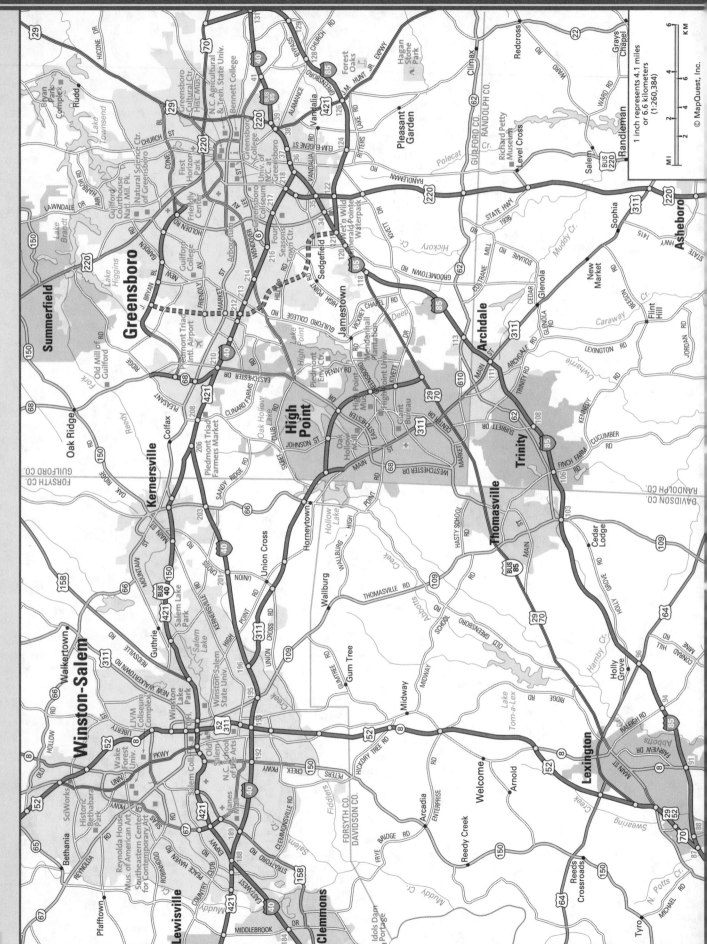

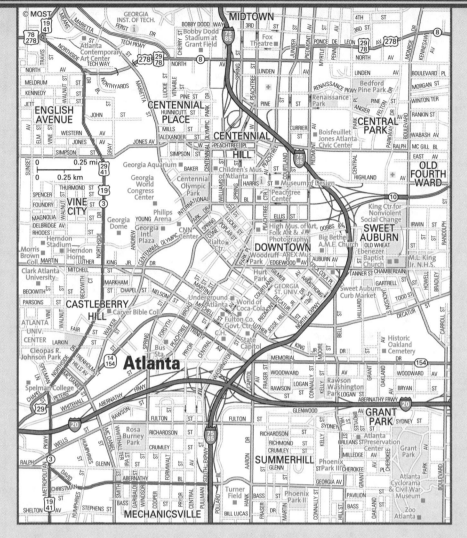

Atlanta

ENGLISH AVENUE

CENTENNIAL PLACE

CENTENNIAL HILL

CENTRAL PARK

OLD FOURTH WARD

VINE CITY

DOWNTOWN

SWEET AUBURN

CASTLEBERRY HILL

ATLANTA UNIV. CENTER

Atlanta

GRANT PARK

SUMMERHILL

MECHANICSVILLE

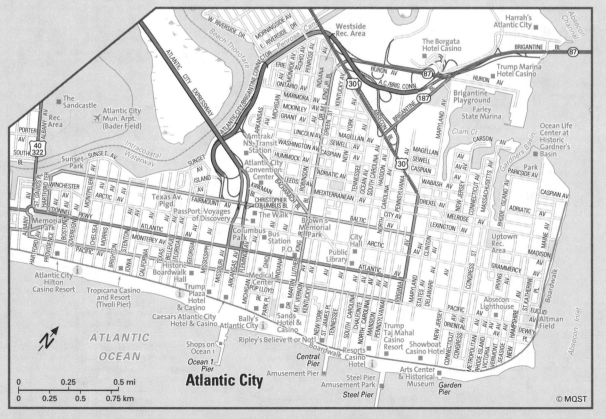

Atlantic City

ATLANTIC OCEAN

Atlantic City

0   0.25   0.5 mi

0   0.25   0.5   0.75 km

© MQST

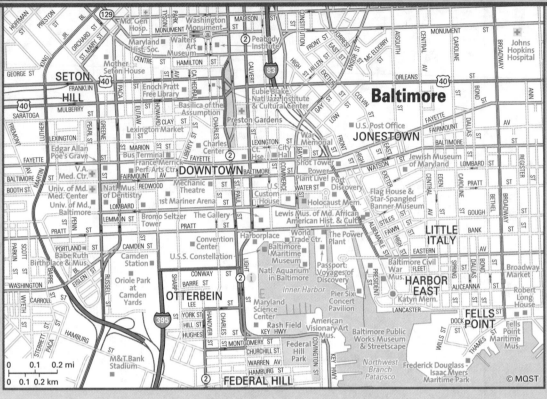

Baltimore

SETON HILL

DOWNTOWN

JONESTOWN

LITTLE ITALY

HARBOR EAST

FELLS POINT

OTTERBEIN

FEDERAL HILL

Inner Harbor

Md. Gen. Hosp.
Washington Monument
Maryland Hist. Soc.
Walters Art Museum
Peabody Institute
Mother Seton House
Enoch Pratt Free Library
Basilica of the Assumption
Preston Gardens
Eubie Blake Natl. Jazz Institute & Cultural Center
Johns Hopkins Hospital
U.S. Post Office
Lexington Market
Charles Center
Bus Terminal
France-Merrick Perf. Arts Ctr.
War Memorial
City Hall
Shot Tower
Power Plant Live!
Port Discovery
Jewish Museum of Maryland
Edgar Allan Poe's Grave
V.A. Med. Ctr.
Univ. of Md. Med. Center
Univ. of Md., Baltimore
Natl. Mus. of Dentistry
1st Mariner Arena
Mechanic Theatre
Holocaust Mem.
U.S. Custom House
Flag House & Star-Spangled Banner Museum
Bromo Seltzer Tower
The Gallery
Lewis Mus. of Md. African American Hist. & Cult.
Babe Ruth Birthplace & Mus.
Convention Center
Harborplace
World Trade Ctr.
The Power Plant
Baltimore Maritime Museum
Natl. Aquarium in Baltimore
Baltimore Civil War Mus.
Camden Station
U.S.S. Constellation
Passport: Voyages of Discovery
Katyn Mem.
Broadway Market
Oriole Park at Camden Yards
Maryland Science Center
Rash Field
Pier Six Concert Pavilion
Robert Long House
American Visionary Art Mus.
Baltimore Public Works Museum & Streetscape
Fells Point Maritime Mus.
M&T Bank Stadium
Federal Hill Park
Northwest Branch Patapsco
Frederick Douglass-Isaac Myers Maritime Park

© MQST

0 0.1 0.2 mi
0 0.1 0.2 km

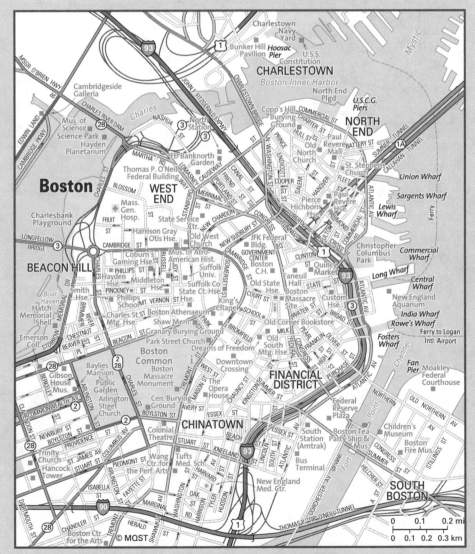

Boston

CHARLESTOWN

NORTH END

WEST END

BEACON HILL

FINANCIAL DISTRICT

CHINATOWN

SOUTH BOSTON

Boston Inner Harbor

Charlestown Navy Yard
Bunker Hill Pavilion
Hoosac Pier
U.S.S. Constitution
Cambridgeside Galleria
Mus. of Science
Science Park
Hayden Planetarium
North End Plgd.
U.S.C.G. Piers
Copp's Hill Burying Ground
Charles River Dam
TD Banknorth Garden
North Station
Old North Church
St. Stephen's Church
Union Wharf
Thomas P. O'Neill Federal Building
Paul Revere Mall
Sargents Wharf
Mass. Gen. Hosp.
State Service Ctr.
Pierce Hichborn Hse.
Paul Revere Hse.
Lewis Wharf
Charlesbank Playground
Harrison Gray Otis Hse.
Old West Church
JFK Federal Bldg.
Christopher Columbus Park
Commercial Wharf
Coburn's Gaming Hse.
Mus. of Afro-American Hist.
Boston C.H.
Quincy Market
Long Wharf
Boat Haven
Hayden Hse.
Phillips Hse.
Middleton Hse.
Suffolk Univ.
Suffolk Co. Ct. Hse.
Faneuil Hall
Custom Hse.
Central Wharf
New England Aquarium
Smith Hse.
Phillips School
Old State Hse.
Boston Massacre Site
King's Chapel
Old Corner Bookstore
India Wharf
Rowe's Wharf
Boston Athenaeum
Charles St. Mtg. Hse.
Shaw Mem.
Granary Burying Ground
Park Street Church
Old South Mtg. Hse.
Fosters Wharf
Ferry to Logan Intl. Airport
Emerson Coll.
Dreams of Freedom
Boston Common
Boston Massacre Monument
Downtown Crossing
The Opera House
Fan Pier
Moakley Federal Courthouse
Baylies Mansion
Gibson House Mus.
Public Garden
Arlington Street Church
Cen. Burying Ground
Colonial Theatre
Federal Reserve Plaza
Children's Museum
Boston Fire Mus.
Boston Tea Party Ship & Mus.
Trinity Church
Hancock Tower
Newbury
Wang Ctr. for the Perf. Arts
Tufts Med. Ctr.
South Station (Amtrak)
Bus Terminal
New England Med. Ctr.
Boston Ctr. for the Arts
Thomas P. O'Neill Tunnel

© MQST

0 0.1 0.2 mi
0 0.1 0.2 0.3 km

Goose Island

RIVER NORTH

NEAR NORTH

Seward Park

Newberry Library

Washington Square

Peace Mus.

Moody Bible Institute

Chicago Ctr. for the Performing Arts

900 N. Michigan Av. Shops

Water Tower

John Hancock Ctr.

Oak Street Beach

Outer Harbor

Museum of Contemporary Art

Northwestern Univ. (Chicago Campus)

Lake Shore Pk.

Seneca Pk.

Northwestern Mem. Hosp.

V.A. Med. Ctr.

Jane Addams Mem. Park

Chicago Children's Museum

Smith Mus. of Stained Glass Windows

NAVY PIER

Wrigley Bldg.

Tribune Tower

Merchandise Mart

Mus. of Broadcast Journalism (u.c.)

River East Plaza

River Esplanade Park

Centennial Fountain & Arc

Union Station

James R. Thompson Ctr.

City Hall

Civic Opera House

Chicago Mercantile Exchange

GREEK TOWN

Ford Ctr. for the Perf. Arts

Daley Plaza

Chicago Athenaeum

LaSalle Bank Theatre

THE LOOP

Chicago Theatre

Hellenic Museum & Cultural Center

Harris Theater

Pritzker Pavilion

Chicago Cultural Ctr.

Cloud Gate

Millennium Park

Grant

Chicago Yacht Club

Sears Tower

Symphony Center

Art Inst. of Chicago

Park

Chicago Harbor

Chicago

Petrillo Band Shell

Chicago Board of Trade

Monadnock Building

De Paul Center

Chicago Stock Exchange

Auditorium Building

Buckingham Fountain

LAKE MICHIGAN

Univ. of Illinois at Chicago

Harold Washington Library Center

Chicago Main Post Office

Spertus Mus.

PRINTER'S ROW

Mus. of Contemporary Photography

Grant Park

Jane Addams' Hull House Museum

Chicago Fire Marker

Dearborn Station

John G. Shedd Aquarium

Adler Planetarium & Astronomy Mus.

New Maxwell Street Market

The Field Mus.

Northerly Island

Soldier Field

Burnham Park

12th Street Beach

LITTLE ITALY

Natl. Vietnam Veterans Art Museum

Prairie Av. Historic District

Northerly Island Park

Burnham Park Yacht Harbor

Branch Grove

CHINATOWN

MC CORMICK PLACE

Burnham Park

Mercy Hosp. & Med. Ctr.

© MQST

N

P 43
Ohio

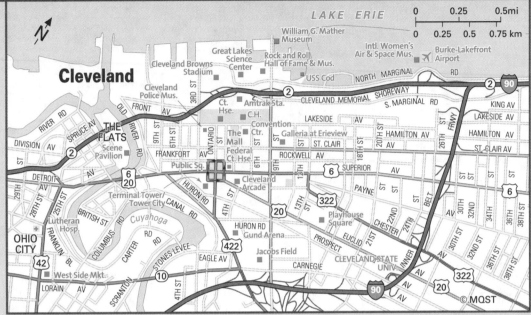

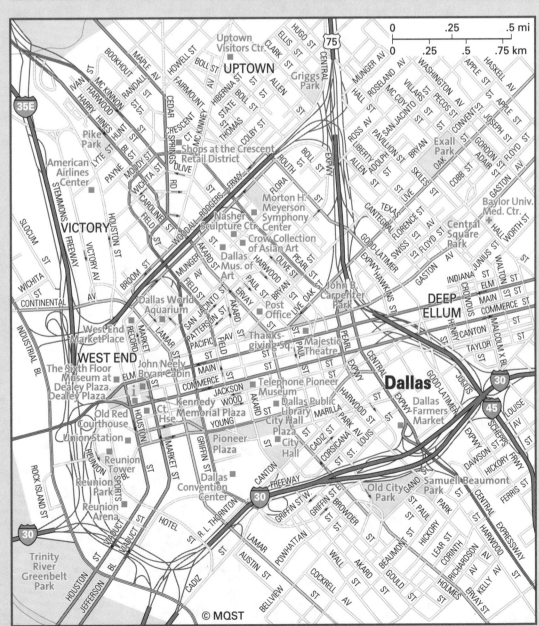

P 48
Texas

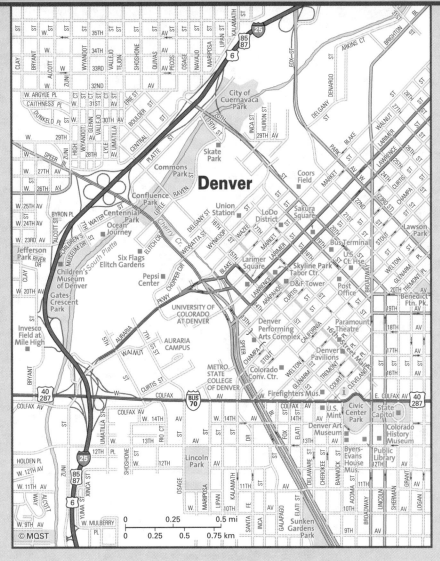

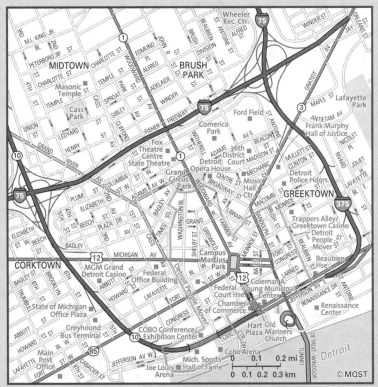

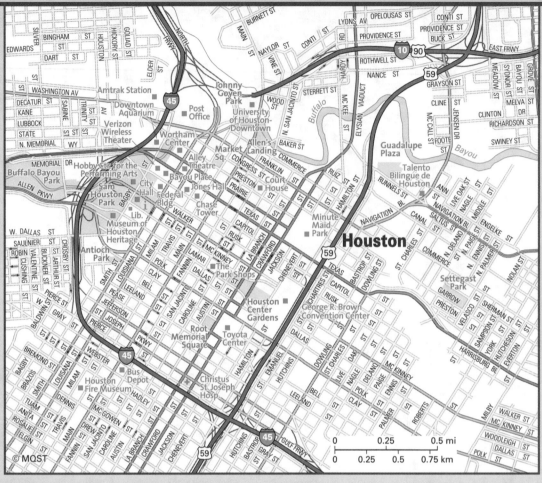

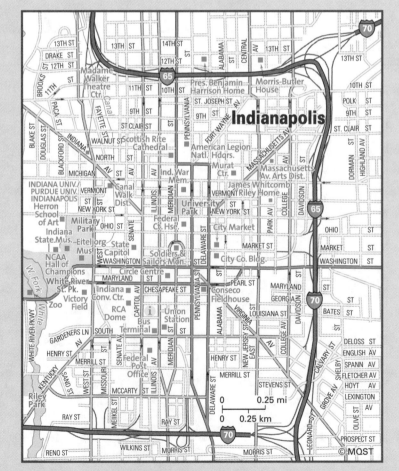

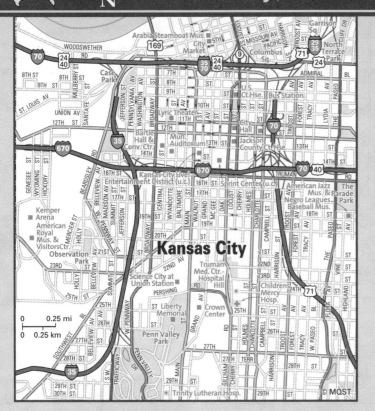

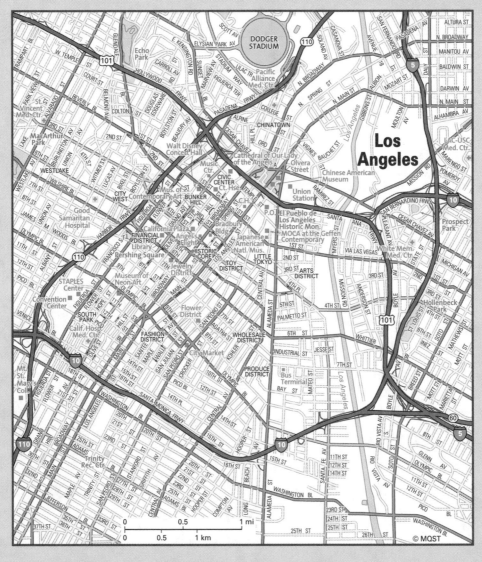

P 31
Missouri

P 34
Nevada

P 11
California

© MQST

Miami (top map)

N.W. 19TH AV · N.W. 22ND AV · N.W. 17TH ST · N.W. 16TH ST · N.W. 15TH ST RD · V.A. Med. Ctr. · N. 16TH ST · Highland Park · N.W. 17TH ST · OVERTOWN · Dorsey Park · Sanford & Dolores Ziff Ballet Opera House · VENETIAN CAUSEWAY · Miami Herald Building · Biscayne I.

Jackson Mem. Hosp. · N.W. 15TH ST · N.W. 14TH ST · Carnival Symphony Hall · Children's Museum · Parrot Jungle Island · Watson I.

Cedars Med. Ctr. · N.W. 14TH ST · N.W.12TH ST · N.W. 11TH · Bicentennial Park · American Airlines Arena · Watson Park · Watson Island Intl. Seaplane Base

N. RIVER DR · Miami · N.W. 10TH ST · N.W. 9TH ST · N.W. 8TH ST · N.W. 7TH ST · N.W. 6TH ST · N.W. 5TH ST · Miami Arena · Freedom Tower · Dodge I.

Orange Bowl · Henderson Park · Lummus Park · Bus Station · DOWN-TOWN · Bayside Marketplace · Port of Miami · PORT BOULEVARD

W. FLAGLER ST · Miami-Dade Cultural Ctr. Hist. Mus. of S. Florida · W. Flagler St · Amphitheatre · Bayfront Park · **Miami**

LITTLE HAVANA · Riverside Park · José Martí Park · Ct. Hse. · Gusman Ctr. · Flagler Palm Cottage · James L. Knight Center · Brickell Key

Juan J. Peruyero Mus. & Manuel F. Artime Lib. · Tower Theater · Triangle Park · Southside Park · FINANCIAL DISTRICT · Brickell Park · Intracoastal · Biscayne

0 · 0.5 · 1 mi
0 · 0.5 · 1 km

Milwaukee (bottom map)

W. CHERRY ST · E. KEWAUNEE ST · Wisc. Conserv. of Music · W. VLIET ST · Martin Luther King Park · McKINLEY AV · W. WINNEBAGO ST · W. JUNEAU AV · E. PLEASANT ST · E. LYON ST · E. OGDEN AV · MILWAUKEE SCHOOL OF ENGINEERING · Veteran's Park

W. HIGHLAND · E. KNAPP · Marcus Ctr. for the Performing Arts · Juneau Park · E. HIGHLAND

W. STATE ST · Bradley Center · Red Arrow Park · Cathedral Sq. · Milwaukee Art Mus. & War Memorial Ctr.

Sinai Samaritan Med. Ctr. · Ct. Hse. · Mac Arthur Square · U.S. Cellular Arena · Pabst Theater · E. KILBOURN · WELLS ST

W. KILBOURN · Discovery World Mus. · Milw. Theatre · St. Office Bldg. · Milw. Co. Hist. Ctr. · Marquette University · C.H. · MASON · Betty Brinn Children's Museum

W. WELLS ST · Milw. Pub. Mus. · IMAX · Midwest Airlines Center · Federal Plaza

W. WISCONSIN AV · MARQUETTE UNIVERSITY · St. Joan of Arc Chapel · Haggerty Mus. of Art · Intercity Bus Depot · The Shops of Grand Av. MICHIGAN · Zeidler Park · EVERETT ST · Grain Exchange · **Milwaukee** · Pier Wisconsin (to open early 2006)

CLYBOURN ST · Helfaer Theatre · CLYBOURN · LAKE MICHIGAN

W. ST. PAUL · W. MT. VERNON AV · Amtrak Station · Post Office · Milwaukee Public Mkt. · Hist. Third Ward · E. BUFFALO · MAIER FESTIVAL PARK

Potawatomi Bingo & Casino · W. CANAL · Menomonee · William Eisner Mus. of Advertising & Design · E. CHICAGO · Broadway Theatre Ctr. · Lakeshore State Park

PITTSBURGH AV · Milwaukee Inst. of Art & Design · SEEBOTH ST · E. MENOMONEE · CORCORAN · POLK ST · Marcus Amphitheater

VIRGINIA · FLORIDA · E. BRUCE ST · Marcus Amphitheater

0 · 0.25 mi
0 · 0.25 km

© MQST

Minneapolis

Nicollet I.

Mississippi

St. Anthony Falls

St. Anthony Main

Central Library (u.c.)

The Depot

Mill City Mus.

Guthrie Theater (u.c.)

Target Center

Orpheum Theatre

IDS Ctr.

Gaviidae Common

State Theatre

C.H.

HHH Metrodome

Orchestra Hall

Loring Park

Guthrie Theater

Walker Art Ctr.

Conv. Ctr.

Elliot Park

N. Central Univ.

Stevens Square

Hennepin Hist. Mus.

Morrison Park

Minn. Inst. of Arts

Bell-Museum of Natural History

Mariucci Arena

Williams Arena

Weisman Art Mus.

UNIV. OF MINNESOTA

Univ. Hosp.

UNIVERSITY OF MINNESOTA

Fairview Riverside Hosp.

Riverside Park

Augsburg Coll

Van Cleve Park

New Orleans

FRENCH QUARTER (VIEUX CARRÉ)

Mahalia Jackson Theatre for the Performing Arts

Louis Armstrong Park

Morris Jeff Mun. Auditorium

New Orleans Jazz N.H.P. Visitor Center

Old U.S. Mint

Washington Square

Pontalba Bldgs.

St. Louis Cathedral

The Cabildo

The Presbytère

Jackson Square

Moonwalk

Saenger Theatre

Musée Conti Wax Mus.

Orpheum Theatre

Jean Lafitte N.H.P. (Visitor Ctr.)

St. Charles Ave. Streetcar

U.S. Customs House

Woldenberg Riverfront Park

Aquarium of the Americas

Med. Ctr. of La.-Univ. Campus

Med. Ctr. of La.

Tulane Univ. Hosp.

V.A. Med. Ctr.

Public Library

City Hall

Louisiana Superdome

New Orleans Centre

New Orleans Arena

P.O. & Fed. Bldg.

Union Passenger Terminal

Lafayette Square

Harrah's

Creole Queen

World Trade Center

Canal Street-Algiers Ferry

Mississippi

Riverwalk

Louisiana Children's Mus.

Ogden Museum

Contemp. Arts Ctr.

Lee Circle

Confederate Museum

Natl. D-Day Mus.

Ernest N. Morial Convention Center

© MQST

© MQST

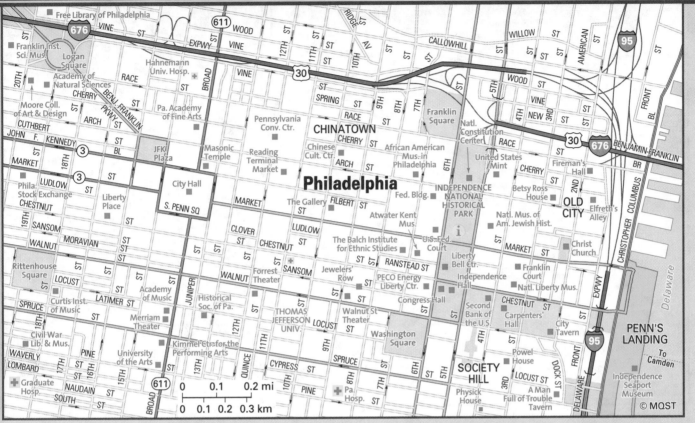

Philadelphia

Free Library of Philadelphia
676 VINE ST
611 WOOD ST
RIDGE
WILLOW ST
AMERICAN
95
Franklin Inst.
Sci. Mus.
VINE EXPWY
VINE ST
12TH
11TH
10TH
CALLOWHILL ST
WOOD
FRONT
Logan
Square
30
ST
9TH
8TH
7TH
5TH
VINE
NEW 3RD
ST
Academy of
Natural Sciences
20TH
RACE
SPRING ST
Franklin
Square
4TH
30
676
BENJAMIN-FRANKLIN BR
Moore Coll.
of Art & Design
CHERRY
BEN. FRANKLIN PKWY
ST
RACE
ST
Natl.
Constitution
Center
CHERRY
ST
Fireman's
Hall
2ND
CHRISTOPHER COLUMBUS
Pa. Academy
of Fine Arts
Hahnemann
Univ. Hosp.
VINE
BROAD
CHINATOWN
Pennsylvania
Conv. Ctr.
African American
Mus. in
Philadelphia
6TH
United States
Mint
Betsy Ross
House
OLD
CITY
CUTHBERT
ARCH ST
Chinese
Cult. Ctr.
CHERRY
ARCH
Fed. Bldg.
Natl. Mus. of
Am. Jewish Hist.
Elfreth's
Alley
JOHN F. KENNEDY
3
BL
JFK
Plaza
Masonic
Temple
Reading
Terminal
Market
INDEPENDENCE
NATIONAL
HISTORICAL
PARK
Christ
Church
MARKET
3
ST
18TH
City Hall
The Gallery
FILBERT
ST
Liberty
Bell Ctr.
MARKET ST
Franklin
Court
Phila.
Stock Exchange
LUDLOW
ST
S. PENN SQ
Atwater Kent
Mus.
The Balch Institute
for Ethnic Studies
U.S. Fed.
Court
Independence
Hall
Natl. Liberty Mus.
CHESTNUT
19TH
Liberty
Place
CLOVER
LUDLOW
RANSTEAD ST
Jewelers'
Row
PECO Energy
Liberty Ctr.
Independence
Hall
CHESTNUT
Carpenters'
Hall
City
Tavern
95
PENN'S
LANDING
SANSOM
CHESTNUT ST
Forrest
Theater
SANSOM
Congress
Hall
Second
Bank of
the U.S.
4TH
WALNUT
Rittenhouse
Square
LOCUST
Academy
of Music
JUNIPER
Historical
Soc. of Pa.
WALNUT
Walnut St
Theater
DOCK ST
Powel
House
To
Camden
SPRUCE
18TH
Curtis Inst.
of Music
LATIMER ST
THOMAS
JEFFERSON
UNIV.
LOCUST
Washington
Square
SOCIETY
HILL
LOCUST ST
A Man
Full of Trouble
Tavern
Independence
Seaport
Museum
Civil War
Lib. & Mus.
Merriam
Theater
Kimmel Ctr. for the
Performing Arts
11TH
WAVERLY
PINE
University
of the Arts
13TH
CYPRESS ST
SPRUCE
6TH
5TH
4TH
3RD
Physick
House
Delaware
LOMBARD
17TH
16TH
15TH
611
QUINCE
PINE
8TH
7TH
Pa.
Hosp.
© MQST
Graduate
Hosp.
NAUDAIN
SOUTH
ST
BROAD
0   0.1   0.2 mi
0 0.1 0.2 0.3 km

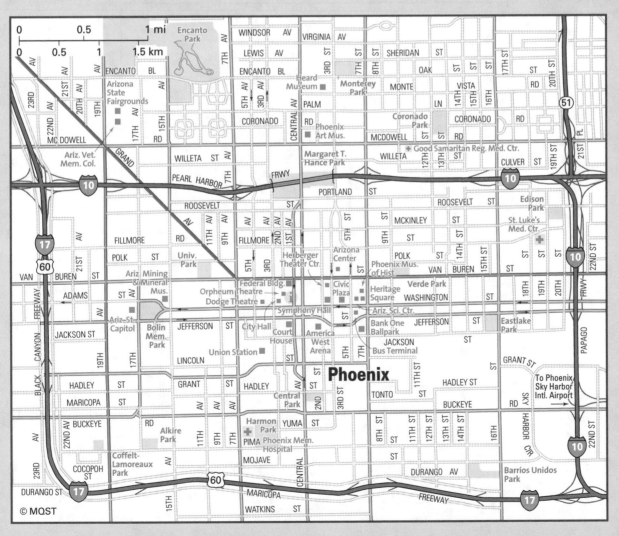

Phoenix

0   0.5   1 mi
0   0.5   1   1.5 km
Encanto
Park
WINDSOR AV
VIRGINIA AV
7TH
95
23RD
21ST
20TH
19TH
ENCANTO BL
LEWIS AV
ENCANTO BL
3RD
7TH
8TH
SHERIDAN ST
17TH
20TH ST
51
22ND
MC DOWELL
Arizona State
Fairgrounds
17TH
15TH RD
Heard
Museum
Monterey
Park
CENTRAL
MONTE
OAK
VISTA
14TH
15TH
16TH
RD
Ariz. Vet.
Mem. Col.
CORONADO
5TH
3RD
PALM
Phoenix
Art Mus.
Coronado
Park
CORONADO
RD
19TH ST
21ST PL
GRAND
WILLETA ST
Margaret T.
Hance Park
MCDOWELL
12TH
13TH
Good Samaritan Reg. Med. Ctr.
WILLETA
CULVER
10
PEARL HARBOR
7TH
FRWY
PORTLAND ST
10
17
ROOSEVELT
ST
ROOSEVELT ST
Edison
Park
60
FILLMORE
RD
11TH
9TH
MCKINLEY
5TH
14TH
15TH ST
St. Luke's
Med. Ctr.
10
VAN
BUREN
POLK
Univ.
Park
FILLMORE
2ND
1ST
POLK
VAN BUREN
18TH
19TH
20TH
22ND ST
Ariz. Mining
& Mineral
Mus.
Herberger
Theater Ctr.
Arizona
Center
Phoenix Mus.
of Hist.
10
ADAMS
Ariz. St.
Capitol
Bolin
Mem.
Park
Orpheum Theatre
Dodge Theatre
Federal Bldg.
Civic
Plaza
Heritage
Square
Verde Park
WASHINGTON
PAPAGO
JACKSON ST
JEFFERSON
Symphony Hall
Ariz. Sci. Ctr.
Bank One
Ballpark
JEFFERSON
Eastlake
Park
America
West
Arena
LINCOLN
Union Station
Court
House
5TH
7TH
JACKSON
Bus Terminal
GRANT ST
To Phoenix
Sky Harbor
Intl. Airport
Phoenix
HADLEY
GRANT
HADLEY
TONTO
11TH
HADLEY ST
SKY HARBOR CIR
Central
Park
2ND
3RD ST
BUCKEYE
MARICOPA
BUCKEYE
YUMA
8TH
11TH
12TH
13TH
14TH
16TH
10
Harmon
Park
22ND AV
Alkire
Park
11TH
9TH
PIMA
Phoenix Mem.
Hospital
MOJAVE
23RD
COCOPOH
Coffelt-
Lamoreaux
Park
60
MARICOPA
CENTRAL
DURANGO AV
Barrios Unidos
Park
17
DURANGO ST
17
WATKINS
FREEWAY
© MQST

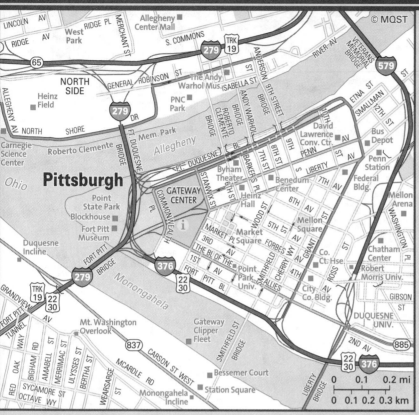

Pittsburgh

NORTH SIDE

Allegheny Center Mall
West Park
S. COMMONS
LINCOLN AV
RIDGE PL
RIDGE AV
MERCHANT ST
65
279
TRK 19
579
The Andy Warhol Mus.
S. COMMONS
ANDERSON ST
ISABELLA ST
9TH ST
RIVER AV
VETERANS MEMORIAL BRIDGE
© MQST
GENERAL ROBINSON ST
ALLEGHENY AV
Heinz Field
PNC Park
279 DR
ETNA ST
SMALLMAN
12TH ST
10TH ST
NORTH SHORE
NORTH
Mem. Park
David L. Lawrence Conv. Ctr.
PENN AV
Bus Depot
Carnegie Science Center
Roberto Clemente
Allegheny
FT. DUQUESNE BRIDGE
ROBERTO CLEMENTE BRIDGE
ANDY WARHOL BRIDGE
7TH ST
8TH ST
9TH ST
LIBERTY AV
Penn Station
Federal Bldg.
Ohio
279
Point State Park
Blockhouse
Fort Pitt Museum
Duquesne Incline
FORT PITT BRIDGE
COMMONWEALTH PL
Byham Theater
BARKER'S PL
STANWIX ST
Heinz Hall
GATEWAY CENTER
WOOD ST
5TH AV
6TH AV
Benedum Center
Mellon Square
Mellon Arena
Washington
Chatham Center
Robert Morris Univ.
376
Monongahela
22 30
FORT PITT BL
Market Square
MARKET PL
3RD AV
THE BL OF THE ALLIES
SMITHFIELD ST
FORBES AV
GRANT ST
CHERRY WY
ROSS ST
Co. Ct. Hse.
City Co. Bldg.
Point Park Univ.
GIBSON ST
DUQUESNE UNIV.
FORT PITT TUNNEL
GRANDVIEW AV
TRK 19
22 30
RED OAK WAY
BIGHAM ST
AMABELL ST
MERRIMAC ST
ULYSSES ST
BERTHA ST
SYCAMORE ST
OCTAVE WY
WEARSARGE ST
MCARDLE RD
837
CARSON ST WEST
Mt. Washington Overlook
Gateway Clipper Fleet
SMITHFIELD ST BRIDGE
Bessemer Court
Station Square
Monongahela Incline
2ND AV
885
LIBERTY BRIDGE
22 30
376

0 0.1 0.2 mi
0 0.1 0.2 0.3 km

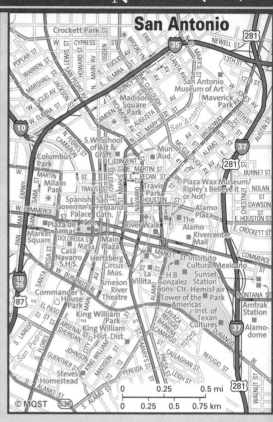

San Antonio

Crockett Park
CYPRESS
281
NEWELL AV
35
© MQST
POPLAR ST
WARREN ST
MARSHALL ST
JACKSON ST
W. EUCLID AV
W. ELMIRA ST
San Antonio Museum of Art
Maverick Park
San Antonio River
BROADWAY
Columbus Park
S.W. School of Art & Craft
Mun. Aud.
37
281
BURNET ST
NOLAN
CHESTNUT
DAWSON
E. HOUSTON ST
E. CROCKETT ST
E. COMMERCE ST
W. EXPWY
Martin Milam Park
W. MARTIN ST
TRAVIS
Travis Park
W. HOUSTON
Spanish Governor's Palace
San Fernando Cath.
River Walk
The Alamo
Plaza
Alamo Plaza Rivercenter Mall
Ripley's Believe It or Not!
Plaza Wax Museum/
W. COMMERCE
Market Square
DOLOROSA ST
NUEVA ST
Plaza de las Islas
Main Plaza
Casa Navarro S.H.S.
Hertzberg Circus Mus.
La Villita
MARKET ST
Instituto Cultural Mexicano
H.B. Gonzalez Conv. Ctr.
Sunset Station
10 35
87
W. DURANGO ST
Commander's House
S. EL PASO ST
Arneson River Theatre
HemisFair Park
Tower of the Americas
Inst. of Texan Cultures
DURANGO
Amtrak Station
37
MONTANA ST
King William Park
King William Hist. Dist.
S. LAREDO ST
S. PEDRO ST
ARSENAL ST
SHERIDAN
KING WILLIAM ST
GUENTHER ST
JOHNSON ST
S. ST. MARY'S ST
LAVACA ST
BARRERA ST
CAMARGO ST
MADISON ST
Alamodome
Steves Homestead
S. ALAMO ST
PEREIDA ST
LEIGH ST
CALLAGHAN ST
REFUGIO ST
281
WALNUT ST
© MQST 536

0 0.25 0.5 mi
0 0.25 0.5 0.75 km

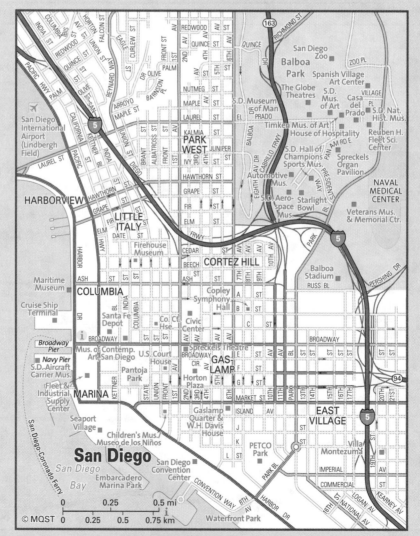

San Diego

San Diego International Airport (Lindbergh Field)
COLUMBIA ST
INDIA ST
HORTON ST
REYNARD WAY
REDWOOD ST
QUINCE ST
PALM ST
OLIVE ST
NUTMEG ST
MAPLE ST
LAUREL ST
5
163
REDWOOD
QUINCE
163
QUINCE ST
San Diego Zoo
ZOO PL
Balboa Park
Spanish Village Art Center
The Globe Theatres
S.D. Museum of Man
El Prado
S.D. Mus. of Art
Casa del Prado
VILLAGE PL
S.D. Nat. Hist. Mus.
PARK WEST
KALMIA ST
IVY ST
JUNIPER ST
HAWTHORN ST
GRAPE ST
FIR ST
ELM ST
Timken Mus. of Art
House of Hospitality
CABRILLO FRWY
BALBOA DR
PAN AM RD E.
Reuben H. Fleet Sci. Center
S.D. Hall of Champions Sports Mus.
Automotive Mus.
S.D. Aero-space Mus.
EIGHTH AV
PRESIDENTS WAY
Spreckels Organ Pavilion
NAVAL MEDICAL CENTER
HARBORVIEW
LITTLE ITALY
DATE
Firehouse Museum
CEDAR ST
BEECH ST
CORTEZ HILL
7TH 8TH 9TH
Balboa Stadium
RUSS BL
PARK BL
PERSHING DR
Starlight Bowl
Veterans Mus. & Memorial Ctr.
Maritime Museum
COLUMBIA
ASH ST
Copley Symphony Hall
A ST
Cruise Ship Terminal
HARBOR DR
Santa Fe Depot
Co. Ct. Hse.
Civic Center
B ST
C ST
BROADWAY
Mus. of Contemp. Art San Diego
U.S. Court House
Spreckels Theatre
BROADWAY CIR.
GAS LAMP
Broadway Pier
Navy Pier
S.D. Aircraft Carrier Mus.
Fleet & Industrial Supply Center
MARINA
Pantoja Park
Horton Plaza
STATE
UNION
FRONT
1ST
2ND
3RD
4TH
5TH
6TH
F ST
G ST
Seaport Village
Children's Mus./ Museo de los Niños
Gaslamp Quarter & W.H. Davis House
ISLAND AV
J ST
PETCO Park
Villa Montezuma
EAST VILLAGE
5
94
San Diego Bay
Embarcadero Marina Park
San Diego Convention Center
San Diego-Coronado Ferry
CONVENTION WAY
8TH AV
HARBOR DR
Waterfront Park
IMPERIAL AV
COMMERCIAL ST
LOGAN AV
KEARNEY AV
NATIONAL AV

0 0.25 0.5 mi
0 0.25 0.5 0.75 km
© MQST

N

to Tiburon & Vallejo

to Sausalito & Larkspur

to Sausalito, Tiburon, & Vallejo

to Alcatraz Island & Angel Island

to Oakland & Alameda

to Oakland & Alameda

San Francisco Bay

San Francisco Bay

San Francisco

Rincon Point

China Basin

Central Basin

CITY FRONT

SOUTH BEACH

SHOWPLACE SQUARE DESIGN DISTRICT

NORTH BEACH

TELEGRAPH HILL

CHINATOWN

NOB HILL

RUSSIAN HILL

SOUTH OF MARKET (SOMA)

MARINA

CIVIC CENTER

HAYES VALLEY

PACIFIC HEIGHTS

WESTERN ADDITION

HAIGHT-ASHBURY

RICHMOND

THE PRESIDIO

GOLDEN GATE NATIONAL RECREATION AREA

0.5 mi

0.75 km

0.25   0.5

0.25   0.5

0   0

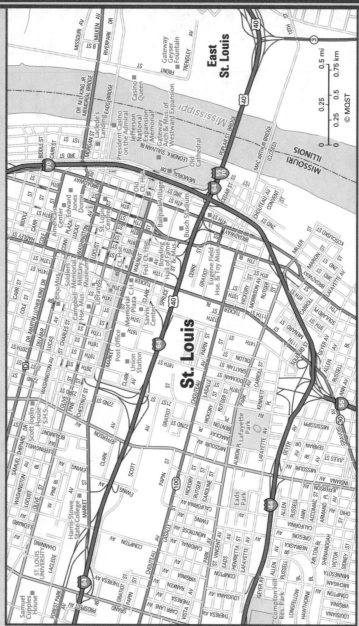

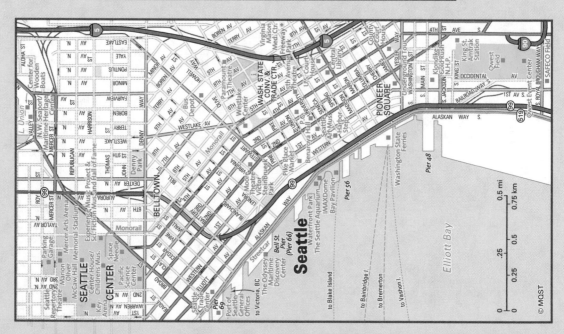

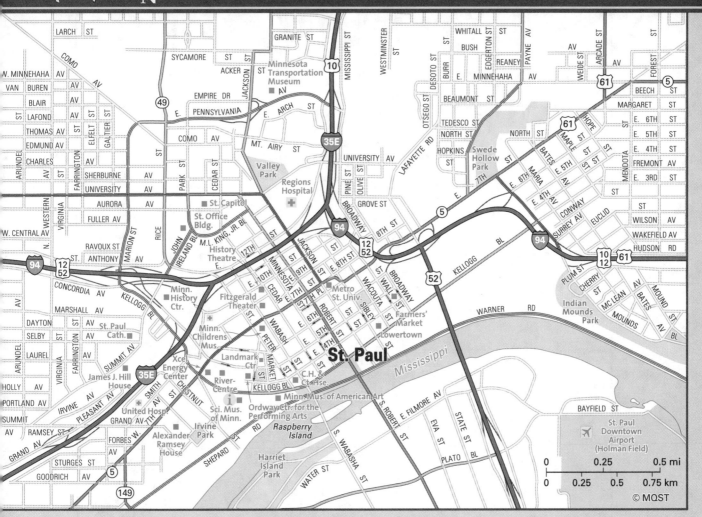

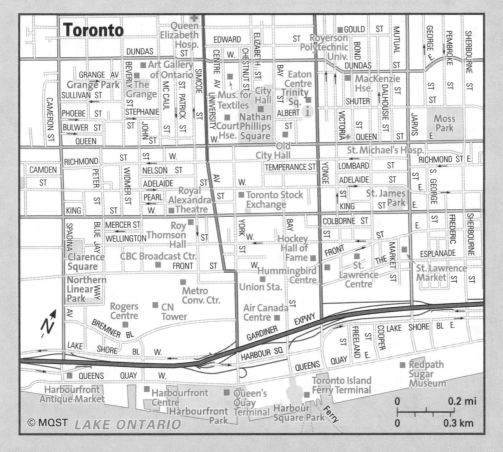

P 27
Minnesota

P 62
Ontario

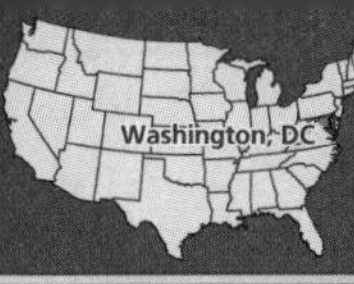

Washington

GEORGETOWN

NORTH CAPITOL

CHINATOWN

DOWNTOWN

CAPITOL HILL

NEAR SOUTHEAST

SW/WATERFRONT

FOGGY BOTTOM

LAFAYETTE SQUARE

ROSSLYN

Points of interest

- Bus Depot
- Union Station
- National Postal Museum
- Government Printing Office
- Georgetown University Law Center
- Union Station Plaza
- Taft Memorial Carillon
- Sewall-Belmont House
- Senate Office Buildings
- The Supreme Court
- Thomas Jefferson Building
- Library of Congress
- James Madison Building
- John Adams Building
- U.S. Capitol
- U.S. Grant Memorial
- U.S. Botanic Garden
- Capitol Reflecting Pool
- House Office Buildings
- Natl. Museum of the American Indian
- Dept. of Health, Education & Human Services
- The Washington Design Ctr.
- Southeastern University
- Waterside Mall
- Washington Convention Center
- National Building Museum
- Marian Koshland Science Mus.
- Judiciary Square
- Department of Labor
- John Marshall Park
- U.S. District Court Hse.
- National Portrait Gallery
- Smithsonian Am. Art Mus. (closed for renovation)
- Friendship Archway
- MCI Center
- U.S. Navy Memorial & Naval Heritage Ctr.
- The National Archives
- Natl. Gallery of Art West Bldg.
- Natl. Gallery of Art East Bldg.
- Natl. Air & Space Museum
- Dept. of Transportation
- L'Enfant Plaza
- Dept. of Health & Human Services
- Benjamin Banneker Park
- City Mus. of Wash. DC
- National Museum of Women in the Arts
- Martin Luther King, Jr. Mem. Library
- Warner Theatre
- Ford's Theatre N.H.S.
- Int'l. Spy Mus.
- Shakespeare Th.
- Dept. of Justice
- J. Edgar Hoover FBI Building
- I.R.S.
- Natl. Mus. of Natural History
- The Hirshhorn Museum and Sculpture Garden
- Arts & Industries Building
- Smithsonian Institution Castle
- Natl. Mus. of African Art
- Arthur M. Sackler Gallery
- Freer Gallery of Art
- Ice Skating Rink
- NASA
- U.S. Postal Service Headquarters
- Thomas Circle
- Franklin Park
- National Theatre
- Old Post Office Pavilion
- Environmental Protection Agency
- Dept. of Agriculture
- U.S. Holocaust Memorial Museum
- Washington Post
- B'nai B'rith Klutznick National Jewish Mus.
- National Geographic Society & Explorers Hall
- McPherson Square
- Department of Veterans Affairs
- Claims Court
- Dept. of the Treasury
- The White House (CLOSED TO VEHICLES)
- Pershing Park
- The National Aquarium
- Ronald Reagan Bldg. and Int'l. Trade Center
- Dept. of Commerce
- National Museum of American History
- Washington Monument
- St. Matthew's Cathedral
- Wilderness Society
- Lafayette Square
- Blair-Lee House (CLOSED TO VEHICLES)
- Corcoran Gallery of Art
- American Red Cross
- D.A.R.
- Art Mus. of the Americas
- Zero Milestone
- The Ellipse
- SOUTH PLACE
- Parking
- Natl. World War II Memorial
- Decatur House
- Edward R. Murrow Park
- Renwick Gallery
- Octagon House
- Department of the Interior
- Organization of American States
- Constitution Hall
- Signers of the Declaration of Independence Memorial
- Rainbow Pool
- D.C. War Memorial
- James Monroe Park
- George Washington Univ. Hosp.
- George Washington University
- Department of State
- Constitution Gardens
- Vietnam Veterans Memorial
- Reflecting Pool
- West Potomac Park
- Korean War Veterans Memorial
- Franklin Delano Roosevelt Memorial
- Lincoln Memorial
- F.D.R. Mem. Park
- U.S. Navy Bureau of Medicine and Surgery
- John F. Kennedy Center for the Performing Arts
- Rock Creek Park
- The Shops at Georgetown Park
- Georgetown Park
- C & O Canal N.H.P.
- Old Stone House
- Washington Harbour
- Georgetown Waterfront Park
- Theodore Roosevelt Memorial
- Theodore Roosevelt Island
- Tidal Basin
- Thomas Jefferson Memorial
- Bureau of Engraving & Printing
- East Potomac Park
- Columbia Island
- Lady Bird Johnson Park
- Lyndon B. Johnson Memorial Grove
- Navy and Marine Memorial
- Marine Corps War Memorial
- The Netherlands Carillon
- United Spanish War Veterans Mem.
- U.S. Navy Mem.
- Women in Military Service for America Mem.
- Seabees of the U.S. Navy
- Arlington National Cemetery
- John F. Kennedy Gravesite
- Tomb of the Unknowns
- North Parking Area for the Pentagon

Rivers and channels

- Potomac River
- Georgetown Channel
- Washington Channel
- Little River
- Rock Creek
- Boundary Channel

Scale

0.5 mi — 0.75 km
0.25 — 0.5
0 — 0.25

DIST. OF COLUMBIA
VIRGINIA
D.C. VA.

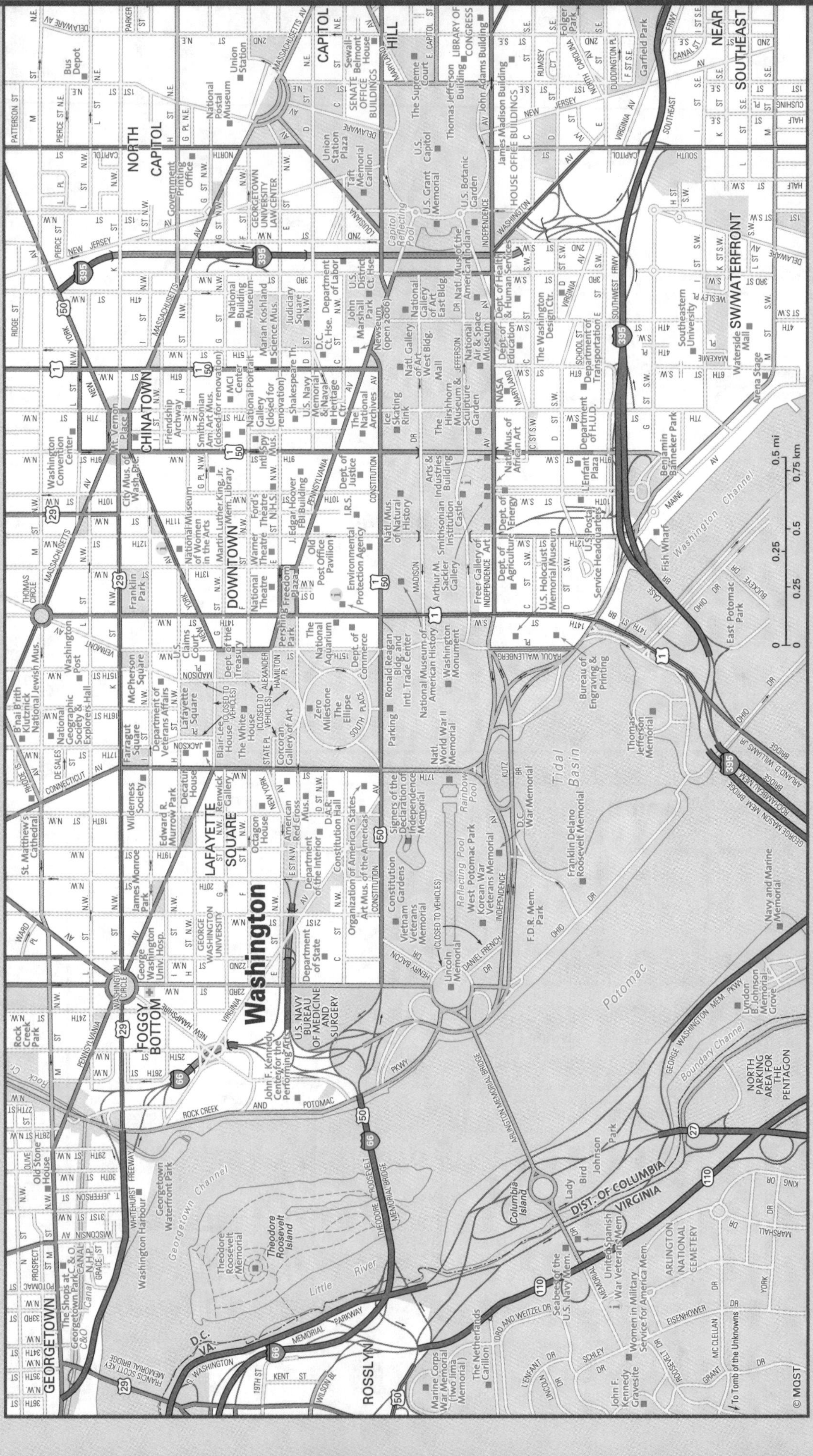

© MOST

American Map®

Business Road Atlas

Reference Section

▪ Features of this Section

These information-packed pages offer important demographic data ranked by a variety of categories for two kinds of marketing units: United States Core Based Statistical Areas (CBSAs), as defined by the U.S. Office of Managements and Budget (OMB); and three-digit ZIP Code Areas, as defined by the U.S. Postal Service. You will also find a number of convenient daily planning aids, such as area code listings, time zones, international dial codes, mileage charts, and more.

▪ Contents

▪ Notes on CBSA and Three-Digit ZIP Code Areas:

CBSAs: These areas are constituted of one or more entire counties. The two types of CBSAs are metropolitan statistical areas, as defined by the OMB. Metropolitan statistical areas contain at least one "urbanized area" with a population of 50,000 or more. Micropolitan statistical areas contain at least one "urban cluster" with a population of at least 10,000 but less than 50,000. For more information, see <www.census.gov/population/www/estimates/aboutmetro.html>.

Three-Digit ZIP Code Areas: The first digit of a three-digit ZIP Code area identifies one of the 10 national ZIP Code areas (see map on pages 158-159). The next two digits break down the national areas into smaller geographical units. Combined, these three digits identify units that are served by Sectional Centers that are responsible for the distribution of mail to smaller post offices in the area. Due to their population density, some large cities have their own three-digit ZIP code. (Fourth and fifth digits - not included in this publication - when added to the three above, form the five digit code used to identify local delivery areas.)

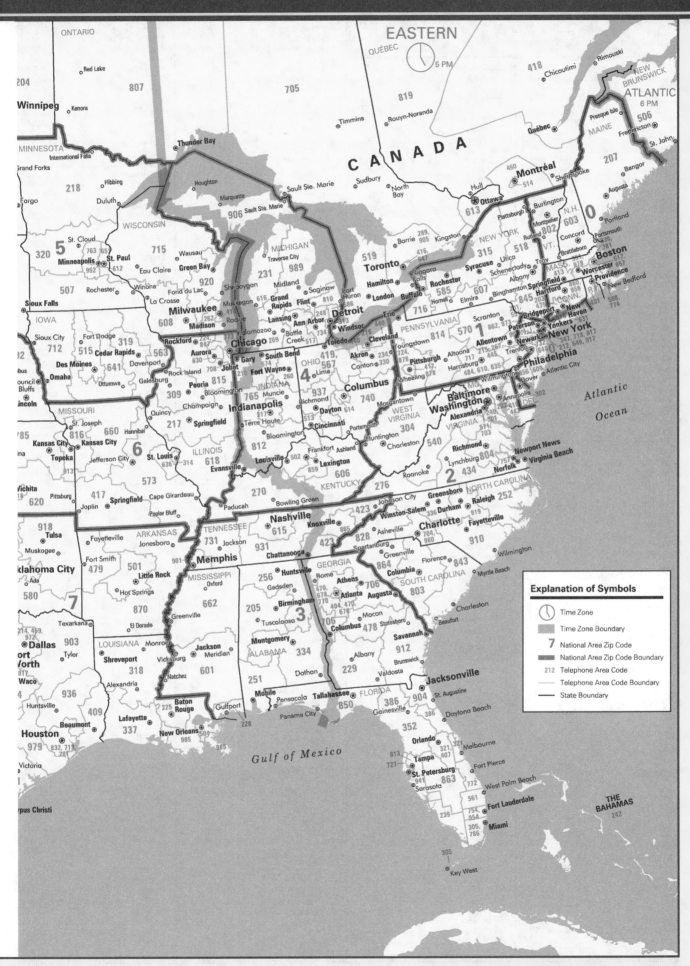

Frequently Called Cities in the U. S., Canada, and the Caribbean

Alabama
Birmingham 205
Mobile 251
Montgomery 334

Alaska
all points 907

Arizona
Phoenix 602
Tucson 520

Arkansas
Little Rock 501
Pine Bluff 870

California
Anaheim 714
Bakersfield 661
Beverly Hills 818
Burbank 818
Fresno 559
Los Angeles: Downtown 213
  Greater Metro Area 323
Oakland 510
Palo Alto 650
Palm Springs 760
Pasadena 626
Redding 530
Sacramento 916
San Bernardino 909
San Diego 619
San Francisco 415
San Jose 408
Santa Rosa 707

Colorado
Colorado Springs 719
Denver ....303 & 720
Grand Junction 970

Connecticut
Hartford ....860 & 959
New Haven ....203 & 475
Stamford ....203 & 475

Delaware
all points 302

District of Columbia
Washington, D.C. 202

Florida
Fort Lauderdale ....754 & 954
Gainesville 352
Jacksonville 904
Miami ....305 & 786
Orlando ....321 & 407
St. Petersburg 727
Sarasota 941
Tallahassee 850
Tampa 813
West Palm Beach 561

Georgia
Albany 229
Atlanta:
  Central ....404, 678 & 770
  Greater
    Metro Area ....470, 678 & 770
Augusta 706
Columbus 706
Macon 478
Savannah 912

Hawaii
all points 808

Idaho
all points 208

Illinois
Bloomington 309
Champaign 217
Chicago: Inner 312
  Outer ....224, 773 & 847

East St. Louis 618
Peoria 309
Rockford 815
Springfield 217

Indiana
Evansville 812
Fort Wayne 260
Gary 219
Indianapolis 317
Muncie 765
South Bend 574

Iowa
Cedar Rapids 319
Council Bluffs 712
Davenport 563
Des Moines 515
Sioux City 712

Kansas
Kansas City 913
Topeka 785

Kentucky
Covington 859
Lexington-Fayette 859
Louisville 502
Owensboro 270

Louisiana
Baton Rouge 225
Lafayette 337
New Orleans 504
Shreveport 318

Maine
all points 207

Maryland
Annapolis ....410 & 443
Baltimore ....410 & 443
Bethesda ....240 & 301

Massachusetts
Boston ....617 & 857
Lawrence ....351 & 978
Lowell ....351 & 978
New Bedford ....508 & 774
Springfield 413
Weymouth ....339 & 781
Worcester ....508 & 774

Michigan
Ann Arbor 734
Detroit 313
Grand Rapids 616
Lansing 517
Pontiac 248
Saginaw 989

Minnesota
Duluth 218
Minneapolis 612
Rochester 507
St. Cloud 320
St. Paul 651

Mississippi
Gulfport 228
Jackson 601

Missouri
Columbia 573
Kansas City 816
St. Louis 314
  Suburbs 336
Springfield 417

Montana
all points 406

Nebraska
Lincoln 402
North Platte 308
Omaha 402

Nevada
Carson City 775
Las Vegas 702
Reno 775

New Hampshire
all points 603

New Jersey
Atlantic City 609
Camden 856
Elizabeth 908
Jersey City ....201 & 551
Middletown ....732 & 848
Newark ....862 & 973
Paterson ....862 & 973
Trenton 609

New Mexico
all points 505

New York
Albany 518
Binghamton 607
Buffalo 716
Long Island: Nassau Co. 516
  Suffolk Co. 631
New York City:
  Bronx ....347, 718 & 917
  Brooklyn ....347, 718 & 917
  Manhattan ....212, 646 & 917
  Queens.............347, 718 & 917
  Staten Island .....347, 718 & 917
Plattsburgh 518
Poughkeepsie 845
Rochester 585
Syracuse 315
White Plains 914
Yonkers 914

North Carolina
Asheville 828
Charlotte ....704 & 980
Durham 919
Greensboro 336
Raleigh 919
Rocky Mount 252
Wilmington 910
Winston-Salem 336

North Dakota
all points 701

Ohio
Akron ....234 & 330
Cincinnati 513
Cleveland 216
Columbus 614
Dayton 937
Lorain 440
Toledo ....419 & 567
Youngstown ....234 & 330

Oklahoma
Enid 580
Oklahoma City 405
Tulsa 918

Oregon
Eugene 541
Portland ....503 & 971
Salem ....503 & 971

Pennsylvania
Allentown ....484, 610 & 835
Bethel Park ....412 & 878
Erie 814
Harrisburg 717
Philadelphia ....215, 267 & 445
Pittsburgh ....412 & 878
Scranton 570

Rhode Island
all points 401

South Carolina
Charleston 843
Columbia 803
Greenville 864

South Dakota
all points 605

Tennessee
Chattanooga 423
Knoxville 865
Memphis 901
Nashville 615

Texas
Abilene 915
Amarillo 806
Austin 512
Corpus Christi 361
Dallas...................214, 469 & 972
El Paso 915
Fort Worth ....682 & 817
Galveston 409
Houston ....281, 713 & 832
Lubbock 806
Odessa 915
San Antonio 210
Tyler 903
Waco 254

Utah
Cedar City 435
Salt Lake City 801

Vermont
all points 802

Virginia
Arlington ....571 & 703
Norfolk 757
Richmond 804
Roanoke 540

Washington
Olympia 360
Seattle 206
Spokane 509
Tacoma 253

West Virginia
all points 304

Wisconsin
Eau Claire 715
Green Bay 920
Madison 608
Milwaukee 414

Wyoming
all points 307

Canada
Calgary 403
Edmonton 780
Hamilton ....289 & 905
Halifax 902
Montréal 450
Ottawa 613
Québec City 418
Regina 306
St. John's 709
Thunder Bay 807
Toronto ....416 & 647
Vancouver ....604 & 778
Victoria 250
Windsor 519
Winnipeg 204

Caribbean
Anguilla 264
Antigua & Barbuda 268
Bahamas 242
Barbados 246
Bermuda 441
British Virgin Islands 284
Cayman Islands 345
Dominica 767
Dominican Republic 809
Grenada 473
Jamaica 876
Montserrat 664
Puerto Rico ....787 & 939
St. Kitts & Nevis 869
St. Lucia 758
St. Vincent & Grenadines 784
Trinidad & Tobago 868
Turks & Caicos 649
U.S. Virgin Islands 340

Area Codes: Numerical Listing for the United States, Canada, and the Caribbean

201	New Jersey - Northeastern (shared with 551)
202	District of Columbia
203	Connecticut - Southwestern (shared with 475)
204	Canada - Manitoba Province
205	Alabama - West Central
206	Washington - Seattle Metro Area
207	Maine
208	Idaho
209	California - Upper Central
210	Texas - San Antonio Metro Area
212	New York - New York City, Manhattan (shared with 646 & 917)
213	California - Downtown Los Angeles
214	Texas - Dallas Metro & Outlying Area (shared with 469 & 972)
215	Pennsylvania - Philadelphia Metro Area (shared with 267 & 445)
216	Ohio - Cleveland Metro Area
217	Illinois - Central
218	Minnesota - northern third
219	Indiana - Northern
224	Illinois - Northwest (Outer) Chicago & Outlying Area (shared with 847)
225	Louisiana - Baton Rouge General Area
228	Mississippi - Gulf Coast
229	Georgia - Southeastern (shared with 912)
231	Michigan - Northwestern
234	Ohio - East Central (shared with 330)
239	Florida - Southwestern
240	Maryland - Western Half (shared with 301)
242	Caribbean - Bahamas
246	Caribbean - Barbados
248	Michigan - Detroit Metro Outlying Area
250	Canada - British Columbia Province (Excluding Vancouver Metro Area)
251	Alabama - Mobile Metro and Outlying Area
252	North Carolina - Northeastern
253	Washington - Tacoma Metro Area
254	Texas - Central
256	Alabama - North & East Central
260	Indiana - Northwestern
262	Wisconsin - Southeastern
264	Caribbean - Anguilla
267	Pennsylvania - Philadelphia Metro Area (shared with 215 & 445)
268	Caribbean - Antigua & Barbuda
269	Michigan - Southwestern (shared with 616)
270	Kentucky - Western Half
276	Virginia - Southwestern
281	Texas - Houston Metro & Outlying Area (shared with 713 & 832)
284	Caribbean - British Virgin Islands
289	Canada - Lake Ontario Coastal Area (Excluding Toronto Metro area), Ontario Province (shared with 905)
301	Maryland - Western Half (shared with 240)
302	Delaware
303	Colorado - Denver Metro Area (shared with 720)
304	West Virginia
305	Florida - Southern (shared with 786)
306	Canada - Saskatchewan Province
307	Wyoming
308	Nebraska - Western Half
309	Illinois - West Central
310	California - Malibu/Santa Monica Area (shared with 424)
312	Illinois - Inner Chicago
313	Michigan - Detroit Metro Area
314	Missouri - St. Louis Metro Area
315	New York - North Central
316	Kansas - Wichita Metro Area
317	Indiana - Central
318	Louisiana - Northern & Central
319	Iowa - Eastern
320	Minnesota - Central Third
321	Florida - East Central (shared with 407)
323	California - Los Angeles Metro Area
330	Ohio - East Central (shared with 234)
334	Alabama - South Central & Southeastern
336	North Carolina - Northwestern
337	Louisiana - Southwestern
339	Massachusetts - Boston Metro Outlying Area (shared with 781)
340	Caribbean - United States Virgin Islands
345	Caribbean - Cayman Islands
347	New York - New York City, Outer Boroughs (shared with 718 & 917)
351	Massachusetts - Northeastern (shared with 978)
352	Florida - Upper West Central

360	Washington - Western Half (Excluding Seattle-Tacoma Metro Area)
361	Texas - Lower Gulf Coast
385	Utah (Excluding Salt Lake City Metro Area)
386	Florida - Northern
401	Rhode Island
402	Nebraska - Eastern Half
403	Canada - Southern Alberta Province
404	Georgia - Central Atlanta (shared with 678 & 470)
405	Oklahoma - Oklahoma City Metro Area
406	Montana
407	Florida - East Central (Partially Shared with 321)
408	California - San Jose Area (shared with 669)
409	Texas - Southeastern (Excluding Houston General Area)
410	Maryland - Eastern Half (shared with 443)
412	Pennsylvania - Pittsburgh Metro Area (shared with 878)
413	Massachusetts - Western
414	Wisconsin - Milwaukee Metro Area
415	California - San Francisco Metro Area
416	Canada - Toronto Metro Area, Ontario Province (shared with 647)
417	Missouri - Southwestern
418	Canada - Eastern Québec Province
419	Ohio - Northwestern (shared with 567)
423	Tennessee - Northeastern & Southeastern
424	California - Malibu/Santa Monica Area (shared with 310)
425	Washington - Seattle-Tacoma Metro Outlying Area
434	Virginia - South Central
435	Utah - (Excluding Salt Lake City Metro Area)
440	Ohio - Northeastern
441	Caribbean - Bermuda
443	Maryland - Eastern Half (shared with 410)
445	Pennsylvania - Metro Area (shared with 215 & 267)
450	Canada - Montréal Metro Area, Québec Province
469	Texas - Dallas Metro & Outlying Area (shared with 214 & 972)
470	Georgia - Central Atlanta (shared with 404, 678 & 770)
473	Caribbean - Grenada
475	Connecticut - Southwestern (shared with 203)
478	Georgia - Central
479	Arkansas - Northwestern
480	Arizona - Phoenix Metro Outlying Area
484	Pennsylvania - Philadelphia Metro Outlying Area (shared with 610 & 835)
501	Arkansas - Northwestern
502	Kentucky - North Central
503	Oregon - Portland-Salem Metro Area (shared with 971)
504	Louisiana - New Orleans Metro Area
505	New Mexico
506	Canada - New Brunswick Province
507	Minnesota - Southern
508	Massachusetts - Southeastern (shared with 774)
509	Washington - Eastern Half
510	California - Oakland-Berkeley Metro Area
512	Texas - Austin General Area
513	Ohio - Southwestern
514	Canada - Montréal Outlying Area
515	Iowa - Central
516	New York - Nassau County, Long Island
517	Michigan - South Central
518	New York - Upstate, Eastern Half
519	Canada - Southwestern Ontario Province
520	Arizona - Southeastern
530	California - Northeastern
540	Virginia - Western
541	Oregon - (Excluding Portland-Salem Metro Area)
551	New Jersey - Northeastern (shared with 201)
559	California - Central
561	Florida - Lower East Central
562	California - Long Beach Area
563	Iowa - Eastern
567	Ohio - Northwestern (shared with 419)
570	Pennsylvania - Northeastern
571	Virginia - Northeastern (shared with 703)
573	Missouri - Eastern (Excluding Northeast and St. Louis General Area)
574	Indiana - North
580	Oklahoma - Western & Southeastern
585	New York - Southwestern (shared with 716)
586	Michigan - East Central (shared with 810)
601	Mississippi - Southern Half (Excluding Gulf Coast)
602	Arizona - Phoenix Metro Area
603	New Hampshire
604	Canada - Vancouver Metro Area, British Columbia Province (shared with 778)
605	South Dakota
606	Kentucky - Eastern
607	New York - South Central
608	Wisconsin - Southwestern

609	New Jersey - Central & Southeastern
610	Pennsylvania - Philadelphia Metro Outlying Area (shared with 484 & 835)
612	Minnesota - Western Minneapolis-St. Paul Metro Area
613	Canada - Southeastern Ontario Province (Excluding Toronto Metro Area)
614	Ohio - Columbus Metro Area
615	Tennessee - Nashville General Area
616	Michigan - Southwestern (shared with 269)
617	Massachusetts - Boston Metro Area (shared with 857)
618	Illinois - Southern
619	California - San Diego Metro Area
620	Kansas - Southern Half (Excluding Wichita Metro Area)
623	Arizona - Phoenix Metro Outlying Area
626	California - Pasadena Area
630	Illinois - West Side (Outer) Chicago & Outlying Area
631	New York - Suffolk County, Long Island
636	Missouri - St. Louis Metro Outlying Area
641	Iowa - Central
646	New York - New York City, Manhattan (shared with 212 & 917)
647	Canada - Toronto Metro Area, Ontario Province (shared with 416)
649	Caribbean - Turks & Caicos Islands
650	California - South Bay Area
651	Minnesota - Eastern Minneapolis-St. Paul Metro Area
660	Missouri - Northwestern
661	California - Bakersfield Area
662	Mississippi - Northern Half
664	Caribbean - Montserrat
669	California - San Jose Area (shared with 408)
671	Guam
678	Georgia - Atlanta Metro Outlying Area (shared with 470 & 770)
682	Texas - Ft. Worth Metro Area (shared with 817)
701	North Dakota
702	Nevada - Far Southeastern (Las Vegas General Area)
703	Virginia - Northeastern (shared with 571)
704	North Carolina - South Central (shared with 980)
705	Canada - Central Southeastern Ontario Province
706	Georgia - Northern Half (Excluding Atlanta General Area)
707	California - Northwestern
708	Illinois - South Side (Outer) Chicago & Outlying Area
709	Canada - Newfoundland Province
712	Iowa - Western
713	Texas - Houston Metro & Outlying Area (shared with 281 & 832)
714	California - Anaheim & Santa Ana Area
715	Wisconsin - Northern
716	New York - Western
717	Pennsylvania - Southeastern (Excluding Philadelphia General Area)
718	New York - New York City, Outer Boroughs (shared with 347 & 917)
719	Colorado - Southeastern
720	Colorado - Denver Metro Area (shared with 303)
724	Pennsylvania - Southwestern (Excluding Pittsburgh Metro Area) (shared with 878)
727	Florida - West Central Coastal Area
731	Tennessee - Eastern Third (Excluding Memphis Metro Area)
732	New Jersey - East Central (shared with 848)
734	Michigan - Southeastern
740	Ohio - Southeastern
754	Florida - Ft. Lauderdale Area (shared with 954)
757	Virginia - Southeastern
758	Caribbean - St. Lucia
760	California - Southern & Desert Area (Excluding San Diego Metro Area)
763	Minnesota - Minneapolis-St. Paul Metro Outlying Area
765	Indiana - East Central
767	Caribbean - Dominica
770	Georgia - Atlanta Metro Outlying Area (shared with 470 & 678)
772	Florida - Lower East Central (shared with 561)
773	Illinois - Chicago Outer Metro Area
774	Massachusetts - Southeastern (shared with 508)
775	Nevada - (Excluding Far Southeast, Las Vegas General Area)
778	Canada - Vancouver Metro Area, British Columbia Province (shared with 604)
780	Canada - Northern Alberta Province
781	Massachusetts - Boston Metro Outlying Area (shared With 339)
784	Caribbean - St. Vincent and the Grenadines
785	Kansas - Northern Half
786	Florida - Southern (shared with 305)
787	Caribbean - Puerto Rico (shared with 939)
801	Utah - Salt Lake City Metro Area
802	Vermont
803	South Carolina - Central
804	Virginia - East Central
805	California - Santa Barbara Area
806	Texas - Panhandle
807	Canada - Western Ontario Province

808	Hawaii
809	Caribbean - Dominican Republic
810	Michigan - East Central
812	Indiana - Southern
813	Florida - Tampa Area
814	Pennsylvania - Central Western
815	Illinois - Northwestern
816	Missouri - Kansas City Metro Area
817	Texas - Ft. Worth Metro Area (shared with 682)
818	California - Burbank Area
819	Canada - Southern & Western Québec Province
828	North Carolina - Southwestern
830	Texas - Southwestern (Excluding San Antonio Metro Area)
831	California - Monterey Area
832	Texas - Houston Metro & Outlying Area (shared with 281 & 713)
835	Pennsylvania - Philadelphia Metro Outlying Area (shared with 484 & 610)
843	South Carolina - Eastern
845	New York - Southeastern (Excluding New York City, Long Island and Westchester County)
847	Illinois - Northwest (Outer) Chicago & Outlying Area (shared with 224)
848	New Jersey - East Central (shared with 732)
850	Florida - Panhandle
856	New Jersey - Southwestern
857	Massachusetts - Boston Metro Area (shared with 617)
858	California - Northwestern San Diego Metro Outlying Area
859	Kentucky - North Central
860	Connecticut - (Excluding Southwestern Corridor) (shared with 959)
862	New Jersey - North Central (shared with 973)
863	Florida - Lower Central
864	South Carolina - Northwestern
865	Tennessee - East Central
867	Canada - Northwest Territories, Nunavut & Yukon Province
868	Caribbean - Trinidad and Tobago
869	Caribbean - St. Kitts and Nevis
870	Arkansas - (Excluding Northwestern)
876	Caribbean - Jamaica
878	Pennsylvania - Southwestern (shared with 412 & 724)
901	Tennessee - Memphis Metro Area
902	Canada - Nova Scotia & Prince Edward Island Provinces
903	Texas - Northeastern
904	Florida - Northeastern
905	Canada - Lake Ontario Coastal Area (Excluding Toronto Metro Area), Ontario Province (shared with 289)
906	Michigan - Upper Peninsula
907	Alaska
908	New Jersey - Northwestern
909	California - San Bernardino Metro Area
910	North Carolina - Southeastern
912	Georgia - Southeastern
913	Kansas - Kansas City Metro Area
914	New York - Southeastern (Excluding New York City and Long Island)
915	Texas - Central Western
916	California - Upper Central
917	New York - New York City (shared with 212, 347, 646 & 718)
918	Oklahoma - Northeastern
919	North Carolina - North Central
920	Wisconsin - Eastern
925	California - Fairfield Area
928	Arizona - Excluding Phoenix Metro Area and Southeast
931	Tennessee - Central (Excluding Nashville General Area)
935	California - Southern San Diego Metro Outlying Area
936	Texas - East Central
937	Ohio - South Central
939	Caribbean - Puerto Rico (shared with 787)
940	Texas - North Central
941	Florida - Southwestern
949	California - Irvine Area, Southern Orange County
952	Minnesota - Minneapolis-St. Paul Metro Outlying Area
954	Florida - Ft. Lauderdale Area/Broward County
956	Texas - Lower Southwestern
959	Connecticut - (Excluding Southwestern Corridor) (shared with 860)
970	Colorado - Northern & Western
971	Oregon - Portland-Salem Metro Area (shared with 503)
972	Texas - Dallas Metro and Outlying Area (shared with 214 & 469)
973	New Jersey - North Central (shared with 862)
978	Massachusetts - Northeastern (shared with 351)
979	Texas - Southeastern
980	North Carolina - South Central (shared with 704)
985	Louisiana - Southwestern
989	Michigan - Northeastern and Central

Dialing International Calls

FOR CODES OF PLACES NOT LISTED, DIAL "0" (OPERATOR)

For example, a call to Cape Town, South Africa, would be dialed:

011 + 27 + 21 + 123456

INTERNATIONAL ACCESS CODE	COUNTRY CODE	CITY ROUTING CODE	LOCAL NUMBER
011	27	21	123456

Algeria	**213**
American Samoa •	**684**
Argentina	**54**
Buenos Aires	11
Cordoba	351
La Plata	221
Rosario	341
Armenia	**374**
Aruba •	**297**
All Points	8
Ascension Island •	**247**
Australia	**61**
Adelaide	8
Brisbane	7
Canberra	2
Melbourne	3
Perth	8
Sydney	2
Austria	**43**
Graz	316
Innsbruck	512
Salzburg	662
Vienna	1
Azerbaijan	**994**
Baku	12
Bahrain •	**973**
Bangladesh	**880**
Dhaka	2
Belarus	**375**
Minsk	17
Belgium	**32**
Antwerp	3
Brussels	2
Belize	**501**
Belize City	2
Belmopan	8
Bolivia	**591**
La Paz	2
Bosnia & Herzegovina	**387**
Sarajevo	33
Botswana •	**267**
Brazil	**55**
Brasilia	61
Rio de Janeiro	21
São Paulo	11
Brunei	**673**
Bandar Seri Begawan	2
Bulgaria	**359**
Sofia	2
Cameroon •	**237**
Cape Verde Is. •	**238**
Chile	**56**
Concepcion	41
Santiago	2
Valparaiso	32
China	**86**
Beijing	10
Fuzhou	591
Guangzhou	20
Hong Kong ★	852
Macau ★	853
Shanghai	21

Côte D'Ivoire •	**225**
Colombia	**57**
Barranquilla	5
Bogota	1
Cali	2
Cartegena	5
Medellin	4
Costa Rica •	**506**
Croatia	**385**
Zagreb	1
Cyprus	**357**
Nicosia	2
Czech Republic	**420**
Brno	5
Prague	2
Dem. Rep. of Congo	**243**
Kinshasa	12
Denmark •	**45**
Djibouti •	**253**
Ecuador	**593**
Cuenca	7
Guayaquil	4
Quito	2
Egypt	**20**
Alexandria	3
Cairo	2
Port Said	66
El Salvador •	**503**
Estonia	**372**
Tallinn	2
Ethiopia	**251**
Addis Ababa	1
Faeroe Islands •	**298**
Fiji •	**679**
Finland	**358**
Helsinki	9
France	**33**
Bordeaux	556
Cannes	493
Lyon	478
Marseille	491
Nice	493
Paris	1
Rouen	235
Toulouse	561
French Antilles	**596**
French Guiana •	**594**
French Polynesia •	**689**
Gabon •	**241**
Georgia	**995**
T'bilisi	32
Germany	**49**
Berlin	30
Bonn	228
Bremen	421
Cologne	221
Dresden	351
Dusseldorf	211
Frankfurt	69
Hamburg	40
Leipzig	341
Munich	89
Stuttgart	711

Ghana	**233**
Accra	21
Gibraltar •	**350**
Greece	**30**
Athens	210
Greenland (Kalaallit Nunaat)	**299**
Godthab (Nuuk)	2
Guam •	**671**
Guantanamo Bay •	**5399**
Guatemala	**502**
Guatemala City	2
All other places	9
Guinea	**224**
Conakry	4
Guyana	**592**
Georgetown	2
Haiti •	**509**
Honduras •	**504**
Hungary	**36**
Budapest	1
Iceland •	**354**
India	**91**
Kolkata (Calcutta)	33
Mumbai (Bombay)	22
New Delhi	11
Indonesia	**62**
Jakarta	21
Iraq	**964**
Baghdad	1
Ireland	**353**
Cork	21
Dublin	1
Israel	**972**
Haifa	4
Jerusalem	2
Tel Aviv	3
Italy	**39**
Bologna	051
Florence	055
Genoa	010
Milan	02
Naples	081
Palermo	091
Rome	06
Venice	041
Japan	**81**
Hiroshima	82
Kobe	78
Kyoto	75
Osaka	6
Sapporo	11
Tokyo	3
Yokohama	45
Jordan	**962**
Amman	6
Kazakhstan	**7**
Almaty	3273
Astana	3172
Kenya	**254**
Nairobi	2
Korea (Rep of)	**82**
Inchon	32
Pusan	51
Seoul	2

Kuwait •	**965**
Kyrgyz Republic	**996**
Bishkek	312
Latvia •	**371**
Lesotho •	**266**
Liberia •	**231**
Libya	**218**
Tripoli	21
Liechtenstein	**423**
All places	75
Lithuania	**370**
Vilnius	2
Luxembourg •	**352**
Macedonia	**389**
Skopje	2
Malaysia	**60**
Kuala Lumpur	3
Malta •	**356**
Marshall Islands	**692**
Majuro	625
Mexico	**52**
Acapulco	744
Guadalajara	33
Mexico	55
Monterrey	81
Micronesia	**691**
Ponape	320
Moldova	**373**
Kishinev	2
Monaco •	**377**
Morocco	**212**
Marrakech	44
Tanger	399
Namibia	**264**
Windhoek	61
Nepal	**977**
Kathmandu	1
Netherlands	**31**
Amsterdam	20
Rotterdam	10
The Hague	70
Netherlands Antilles	**599**
Bonaire	717
Curacao	9
St. Maarten	5
New Caledonia •	**687**
New Zealand	**64**
Auckland	9
Wellington	4
Nicaragua	**505**
Managua	2
Niger •	**227**
Nigeria	**234**
Lagos	1
Norway	**47**
Oslo	22
Oman •	**968**

Pakistan	**92**
Islamabad	51
Karachi	21
Palau •	**680**
Panama •	**507**
Papua New Guinea •	**675**
Paraguay	**595**
Asuncion	21
Peru	**51**
Lima	1
Philippines	**63**
Manila	2
Poland	**48**
Krakow	12
Warsaw	22
Portugal	**351**
Lisbon	21
Qatar •	**974**
Romania •	**40**
Russia	**7**
Moscow	095
St. Pierre and Miquelon •	**508**
San Marino •	**378**
Saudi Arabia	**966**
Jeddah	2
Mecca	2
Medina	4
Riyadh	1
Senegal •	**221**
Serbia & Montenegro	**381**
Belgrade	11
Sierra Leone	**232**
Freetown	22
Singapore •	**65**
Slovakia	**421**
Bratislava	2
Presov	51
Slovenia	**386**
Ljubijana	1
South Africa	**27**
Cape Town	21
Johannesburg	11
Pretoria	12
Spain	**34**
Barcelona	93
Madrid	91
Valencia	96
Sri Lanka	**94**
Colombo	1
Suriname •	**597**
Sweden	**46**
Stockholm	8
Switzerland	**41**
Berne	31
Geneva	22
Zurich	1
Taiwan	**886**
Taipei	2

Tajikistan	**992**
Dushanbe	372
Tanzania	**255**
Dar es Salaam	22
Thailand	**66**
Bangkok	2
Togo •	**228**
Tunisia	**216**
Tunis	1
Turkey	**90**
Ankara	312
Istanbul	212, 216
Izmir	232
Turkmenistan	**993**
Ashgabat	12
Uganda	**256**
Entebbe	42
Kampala	41
Ukraine	**380**
Kiev	44
United Arab Emirates	**971**
Abu Dhabi	2
Dubai	4
United Kingdom	**44**
Belfast	2890
Birmingham	121
Edinburgh	131
Glasgow	141
Liverpool	151
London	207, 208
Manchester	161
Sheffield	114
Southampton	2380
Uruguay	**598**
Montevideo	2
Uzbekistan	**998**
Tashkent	71
Vatican City	**39**
All places	6
Venezuela	**58**
Caracas	212
Maracaibo	261
Vietnam	**84**
Hanoi	4
Yemen	**967**
Sanaa	1
Zambia	**260**
Lusaka	1
Zimbabwe	**263**
Harare	4

★ = No country code required

• = No city routing code required

Note: City routing codes change frequently. The information above was current at the time of publication.

CBSA	POPULATION	RANK
New York-Newark-Edison, NY-NJ-PA Metro	18,736,586	1
Los Angeles-Long Beach-Santa Ana, CA Metro	13,006,527	2
Chicago-Naperville-Joliet, IL-IN-WI Metro	9,398,294	3
Philadelphia-Camden-Wilmington, PA-NJ-DE-MD Metro	5,800,413	4
Dallas-Fort Worth-Arlington, TX Metro	5,705,118	5
Miami-Fort Lauderdale-Miami Beach, FL Metro	5,346,010	6
Washington-Arlington-Alexandria, DC-VA-MD-WV Metro	5,189,088	7
Houston-Baytown-Sugar Land, TX Metro	5,130,511	8
Atlanta-Sandy Springs-Marietta, GA Metro	4,704,390	9
Detroit-Warren-Livonia, MI Metro	4,496,259	10
Boston-Cambridge-Quincy, MA-NH Metro	4,455,761	11
San Francisco-Oakland-Fremont, CA Metro	4,215,610	12
Phoenix-Mesa-Scottsdale, AZ Metro	3,654,002	13
Riverside-San Bernardino-Ontario, CA Metro	3,648,841	14
Seattle-Tacoma-Bellevue, WA Metro	3,183,926	15
Minneapolis-St. Paul-Bloomington, MN-WI Metro	3,115,214	16
San Diego-Carlsbad-San Marcos, CA Metro	2,972,165	17
St. Louis, MO-IL Metro	2,773,681	18
Baltimore-Towson, MD Metro	2,628,688	19
Tampa-St. Petersburg-Clearwater, FL Metro	2,563,390	20
Pittsburgh, PA Metro	2,412,526	21
Denver-Aurora, CO Metro	2,321,714	22
Cleveland-Elyria-Mentor, OH Metro	2,145,947	23
Portland-Vancouver-Beaverton, OR-WA Metro	2,062,457	24
Cincinnati-Middletown, OH-KY-IN Metro	2,060,020	25
Sacramento-Arden-Arcade-Roseville, CA Metro	1,990,366	26
Kansas City, MO-KS Metro	1,926,239	27
Orlando, FL Metro	1,851,675	28
San Antonio, TX Metro	1,832,456	29
San Jose-Sunnyvale-Santa Clara, CA Metro	1,756,162	30
Columbus, OH Metro	1,688,256	31
Providence-New Bedford-Fall River, RI-MA Metro	1,630,098	32
Virginia Beach-Norfolk-Newport News, VA-NC Metro	1,629,048	33
Las Vegas-Paradise, NV Metro	1,623,935	34
Indianapolis, IN Metro	1,611,194	35
Milwaukee-Waukesha-West Allis, WI Metro	1,517,694	36
Charlotte-Gastonia-Concord, NC-SC Metro	1,462,001	37
Austin-Round Rock, TX Metro	1,413,673	38
Nashville-Davidson-Murfreesboro, TN Metro	1,382,124	39
New Orleans-Metairie-Kenner, LA Metro	1,319,314	40
Memphis, TN-MS-AR Metro	1,250,399	41
Jacksonville, FL Metro	1,221,806	42
Louisville, KY-IN Metro	1,199,236	43
Hartford-West Hartford-East Hartford, CT Metro	1,182,417	44
Buffalo-Cheektowaga-Tonawanda, NY Metro	1,156,647	45
Richmond, VA Metro	1,145,408	46
Oklahoma City, OK Metro	1,140,319	47
Birmingham-Hoover, AL Metro	1,078,768	48
Rochester, NY Metro	1,044,679	49
Salt Lake City, UT Metro	1,017,152	50
Tucson, AZ Metro	913,496	51
Honolulu, HI Metro	911,333	52
Bridgeport-Stamford-Norwalk, CT Metro	905,906	53
Raleigh-Cary, NC Metro	898,752	54
Tulsa, OK Metro	890,907	55
Fresno, CA Metro	853,658	56
Dayton, OH Metro	845,398	57
New Haven-Milford, CT Metro	844,458	58
Albany-Schenectady-Troy, NY Metro	841,528	59
Oxnard-Thousand Oaks-Ventura, CA Metro	800,010	60
Omaha-Council Bluffs, NE-IA Metro	798,434	61
Worcester, MA Metro	779,512	62
Albuquerque, NM Metro	775,040	63
Allentown-Bethlehem-Easton, PA-NJ Metro	771,039	64
Grand Rapids-Wyoming, MI Metro	768,280	65
Baton Rouge, LA Metro	726,686	66
Bakersfield, CA Metro	713,645	67
El Paso, TX Metro	710,212	68
Akron, OH Metro	703,010	69
Springfield, MA Metro	685,943	70
Columbia, SC Metro	676,731	71
Greensboro-High Point, NC Metro	665,937	72
Poughkeepsie-Newburgh-Middletown, NY Metro	659,398	73
Toledo, OH Metro	658,597	74
Syracuse, NY Metro	654,615	75
McAllen-Edinburg-Pharr, TX Metro	642,074	76
Sarasota-Bradenton-Venice, FL Metro	641,420	77
Knoxville, TN Metro	640,696	78
Stockton, CA Metro	635,646	79
Little Rock-North Little Rock, AR Metro	632,290	80
Youngstown-Warren-Boardman, OH-PA Metro	591,161	81
Wichita, KS Metro	588,401	82
Greenville, SC Metro	585,298	83
Colorado Springs, CO Metro	575,170	84
Charleston-North Charleston, SC Metro	573,903	85
Scranton-Wilkes-Barre, PA Metro	548,725	86
Madison, WI Metro	529,311	87
Boise City-Nampa, ID Metro	523,298	88
Harrisburg-Carlisle, PA Metro	519,672	89
Lakeland-Winter Haven, FL Metro	513,989	90
Augusta-Richmond County, GA-SC Metro	512,617	91
Jackson, MS Metro	511,491	92
Portland-South Portland, ME Metro	511,203	93
Palm Bay-Melbourne-Titusville, FL Metro	509,694	94
Des Moines, IA Metro	509,346	95
Cape Coral-Fort Myers, FL Metro	503,053	96
Modesto, CA Metro	497,718	97
Chattanooga, TN-GA Metro	487,340	98
Lancaster, PA Metro	484,729	99
Deltona-Daytona Beach-Ormond Beach, FL Metro	472,690	100
Santa Rosa-Petaluma, CA Metro	472,358	101
Ogden-Clearfield, UT Metro	470,689	102
Lansing-East Lansing, MI Metro	457,201	103
Durham, NC Metro	456,102	104
Flint, MI Metro	444,695	105
Winston-Salem, NC Metro	441,047	106
Pensacola-Ferry Pass-Brent, FL Metro	434,400	107
Spokane, WA Metro	433,726	108
Lexington-Fayette, KY Metro	422,530	109
Salinas, CA Metro	418,102	110
Vallejo-Fairfield, CA Metro	416,654	111
Provo-Orem, UT Metro	415,207	112
Corpus Christi, TX Metro	409,361	113
Santa Barbara-Santa Maria-Goleta, CA Metro	407,310	114
Canton-Massillon, OH Metro	406,864	115
Fort Wayne, IN Metro	401,828	116
Mobile, AL Metro	399,912	117
Manchester-Nashua, NH Metro	398,500	118
York-Hanover, PA Metro	394,849	119
Visalia-Porterville, CA Metro	390,116	120
Reading, PA Metro	388,557	121
Springfield, MO Metro	386,298	122
Beaumont-Port Arthur, TX Metro	384,714	123
Asheville, NC Metro	384,686	124
Fayetteville-Springdale-Rogers, AR-MO Metro	382,973	125
Reno-Sparks, NV Metro	382,377	126
Shreveport-Bossier City, LA Metro	380,015	127
Davenport-Moline-Rock Island, IA-IL Metro	374,746	128
Brownsville-Harlingen, TX Metro	366,128	129
Peoria, IL Metro	365,345	130
Trenton-Ewing, NJ Metro	364,545	131
Salem, OR Metro	363,889	132
Huntsville, AL Metro	362,096	133
Montgomery, AL Metro	354,959	134
Hickory-Morganton-Lenoir, NC Metro	352,697	135
Port St. Lucie-Fort Pierce, FL Metro	349,682	136
Killeen-Temple-Fort Hood, TX Metro	347,446	137
Evansville, IN-KY Metro	345,888	138
Anchorage, AK Metro	343,612	139
Ann Arbor, MI Metro	341,745	140
Fayetteville, NC Metro	341,368	141
Tallahassee, FL Metro	337,061	142
Eugene-Springfield, OR Metro	331,900	143
Rockford, IL Metro	331,791	144
Kalamazoo-Portage, MI Metro	321,457	145
South Bend-Mishawaka, IN-MI Metro	319,986	146
Charleston, WV Metro	306,202	147
Savannah, GA Metro	304,469	148
Naples-Marco Island, FL Metro	297,619	149
Utica-Rome, NY Metro	297,598	150
Wilmington, NC Metro	295,406	151
Green Bay, WI Metro	294,254	152
Roanoke, VA Metro	292,819	153
Huntington-Ashland, WV-KY-OH Metro	285,666	154
Columbus, GA-AL Metro	283,657	155
Ocala, FL Metro	282,475	156
Fort Smith, AR-OK Metro	282,235	157
Boulder, CO Metro	280,996	158
Lincoln, NE Metro	280,381	159
Erie, PA Metro	280,152	160
Duluth, MN-WI Metro	275,129	161
Fort Collins-Loveland, CO Metro	269,231	162
Norwich-New London, CT Metro	265,569	163
Atlantic City, NJ Metro	264,055	164
Spartanburg, SC Metro	263,251	165
Lubbock, TX Metro	257,656	166
San Luis Obispo-Paso Robles, CA Metro	256,929	167
Santa Cruz-Watsonville, CA Metro	254,831	168
Gulfport-Biloxi, MS Metro	252,678	169
Binghamton, NY Metro	251,740	170
Holland-Grand Haven, MI Metro	249,988	171
Gainesville, FL Metro	246,884	172
Lafayette, LA Metro	246,050	173
Cedar Rapids, IA Metro	244,664	174
Bremerton-Silverdale, WA Metro	239,770	175
Hagerstown-Martinsburg, MD-WV Metro	237,013	176
Clarksville, TN-KY Metro	236,974	177
Amarillo, TX Metro	235,502	178
Kingsport-Bristol, TN-VA Metro	232,512	179
Barnstable Town, MA Metro	231,906	180
Merced, CA Metro	231,717	181
Lynchburg, VA Metro	231,010	182
Yakima, WA Metro	227,285	183
Macon, GA Metro	227,171	184
Topeka, KS Metro	226,163	185
Olympia, WA Metro	221,297	186
Waco, TX Metro	220,818	187
Laredo, TX Metro	217,923	188
Greeley, CO Metro	217,652	189
Champaign-Urbana, IL Metro	215,808	190
Appleton, WI Metro	213,079	191
Myrtle Beach-Conway-North Myrtle Beach, SC Metro	212,770	192
Chico, CA Metro	212,004	193
Kennewick-Richland-Pasco, WA Metro	210,844	194
Saginaw-Saginaw Township North, MI Metro	209,916	195
Burlington-South Burlington, VT Metro	205,324	196
Springfield, IL Metro	204,222	197
Longview, TX Metro	200,941	198
Sioux Falls, SD Metro	199,881	199
Houma-Bayou Cane-Thibodaux, LA Metro	199,245	200
Florence, SC Metro	196,985	201
Tuscaloosa, AL Metro	194,927	202
College Station-Bryan, TX Metro	194,037	203
Lake Charles, LA Metro	193,280	204
Medford, OR Metro	191,768	205
Racine, WI Metro	191,653	206
Torrington, CT Micro	189,803	207
Elkhart-Goshen, IN Metro	188,770	208
Prescott, AZ Metro	187,647	209
Tyler, TX Metro	186,264	210
Johnson City, TN Metro	185,518	211
Lafayette, IN Metro	183,783	212
Charlottesville, VA Metro	183,357	213
Las Cruces, NM Metro	182,035	214
Kingston, NY Metro	181,647	215
Fort Walton Beach-Crestview-Destin, FL Metro	181,471	216
Fargo, ND-MN Metro	179,489	217
Bellingham, WA Metro	178,551	218
Bloomington, IN Metro	178,253	219
St. Cloud, MN Metro	175,809	220
Redding, CA Metro	175,646	221
Athens-Clarke County, GA Metro	174,192	222
Rochester, MN Metro	174,190	223
Yuma, AZ Metro	174,159	224
Anderson, SC Metro	173,679	225
Lake Havasu City-Kingman, AZ Micro	173,567	226
Muskegon-Norton Shores, MI Metro	172,532	227
Lebanon, NH-VT Micro	171,437	228
Monroe, LA Metro	171,062	229
Terre Haute, IN Metro	169,499	230
Seaford, DE Micro	169,340	231
Parkersburg-Marietta, WV-OH Metro	163,138	232
Waterloo-Cedar Falls, IA Metro	162,804	233
Jackson, MI Metro	162,521	234
Joplin, MO Metro	162,424	235
Niles-Benton Harbor, MI Metro	162,229	236
Albany, GA Metro	160,614	237
Gainesville, GA Metro	160,370	238
Abilene, TX Metro	159,905	239
Oshkosh-Neenah, WI Metro	159,847	240
Greenville, NC Metro	159,353	241
Hilo, HI Micro	159,160	242
Bloomington-Normal, IL Metro	157,428	243
East Stroudsburg, PA Micro	156,276	244
Panama City-Lynn Haven, FL Metro	155,312	245
Janesville, WI Metro	154,741	246
Pascagoula, MS Metro	154,275	247
Punta Gorda, FL Metro	154,137	248
Hilton Head Island-Beaufort, SC Micro	154,110	249
Lexington-Thomasville, NC Micro	153,550	250
Blacksburg-Christiansburg-Radford, VA Metro	153,421	251
Ottawa-Streator, IL Micro	153,346	252
Daphne-Fairhope, AL Micro	152,986	253
Eau Claire, WI Metro	152,787	254
Columbia, MO Metro	152,440	255
Wichita Falls, TX Metro	151,616	256
Monroe, MI Metro	151,207	257
El Centro, CA Metro	150,768	258
Pueblo, CO Metro	149,472	259
Wheeling, WV-OH Metro	149,422	260
Johnstown, PA Metro	149,133	261
Jacksonville, NC Metro	148,621	262
Vineland-Millville-Bridgeton, NJ Metro	148,511	263
Yuba City-Marysville, CA Metro	148,101	264
Pottsville, PA Micro	147,359	265
Bangor, ME Metro	147,304	266
Decatur, AL Metro	146,537	267
Alexandria, LA Metro	146,386	268
Rocky Mount, NC Metro	145,019	269
Concord, NH Micro	144,687	270
Billings, MT Metro	144,236	271
Jefferson City, MO Metro	143,882	272
Sioux City, IA-NE-SD Metro	142,937	273
Springfield, OH Metro	142,396	274
Florence, AL Metro	141,259	275
State College, PA Metro	140,720	276
Traverse City, MI Micro	140,141	277
Burlington, NC Metro	138,987	278
Santa Fe, NM Metro	138,986	279
Battle Creek, MI Metro	138,480	280
Hanford-Corcoran, CA Metro	138,034	281
Iowa City, IA Metro	138,031	282
Kahului-Wailuku, HI Micro	137,520	283
Jamestown-Dunkirk-Fredonia, NY Micro	137,259	284
Salisbury, NC Micro	135,038	285
Statesville-Mooresville, NC Micro	134,830	286
Dover, DE Metro	134,615	287
Madera, CA Metro	134,194	288
Bend, OR Metro	133,644	289
Chambersburg, PA Micro	133,417	290
Texarkana, TX-Texarkana, AR Metro	132,584	291
Dothan, AL Metro	132,199	292
Napa, CA Metro	132,101	293
Pittsfield, MA Metro	131,892	294
Anderson, IN Metro	131,542	295
Hattiesburg, MS Metro	128,925	296
Dalton, GA Metro	128,843	297
La Crosse, WI-MN Metro	128,623	298
Weirton-Steubenville, WV-OH Metro	128,499	299
Tupelo, MS Micro	128,328	300
Wausau, WI Metro	128,152	301
Eureka-Arcata-Fortuna, CA Micro	127,570	302
Flagstaff, AZ Metro	127,438	303
Mansfield, OH Metro	127,432	304
Homosassa Springs, FL Micro	127,430	305
Morristown, TN Metro	127,072	306

CBSA	POPULATION	RANK
Altoona, PA Metro	126,915	307
Lumberton, NC Micro	126,599	308
Farmington, NM Metro	125,927	309
Glens Falls, NY Metro	125,441	310
Sierra Vista-Douglas, AZ Micro	125,157	311
Grand Junction, CO Metro	125,010	312
Odessa, TX Metro	122,701	313
Valdosta, GA Metro	122,590	314
Vero Beach, FL Metro	122,283	315
Lebanon, PA Metro	121,920	316
St. Joseph, MO-KS Metro	121,463	317
Warner Robins, GA Metro	121,393	318
Auburn-Opelika, AL Metro	120,228	319
Augusta-Waterville, ME Micro	119,426	320
Williamsport, PA Metro	118,535	321
Midland, TX Metro	118,434	322
Coeur d'Alene, ID Metro	118,402	323
Muncie, IN Metro	117,650	324
Rapid City, SD Metro	117,243	325
Sherman-Denison, TX Metro	116,045	326
Victoria, TX Metro	114,605	327
New Bern, NC Micro	114,482	328
Morgantown, WV Metro	113,860	329
Sheboygan, WI Metro	113,439	330
Wooster, OH Micro	113,407	331
Salisbury, MD Metro	113,323	332
Willimantic, CT Micro	113,250	333
Lawton, OK Metro	113,237	334
Goldsboro, NC Metro	112,487	335
Harrisonburg, VA Metro	112,290	336
Winchester, VA-WV Metro	112,008	337
Anniston-Oxford, AL Metro	111,715	338
East Liverpool-Salem, OH Micro	111,661	339
Allegan, MI Micro	111,572	340
Staunton-Waynesboro, VA Micro	111,277	341
Owensboro, KY Metro	110,872	342
Jonesboro, AR Metro	110,853	343
Michigan City-La Porte, IN Metro	110,712	344
Ogdensburg-Massena, NY Micro	110,514	345
Jackson, TN Metro	110,481	346
Elizabethtown, KY Metro	110,232	347
Decatur, IL Metro	109,831	348
Bay City, MI Metro	109,352	349
Danville, VA Metro	108,899	350
Mount Vernon-Anacortes, WA Metro	108,838	351
Bowling Green, KY Metro	108,545	352
Logan, UT-ID Metro	108,468	353
Idaho Falls, ID Metro	108,253	354
Lima, OH Metro	107,679	355
Cleveland, TN Metro	107,102	356
St. George, UT Metro	106,324	357
Sumter, SC Metro	106,232	358
Meridian, MS Micro	106,123	359
Lewiston-Auburn, ME Metro	106,087	360
Albany-Lebanon, OR Micro	105,925	361
Bluefield, WV-VA Micro	105,645	362
San Angelo, TX Metro	105,365	363
Pine Bluff, AR Metro	105,345	364
Kankakee-Bradley, IL Metro	105,097	365
Watertown-Fort Drum, NY Micro	105,082	366
Manhattan, KS Micro	104,432	367
Hammond, LA Micro	104,133	368
Lawrence, KS Metro	103,860	369
Gadsden, AL Metro	103,075	370
Ashtabula, OH Micro	102,352	371
Roseburg, OR Micro	102,107	372
Wenatchee, WA Metro	101,961	373
Ocean City, NJ Metro	101,481	374
Kokomo, IN Metro	101,371	375
Dunn, NC Micro	101,287	376
Adrian, MI Micro	100,933	377
Cumberland, MD-WV Metro	100,915	378
Ithaca, NY Metro	100,857	379
Missoula, MT Metro	100,706	380
Corning, NY Micro	99,381	381
Shelby, NC Micro	98,839	382
Whitewater, WI Micro	98,753	383
Fond du Lac, WI Metro	98,632	384
Bismarck, ND Metro	98,224	385
Cookeville, TN Micro	97,432	386
Tullahoma, TN Micro	97,093	387
Paducah, KY-IL Micro	96,978	388
Gettysburg, PA Micro	96,848	389
Brunswick, GA Metro	96,546	390
Truckee-Grass Valley, CA Micro	96,434	391
Longview-Kelso, WA Metro	95,725	392
Grand Forks, ND-MN Metro	95,531	393
Rome, GA Metro	94,242	394
New Castle, PA Micro	93,898	395
Enterprise-Ozark, AL Micro	93,559	396
Lexington Park, MD Micro	93,082	397
Sunbury, PA Micro	92,652	398
Richmond, KY Micro	92,112	399
New Philadelphia-Dover, OH Micro	91,853	400
Cape Girardeau-Jackson, MO-IL Micro	91,813	401
Hot Springs, AR Metro	91,562	402
Clarksburg, WV Micro	91,518	403
Sebring, FL Micro	91,200	404
Orangeburg, SC Micro	91,048	405
Elmira, NY Metro	90,197	406
Dubuque, IA Metro	89,898	407
Meadville, PA Micro	89,516	408
Opelousas-Eunice, LA Micro	88,639	409
Indiana, PA Micro	88,270	410
Mankato-North Mankato, MN Micro	88,122	411
Ukiah, CA Micro	87,696	412
Beaver Dam, WI Micro	87,528	413
Brainerd, MN Micro	86,569	414
Twin Falls, ID Micro	86,175	415
Fairbanks, AK Metro	86,098	416
Zanesville, OH Micro	85,840	417
Albertville, AL Micro	84,900	418
Midland, MI Micro	84,685	419
Pendleton-Hermiston, OR Micro	83,876	420
Cheyenne, WY Metro	83,743	421
Pocatello, ID Metro	83,718	422
Laurel, MS Micro	83,494	423
DuBois, PA Micro	83,240	424
Manitowoc, WI Micro	82,952	425
Olean, NY Micro	82,761	426
Danville, IL Metro	82,494	427
Lufkin, TX Micro	82,326	428
Bloomsburg-Berwick, PA Micro	82,315	429
Plattsburgh, NY Micro	81,857	430
Auburn, NY Micro	81,381	431
Ames, IA Metro	81,363	432
Talladega-Sylacauga, AL Micro	80,988	433
Key West-Marathon, FL Micro	80,915	434
Southern Pines, NC Micro	80,480	435
Corvallis, OR Metro	80,361	436
Kalispell, MT Micro	79,767	437
Beckley, WV Micro	79,711	438
Great Falls, MT Metro	79,462	439
Grants Pass, OR Micro	79,233	440
Somerset, PA Micro	79,217	441
Moses Lake, WA Micro	79,156	442
Sandusky, OH Metro	78,746	443
Cullman, AL Micro	78,353	444
Athens, TX Micro	77,836	445
Roanoke Rapids, NC Micro	77,641	446
Quincy, IL-MO Micro	77,524	447
Russellville, AR Micro	77,445	448
Portsmouth, OH Micro	77,230	449
Sevierville, TN Micro	76,676	450
Oak Harbor, WA Micro	76,268	451
Watertown-Fort Atkinson, WI Micro	76,161	452
Keene, NH Micro	76,132	453
Wilson, NC Micro	75,798	454
Warsaw, IN Micro	75,242	455
Wisconsin Rapids-Marshfield, WI Micro	75,197	456
Chillicothe, OH Micro	75,187	457
New Iberia, LA Micro	74,421	458
Bozeman, MT Micro	73,968	459
Columbia, TN Micro	73,440	460
Hinesville-Fort Stewart, GA Metro	73,242	461
Findlay, OH Micro	72,906	462
Mount Airy, NC Micro	72,805	463
Gallup, NM Micro	72,707	464
Galesburg, IL Micro	72,399	465
Owosso, MI Micro	72,221	466
Palatka, FL Micro	71,876	467
Martinsville, VA Micro	71,609	468
Columbus, IN Metro	71,588	469
Marion, IN Micro	71,447	470
Branson, MO Micro	71,383	471
Centralia, WA Micro	70,884	472
Searcy, AR Micro	70,781	473
Stillwater, OK Micro	70,592	474
Richmond, IN Micro	70,394	475
Muskogee, OK Micro	70,263	476
Aberdeen, WA Micro	69,290	477
Seneca, SC Micro	69,240	478
Marinette, WI-MI Micro	68,662	479
Bristol, VA Metro	68,596	480
Lincolnton, NC Micro	68,521	481
Greenwood, SC Micro	68,364	482
Grand Island, NE Micro	68,335	483
Frankfort, KY Micro	68,324	484
Helena, MT Micro	68,271	485
Stevens Point, WI Micro	68,120	486
Casper, WY Metro	67,821	487
Shawnee, OK Micro	67,467	488
North Wilkesboro, NC Micro	67,268	489
Port Angeles, WA Micro	66,960	490
Marion, OH Micro	65,891	491
Mount Pleasant, MI Micro	65,334	492
Klamath Falls, OR Micro	65,097	493
The Villages, FL Micro	64,844	494
Minot, ND Micro	64,465	495
Greeneville, TN Micro	64,434	496
Marquette, MI Micro	63,977	497
Athens, OH Micro	63,898	498
Hudson, NY Micro	63,894	499
Huntsville, TX Micro	63,455	500
Forest City, NC Micro	63,299	501
Rutland, VT Micro	63,118	502
Lancaster, SC Micro	63,001	503
Clearlake, CA Micro	62,990	504
Palm Coast, FL Micro	62,950	505
Charleston-Mattoon, IL Micro	62,945	506
Coos Bay, OR Micro	62,936	507
Sayre, PA Micro	62,904	508
Hutchinson, KS Micro	62,888	509
Marshall, TX Micro	62,672	510
Oneonta, NY Micro	62,334	511
Sturgis, MI Micro	62,141	512
Marion-Herrin, IL Micro	61,848	513
Fremont, OH Micro	61,571	514
Alamogordo, NM Micro	61,534	515
Kapaa, HI Micro	61,060	516
Laconia, NH Micro	60,904	517
Morehead City, NC Micro	60,739	518
Columbus, MS Micro	60,631	519
Norwalk, OH Micro	60,472	520
Salina, KS Micro	60,458	521
Nacogdoches, TX Micro	60,278	522
Greenville, MS Micro	60,195	523
Georgetown, SC Micro	60,170	524
LaGrange, GA Micro	60,165	525
Sterling, IL Micro	59,935	526
Faribault-Northfield, MN Micro	59,842	527
Carbondale, IL Micro	59,786	528
Roswell, NM Micro	59,597	529
Lake City, FL Micro	59,502	530
Batavia, NY Micro	59,348	531
Barre, VT Micro	59,305	532
Crowley, LA Micro	59,152	533
Kinston, NC Micro	58,643	534
Fergus Falls, MN Micro	58,521	535
Albemarle, NC Micro	58,476	536
Statesboro, GA Micro	58,027	537
Rio Grande City, TX Micro	58,014	538
Red Bluff, CA Micro	57,995	539
Somerset, KY Micro	57,945	540
Lewiston, ID-WA Metro	57,912	541
Ruston, LA Micro	57,801	542
Farmington, MO Micro	57,733	543
Point Pleasant, WV-OH Micro	57,580	544
Tiffin-Fostoria, OH Micro	57,538	545
Mount Vernon, OH Micro	57,055	546
Enid, OK Micro	56,971	547
Baraboo, WI Micro	56,960	548
Fairmont, WV Micro	56,794	549
Walla Walla, WA Micro	56,654	550
Phoenix Lake-Cedar Ridge, CA Micro	56,610	551
Oil City, PA Micro	56,378	552
Hobbs, NM Micro	56,320	553
Carson City, NV Metro	55,832	554
Ardmore, OK Micro	55,750	555
London, KY Micro	55,550	556
Elizabeth City, NC Micro	55,421	557
Edwards, CO Micro	55,398	558
Dublin, GA Micro	55,386	559
Palestine, TX Micro	55,064	560
Gloversville, NY Micro	55,049	561
Milledgeville, GA Micro	54,798	562
Muscatine, IA Micro	54,678	563
Abbeville, LA Micro	54,576	564
Gaffney, SC Micro	54,274	565
Scottsboro, AL Micro	54,006	566
Jasper, IN Micro	53,300	567
Ontario, OR-ID Micro	53,210	568
Granbury, TX Micro	53,173	569
Ashland, OH Micro	53,040	570
Natchez, MS-LA Micro	52,915	571
Payson, AZ Micro	52,882	572
Harriman, TN Micro	52,785	573
Rochelle, IL Micro	52,769	574
Greenville, OH Micro	52,725	575
Danville, KY Micro	52,685	576
McComb, MS Micro	52,463	577
Mason City, IA Micro	52,440	578
Morgan City, LA Micro	51,938	579
Waycross, GA Micro	51,814	580
Picayune, MS Micro	51,719	581
Shelton, WA Micro	51,394	582
Carlsbad-Artesia, NM Micro	51,228	583
Norfolk, NE Micro	51,228	584
Warrensburg, MO Micro	50,784	585
Athens, TN Micro	50,748	586
Malone, NY Micro	50,748	587
Eagle Pass, TX Micro	50,391	588
Kearney, NE Micro	50,187	589
Crossville, TN Micro	50,021	590
Ocean Pines, MD Micro	49,870	591
Platteville, WI Micro	49,577	592
Fort Polk South, LA Micro	49,495	593
Clinton, IA Micro	49,442	594
Paris, TX Micro	49,425	595
Bartlesville, OK Micro	49,390	596
Vicksburg, MS Micro	49,360	597
Sanford, NC Micro	49,320	598
Blytheville, AR Micro	49,273	599
Glasgow, KY Micro	49,247	600
Amsterdam, NY Micro	49,105	601
Cortland, NY Micro	48,922	602
Burlington, IA-IL Micro	48,887	603
Winona, MN Micro	48,856	604
Sidney, OH Micro	48,807	605
Mount Vernon, IL Micro	48,709	606
Jacksonville, TX Micro	48,351	607
Corsicana, TX Micro	48,087	608
Calhoun, GA Micro	47,930	609
Canon City, CO Micro	47,870	610
New Castle, IN Micro	47,682	611
Ponca City, OK Micro	47,663	612
Kendallville, IN Micro	47,621	613
Freeport, IL Micro	47,418	614
Oak Hill, WV Micro	47,206	615
Greenwood, MS Micro	47,079	616
Madisonville, KY Micro	46,981	617
Rockingham, NC Micro	46,961	618

CBSA	POPULATION	RANK
Del Rio, TX Micro	46,897	619
Durango, CO Micro	46,890	620
Douglas, GA Micro	46,673	621
Coldwater, MI Micro	46,538	622
Bellefontaine, OH Micro	46,473	623
Lewistown, PA Micro	46,395	624
Bedford, IN Micro	46,302	625
Wapakoneta, OH Micro	46,239	626
Cadillac, MI Micro	46,199	627
Plymouth, IN Micro	46,162	628
Bucyrus, OH Micro	46,009	629
Washington, NC Micro	45,937	630
Huntingdon, PA Micro	45,843	631
Kerrville, TX Micro	45,752	632
Elko, NV Micro	45,376	633
Red Wing, MN Micro	45,345	634
El Dorado, AR Micro	45,320	635
Clovis, NM Micro	45,228	636
St. Marys, GA Micro	45,164	637
Henderson, NC Micro	45,127	638
Selma, AL Micro	45,032	639
Gardnerville Ranchos, NV Micro	44,695	640
Brigham City, UT Micro	44,484	641
McAlester, OK Micro	44,326	642
Bradford, PA Micro	44,250	643
Fort Leonard Wood, MO Micro	44,144	644
Tahlequah, OK Micro	44,095	645
Bogalusa, LA Micro	43,947	646
Harrison, AR Micro	43,738	647
Keokuk-Fort Madison, IA-MO Micro	43,548	648
Moultrie, GA Micro	43,296	649
Blackfoot, ID Micro	43,175	650
Thomasville, GA Micro	43,072	651
Warren, PA Micro	42,810	652
Boone, NC Micro	42,790	653
Starkville, MS Micro	42,642	654
Alma, MI Micro	42,364	655
Duncan, OK Micro	42,283	656
Mount Sterling, KY Micro	42,259	657
Big Rapids, MI Micro	42,172	658
Lewisburg, PA Micro	42,112	659
Rolla, MO Micro	41,948	660
El Campo, TX Micro	41,908	661
Bemidji, MN Micro	41,851	662
Seymour, IN Micro	41,786	663
Minden, LA Micro	41,490	664
Safford, AZ Micro	41,410	665
Menomonie, WI Micro	41,383	666
Burley, ID Micro	41,373	667
Wilmington, OH Micro	41,363	668
Jacksonville, IL Micro	41,267	669
Rockland, ME Micro	41,261	670
Cambridge, OH Micro	41,118	671
Lawrenceburg, TN Micro	41,045	672
Pullman, WA Micro	41,021	673
Espanola, NM Micro	41,006	674
Nogales, AZ Micro	40,937	675
Poplar Bluff, MO Micro	40,827	676
Auburn, IN Micro	40,782	677
Willmar, MN Micro	40,756	678
Celina, OH Micro	40,747	679
Shelbyville, TN Micro	40,687	680
Alice, TX Micro	40,633	681
Logansport, IN Micro	40,495	682
Centralia, IL Micro	40,466	683
Cedartown, GA Micro	40,292	684
La Follette, TN Micro	40,208	685
Rexburg, ID Micro	40,177	686
Sikeston, MO Micro	40,133	687
Oxford, MS Micro	40,100	688
Tifton, GA Micro	40,031	689
Union City, TN-KY Micro	39,749	690
Berlin, NH-VT Micro	39,688	691
Marshalltown, IA Micro	39,677	692
Sedalia, MO Micro	39,580	693
Fort Dodge, IA Micro	39,522	694
Pontiac, IL Micro	39,476	695
Sault Ste. Marie, MI Micro	39,265	696
Cornelia, GA Micro	39,258	697
Urbana, OH Micro	39,247	698
McMinnville, TN Micro	39,239	699
Walterboro, SC Micro	39,197	700
Cleveland, MS Micro	39,154	701
Defiance, OH Micro	39,140	702
Mountain Home, AR Micro	39,036	703
Aberdeen, SD Micro	38,995	704
Austin, MN Micro	38,876	705
Garden City, KS Micro	38,868	706
Gainesville, TX Micro	38,714	707
Huntington, IN Micro	38,592	708
Emporia, KS Micro	38,581	709
Paragould, AR Micro	38,537	710
Natchitoches, LA Micro	38,517	711
Brownwood, TX Micro	38,511	712
Bay City, TX Micro	38,423	713
Hastings, NE Micro	38,253	714
Crawfordsville, IN Micro	38,216	715
Vincennes, IN Micro	38,204	716
Escanaba, MI Micro	38,158	717
Selinsgrove, PA Micro	38,021	718
Houghton, MI Micro	38,011	719
Gillette, WY Micro	38,006	720
Pittsburg, KS Micro	37,774	721
Newberry, SC Micro	37,601	722
Scottsbluff, NE Micro	37,596	723
Hannibal, MO Micro	37,551	724
Newton, IA Micro	37,505	725
Lock Haven, PA Micro	37,498	726
Durant, OK Micro	37,493	727
Mayfield, KY Micro	37,452	728
West Plains, MO Micro	37,409	729
Okeechobee, FL Micro	37,397	730
Canton, IL Micro	37,340	731
Americus, GA Micro	37,310	732
Rock Springs, WY Micro	37,302	733
Bennington, VT Micro	37,264	734
Corbin, KY Micro	37,167	735
Coshocton, OH Micro	36,875	736
Dyersburg, TN Micro	36,850	737
Winfield, KS Micro	36,788	738
Clewiston, FL Micro	36,679	739
Montrose, CO Micro	36,474	740
Riverton, WY Micro	36,370	741
Astoria, OR Micro	36,328	742
Peru, IN Micro	36,252	743
Cedar City, UT Micro	36,232	744
Laurinburg, NC Micro	36,058	745
Dixon, IL Micro	35,997	746
Valley, AL Micro	35,973	747
Plainview, TX Micro	35,965	748
Pahrump, NV Micro	35,937	749
Fremont, NE Micro	35,905	750
Hutchinson, MN Micro	35,756	751
Moscow, ID Micro	35,619	752
Ottumwa, IA Micro	35,558	753
North Platte, NE Micro	35,538	754
Seneca Falls, NY Micro	35,530	755
Ellensburg, WA Micro	35,498	756
Taylorville, IL Micro	35,098	757
Corinth, MS Micro	34,825	758
Owatonna, MN Micro	34,792	759
Ada, OK Micro	34,750	760
Newport, TN Micro	34,650	761
Monroe, WI Micro	34,590	762
Batesville, AR Micro	34,587	763
Murray, KY Micro	34,578	764
Coffeyville, KS Micro	34,549	765
Wabash, IN Micro	34,544	766
Easton, MD Micro	34,487	767
Chester, SC Micro	34,347	768
Effingham, IL Micro	34,214	769
Alexandria, MN Micro	34,196	770
Frankfort, IN Micro	34,020	771
St. Marys, PA Micro	33,969	772
Kill Devil Hills, NC Micro	33,644	773
Brookhaven, MS Micro	33,635	774
De Ridder, LA Micro	33,586	775
Big Spring, TX Micro	33,585	776
Decatur, IN Micro	33,479	777
Angola, IN Micro	33,444	778
Indianola, MS Micro	33,441	779
Stephenville, TX Micro	33,252	780
Arcadia, FL Micro	33,137	781
Hope, AR Micro	33,116	782
Camden, AR Micro	33,018	783
Butte-Silver Bow, MT Micro	32,966	784
Lebanon, MO Micro	32,825	785
Miami, OK Micro	32,774	786
Dodge City, KS Micro	32,760	787
Kennett, MO Micro	32,578	788
Macomb, IL Micro	32,469	789
Beeville, TX Micro	32,399	790
Iron Mountain, MI-WI Micro	32,365	791
Madison, IN Micro	32,352	792
Sulphur Springs, TX Micro	32,316	793
Central City, KY Micro	31,663	794
Kingsville, TX Micro	31,609	795
Albert Lea, MN Micro	31,606	796
Watertown, SD Micro	31,491	797
Taos, NM Micro	31,483	798
Laramie, WY Micro	31,441	799
Paris, TN Micro	31,314	800
Jennings, LA Micro	31,123	801
Brenham, TX Micro	31,043	802
Dillon, SC Micro	31,009	803
Columbus, NE Micro	30,974	804
Juneau, AK Micro	30,891	805
Maysville, KY Micro	30,863	806
Alpena, MI Micro	30,711	807
Middlesborough, KY Micro	30,447	808
Lincoln, IL Micro	30,268	809
Cambridge, MD Micro	30,238	810
Bastrop, LA Micro	30,146	811
Washington, IN Micro	30,020	812
Merrill, WI Micro	30,006	813
Mountain Home, ID Micro	29,954	814
Clarksdale, MS Micro	29,871	815
Silver City, NM Micro	29,629	816
Brevard, NC Micro	29,587	817
Troy, AL Micro	29,578	818
Las Vegas, NM Micro	29,483	819
Kirksville, MO Micro	29,266	820
Union, SC Micro	29,252	821
McPherson, KS Micro	29,221	822
Van Wert, OH Micro	29,206	823
Mount Pleasant, TX Micro	28,982	824
Bennettsville, SC Micro	28,643	825
Brookings, SD Micro	28,625	826
North Vernon, IN Micro	28,616	827
Forrest City, AR Micro	28,524	828
Yazoo City, MS Micro	28,389	829
Bainbridge, GA Micro	28,269	830
Washington, OH Micro	28,004	831
Fort Morgan, CO Micro	27,973	832
Mineral Wells, TX Micro	27,884	833
Wauchula, FL Micro	27,853	834
Thomaston, GA Micro	27,767	835
Crescent City North, CA Micro	27,586	836
Great Bend, KS Micro	27,458	837
Fitzgerald, GA Micro	27,377	838
Jesup, GA Micro	27,314	839
Sheridan, WY Micro	27,134	840
Hays, KS Micro	27,064	841
Silverthorne, CO Micro	27,030	842
Uvalde, TX Micro	26,953	843
Grants, NM Micro	26,815	844
Lexington, NE Micro	26,734	845
Summerville, GA Micro	26,573	846
Vernal, UT Micro	26,484	847
New Ulm, MN Micro	26,435	848
Altus, OK Micro	26,426	849
Jackson, WY-ID Micro	26,217	850
Boone, IA Micro	26,111	851
Toccoa, GA Micro	25,901	852
Harrisburg, IL Micro	25,647	853
Mexico, MO Micro	25,626	854
Deming, NM Micro	25,542	855
Magnolia, AR Micro	25,289	856
Connersville, IN Micro	25,113	857
Marshall, MN Micro	24,877	858
La Grande, OR Micro	24,685	859
Moberly, MO Micro	24,679	860
Greensburg, IN Micro	24,622	861
Fort Valley, GA Micro	24,586	862
Wahpeton, ND-MN Micro	24,228	863
West Helena, AR Micro	23,963	864
Fallon, NV Micro	23,837	865
City of The Dalles, OR Micro	23,713	866
Scottsburg, IN Micro	23,577	867
Campbellsville, KY Micro	23,546	868
Liberal, KS Micro	23,545	869
Tuskegee, AL Micro	23,451	870
Arkadelphia, AR Micro	23,445	871
Beatrice, NE Micro	23,242	872
Pierre Part, LA Micro	23,194	873
Borger, TX Micro	23,086	874
Pampa, TX Micro	22,953	875
Dickinson, ND Micro	22,759	876
Grenada, MS Micro	22,735	877
Levelland, TX Micro	22,487	878
Marshall, MO Micro	22,437	879
Mitchell, SD Micro	22,352	880
Oskaloosa, IA Micro	22,116	881
Parsons, KS Micro	21,927	882
Cordele, GA Micro	21,895	883
Sterling, CO Micro	21,889	884
Spearfish, SD Micro	21,573	885
Brookings, OR Micro	21,502	886
Maryville, MO Micro	21,479	887
Yankton, SD Micro	21,414	888
Jamestown, ND Micro	20,906	889
Hood River, OR Micro	20,890	890
Fairmont, MN Micro	20,875	891
Prineville, OR Micro	20,716	892
Dumas, TX Micro	20,617	893
Storm Lake, IA Micro	20,462	894
Raymondville, TX Micro	20,292	895
Guymon, OK Micro	20,193	896
Worthington, MN Micro	20,090	897
Evanston, WY Micro	19,965	898
Pierre, SD Micro	19,823	899
Williston, ND Micro	19,637	900
Price, UT Micro	19,501	901
Brownsville, TN Micro	19,449	902
Los Alamos, NM Micro	18,796	903
Woodward, OK Micro	18,472	904
Bishop, CA Micro	18,287	905
Hereford, TX Micro	18,227	906
Portales, NM Micro	18,191	907
Spencer, IA Micro	16,839	908
Spirit Lake, IA Micro	16,582	909
Atchison, KS Micro	16,551	910
Havre, MT Micro	16,248	911
Huron, SD Micro	16,240	912
Snyder, TX Micro	15,677	913
Sweetwater, TX Micro	14,979	914
Lamesa, TX Micro	14,521	915
Vernon, TX Micro	14,004	916
Kodiak, AK Micro	13,751	917
Ketchikan, AK Micro	13,346	918
Tallulah, LA Micro	13,089	919
Andrews, TX Micro	13,026	920
Vermillion, SD Micro	12,893	921
Pecos, TX Micro	12,169	922

CBSA Total	272,949,244
United States Total	292,936,668
CBSA (% of U. S. Total)	93.18

CBSA	POPULATION	RANK
New York-Newark-Edison, NY-NJ-PA Metro	2,385,135	1
Los Angeles-Long Beach-Santa Ana, CA Metro	1,297,685	2
Chicago-Naperville-Joliet, IL-IN-WI Metro	1,020,861	3
Miami-Fort Lauderdale-Miami Beach, FL Metro	859,686	4
Philadelphia-Camden-Wilmington, PA-NJ-DE-MD Metro	774,060	5
Boston-Cambridge-Quincy, MA-NH Metro	566,934	6
Detroit-Warren-Livonia, MI Metro	541,985	7
San Francisco-Oakland-Fremont, CA Metro	500,865	8
Washington-Arlington-Alexandria, DC-VA-MD-WV Metro	477,226	9
Tampa-St. Petersburg-Clearwater, FL Metro	468,201	10
Dallas-Fort Worth-Arlington, TX Metro	457,052	11
Phoenix-Mesa-Scottsdale, AZ Metro	428,944	12
Pittsburgh, PA Metro	424,992	13
Houston-Baytown-Sugar Land, TX Metro	414,592	14
Riverside-San Bernardino-Ontario, CA Metro	379,370	15
Atlanta-Sandy Springs-Marietta, GA Metro	371,595	16
St. Louis, MO-IL Metro	360,251	17
San Diego-Carlsbad-San Marcos, CA Metro	334,361	18
Seattle-Tacoma-Bellevue, WA Metro	325,927	19
Baltimore-Towson, MD Metro	318,255	20
Cleveland-Elyria-Mentor, OH Metro	313,227	21
Minneapolis-St. Paul-Bloomington, MN-WI Metro	303,887	22
Cincinnati-Middletown, OH-KY-IN Metro	242,262	23
Providence-New Bedford-Fall River, RI-MA Metro	231,968	24
Orlando, FL Metro	228,771	25
Sacramento-Arden-Arcade-Roseville, CA Metro	224,624	26
Kansas City, MO-KS Metro	221,360	27
Denver-Aurora, CO Metro	212,564	28
Portland-Vancouver-Beaverton, OR-WA Metro	210,782	29
San Antonio, TX Metro	200,352	30
Milwaukee-Waukesha-West Allis, WI Metro	190,773	31
Buffalo-Cheektowaga-Tonawanda, NY Metro	183,941	32
Las Vegas-Paradise, NV Metro	176,744	33
San Jose-Sunnyvale-Santa Clara, CA Metro	175,333	34
Sarasota-Bradenton-Venice, FL Metro	174,791	35
Virginia Beach-Norfolk-Newport News, VA-NC Metro	172,790	36
Columbus, OH Metro	170,970	37
Indianapolis, IN Metro	170,929	38
Hartford-West Hartford-East Hartford, CT Metro	164,983	39
New Orleans-Metairie-Kenner, LA Metro	152,337	40
Louisville, KY-IN Metro	148,489	41
Nashville-Davidson-Murfreesboro, TN Metro	143,305	42
Charlotte-Gastonia-Concord, NC-SC Metro	142,787	43
Birmingham-Hoover, AL Metro	138,594	44
Rochester, NY Metro	136,435	45
Jacksonville, FL Metro	135,337	46
Oklahoma City, OK Metro	131,915	47
Richmond, VA Metro	131,163	48
Tucson, AZ Metro	130,758	49
Honolulu, HI Metro	125,746	50
Memphis, TN-MS-AR Metro	125,545	51
Cape Coral-Fort Myers, FL Metro	121,746	52
New Haven-Milford, CT Metro	121,006	53
Bridgeport-Stamford-Norwalk, CT Metro	120,988	54
Allentown-Bethlehem-Easton, PA-NJ Metro	119,260	55
Albany-Schenectady-Troy, NY Metro	116,783	56
Dayton, OH Metro	115,892	57
Tulsa, OK Metro	108,627	58
Austin-Round Rock, TX Metro	105,831	59
Scranton-Wilkes-Barre, PA Metro	104,503	60
Palm Bay-Melbourne-Titusville, FL Metro	102,139	61
Deltona-Daytona Beach-Ormond Beach, FL Metro	101,898	62
Youngstown-Warren-Boardman, OH-PA Metro	101,769	63
Worcester, MA Metro	99,636	64
Akron, OH Metro	95,315	65
Springfield, MA Metro	94,468	66
Lakeland-Winter Haven, FL Metro	92,029	67
Albuquerque, NM Metro	89,851	68
Omaha-Council Bluffs, NE-IA Metro	88,542	69
Knoxville, TN Metro	87,888	70
Syracuse, NY Metro	87,087	71
Toledo, OH Metro	84,921	72
Port St. Lucie-Fort Pierce, FL Metro	84,741	73
Fresno, CA Metro	84,593	74
Oxnard-Thousand Oaks-Ventura, CA Metro	83,672	75
Salt Lake City, UT Metro	83,138	76
Greensboro-High Point, NC Metro	83,045	77
Grand Rapids-Wyoming, MI Metro	81,967	78
Harrisburg-Carlisle, PA Metro	75,508	79
Little Rock-North Little Rock, AR Metro	73,263	80
Columbia, SC Metro	73,131	81
Poughkeepsie-Newburgh-Middletown, NY Metro	73,109	82
El Paso, TX Metro	72,894	83
Raleigh-Cary, NC Metro	72,291	84
Baton Rouge, LA Metro	71,591	85
Naples-Marco Island, FL Metro	71,362	86
Wichita, KS Metro	71,080	87
Greenville, SC Metro	70,609	88
Lancaster, PA Metro	69,053	89
Ocala, FL Metro	68,917	90
Portland-South Portland, ME Metro	68,779	91
Asheville, NC Metro	67,813	92
Bakersfield, CA Metro	67,142	93
Chattanooga, TN-GA Metro	66,791	94
Stockton, CA Metro	64,635	95
McAllen-Edinburg-Pharr, TX Metro	62,169	96
Canton-Massillon, OH Metro	61,471	97
Charleston-North Charleston, SC Metro	61,333	98
Santa Rosa-Petaluma, CA Metro	60,413	99
Des Moines, IA Metro	58,455	100
Reading, PA Metro	57,994	101
Augusta-Richmond County, GA-SC Metro	57,792	102
Winston-Salem, NC Metro	57,180	103
Pensacola-Ferry Pass-Brent, FL Metro	56,415	104
Jackson, MS Metro	55,684	105
York-Hanover, PA Metro	54,279	106
Peoria, IL Metro	54,274	107
Barnstable Town, MA Metro	54,009	108
Spokane, WA Metro	53,878	109
Madison, WI Metro	53,555	110
Flint, MI Metro	53,403	111
Davenport-Moline-Rock Island, IA-IL Metro	52,422	112
Santa Barbara-Santa Maria-Goleta, CA Metro	52,405	113
Punta Gorda, FL Metro	52,138	114
Boise City-Nampa, ID Metro	51,849	115
Beaumont-Port Arthur, TX Metro	51,616	116
Springfield, MO Metro	51,313	117
Colorado Springs, CO Metro	51,043	118
Modesto, CA Metro	51,007	119
Shreveport-Bossier City, LA Metro	49,825	120
Corpus Christi, TX Metro	48,958	121
Evansville, IN-KY Metro	48,956	122
Mobile, AL Metro	48,806	123
Utica-Rome, NY Metro	48,698	124
Lansing-East Lansing, MI Metro	47,523	125
Fort Wayne, IN Metro	47,188	126
Charleston, WV Metro	47,100	127
Durham, NC Metro	46,948	128
Hickory-Morganton-Lenoir, NC Metro	46,063	129
Roanoke, VA Metro	45,972	130
Fayetteville-Springdale-Rogers, AR-MO Metro	45,917	131
Trenton-Ewing, NJ Metro	45,820	132
Salem, OR Metro	45,497	133
Eugene-Springfield, OR Metro	44,509	134
Huntington-Ashland, WV-KY-OH Metro	44,386	135
Lexington-Fayette, KY Metro	44,190	136
South Bend-Mishawaka, IN-MI Metro	43,369	137
Duluth, MN-WI Metro	42,987	138
Manchester-Nashua, NH Metro	42,733	139
Wilmington, NC Metro	42,493	140
Ogden-Clearfield, UT Metro	42,339	141
Salinas, CA Metro	42,203	142
Huntsville, AL Metro	41,781	143
Vallejo-Fairfield, CA Metro	41,423	144
Rockford, IL Metro	41,384	145
Montgomery, AL Metro	41,288	146
Prescott, AZ Metro	41,105	147
Brownsville-Harlingen, TX Metro	40,796	148
Reno-Sparks, NV Metro	40,659	149
Erie, PA Metro	40,424	150
Homosassa Springs, FL Micro	40,072	151
Binghamton, NY Metro	39,906	152
Kalamazoo-Portage, MI Metro	38,019	153
Visalia-Porterville, CA Metro	37,902	154
San Luis Obispo-Paso Robles, CA Metro	37,506	155
Kingsport-Bristol, TN-VA Metro	37,254	156
Fort Smith, AR-OK Metro	37,038	157
Atlantic City, NJ Metro	35,931	158
Lake Havasu City-Kingman, AZ Micro	35,821	159
Savannah, GA Metro	35,711	160
Norwich-New London, CT Metro	34,734	161
Vero Beach, FL Metro	34,571	162
Lynchburg, VA Metro	34,381	163
Green Bay, WI Metro	34,027	164
Spartanburg, SC Metro	33,488	165
Columbus, GA-AL Metro	33,084	166
Chico, CA Metro	32,724	167
Myrtle Beach-Conway-North Myrtle Beach, SC Metro	32,522	168
Seaford, DE Micro	32,198	169
Cedar Rapids, IA Metro	31,984	170
Topeka, KS Metro	31,888	171
Tallahassee, FL Metro	31,715	172
Hagerstown-Martinsburg, MD-WV Metro	31,370	173
Medford, OR Metro	30,663	174
Killeen-Temple-Fort Hood, TX Metro	30,596	175
Gulfport-Biloxi, MS Metro	30,314	176
Yuma, AZ Metro	30,148	177
Lincoln, NE Metro	29,937	178
Lubbock, TX Metro	29,378	179
Sebring, FL Micro	29,227	180
Johnstown, PA Metro	29,195	181
Saginaw-Saginaw Township North, MI Metro	29,157	182
Pottsville, PA Micro	29,047	183
Amarillo, TX Metro	28,960	184
Ann Arbor, MI Metro	28,824	185
Fayetteville, NC Metro	28,741	186
Longview, TX Metro	28,510	187
Waco, TX Metro	28,431	188
Johnson City, TN Metro	27,837	189
Springfield, IL Metro	27,640	190
Provo-Orem, UT Metro	27,397	191
Macon, GA Metro	27,220	192
Torrington, CT Micro	26,819	193
Tyler, TX Metro	26,756	194
Wheeling, WV-OH Metro	26,634	195
Redding, CA Metro	26,390	196
Bremerton-Silverdale, WA Metro	26,343	197
Fort Collins-Loveland, CO Metro	26,325	198
Holland-Grand Haven, MI Metro	26,017	199
Santa Cruz-Watsonville, CA Metro	25,831	200
Yakima, WA Metro	25,694	201
Ottawa-Streator, IL Micro	25,407	202
Olympia, WA Metro	25,382	203
Parkersburg-Marietta, WV-OH Metro	25,247	204
Gainesville, FL Metro	25,032	205
Lafayette, LA Metro	24,685	206
Lebanon, NH-VT Micro	24,618	207
Terre Haute, IN Metro	24,381	208
Daphne-Fairhope, AL Micro	24,295	209
Hilton Head Island-Beaufort, SC Micro	24,280	210
Anderson, SC Metro	24,083	211
Kingston, NY Metro	24,078	212
Florence, SC Metro	24,060	213
Waterloo-Cedar Falls, IA Metro	23,995	214
Weirton-Steubenville, WV-OH Metro	23,933	215
Champaign-Urbana, IL Metro	23,866	216
Racine, WI Metro	23,815	217
Pittsfield, MA Metro	23,803	218
Appleton, WI Metro	23,631	219
Niles-Benton Harbor, MI Metro	23,629	220
Lake Charles, LA Metro	23,617	221
Fort Walton Beach-Crestview-Destin, FL Metro	23,276	222
Sioux Falls, SD Metro	22,865	223
Tuscaloosa, AL Metro	22,840	224
Clarksville, TN-KY Metro	22,761	225
Boulder, CO Metro	22,740	226
Joplin, MO Metro	22,478	227
Altoona, PA Metro	22,391	228
Pueblo, CO Metro	22,370	229
Florence, AL Metro	22,292	230
Charlottesville, VA Metro	22,266	231
Muskegon-Norton Shores, MI Metro	22,062	232
Jamestown-Dunkirk-Fredonia, NY Micro	22,007	233
Chambersburg, PA Micro	21,875	234
Anchorage, AK Metro	21,859	235
Hilo, HI Micro	21,703	236
Houma-Bayou Cane-Thibodaux, LA Metro	21,651	237
Monroe, LA Metro	21,434	238
Merced, CA Metro	21,367	239
Abilene, TX Metro	21,297	240
Panama City-Lynn Haven, FL Metro	21,280	241
Burlington-South Burlington, VT Metro	21,069	242
Bellingham, WA Metro	21,055	243
Springfield, OH Metro	21,025	244
Jackson, MI Metro	20,955	245
Kennewick-Richland-Pasco, WA Metro	20,727	246
Elkhart-Goshen, IN Metro	20,719	247
Ocean City, NJ Metro	20,611	248
Traverse City, MI Micro	20,578	249
Las Cruces, NM Metro	20,412	250
Rochester, MN Metro	20,317	251
Lexington-Thomasville, NC Micro	20,276	252
Oshkosh-Neenah, WI Metro	20,268	253
Wichita Falls, TX Metro	20,259	254
Lebanon, PA Metro	20,135	255
Anderson, IN Metro	20,094	256
Eau Claire, WI Metro	20,065	257
Bloomington, IN Metro	19,919	258
Janesville, WI Metro	19,918	259
Billings, MT Metro	19,809	260
Napa, CA Metro	19,780	261
Bangor, ME Metro	19,615	262
Burlington, NC Metro	19,530	263
St. Cloud, MN Metro	19,505	264
Fargo, ND-MN Metro	19,436	265
Dothan, AL Metro	19,435	266
Grand Junction, CO Metro	19,226	267
Williamsport, PA Metro	19,212	268
Vineland-Millville-Bridgeton, NJ Metro	19,207	269
Hot Springs, AR Metro	19,163	270
Alexandria, LA Metro	19,156	271
Sierra Vista-Douglas, AZ Micro	19,118	272
Battle Creek, MI Metro	19,097	273
Salisbury, NC Micro	18,768	274
East Stroudsburg, PA Micro	18,744	275
Greeley, CO Metro	18,669	276
Roseburg, OR Micro	18,606	277
Mansfield, OH Metro	18,564	278
Decatur, AL Metro	18,540	279
Sioux City, IA-NE-SD Metro	18,533	280
Glens Falls, NY Metro	18,471	281
Rocky Mount, NC Metro	18,364	282
Lafayette, IN Metro	18,321	283
Danville, VA Metro	18,280	284
New Castle, PA Micro	18,166	285
St. Joseph, MO-KS Metro	18,099	286
St. George, UT Metro	18,071	287
Albany, GA Metro	18,007	288
Texarkana, TX-Texarkana, AR Metro	17,949	289
Bluefield, WV-VA Micro	17,820	290
Sunbury, PA Micro	17,786	291
Concord, NH Micro	17,641	292
Southern Pines, NC Micro	17,608	293
Bend, OR Metro	17,446	294
Sherman-Denison, TX Metro	17,405	295
Cumberland, MD-WV Metro	17,326	296
Yuba City-Marysville, CA Metro	17,290	297
Blacksburg-Christiansburg-Radford, VA Metro	17,236	298
Palm Coast, FL Micro	17,191	299
Monroe, MI Metro	17,187	300
Morristown, TN Metro	17,083	301
East Liverpool-Salem, OH Micro	17,081	302
Decatur, IL Metro	17,075	303
Laredo, TX Metro	17,058	304
Jefferson City, MO Metro	17,011	305
New Bern, NC Micro	16,995	306
La Crosse, WI-MN Metro	16,983	307
Augusta-Waterville, ME Micro	16,979	308

CBSA	POPULATION	RANK	CBSA	POPULATION	RANK	CBSA	POPULATION	RANK
Pascagoula, MS Metro	16,918	309	Beaver Dam, WI Micro	12,170	413	Harriman, TN Micro	8,781	517
Wausau, WI Metro	16,904	310	Marinette, WI-MI Micro	12,168	414	Batavia, NY Micro	8,767	518
College Station-Bryan, TX Metro	16,844	311	Bowling Green, KY Metro	12,013	415	Salina, KS Micro	8,723	519
Staunton-Waynesboro, VA Micro	16,789	312	Martinsville, VA Micro	11,959	416	Casper, WY Metro	8,720	520
Gadsden, AL Metro	16,683	313	Twin Falls, ID Micro	11,945	417	New Iberia, LA Micro	8,660	521
The Villages, FL Micro	16,640	314	Grand Forks, ND-MN Metro	11,923	418	Lawrence, KS Metro	8,649	522
Statesville-Mooresville, NC Micro	16,606	315	Wisconsin Rapids-Marshfield, WI Micro	11,908	419	Charleston-Mattoon, IL Micro	8,630	523
Bay City, MI Metro	16,428	316	Bristol, VA Metro	11,891	420	Logan, UT-ID Metro	8,582	524
Truckee-Grass Valley, CA Micro	16,357	317	Opelousas-Eunice, LA Micro	11,877	421	Lexington Park, MD Micro	8,561	525
Anniston-Oxford, AL Metro	16,183	318	Auburn, NY Micro	11,854	422	Lake City, FL Micro	8,560	526
Muncie, IN Metro	16,124	319	Ukiah, CA Micro	11,854	423	Corvallis, OR Metro	8,529	527
Eureka-Arcata-Fortuna, CA Micro	16,057	320	Elizabethtown, KY Metro	11,796	424	Albemarle, NC Micro	8,527	528
Athens-Clarke County, GA Metro	16,006	321	Warner Robins, GA Metro	11,787	425	Kapaa, HI Micro	8,500	529
Dover, DE Metro	16,000	322	Farmington, NM Metro	11,773	426	Farmington, MO Micro	8,497	530
Greenville, NC Metro	15,980	323	Laurel, MS Micro	11,759	427	Carson City, NV Metro	8,478	531
Sheboygan, WI Metro	15,866	324	Portsmouth, OH Micro	11,698	428	Baraboo, WI Micro	8,441	532
Grants Pass, OR Micro	15,858	325	Cullman, AL Micro	11,679	429	Shelton, WA Micro	8,429	533
Tupelo, MS Micro	15,853	326	Key West-Marathon, FL Micro	11,659	430	Walla Walla, WA Micro	8,417	534
Kahului-Wailuku, HI Micro	15,836	327	Lawton, OK Metro	11,652	431	Point Pleasant, WV-OH Micro	8,393	535
Mount Vernon-Anacortes, WA Metro	15,833	328	Great Falls, MT Metro	11,520	432	Natchez, MS-LA Micro	8,384	536
Santa Fe, NM Metro	15,731	329	Mount Airy, NC Micro	11,446	433	Burlington, IA-IL Micro	8,277	537
Paducah, KY-IL Micro	15,695	330	Kerrville, TX Micro	11,335	434	Elizabeth City, NC Micro	8,256	538
El Centro, CA Metro	15,525	331	Hammond, LA Micro	11,246	435	Tiffin-Fostoria, OH Micro	8,240	539
Albany-Lebanon, OR Micro	15,418	332	Seneca, SC Micro	11,237	436	Lincolnton, NC Micro	8,231	540
Meridian, MS Micro	15,392	333	Idaho Falls, ID Metro	11,189	437	Frankfort, KY Micro	8,212	541
Owensboro, KY Metro	15,378	334	Centralia, WA Micro	11,187	438	Greenville, OH Micro	8,175	542
Bloomington-Normal, IL Metro	15,292	335	Marion, IN Micro	11,136	439	Ames, IA Metro	8,165	543
Lima, OH Metro	15,244	336	Richmond, IN Micro	11,117	440	Marshall, TX Micro	8,162	544
Lewiston-Auburn, ME Metro	15,187	337	Fergus Falls, MN Micro	11,087	441	Sturgis, MI Micro	8,135	545
Coeur d'Alene, ID Metro	15,130	338	Clearlake, CA Micro	11,073	442	Lewistown, PA Micro	8,102	546
Michigan City-La Porte, IN Metro	15,057	339	Jacksonville, NC Metro	10,927	443	Helena, MT Micro	8,050	547
State College, PA Metro	15,036	340	Talladega-Sylacauga, AL Micro	10,867	444	Freeport, IL Micro	8,030	548
Victoria, TX Metro	14,951	341	Oak Harbor, WA Micro	10,849	445	Ponca City, OK Micro	8,003	549
Brainerd, MN Micro	14,932	342	Crossville, TN Micro	10,846	446	Alamogordo, NM Micro	7,858	550
Ashtabula, OH Micro	14,893	343	Payson, AZ Micro	10,745	447	Platteville, WI Micro	7,828	551
Gainesville, GA Metro	14,854	344	Muskogee, OK Micro	10,710	448	Lancaster, SC Micro	7,811	552
Corning, NY Micro	14,835	345	Morehead City, NC Micro	10,679	449	Clinton, IA Micro	7,793	553
Madera, CA Micro	14,808	346	Lufkin, TX Micro	10,672	450	Oak Hill, WV Micro	7,760	554
Clarksburg, WV Micro	14,805	347	Russellville, AR Micro	10,665	451	Paris, TX Micro	7,743	555
Salisbury, MD Metro	14,788	348	Keene, NH Micro	10,577	452	Mount Vernon, IL Micro	7,724	556
Ogdensburg-Massena, NY Micro	14,719	349	Hudson, NY Micro	10,576	453	Duncan, OK Micro	7,711	557
Tullahoma, TN Micro	14,659	350	Midland, MI Micro	10,543	454	Mount Vernon, OH Micro	7,702	558
Somerset, PA Micro	14,623	351	Kalispell, MT Micro	10,536	455	Barre, VT Micro	7,696	559
San Angelo, TX Metro	14,529	352	Aberdeen, WA Micro	10,440	456	McComb, MS Micro	7,683	560
DuBois, PA Micro	14,505	353	Hutchinson, KS Micro	10,431	457	Stevens Point, WI Micro	7,680	561
Port Angeles, WA Micro	14,451	354	Mountain Home, AR Micro	10,398	458	Scottsboro, AL Micro	7,670	562
Midland, TX Metro	14,442	355	Forest City, NC Micro	10,356	459	Dublin, GA Micro	7,593	563
Wooster, OH Micro	14,338	356	Missoula, MT Metro	10,304	460	Waycross, GA Micro	7,563	564
Fond du Lac, WI Metro	14,314	357	Marion-Herrin, IL Micro	10,286	461	McAlester, OK Micro	7,559	565
Athens, TX Micro	14,288	358	Dunn, NC Micro	10,280	462	Stillwater, OK Micro	7,559	566
Kokomo, IN Metro	14,225	359	Sevierville, TN Micro	10,243	463	New Castle, IN Micro	7,552	567
Columbia, MO Metro	14,192	360	Mankato-North Mankato, MN Metro	10,232	464	Carlsbad-Artesia, NM Micro	7,532	568
Meadville, PA Micro	14,046	361	Phoenix Lake-Cedar Ridge, CA Micro	10,223	465	Norwalk, OH Micro	7,496	569
Elmira, NY Metro	14,018	362	Hanford-Corcoran, CA Micro	10,191	466	Abbeville, SC Micro	7,494	570
Hattiesburg, MS Metro	13,999	363	Pendleton-Hermiston, OR Micro	10,141	467	Austin, MN Micro	7,468	571
Winchester, VA-WV Metro	13,999	364	Ocean Pines, MD Micro	10,136	468	LaGrange, GA Micro	7,443	572
Rapid City, SD Metro	13,912	365	Sayre, PA Micro	10,098	469	Glasgow, KY Micro	7,440	573
Wenatchee, WA Metro	13,909	366	Auburn-Opelika, AL Metro	10,083	470	Ashland, OH Micro	7,432	574
Willimantic, CT Micro	13,878	367	Fairmont, WV Micro	10,079	471	Ruston, LA Micro	7,421	575
Jonesboro, AR Metro	13,873	368	Grand Island, NE Micro	9,961	472	Norfolk, NE Micro	7,420	576
New Philadelphia-Dover, OH Micro	13,871	369	Plattsburgh, NY Micro	9,961	473	Bradford, PA Micro	7,418	577
Odessa, TX Metro	13,847	370	Cheyenne, WY Metro	9,941	474	Nacogdoches, TX Micro	7,410	578
Kankakee-Bradley, IL Metro	13,831	371	Greeneville, TN Micro	9,892	475	Washington, NC Micro	7,382	579
Jackson, TN Metro	13,817	372	Klamath Falls, OR Micro	9,888	476	Athens, TN Micro	7,371	580
Cookeville, TN Micro	13,662	373	Richmond, KY Micro	9,878	477	Crowley, LA Micro	7,344	581
Cleveland, TN Metro	13,610	374	Sterling, IL Micro	9,863	478	Harrison, AR Micro	7,326	582
Gettysburg, PA Micro	13,580	375	Wilson, NC Micro	9,849	479	Pahrump, NV Micro	7,270	583
Quincy, IL-MO Micro	13,575	376	Lewiston, ID-WA Metro	9,778	480	Jasper, IN Micro	7,259	584
Shelby, NC Micro	13,553	377	Searcy, AR Micro	9,776	481	Keokuk-Fort Madison, IA-MO Micro	7,259	585
Pine Bluff, AR Metro	13,539	378	Manhattan, KS Metro	9,761	482	Jacksonville, TX Micro	7,250	586
Harrisonburg, VA Metro	13,517	379	Ithaca, NY Metro	9,758	483	El Dorado, AR Micro	7,237	587
Goldsboro, NC Metro	13,488	380	North Wilkesboro, NC Micro	9,710	484	Warren, PA Micro	7,231	588
Morgantown, WV Metro	13,443	381	Findlay, OH Micro	9,678	485	Bucyrus, OH Micro	7,187	589
Dubuque, IA Metro	13,317	382	Oil City, PA Micro	9,567	486	Ontario, OR-ID Micro	7,179	590
Bloomsburg-Berwick, PA Micro	13,310	383	Watertown-Fort Atkinson, WI Micro	9,529	487	Easton, MD Micro	7,171	591
Danville, IL Metro	13,236	384	Rutland, VT Micro	9,504	488	Columbus, MS Micro	7,170	592
Bismarck, ND Metro	13,228	385	Flagstaff, AZ Metro	9,497	489	Gardnerville Ranchos, NV Micro	7,162	593
Indiana, PA Micro	13,133	386	Greenwood, SC Micro	9,493	490	Danville, KY Micro	7,150	594
Palatka, FL Micro	13,091	387	Georgetown, SC Micro	9,451	491	Berlin, NH-VT Micro	7,132	595
Cape Girardeau-Jackson, MO-IL Micro	13,038	388	Mason City, IA Micro	9,427	492	Muscatine, IA Micro	7,119	596
Rome, GA Metro	13,037	389	Granbury, TX Micro	9,394	493	Rockland, ME Micro	7,088	597
Brunswick, GA Metro	13,007	390	Shawnee, OK Micro	9,323	494	Madisonville, KY Micro	6,986	598
Adrian, MI Micro	12,912	391	Amsterdam, NY Micro	9,293	495	Greenville, MS Micro	6,984	599
Manitowoc, WI Micro	12,902	392	Laconia, NH Micro	9,271	496	Bedford, IN Micro	6,978	600
Sandusky, OH Metro	12,873	393	Minot, ND Micro	9,257	497	Rochelle, IL Micro	6,976	601
Lumberton, NC Micro	12,832	394	Enid, OK Micro	9,255	498	Hobbs, NM Micro	6,959	602
Longview-Kelso, WA Metro	12,784	395	Chillicothe, OH Micro	9,245	499	Huntingdon, PA Micro	6,904	603
Branson, MO Micro	12,723	396	Oneonta, NY Micro	9,223	500	Fort Dodge, IA Micro	6,876	604
Dalton, GA Metro	12,695	397	Warsaw, IN Micro	9,205	501	Faribault-Northfield, MN Micro	6,867	605
Iowa City, IA Metro	12,688	398	Moses Lake, WA Micro	9,128	502	Canton, IL Micro	6,864	606
Whitewater, WI Micro	12,591	399	Somerset, KY Micro	9,048	503	Gaffney, SC Micro	6,861	607
Galesburg, IL Micro	12,536	400	Red Bluff, CA Micro	9,035	504	Centralia, IL Micro	6,844	608
Allegan, MI Micro	12,469	401	Ardmore, OK Micro	9,022	505	Wapakoneta, OH Micro	6,844	609
Zanesville, OH Micro	12,464	402	Columbia, TN Micro	9,003	506	Poplar Bluff, MO Micro	6,843	610
Valdosta, GA Metro	12,411	403	Gloversville, NY Micro	8,983	507	Canon City, CO Micro	6,787	611
Roanoke Rapids, NC Micro	12,403	404	Columbus, IN Metro	8,948	508	Cadillac, MI Micro	6,776	612
Sumter, SC Metro	12,399	405	Owosso, MI Micro	8,915	509	Minden, LA Micro	6,752	613
Watertown-Fort Drum, NY Micro	12,396	406	Fremont, OH Micro	8,910	510	Picayune, MS Micro	6,717	614
Enterprise-Ozark, AL Micro	12,373	407	Marion, OH Micro	8,891	511	Aberdeen, SD Micro	6,685	615
Orangeburg, SC Micro	12,296	408	Kinston, NC Micro	8,888	512	Red Wing, MN Micro	6,661	616
Olean, NY Micro	12,240	409	Marquette, MI Micro	8,850	513	Escanaba, MI Micro	6,624	617
Beckley, WV Micro	12,223	410	Roswell, NM Micro	8,842	514	Corsicana, TX Micro	6,587	618
Albertville, AL Micro	12,191	411	Pocatello, ID Metro	8,808	515	Carbondale, IL Micro	6,572	619
Coos Bay, OR Micro	12,182	412	Bartlesville, OK Micro	8,796	516	London, KY Micro	6,571	620

CBSA	POPULATION	RANK
Scottsbluff, NE Micro	6,556	621
Jacksonville, IL Micro	6,539	622
Sanford, NC Micro	6,521	623
Rockingham, NC Micro	6,514	624
Bellefontaine, OH Micro	6,481	625
Brevard, NC Micro	6,476	626
Winona, MN Micro	6,437	627
Marshalltown, IA Micro	6,410	628
Lock Haven, PA Micro	6,402	629
West Plains, MO Micro	6,389	630
Malone, NY Micro	6,382	631
Bennington, VT Micro	6,366	632
Bozeman, MT Micro	6,340	633
La Follette, TN Micro	6,319	634
Union City, TN-KY Micro	6,315	635
Ottumwa, IA Micro	6,311	636
Fremont, NE Micro	6,294	637
Bogalusa, LA Micro	6,288	638
Coffeyville, KS Micro	6,285	639
Selma, AL Micro	6,279	640
Coldwater, MI Micro	6,237	641
Brownwood, TX Micro	6,224	642
Palestine, TX Micro	6,219	643
Blytheville, AR Micro	6,216	644
Kearney, NE Micro	6,208	645
Willmar, MN Micro	6,200	646
Sedalia, MO Micro	6,175	647
Plymouth, IN Micro	6,146	648
Hastings, NE Micro	6,116	649
Alexandria, MN Micro	6,112	650
Mount Pleasant, MI Micro	6,112	651
Cortland, NY Micro	6,074	652
Lawrenceburg, TN Micro	6,049	653
Morgan City, LA Micro	6,049	654
Taylorville, IL Micro	6,040	655
Milledgeville, GA Micro	6,038	656
Okeechobee, FL Micro	6,015	657
Albert Lea, MN Micro	6,012	658
Celina, OH Micro	6,005	659
Athens, OH Micro	6,004	660
St. Marys, PA Micro	5,992	661
Hannibal, MO Micro	5,965	662
Arcadia, FL Micro	5,962	663
Cambridge, OH Micro	5,955	664
Newton, IA Micro	5,947	665
Pontiac, IL Micro	5,947	666
Thomasville, GA Micro	5,943	667
Mayfield, KY Micro	5,933	668
Sidney, OH Micro	5,918	669
Huntsville, TX Micro	5,910	670
Logansport, IN Micro	5,909	671
El Campo, TX Micro	5,865	672
Alma, MI Micro	5,852	673
Valley, AL Micro	5,848	674
Iron Mountain, MI-WI Micro	5,837	675
Vicksburg, MS Micro	5,824	676
Vincennes, IN Micro	5,811	677
Winfield, KS Micro	5,801	678
Rolla, MO Micro	5,798	679
Astoria, OR Micro	5,726	680
Durant, OK Micro	5,724	681
Greenwood, MS Micro	5,722	682
Houghton, MI Micro	5,715	683
Lewisburg, PA Micro	5,702	684
Del Rio, TX Micro	5,699	685
Seymour, IN Micro	5,674	686
Brookings, OR Micro	5,667	687
Paris, TN Micro	5,661	688
Big Rapids, MI Micro	5,654	689
Gainesville, TX Micro	5,634	690
Statesboro, GA Micro	5,627	691
Pittsburg, KS Micro	5,617	692
Wabash, IN Micro	5,608	693
McMinnville, TN Micro	5,601	694
Henderson, NC Micro	5,599	695
North Platte, NE Micro	5,590	696
Mount Sterling, KY Micro	5,583	697
Miami, OK Micro	5,569	698
Burley, ID Micro	5,547	699
Montrose, CO Micro	5,547	700
Camden, AR Micro	5,545	701
Cornelia, GA Micro	5,545	702
Huntington, IN Micro	5,526	703
Sikeston, MO Micro	5,509	704
Newberry, SC Micro	5,503	705
Alpena, MI Micro	5,498	706
Gallup, NM Micro	5,471	707
Butte-Silver Bow, MT Micro	5,427	708
Selinsgrove, PA Micro	5,398	709
Kennett, MO Micro	5,393	710
Moultrie, GA Micro	5,392	711
Coshocton, OH Micro	5,385	712
Tahlequah, OK Micro	5,375	713
Paragould, AR Micro	5,359	714
Crawfordsville, IN Micro	5,352	715
Cambridge, MD Micro	5,331	716
Clovis, NM Micro	5,322	717
Dixon, IL Micro	5,306	718
Kendallville, IN Micro	5,284	719
Brenham, TX Micro	5,240	720
Cedartown, GA Micro	5,230	721
Defiance, OH Micro	5,218	722
Silver City, NM Micro	5,189	723
Corinth, MS Micro	5,184	724
Murray, KY Micro	5,181	725
Seneca Falls, NY Micro	5,143	726
Batesville, AR Micro	5,131	727
Ada, OK Micro	5,126	728
McPherson, KS Micro	5,118	729
Rio Grande City, TX Micro	5,105	730
Calhoun, GA Micro	5,103	731
Alice, TX Micro	5,097	732
Monroe, WI Micro	5,087	733
Walterboro, SC Micro	5,081	734
Shelbyville, TN Micro	5,078	735
Urbana, OH Micro	5,043	736
Wilmington, OH Micro	5,036	737
Eagle Pass, TX Micro	5,029	738
Riverton, WY Micro	5,023	739
Sault Ste. Marie, MI Micro	5,010	740
Dyersburg, TN Micro	4,999	741
Merrill, WI Micro	4,986	742
Hutchinson, MN Micro	4,981	743
Central City, KY Micro	4,966	744
Newport, TN Micro	4,941	745
Bay City, TX Micro	4,916	746
Great Bend, KS Micro	4,905	747
Frankfort, IN Micro	4,878	748
Harrisburg, IL Micro	4,872	749
Sulphur Springs, TX Micro	4,871	750
Bemidji, MN Micro	4,861	751
Brigham City, UT Micro	4,852	752
Union, SC Micro	4,838	753
Warrensburg, MO Micro	4,836	754
Plainview, TX Micro	4,833	755
Safford, AZ Micro	4,832	756
Hope, AR Micro	4,826	757
Deming, NM Micro	4,803	758
Big Spring, TX Micro	4,798	759
Effingham, IL Micro	4,783	760
Boone, NC Micro	4,780	761
Tifton, GA Micro	4,775	762
Lebanon, MO Micro	4,750	763
Espanola, NM Micro	4,733	764
Corbin, KY Micro	4,730	765
Auburn, IN Micro	4,727	766
Watertown, SD Micro	4,713	767
Emporia, KS Micro	4,695	768
Peru, IN Micro	4,683	769
Brookhaven, MS Micro	4,665	770
Owatonna, MN Micro	4,623	771
Bastrop, LA Micro	4,618	772
Kill Devil Hills, NC Micro	4,617	773
Blackfoot, ID Micro	4,615	774
New Ulm, MN Micro	4,611	775
Natchitoches, LA Micro	4,606	776
Americus, GA Micro	4,605	777
Douglas, GA Micro	4,597	778
Macomb, IL Micro	4,596	779
Durango, CO Micro	4,590	780
Stephenville, TX Micro	4,586	781
Menomonie, WI Micro	4,567	782
Fairbanks, AK Metro	4,556	783
Van Wert, OH Micro	4,554	784
Mineral Wells, TX Micro	4,552	785
Nogales, AZ Micro	4,544	786
Decatur, IN Micro	4,518	787
Lincoln, IL Micro	4,492	788
Chester, SC Micro	4,487	789
Maysville, KY Micro	4,383	790
Washington, IN Micro	4,370	791
Beatrice, NE Micro	4,330	792
Cleveland, MS Micro	4,295	793
Madison, IN Micro	4,246	794
Middlesborough, KY Micro	4,239	795
Fort Polk South, LA Micro	4,234	796
Ellensburg, WA Micro	4,222	797
Mexico, MO Micro	4,216	798
Sheridan, WY Micro	4,209	799
Jennings, LA Micro	4,206	800
Laurinburg, NC Micro	4,187	801
Boone, IA Micro	4,183	802
Fairmont, MN Micro	4,167	803
Taos, NM Micro	4,153	804
Pampa, TX Micro	4,123	805
Thomaston, GA Micro	4,115	806
Toccoa, GA Micro	4,094	807
De Ridder, LA Micro	4,091	808
Washington, OH Micro	4,086	809
Columbus, NE Micro	4,078	810
City of The Dalles, OR Micro	4,073	811
Oxford, MS Micro	4,070	812
Angola, IN Micro	4,063	813
Connersville, IN Micro	3,999	814
Magnolia, AR Micro	3,944	815
Hays, KS Micro	3,922	816
Lexington, NE Micro	3,899	817
Kirksville, MO Micro	3,872	818
Pullman, WA Micro	3,863	819
Wauchula, FL Micro	3,809	820
Parsons, KS Micro	3,805	821
Starkville, MS Micro	3,803	822
Bainbridge, GA Micro	3,798	823
Jamestown, ND Micro	3,797	824
Fitzgerald, GA Micro	3,795	825
Wahpeton, ND-MN Micro	3,795	826
Summerville, GA Micro	3,783	827
Troy, AL Micro	3,776	828
Clewiston, FL Micro	3,760	829
Uvalde, TX Micro	3,742	830
La Grande, OR Micro	3,734	831
Marshall, MO Micro	3,712	832
Fort Morgan, CO Micro	3,675	833
Las Vegas, NM Micro	3,657	834
Marshall, MN Micro	3,655	835
Dickinson, ND Micro	3,647	836
Borger, TX Micro	3,625	837
Campbellsville, KY Micro	3,624	838
Bennettsville, SC Micro	3,617	839
Moberly, MO Micro	3,609	840
Mitchell, SD Micro	3,599	841
Dillon, SC Micro	3,589	842
Fort Leonard Wood, MO Micro	3,568	843
Clarksdale, MS Micro	3,561	844
Mount Pleasant, TX Micro	3,553	845
Oskaloosa, IA Micro	3,529	846
Kingsville, TX Micro	3,508	847
Dodge City, KS Micro	3,484	848
Moscow, ID Micro	3,467	849
Worthington, MN Micro	3,461	850
Hinesville-Fort Stewart, GA Metro	3,426	851
Spirit Lake, IA Micro	3,411	852
Crescent City North, CA Micro	3,408	853
West Helena, AR Micro	3,404	854
Yazoo City, MS Micro	3,396	855
Arkadelphia, AR Micro	3,391	856
Storm Lake, IA Micro	3,359	857
Williston, ND Micro	3,350	858
Greensburg, IN Micro	3,336	859
Rexburg, ID Micro	3,332	860
Forrest City, AR Micro	3,324	861
Tuskegee, AL Micro	3,294	862
Bishop, CA Micro	3,272	863
Spearfish, SD Micro	3,269	864
Grenada, MS Micro	3,264	865
Elko, NV Micro	3,251	866
Cedar City, UT Micro	3,239	867
Altus, OK Micro	3,228	868
Rock Springs, WY Micro	3,210	869
Huron, SD Micro	3,197	870
Yankton, SD Micro	3,173	871
Jesup, GA Micro	3,162	872
Indianola, MS Micro	3,135	873
Brookings, SD Micro	3,132	874
Prineville, OR Micro	3,101	875
Grants, NM Micro	3,081	876
Sterling, CO Micro	3,071	877
North Vernon, IN Micro	3,064	878
Beeville, TX Micro	3,062	879
Spencer, IA Micro	3,035	880
Fallon, NV Micro	3,017	881
Garden City, KS Micro	2,947	882
Levelland, TX Micro	2,936	883
Maryville, MO Micro	2,929	884
Pierre, SD Micro	2,844	885
Cordele, GA Micro	2,805	886
Vernal, UT Micro	2,790	887
Laramie, WY Micro	2,739	888
Woodward, OK Micro	2,712	889
Hood River, OR Micro	2,711	890
St. Marys, GA Micro	2,689	891
Brownsville, TN Micro	2,657	892
Atchison, KS Micro	2,654	893
Price, UT Micro	2,626	894
Scottsburg, IN Micro	2,616	895
Pierre Part, LA Micro	2,565	896
Sweetwater, TX Micro	2,554	897
Fort Valley, GA Micro	2,521	898
Snyder, TX Micro	2,412	899
Los Alamos, NM Micro	2,329	900
Raymondville, TX Micro	2,328	901
Vernon, TX Micro	2,289	902
Hereford, TX Micro	2,277	903
Edwards, CO Micro	2,258	904
Portales, NM Micro	2,229	905
Dumas, TX Micro	2,220	906
Mountain Home, ID Micro	2,183	907
Gillette, WY Micro	2,156	908
Juneau, AK Micro	2,104	909
Havre, MT Micro	2,081	910
Liberal, KS Micro	2,029	911
Guymon, OK Micro	2,016	912
Lamesa, TX Micro	1,967	913
Jackson, WY-ID Micro	1,929	914
Andrews, TX Micro	1,642	915
Pecos, TX Micro	1,629	916
Tallulah, LA Micro	1,518	917
Evanston, WY Micro	1,496	918
Vermillion, SD Micro	1,322	919
Ketchikan, AK Micro	1,139	920
Silverthorne, CO Micro	1,091	921
Kodiak, AK Micro	775	922

CBSA Total	33,373,235	
United States Total	36,555,990	
CBSA (% of U.S. Total)	91.3	

CBSA	POPULATION	RANK
New York-Newark-Edison, NY-NJ-PA Metro	3,395,678	1
Chicago-Naperville-Joliet, IL-IN-WI Metro	1,706,696	2
Atlanta-Sandy Springs-Marietta, GA Metro	1,355,188	3
Washington-Arlington-Alexandria, DC-VA-MD-WV Metro	1,323,322	4
Philadelphia-Camden-Wilmington, PA-NJ-DE-MD Metro	1,166,867	5
Miami-Fort Lauderdale-Miami Beach, FL Metro	1,061,817	6
Detroit-Warren-Livonia, MI Metro	1,029,919	7
Los Angeles-Long Beach-Santa Ana, CA Metro	988,141	8
Houston-Baytown-Sugar Land, TX Metro	838,124	9
Dallas-Fort Worth-Arlington, TX Metro	781,615	10
Baltimore-Towson, MD Metro	713,793	11
Memphis, TN-MS-AR Metro	561,394	12
Virginia Beach-Norfolk-Newport News, VA-NC Metro	519,730	13
New Orleans-Metairie-Kenner, LA Metro	497,992	14
St. Louis, MO-IL Metro	497,000	15
Cleveland-Elyria-Mentor, OH Metro	416,850	16
San Francisco-Oakland-Fremont, CA Metro	381,603	17
Richmond, VA Metro	351,415	18
Charlotte-Gastonia-Concord, NC-SC Metro	339,370	19
Birmingham-Hoover, AL Metro	304,006	20
Tampa-St. Petersburg-Clearwater, FL Metro	290,007	21
Riverside-San Bernardino-Ontario, CA Metro	284,036	22
Boston-Cambridge-Quincy, MA-NH Metro	283,482	23
Jacksonville, FL Metro	279,275	24
Orlando, FL Metro	279,015	25
Baton Rouge, LA Metro	249,377	26
Milwaukee-Waukesha-West Allis, WI Metro	246,216	27
Kansas City, MO-KS Metro	239,150	28
Jackson, MS Metro	236,613	29
Cincinnati-Middletown, OH-KY-IN Metro	235,469	30
Columbia, SC Metro	230,933	31
Indianapolis, IN Metro	229,998	32
Columbus, OH Metro	225,041	33
Nashville-Davidson-Murfreesboro, TN Metro	205,339	34
Pittsburgh, PA Metro	193,122	35
Charleston-North Charleston, SC Metro	181,236	36
Augusta-Richmond County, GA-SC Metro	178,610	37
Raleigh-Cary, NC Metro	178,177	38
Minneapolis-St. Paul-Bloomington, MN-WI Metro	173,204	39
Seattle-Tacoma-Bellevue, WA Metro	165,745	40
San Diego-Carlsbad-San Marcos, CA Metro	161,812	41
Greensboro-High Point, NC Metro	157,824	42
Louisville, KY-IN Metro	156,907	43
Shreveport-Bossier City, LA Metro	147,720	44
Montgomery, AL Metro	147,489	45
Sacramento-Arden-Arcade-Roseville, CA Metro	145,084	46
Buffalo-Cheektowaga-Tonawanda, NY Metro	144,347	47
Little Rock-North Little Rock, AR Metro	141,975	48
Las Vegas-Paradise, NV Metro	139,722	49
Mobile, AL Metro	138,232	50
Phoenix-Mesa-Scottsdale, AZ Metro	137,303	51
Durham, NC Metro	129,464	52
Denver-Aurora, CO Metro	128,670	53
Fayetteville, NC Metro	127,001	54
Oklahoma City, OK Metro	122,958	55
Dayton, OH Metro	121,933	56
Rochester, NY Metro	120,500	57
Hartford-West Hartford-East Hartford, CT Metro	117,460	58
Columbus, GA-AL Metro	113,179	59
Tallahassee, FL Metro	112,408	60
San Antonio, TX Metro	105,994	61
Austin-Round Rock, TX Metro	105,706	62
Savannah, GA Metro	103,687	63
Greenville, SC Metro	101,854	64
New Haven-Milford, CT Metro	101,700	65
Beaumont-Port Arthur, TX Metro	97,386	66
Macon, GA Metro	96,005	67
Bridgeport-Stamford-Norwalk, CT Metro	92,172	68
Flint, MI Metro	88,950	69
Winston-Salem, NC Metro	88,705	70
Florence, SC Metro	81,167	71
Tulsa, OK Metro	79,441	72
Toledo, OH Metro	79,004	73
Albany, GA Metro	78,940	74
Akron, OH Metro	78,211	75
Pensacola-Ferry Pass-Brent, FL Metro	77,071	76
Huntsville, AL Metro	77,052	77
Lakeland-Winter Haven, FL Metro	74,627	78
Trenton-Ewing, NJ Metro	73,230	79
Tuscaloosa, AL Metro	68,997	80
Chattanooga, TN-GA Metro	67,704	81
Providence-New Bedford-Fall River, RI-MA Metro	64,942	82
Lafayette, LA Metro	64,736	83
Poughkeepsie-Newburgh-Middletown, NY Metro	64,735	84
Rocky Mount, NC Metro	64,222	85
Vallejo-Fairfield, CA Metro	63,213	86
Killeen-Temple-Fort Hood, TX Metro	63,022	87
Youngstown-Warren-Boardman, OH-PA Metro	62,827	88
Omaha-Council Bluffs, NE-IA Metro	61,059	89
Albany-Schenectady-Troy, NY Metro	60,535	90
Grand Rapids-Wyoming, MI Metro	58,283	91
Monroe, LA Metro	56,790	92
Orangeburg, SC Micro	56,713	93
Portland-Vancouver-Beaverton, OR-WA Metro	56,422	94
Greenville, NC Metro	55,996	95
Spartanburg, SC Metro	55,589	96
Sumter, SC Metro	52,231	97
Gainesville, FL Metro	50,061	98
Syracuse, NY Metro	49,926	99
Gulfport-Biloxi, MS Metro	49,488	100
Harrisburg-Carlisle, PA Metro	49,054	101
Pine Bluff, AR Metro	48,951	102
Wilmington, NC Metro	48,347	103
Stockton, CA Metro	47,616	104
Deltona-Daytona Beach-Ormond Beach, FL Metro	46,769	105
Clarksville, TN-KY Metro	46,633	106
Lake Charles, LA Metro	46,308	107
Fresno, CA Metro	45,685	108
Palm Bay-Melbourne-Titusville, FL Metro	45,358	109
Atlantic City, NJ Metro	45,183	110
Wichita, KS Metro	45,084	111
Lexington-Fayette, KY Metro	43,939	112
Springfield, MA Metro	43,481	113
Meridian, MS Micro	43,388	114
Hilton Head Island-Beaufort, SC Micro	43,309	115
Lynchburg, VA Metro	43,218	116
Roanoke Rapids, NC Micro	42,780	117
San Jose-Sunnyvale-Santa Clara, CA Metro	42,647	118
Bakersfield, CA Metro	42,195	119
Sarasota-Bradenton-Venice, FL Metro	42,068	120
Port St. Lucie-Fort Pierce, FL Metro	41,913	121
Alexandria, LA Metro	41,825	122
Ann Arbor, MI Metro	40,798	123
Greenville, MS Micro	40,067	124
Saginaw-Saginaw Township North, MI Metro	40,045	125
Knoxville, TN Metro	39,789	126
Valdosta, GA Metro	39,304	127
Fort Wayne, IN Metro	38,544	128
Lansing-East Lansing, MI Metro	38,263	129
Goldsboro, NC Metro	37,934	130
Colorado Springs, CO Metro	37,680	131
Opelousas-Eunice, LA Micro	37,499	132
Cape Coral-Fort Myers, FL Metro	36,939	133
Roanoke, VA Metro	36,800	134
Danville, VA Metro	36,345	135
Longview, TX Metro	35,833	136
Tyler, TX Metro	34,534	137
Athens-Clarke County, GA Metro	34,517	138
Hattiesburg, MS Metro	34,367	139
Myrtle Beach-Conway-North Myrtle Beach, SC Metro	33,854	140
Ocala, FL Metro	33,659	141
South Bend-Mishawaka, IN-MI Metro	33,135	142
Jackson, TN Metro	32,881	143
Waco, TX Metro	32,737	144
Peoria, IL Metro	31,917	145
Texarkana, TX-Texarkana, AR Metro	31,845	146
Lumberton, NC Micro	31,704	147
Rockford, IL Metro	31,609	148
Pascagoula, MS Metro	31,427	149
Houma-Bayou Cane-Thibodaux, LA Metro	31,316	150
Dothan, AL Metro	31,023	151
Vineland-Millville-Bridgeton, NJ Metro	30,604	152
Salisbury, MD Metro	30,499	153
Wilson, NC Micro	30,142	154
Hammond, LA Micro	29,968	155
Warner Robins, GA Metro	29,809	156
Selma, AL Micro	29,624	157
Anderson, SC Metro	29,607	158
New Bern, NC Micro	29,562	159
Greenwood, MS Micro	29,310	160
Auburn-Opelika, AL Metro	28,001	161
Honolulu, HI Metro	27,572	162
Laurel, MS Micro	27,559	163
Milledgeville, GA Micro	27,392	164
Canton-Massillon, OH Metro	27,371	165
Kalamazoo-Portage, MI Metro	27,353	166
Dover, DE Metro	27,324	167
Jacksonville, NC Metro	26,593	168
Hinesville-Fort Stewart, GA Metro	26,385	169
Columbus, MS Micro	26,152	170
Tucson, AZ Metro	26,143	171
Tupelo, MS Micro	26,070	172
Cleveland, MS Micro	25,886	173
Talladega-Sylacauga, AL Micro	25,801	174
Burlington, NC Metro	25,762	175
Natchez, MS-LA Micro	25,740	176
Worcester, MA Metro	25,512	177
Charlottesville, VA Metro	25,102	178
McComb, MS Micro	25,066	179
Niles-Benton Harbor, MI Metro	24,788	180
Indianola, MS Micro	24,226	181
Kinston, NC Micro	24,104	182
Muskegon-Norton Shores, MI Metro	23,959	183
Allentown-Bethlehem-Easton, PA-NJ Metro	23,848	184
Hickory-Morganton-Lenoir, NC Metro	23,756	185
New Iberia, LA Micro	23,209	186
Dunn, NC Micro	23,193	187
College Station-Bryan, TX Metro	23,155	188
Seaford, DE Micro	23,066	189
Lawton, OK Metro	22,772	190
Henderson, NC Micro	22,585	191
Brunswick, GA Metro	22,492	192
Vicksburg, MS Micro	22,477	193
Davenport-Moline-Rock Island, IA-IL Metro	22,332	194
Georgetown, SC Micro	22,164	195
Clarksdale, MS Micro	21,895	196
Greenwood, SC Micro	21,876	197
Anniston-Oxford, AL Metro	21,626	198
Ruston, LA Micro	21,003	199
Salisbury, NC Micro	20,798	200
Shelby, NC Micro	20,752	201
Champaign-Urbana, IL Metro	20,573	202
Racine, WI Metro	20,319	203
Albuquerque, NM Metro	19,706	204
Springfield, IL Metro	19,600	205
Tuskegee, AL Micro	19,596	206
Martinsville, VA Micro	19,563	207
Asheville, NC Metro	19,368	208
Evansville, IN-KY Metro	19,219	209
Dublin, GA Micro	19,187	210
LaGrange, GA Micro	19,167	211
Lubbock, TX Metro	19,124	212
Des Moines, IA Metro	18,990	213
Elizabeth City, NC Micro	18,890	214
Madison, WI Metro	18,484	215
Enterprise-Ozark, AL Micro	18,427	216
Americus, GA Micro	17,807	217
Statesville-Mooresville, NC Micro	17,687	218
Florence, AL Metro	17,615	219
Decatur, AL Metro	17,427	220
Erie, PA Metro	17,335	221
Fort Walton Beach-Crestview-Destin, FL Metro	17,334	222
Lancaster, SC Micro	17,294	223
Blytheville, AR Micro	17,115	224
Panama City-Lynn Haven, FL Metro	16,988	225
El Paso, TX Metro	16,947	226
Morgan City, LA Micro	16,897	227
Anchorage, AK Metro	16,886	228
Thomasville, GA Micro	16,847	229
Statesboro, GA Micro	16,472	230
Kankakee-Bradley, IL Metro	16,323	231
Walterboro, SC Micro	16,275	232
Starkville, MS Micro	16,175	233
Decatur, IL Metro	15,881	234
Topeka, KS Metro	15,819	235
Yazoo City, MS Micro	15,598	236
Norwich-New London, CT Metro	15,392	237
Oxnard-Thousand Oaks-Ventura, CA Metro	15,346	238
El Dorado, AR Micro	15,223	239
Hagerstown-Martinsburg, MD-WV Metro	15,168	240
West Helena, AR Micro	15,149	241
Daphne-Fairhope, AL Micro	15,129	242
Gadsden, AL Metro	15,104	243
Natchitoches, LA Micro	15,076	244
Naples-Marco Island, FL Metro	14,965	245
Reading, PA Metro	14,951	246
Battle Creek, MI Metro	14,928	247
York-Hanover, PA Metro	14,906	248
Utica-Rome, NY Metro	14,861	249
Huntsville, TX Micro	14,812	250
Bennettsville, SC Micro	14,805	251
Salinas, CA Metro	14,710	252
Marshall, TX Micro	14,619	253
Charleston, WV Metro	14,483	254
Forrest City, AR Micro	14,402	255
Modesto, CA Metro	14,285	256
Rockingham, NC Micro	14,276	257
Dillon, SC Micro	14,211	258
Valley, AL Micro	14,074	259
Bogalusa, LA Micro	13,994	260
Lancaster, PA Metro	13,898	261
Minden, LA Micro	13,675	262
Laurinburg, NC Micro	13,636	263
East Stroudsburg, PA Micro	13,516	264
Chester, SC Micro	13,425	265
Lexington-Thomasville, NC Micro	13,396	266
Bastrop, LA Micro	13,362	267
Corpus Christi, TX Metro	13,307	268
Amarillo, TX Metro	13,225	269
Washington, NC Micro	13,043	270
Lima, OH Metro	12,968	271
Columbia, MO Metro	12,786	272
Palatka, FL Micro	12,729	273
Wichita Falls, TX Metro	12,500	274
Newberry, SC Micro	12,397	275
Rome, GA Metro	12,303	276
Jackson, MI Metro	12,279	277
Springfield, OH Metro	12,242	278
Camden, AR Micro	12,178	279
Southern Pines, NC Micro	12,160	280
Elizabethtown, KY Metro	12,090	281
Palestine, TX Micro	12,084	282
Lufkin, TX Micro	12,070	283
Lexington Park, MD Micro	12,037	284
Mansfield, OH Metro	11,962	285
Salt Lake City, UT Metro	11,644	286
Douglas, GA Micro	11,618	287
Hanford-Corcoran, CA Metro	11,561	288
Waycross, GA Micro	11,349	289
Gaffney, SC Micro	11,323	290
Bainbridge, GA Micro	11,237	291
Troy, AL Micro	11,187	292
Kingston, NY Metro	10,982	293
Tifton, GA Micro	10,876	294
Gainesville, GA Metro	10,861	295
Watertown-Fort Drum, NY Micro	10,846	296
Michigan City-La Porte, IN Metro	10,747	297
Crowley, LA Micro	10,729	298
Fort Valley, GA Micro	10,693	299
Waterloo-Cedar Falls, IA Metro	10,617	300
Lake City, FL Micro	10,528	301
Brookhaven, MS Micro	10,348	302
Anderson, IN Metro	10,331	303
Fort Smith, AR-OK Metro	10,331	304
Vero Beach, FL Metro	10,296	305
Hope, AR Micro	10,230	306
Bloomington-Normal, IL Metro	10,190	307
Oxford, MS Micro	10,185	308

CBSA	POPULATION	RANK
Jefferson City, MO Metro	10,155	309
Nacogdoches, TX Micro	10,129	310
Abilene, TX Metro	10,051	311
Jonesboro, AR Metro	9,934	312
Columbia, TN Micro	9,886	313
Moultrie, GA Micro	9,783	314
Brownsville, TN Micro	9,715	315
Grenada, MS Micro	9,624	316
Sanford, NC Micro	9,606	317
Magnolia, AR Micro	9,553	318
Union, SC Micro	9,541	319
Cordele, GA Micro	9,449	320
The Villages, FL Micro	9,286	321
Elkhart-Goshen, IN Metro	9,212	322
Sebring, FL Micro	9,093	323
Muskogee, OK Micro	9,011	324
Santa Barbara-Santa Maria-Goleta, CA Metro	8,995	325
Fort Polk South, LA Micro	8,951	326
Danville, IL Metro	8,939	327
Manhattan, KS Micro	8,887	328
Scranton-Wilkes-Barre, PA Metro	8,855	329
St. Marys, GA Micro	8,676	330
Bowling Green, KY Metro	8,507	331
Merced, CA Metro	8,449	332
Binghamton, NY Metro	8,398	333
Paducah, KY-IL Micro	8,304	334
Cambridge, MD Micro	8,237	335
Tallulah, LA Micro	8,092	336
Fitzgerald, GA Micro	8,016	337
Thomaston, GA Micro	7,937	338
Midland, TX Metro	7,852	339
Abbeville, LA Micro	7,805	340
Staunton-Waynesboro, VA Micro	7,794	341
Muncie, IN Metro	7,758	342
Carbondale, IL Micro	7,704	343
Corsicana, TX Micro	7,648	344
Lincoln, NE Metro	7,635	345
Punta Gorda, FL Metro	7,565	346
Jacksonville, TX Micro	7,441	347
Cape Girardeau-Jackson, MO-IL Micro	7,381	348
Hot Springs, AR Metro	7,380	349
Pierre Part, LA Micro	7,229	350
Janesville, WI Metro	7,086	351
Terre Haute, IN Metro	7,086	352
Spokane, WA Metro	7,048	353
Ocean Pines, MD Micro	7,022	354
Beckley, WV Micro	6,981	355
Forest City, NC Micro	6,935	356
Huntington-Ashland, WV-KY-OH Metro	6,837	357
Blacksburg-Christiansburg-Radford, VA Metro	6,725	358
Sandusky, OH Metro	6,689	359
Albemarle, NC Micro	6,684	360
Santa Rosa-Petaluma, CA Metro	6,621	361
Reno-Sparks, NV Metro	6,493	362
Paris, TX Micro	6,465	363
Springfield, MO Metro	6,450	364
Visalia-Porterville, CA Metro	6,374	365
Picayune, MS Micro	6,306	366
Victoria, TX Metro	6,244	367
Bremerton-Silverdale, WA Metro	6,232	368
Sherman-Denison, TX Metro	6,144	369
Manchester-Nashua, NH Metro	6,118	370
Ogden-Clearfield, UT Metro	5,984	371
Elmira, NY Metro	5,982	372
El Campo, TX Micro	5,967	373
Cedar Rapids, IA Metro	5,912	374
Seneca, SC Micro	5,876	375
Kokomo, IN Metro	5,735	376
Olympia, WA Metro	5,628	377
Fayetteville-Springdale-Rogers, AR-MO Metro	5,626	378
Palm Coast, FL Micro	5,561	379
El Centro, CA Metro	5,514	380
Brenham, TX Micro	5,511	381
Fairbanks, AK Metro	5,384	382
Odessa, TX Metro	5,343	383
Cedartown, GA Micro	5,312	384
Jennings, LA Micro	5,309	385
Arkadelphia, AR Micro	5,298	386
Clewiston, FL Micro	5,239	387
Jesup, GA Micro	5,189	388
Fort Leonard Wood, MO Micro	5,120	389
San Luis Obispo-Paso Robles, CA Metro	5,069	390
St. Joseph, MO-KS Metro	5,031	391
Weirton-Steubenville, WV-OH Metro	5,030	392
Marion, IN Micro	5,023	393
Bluefield, WV-VA Micro	5,009	394
Easton, MD Micro	4,953	395
Frankfort, KY Micro	4,927	396
Williamsport, PA Metro	4,908	397
Union City, TN-KY Micro	4,879	398
Johnson City, TN Metro	4,852	399
Athens, TX Micro	4,848	400
Madera, CA Metro	4,812	401
Dyersburg, TN Micro	4,806	402
Winchester, VA-WV Metro	4,775	403
Ocean City, NJ Metro	4,700	404
Sikeston, MO Micro	4,644	405
De Ridder, LA Micro	4,612	406
Bay City, TX Micro	4,607	407
Cumberland, MD-WV Metro	4,605	408
Johnstown, PA Metro	4,505	409
Portland-South Portland, ME Metro	4,487	410
Wheeling, WV-OH Metro	4,465	411
Chillicothe, OH Micro	4,455	412
Lincolnton, NC Micro	4,334	413
Sierra Vista-Douglas, AZ Micro	4,302	414
Owensboro, KY Metro	4,249	415
Barnstable Town, MA Metro	4,216	416
Morehead City, NC Micro	4,198	417
Tullahoma, TN Micro	4,192	418
Kingsport-Bristol, TN-VA Metro	4,095	419
Lawrence, KS Metro	4,042	420
Arcadia, FL Micro	3,944	421
Corinth, MS Micro	3,906	422
Ithaca, NY Metro	3,905	423
Galesburg, IL Micro	3,874	424
Marion, OH Micro	3,845	425
Key West-Marathon, FL Micro	3,827	426
Harrisonburg, VA Metro	3,815	427
Lafayette, IN Metro	3,750	428
Yuba City-Marysville, CA Metro	3,742	429
Cleveland, TN Metro	3,719	430
Malone, NY Micro	3,719	431
Ardmore, OK Micro	3,714	432
San Angelo, TX Metro	3,679	433
State College, PA Metro	3,655	434
Freeport, IL Micro	3,620	435
Iowa City, IA Metro	3,616	436
Pottsville, PA Micro	3,553	437
Morristown, TN Metro	3,536	438
Richmond, IN Micro	3,533	439
New Castle, PA Micro	3,510	440
Rochester, MN Metro	3,508	441
Zanesville, OH Micro	3,501	442
Dalton, GA Metro	3,429	443
Auburn, NY Micro	3,392	444
Green Bay, WI Metro	3,385	445
Bloomington, IN Metro	3,313	446
Jamestown-Dunkirk-Fredonia, NY Micro	3,286	447
Chambersburg, PA Micro	3,282	448
Homosassa Springs, FL Micro	3,268	449
Richmond, KY Micro	3,261	450
Mount Vernon, IL Micro	3,236	451
Ashtabula, OH Micro	3,223	452
Clovis, NM Micro	3,191	453
Lewisburg, PA Micro	3,167	454
Salem, OR Metro	3,164	455
Shelbyville, TN Micro	3,117	456
Danville, KY Micro	3,109	457
Beeville, TX Micro	3,095	458
Toccoa, GA Micro	3,073	459
Plattsburgh, NY Micro	3,065	460
Morgantown, WV Metro	3,051	461
Ogdensburg-Massena, NY Micro	3,043	462
Yuma, AZ Metro	3,041	463
Mount Pleasant, TX Micro	3,008	464
Kennett, MO Micro	3,007	465
Boise City-Nampa, ID Metro	3,003	466
Chico, CA Metro	2,986	467
Kennewick-Richland-Pasco, WA Metro	2,982	468
Madisonville, KY Micro	2,980	469
Sioux Falls, SD Metro	2,965	470
Hudson, NY Micro	2,963	471
Pueblo, CO Metro	2,947	472
Okeechobee, FL Micro	2,917	473
Mount Airy, NC Micro	2,899	474
Las Cruces, NM Metro	2,876	475
Pittsfield, MA Metro	2,865	476
Holland-Grand Haven, MI Metro	2,863	477
Monroe, MI Metro	2,804	478
Searcy, AR Micro	2,799	479
North Wilkesboro, NC Micro	2,754	480
McAllen-Edinburg-Pharr, TX Metro	2,719	481
Paris, TN Micro	2,653	482
Hobbs, NM Micro	2,646	483
Summerville, GA Micro	2,610	484
Eugene-Springfield, OR Metro	2,604	485
Boulder, CO Metro	2,507	486
Sulphur Springs, TX Micro	2,498	487
Quincy, IL-MO Micro	2,480	488
Cheyenne, WY Metro	2,455	489
Canon City, CO Micro	2,446	490
Oak Hill, WV Micro	2,434	491
Santa Cruz-Watsonville, CA Metro	2,398	492
Napa, CA Metro	2,397	493
Alamogordo, NM Micro	2,394	494
Duluth, MN-WI Metro	2,389	495
Glens Falls, NY Metro	2,370	496
Huntingdon, PA Micro	2,367	497
Stillwater, OK Micro	2,336	498
East Liverpool-Salem, OH Micro	2,323	499
Yakima, WA Metro	2,313	500
Altus, OK Micro	2,311	501
Athens, TN Micro	2,296	502
Joplin, MO Metro	2,287	503
Wauchula, FL Micro	2,279	504
Sioux City, IA-NE-SD Metro	2,264	505
St. Cloud, MN Metro	2,252	506
Poplar Bluff, MO Micro	2,205	507
Seneca Falls, NY Micro	2,161	508
Willimantic, CT Micro	2,139	509
Beaver Dam, WI Micro	2,138	510
Pontiac, IL Micro	2,138	511
Adrian, MI Micro	2,125	512
Fort Collins-Loveland, CO Metro	2,104	513
Torrington, CT Micro	2,095	514
Coffeyville, KS Micro	2,093	515
Ottawa-Streator, IL Micro	2,062	516
Warrensburg, MO Micro	2,058	517
Sault Ste. Marie, MI Micro	2,039	518
Portsmouth, OH Micro	2,025	519
Lincoln, IL Micro	2,005	520
Corning, NY Micro	1,973	521
Fairmont, WV Micro	1,934	522
Russellville, AR Micro	1,927	523
Scottsboro, AL Micro	1,924	524
Jacksonville, IL Micro	1,868	525
Mexico, MO Micro	1,840	526
Plainview, TX Micro	1,808	527
Sturgis, MI Micro	1,800	528
Shawnee, OK Micro	1,792	529
Bristol, VA Metro	1,763	530
Enid, OK Micro	1,746	531
Dixon, IL Micro	1,744	532
Salina, KS Micro	1,732	533
Oshkosh-Neenah, WI Metro	1,714	534
Oak Harbor, WA Micro	1,704	535
Fargo, ND-MN Metro	1,697	536
Fremont, OH Micro	1,695	537
Wooster, OH Micro	1,689	538
Burlington-South Burlington, VT Metro	1,682	539
Mayfield, KY Micro	1,678	540
Moberly, MO Micro	1,655	541
Minot, ND Micro	1,650	542
Parkersburg-Marietta, WV-OH Metro	1,650	543
Centralia, IL Micro	1,647	544
Alma, MI Micro	1,637	545
Allegan, MI Micro	1,628	546
Glasgow, KY Micro	1,626	547
Brownsville-Harlingen, TX Metro	1,607	548
Marion-Herrin, IL Micro	1,602	549
McAlester, OK Micro	1,572	550
Cornelia, GA Micro	1,569	551
Hannibal, MO Micro	1,553	552
Big Rapids, MI Micro	1,551	553
Clearlake, CA Micro	1,551	554
Lebanon, PA Metro	1,550	555
Calhoun, GA Micro	1,547	556
Rapid City, SD Metro	1,542	557
Sunbury, PA Micro	1,541	558
Ames, IA Metro	1,513	559
Hutchinson, KS Micro	1,512	560
Redding, CA Metro	1,510	561
Brownwood, TX Micro	1,490	562
Batavia, NY Micro	1,480	563
Provo-Orem, UT Metro	1,477	564
Burlington, IA-IL Micro	1,472	565
Altoona, PA Metro	1,463	566
Bay City, MI Metro	1,455	567
DuBois, PA Micro	1,444	568
Canton, IL Micro	1,437	569
Greeley, CO Metro	1,425	570
Somerset, PA Micro	1,421	571
Clarksburg, WV Micro	1,417	572
Coldwater, MI Micro	1,406	573
Meadville, PA Micro	1,383	574
Big Spring, TX Micro	1,374	575
Harriman, TN Micro	1,370	576
Albertville, AL Micro	1,358	577
Central City, KY Micro	1,352	578
Athens, OH Micro	1,349	579
Bellingham, WA Metro	1,342	580
McMinnville, TN Micro	1,340	581
Indiana, PA Micro	1,333	582
Cookeville, TN Micro	1,324	583
Murray, KY Micro	1,322	584
Pampa, TX Micro	1,301	585
Lamesa, TX Micro	1,296	586
Columbus, IN Metro	1,291	587
Fort Dodge, IA Micro	1,290	588
Charleston-Mattoon, IL Micro	1,287	589
Sedalia, MO Micro	1,277	590
Oneonta, NY Micro	1,275	591
Greeneville, TN Micro	1,266	592
Maysville, KY Micro	1,263	593
Bartlesville, OK Micro	1,262	594
Appleton, WI Metro	1,257	595
Mount Pleasant, MI Micro	1,252	596
Phoenix Lake-Cedar Ridge, CA Micro	1,212	597
Eureka-Arcata-Fortuna, CA Micro	1,206	598
Sheboygan, WI Metro	1,206	599
Grand Forks, ND-MN Metro	1,204	600
Campbellsville, KY Micro	1,191	601
Macomb, IL Micro	1,186	602
Gloversville, NY Micro	1,185	603
La Crosse, WI-MN Metro	1,179	604
Gettysburg, PA Micro	1,170	605
Brevard, NC Micro	1,168	606
Roswell, NM Micro	1,162	607
Mountain Home, ID Micro	1,161	608
Gainesville, TX Micro	1,152	609
Crescent City North, CA Micro	1,145	610
Flagstaff, AZ Metro	1,132	611
Great Falls, MT Metro	1,122	612
Farmington, MO Micro	1,116	613
Clinton, IA Micro	1,112	614
Vernon, TX Micro	1,095	615
Parsons, KS Micro	1,081	616
Olean, NY Micro	1,078	617
Mount Sterling, KY Micro	1,073	618
Kingsville, TX Micro	1,069	619
Harrisburg, IL Micro	1,057	620

CBSA	POPULATION	RANK
Midland, MI Micro	1,052	621
Marshall, MO Micro	1,050	622
Winfield, KS Micro	1,044	623
Santa Fe, NM Metro	1,021	624
Duncan, OK Micro	1,015	625
Mankato-North Mankato, MN Micro	1,004	626
Fond du Lac, WI Metro	999	627
Tiffin-Fostoria, OH Micro	997	628
Traverse City, MI Micro	995	629
Dubuque, IA Metro	990	630
Walla Walla, WA Micro	990	631
Snyder, TX Micro	974	632
Marquette, MI Micro	973	633
Point Pleasant, WV-OH Micro	962	634
Findlay, OH Micro	951	635
Keokuk-Fort Madison, IA-MO Micro	949	636
Atchison, KS Micro	933	637
Lake Havasu City-Kingman, AZ Micro	924	638
Peru, IN Micro	906	639
Hilo, HI Micro	899	640
Lebanon, NH-VT Micro	889	641
Urbana, OH Micro	889	642
Carson City, NV Metro	885	643
Carlsbad-Artesia, NM Micro	872	644
Ponca City, OK Micro	872	645
Lewiston-Auburn, ME Metro	864	646
Medford, OR Metro	864	647
Kill Devil Hills, NC Micro	853	648
Concord, NH Micro	846	649
Levelland, TX Micro	840	650
Wilmington, OH Micro	835	651
Bloomsburg-Berwick, PA Micro	830	652
Moses Lake, WA Micro	830	653
Taylorville, IL Micro	804	654
Amsterdam, NY Micro	788	655
Batesville, AR Micro	776	656
Emporia, KS Micro	774	657
Bellefontaine, OH Micro	767	658
Liberal, KS Micro	764	659
Boone, NC Micro	760	660
Sterling, IL Micro	753	661
Eau Claire, WI Metro	750	662
Kerrville, TX Micro	749	663
Norfolk, NE Micro	747	664
Vincennes, IN Micro	746	665
Sidney, OH Micro	743	666
Bangor, ME Metro	733	667
Cullman, AL Micro	728	668
Laredo, TX Metro	726	669
Middlesborough, KY Micro	724	670
Newport, TN Micro	721	671
Whitewater, WI Micro	712	672
Prescott, AZ Metro	708	673
Oil City, PA Micro	699	674
Faribault-Northfield, MN Micro	698	675
Corvallis, OR Metro	696	676
Rolla, MO Micro	693	677
Pittsburg, KS Micro	691	678
Billings, MT Metro	690	679
Bradford, PA Micro	685	680
Safford, AZ Micro	685	681
Borger, TX Micro	674	682
Sweetwater, TX Micro	669	683
Pendleton-Hermiston, OR Micro	660	684
Kahului-Wailuku, HI Micro	658	685
Lawrenceburg, TN Micro	658	686
New Philadelphia-Dover, OH Micro	658	687
Grand Junction, CO Metro	646	688
Cambridge, OH Micro	640	689
Defiance, OH Micro	640	690
Ada, OK Micro	635	691
Somerset, KY Micro	623	692
Durant, OK Micro	614	693
Cortland, NY Micro	606	694
Mineral Wells, TX Micro	605	695
Casper, WY Metro	601	696
Longview-Kelso, WA Metro	601	697
Ukiah, CA Micro	601	698
Farmington, NM Metro	599	699
Idaho Falls, ID Metro	597	700
Port Angeles, WA Micro	586	701
Shelton, WA Micro	585	702
Pullman, WA Micro	577	703
Washington, OH Micro	577	704
Del Rio, TX Micro	563	705
Pahrump, NV Micro	550	706
Logansport, IN Micro	540	707
Augusta-Waterville, ME Micro	538	708
Mount Vernon-Anacortes, WA Metro	518	709
Norwalk, OH Micro	512	710
Warsaw, IN Micro	505	711
Pocatello, ID Metro	501	712
Sterling, CO Micro	489	713
Klamath Falls, OR Micro	472	714
Garden City, KS Micro	467	715
Tahlequah, OK Micro	467	716
Great Bend, KS Micro	463	717
Raymondville, TX Micro	462	718
Dodge City, KS Micro	457	719
Madison, IN Micro	457	720
Mount Vernon, OH Micro	455	721
Ashland, OH Micro	453	722
Coshocton, OH Micro	447	723
Ontario, OR-ID Micro	444	724
Logan, UT-ID Metro	439	725
Selinsgrove, PA Micro	428	726
Sevierville, TN Micro	426	727
Bend, OR Metro	424	728
Marshalltown, IA Micro	411	729
Mason City, IA Micro	410	730
New Castle, IN Micro	409	731
Platteville, WI Micro	405	732
Muscatine, IA Micro	404	733
Owatonna, MN Micro	403	734
Branson, MO Micro	401	735
Houghton, MI Micro	398	736
Wausau, WI Metro	397	737
Ottumwa, IA Micro	396	738
Connersville, IN Micro	393	739
Austin, MN Micro	384	740
Laramie, WY Micro	377	741
Lewistown, PA Micro	356	742
Red Wing, MN Micro	355	743
Winona, MN Micro	353	744
Missoula, MT Metro	346	745
Bismarck, ND Metro	343	746
Crawfordsville, IN Micro	343	747
London, KY Micro	339	748
Manitowoc, WI Micro	337	749
Kirksville, MO Micro	334	750
Keene, NH Micro	331	751
Newton, IA Micro	326	752
Wenatchee, WA Metro	326	753
Rock Springs, WY Micro	324	754
Granbury, TX Micro	319	755
Barre, VT Micro	317	756
Rochelle, IL Micro	317	757
Brainerd, MN Micro	315	758
Portales, NM Micro	315	759
St. George, UT Metro	314	760
Alice, TX Micro	309	761
Red Bluff, CA Micro	308	762
Gallup, NM Micro	304	763
Yankton, SD Micro	302	764
Grand Island, NE Micro	298	765
Maryville, MO Micro	298	766
Sayre, PA Micro	298	767
Aberdeen, WA Micro	297	768
Bozeman, MT Micro	296	769
Fallon, NV Micro	286	770
Seymour, IN Micro	282	771
Centralia, WA Micro	280	772
Marshall, MN Micro	280	773
Albany-Lebanon, OR Micro	279	774
Bucyrus, OH Micro	278	775
Stephenville, TX Micro	276	776
Coeur d'Alene, ID Metro	275	777
Washington, IN Micro	274	778
Van Wert, OH Micro	270	779
Pecos, TX Micro	266	780
Andrews, TX Micro	261	781
Grants, NM Micro	261	782
Kendallville, IN Micro	261	783
Grants Pass, OR Micro	258	784
Kearney, NE Micro	258	785
Twin Falls, ID Micro	257	786
Lock Haven, PA Micro	256	787
Hereford, TX Micro	255	788
Moscow, ID Micro	255	789
Rutland, VT Micro	255	790
Miami, OK Micro	253	791
Silverthorne, CO Micro	252	792
Hastings, NE Micro	250	793
Warren, PA Micro	246	794
Deming, NM Micro	244	795
Kalispell, MT Micro	244	796
Truckee-Grass Valley, CA Micro	243	797
Juneau, AK Micro	242	798
Watertown-Fort Atkinson, WI Micro	242	799
Cadillac, MI Micro	241	800
Marinette, WI-MI Micro	240	801
Kapaa, HI Micro	239	802
North Platte, NE Micro	238	803
Fergus Falls, MN Micro	234	804
Las Vegas, NM Micro	234	805
McPherson, KS Micro	234	806
Oskaloosa, IA Micro	231	807
Stevens Point, WI Micro	231	808
Ellensburg, WA Micro	228	809
Bennington, VT Micro	227	810
Astoria, OR Micro	223	811
Wisconsin Rapids-Marshfield, WI Micro	223	812
Dumas, TX Micro	222	813
Wabash, IN Micro	219	814
North Vernon, IN Micro	216	815
Edwards, CO Micro	212	816
Woodward, OK Micro	211	817
Silver City, NM Micro	209	818
Payson, AZ Micro	207	819
Elko, NV Micro	205	820
Lebanon, MO Micro	205	821
Corbin, KY Micro	204	822
Durango, CO Micro	202	823
Owosso, MI Micro	199	824
Scottsbluff, NE Micro	196	825
Laconia, NH Micro	195	826
Cedar City, UT Micro	191	827
Greenville, OH Micro	189	828
Plymouth, IN Micro	189	829
Roseburg, OR Micro	188	830
Coos Bay, OR Micro	187	831
Bemidji, MN Micro	184	832
Hays, KS Micro	183	833
Lewiston, ID-WA Metro	181	834
Espanola, NM Micro	180	835
Fremont, NE Micro	179	836
Eagle Pass, TX Micro	178	837
Menomonie, WI Micro	176	838
Worthington, MN Micro	171	839
Willmar, MN Micro	164	840
Columbus, NE Micro	162	841
Merrill, WI Micro	162	842
Nogales, AZ Micro	155	843
Brookings, SD Micro	149	844
Vermillion, SD Micro	149	845
Huron, SD Micro	148	846
Helena, MT Micro	147	847
Baraboo, WI Micro	145	848
Kodiak, AK Micro	143	849
Albert Lea, MN Micro	140	850
Taos, NM Micro	140	851
La Follette, TN Micro	138	852
Hood River, OR Micro	136	853
Bedford, IN Micro	135	854
La Grande, OR Micro	135	855
Guymon, OK Micro	130	856
Aberdeen, SD Micro	129	857
Auburn, IN Micro	128	858
Crossville, TN Micro	128	859
Uvalde, TX Micro	126	860
Angola, IN Micro	124	861
Montrose, CO Micro	124	862
Monroe, WI Micro	123	863
Hutchinson, MN Micro	122	864
Paragould, AR Micro	116	865
Boone, IA Micro	112	866
Gardnerville Ranchos, NV Micro	112	867
Mountain Home, AR Micro	112	868
Wahpeton, ND-MN Micro	112	869
Brigham City, UT Micro	111	870
Frankfort, IN Micro	111	871
Gillette, WY Micro	111	872
Harrison, AR Micro	107	873
Wapakoneta, OH Micro	107	874
Los Alamos, NM Micro	106	875
Rexburg, ID Micro	105	876
Burley, ID Micro	104	877
Fort Morgan, CO Micro	104	878
Storm Lake, IA Micro	100	879
Riverton, WY Micro	99	880
Rockland, ME Micro	99	881
Alpena, MI Micro	97	882
West Plains, MO Micro	97	883
Alexandria, MN Micro	91	884
Jasper, IN Micro	90	885
Ketchikan, AK Micro	89	886
Beatrice, NE Micro	87	887
Jamestown, ND Micro	87	888
Rio Grande City, TX Micro	86	889
Blackfoot, ID Micro	84	890
Effingham, IL Micro	84	891
Lexington, NE Micro	81	892
Sheridan, WY Micro	81	893
Huntington, IN Micro	77	894
Mitchell, SD Micro	77	895
City of The Dalles, OR Micro	76	896
Fairmont, MN Micro	73	897
Price, UT Micro	73	898
Butte-Silver Bow, MT Micro	72	899
Spearfish, SD Micro	71	900
Decatur, IN Micro	69	901
Escanaba, MI Micro	67	902
St. Marys, PA Micro	67	903
Berlin, NH-VT Micro	62	904
Celina, OH Micro	57	905
Dickinson, ND Micro	56	906
Brookings, OR Micro	53	907
Iron Mountain, MI-WI Micro	51	908
Jackson, WY-ID Micro	51	909
Watertown, SD Micro	51	910
Pierre, SD Micro	50	911
New Ulm, MN Micro	49	912
Spirit Lake, IA Micro	47	913
Spencer, IA Micro	46	914
Williston, ND Micro	46	915
Vernal, UT Micro	45	916
Greensburg, IN Micro	41	917
Bishop, CA Micro	36	918
Evanston, WY Micro	35	919
Havre, MT Micro	24	920
Scottsburg, IN Micro	16	921
Prineville, OR Micro	10	922

CBSA Total	34,584,936
United States Total	36,299,387
CBSA (% of U.S. Total)	95.28

CBSA	POPULATION	RANK
Los Angeles-Long Beach-Santa Ana, CA Metro	5,745,884	1
New York-Newark-Edison, NY-NJ-PA Metro	3,975,570	2
Miami-Fort Lauderdale-Miami Beach, FL Metro	2,009,210	3
Chicago-Naperville-Joliet, IL-IN-WI Metro	1,730,299	4
Houston-Baytown-Sugar Land, TX Metro	1,625,781	5
Riverside-San Bernardino-Ontario, CA Metro	1,517,351	6
Dallas-Fort Worth-Arlington, TX Metro	1,415,900	7
Phoenix-Mesa-Scottsdale, AZ Metro	1,049,210	8
San Antonio, TX Metro	970,605	9
San Diego-Carlsbad-San Marcos, CA Metro	880,154	10
San Francisco-Oakland-Fremont, CA Metro	818,764	11
El Paso, TX Metro	583,708	12
McAllen-Edinburg-Pharr, TX Metro	576,227	13
Washington-Arlington-Alexandria, DC-VA-MD-WV Metro	555,330	14
Denver-Aurora, CO Metro	480,685	15
San Jose-Sunnyvale-Santa Clara, CA Metro	454,665	16
Austin-Round Rock, TX Metro	409,714	17
Las Vegas-Paradise, NV Metro	404,676	18
Fresno, CA Metro	400,140	19
Atlanta-Sandy Springs-Marietta, GA Metro	385,521	20
Orlando, FL Metro	361,521	21
Sacramento-Arden-Arcade-Roseville, CA Metro	347,929	22
Albuquerque, NM Metro	333,875	23
Boston-Cambridge-Quincy, MA-NH Metro	320,284	24
Philadelphia-Camden-Wilmington, PA-NJ-DE-MD Metro	315,485	25
Brownsville-Harlingen, TX Metro	313,895	26
Tampa-St. Petersburg-Clearwater, FL Metro	313,614	27
Bakersfield, CA Metro	301,126	28
Tucson, AZ Metro	297,778	29
Oxnard-Thousand Oaks-Ventura, CA Metro	287,341	30
Corpus Christi, TX Metro	228,160	31
Stockton, CA Metro	215,480	32
Visalia-Porterville, CA Metro	213,304	33
Salinas, CA Metro	211,902	34
Laredo, TX Metro	207,727	35
Seattle-Tacoma-Bellevue, WA Metro	204,658	36
Portland-Vancouver-Beaverton, OR-WA Metro	186,903	37
Modesto, CA Metro	184,384	38
Santa Barbara-Santa Maria-Goleta, CA Metro	149,858	39
Detroit-Warren-Livonia, MI Metro	146,058	40
Salt Lake City, UT Metro	136,846	41
Providence-New Bedford-Fall River, RI-MA Metro	128,006	42
Minneapolis-St. Paul-Bloomington, MN-WI Metro	122,484	43
Hartford-West Hartford-East Hartford, CT Metro	120,682	44
Las Cruces, NM Metro	119,011	45
Bridgeport-Stamford-Norwalk, CT Metro	118,687	46
Merced, CA Metro	116,819	47
El Centro, CA Metro	114,157	48
Kansas City, MO-KS Metro	112,202	49
Milwaukee-Waukesha-West Allis, WI Metro	107,283	50
Charlotte-Gastonia-Concord, NC-SC Metro	100,965	51
New Haven-Milford, CT Metro	95,897	52
Yuma, AZ Metro	95,565	53
Santa Rosa-Petaluma, CA Metro	94,305	54
Yakima, WA Metro	87,507	55
Oklahoma City, OK Metro	86,353	56
Springfield, MA Metro	86,320	57
Vallejo-Fairfield, CA Metro	84,526	58
Cleveland-Elyria-Mentor, OH Metro	79,208	59
Lubbock, TX Metro	78,185	60
Poughkeepsie-Newburgh-Middletown, NY Metro	77,640	61
Santa Cruz-Watsonville, CA Metro	72,160	62
Reno-Sparks, NV Metro	71,965	63
Naples-Marco Island, FL Metro	70,520	64
Santa Fe, NM Metro	69,690	65
Colorado Springs, CO Metro	67,475	66
Raleigh-Cary, NC Metro	67,242	67
Greeley, CO Metro	67,062	68
Salem, OR Metro	66,830	69
Madera, CA Metro	64,136	70
Allentown-Bethlehem-Easton, PA-NJ Metro	63,991	71
Hanford-Corcoran, CA Metro	63,934	72
New Orleans-Metairie-Kenner, LA Metro	63,611	73
Cape Coral-Fort Myers, FL Metro	62,024	74
Killeen-Temple-Fort Hood, TX Metro	61,126	75
Honolulu, HI Metro	59,591	76
Worcester, MA Metro	59,335	77
Pueblo, CO Metro	59,247	78
Lakeland-Winter Haven, FL Metro	58,123	79
Odessa, TX Metro	56,870	80
Rio Grande City, TX Micro	56,673	81
Baltimore-Towson, MD Metro	56,435	82
Rochester, NY Metro	54,975	83
Nashville-Davidson-Murfreesboro, TN Metro	54,883	84
Indianapolis, IN Metro	54,669	85
Grand Rapids-Wyoming, MI Metro	54,241	86
Boise City-Nampa, ID Metro	53,776	87
Virginia Beach-Norfolk-Newport News, VA-NC Metro	51,376	88
Sarasota-Bradenton-Venice, FL Metro	50,789	89
Jacksonville, FL Metro	50,710	90
Amarillo, TX Metro	50,363	91
Wichita, KS Metro	49,988	92
Kennewick-Richland-Pasco, WA Metro	49,546	93
Eagle Pass, TX Micro	48,267	94
Tulsa, OK Metro	47,567	95
Omaha-Council Bluffs, NE-IA Metro	47,551	96
St. Louis, MO-IL Metro	47,413	97
Victoria, TX Metro	47,357	98
San Luis Obispo-Paso Robles, CA Metro	44,984	99
Waco, TX Metro	44,549	100
Ogden-Clearfield, UT Metro	44,089	101
Reading, PA Metro	41,449	102
Sierra Vista-Douglas, AZ Micro	41,179	103
Trenton-Ewing, NJ Metro	40,265	104
Buffalo-Cheektowaga-Tonawanda, NY Metro	39,449	105
Durham, NC Metro	39,015	106
Fayetteville-Springdale-Rogers, AR-MO Metro	38,498	107
Midland, TX Metro	38,077	108
Greensboro-High Point, NC Metro	37,643	109
Deltona-Daytona Beach-Ormond Beach, FL Metro	37,613	110
College Station-Bryan, TX Metro	37,589	111
Gainesville, GA Metro	37,335	112
Del Rio, TX Micro	37,002	113
San Angelo, TX Metro	35,659	114
Napa, CA Metro	35,293	115
Atlantic City, NJ Metro	35,016	116
Columbus, OH Metro	34,811	117
Boulder, CO Metro	34,251	118
Beaumont-Port Arthur, TX Metro	33,969	119
Memphis, TN-MS-AR Metro	33,867	120
Yuba City-Marysville, CA Metro	33,764	121
Nogales, AZ Micro	33,552	122
Winston-Salem, NC Metro	33,437	123
Port St. Lucie-Fort Pierce, FL Metro	31,892	124
Rockford, IL Metro	31,783	125
Provo-Orem, UT Metro	31,484	126
Vineland-Millville-Bridgeton, NJ Metro	31,407	127
Alice, TX Micro	31,237	128
Toledo, OH Metro	30,756	129
Abilene, TX Metro	30,568	130
Richmond, VA Metro	30,419	131
Espanola, NM Micro	30,086	132
Lancaster, PA Metro	29,756	133
Roswell, NM Micro	28,085	134
Albany-Schenectady-Troy, NY Metro	27,478	135
Dalton, GA Metro	26,776	136
Palm Bay-Melbourne-Titusville, FL Metro	26,676	137
Moses Lake, WA Micro	26,460	138
Cincinnati-Middletown, OH-KY-IN Metro	25,732	139
Louisville, KY-IN Metro	25,197	140
Greenville, SC Metro	25,184	141
Chico, CA Metro	24,698	142
Fort Collins-Loveland, CO Metro	24,502	143
Hobbs, NM Micro	24,468	144
Birmingham-Hoover, AL Metro	24,193	145
Tyler, TX Metro	23,989	146
Des Moines, IA Metro	23,755	147
Las Vegas, NM Micro	23,033	148
Lansing-East Lansing, MI Metro	22,995	149
Davenport-Moline-Rock Island, IA-IL Metro	22,919	150
Kingsville, TX Micro	21,964	151
Alamogordo, NM Micro	21,106	152
Elkhart-Goshen, IN Metro	20,858	153
Carlsbad-Artesia, NM Micro	20,660	154
Wenatchee, WA Metro	20,631	155
Prescott, AZ Metro	19,791	156
Ocala, FL Metro	19,710	157
Farmington, NM Metro	19,556	158
Anchorage, AK Metro	19,468	159
Lake Havasu City-Kingman, AZ Micro	19,310	160
Wichita Falls, TX Metro	18,997	161
Fayetteville, NC Metro	18,895	162
Holland-Grand Haven, MI Metro	18,738	163
Columbia, SC Metro	18,589	164
Madison, WI Metro	18,447	165
Longview, TX Metro	18,444	166
Beeville, TX Micro	18,306	167
Hickory-Morganton-Lenoir, NC Metro	18,272	168
Uvalde, TX Micro	18,228	169
Hilo, HI Micro	18,219	170
Plainview, TX Micro	18,014	171
Taos, NM Micro	17,977	172
Syracuse, NY Metro	17,772	173
Fort Wayne, IN Metro	17,702	174
Raymondville, TX Micro	17,593	175
Pittsburgh, PA Metro	17,344	176
Eugene-Springfield, OR Metro	17,189	177
Garden City, KS Micro	16,767	178
Racine, WI Metro	16,671	179
Ukiah, CA Micro	16,594	180
Edwards, CO Micro	16,301	181
Pendleton-Hermiston, OR Micro	16,061	182
Clewiston, FL Micro	15,784	183
Sioux City, IA-NE-SD Metro	15,638	184
South Bend-Mishawaka, IN-MI Metro	15,432	185
Fort Smith, AR-OK Metro	15,323	186
Clovis, NM Micro	15,193	187
Asheville, NC Metro	15,155	188
Key West-Marathon, FL Micro	15,144	189
Deming, NM Micro	15,073	190
Lexington-Fayette, KY Metro	15,007	191
Topeka, KS Metro	14,921	192
Norwich-New London, CT Metro	14,779	193
Manchester-Nashua, NH Metro	14,654	194
Silver City, NM Micro	14,644	195
Saginaw-Saginaw Township North, MI Metro	14,496	196
Harrisburg-Carlisle, PA Metro	14,414	197
Charleston-North Charleston, SC Metro	14,413	198
Spokane, WA Metro	14,256	199
Medford, OR Metro	14,230	200
Flagstaff, AZ Metro	14,181	201
Baton Rouge, LA Metro	14,140	202
Little Rock-North Little Rock, AR Metro	14,042	203
El Campo, TX Micro	14,031	204
Dodge City, KS Micro	13,951	205
Mount Vernon-Anacortes, WA Metro	13,934	206
Gainesville, FL Metro	13,426	207
Kalamazoo-Portage, MI Metro	13,398	208
Bay City, TX Micro	13,380	209
Big Spring, TX Micro	13,377	210
Lufkin, TX Micro	13,084	211
Burlington, NC Metro	13,041	212
Grand Junction, CO Metro	12,960	213
Tallahassee, FL Metro	12,945	214
Safford, AZ Micro	12,926	215
Kingston, NY Metro	12,890	216
Sebring, FL Micro	12,708	217
East Stroudsburg, PA Micro	12,519	218
York-Hanover, PA Metro	12,443	219
Hilton Head Island-Beaufort, SC Micro	12,398	220
Redding, CA Metro	12,150	221
Liberal, KS Micro	12,102	222
Twin Falls, ID Micro	11,891	223
Ontario, OR-ID Micro	11,450	224
Bremerton-Silverdale, WA Metro	11,249	225
Hereford, TX Micro	11,198	226
Augusta-Richmond County, GA-SC Metro	11,106	227
Green Bay, WI Metro	10,940	228
Red Bluff, CA Micro	10,834	229
Flint, MI Metro	10,769	230
Olympia, WA Metro	10,764	231
Kahului-Wailuku, HI Micro	10,754	232
Lincoln, NE Metro	10,701	233
Wauchula, FL Micro	10,475	234
Utica-Rome, NY Metro	10,370	235
Youngstown-Warren-Boardman, OH-PA Metro	10,300	236
Lafayette, IN Metro	10,188	237
Bellingham, WA Metro	10,170	238
Athens-Clarke County, GA Metro	10,102	239
Dumas, TX Micro	9,948	240
Cheyenne, WY Metro	9,904	241
Columbus, GA-AL Metro	9,886	242
Dayton, OH Metro	9,873	243
Eureka-Arcata-Fortuna, CA Micro	9,802	244
Ann Arbor, MI Metro	9,792	245
Arcadia, FL Micro	9,718	246
Kerrville, TX Micro	9,662	247
Burley, ID Micro	9,661	248
Mount Pleasant, TX Micro	9,602	249
Knoxville, TN Metro	9,519	250
Spartanburg, SC Metro	9,491	251
Pensacola-Ferry Pass-Brent, FL Metro	9,378	252
Walla Walla, WA Micro	9,297	253
Gallup, NM Micro	9,268	254
Sherman-Denison, TX Metro	9,241	255
Vero Beach, FL Metro	9,196	256
Huntsville, TX Micro	9,133	257
Grants, NM Micro	9,107	258
Corsicana, TX Micro	9,082	259
Pecos, TX Micro	9,063	260
Clarksville, TN-KY Metro	9,026	261
Elko, NV Micro	9,012	262
Grand Island, NE Micro	8,999	263
Ottawa-Streator, IL Micro	8,993	264
Idaho Falls, ID Metro	8,961	265
Levelland, TX Micro	8,918	266
Carson City, NV Metro	8,836	267
Clearlake, CA Micro	8,760	268
Payson, AZ Micro	8,730	269
Huntsville, AL Metro	8,643	270
Willimantic, CT Micro	8,501	271
Fort Morgan, CO Micro	8,493	272
Wilmington, NC Metro	8,389	273
Seaford, DE Micro	8,345	274
Logan, UT-ID Metro	8,282	275
Shreveport-Bossier City, LA Metro	7,985	276
Lumberton, NC Micro	7,963	277
Jacksonville, NC Metro	7,956	278
Watertown-Fort Drum, NY Micro	7,948	279
Lawton, OK Metro	7,942	280
Scranton-Wilkes-Barre, PA Metro	7,892	281
Okeechobee, FL Micro	7,819	282
Nacogdoches, TX Micro	7,714	283
Chattanooga, TN-GA Metro	7,672	284
Fort Walton Beach-Crestview-Destin, FL Metro	7,662	285
Dunn, NC Micro	7,659	286
Whitewater, WI Micro	7,529	287
Jacksonville, TX Micro	7,407	288
Adrian, MI Micro	7,318	289
Harrisonburg, VA Metro	7,230	290
Lexington, NE Micro	7,227	291
Lamesa, TX Micro	7,226	292
Palestine, TX Micro	7,194	293
Champaign-Urbana, IL Metro	7,116	294
Greenville, NC Metro	7,114	295
Jamestown-Dunkirk-Fredonia, NY Micro	7,086	296
Myrtle Beach-Conway-North Myrtle Beach, SC Metro	7,042	297
Sanford, NC Micro	7,019	298
Salisbury, NC Micro	7,002	299
Janesville, WI Metro	6,977	300
Muscatine, IA Micro	6,812	301
Emporia, KS Micro	6,806	302
Peoria, IL Metro	6,665	303
Guymon, OK Micro	6,624	304
Brownwood, TX Micro	6,618	305
Albertville, AL Micro	6,518	306
Springfield, MO Metro	6,510	307
Allegan, MI Micro	6,491	308

CBSA	POPULATION	RANK	CBSA	POPULATION	RANK	CBSA	POPULATION	RANK
Lebanon, PA Metro	6,427	309	Rock Springs, WY Micro	3,749	413	Salisbury, MD Metro	2,183	517
Akron, OH Metro	6,404	310	Salina, KS Micro	3,722	414	Hudson, NY Micro	2,165	518
Lexington-Thomasville, NC Micro	6,391	311	Ocean City, NJ Metro	3,694	415	Kinston, NC Micro	2,151	519
Portales, NM Micro	6,375	312	Cedartown, GA Micro	3,692	416	Anderson, SC Metro	2,144	520
Muskegon-Norton Shores, MI Metro	6,344	313	Palm Coast, FL Micro	3,651	417	Duluth, MN-WI Metro	2,124	521
Rome, GA Metro	6,310	314	Cornelia, GA Micro	3,629	418	Cullman, AL Metro	2,122	522
Erie, PA Metro	6,306	315	Elizabethtown, KY Metro	3,627	419	Beaver Dam, WI Micro	2,116	523
Gulfport-Biloxi, MS Metro	6,237	316	Sulphur Springs, TX Micro	3,553	420	Muskogee, OK Micro	2,111	524
Goldsboro, NC Metro	6,212	317	Canton-Massillon, OH Metro	3,551	421	Malone, NY Micro	2,106	525
Scottsbluff, NE Micro	6,154	318	Watertown-Fort Atkinson, WI Micro	3,527	422	Blacksburg-Christiansburg-Radford, VA Metro	2,099	526
Truckee-Grass Valley, CA Micro	6,093	319	Tifton, GA Micro	3,517	423	Jackson, TN Metro	2,098	527
Blackfoot, ID Micro	6,065	320	Cedar Rapids, IA Metro	3,513	424	Newberry, SC Micro	2,082	528
Kankakee-Bradley, IL Metro	6,042	321	Fargo, ND-MN Metro	3,475	425	Burlington-South Burlington, VT Metro	2,065	529
St. George, UT Metro	5,993	322	Logansport, IN Micro	3,434	426	Huntington-Ashland, WV-KY-OH Metro	2,050	530
Athens, TX Micro	5,959	323	Hagerstown-Martinsburg, MD-WV Metro	3,424	427	Elmira, NY Metro	2,048	531
Binghamton, NY Metro	5,860	324	Roseburg, OR Micro	3,421	428	Anniston-Oxford, AL Metro	2,034	532
Joplin, MO Metro	5,787	325	Frankfort, IN Micro	3,413	429	Dothan, AL Metro	2,032	533
Savannah, GA Metro	5,753	326	Plymouth, IN Micro	3,406	430	Seneca, SC Micro	2,028	534
Klamath Falls, OR Micro	5,752	327	Casper, WY Metro	3,393	431	Auburn-Opelika, AL Metro	2,013	535
Morristown, TN Metro	5,748	328	Daphne-Fairhope, AL Micro	3,389	432	Fallon, NV Micro	2,011	536
Jackson, MS Metro	5,743	329	Oshkosh-Neenah, WI Metro	3,389	433	Laurel, MS Micro	2,005	537
Statesville-Mooresville, NC Micro	5,743	330	Pampa, TX Micro	3,387	434	Great Falls, MT Metro	1,989	538
Sterling, IL Micro	5,711	331	Houma-Bayou Cane-Thibodaux, LA Metro	3,374	435	Ellensburg, WA Micro	1,988	539
Montrose, CO Micro	5,701	332	Brenham, TX Micro	3,341	436	Albany, GA Metro	1,986	540
Bend, OR Metro	5,689	333	Pahrump, NV Micro	3,310	437	Tahlequah, OK Micro	1,986	541
Niles-Benton Harbor, MI Metro	5,678	334	Grants Pass, OR Micro	3,291	438	Gadsden, AL Metro	1,970	542
Punta Gorda, FL Metro	5,672	335	Warner Robins, GA Micro	3,287	439	Tiffin-Fostoria, OH Micro	1,967	543
Mount Airy, NC Micro	5,646	336	Willmar, MN Micro	3,285	440	Sedalia, MO Micro	1,965	544
Pocatello, ID Metro	5,582	337	Storm Lake, IA Micro	3,264	441	Fremont, NE Micro	1,964	545
Billings, MT Metro	5,519	338	Barnstable Town, MA Metro	3,256	442	Kingsport-Bristol, TN-VA Metro	1,946	546
Andrews, TX Micro	5,502	339	New Bern, NC Micro	3,231	443	Springfield, OH Metro	1,944	547
Moultrie, GA Micro	5,419	340	Monroe, MI Metro	3,200	444	Albert Lea, MN Micro	1,940	548
Mobile, AL Metro	5,381	341	North Wilkesboro, NC Micro	3,156	445	Ardmore, OK Micro	1,935	549
Wilson, NC Micro	5,353	342	Coeur d'Alene, ID Metro	3,147	446	Ottumwa, IA Micro	1,935	550
Decatur, AL Metro	5,290	343	Vernon, TX Micro	3,114	447	Florence, SC Metro	1,934	551
Hood River, OR Micro	5,280	344	Oak Harbor, WA Micro	3,054	448	Paris, TX Micro	1,932	552
Stephenville, TX Micro	5,277	345	Rapid City, SD Metro	3,037	449	Columbus, IN Metro	1,913	553
Bloomington-Normal, IL Metro	5,219	346	Panama City-Lynn Haven, FL Metro	3,008	450	Price, UT Micro	1,872	554
Portland-South Portland, ME Metro	5,208	347	Columbia, TN Micro	2,997	451	Jefferson City, MO Metro	1,870	555
Manhattan, KS Micro	5,184	348	Pascagoula, MS Metro	2,969	452	Hammond, LA Micro	1,866	556
Kapaa, HI Micro	5,102	349	Bloomington, IN Metro	2,949	453	Staunton-Waynesboro, VA Micro	1,865	557
Phoenix Lake-Cedar Ridge, CA Micro	5,057	350	Fort Polk South, LA Micro	2,938	454	Marion, IN Micro	1,855	558
Longview-Kelso, WA Metro	5,029	351	Waterloo-Cedar Falls, IA Metro	2,936	455	Hastings, NE Micro	1,843	559
Lincolnton, NC Micro	4,988	352	Columbia, MO Metro	2,916	456	Auburn, NY Micro	1,829	560
Albany-Lebanon, OR Micro	4,912	353	Bishop, CA Micro	2,915	457	Shawnee, OK Micro	1,829	561
Calhoun, GA Micro	4,900	354	Macon, GA Metro	2,912	458	Lexington Park, MD Micro	1,809	562
Texarkana, TX-Texarkana, AR Metro	4,891	355	Great Bend, KS Micro	2,902	459	Sandusky, OH Metro	1,801	563
Canon City, CO Micro	4,884	356	Gardnerville Ranchos, NV Micro	2,896	460	Kokomo, IN Metro	1,793	564
Snyder, TX Micro	4,789	357	Sturgis, MI Micro	2,895	461	Gillette, WY Micro	1,786	565
Montgomery, AL Metro	4,788	358	Brigham City, UT Micro	2,891	462	Pottsville, PA Micro	1,777	566
Charlottesville, VA Metro	4,755	359	Martinsville, VA Micro	2,856	463	Carbondale, IL Micro	1,775	567
Durango, CO Micro	4,750	360	St. Cloud, MN Metro	2,856	464	Tupelo, MS Micro	1,775	568
Russellville, AR Micro	4,750	361	Galesburg, IL Micro	2,834	465	Riverton, WY Micro	1,774	569
The Villages, FL Micro	4,731	362	Cookeville, TN Micro	2,832	466	Alma, MI Micro	1,758	570
Hinesville-Fort Stewart, GA Metro	4,712	363	Winfield, KS Micro	2,831	467	Missoula, MT Metro	1,743	571
Rocky Mount, NC Metro	4,689	364	Defiance, OH Micro	2,828	468	Hattiesburg, MS Metro	1,718	572
Norfolk, NE Micro	4,660	365	Jackson, WY-ID Micro	2,786	469	Lake City, FL Micro	1,708	573
Granbury, TX Micro	4,629	366	Lake Charles, LA Metro	2,757	470	Lewisburg, PA Micro	1,708	574
Sheboygan, WI Metro	4,622	367	Danville, IL Metro	2,752	471	Duncan, OK Micro	1,684	575
Dover, DE Metro	4,572	368	Enterprise-Ozark, AL Micro	2,718	472	Rockingham, NC Micro	1,673	576
Amsterdam, NY Micro	4,556	369	Tuscaloosa, AL Metro	2,716	473	Terre Haute, IN Metro	1,673	577
Gainesville, TX Micro	4,517	370	Pittsfield, MA Metro	2,702	474	Astoria, OR Micro	1,670	578
Palatka, FL Micro	4,511	371	Ashtabula, OH Micro	2,689	475	Mankato-North Mankato, MN Micro	1,651	579
Fremont, OH Micro	4,499	372	Fort Leonard Wood, MO Micro	2,687	476	Sumter, SC Metro	1,649	580
Battle Creek, MI Metro	4,491	373	Shelton, WA Micro	2,684	477	Charleston, WV Metro	1,640	581
Douglas, GA Micro	4,472	374	Columbus, NE Micro	2,677	478	Albemarle, NC Micro	1,625	582
Torrington, CT Micro	4,431	375	Ogdensburg-Massena, NY Micro	2,663	479	Mount Pleasant, MI Micro	1,621	583
Altus, OK Micro	4,418	376	Enid, OK Micro	2,661	480	North Platte, NE Micro	1,618	584
Appleton, WI Metro	4,405	377	Sterling, CO Micro	2,639	481	Florence, AL Metro	1,590	585
Rochester, MN Metro	4,404	378	Hot Springs, AR Metro	2,593	482	Lebanon, NH-VT Micro	1,570	586
Sweetwater, TX Micro	4,396	379	Greenwood, SC Micro	2,578	483	Stillwater, OK Micro	1,546	587
Bay City, MI Metro	4,384	380	Johnson City, TN Metro	2,565	484	Oneonta, NY Micro	1,531	588
Kendallville, IN Micro	4,254	381	Springfield, IL Metro	2,550	485	Concord, NH Micro	1,524	589
Shelbyville, TN Micro	4,216	382	Rexburg, ID Micro	2,529	486	Lima, OH Metro	1,514	590
Marshall, TX Micro	4,195	383	Grand Forks, ND-MN Metro	2,528	487	Cedar City, UT Micro	1,509	591
Warsaw, IN Micro	4,181	384	Glens Falls, NY Metro	2,497	488	Searcy, AR Micro	1,490	592
Marshalltown, IA Micro	4,159	385	Port Angeles, WA Micro	2,483	489	Coldwater, MI Micro	1,484	593
Corvallis, OR Metro	4,150	386	Norwalk, OH Micro	2,468	490	Branson, MO Micro	1,475	594
Lawrence, KS Metro	4,113	387	Brunswick, GA Metro	2,464	491	Owosso, MI Micro	1,474	595
Centralia, WA Micro	4,108	388	Monroe, LA Metro	2,452	492	Bartlesville, OK Micro	1,456	596
Crescent City North, CA Micro	4,105	389	Fond du Lac, WI Metro	2,451	493	Miami, OK Micro	1,446	597
Roanoke, VA Metro	4,104	390	Chambersburg, PA Micro	2,431	494	Danville, VA Metro	1,444	598
Michigan City-La Porte, IN Metro	4,044	391	Jonesboro, AR Micro	2,407	495	Jasper, IN Micro	1,432	599
Lafayette, LA Metro	4,025	392	Hope, AR Micro	2,402	496	Seymour, IN Micro	1,431	600
Mineral Wells, TX Micro	3,966	393	Los Alamos, NM Micro	2,402	497	Washington, NC Micro	1,429	601
Sioux Falls, SD Metro	3,958	394	Traverse City, MI Micro	2,402	498	East Liverpool-Salem, OH Micro	1,428	602
Borger, TX Micro	3,953	395	Laramie, WY Micro	2,389	499	Kalispell, MT Micro	1,415	603
Fairbanks, AK Metro	3,953	396	City of The Dalles, OR Micro	2,360	500	Ames, IA Metro	1,413	604
Iowa City, IA Metro	3,951	397	Cleveland, TN Metro	2,360	501	Muncie, IN Metro	1,400	605
Faribault-Northfield, MN Micro	3,940	398	Plattsburgh, NY Micro	2,359	502	Forrest City, AR Micro	1,397	606
Mountain Home, ID Micro	3,933	399	Alexandria, LA Metro	2,347	503	Gaffney, SC Micro	1,391	607
Gettysburg, PA Micro	3,932	400	St. Joseph, MO-KS Metro	2,347	504	Yazoo City, MS Micro	1,384	608
Jackson, MI Metro	3,925	401	Lynchburg, VA Metro	2,324	505	Pullman, WA Micro	1,382	609
Hutchinson, KS Micro	3,855	402	Worthington, MN Micro	2,322	506	Johnstown, PA Metro	1,377	610
Bowling Green, KY Metro	3,850	403	Kearney, NE Micro	2,279	507	Owatonna, MN Micro	1,370	611
Evansville, IN-KY Metro	3,836	404	Tullahoma, TN Micro	2,261	508	Hutchinson, MN Micro	1,362	612
Homosassa Springs, FL Micro	3,831	405	Findlay, OH Micro	2,248	509	Manitowoc, WI Micro	1,349	613
Silverthorne, CO Micro	3,815	406	Anderson, IN Metro	2,237	510	Corning, NY Micro	1,327	614
Southern Pines, NC Micro	3,798	407	Ponca City, OK Micro	2,231	511	Shelby, NC Micro	1,326	615
Valdosta, GA Metro	3,792	408	McMinnville, TN Micro	2,224	512	Mayfield, KY Micro	1,325	616
Aberdeen, WA Micro	3,787	409	Coos Bay, OR Micro	2,214	513	Mason City, IA Micro	1,322	617
Winchester, VA-WV Metro	3,781	410	Henderson, NC Micro	2,211	514	Midland, MI Micro	1,294	618
Ithaca, NY Metro	3,777	411	State College, PA Metro	2,195	515	Seneca Falls, NY Micro	1,287	619
Rochelle, IL Micro	3,753	412	Austin, MN Micro	2,189	516	Olean, NY Micro	1,269	620

CBSA	POPULATION	RANK	CBSA	POPULATION	RANK	CBSA	POPULATION	RANK
Meridian, MS Micro	1,259	621	Cortland, NY Micro	737	725	Sayre, PA Micro	383	829
Decatur, IL Metro	1,258	622	Kodiak, AK Micro	737	726	Selinsgrove, PA Micro	383	830
Prineville, OR Micro	1,252	623	Red Wing, MN Micro	735	727	Wapakoneta, OH Micro	381	831
Morgan City, LA Micro	1,247	624	La Grande, OR Micro	726	728	Kirksville, MO Micro	380	832
Bozeman, MT Micro	1,242	625	Arkadelphia, AR Micro	725	729	New Castle, IN Micro	377	833
Dixon, IL Micro	1,225	626	Auburn, IN Micro	714	730	Harriman, TN Micro	369	834
St. Marys, GA Micro	1,223	627	New Philadelphia-Dover, OH Micro	706	731	Ketchikan, AK Micro	368	835
Warrensburg, MO Micro	1,223	628	Walterboro, SC Micro	705	732	Spearfish, SD Micro	367	836
Pine Bluff, AR Metro	1,201	629	Wheeling, WV-OH Metro	705	733	Mountain Home, AR Micro	359	837
Eau Claire, WI Metro	1,200	630	El Dorado, AR Micro	694	734	Washington, NC Micro	353	838
Waycross, GA Micro	1,184	631	Columbus, MS Micro	692	735	Jennings, LA Micro	351	839
Lancaster, SC Micro	1,173	632	Cumberland, MD-WV Metro	681	736	Lebanon, MO Micro	351	840
Minot, ND Micro	1,171	633	Parsons, KS Micro	679	737	London, KY Micro	349	841
LaGrange, GA Micro	1,166	634	Sheridan, WY Micro	679	738	Ashland, OH Micro	347	842
Lewiston, ID-WA Metro	1,153	635	Easton, MD Micro	678	739	Effingham, IL Micro	347	843
New Iberia, LA Micro	1,153	636	Wisconsin Rapids-Marshfield, WI Micro	675	740	Thomaston, GA Micro	347	844
Forest City, NC Micro	1,149	637	Brownsville, TN Micro	671	741	Magnolia, AR Micro	346	845
Sevierville, TN Micro	1,143	638	Clinton, IA Micro	658	742	Newport, TN Micro	346	846
Pittsburg, KS Micro	1,142	639	Dillon, SC Micro	657	743	Menomonie, WI Micro	344	847
Wausau, WI Metro	1,134	640	Milledgeville, GA Micro	655	744	Paris, TN Micro	343	848
Fitzgerald, GA Micro	1,124	641	Brainerd, MN Micro	652	745	Watertown, SD Micro	342	849
Georgetown, SC Micro	1,120	642	Athens, OH Micro	650	746	Cambridge, OH Micro	341	850
La Crosse, WI-MN Metro	1,119	643	Batesville, AR Micro	647	747	Corbin, KY Micro	341	851
Mansfield, OH Metro	1,114	644	De Ridder, LA Micro	636	748	Huntington, IN Micro	341	852
Batavia, NY Micro	1,089	645	Keene, NH Micro	634	749	Bellefontaine, OH Micro	337	853
Evanston, WY Micro	1,088	646	Angola, IN Micro	631	750	Camden, AR Micro	336	854
Decatur, IN Micro	1,086	647	Winona, MN Micro	627	751	Brevard, NC Micro	335	855
Juneau, AK Micro	1,086	648	Murray, KY Micro	625	752	Madison, IN Micro	333	856
Gloversville, NY Micro	1,078	649	Mount Vernon, IL Micro	621	753	Bemidji, MN Micro	332	857
Americus, GA Micro	1,077	650	Ocean Pines, MD Micro	621	754	Urbana, OH Micro	330	858
Owensboro, KY Metro	1,075	651	Somerset, KY Micro	602	755	Point Pleasant, WV-OH Micro	328	859
Lewiston-Auburn, ME Metro	1,068	652	New Castle, PA Micro	599	756	Oil City, PA Micro	320	860
Helena, MT Micro	1,054	653	Huntingdon, PA Micro	585	757	Vincennes, IN Micro	320	861
Sunbury, PA Micro	1,052	654	McPherson, KS Micro	582	758	Platteville, WI Micro	314	862
Blytheville, AR Micro	1,044	655	Natchez, MS-LA Micro	582	759	Atchison, KS Micro	309	863
Pontiac, IL Micro	1,038	656	Natchitoches, LA Micro	581	760	Selma, AL Micro	309	864
Ada, OK Micro	1,036	657	Crossville, TN Micro	578	761	Valley, AL Micro	308	865
Durant, OK Micro	1,033	658	New Ulm, MN Micro	570	762	Pierre Part, LA Micro	305	866
Jesup, GA Micro	1,031	659	Corinth, MS Micro	565	763	Oak Hill, WV Micro	301	867
Paducah, KY-IL Micro	1,026	660	Lincoln, IL Micro	565	764	West Helena, AR Micro	300	868
Charleston-Mattoon, IL Micro	1,025	661	Meadville, PA Micro	564	765	Alexandria, MN Micro	296	869
Woodward, OK Micro	1,020	662	Big Rapids, MI Micro	554	766	Houghton, MI Micro	291	870
Baraboo, WI Micro	1,015	663	Crowley, LA Micro	551	767	Lewistown, PA Micro	290	871
Augusta-Waterville, ME Micro	1,012	664	Marinette, WI-MI Micro	550	768	Wahpeton, ND-MN Micro	290	872
Orangeburg, SC Micro	1,011	665	Van Wert, OH Micro	544	769	Moberly, MO Micro	288	873
Richmond, IN Micro	1,005	666	Somerset, PA Micro	536	770	Clarksdale, MS Micro	286	874
Talladega-Sylacauga, AL Micro	999	667	Oxford, MS Micro	535	771	Aberdeen, SD Micro	285	875
McAlester, OK Micro	998	668	Elizabeth City, NC Micro	534	772	Harrisburg, IL Micro	285	876
Morehead City, NC Micro	998	669	Bristol, VA Metro	532	773	La Follette, TN Micro	281	877
Vernal, UT Micro	996	670	Canton, IL Micro	531	774	Toccoa, GA Micro	281	878
Dubuque, IA Metro	992	671	Macomb, IL Micro	531	775	Middlesborough, KY Micro	279	879
Freeport, IL Micro	989	672	Bluefield, WV-VA Micro	528	776	Wilmington, OH Micro	273	880
Morgantown, WV Metro	986	673	Portsmouth, OH Micro	522	777	Bastrop, LA Micro	263	881
Statesboro, GA Micro	986	674	Starkville, MS Micro	522	778	Pierre, SD Micro	263	882
Richmond, KY Micro	983	675	Jacksonville, IL Micro	517	779	Mexico, MO Micro	258	883
Fort Valley, GA Micro	982	676	Bogalusa, LA Micro	510	780	Brookhaven, MS Micro	251	884
Frankfort, KY Micro	975	677	Poplar Bluff, MO Micro	505	781	Monroe, WI Micro	251	885
Butte-Silver Bow, MT Micro	966	678	Vicksburg, MS Micro	504	782	Maysville, KY Micro	250	886
Abbeville, LA Micro	961	679	Cadillac, MI Micro	498	783	Coshocton, OH Micro	249	887
Kennett, MO Micro	958	680	Celina, OH Micro	495	784	Hannibal, MO Micro	248	888
Marion-Herrin, IL Micro	945	681	Marquette, MI Micro	495	785	Rockland, ME Micro	245	889
Bangor, ME Metro	941	682	DuBois, PA Micro	493	786	Oskaloosa, IA Micro	241	890
Athens, TN Micro	939	683	Indianola, MS Micro	492	787	Dickinson, ND Micro	239	891
Brookings, OR Micro	933	684	Minden, LA Micro	491	788	Central City, KY Micro	238	892
Fort Dodge, IA Micro	919	685	Altoona, PA Metro	489	789	Beatrice, NE Micro	235	893
Opelousas-Eunice, LA Micro	918	686	Rutland, VT Micro	488	790	Brookings, SD Micro	235	894
Coffeyville, KS Micro	917	687	Greenville, MS Micro	486	791	Scottsburg, IN Micro	234	895
Wooster, OH Micro	912	688	Mount Vernon, OH Micro	486	792	Iron Mountain, MI-WI Micro	231	896
Bloomsburg-Berwick, PA Micro	911	689	Rolla, MO Micro	483	793	Williston, ND Micro	231	897
Stevens Point, WI Micro	901	690	Greenville, OH Micro	476	794	Jamestown, ND Micro	228	898
Keokuk-Fort Madison, IA-MO Micro	884	691	Laconia, NH Micro	472	795	Lock Haven, PA Micro	228	899
Marshall, MN Micro	884	692	McComb, MS Micro	472	796	Spencer, IA Micro	221	900
Bainbridge, GA Micro	870	693	Mount Sterling, KY Micro	471	797	Campbellsville, KY Micro	220	901
Picayune, MS Micro	862	694	Glasgow, KY Micro	467	798	Boone, IA Micro	217	902
Greenwood, MS Micro	839	695	Madisonville, KY Micro	467	799	Merrill, WI Micro	217	903
Scottsboro, AL Micro	838	696	Cordele, GA Micro	460	800	Berlin, NH-VT Micro	213	904
Burlington, IA-IL Micro	833	697	Dyersburg, TN Micro	457	801	Chester, SC Micro	213	905
Weirton-Steubenville, WV-OH Micro	830	698	Sikeston, MO Micro	453	802	Havre, MT Micro	212	906
Moscow, ID Micro	824	699	Wabash, IN Micro	450	803	Bennettsville, SC Micro	204	907
Parkersburg-Marietta, WV-OH Metro	824	700	Troy, AL Micro	448	804	Union, SC Micro	204	908
Union City, TN-KY Micro	821	701	West Plains, MO Micro	447	805	North Vernon, IN Micro	201	909
Clarksburg, WV Micro	817	702	Bradford, PA Micro	445	806	Alpena, MI Micro	192	910
Fergus Falls, MN Micro	817	703	Indiana, PA Micro	443	807	Mitchell, SD Micro	192	911
Kill Devil Hills, NC Micro	816	704	Peru, IN Micro	438	808	Tuskegee, AL Micro	181	912
Crawfordsville, IN Micro	804	705	Cleveland, MS Micro	433	809	Escanaba, MI Micro	179	913
Marion, OH Micro	800	706	Taylorville, IL Micro	431	810	Huron, SD Micro	179	914
Boone, NC Micro	786	707	Zanesville, OH Micro	431	811	Greensburg, IN Micro	162	915
Greeneville, TN Micro	786	708	Farmington, MO Micro	430	812	St. Marys, PA Micro	161	916
Quincy, IL-MO Micro	784	709	Laurinburg, NC Micro	427	813	Maryville, MO Micro	159	917
Summerville, GA Micro	775	710	Chillicothe, OH Micro	425	814	Grenada, MS Micro	153	918
Hays, KS Micro	773	711	Sidney, OH Micro	424	815	Warren, PA Micro	152	919
Washington, IN Micro	769	712	Tallulah, LA Micro	424	816	Vermillion, SD Micro	148	920
Ruston, LA Micro	768	713	Cambridge, MD Micro	423	817	Connersville, IN Micro	141	921
Cape Girardeau-Jackson, MO-IL Micro	767	714	Centralia, IL Micro	417	818	Spirit Lake, IA Micro	134	922
Thomasville, GA Micro	766	715	Bedford, IN Micro	415	819			
Beckley, WV Micro	753	716	Yankton, SD Micro	413	820	CBSA Total	40,201,359	
Danville, KY Micro	749	717	Fairmont, WV Micro	409	821	United States Total	41,143,351	
Bismarck, ND Metro	747	718	Harrison, AR Micro	409	822	CBSA (% of U.S. Total)	97.71	
Marshall, MO Micro	746	719	Lawrenceburg, TN Micro	409	823			
Roanoke Rapids, NC Micro	740	720	Bennington, VT Micro	408	824			
Williamsport, PA Metro	740	721	Bucyrus, OH Micro	405	825			
Sault Ste. Marie, MI Micro	739	722	Fairmont, MN Micro	395	826			
Dublin, GA Micro	738	723	Newton, IA Micro	392	827			
Barre, VT Micro	737	724	Paragould, AR Micro	391	828			

Total Households

CBSA	HOUSEHOLDS	RANK
New York-Newark-Edison, NY-NJ-PA Metro	6,818,599	1
Los Angeles-Long Beach-Santa Ana, CA Metro	4,257,854	2
Chicago-Naperville-Joliet, IL-IN-WI Metro	3,384,057	3
Philadelphia-Camden-Wilmington, PA-NJ-DE-MD Metro	2,185,750	4
Dallas-Fort Worth-Arlington, TX Metro	2,071,180	5
Miami-Fort Lauderdale-Miami Beach, FL Metro	2,023,093	6
Washington-Arlington-Alexandria, DC-VA-MD-WV Metro	1,949,290	7
Houston-Baytown-Sugar Land, TX Metro	1,794,422	8
Detroit-Warren-Livonia, MI Metro	1,723,533	9
Boston-Cambridge-Quincy, MA-NH Metro	1,712,655	10
Atlanta-Sandy Springs-Marietta, GA Metro	1,711,283	11
San Francisco-Oakland-Fremont, CA Metro	1,578,017	12
Phoenix-Mesa-Scottsdale, AZ Metro	1,334,212	13
Seattle-Tacoma-Bellevue, WA Metro	1,251,502	14
Minneapolis-St. Paul-Bloomington, MN-WI Metro	1,193,593	15
Riverside-San Bernardino-Ontario, CA Metro	1,150,039	16
St. Louis, MO-IL Metro	1,081,946	17
Tampa-St. Petersburg-Clearwater, FL Metro	1,079,049	18
San Diego-Carlsbad-San Marcos, CA Metro	1,051,344	19
Baltimore-Towson, MD Metro	1,008,010	20
Pittsburgh, PA Metro	993,772	21
Denver-Aurora, CO Metro	901,339	22
Cleveland-Elyria-Mentor, OH Metro	856,502	23
Cincinnati-Middletown, OH-KY-IN Metro	803,625	24
Portland-Vancouver-Beaverton, OR-WA Metro	796,287	25
Kansas City, MO-KS Metro	755,705	26
Sacramento-Arden-Arcade-Roseville, CA Metro	735,636	27
Orlando, FL Metro	705,005	28
Columbus, OH Metro	671,120	29
San Antonio, TX Metro	645,578	30
Providence-New Bedford-Fall River, RI-MA Metro	636,851	31
Indianapolis, IN Metro	629,264	32
Virginia Beach-Norfolk-Newport News, VA-NC Metro	604,810	33
Las Vegas-Paradise, NV Metro	600,039	34
Milwaukee-Waukesha-West Allis, WI Metro	599,727	35
San Jose-Sunnyvale-Santa Clara, CA Metro	584,841	36
Charlotte-Gastonia-Concord, NC-SC Metro	561,868	37
Nashville-Davidson-Murfreesboro, TN Metro	538,501	38
Austin-Round Rock, TX Metro	530,399	39
New Orleans-Metairie-Kenner, LA Metro	502,165	40
Louisville, KY-IN Metro	480,222	41
Jacksonville, FL Metro	473,296	42
Memphis, TN-MS-AR Metro	468,409	43
Buffalo-Cheektowaga-Tonawanda, NY Metro	465,606	44
Hartford-West Hartford-East Hartford, CT Metro	461,926	45
Oklahoma City, OK Metro	449,223	46
Richmond, VA Metro	444,509	47
Birmingham-Hoover, AL Metro	425,136	48
Rochester, NY Metro	401,432	49
Tucson, AZ Metro	359,967	50
Tulsa, OK Metro	349,541	51
Raleigh-Cary, NC Metro	344,684	52
Dayton, OH Metro	340,176	53
Albany-Schenectady-Troy, NY Metro	339,518	54
Salt Lake City, UT Metro	333,069	55
Bridgeport-Stamford-Norwalk, CT Metro	332,533	56
New Haven-Milford, CT Metro	328,465	57
Omaha-Council Bluffs, NE-IA Metro	307,833	58
Honolulu, HI Metro	300,269	59
Albuquerque, NM Metro	300,091	60
Allentown-Bethlehem-Easton, PA-NJ Metro	298,684	61
Worcester, MA Metro	296,987	62
Sarasota-Bradenton-Venice, FL Metro	285,475	63
Grand Rapids-Wyoming, MI Metro	283,695	64
Akron, OH Metro	279,711	65
Fresno, CA Metro	267,644	66
Greensboro-High Point, NC Metro	265,766	67
Baton Rouge, LA Metro	265,763	68
Springfield, MA Metro	265,464	69
Knoxville, TN Metro	265,037	70
Toledo, OH Metro	262,264	71
Columbia, SC Metro	259,429	72
Oxnard-Thousand Oaks-Ventura, CA Metro	258,235	73
Syracuse, NY Metro	256,686	74
Little Rock-North Little Rock, AR Metro	251,478	75
Youngstown-Warren-Boardman, OH-PA Metro	235,058	76
Poughkeepsie-Newburgh-Middletown, NY Metro	228,858	77
Greenville, SC Metro	228,501	78
Wichita, KS Metro	227,273	79
Scranton-Wilkes-Barre, PA Metro	224,599	80
Bakersfield, CA Metro	222,088	81
Charleston-North Charleston, SC Metro	221,207	82
El Paso, TX Metro	220,591	83
Cape Coral-Fort Myers, FL Metro	216,340	84
Madison, WI Metro	215,901	85
Colorado Springs, CO Metro	214,763	86
Palm Bay-Melbourne-Titusville, FL Metro	213,296	87
Portland-South Portland, ME Metro	208,429	88
Harrisburg-Carlisle, PA Metro	207,363	89
Stockton, CA Metro	204,446	90
Des Moines, IA Metro	200,761	91
Lakeland-Winter Haven, FL Metro	199,053	92
Deltona-Daytona Beach-Ormond Beach, FL Metro	197,286	93
Chattanooga, TN-GA Metro	195,114	94
Boise City-Nampa, ID Metro	191,380	95
Augusta-Richmond County, GA-SC Metro	190,452	96
Jackson, MS Metro	186,694	97
Durham, NC Metro	180,698	98
Lancaster, PA Metro	178,632	99
Lansing-East Lansing, MI Metro	178,559	100
Winston-Salem, NC Metro	177,559	101
McAllen-Edinburg-Pharr, TX Metro	177,551	102
Santa Rosa-Petaluma, CA Metro	176,599	103
Flint, MI Metro	174,489	104
Lexington-Fayette, KY Metro	170,741	105
Spokane, WA Metro	169,538	106
Pensacola-Ferry Pass-Brent, FL Metro	162,547	107
Asheville, NC Metro	161,504	108
Canton-Massillon, OH Metro	160,434	109
Modesto, CA Metro	160,415	110
Fort Wayne, IN Metro	156,340	111
York-Hanover, PA Metro	153,899	112
Springfield, MO Metro	152,912	113
Manchester-Nashua, NH Metro	151,862	114
Mobile, AL Metro	151,277	115
Davenport-Moline-Rock Island, IA-IL Metro	149,860	116
Ogden-Clearfield, UT Metro	148,272	117
Reno-Sparks, NV Metro	148,113	118
Reading, PA Metro	147,094	119
Shreveport-Bossier City, LA Metro	146,784	120
Port St. Lucie-Fort Pierce, FL Metro	145,448	121
Fayetteville-Springdale-Rogers, AR-MO Metro	145,320	122
Corpus Christi, TX Metro	144,438	123
Peoria, IL Metro	143,490	124
Huntsville, AL Metro	143,481	125
Beaumont-Port Arthur, TX Metro	141,112	126
Hickory-Morganton-Lenoir, NC Metro	138,637	127
Santa Barbara-Santa Maria-Goleta, CA Metro	138,606	128
Evansville, IN-KY Metro	138,434	129
Vallejo-Fairfield, CA Metro	137,495	130
Eugene-Springfield, OR Metro	134,908	131
Ann Arbor, MI Metro	134,260	132
Montgomery, AL Metro	133,444	133
Tallahassee, FL Metro	132,939	134
Trenton-Ewing, NJ Metro	130,580	135
Salem, OR Metro	130,238	136
Charleston, WV Metro	129,170	137
Rockford, IL Metro	127,111	138
Salinas, CA Metro	125,049	139
Kalamazoo-Portage, MI Metro	124,866	140
Wilmington, NC Metro	124,617	141
Anchorage, AK Metro	123,965	142
Roanoke, VA Metro	122,425	143
Naples-Marco Island, FL Metro	122,207	144
South Bend-Mishawaka, IN-MI Metro	122,015	145
Fayetteville, NC Metro	121,880	146
Killeen-Temple-Fort Hood, TX Metro	118,221	147
Huntington-Ashland, WV-KY-OH Metro	117,795	148
Ocala, FL Metro	117,038	149
Utica-Rome, NY Metro	116,332	150
Visalia-Porterville, CA Metro	116,039	151
Savannah, GA Metro	115,982	152
Green Bay, WI Metro	114,160	153
Provo-Orem, UT Metro	113,246	154
Duluth, MN-WI Metro	112,854	155
Lincoln, NE Metro	111,135	156
Boulder, CO Metro	110,947	157
Fort Smith, AR-OK Metro	108,185	158
Brownsville-Harlingen, TX Metro	106,936	159
Erie, PA Metro	106,539	160
Columbus, GA-AL Metro	105,262	161
Fort Collins-Loveland, CO Metro	104,401	162
Norwich-New London, CT Metro	103,670	163
Spartanburg, SC Metro	102,011	164
Binghamton, NY Metro	101,094	165
Barnstable Town, MA Metro	99,372	166
Atlantic City, NJ Metro	99,202	167
Lubbock, TX Metro	98,941	168
Gainesville, FL Metro	98,712	169
Cedar Rapids, IA Metro	97,562	170
Kingsport-Bristol, TN-VA Metro	97,347	171
San Luis Obispo-Paso Robles, CA Metro	96,888	172
Gulfport-Biloxi, MS Metro	96,531	173
Lafayette, LA Metro	92,820	174
Lynchburg, VA Metro	91,501	175
Hagerstown-Martinsburg, MD-WV Metro	91,444	176
Topeka, KS Metro	90,579	177
Santa Cruz-Watsonville, CA Metro	90,323	178
Myrtle Beach-Conway-North Myrtle Beach, SC Metro	89,887	179
Bremerton-Silverdale, WA Metro	89,605	180
Amarillo, TX Metro	88,096	181
Olympia, WA Metro	87,452	182
Macon, GA Metro	86,732	183
Clarksville, TN-KY Metro	86,444	184
Champaign-Urbana, IL Metro	86,265	185
Holland-Grand Haven, MI Metro	85,966	186
Springfield, IL Metro	85,236	187
Chico, CA Metro	82,914	188
Waco, TX Metro	81,398	189
Saginaw-Saginaw Township North, MI Metro	80,784	190
Appleton, WI Metro	80,527	191
Burlington-South Burlington, VT Metro	79,136	192
Prescott, AZ Metro	78,686	193
Johnson City, TN Metro	77,746	194
Sioux Falls, SD Metro	77,565	195
Tuscaloosa, AL Metro	77,070	196
Longview, TX Metro	75,892	197
Greeley, CO Metro	75,819	198
Medford, OR Metro	75,814	199
Florence, SC Metro	75,346	200
Torrington, CT Micro	75,019	201
Yakima, WA Metro	74,815	202
Kennewick-Richland-Pasco, WA Metro	73,975	203
Fargo, ND-MN Metro	72,974	204
Lake Charles, LA Metro	72,564	205
Racine, WI Metro	72,129	206
Charlottesville, VA Metro	71,517	207
Fort Walton Beach-Crestview-Destin, FL Metro	71,255	208
College Station-Bryan, TX Metro	71,208	209
Lake Havasu City-Kingman, AZ Micro	70,724	210
Houma-Bayou Cane-Thibodaux, LA Metro	70,460	211
Bloomington, IN Metro	70,435	212
Tyler, TX Metro	70,020	213
Punta Gorda, FL Metro	70,010	214
Merced, CA Metro	69,981	215
Lafayette, IN Metro	69,298	216
Kingston, NY Metro	69,261	217
Anderson, SC Metro	69,256	218
Bellingham, WA Metro	69,217	219
Lebanon, NH-VT Micro	69,077	220
Redding, CA Metro	68,553	221
Elkhart-Goshen, IN Metro	68,266	222
Seaford, DE Micro	68,079	223
Rochester, MN Metro	66,877	224
Athens-Clarke County, GA Metro	66,842	225
Parkersburg-Marietta, WV-OH Metro	66,555	226
Terre Haute, IN Metro	65,263	227
Monroe, LA Metro	65,175	228
St. Cloud, MN Metro	64,612	229
Muskegon-Norton Shores, MI Metro	64,424	230
Niles-Benton Harbor, MI Metro	63,799	231
Joplin, MO Metro	63,459	232
Waterloo-Cedar Falls, IA Metro	63,424	233
Panama City-Lynn Haven, FL Metro	62,985	234
Oshkosh-Neenah, WI Metro	62,567	235
Las Cruces, NM Metro	62,310	236
Greenville, NC Metro	62,219	237
Lexington-Thomasville, NC Micro	60,888	238
Wheeling, WV-OH Metro	60,823	239
Daphne-Fairhope, AL Micro	60,803	240
Columbia, MO Metro	60,272	241
Bangor, ME Metro	60,233	242
Ottawa-Streator, IL Micro	60,222	243
Jackson, MI Metro	59,967	244
Blacksburg-Christiansburg-Radford, VA Metro	59,933	245
Bloomington-Normal, IL Metro	59,927	246
Janesville, WI Metro	59,836	247
Eau Claire, WI Metro	59,522	248
Johnstown, PA Metro	59,445	249
Pottsville, PA Micro	58,987	250
Albany, GA Metro	58,700	251
Yuma, AZ Metro	58,575	252
Billings, MT Metro	58,533	253
Florence, AL Metro	58,428	254
Abilene, TX Metro	57,970	255
Decatur, AL Metro	57,939	256
Hilton Head Island-Beaufort, SC Micro	57,801	257
Pueblo, CO Metro	57,733	258
Laredo, TX Metro	57,447	259
Santa Fe, NM Metro	57,131	260
Homosassa Springs, FL Micro	57,090	261
Hilo, HI Micro	57,079	262
Monroe, MI Metro	56,366	263
Springfield, OH Metro	56,234	264
Pascagoula, MS Metro	56,028	265
Traverse City, MI Micro	55,781	266
East Stroudsburg, PA Micro	55,735	267
Wichita Falls, TX Metro	55,728	268
Alexandria, LA Metro	55,517	269
Pittsfield, MA Metro	55,410	270
Iowa City, IA Metro	55,380	271
Concord, NH Micro	55,291	272
Rocky Mount, NC Metro	54,927	273
Burlington, NC Metro	54,796	274
Battle Creek, MI Metro	54,614	275
Dothan, AL Metro	53,986	276
Gainesville, GA Metro	53,876	277
Jamestown-Dunkirk-Fredonia, NY Micro	53,751	278
Weirton-Steubenville, WV-OH Metro	53,697	279
Sioux City, IA-NE-SD Metro	53,554	280
Vero Beach, FL Metro	53,514	281
Jefferson City, MO Metro	53,131	282
Bend, OR Metro	52,975	283
Anderson, IN Metro	52,740	284
Chambersburg, PA Micro	52,633	285
Statesville-Mooresville, NC Micro	52,136	286
Eureka-Arcata-Fortuna, CA Micro	52,019	287
State College, PA Metro	51,791	288
Salisbury, NC Micro	51,633	289
Altoona, PA Metro	50,858	290
Dover, DE Metro	50,674	291
Morristown, TN Metro	50,609	292
Yuba City-Marysville, CA Metro	50,433	293
La Crosse, WI-MN Metro	50,257	294
Jacksonville, NC Metro	50,133	295
Texarkana, TX-Texarkana, AR Metro	49,479	296
Tupelo, MS Micro	49,466	297
Augusta-Waterville, ME Micro	49,429	298
Grand Junction, CO Metro	49,380	299
Glens Falls, NY Metro	49,304	300
Vineland-Millville-Bridgeton, NJ Metro	49,287	301
Wausau, WI Metro	49,066	302
Mansfield, OH Metro	48,915	303
Napa, CA Metro	48,166	304
Auburn-Opelika, AL Metro	48,130	305
Hattiesburg, MS Metro	48,046	306
Lebanon, PA Metro	47,396	307

CBSA	HOUSEHOLDS	RANK
Muncie, IN Metro	47,235	308
Sierra Vista-Douglas, AZ Micro	47,164	309
Kahului-Wailuku, HI Micro	46,981	310
Morgantown, WV Metro	46,683	311
Williamsport, PA Metro	46,544	312
Anniston-Oxford, AL Metro	46,110	313
St. Joseph, MO-KS Metro	45,910	314
Rapid City, SD Metro	45,683	315
Flagstaff, AZ Metro	45,615	316
Dalton, GA Metro	45,544	317
Danville, VA Metro	45,267	318
Lumberton, NC Micro	45,017	319
Warner Robins, GA Metro	44,966	320
Sherman-Denison, TX Metro	44,937	321
Coeur d'Alene, ID Metro	44,828	322
Decatur, IL Metro	44,768	323
Bluefield, WV-VA Micro	44,703	324
Odessa, TX Metro	44,520	325
Sheboygan, WI Metro	44,118	326
Staunton-Waynesboro, VA Micro	44,110	327
Bay City, MI Metro	44,046	328
Owensboro, KY Metro	43,947	329
New Bern, NC Micro	43,868	330
Winchester, VA-WV Metro	43,852	331
Jonesboro, AR Metro	43,792	332
Valdosta, GA Metro	43,784	333
Midland, TX Metro	43,670	334
Lewiston-Auburn, ME Metro	43,539	335
Goldsboro, NC Metro	42,985	336
Willimantic, CT Micro	42,964	337
East Liverpool-Salem, OH Micro	42,750	338
Jackson, TN Metro	42,499	339
Cleveland, TN Metro	42,279	340
Farmington, NM Metro	42,209	341
Salisbury, MD Metro	42,120	342
Ocean City, NJ Metro	42,066	343
Elizabethtown, KY Metro	41,834	344
Bowling Green, KY Metro	41,810	345
Gadsden, AL Metro	41,713	346
Kokomo, IN Metro	41,584	347
Michigan City-La Porte, IN Metro	41,550	348
Wooster, OH Micro	41,362	349
Victoria, TX Metro	41,299	350
Meridian, MS Micro	40,910	351
Mount Vernon-Anacortes, WA Metro	40,899	352
Roseburg, OR Micro	40,876	353
Paducah, KY-IL Micro	40,862	354
Albany-Lebanon, OR Micro	40,692	355
El Centro, CA Metro	40,674	356
Lima, OH Metro	40,608	357
Missoula, MT Metro	40,569	358
San Angelo, TX Metro	40,552	359
Allegan, MI Micro	40,536	360
Ogdensburg-Massena, NY Micro	40,438	361
Lawrence, KS Metro	40,320	362
Harrisonburg, VA Metro	39,925	363
Corning, NY Micro	39,775	364
Sumter, SC Metro	39,593	365
Ashtabula, OH Micro	39,583	366
Hot Springs, AR Metro	39,481	367
Cumberland, MD-WV Metro	39,447	368
Cookeville, TN Micro	39,404	369
Bismarck, ND Metro	39,394	370
Lawton, OK Metro	39,243	371
Sebring, FL Micro	39,042	372
Truckee-Grass Valley, CA Micro	38,868	373
Kankakee-Bradley, IL Metro	38,779	374
Ithaca, NY Metro	38,776	375
Brunswick, GA Metro	38,637	376
Manhattan, KS Micro	38,551	377
Madera, CA Metro	38,505	378
Hammond, LA Micro	38,213	379
Shelby, NC Micro	38,108	380
Sunbury, PA Micro	38,041	381
Tullahoma, TN Micro	37,910	382
Watertown-Fort Drum, NY Micro	37,806	383
Fond du Lac, WI Metro	37,698	384
Dunn, NC Micro	37,645	385
Pine Bluff, AR Metro	37,514	386
Wenatchee, WA Metro	37,414	387
Grand Forks, ND-MN Metro	37,295	388
Enterprise-Ozark, AL Micro	37,176	389
Idaho Falls, ID Metro	37,162	390
New Castle, PA Micro	37,053	391
Clarksburg, WV Micro	37,040	392
Adrian, MI Micro	36,976	393
Longview-Kelso, WA Metro	36,913	394
Whitewater, WI Micro	36,259	395
New Philadelphia-Dover, OH Micro	36,238	396
Richmond, KY Micro	36,216	397
Cape Girardeau-Jackson, MO-IL Micro	36,117	398
Key West-Marathon, FL Micro	35,974	399
Gettysburg, PA Micro	35,897	400
Hanford-Corcoran, CA Metro	35,867	401
St. George, UT Metro	35,617	402
Rome, GA Metro	35,407	403
Brainerd, MN Micro	35,191	404
Elmira, NY Metro	34,917	405
Orangeburg, SC Micro	34,527	406
Meadville, PA Micro	34,431	407
Dubuque, IA Metro	34,356	408
Indiana, PA Micro	34,183	409
Ukiah, CA Micro	33,943	410
Albertville, AL Micro	33,653	411
Lexington Park, MD Micro	33,524	412
Opelousas-Eunice, LA Micro	33,166	413
Southern Pines, NC Micro	33,153	414
Zanesville, OH Micro	33,138	415
Manitowoc, WI Micro	33,105	416
Danville, IL Metro	33,025	417
Mankato-North Mankato, MN Micro	33,023	418
Cheyenne, WY Metro	32,763	419
DuBois, PA Micro	32,746	420
Logan, UT-ID Metro	32,745	421
Midland, MI Micro	32,742	422
Grants Pass, OR Micro	32,582	423
Great Falls, MT Metro	32,471	424
Bloomsburg-Berwick, PA Micro	32,278	425
Beaver Dam, WI Micro	32,164	426
Beckley, WV Micro	32,081	427
Olean, NY Micro	31,913	428
Kalispell, MT Micro	31,878	429
Sandusky, OH Metro	31,715	430
Twin Falls, ID Micro	31,443	431
Corvallis, OR Metro	31,383	432
Laurel, MS Micro	31,342	433
Fairbanks, AK Metro	31,329	434
Cullman, AL Micro	31,328	435
Talladega-Sylacauga, AL Micro	31,265	436
Sevierville, TN Micro	30,951	437
Somerset, PA Micro	30,904	438
Plattsburgh, NY Micro	30,869	439
Auburn, NY Micro	30,635	440
Athens, TX Micro	30,609	441
Quincy, IL-MO Micro	30,407	442
Roanoke Rapids, NC Micro	30,402	443
Portsmouth, OH Micro	30,387	444
Wisconsin Rapids-Marshfield, WI Micro	30,378	445
Ames, IA Metro	30,283	446
Oak Harbor, WA Micro	30,149	447
Martinsville, VA Micro	30,009	448
Pocatello, ID Metro	29,971	449
Watertown-Fort Atkinson, WI Micro	29,577	450
Wilson, NC Micro	29,490	451
Pendleton-Hermiston, OR Micro	29,440	452
Keene, NH Micro	29,424	453
Lufkin, TX Micro	29,400	454
Russellville, AR Micro	29,395	455
Bristol, VA Metro	29,235	456
Branson, MO Micro	29,175	457
Mount Airy, NC Micro	29,089	458
Bozeman, MT Micro	28,882	459
Seneca, SC Micro	28,865	460
Findlay, OH Micro	28,731	461
Palatka, FL Micro	28,547	462
Richmond, IN Micro	28,454	463
Port Angeles, WA Micro	28,412	464
Marinette, WI-MI Micro	28,373	465
Galesburg, IL Micro	28,256	466
Chillicothe, OH Micro	28,167	467
Columbus, IN Metro	28,142	468
Frankfort, KY Micro	28,055	469
Columbia, TN Micro	27,986	470
Helena, MT Micro	27,844	471
Warsaw, IN Micro	27,842	472
Aberdeen, WA Micro	27,686	473
Stillwater, OK Micro	27,620	474
Marion, IN Micro	27,604	475
North Wilkesboro, NC Micro	27,558	476
Casper, WY Metro	27,477	477
Owosso, MI Micro	27,383	478
Centralia, WA Micro	27,245	479
Palm Coast, FL Micro	27,096	480
Muskogee, OK Micro	26,914	481
Greeneville, TN Micro	26,727	482
Searcy, AR Micro	26,656	483
Greenwood, SC Micro	26,596	484
Coos Bay, OR Micro	26,478	485
Moses Lake, WA Micro	26,345	486
Grand Island, NE Micro	26,122	487
Marquette, MI Micro	26,118	488
Morehead City, NC Micro	26,033	489
Clearlake, CA Micro	25,920	490
New Iberia, LA Micro	25,913	491
Rutland, VT Micro	25,906	492
Lincolnton, NC Micro	25,872	493
Klamath Falls, OR Micro	25,831	494
Minot, ND Micro	25,770	495
Stevens Point, WI Micro	25,765	496
Marion-Herrin, IL Micro	25,737	497
The Villages, FL Micro	25,497	498
Forest City, NC Micro	25,422	499
Hudson, NY Micro	25,302	500
Shawnee, OK Micro	25,264	501
Charleston-Mattoon, IL Micro	25,208	502
Sayre, PA Micro	24,774	503
Hutchinson, KS Micro	24,730	504
Carbondale, IL Micro	24,664	505
Barre, VT Micro	24,549	506
Laconia, NH Micro	24,484	507
Marion, OH Micro	24,359	508
Salina, KS Micro	24,058	509
Fairmont, WV Micro	23,998	510
Fremont, OH Micro	23,912	511
Lancaster, SC Micro	23,901	512
Hinesville-Fort Stewart, GA Metro	23,835	513
Georgetown, SC Micro	23,818	514
Oneonta, NY Micro	23,794	515
Somerset, KY Micro	23,695	516
Lewiston, ID-WA Metro	23,690	517
Kinston, NC Micro	23,640	518
Mount Pleasant, MI Micro	23,596	519
Sterling, IL Micro	23,536	520
Athens, OH Micro	23,519	521
Marshall, TX Micro	23,424	522
Sturgis, MI Micro	23,357	523
Fergus Falls, MN Micro	23,350	524
Point Pleasant, WV-OH Micro	23,168	525
Alamogordo, NM Micro	22,951	526
Enid, OK Micro	22,879	527
Norwalk, OH Micro	22,864	528
Batavia, NY Micro	22,574	529
Columbus, MS Micro	22,567	530
Baraboo, WI Micro	22,490	531
LaGrange, GA Micro	22,486	532
Nacogdoches, TX Micro	22,465	533
Oil City, PA Micro	22,460	534
Albemarle, NC Micro	22,314	535
Tiffin-Fostoria, OH Micro	22,165	536
Ardmore, OK Micro	22,066	537
Roswell, NM Micro	22,043	538
Phoenix Lake-Cedar Ridge, CA Micro	21,978	539
Lake City, FL Micro	21,971	540
Mason City, IA Micro	21,931	541
Gloversville, NY Micro	21,904	542
Scottsboro, AL Micro	21,902	543
London, KY Micro	21,774	544
Statesboro, GA Micro	21,750	545
Ruston, LA Micro	21,741	546
Harriman, TN Micro	21,738	547
Red Bluff, CA Micro	21,722	548
Farmington, MO Micro	21,686	549
Kapaa, HI Micro	21,445	550
Greenville, MS Micro	21,406	551
Crowley, LA Micro	21,405	552
Gaffney, SC Micro	21,393	553
Carson City, NV Metro	21,337	554
Ocean Pines, MD Micro	21,298	555
Crossville, TN Micro	21,179	556
Elizabeth City, NC Micro	21,158	557
Dublin, GA Micro	21,106	558
Gallup, NM Micro	21,064	559
Mount Vernon, OH Micro	20,953	560
Payson, AZ Micro	20,813	561
Granbury, TX Micro	20,747	562
Natchez, MS-LA Micro	20,739	563
Muscatine, IA Micro	20,737	564
Athens, TN Micro	20,593	565
Danville, KY Micro	20,567	566
Bartlesville, OK Micro	20,460	567
Greenville, OH Micro	20,418	568
Jasper, IN Micro	20,394	569
Abbeville, LA Micro	20,255	570
McComb, MS Micro	20,225	571
Edwards, CO Micro	20,089	572
Burlington, IA-IL Micro	20,035	573
Walla Walla, WA Micro	20,027	574
Glasgow, KY Micro	20,016	575
Hobbs, NM Micro	20,010	576
Rochelle, IL Micro	19,989	577
Faribault-Northfield, MN Micro	19,957	578
Clinton, IA Micro	19,955	579
Amsterdam, NY Micro	19,930	580
Ashland, OH Micro	19,816	581
Waycross, GA Micro	19,812	582
Shelton, WA Micro	19,651	583
Paris, TX Micro	19,544	584
Norfolk, NE Micro	19,406	585
Picayune, MS Micro	19,401	586
Carlsbad-Artesia, NM Micro	19,374	587
New Castle, IN Micro	19,292	588
Freeport, IL Micro	19,231	589
Madisonville, KY Micro	19,197	590
Kearney, NE Micro	19,051	591
Morgan City, LA Micro	19,050	592
Ponca City, OK Micro	18,989	593
Washington, NC Micro	18,972	594
Bedford, IN Micro	18,930	595
Oak Hill, WV Micro	18,900	596
Kerrville, TX Micro	18,801	597
Vicksburg, MS Micro	18,788	598
Bucyrus, OH Micro	18,752	599
Durango, CO Micro	18,727	600
Platteville, WI Micro	18,696	601
Warrensburg, MO Micro	18,614	602
Cortland, NY Micro	18,592	603
Mount Vernon, IL Micro	18,566	604
Blytheville, AR Micro	18,537	605
Huntsville, TX Micro	18,527	606
Sanford, NC Micro	18,524	607
Lewistown, PA Micro	18,489	608
Winona, MN Micro	18,484	609
Bellefontaine, OH Micro	18,262	610
Sidney, OH Micro	18,184	611
Rockingham, NC Micro	18,035	612
Harrison, AR Micro	18,000	613
El Dorado, AR Micro	17,976	614
Milledgeville, GA Micro	17,968	615
Fort Polk South, LA Micro	17,927	616
Gardnerville Ranchos, NV Micro	17,905	617
Cadillac, MI Micro	17,854	618
Selma, AL Micro	17,662	619

CBSA	HOUSEHOLDS	RANK
Calhoun, GA Micro	17,599	620
Red Wing, MN Micro	17,565	621
Corsicana, TX Micro	17,516	622
Rockland, ME Micro	17,515	623
Malone, NY Micro	17,503	624
Warren, PA Micro	17,465	625
Ontario, OR-ID Micro	17,456	626
Keokuk-Fort Madison, IA-MO Micro	17,447	627
Bradford, PA Micro	17,422	628
Mountain Home, AR Micro	17,408	629
Wapakoneta, OH Micro	17,331	630
Kendallville, IN Micro	17,239	631
McAlester, OK Micro	17,197	632
Duncan, OK Micro	17,160	633
Henderson, NC Micro	17,148	634
Jacksonville, TX Micro	17,136	635
Huntingdon, PA Micro	16,964	636
Plymouth, IN Micro	16,964	637
Clovis, NM Micro	16,954	638
Mount Sterling, KY Micro	16,894	639
Berlin, NH-VT Micro	16,827	640
Tahlequah, OK Micro	16,819	641
Poplar Bluff, MO Micro	16,799	642
Rolla, MO Micro	16,705	643
Douglas, GA Micro	16,611	644
Bogalusa, LA Micro	16,602	645
Boone, NC Micro	16,591	646
Thomasville, GA Micro	16,527	647
La Follette, TN Micro	16,514	648
Minden, LA Micro	16,500	649
Coldwater, MI Micro	16,488	650
Seymour, IN Micro	16,360	651
Cambridge, OH Micro	16,354	652
Union City, TN-KY Micro	16,308	653
Greenwood, MS Micro	16,306	654
Starkville, MS Micro	16,167	655
Centralia, IL Micro	16,156	656
Aberdeen, SD Micro	16,149	657
Moultrie, GA Micro	16,107	658
Lawrenceburg, TN Micro	15,994	659
Big Rapids, MI Micro	15,988	660
Jacksonville, IL Micro	15,927	661
Willmar, MN Micro	15,925	662
Escanaba, MI Micro	15,894	663
Wilmington, OH Micro	15,818	664
Rio Grande City, TX Micro	15,765	665
Austin, MN Micro	15,695	666
Elko, NV Micro	15,670	667
Pullman, WA Micro	15,648	668
McMinnville, TN Micro	15,640	669
Sikeston, MO Micro	15,602	670
Sedalia, MO Micro	15,597	671
Logansport, IN Micro	15,546	672
Marshalltown, IA Micro	15,505	673
Fort Dodge, IA Micro	15,477	674
Auburn, IN Micro	15,445	675
St. Marys, GA Micro	15,421	676
Bemidji, MN Micro	15,293	677
Paragould, AR Micro	15,277	678
Vincennes, IN Micro	15,267	679
Espanola, NM Micro	15,255	680
Scottsbluff, NE Micro	15,229	681
Defiance, OH Micro	15,226	682
Pittsburg, KS Micro	15,226	683
Urbana, OH Micro	15,218	684
Bennington, VT Micro	15,134	685
El Campo, TX Micro	15,083	686
Canon City, CO Micro	15,070	687
Menomonie, WI Micro	15,066	688
Walterboro, SC Micro	15,060	689
Astoria, OR Micro	15,054	690
Palestine, TX Micro	15,050	691
Oxford, MS Micro	15,022	692
Mayfield, KY Micro	15,006	693
Shelbyville, TN Micro	14,959	694
Hastings, NE Micro	14,924	695
Pahrump, NV Micro	14,919	696
Del Rio, TX Micro	14,887	697
Celina, OH Micro	14,872	698
Fort Leonard Wood, MO Micro	14,860	699
West Plains, MO Micro	14,852	700
Crawfordsville, IN Micro	14,848	701
Emporia, KS Micro	14,839	702
Durant, OK Micro	14,831	703
Cedartown, GA Micro	14,769	704
Newton, IA Micro	14,747	705
Newberry, SC Micro	14,735	706
Lock Haven, PA Micro	14,723	707
Houghton, MI Micro	14,719	708
Hannibal, MO Micro	14,652	709
Tifton, GA Micro	14,642	710
Easton, MD Micro	14,635	711
Dyersburg, TN Micro	14,605	712
Cornelia, GA Micro	14,583	713
Brownwood, TX Micro	14,565	714
Ottumwa, IA Micro	14,565	715
Coshocton, OH Micro	14,540	716
North Platte, NE Micro	14,535	717
Gainesville, TX Micro	14,527	718
Huntington, IN Micro	14,504	719
Corinth, MS Micro	14,459	720
Valley, AL Micro	14,444	721
Corbin, KY Micro	14,437	722
Pontiac, IL Micro	14,412	723
Newport, TN Micro	14,398	724
Fremont, NE Micro	14,392	725
Canton, IL Micro	14,391	726
Kill Devil Hills, NC Micro	14,338	727
Ellensburg, WA Micro	14,332	728
Winfield, KS Micro	14,292	729
Montrose, CO Micro	14,263	730
Murray, KY Micro	14,254	731
Coffeyville, KS Micro	14,238	732
Alma, MI Micro	14,235	733
Natchitoches, LA Micro	14,187	734
Rock Springs, WY Micro	14,159	735
Bay City, TX Micro	14,136	736
Eagle Pass, TX Micro	14,039	737
Burley, ID Micro	13,999	738
Alexandria, MN Micro	13,985	739
Gillette, WY Micro	13,966	740
Selinsgrove, PA Micro	13,950	741
Riverton, WY Micro	13,925	742
Hutchinson, MN Micro	13,903	743
Blackfoot, ID Micro	13,893	744
Ada, OK Micro	13,887	745
Peru, IN Micro	13,846	746
St. Marys, PA Micro	13,839	747
Sault Ste. Marie, MI Micro	13,786	748
Butte-Silver Bow, MT Micro	13,742	749
Brigham City, UT Micro	13,737	750
Taylorville, IL Micro	13,695	751
Americus, GA Micro	13,693	752
Batesville, AR Micro	13,680	753
Monroe, WI Micro	13,664	754
Laurinburg, NC Micro	13,590	755
Seneca Falls, NY Micro	13,579	756
Taos, NM Micro	13,579	757
Iron Mountain, MI-WI Micro	13,571	758
Alice, TX Micro	13,493	759
Camden, AR Micro	13,467	760
Cleveland, MS Micro	13,404	761
Owatonna, MN Micro	13,368	762
Moscow, ID Micro	13,298	763
Kennett, MO Micro	13,216	764
Laramie, WY Micro	13,201	765
Dixon, IL Micro	13,184	766
Wabash, IN Micro	13,178	767
Paris, TN Micro	13,163	768
Chester, SC Micro	13,136	769
Okeechobee, FL Micro	13,127	770
Effingham, IL Micro	13,107	771
Albert Lea, MN Micro	13,059	772
Lewisburg, PA Micro	12,976	773
Lebanon, MO Micro	12,945	774
Safford, AZ Micro	12,932	775
Angola, IN Micro	12,888	776
Miami, OK Micro	12,791	777
Brookhaven, MS Micro	12,786	778
Hope, AR Micro	12,714	779
Alpena, MI Micro	12,693	780
Nogales, AZ Micro	12,687	781
Brevard, NC Micro	12,629	782
Cambridge, MD Micro	12,590	783
Frankfort, IN Micro	12,589	784
Stephenville, TX Micro	12,570	785
Macomb, IL Micro	12,535	786
Madison, IN Micro	12,519	787
Watertown, SD Micro	12,499	788
De Ridder, LA Micro	12,486	789
Sulphur Springs, TX Micro	12,445	790
Middlesborough, KY Micro	12,372	791
Maysville, KY Micro	12,368	792
Garden City, KS Micro	12,335	793
Central City, KY Micro	12,318	794
Troy, AL Micro	12,144	795
Union, SC Micro	11,996	796
Merrill, WI Micro	11,968	797
Columbus, NE Micro	11,902	798
Decatur, IN Micro	11,870	799
Silver City, NM Micro	11,838	800
Juneau, AK Micro	11,624	801
Brenham, TX Micro	11,586	802
Kirksville, MO Micro	11,585	803
Plainview, TX Micro	11,554	804
Van Wert, OH Micro	11,537	805
Sheridan, WY Micro	11,518	806
Cedar City, UT Micro	11,483	807
Jennings, LA Micro	11,481	808
Dillon, SC Micro	11,463	809
Rexburg, ID Micro	11,365	810
Bastrop, LA Micro	11,190	811
Great Bend, KS Micro	11,143	812
Hays, KS Micro	11,094	813
McPherson, KS Micro	11,078	814
Las Vegas, NM Micro	11,066	815
Big Spring, TX Micro	11,045	816
Mineral Wells, TX Micro	11,016	817
Kingsville, TX Micro	10,985	818
Washington, IN Micro	10,975	819
Brookings, SD Micro	10,973	820
Washington, OH Micro	10,970	821
Arcadia, FL Micro	10,895	822
Thomaston, GA Micro	10,855	823
Dodge City, KS Micro	10,804	824
Clewiston, FL Micro	10,665	825
Lincoln, IL Micro	10,643	826
North Vernon, IN Micro	10,625	827
Jackson, WY-ID Micro	10,555	828
Harrisburg, IL Micro	10,517	829
Bainbridge, GA Micro	10,486	830
Bennettsville, SC Micro	10,447	831
New Ulm, MN Micro	10,432	832
Clarksdale, MS Micro	10,364	833
Boone, IA Micro	10,361	834
Fitzgerald, GA Micro	10,336	835
Silverthorne, CO Micro	10,335	836
Toccoa, GA Micro	10,141	837
Connersville, IN Micro	10,083	838
Magnolia, AR Micro	9,918	839
Altus, OK Micro	9,889	840
Summerville, GA Micro	9,877	841
La Grande, OR Micro	9,868	842
Brookings, OR Micro	9,798	843
Mount Pleasant, TX Micro	9,760	844
Fort Morgan, CO Micro	9,712	845
Lexington, NE Micro	9,612	846
Marshall, MN Micro	9,597	847
Deming, NM Micro	9,589	848
Mexico, MO Micro	9,585	849
Greensburg, IN Micro	9,556	850
Campbellsville, KY Micro	9,537	851
Forrest City, AR Micro	9,511	852
Beatrice, NE Micro	9,473	853
Jesup, GA Micro	9,466	854
Wahpeton, ND-MN Micro	9,390	855
City of The Dalles, OR Micro	9,341	856
Moberly, MO Micro	9,208	857
Scottsburg, IN Micro	9,189	858
Indianola, MS Micro	9,094	859
Dickinson, ND Micro	9,083	860
Borger, TX Micro	9,048	861
Crescent City North, CA Micro	9,019	862
Yazoo City, MS Micro	9,004	863
Mountain Home, ID Micro	9,003	864
Uvalde, TX Micro	8,926	865
Arkadelphia, AR Micro	8,894	866
Mitchell, SD Micro	8,890	867
Fort Valley, GA Micro	8,879	868
Spearfish, SD Micro	8,873	869
West Helena, AR Micro	8,866	870
Oskaloosa, IA Micro	8,852	871
Tuskegee, AL Micro	8,852	872
Fallon, NV Micro	8,850	873
Parsons, KS Micro	8,842	874
Grants, NM Micro	8,824	875
Fairmont, MN Micro	8,749	876
Vernal, UT Micro	8,732	877
Grenada, MS Micro	8,706	878
Pampa, TX Micro	8,697	879
Jamestown, ND Micro	8,566	880
Marshall, MO Micro	8,480	881
Cordele, GA Micro	8,359	882
Pierre Part, LA Micro	8,306	883
Wauchula, FL Micro	8,236	884
Williston, ND Micro	8,162	885
Beeville, TX Micro	8,125	886
Yankton, SD Micro	8,091	887
Maryville, MO Micro	8,035	888
Levelland, TX Micro	8,016	889
Bishop, CA Micro	7,938	890
Prineville, OR Micro	7,924	891
Sterling, CO Micro	7,861	892
Pierre, SD Micro	7,846	893
Los Alamos, NM Micro	7,722	894
Liberal, KS Micro	7,653	895
Worthington, MN Micro	7,652	896
Brownsville, TN Micro	7,506	897
Storm Lake, IA Micro	7,471	898
Hood River, OR Micro	7,279	899
Spirit Lake, IA Micro	7,251	900
Woodward, OK Micro	7,184	901
Price, UT Micro	7,141	902
Guymon, OK Micro	7,092	903
Spencer, IA Micro	7,085	904
Evanston, WY Micro	7,037	905
Huron, SD Micro	6,945	906
Dumas, TX Micro	6,920	907
Portales, NM Micro	6,769	908
Havre, MT Micro	6,401	909
Atchison, KS Micro	6,242	910
Hereford, TX Micro	6,105	911
Sweetwater, TX Micro	5,902	912
Raymondville, TX Micro	5,561	913
Snyder, TX Micro	5,500	914
Vernon, TX Micro	5,249	915
Ketchikan, AK Micro	5,174	916
Vermillion, SD Micro	4,688	917
Andrews, TX Micro	4,673	918
Kodiak, AK Micro	4,439	919
Lamesa, TX Micro	4,267	920
Tallulah, LA Micro	4,098	921
Pecos, TX Micro	3,748	922

CBSA Total	102,191,978	
United States Total	109,949,228	
CBSA (% of U.S. Total)	92.94	

CBSA	INCOME ($)	RANK
Los Alamos, NM Micro	87,091	1
San Jose-Sunnyvale-Santa Clara, CA Metro	84,410	2
Bridgeport-Stamford-Norwalk, CT Metro	72,694	3
Washington-Arlington-Alexandria, DC-VA-MD-WV Metro	70,274	4
San Francisco-Oakland-Fremont, CA Metro	70,241	5
Edwards, CO Micro	66,908	6
Oxnard-Thousand Oaks-Ventura, CA Metro	66,393	7
Juneau, AK Micro	65,908	8
Trenton-Ewing, NJ Metro	64,505	9
Boulder, CO Metro	63,564	10
Silverthorne, CO Micro	62,938	11
Boston-Cambridge-Quincy, MA-NH Metro	62,499	12
Santa Cruz-Watsonville, CA Metro	62,070	13
Lexington Park, MD Micro	61,912	14
Vallejo-Fairfield, CA Metro	61,825	15
Minneapolis-St. Paul-Bloomington, MN-WI Metro	61,567	16
Torrington, CT Micro	61,086	17
Santa Rosa-Petaluma, CA Metro	60,993	18
Manchester-Nashua, NH Metro	60,207	19
Anchorage, AK Metro	59,559	20
Denver-Aurora, CO Metro	59,519	21
Napa, CA Metro	59,311	22
Poughkeepsie-Newburgh-Middletown, NY Metro	59,157	23
Raleigh-Cary, NC Metro	58,064	24
Hartford-West Hartford-East Hartford, CT Metro	57,991	25
Atlanta-Sandy Springs-Marietta, GA Metro	57,620	26
Gardnerville Ranchos, NV Micro	57,535	27
Jackson, WY-ID Micro	57,485	28
Kodiak, AK Micro	57,352	29
Ann Arbor, MI Metro	57,216	30
Gillette, WY Micro	57,012	31
Chicago-Naperville-Joliet, IL-IN-WI Metro	56,906	32
Holland-Grand Haven, MI Metro	56,732	33
Appleton, WI Metro	56,482	34
Honolulu, HI Metro	56,161	35
Fort Collins-Loveland, CO Metro	56,018	36
Monroe, MI Metro	55,864	37
Rochester, MN Metro	55,832	38
Norwich-New London, CT Metro	55,734	39
Ogden-Clearfield, UT Metro	55,473	40
New York-Newark-Edison, NY-NJ-PA Metro	55,471	41
Baltimore-Towson, MD Metro	55,412	42
Seattle-Tacoma-Bellevue, WA Metro	55,379	43
Salt Lake City, UT Metro	55,244	44
Concord, NH Micro	54,622	45
Salinas, CA Metro	54,609	46
Madison, WI Metro	54,499	47
Austin-Round Rock, TX Metro	54,475	48
Ketchikan, AK Micro	54,385	49
Detroit-Warren-Livonia, MI Metro	53,992	50
Worcester, MA Metro	53,813	51
Fairbanks, AK Metro	53,775	52
Faribault-Northfield, MN Micro	53,637	53
Kahului-Wailuku, HI Micro	53,606	54
Philadelphia-Camden-Wilmington, PA-NJ-DE-MD Metro	53,444	55
San Diego-Carlsbad-San Marcos, CA Metro	53,333	56
Colorado Springs, CO Metro	53,147	57
Naples-Marco Island, FL Metro	53,126	58
Dallas-Fort Worth-Arlington, TX Metro	53,099	59
Red Wing, MN Micro	52,879	60
New Haven-Milford, CT Metro	52,707	61
Truckee-Grass Valley, CA Micro	52,588	62
Racine, WI Metro	52,474	63
Olympia, WA Metro	52,393	64
Portland-Vancouver-Beaverton, OR-WA Metro	52,291	65
Santa Barbara-Santa Maria-Goleta, CA Metro	52,194	66
East Stroudsburg, PA Micro	52,192	67
Charlotte-Gastonia-Concord, NC-SC Metro	52,186	68
Watertown-Fort Atkinson, WI Micro	52,072	69
Bremerton-Silverdale, WA Metro	52,070	70
Bloomington-Normal, IL Metro	51,857	71
Burlington-South Burlington, VT Metro	51,855	72
Sacramento-Arden-Arcade-Roseville, CA Metro	51,447	73
Reno-Sparks, NV Metro	51,374	74
Provo-Orem, UT Metro	51,203	75
Whitewater, WI Micro	51,145	76
Elko, NV Micro	51,058	77
Des Moines, IA Metro	50,872	78
Rock Springs, WY Micro	50,832	79
Sheboygan, WI Metro	50,687	80
Indianapolis, IN Metro	50,664	81
Kansas City, MO-KS Metro	50,485	82
Richmond, VA Metro	50,427	83
Barnstable Town, MA Metro	50,419	84
Allegan, MI Micro	50,340	85
Milwaukee-Waukesha-West Allis, WI Metro	50,049	86
Hilton Head Island-Beaufort, SC Micro	49,999	87
Owatonna, MN Micro	49,924	88
Kennewick-Richland-Pasco, WA Metro	49,857	89
Green Bay, WI Metro	49,856	90
Fond du Lac, WI Metro	49,771	91
Los Angeles-Long Beach-Santa Ana, CA Metro	49,766	92
Wausau, WI Metro	49,728	93
Houston-Baytown-Sugar Land, TX Metro	49,691	94
Hutchinson, MN Micro	49,595	95
Phoenix-Mesa-Scottsdale, AZ Metro	49,524	96
Laconia, NH Micro	49,436	97
Lancaster, PA Metro	49,430	98
Cincinnati-Middletown, OH-KY-IN Metro	49,414	99
Beaver Dam, WI Micro	49,404	100
Omaha-Council Bluffs, NE-IA Metro	49,358	101
Cedar Rapids, IA Metro	49,289	102
Oak Harbor, WA Micro	49,244	103
Willimantic, CT Micro	49,197	104
Allentown-Bethlehem-Easton, PA-NJ Metro	49,182	105
Columbus, OH Metro	49,175	106
Evanston, WY Micro	49,139	107
Adrian, MI Micro	49,050	108
Kill Devil Hills, NC Micro	48,980	109
York-Hanover, PA Metro	48,956	110
Rochelle, IL Micro	48,932	111
Grand Rapids-Wyoming, MI Metro	48,907	112
Albany-Schenectady-Troy, NY Metro	48,872	113
Gainesville, GA Metro	48,752	114
Stevens Point, WI Micro	48,752	115
Oshkosh-Neenah, WI Metro	48,661	116
Easton, MD Micro	48,608	117
Midland, MI Micro	48,504	118
Janesville, WI Metro	48,489	119
Reading, PA Metro	48,434	120
Las Vegas-Paradise, NV Metro	48,431	121
Portland-South Portland, ME Metro	48,431	122
St. Louis, MO-IL Metro	48,421	123
Brigham City, UT Micro	48,355	124
Charlottesville, VA Metro	48,276	125
Kapaa, HI Micro	48,088	126
Granbury, TX Micro	48,012	127
Springfield, IL Metro	47,974	128
Lansing-East Lansing, MI Metro	47,920	129
Harrisburg-Carlisle, PA Metro	47,877	130
Gettysburg, PA Micro	47,866	131
Nashville-Davidson-Murfreesboro, TN Metro	47,767	132
Auburn, IN Micro	47,684	133
Warner Robins, GA Metro	47,678	134
San Luis Obispo-Paso Robles, CA Metro	47,615	135
Rochester, NY Metro	47,537	136
Greeley, CO Metro	47,520	137
Monroe, WI Micro	47,505	138
Sidney, OH Micro	47,471	139
Rockford, IL Metro	47,416	140
Defiance, OH Micro	47,401	141
Huntsville, AL Metro	47,396	142
Manitowoc, WI Micro	47,347	143
Findlay, OH Micro	47,316	144
Sioux Falls, SD Metro	47,287	145
Wapakoneta, OH Micro	47,130	146
Keene, NH Micro	47,120	147
Santa Fe, NM Metro	47,120	148
Baraboo, WI Micro	47,101	149
Durham, NC Metro	47,091	150
Providence-New Bedford-Fall River, RI-MA Metro	47,051	151
Virginia Beach-Norfolk-Newport News, VA-NC Metro	47,002	152
St. Cloud, MN Metro	46,993	153
Warsaw, IN Micro	46,957	154
Atlantic City, NJ Metro	46,951	155
Hudson, NY Micro	46,867	156
Mount Vernon-Anacortes, WA Metro	46,851	157
Jacksonville, FL Metro	46,841	158
Corvallis, OR Metro	46,835	159
Elkhart-Goshen, IN Metro	46,769	160
Urbana, OH Micro	46,756	161
Akron, OH Metro	46,746	162
Key West-Marathon, FL Micro	46,741	163
Pierre, SD Micro	46,676	164
Bend, OR Metro	46,674	165
Peoria, IL Metro	46,641	166
Jackson, MI Metro	46,582	167
Lincoln, NE Metro	46,508	168
Angola, IN Micro	46,507	169
Kokomo, IN Metro	46,488	170
Kingston, NY Metro	46,468	171
Barre, VT Micro	46,440	172
Columbus, IN Metro	46,419	173
Riverside-San Bernardino-Ontario, CA Metro	46,419	174
Wichita, KS Metro	46,286	175
Cleveland-Elyria-Mentor, OH Metro	46,266	176
Celina, OH Micro	46,233	177
Ocean City, NJ Metro	46,225	178
Boise City-Nampa, ID Metro	46,200	179
Traverse City, MI Micro	46,191	180
Carson City, NV Metro	46,163	181
Cape Coral-Fort Myers, FL Metro	46,069	182
Fort Wayne, IN Metro	46,063	183
Fort Walton Beach-Crestview-Destin, FL Metro	46,040	184
Boone, IA Micro	45,983	185
Sandusky, OH Metro	45,979	186
Kankakee-Bradley, IL Metro	45,965	187
Jasper, IN Micro	45,811	188
Durango, CO Micro	45,738	189
Orlando, FL Metro	45,698	190
Lebanon, NH-VT Micro	45,684	191
Statesville-Mooresville, NC Micro	45,649	192
Mankato-North Mankato, MN Micro	45,643	193
Kendallville, IN Micro	45,528	194
Frankfort, KY Micro	45,520	195
Stockton, CA Metro	45,427	196
Newton, IA Micro	45,401	197
Southern Pines, NC Micro	45,379	198
Winchester, VA-WV Metro	45,360	199
Plymouth, IN Micro	45,343	200
Dayton, OH Metro	45,312	201
Sarasota-Bradenton-Venice, FL Metro	45,298	202
Idaho Falls, ID Metro	45,126	203
Owosso, MI Micro	45,124	204
Fallon, NV Micro	45,088	205
Ames, IA Metro	45,069	206
Bellefontaine, OH Micro	45,028	207
Topeka, KS Metro	45,022	208
Lebanon, PA Metro	45,018	209
Wisconsin Rapids-Marshfield, WI Micro	44,958	210
McPherson, KS Micro	44,950	211
Louisville, KY-IN Metro	44,943	212
Daphne-Fairhope, AL Micro	44,932	213
Bismarck, ND Metro	44,931	214
Springfield, MA Metro	44,910	215
Huntington, IN Micro	44,892	216
Columbia, TN Micro	44,888	217
Muscatine, IA Micro	44,868	218
New Ulm, MN Micro	44,856	219
Dixon, IL Micro	44,804	220
Crawfordsville, IN Micro	44,802	221
Pontiac, IL Micro	44,783	222
Ottawa-Streator, IL Micro	44,637	223
Columbia, SC Metro	44,607	224
Jefferson City, MO Metro	44,568	225
Michigan City-La Porte, IN Metro	44,563	226
Winston-Salem, NC Metro	44,550	227
Wooster, OH Micro	44,494	228
St. Marys, GA Micro	44,465	229
Ocean Pines, MD Micro	44,421	230
Davenport-Moline-Rock Island, IA-IL Metro	44,415	231
Kalamazoo-Portage, MI Metro	44,404	232
Iowa City, IA Metro	44,366	233
Palm Coast, FL Micro	44,299	234
Lincolnton, NC Micro	44,277	235
Bennington, VT Micro	44,271	236
Salem, OR Metro	44,197	237
Dover, DE Metro	44,155	238
Frankfort, IN Micro	44,142	239
Flint, MI Metro	44,141	240
Fremont, OH Micro	44,046	241
Cheyenne, WY Metro	44,045	242
Lexington-Fayette, KY Metro	44,010	243
Palm Bay-Melbourne-Titusville, FL Metro	43,979	244
Batavia, NY Micro	43,929	245
La Crosse, WI-MN Metro	43,911	246
Miami-Fort Lauderdale-Miami Beach, FL Metro	43,901	247
Modesto, CA Metro	43,894	248
Chambersburg, PA Micro	43,863	249
Wilmington, OH Micro	43,850	250
Hagerstown-Martinsburg, MD-WV Metro	43,834	251
Dubuque, IA Metro	43,825	252
Charleston-North Charleston, SC Metro	43,792	253
South Bend-Mishawaka, IN-MI Metro	43,755	254
Willmar, MN Micro	43,732	255
Lewisburg, PA Micro	43,695	256
Greensburg, IN Micro	43,694	257
Phoenix Lake-Cedar Ridge, CA Micro	43,628	258
Seaford, DE Micro	43,596	259
Bozeman, MT Micro	43,591	260
Greensboro-High Point, NC Metro	43,587	261
Norwalk, OH Micro	43,460	262
Vero Beach, FL Metro	43,418	263
San Antonio, TX Metro	43,387	264
Memphis, TN-MS-AR Metro	43,381	265
Hilo, HI Micro	43,355	266
Savannah, GA Metro	43,336	267
Albuquerque, NM Metro	43,313	268
Syracuse, NY Metro	43,296	269
Eau Claire, WI Metro	43,274	270
Sterling, IL Micro	43,257	271
Mount Vernon, OH Micro	43,252	272
Bellingham, WA Metro	43,156	273
Lincoln, IL Micro	43,150	274
Wabash, IN Micro	43,149	275
Logan, UT-ID Metro	43,137	276
Springfield, OH Metro	43,050	277
Hood River, OR Micro	43,044	278
Little Rock-North Little Rock, AR Metro	43,025	279
Columbus, NE Micro	42,963	280
Effingham, IL Micro	42,923	281
Canton-Massillon, OH Metro	42,914	282
Longview-Kelso, WA Metro	42,908	283
Greenville, OH Micro	42,860	284
Wilmington, NC Metro	42,782	285
Greenville, SC Metro	42,778	286
Midland, TX Metro	42,770	287
Marshall, MN Micro	42,769	288
Freeport, IL Micro	42,718	289
Spirit Lake, IA Micro	42,718	290
Lafayette, IN Metro	42,701	291
Flagstaff, AZ Metro	42,687	292
Pittsfield, MA Metro	42,652	293
Toledo, OH Metro	42,651	294
Seymour, IN Micro	42,640	295
Evansville, IN-KY Metro	42,607	296
Port St. Lucie-Fort Pierce, FL Metro	42,598	297
Menomonie, WI Micro	42,562	298
Champaign-Urbana, IL Metro	42,538	299
Sioux City, IA-NE-SD Metro	42,510	300
Morehead City, NC Micro	42,492	301
Lawrence, KS Metro	42,456	302
Merrill, WI Micro	42,409	303
Staunton-Waynesboro, VA Micro	42,408	304
Shelton, WA Micro	42,386	305
Peru, IN Micro	42,347	306
Birmingham-Hoover, AL Metro	42,332	307
Waterloo-Cedar Falls, IA Metro	42,254	308
Logansport, IN Micro	42,239	309

CBSA	INCOME ($)	RANK
Sanford, NC Micro	42,230	310
Anderson, IN Metro	42,221	311
Marion, OH Micro	42,212	312
Madison, IN Micro	42,183	313
North Vernon, IN Micro	42,172	314
Coldwater, MI Micro	42,124	315
Fargo, ND-MN Metro	42,123	316
Washington, OH Micro	42,118	317
Sturgis, MI Micro	42,091	318
Glens Falls, NY Metro	42,071	319
Roanoke, VA Metro	42,065	320
Vernal, UT Micro	42,028	321
Alexandria, MN Micro	41,997	322
Winona, MN Micro	41,988	323
Rockland, ME Micro	41,980	324
Tampa-St. Petersburg-Clearwater, FL Metro	41,979	325
Decatur, IN Micro	41,970	326
St. George, UT Metro	41,935	327
Vineland-Millville-Bridgeton, NJ Metro	41,927	328
Coeur d'Alene, ID Metro	41,911	329
Wenatchee, WA Metro	41,884	330
Buffalo-Cheektowaga-Tonawanda, NY Metro	41,879	331
Helena, MT Micro	41,869	332
Tulsa, OK Metro	41,859	333
Pascagoula, MS Metro	41,749	334
Burlington, NC Metro	41,744	335
Casper, WY Metro	41,711	336
Marshalltown, IA Micro	41,711	337
New Castle, IN Micro	41,685	338
Van Wert, OH Micro	41,670	339
Auburn, NY Micro	41,621	340
Bay City, MI Metro	41,620	341
Ashland, OH Micro	41,600	342
Battle Creek, MI Metro	41,579	343
Gainesville, TX Micro	41,547	344
Elizabethtown, KY Metro	41,466	345
Brainerd, MN Micro	41,426	346
Muskegon-Norton Shores, MI Metro	41,423	347
Lexington-Thomasville, NC Micro	41,408	348
Oskaloosa, IA Micro	41,356	349
Tyler, TX Metro	41,310	350
Dalton, GA Metro	41,292	351
Niles-Benton Harbor, MI Metro	41,275	352
Rapid City, SD Metro	41,184	353
Killeen-Temple-Fort Hood, TX Metro	41,182	354
Pittsburgh, PA Metro	41,145	355
Calhoun, GA Micro	41,107	356
Kearney, NE Micro	41,091	357
Victoria, TX Metro	41,079	358
Pensacola-Ferry Pass-Brent, FL Metro	41,059	359
Spokane, WA Metro	41,033	360
Connersville, IN Micro	41,020	361
Fayetteville, NC Metro	40,975	362
Albany-Lebanon, OR Micro	40,965	363
Billings, MT Metro	40,962	364
Montgomery, AL Metro	40,931	365
Austin, MN Micro	40,912	366
Sherman-Denison, TX Metro	40,874	367
Burlington, IA-IL Micro	40,857	368
Plattsburgh, NY Micro	40,848	369
Augusta-Richmond County, GA-SC Metro	40,837	370
St. Marys, PA Micro	40,823	371
Clinton, IA Micro	40,816	372
Salina, KS Micro	40,816	373
Oklahoma City, OK Metro	40,795	374
Jackson, MS Metro	40,729	375
Saginaw-Saginaw Township North, MI Metro	40,727	376
Ithaca, NY Metro	40,690	377
Knoxville, TN Metro	40,678	378
Spartanburg, SC Metro	40,662	379
Baton Rouge, LA Metro	40,661	380
Tiffin-Fostoria, OH Micro	40,657	381
Fayetteville-Springdale-Rogers, AR-MO Metro	40,626	382
Albert Lea, MN Micro	40,620	383
Hickory-Morganton-Lenoir, NC Metro	40,598	384
Salisbury, NC Micro	40,591	385
Rutland, VT Micro	40,583	386
Columbia, MO Metro	40,531	387
Tucson, AZ Metro	40,520	388
Mansfield, OH Metro	40,505	389
Harrisonburg, VA Metro	40,491	390
Ukiah, CA Micro	40,489	391
Brevard, NC Micro	40,451	392
Chattanooga, TN-GA Metro	40,433	393
Medford, OR Metro	40,433	394
Punta Gorda, FL Metro	40,395	395
Corning, NY Micro	40,393	396
Salisbury, MD Metro	40,379	397
Fremont, NE Micro	40,348	398
Dodge City, KS Micro	40,306	399
Decatur, IL Metro	40,304	400
Eugene-Springfield, OR Metro	40,290	401
Seneca, SC Micro	40,241	402
Fairmont, MN Micro	40,226	403
Pendleton-Hermiston, OR Micro	40,169	404
Myrtle Beach-Conway-North Myrtle Beach, SC Metro	40,166	405
Anderson, SC Metro	40,083	406
Grand Junction, CO Metro	40,073	407
Jackson, TN Metro	40,062	408
Jacksonville, IL Micro	40,057	409
Borger, TX Micro	40,032	410
Garden City, KS Micro	40,018	411
Chillicothe, OH Micro	40,013	412
Blackfoot, ID Micro	40,006	413
Brenham, TX Micro	39,986	414
Houma-Bayou Cane-Thibodaux, LA Metro	39,938	415
Duluth, MN-WI Metro	39,911	416
Lynchburg, VA Metro	39,911	417
Georgetown, SC Micro	39,876	418
Port Angeles, WA Micro	39,869	419
Elmira, NY Metro	39,851	420
Pocatello, ID Metro	39,841	421
Owensboro, KY Metro	39,835	422
Shelbyville, TN Micro	39,815	423
Seneca Falls, NY Micro	39,800	424
Grand Island, NE Micro	39,793	425
Watertown, SD Micro	39,791	426
Hanford-Corcoran, CA Metro	39,780	427
State College, PA Metro	39,751	428
Montrose, CO Micro	39,687	429
Taylorville, IL Micro	39,687	430
Selinsgrove, PA Micro	39,686	431
Madera, CA Metro	39,664	432
Albemarle, NC Micro	39,660	433
Lafayette, LA Metro	39,655	434
Beatrice, NE Micro	39,599	435
Panama City-Lynn Haven, FL Metro	39,591	436
Astoria, OR Micro	39,585	437
Grand Forks, ND-MN Metro	39,566	438
Fergus Falls, MN Micro	39,564	439
Clarksville, TN-KY Metro	39,528	440
Asheville, NC Metro	39,490	441
Lakeland-Winter Haven, FL Metro	39,451	442
Alma, MI Micro	39,447	443
Augusta-Waterville, ME Micro	39,407	444
Binghamton, NY Metro	39,403	445
Hastings, NE Micro	39,357	446
Mason City, IA Micro	39,334	447
Lima, OH Metro	39,274	448
Worthington, MN Micro	39,266	449
Liberal, KS Micro	39,236	450
Tallahassee, FL Metro	39,209	451
Wahpeton, ND-MN Micro	39,203	452
Brookings, SD Micro	39,190	453
Spencer, IA Micro	39,174	454
Zanesville, OH Micro	39,151	455
Macon, GA Metro	39,140	456
Lewiston-Auburn, ME Metro	39,136	457
North Platte, NE Micro	39,077	458
Platteville, WI Micro	39,069	459
Galesburg, IL Micro	39,052	460
Yankton, SD Micro	39,045	461
Erie, PA Metro	39,023	462
Escanaba, MI Micro	39,022	463
New Orleans-Metairie-Kenner, LA Metro	38,983	464
Decatur, AL Metro	38,969	465
Corpus Christi, TX Metro	38,957	466
Andrews, TX Micro	38,950	467
Woodward, OK Micro	38,949	468
New Bern, NC Micro	38,943	469
Sheridan, WY Micro	38,889	470
Brunswick, GA Metro	38,861	471
Bedford, IN Micro	38,859	472
Deltona-Daytona Beach-Ormond Beach, FL Metro	38,855	473
Warrensburg, MO Micro	38,849	474
Fort Dodge, IA Micro	38,842	475
Lexington, NE Micro	38,817	476
Gulfport-Biloxi, MS Metro	38,736	477
Hutchinson, KS Micro	38,735	478
Walla Walla, WA Micro	38,734	479
Centralia, WA Micro	38,691	480
Bucyrus, OH Micro	38,690	481
Youngstown-Warren-Boardman, OH-PA Metro	38,661	482
Amarillo, TX Metro	38,644	483
St. Joseph, MO-KS Metro	38,644	484
Bishop, CA Micro	38,621	485
Norfolk, NE Micro	38,614	486
Mountain Home, ID Micro	38,608	487
Cornelia, GA Micro	38,602	488
Guymon, OK Micro	38,593	489
Bakersfield, CA Metro	38,566	490
Prescott, AZ Metro	38,559	491
Aberdeen, SD Micro	38,536	492
Merced, CA Metro	38,534	493
Marquette, MI Micro	38,497	494
Lewiston, ID-WA Metro	38,493	495
Sayre, PA Micro	38,487	496
Warren, PA Micro	38,453	497
Lake Charles, LA Metro	38,440	498
LaGrange, GA Micro	38,433	499
Storm Lake, IA Micro	38,415	500
Tullahoma, TN Micro	38,376	501
Marion, IN Micro	38,332	502
Utica-Rome, NY Metro	38,308	503
Rocky Mount, NC Metro	38,303	504
Bloomsburg-Berwick, PA Micro	38,293	505
New Philadelphia-Dover, OH Micro	38,291	506
Prineville, OR Micro	38,270	507
Beaumont-Port Arthur, TX Metro	38,258	508
Longview, TX Metro	38,234	509
Ashtabula, OH Micro	38,228	510
Keokuk-Fort Madison, IA-MO Micro	38,226	511
Canton, IL Micro	38,213	512
Missoula, MT Metro	38,199	513
Moses Lake, WA Micro	38,185	514
Winfield, KS Micro	38,171	515
Pahrump, NV Micro	38,164	516
Goldsboro, NC Metro	38,137	517
Dunn, NC Micro	38,131	518
Fort Leonard Wood, MO Micro	38,115	519
Kalispell, MT Micro	38,084	520
Washington, IN Micro	38,025	521
City of The Dalles, OR Micro	38,017	522
Fresno, CA Metro	37,960	523
Twin Falls, ID Micro	37,936	524
Manhattan, KS Micro	37,925	525
Rome, GA Metro	37,870	526
Lancaster, SC Micro	37,854	527
Yakima, WA Metro	37,840	528
Vicksburg, MS Micro	37,834	529
Canon City, CO Micro	37,772	530
Fort Morgan, CO Micro	37,747	531
Atchison, KS Micro	37,724	532
North Wilkesboro, NC Micro	37,693	533
Redding, CA Metro	37,643	534
Cadillac, MI Micro	37,612	535
Bartlesville, OK Micro	37,587	536
Lawton, OK Metro	37,577	537
Quincy, IL-MO Micro	37,569	538
Sevierville, TN Micro	37,559	539
Jamestown, ND Micro	37,534	540
Jacksonville, NC Metro	37,525	541
Minot, ND Micro	37,512	542
Yuba City-Marysville, CA Metro	37,482	543
Muncie, IN Metro	37,476	544
Farmington, NM Metro	37,435	545
Bangor, ME Metro	37,423	546
Columbus, GA-AL Metro	37,423	547
Cortland, NY Micro	37,398	548
Cape Girardeau-Jackson, MO-IL Micro	37,382	549
Iron Mountain, MI-WI Micro	37,373	550
Marinette, WI-MI Micro	37,350	551
Cambridge, MD Micro	37,333	552
Scranton-Wilkes-Barre, PA Metro	37,315	553
Bemidji, MN Micro	37,307	554
Visalia-Porterville, CA Metro	37,305	555
Scottsburg, IN Micro	37,286	556
Williamsport, PA Metro	37,275	557
Bowling Green, KY Metro	37,235	558
Tupelo, MS Micro	37,202	559
Mount Pleasant, MI Micro	37,187	560
Richmond, IN Micro	37,166	561
Greenwood, SC Micro	37,165	562
Sault Ste. Marie, MI Micro	37,154	563
Springfield, MO Metro	37,129	564
Coshocton, OH Micro	37,112	565
Wichita Falls, TX Metro	37,052	566
Centralia, IL Micro	37,047	567
Mitchell, SD Micro	36,994	568
Bloomington, IN Metro	36,945	569
La Grande, OR Micro	36,934	570
Watertown-Fort Drum, NY Micro	36,922	571
Dickinson, ND Micro	36,830	572
Shelby, NC Micro	36,827	573
Terre Haute, IN Metro	36,803	574
Kerrville, TX Micro	36,773	575
Dumas, TX Micro	36,769	576
Gloversville, NY Micro	36,760	577
East Liverpool-Salem, OH Micro	36,744	578
Pueblo, CO Metro	36,731	579
Lufkin, TX Micro	36,701	580
Hays, KS Micro	36,692	581
Hannibal, MO Micro	36,681	582
Boone, NC Micro	36,640	583
Cleveland, TN Metro	36,640	584
Riverton, WY Micro	36,632	585
Florence, SC Metro	36,596	586
Alpena, MI Micro	36,573	587
Price, UT Micro	36,529	588
Big Rapids, MI Micro	36,512	589
Aberdeen, WA Micro	36,506	590
Cedar City, UT Micro	36,484	591
Mount Vernon, IL Micro	36,399	592
Marshall, TX Micro	36,373	593
Charleston, WV Metro	36,357	594
Parkersburg-Marietta, WV-OH Metro	36,240	595
Enid, OK Micro	36,234	596
Paducah, KY-IL Micro	36,213	597
Sumter, SC Metro	36,213	598
Mobile, AL Metro	36,153	599
Danville, IL Metro	36,126	600
Greenville, NC Metro	36,118	601
Olean, NY Micro	36,115	602
Oneonta, NY Micro	36,086	603
Sierra Vista-Douglas, AZ Micro	36,084	604
Ellensburg, WA Micro	36,077	605
San Angelo, TX Metro	36,050	606
Athens, TX Micro	36,045	607
Gaffney, SC Micro	35,998	608
New Castle, PA Micro	35,947	609
Williston, ND Micro	35,945	610
Waco, TX Metro	35,933	611
Roseburg, OR Micro	35,926	612
Jamestown-Dunkirk-Fredonia, NY Micro	35,884	613
Bradford, PA Micro	35,832	614
Rexburg, ID Micro	35,829	615
Harriman, TN Micro	35,826	616
Wilson, NC Micro	35,814	617
Athens-Clarke County, GA Metro	35,784	618
Hinesville-Fort Stewart, GA Metro	35,745	619
Meadville, PA Micro	35,743	620
Huntingdon, PA Micro	35,739	621

CBSA	INCOME ($)	RANK
Albany, GA Metro	35,713	622
Great Falls, MT Metro	35,676	623
Shreveport-Bossier City, LA Metro	35,612	624
Moscow, ID Micro	35,534	625
Pottsville, PA Micro	35,528	626
Abilene, TX Metro	35,462	627
Tuscaloosa, AL Metro	35,435	628
Tifton, GA Micro	35,397	629
Mount Airy, NC Micro	35,367	630
Marshall, MO Micro	35,363	631
Fort Valley, GA Micro	35,341	632
Snyder, TX Micro	35,328	633
Mount Pleasant, TX Micro	35,295	634
Newberry, SC Micro	35,288	635
Searcy, AR Micro	35,278	636
Palestine, TX Micro	35,259	637
Sterling, CO Micro	35,255	638
Enterprise-Ozark, AL Micro	35,235	639
Jesup, GA Micro	35,224	640
Great Bend, KS Micro	35,208	641
Amsterdam, NY Micro	35,189	642
Altoona, PA Metro	35,140	643
Carlsbad-Artesia, NM Micro	35,123	644
Pierre Part, LA Micro	35,025	645
Fort Polk South, LA Micro	35,020	646
Joplin, MO Metro	35,017	647
Marion-Herrin, IL Micro	34,996	648
Berlin, NH-VT Micro	34,978	649
Albertville, AL Micro	34,977	650
Ottumwa, IA Micro	34,977	651
Branson, MO Micro	34,966	652
Charleston-Mattoon, IL Micro	34,951	653
Odessa, TX Metro	34,950	654
Chico, CA Metro	34,936	655
Florence, AL Metro	34,914	656
Cullman, AL Micro	34,913	657
Bristol, VA Metro	34,870	658
Emporia, KS Micro	34,864	659
De Ridder, LA Micro	34,794	660
Cedartown, GA Micro	34,789	661
Yuma, AZ Metro	34,782	662
Texarkana, TX-Texarkana, AR Metro	34,779	663
Hot Springs, AR Metro	34,777	664
Milledgeville, GA Micro	34,775	665
Sulphur Springs, TX Micro	34,771	666
Malone, NY Micro	34,769	667
Kingsport-Bristol, TN-VA Metro	34,719	668
The Villages, FL Micro	34,694	669
Duncan, OK Micro	34,691	670
Shawnee, OK Micro	34,687	671
Maryville, MO Micro	34,682	672
Lewistown, PA Micro	34,670	673
Oil City, PA Micro	34,664	674
Pampa, TX Micro	34,659	675
Spearfish, SD Micro	34,652	676
Ocala, FL Metro	34,641	677
Ogdensburg-Massena, NY Micro	34,636	678
Chester, SC Micro	34,634	679
Clewiston, FL Micro	34,627	680
Scottsbluff, NE Micro	34,604	681
Mexico, MO Micro	34,603	682
Red Bluff, CA Micro	34,581	683
Weirton-Steubenville, WV-OH Metro	34,557	684
Blacksburg-Christiansburg-Radford, VA Metro	34,514	685
Morristown, TN Metro	34,509	686
Talladega-Sylacauga, AL Micro	34,433	687
Burley, ID Micro	34,417	688
Dothan, AL Metro	34,417	689
El Campo, TX Micro	34,403	690
El Centro, CA Metro	34,362	691
Macomb, IL Micro	34,353	692
Safford, AZ Micro	34,339	693
Fort Smith, AR-OK Metro	34,309	694
Elizabeth City, NC Micro	34,285	695
Dyersburg, TN Micro	34,262	696
Kinston, NC Micro	34,238	697
Batesville, AR Micro	34,219	698
Ontario, OR-ID Micro	34,202	699
Union, SC Micro	34,191	700
Anniston-Oxford, AL Metro	34,188	701
Hobbs, NM Micro	34,178	702
Scottsboro, AL Micro	34,151	703
Ponca City, OK Micro	34,145	704
Lubbock, TX Metro	34,127	705
Coos Bay, OR Micro	34,095	706
Columbus, MS Micro	34,087	707
Thomasville, GA Micro	34,056	708
Sedalia, MO Micro	34,032	709
Lake Havasu City-Kingman, AZ Micro	34,029	710
Huntsville, TX Micro	34,017	711
Homosassa Springs, FL Micro	33,977	712
Grants Pass, OR Micro	33,968	713
Mineral Wells, TX Micro	33,920	714
Monroe, LA Metro	33,917	715
Vincennes, IN Micro	33,884	716
Klamath Falls, OR Micro	33,840	717
Gainesville, FL Metro	33,826	718
New Iberia, LA Micro	33,824	719
Eureka-Arcata-Fortuna, CA Micro	33,818	720
Athens, TN Micro	33,738	721
Sikeston, MO Micro	33,730	722
Altus, OK Micro	33,713	723
Russellville, AR Micro	33,707	724
DuBois, PA Micro	33,695	725
Sunbury, PA Micro	33,693	726
Payson, AZ Micro	33,660	727
Richmond, KY Micro	33,627	728
Lock Haven, PA Micro	33,621	729
Paragould, AR Micro	33,611	730
Mayfield, KY Micro	33,591	731
Moberly, MO Micro	33,591	732
Pine Bluff, AR Metro	33,571	733
Brownwood, TX Micro	33,554	734
Stephenville, TX Micro	33,543	735
Levelland, TX Micro	33,532	736
Bay City, TX Micro	33,514	737
Madisonville, KY Micro	33,509	738
Huron, SD Micro	33,505	739
Picayune, MS Micro	33,501	740
Johnson City, TN Metro	33,500	741
Coffeyville, KS Micro	33,480	742
El Paso, TX Metro	33,474	743
Union City, TN-KY Micro	33,465	744
Farmington, MO Micro	33,448	745
Paris, TX Micro	33,410	746
Hattiesburg, MS Metro	33,399	747
Washington, NC Micro	33,362	748
Cumberland, MD-WV Metro	33,275	749
Gadsden, AL Metro	33,272	750
Crossville, TN Micro	33,261	751
Valdosta, GA Metro	33,255	752
Big Spring, TX Micro	33,247	753
Corsicana, TX Micro	33,246	754
Danville, KY Micro	33,246	755
Espanola, NM Micro	33,233	756
Plainview, TX Micro	33,189	757
Alamogordo, NM Micro	33,176	758
Somerset, PA Micro	33,153	759
Henderson, NC Micro	33,094	760
Clearlake, CA Micro	33,072	761
Dublin, GA Micro	33,055	762
Forest City, NC Micro	33,048	763
Cambridge, OH Micro	32,958	764
Greeneville, TN Micro	32,920	765
Danville, VA Metro	32,912	766
Okeechobee, FL Micro	32,903	767
Lawrenceburg, TN Micro	32,850	768
Butte-Silver Bow, MT Micro	32,843	769
Brookings, OR Micro	32,821	770
Jonesboro, AR Metro	32,779	771
Wheeling, WV-OH Metro	32,779	772
Laurinburg, NC Micro	32,734	773
Johnstown, PA Metro	32,732	774
Alexandria, LA Metro	32,720	775
El Dorado, AR Micro	32,696	776
Summerville, GA Micro	32,673	777
Parsons, KS Micro	32,594	778
Vernon, TX Micro	32,583	779
Alice, TX Micro	32,546	780
Lebanon, MO Micro	32,545	781
Auburn-Opelika, AL Metro	32,520	782
Abbeville, LA Micro	32,515	783
Sebring, FL Micro	32,500	784
Paris, TN Micro	32,499	785
Thomaston, GA Micro	32,491	786
Murray, KY Micro	32,489	787
Lake City, FL Micro	32,485	788
Arcadia, FL Micro	32,476	789
Clarksburg, WV Micro	32,462	790
Americus, GA Micro	32,413	791
Mountain Home, AR Micro	32,354	792
McMinnville, TN Micro	32,344	793
Martinsville, VA Micro	32,249	794
Nogales, AZ Micro	32,222	795
Orangeburg, SC Micro	32,216	796
Havre, MT Micro	32,175	797
Pittsburg, KS Micro	32,174	798
Ardmore, OK Micro	32,173	799
Indiana, PA Micro	32,156	800
Rolla, MO Micro	32,090	801
Glasgow, KY Micro	32,078	802
Walterboro, SC Micro	32,077	803
College Station-Bryan, TX Metro	32,041	804
Las Cruces, NM Metro	32,024	805
Fairmont, WV Micro	32,018	806
Clovis, NM Micro	31,976	807
Hammond, LA Micro	31,963	808
Wauchula, FL Micro	31,963	809
Toccoa, GA Micro	31,880	810
Harrisburg, IL Micro	31,833	811
Statesboro, GA Micro	31,815	812
Huntington-Ashland, WV-KY-OH Metro	31,805	813
Cookeville, TN Micro	31,787	814
Douglas, GA Micro	31,787	815
Jacksonville, TX Micro	31,763	816
McAlester, OK Micro	31,730	817
Oxford, MS Micro	31,727	818
Houghton, MI Micro	31,669	819
Grants, NM Micro	31,657	820
Beckley, WV Micro	31,616	821
Lamesa, TX Micro	31,591	822
Meridian, MS Micro	31,524	823
Silver City, NM Micro	31,504	824
Valley, AL Micro	31,491	825
Harrison, AR Micro	31,462	826
Arkadelphia, AR Micro	31,457	827
Point Pleasant, WV-OH Micro	31,455	828
Laramie, WY Micro	31,441	829
Mount Sterling, KY Micro	31,407	830
Camden, AR Micro	31,406	831
Campbellsville, KY Micro	31,396	832
Corinth, MS Micro	31,377	833
Crescent City North, CA Micro	31,327	834
Del Rio, TX Micro	31,305	835
Minden, LA Micro	31,265	836
Morgan City, LA Micro	31,233	837
Morgantown, WV Metro	31,211	838
Laredo, TX Metro	31,160	839
Palatka, FL Micro	31,044	840
Beeville, TX Micro	31,019	841
Rockingham, NC Micro	31,006	842
Muskogee, OK Micro	30,999	843
Roswell, NM Micro	30,904	844
Portsmouth, OH Micro	30,842	845
Stillwater, OK Micro	30,832	846
Durant, OK Micro	30,810	847
Magnolia, AR Micro	30,797	848
Kingsville, TX Micro	30,743	849
Laurel, MS Micro	30,706	850
Pullman, WA Micro	30,698	851
Hereford, TX Micro	30,644	852
Bainbridge, GA Micro	30,601	853
Jennings, LA Micro	30,586	854
Hope, AR Micro	30,562	855
Brookhaven, MS Micro	30,527	856
Crowley, LA Micro	30,517	857
Central City, KY Micro	30,493	858
Nacogdoches, TX Micro	30,464	859
Ada, OK Micro	30,437	860
Waycross, GA Micro	30,383	861
Taos, NM Micro	30,370	862
Somerset, KY Micro	30,175	863
Miami, OK Micro	30,040	864
Poplar Bluff, MO Micro	30,025	865
London, KY Micro	29,972	866
Moultrie, GA Micro	29,846	867
Grenada, MS Micro	29,814	868
Vermillion, SD Micro	29,791	869
Las Vegas, NM Micro	29,724	870
Brownsville, TN Micro	29,698	871
Lumberton, NC Micro	29,657	872
Kirksville, MO Micro	29,574	873
Fitzgerald, GA Micro	29,510	874
Blytheville, AR Micro	29,492	875
Uvalde, TX Micro	29,461	876
Bluefield, WV-VA Micro	29,439	877
Athens, OH Micro	29,428	878
Tahlequah, OK Micro	29,416	879
Bennettsville, SC Micro	29,410	880
Ruston, LA Micro	29,263	881
Dillon, SC Micro	29,200	882
Brownsville-Harlingen, TX Metro	28,974	883
Portales, NM Micro	28,937	884
Maysville, KY Micro	28,900	885
Roanoke Rapids, NC Micro	28,777	886
West Plains, MO Micro	28,643	887
Natchitoches, LA Micro	28,504	888
Forrest City, AR Micro	28,057	889
Sweetwater, TX Micro	27,991	890
Carbondale, IL Micro	27,839	891
Oak Hill, WV Micro	27,825	892
Cordele, GA Micro	27,796	893
McComb, MS Micro	27,498	894
Troy, AL Micro	27,478	895
McAllen-Edinburg-Pharr, TX Metro	27,453	896
Bastrop, LA Micro	27,213	897
Greenville, MS Micro	27,178	898
La Follette, TN Micro	27,170	899
Starkville, MS Micro	27,095	900
Newport, TN Micro	27,059	901
Gallup, NM Micro	26,941	902
Yazoo City, MS Micro	26,716	903
Kennett, MO Micro	26,654	904
Indianola, MS Micro	26,511	905
Bogalusa, LA Micro	26,220	906
Natchez, MS-LA Micro	26,087	907
Pecos, TX Micro	25,773	908
Cleveland, MS Micro	25,404	909
Opelousas-Eunice, LA Micro	25,061	910
Clarksdale, MS Micro	24,880	911
Greenwood, MS Micro	24,847	912
Selma, AL Micro	24,823	913
West Helena, AR Micro	24,650	914
Corbin, KY Micro	24,314	915
Tuskegee, AL Micro	23,970	916
Eagle Pass, TX Micro	23,955	917
Raymondville, TX Micro	23,497	918
Deming, NM Micro	23,189	919
Tallulah, LA Micro	23,154	920
Middlesborough, KY Micro	21,122	921
Rio Grande City, TX Micro	18,866	922
CBSA Median	39,034	
United States Median	46,475	

Average Household Income

CBSA	INCOME ($)	RANK
Bridgeport-Stamford-Norwalk, CT Metro	112,345	1
San Jose-Sunnyvale-Santa Clara, CA Metro	111,425	2
Los Alamos, NM Micro	98,853	3
San Francisco-Oakland-Fremont, CA Metro	96,646	4
Washington-Arlington-Alexandria, DC-VA-MD-WV Metro	91,250	5
Edwards, CO Micro	90,722	6
Trenton-Ewing, NJ Metro	87,701	7
Oxnard-Thousand Oaks-Ventura, CA Metro	85,139	8
Boulder, CO Metro	84,363	9
Jackson, WY-ID Micro	83,947	10
Santa Cruz-Watsonville, CA Metro	83,726	11
Boston-Cambridge-Quincy, MA-NH Metro	83,355	12
Naples-Marco Island, FL Metro	80,522	13
Napa, CA Metro	80,490	14
Silverthorne, CO Micro	80,257	15
New York-Newark-Edison, NY-NJ-PA Metro	79,327	16
Santa Rosa-Petaluma, CA Metro	77,976	17
Minneapolis-St. Paul-Bloomington, MN-WI Metro	77,413	18
Torrington, CT Micro	77,259	19
Juneau, AK Micro	77,236	20
Denver-Aurora, CO Metro	77,118	21
Ann Arbor, MI Metro	76,302	22
Chicago-Naperville-Joliet, IL-IN-WI Metro	75,420	23
Atlanta-Sandy Springs-Marietta, GA Metro	75,313	24
Manchester-Nashua, NH Metro	74,597	25
Hartford-West Hartford-East Hartford, CT Metro	74,377	26
Easton, MD Micro	74,194	27
Vallejo-Fairfield, CA Metro	73,984	28
Raleigh-Cary, NC Metro	73,812	29
Santa Barbara-Santa Maria-Goleta, CA Metro	73,600	30
Anchorage, AK Metro	73,599	31
Gardnerville Ranchos, NV Micro	73,249	32
Salinas, CA Metro	72,295	33
San Diego-Carlsbad-San Marcos, CA Metro	72,196	34
Poughkeepsie-Newburgh-Middletown, NY Metro	72,170	35
Dallas-Fort Worth-Arlington, TX Metro	72,036	36
Los Angeles-Long Beach-Santa Ana, CA Metro	71,787	37
Austin-Round Rock, TX Metro	71,667	38
Honolulu, HI Metro	71,560	39
Baltimore-Towson, MD Metro	71,493	40
Lexington Park, MD Micro	71,286	41
Seattle-Tacoma-Bellevue, WA Metro	71,206	42
Philadelphia-Camden-Wilmington, PA-NJ-DE-MD Metro	71,099	43
Hilton Head Island-Beaufort, SC Micro	70,748	44
Fort Collins-Loveland, CO Metro	70,466	45
Detroit-Warren-Livonia, MI Metro	70,323	46
Rochester, MN Metro	70,294	47
Salt Lake City, UT Metro	69,992	48
Kahului-Wailuku, HI Micro	69,417	49
Charlotte-Gastonia-Concord, NC-SC Metro	69,377	50
Truckee-Grass Valley, CA Micro	69,241	51
Houston-Baytown-Sugar Land, TX Metro	69,234	52
Norwich-New London, CT Metro	69,176	53
New Haven-Milford, CT Metro	68,740	54
Worcester, MA Metro	68,588	55
Kodiak, AK Micro	68,509	56
Reno-Sparks, NV Metro	68,130	57
Holland-Grand Haven, MI Metro	67,671	58
Madison, WI Metro	67,669	59
Ogden-Clearfield, UT Metro	67,411	60
Sacramento-Arden-Arcade-Roseville, CA Metro	67,173	61
Concord, NH Micro	67,151	62
Portland-Vancouver-Beaverton, OR-WA Metro	67,071	63
Vero Beach, FL Metro	66,887	64
Colorado Springs, CO Metro	66,680	65
Appleton, WI Metro	66,482	66
Phoenix-Mesa-Scottsdale, AZ Metro	66,404	67
Indianapolis, IN Metro	66,290	68
Midland, MI Micro	66,038	69
Monroe, MI Metro	65,882	70
Barnstable Town, MA Metro	65,816	71
Bloomington-Normal, IL Metro	65,720	72
Richmond, VA Metro	65,649	73
Fairbanks, AK Metro	65,623	74
Bremerton-Silverdale, WA Metro	65,384	75
Kansas City, MO-KS Metro	65,373	76
Ketchikan, AK Micro	65,296	77
Cincinnati-Middletown, OH-KY-IN Metro	65,200	78
Burlington-South Burlington, VT Metro	65,142	79
Santa Fe, NM Metro	65,076	80
Milwaukee-Waukesha-West Allis, WI Metro	65,031	81
Key West-Marathon, FL Micro	65,010	82
Des Moines, IA Metro	64,944	83
Ocean City, NJ Metro	64,763	84
Charlottesville, VA Metro	64,747	85
Durham, NC Metro	64,450	86
Red Wing, MN Micro	64,414	87
Gillette, WY Micro	64,362	88
Cape Coral-Fort Myers, FL Metro	64,142	89
Kill Devil Hills, NC Micro	64,111	90
Columbus, OH Metro	64,065	91
Provo-Orem, UT Metro	64,065	92
Miami-Fort Lauderdale-Miami Beach, FL Metro	63,828	93
Olympia, WA Metro	63,726	94
St. Louis, MO-IL Metro	63,646	95
Sarasota-Bradenton-Venice, FL Metro	63,619	96
Laconia, NH Micro	63,498	97
Nashville-Davidson-Murfreesboro, TN Metro	63,409	98
Faribault-Northfield, MN Micro	63,341	99
San Luis Obispo-Paso Robles, CA Metro	63,332	100
Omaha-Council Bluffs, NE-IA Metro	63,154	101
Racine, WI Metro	63,141	102
Granbury, TX Micro	63,067	103
Las Vegas-Paradise, NV Metro	62,939	104
East Stroudsburg, PA Micro	62,859	105
Kapaa, HI Micro	62,855	106
Gainesville, GA Metro	62,823	107
Albany-Schenectady-Troy, NY Metro	62,673	108
Kennewick-Richland-Pasco, WA Metro	62,548	109
Allentown-Bethlehem-Easton, PA-NJ Metro	62,524	110
Corvallis, OR Metro	62,501	111
Portland-South Portland, ME Metro	62,357	112
Durango, CO Micro	62,307	113
Whitewater, WI Micro	62,110	114
Bend, OR Metro	61,982	115
Jacksonville, FL Metro	61,957	116
Hudson, NY Micro	61,877	117
Springfield, IL Metro	61,839	118
Grand Rapids-Wyoming, MI Metro	61,812	119
Huntsville, AL Metro	61,807	120
Cleveland-Elyria-Mentor, OH Metro	61,522	121
Watertown-Fort Atkinson, WI Micro	61,229	122
Akron, OH Metro	61,145	123
Providence-New Bedford-Fall River, RI-MA Metro	61,102	124
Orlando, FL Metro	60,961	125
Harrisburg-Carlisle, PA Metro	60,903	126
Rochester, NY Metro	60,897	127
Lansing-East Lansing, MI Metro	60,799	128
Lancaster, PA Metro	60,731	129
Mount Vernon-Anacortes, WA Metro	60,619	130
Greeley, CO Metro	60,584	131
Southern Pines, NC Micro	60,513	132
Oak Harbor, WA Micro	60,445	133
Cedar Rapids, IA Metro	60,439	134
Allegan, MI Micro	60,426	135
Green Bay, WI Metro	60,323	136
Wausau, WI Metro	60,254	137
Reading, PA Metro	60,225	138
Savannah, GA Metro	60,200	139
Riverside-San Bernardino-Ontario, CA Metro	60,159	140
Sheboygan, WI Metro	60,124	141
Midland, TX Metro	60,114	142
Iowa City, IA Metro	60,073	143
Stevens Point, WI Micro	60,004	144
Port St. Lucie-Fort Pierce, FL Metro	59,769	145
Atlantic City, NJ Metro	59,669	146
Virginia Beach-Norfolk-Newport News, VA-NC Metro	59,634	147
Boise City-Nampa, ID Metro	59,508	148
Rochelle, IL Micro	59,481	149
Lexington-Fayette, KY Metro	59,447	150
Willimantic, CT Micro	59,436	151
Traverse City, MI Micro	59,418	152
Oshkosh-Neenah, WI Metro	59,381	153
Statesville-Mooresville, NC Micro	59,280	154
Louisville, KY-IN Metro	59,272	155
Rockford, IL Metro	59,191	156
Daphne-Fairhope, AL Micro	59,172	157
Kingston, NY Metro	59,136	158
York-Hanover, PA Metro	59,083	159
Lebanon, NH-VT Micro	58,995	160
Winston-Salem, NC Metro	58,993	161
Adrian, MI Micro	58,945	162
Lincoln, NE Metro	58,945	163
Bennington, VT Micro	58,912	164
Keene, NH Micro	58,904	165
Memphis, TN-MS-AR Metro	58,869	166
Stockton, CA Metro	58,854	167
Fort Walton Beach-Crestview-Destin, FL Metro	58,522	168
Peoria, IL Metro	58,483	169
Ames, IA Metro	58,393	170
Findlay, OH Micro	58,367	171
Rock Springs, WY Micro	58,365	172
Sioux Falls, SD Metro	58,348	173
Birmingham-Hoover, AL Metro	58,281	174
Carson City, NV Metro	58,193	175
Dayton, OH Metro	58,188	176
Columbia, SC Metro	58,109	177
Janesville, WI Metro	58,095	178
St. Cloud, MN Metro	58,062	179
Owatonna, MN Micro	58,033	180
Fort Wayne, IN Metro	58,004	181
Greensboro-High Point, NC Metro	57,988	182
Ocean Pines, MD Micro	57,959	183
Barre, VT Micro	57,940	184
Elkhart-Goshen, IN Metro	57,933	185
Charleston-North Charleston, SC Metro	57,928	186
Wichita, KS Metro	57,743	187
San Antonio, TX Metro	57,677	188
Sandusky, OH Metro	57,668	189
Jackson, MI Metro	57,616	190
Hilo, HI Micro	57,585	191
Pierre, SD Micro	57,561	192
Fond du Lac, WI Metro	57,559	193
Albuquerque, NM Metro	57,552	194
Monroe, WI Micro	57,467	195
Columbus, IN Metro	57,443	196
Kalamazoo-Portage, MI Metro	57,331	197
Lawrence, KS Metro	57,330	198
Tampa-St. Petersburg-Clearwater, FL Metro	57,307	199
Wapakoneta, OH Micro	57,201	200
Warsaw, IN Micro	57,126	201
Beaver Dam, WI Micro	57,105	202
Springfield, MA Metro	57,081	203
Hutchinson, MN Micro	56,955	204
Sidney, OH Micro	56,954	205
Warner Robins, GA Metro	56,954	206
Kankakee-Bradley, IL Metro	56,928	207
Wilmington, NC Metro	56,922	208
Baraboo, WI Micro	56,912	209
Palm Coast, FL Micro	56,900	210
Pittsfield, MA Metro	56,885	211
Greenville, SC Metro	56,868	212
Palm Bay-Melbourne-Titusville, FL Metro	56,811	213
Elko, NV Micro	56,801	214
Modesto, CA Metro	56,737	215
Winchester, VA-WV Metro	56,713	216
Idaho Falls, ID Metro	56,685	217
Fallon, NV Micro	56,574	218
Little Rock-North Little Rock, AR Metro	56,549	219
Ithaca, NY Metro	56,484	220
Mankato-North Mankato, MN Micro	56,452	221
Syracuse, NY Metro	56,432	222
Phoenix Lake-Cedar Ridge, CA Micro	56,378	223
Flint, MI Metro	56,377	224
Kokomo, IN Metro	56,299	225
Seaford, DE Micro	56,163	226
Lewisburg, PA Micro	56,157	227
Tyler, TX Metro	56,115	228
Bellingham, WA Metro	56,096	229
Georgetown, SC Micro	56,064	230
Dubuque, IA Metro	56,007	231
Gettysburg, PA Micro	55,952	232
Tulsa, OK Metro	55,912	233
Angola, IN Micro	55,904	234
Wenatchee, WA Metro	55,857	235
Bozeman, MT Micro	55,845	236
Pittsburgh, PA Metro	55,790	237
Davenport-Moline-Rock Island, IA-IL Metro	55,765	238
Manitowoc, WI Micro	55,765	239
Columbia, TN Micro	55,737	240
La Crosse, WI-MN Metro	55,732	241
South Bend-Mishawaka, IN-MI Metro	55,692	242
Auburn, IN Micro	55,677	243
Bismarck, ND Metro	55,676	244
Champaign-Urbana, IL Metro	55,613	245
Jackson, MS Metro	55,563	246
Toledo, OH Metro	55,476	247
Lebanon, PA Metro	55,456	248
Jasper, IN Micro	55,404	249
Lafayette, IN Metro	55,396	250
Brigham City, UT Micro	55,388	251
Flagstaff, AZ Metro	55,379	252
Topeka, KS Metro	55,356	253
Wisconsin Rapids-Marshfield, WI Micro	55,283	254
Knoxville, TN Metro	55,268	255
Salem, OR Metro	55,255	256
Canton-Massillon, OH Metro	55,214	257
Frankfort, KY Micro	55,178	258
New Orleans-Metairie-Kenner, LA Metro	55,169	259
Tucson, AZ Metro	55,114	260
Morehead City, NC Micro	55,113	261
Owosso, MI Micro	55,094	262
Evanston, WY Micro	55,073	263
Muscatine, IA Micro	55,071	264
New Ulm, MN Micro	55,051	265
Boone, IA Micro	55,029	266
Jefferson City, MO Metro	55,017	267
Defiance, OH Micro	55,006	268
Willmar, MN Micro	54,989	269
Roanoke, VA Metro	54,851	270
Sanford, NC Micro	54,844	271
Spirit Lake, IA Micro	54,802	272
Celina, OH Micro	54,797	273
Cheyenne, WY Metro	54,791	274
Evansville, IN-KY Metro	54,765	275
Buffalo-Cheektowaga-Tonawanda, NY Metro	54,667	276
Ukiah, CA Micro	54,664	277
Fargo, ND-MN Metro	54,644	278
Columbia, MO Metro	54,628	279
Sioux City, IA-NE-SD Metro	54,493	280
Baton Rouge, LA Metro	54,399	281
Niles-Benton Harbor, MI Metro	54,389	282
Urbana, OH Micro	54,383	283
Lafayette, LA Metro	54,372	284
Logan, UT-ID Metro	54,340	285
Medford, OR Metro	54,324	286
Ottawa-Streator, IL Micro	54,318	287
Montgomery, AL Metro	54,287	288
Plymouth, IN Micro	54,272	289
Dixon, IL Micro	54,233	290
Wooster, OH Micro	54,181	291
Huntington, IN Micro	54,117	292
Pensacola-Ferry Pass-Brent, FL Metro	54,110	293
Oklahoma City, OK Metro	54,101	294
Rockland, ME Micro	53,979	295
Victoria, TX Metro	53,924	296
Augusta-Richmond County, GA-SC Metro	53,901	297
Dover, DE Metro	53,900	298
Newton, IA Micro	53,819	299
Waterloo-Cedar Falls, IA Metro	53,819	300
Michigan City-La Porte, IN Metro	53,806	301
Pontiac, IL Micro	53,775	302
Tallahassee, FL Metro	53,767	303
McPherson, KS Micro	53,758	304
Eau Claire, WI Metro	53,746	305
Fremont, OH Micro	53,711	306
Hood River, OR Micro	53,695	307
Lincolnton, NC Micro	53,695	308
Chattanooga, TN-GA Metro	53,652	309

CBSA	INCOME ($)	RANK
Dalton, GA Metro	53,596	310
Bellefontaine, OH Micro	53,524	311
Gainesville, TX Micro	53,513	312
Crawfordsville, IN Micro	53,500	313
Hagerstown-Martinsburg, MD-WV Metro	53,472	314
Spokane, WA Metro	53,439	315
Billings, MT Metro	53,346	316
Vineland-Millville-Bridgeton, NJ Metro	53,338	317
Brunswick, GA Metro	53,325	318
Mount Vernon, OH Micro	53,279	319
Jackson, TN Metro	53,272	320
St. George, UT Metro	53,263	321
Saginaw-Saginaw Township North, MI Metro	53,255	322
Glens Falls, NY Metro	53,250	323
Macon, GA Metro	53,233	324
Springfield, OH Metro	53,199	325
Bay City, MI Metro	53,190	326
Rapid City, SD Metro	53,188	327
Anderson, IN Metro	53,171	328
Casper, WY Metro	53,151	329
Punta Gorda, FL Metro	53,105	330
Fayetteville-Springdale-Rogers, AR-MO Metro	53,097	331
Chambersburg, PA Micro	53,075	332
Sherman-Denison, TX Metro	53,071	333
Effingham, IL Micro	53,035	334
Kendallville, IN Micro	52,913	335
Sheridan, WY Micro	52,864	336
Eugene-Springfield, OR Metro	52,824	337
Hanford-Corcoran, CA Metro	52,754	338
Burlington, NC Metro	52,739	339
Greenville, OH Micro	52,654	340
Prescott, AZ Metro	52,654	341
Spartanburg, SC Metro	52,628	342
State College, PA Metro	52,609	343
Corpus Christi, TX Metro	52,601	344
Austin, MN Micro	52,594	345
Staunton-Waynesboro, VA Micro	52,582	346
Greensburg, IN Micro	52,559	347
Grand Junction, CO Metro	52,541	348
Sterling, IL Micro	52,541	349
Bartlesville, OK Micro	52,475	350
Batavia, NY Micro	52,467	351
Alexandria, MN Micro	52,466	352
Corning, NY Micro	52,465	353
Fresno, CA Metro	52,445	354
Salisbury, MD Metro	52,425	355
Winona, MN Micro	52,417	356
Longview-Kelso, WA Metro	52,336	357
St. Marys, GA Micro	52,329	358
Killeen-Temple-Fort Hood, TX Metro	52,287	359
Wilmington, OH Micro	52,285	360
Brenham, TX Micro	52,228	361
Decatur, IL Metro	52,228	362
Menomonie, WI Micro	52,190	363
Coeur d'Alene, ID Metro	52,152	364
Madera, CA Metro	52,131	365
Myrtle Beach-Conway-N. Myrtle Beach, SC Metro	52,067	366
Columbus, NE Micro	52,009	367
Brainerd, MN Micro	51,941	368
Bakersfield, CA Metro	51,806	369
Washington, OH Micro	51,790	370
Freeport, IL Micro	51,787	371
Battle Creek, MI Metro	51,776	372
Harrisonburg, VA Metro	51,749	373
New Castle, IN Micro	51,700	374
Asheville, NC Metro	51,675	375
Kerrville, TX Micro	51,596	376
Frankfort, IN Micro	51,592	377
Deltona-Daytona Beach-Ormond Beach, FL Metro	51,554	378
Amarillo, TX Metro	51,541	379
Houma-Bayou Cane-Thibodaux, LA Metro	51,535	380
Logansport, IN Micro	51,515	381
Lakeland-Winter Haven, FL Metro	51,512	382
Lincoln, IL Micro	51,507	383
Binghamton, NY Metro	51,503	384
LaGrange, GA Micro	51,482	385
Seymour, IN Micro	51,444	386
Rutland, VT Micro	51,426	387
Marion, OH Micro	51,387	388
Helena, MT Micro	51,358	389
Norwalk, OH Micro	51,348	390
Muskegon-Norton Shores, MI Metro	51,342	391
Lake Charles, LA Metro	51,325	392
Pocatello, ID Metro	51,272	393
Pascagoula, MS Metro	51,248	394
Longview, TX Metro	51,244	395
Marshall, MN Micro	51,243	396
Athens-Clarke County, GA Metro	51,185	397
Shelton, WA Micro	51,171	398
Owensboro, KY Metro	51,168	399
Elizabethtown, KY Metro	51,143	400
Calhoun, GA Micro	51,135	401
Burlington, IA-IL Micro	51,039	402
Mansfield, OH Metro	51,032	403
Lynchburg, VA Metro	51,029	404
Seneca, SC Micro	51,029	405
Panama City-Lynn Haven, FL Metro	51,025	406
Bowling Green, KY Metro	51,006	407
Bishop, CA Micro	50,941	408
Wabash, IN Micro	50,937	409
Auburn, NY Micro	50,920	410
Fayetteville, NC Metro	50,911	411
Vernal, UT Micro	50,891	412
Plattsburgh, NY Micro	50,858	413
Elmira, NY Metro	50,853	414
Beaumont-Port Arthur, TX Metro	50,851	415
Sturgis, MI Micro	50,817	416
Coldwater, MI Micro	50,758	417
Muncie, IN Metro	50,748	418
Hickory-Morganton-Lenoir, NC Metro	50,735	419
Charleston, WV Metro	50,725	420
Visalia-Porterville, CA Metro	50,723	421
Astoria, OR Micro	50,697	422
Decatur, AL Metro	50,695	423
Vicksburg, MS Micro	50,676	424
Anderson, SC Metro	50,656	425
Dodge City, KS Micro	50,593	426
Lexington-Thomasville, NC Micro	50,570	427
Columbus, GA-AL Metro	50,540	428
Kalispell, MT Micro	50,529	429
Kearney, NE Micro	50,527	430
Redding, CA Metro	50,497	431
Peru, IN Micro	50,469	432
Gulfport-Biloxi, MS Metro	50,388	433
Albany-Lebanon, OR Micro	50,386	434
Decatur, IN Micro	50,379	435
Ellensburg, WA Micro	50,357	436
Merced, CA Metro	50,289	437
Gainesville, FL Metro	50,279	438
Yakima, WA Metro	50,256	439
Brevard, NC Micro	50,239	440
Marshalltown, IA Micro	50,210	441
Salisbury, NC Micro	50,210	442
Grand Forks, ND-MN Metro	50,197	443
Port Angeles, WA Micro	50,193	444
Salina, KS Micro	50,187	445
Rome, GA Metro	50,183	446
Garden City, KS Micro	50,173	447
Brookings, SD Micro	50,140	448
Pendleton-Hermiston, OR Micro	50,125	449
Madison, IN Micro	50,110	450
New Bern, NC Micro	50,088	451
Erie, PA Metro	50,081	452
Selinsgrove, PA Micro	50,052	453
Fergus Falls, MN Micro	50,044	454
Zanesville, OH Micro	50,033	455
Ashland, OH Micro	50,012	456
Greenville, NC Metro	50,011	457
Rocky Mount, NC Metro	49,992	458
Hays, KS Micro	49,966	459
Jacksonville, IL Micro	49,934	460
Connersville, IN Micro	49,915	461
Watertown, SD Micro	49,900	462
Yankton, SD Micro	49,881	463
Cornelia, GA Micro	49,862	464
Worthington, MN Micro	49,849	465
Fairmont, MN Micro	49,845	466
Shreveport-Bossier City, LA Metro	49,842	467
Spencer, IA Micro	49,834	468
Yuba City-Marysville, CA Metro	49,829	469
Chillicothe, OH Micro	49,826	470
Waco, TX Metro	49,815	471
Mason City, IA Micro	49,812	472
Duluth, MN-WI Metro	49,796	473
Florence, SC Metro	49,766	474
Lima, OH Metro	49,754	475
Bloomington, IN Metro	49,745	476
Merrill, WI Micro	49,729	477
Missoula, MT Metro	49,712	478
Borger, TX Micro	49,655	479
Walla Walla, WA Micro	49,654	480
Springfield, MO Metro	49,643	481
Liberal, KS Micro	49,623	482
Manhattan, KS Micro	49,592	483
Cambridge, MD Micro	49,587	484
North Vernon, IN Micro	49,574	485
Youngstown-Warren-Boardman, OH-PA Metro	49,531	486
Lewiston-Auburn, ME Metro	49,525	487
Grand Island, NE Micro	49,523	488
Albemarle, NC Micro	49,515	489
Tifton, GA Micro	49,495	490
Albert Lea, MN Micro	49,470	491
Scranton-Wilkes-Barre, PA Metro	49,461	492
Tullahoma, TN Micro	49,455	493
Albany, GA Metro	49,321	494
Bloomsburg-Berwick, PA Micro	49,319	495
Van Wert, OH Micro	49,309	496
Taylorville, IL Micro	49,272	497
St. Joseph, MO-KS Metro	49,256	498
Clarksville, TN-KY Metro	49,237	499
Boone, NC Micro	49,219	500
Hutchinson, KS Micro	49,209	501
Tuscaloosa, AL Metro	49,152	502
Lewiston, ID-WA Metro	49,109	503
Tupelo, MS Micro	49,109	504
Mitchell, SD Micro	49,098	505
Augusta-Waterville, ME Micro	49,083	506
Goldsboro, NC Metro	49,065	507
Utica-Rome, NY Metro	49,060	508
Mobile, AL Metro	49,049	509
Hastings, NE Micro	49,045	510
Twin Falls, ID Micro	49,028	511
Mount Pleasant, MI Micro	49,026	512
Fort Dodge, IA Micro	49,007	513
North Platte, NE Micro	48,987	514
Oskaloosa, IA Micro	48,986	515
Blackfoot, ID Micro	48,941	516
San Angelo, TX Metro	48,939	517
Fremont, NE Micro	48,920	518
Chico, CA Metro	48,903	519
Athens, TX Micro	48,891	520
Cape Girardeau-Jackson, MO-IL Micro	48,872	521
Seneca Falls, NY Micro	48,844	522
Montrose, CO Micro	48,805	523
Pueblo, CO Metro	48,736	524
Woodward, OK Micro	48,710	525
Marquette, MI Micro	48,663	526
Paducah, KY-IL Micro	48,663	527
Marion, IN Micro	48,659	528
Snyder, TX Micro	48,635	529
Aberdeen, SD Micro	48,633	530
Shelbyville, TN Micro	48,626	531
Escanaba, MI Micro	48,589	532
Sayre, PA Micro	48,542	533
Centralia, WA Micro	48,540	534
Cleveland, TN Metro	48,518	535
Moses Lake, WA Micro	48,496	536
Greenwood, SC Micro	48,476	537
Wichita Falls, TX Metro	48,474	538
Warrensburg, MO Micro	48,403	539
Quincy, IL-MO Micro	48,402	540
Harriman, TN Micro	48,337	541
Wilson, NC Micro	48,332	542
Winfield, KS Micro	48,310	543
Bangor, ME Metro	48,237	544
Storm Lake, IA Micro	48,201	545
Bemidji, MN Micro	48,200	546
Clinton, IA Micro	48,199	547
Keokuk-Fort Madison, IA-MO Micro	48,164	548
Lubbock, TX Metro	48,160	549
Williston, ND Micro	48,154	550
Milledgeville, GA Micro	48,108	551
St. Marys, PA Micro	48,099	552
College Station-Bryan, TX Metro	48,093	553
Alma, MI Micro	48,082	554
Mount Pleasant, TX Micro	48,039	555
Monroe, LA Metro	48,027	556
Cortland, NY Micro	48,026	557
North Wilkesboro, NC Micro	48,023	558
Guymon, OK Micro	48,022	559
Williamsport, PA Metro	48,019	560
Tiffin-Fostoria, OH Micro	48,012	561
Dunn, NC Micro	48,007	562
Lexington, NE Micro	48,004	563
Galesburg, IL Micro	48,003	564
Farmington, NM Metro	47,999	565
Platteville, WI Micro	47,920	566
Sulphur Springs, TX Micro	47,888	567
Canton, IL Micro	47,855	568
Texarkana, TX-Texarkana, AR Metro	47,830	569
Andrews, TX Micro	47,819	570
Minot, ND Micro	47,802	571
Lufkin, TX Micro	47,745	572
Washington, IN Micro	47,740	573
Marshall, TX Micro	47,670	574
Riverton, WY Micro	47,617	575
Oneonta, NY Micro	47,603	576
Beatrice, NE Micro	47,591	577
Big Rapids, MI Micro	47,581	578
Sevierville, TN Micro	47,558	579
Canon City, CO Micro	47,534	580
Iron Mountain, MI-WI Micro	47,520	581
Parkersburg-Marietta, WV-OH Metro	47,466	582
Terre Haute, IN Metro	47,459	583
Ashtabula, OH Micro	47,405	584
Hot Springs, AR Metro	47,392	585
Fort Morgan, CO Micro	47,388	586
Jamestown, ND Micro	47,376	587
Warren, PA Micro	47,376	588
Norfolk, NE Micro	47,353	589
Moscow, ID Micro	47,340	590
Shelby, NC Micro	47,323	591
El Centro, CA Metro	47,319	592
Dothan, AL Metro	47,314	593
Pahrump, NV Micro	47,257	594
Cadillac, MI Micro	47,229	595
Sierra Vista-Douglas, AZ Micro	47,166	596
New Philadelphia-Dover, OH Micro	47,152	597
Hattiesburg, MS Metro	47,141	598
Fort Valley, GA Micro	47,124	599
Bristol, VA Metro	47,121	600
Florence, AL Metro	47,112	601
Blacksburg-Christiansburg-Radford, VA Metro	47,063	602
City of The Dalles, OR Micro	47,043	603
Sumter, SC Metro	47,021	604
Enid, OK Micro	46,960	605
Lawton, OK Metro	46,958	606
Ponca City, OK Micro	46,939	607
Yuma, AZ Metro	46,905	608
Vernon, TX Micro	46,859	609
Dumas, TX Micro	46,854	610
Odessa, TX Metro	46,844	611
Oxford, MS Micro	46,839	612
Bedford, IN Micro	46,805	613
Stephenville, TX Micro	46,803	614
Mount Vernon, IL Micro	46,796	615
Richmond, IN Micro	46,790	616
Marion-Herrin, IL Micro	46,743	617
Abilene, TX Metro	46,729	618
Jesup, GA Micro	46,723	619
La Grande, OR Micro	46,689	620
Red Bluff, CA Micro	46,679	621

CBSA	INCOME ($)	RANK	CBSA	INCOME ($)	RANK	CBSA	INCOME ($)	RANK
Prineville, OR Micro	46,664	622	Picayune, MS Micro	44,527	726	Campbellsville, KY Micro	41,921	830
Great Falls, MT Metro	46,651	623	Newberry, SC Micro	44,521	727	Portsmouth, OH Micro	41,808	831
Sterling, CO Micro	46,651	624	Clewiston, FL Micro	44,473	728	Lake City, FL Micro	41,784	832
Albertville, AL Micro	46,628	625	Laurinburg, NC Micro	44,449	729	Del Rio, TX Micro	41,781	833
Nogales, AZ Micro	46,606	626	Huntingdon, PA Micro	44,424	730	Kirksville, MO Micro	41,762	834
Bucyrus, OH Micro	46,576	627	Big Spring, TX Micro	44,415	731	Jacksonville, TX Micro	41,736	835
New Castle, PA Micro	46,571	628	Nacogdoches, TX Micro	44,377	732	Kingsville, TX Micro	41,721	836
Lancaster, SC Micro	46,568	629	Huron, SD Micro	44,365	733	Arkadelphia, AR Micro	41,714	837
El Campo, TX Micro	46,563	630	Morgantown, WV Metro	44,362	734	Walterboro, SC Micro	41,714	838
El Paso, TX Metro	46,522	631	Jonesboro, AR Metro	44,357	735	Poplar Bluff, MO Micro	41,711	839
Searcy, AR Micro	46,510	632	Weirton-Steubenville, WV-OH Metro	44,347	736	Laurel, MS Micro	41,620	840
Huntsville, TX Micro	46,491	633	Atchison, KS Micro	44,331	737	Corinth, MS Micro	41,616	841
Eureka-Arcata-Fortuna, CA Micro	46,476	634	Laredo, TX Metro	44,299	738	Harrison, AR Micro	41,553	842
Jamestown-Dunkirk-Fredonia, NY Micro	46,448	635	Beckley, WV Micro	44,257	739	Harrisburg, IL Micro	41,510	843
Watertown-Fort Drum, NY Micro	46,428	636	Ogdensburg-Massena, NY Micro	44,251	740	Houghton, MI Micro	41,501	844
Spearfish, SD Micro	46,403	637	Elizabeth City, NC Micro	44,235	741	Carbondale, IL Micro	41,468	845
Wahpeton, ND-MN Micro	46,385	638	Henderson, NC Micro	44,232	742	McMinnville, TN Micro	41,468	846
Carlsbad-Artesia, NM Micro	46,377	639	Union City, TN-KY Micro	44,227	743	Point Pleasant, WV-OH Micro	41,353	847
Cedar City, UT Micro	46,366	640	Maryville, MO Micro	44,226	744	Somerset, PA Micro	41,321	848
Pampa, TX Micro	46,361	641	Ottumwa, IA Micro	44,219	745	Morgan City, LA Micro	41,174	849
Kingsport-Bristol, TN-VA Metro	46,351	642	Brownwood, TX Micro	44,165	746	Ruston, LA Micro	41,047	850
Palestine, TX Micro	46,348	643	Wheeling, WV-OH Metro	44,104	747	Brookhaven, MS Micro	41,045	851
Columbus, MS Micro	46,274	644	Butte-Silver Bow, MT Micro	44,098	748	Uvalde, TX Micro	41,020	852
Meadville, PA Micro	46,263	645	Dyersburg, TN Micro	44,003	749	Natchitoches, LA Micro	40,928	853
Centralia, IL Micro	46,206	646	Espanola, NM Micro	44,003	750	Alamogordo, NM Micro	40,912	854
Scottsbluff, NE Micro	46,196	647	Magnolia, AR Micro	43,939	751	Brownsville-Harlingen, TX Metro	40,885	855
Mount Airy, NC Micro	46,193	648	Oil City, PA Micro	43,897	752	Rockingham, NC Micro	40,837	856
Thomasville, GA Micro	46,169	649	Brookings, OR Micro	43,866	753	Havre, MT Micro	40,798	857
Ocala, FL Metro	46,153	650	Scottsboro, AL Micro	43,807	754	Ada, OK Micro	40,769	858
Amsterdam, NY Micro	46,103	651	Pullman, WA Micro	43,759	755	Camden, AR Micro	40,749	859
Jacksonville, NC Metro	46,089	652	Macomb, IL Micro	43,746	756	Jennings, LA Micro	40,746	860
Gloversville, NY Micro	46,086	653	Laramie, WY Micro	43,726	757	Brownsville, TN Micro	40,714	861
Price, UT Micro	46,083	654	Burley, ID Micro	43,716	758	Silver City, NM Micro	40,701	862
Alexandria, LA Metro	46,078	655	Okeechobee, FL Micro	43,710	759	Paris, TN Micro	40,691	863
Branson, MO Micro	46,047	656	Plainview, TX Micro	43,710	760	Somerset, KY Micro	40,647	864
Aberdeen, WA Micro	45,988	657	Wauchula, FL Micro	43,701	761	Cordele, GA Micro	40,459	865
Anniston-Oxford, AL Metro	45,988	658	Emporia, KS Micro	43,680	762	Moultrie, GA Micro	40,459	866
Duncan, OK Micro	45,987	659	Lebanon, MO Micro	43,673	763	London, KY Micro	40,396	867
Joplin, MO Metro	45,964	660	Orangeburg, SC Micro	43,665	764	Parsons, KS Micro	40,389	868
Mountain Home, ID Micro	45,935	661	Vincennes, IN Micro	43,657	765	Valley, AL Micro	40,370	869
Fort Leonard Wood, MO Micro	45,880	662	Fort Polk South, LA Micro	43,625	766	Central City, KY Micro	40,302	870
Charleston-Mattoon, IL Micro	45,866	663	Crossville, TN Micro	43,623	767	Summerville, GA Micro	40,275	871
Marinette, WI-MI Micro	45,846	664	Athens, TN Micro	43,620	768	Grants, NM Micro	40,240	872
Shawnee, OK Micro	45,829	665	Paragould, AR Micro	43,602	769	Hereford, TX Micro	40,227	873
Payson, AZ Micro	45,823	666	Murray, KY Micro	43,586	770	Blytheville, AR Micro	40,061	874
Pierre Part, LA Micro	45,817	667	Las Cruces, NM Metro	43,534	771	Maysville, KY Micro	40,057	875
Lamesa, TX Micro	45,782	668	Thomaston, GA Micro	43,447	772	McComb, MS Micro	40,003	876
Alpena, MI Micro	45,779	669	Mineral Wells, TX Micro	43,440	773	Fitzgerald, GA Micro	39,997	877
Fort Smith, AR-OK Metro	45,742	670	Lock Haven, PA Micro	43,418	774	Portales, NM Micro	39,968	878
Cullman, AL Micro	45,735	671	Hinesville-Fort Stewart, GA Metro	43,355	775	Bluefield, WV-VA Micro	39,896	879
Auburn-Opelika, AL Metro	45,669	672	Danville, VA Micro	43,341	776	Greenville, MS Micro	39,847	880
Coshocton, OH Micro	45,657	673	Hammond, LA Micro	43,339	777	Durant, OK Micro	39,729	881
East Liverpool-Salem, OH Micro	45,628	674	Stillwater, OK Micro	43,308	778	Waycross, GA Micro	39,682	882
Hannibal, MO Micro	45,622	675	Sikeston, MO Micro	43,299	779	Las Vegas, NM Micro	39,612	883
Scottsburg, IN Micro	45,622	676	Sedalia, MO Micro	43,261	780	McAllen-Edinburg-Pharr, TX Metro	39,441	884
Pottsville, PA Micro	45,610	677	Abbeville, LA Micro	43,235	781	Beeville, TX Micro	39,417	885
Clearlake, CA Micro	45,605	678	Clarksburg, WV Micro	43,227	782	Hope, AR Micro	39,318	886
Enterprise-Ozark, AL Micro	45,563	679	Americus, GA Micro	43,199	783	Roanoke Rapids, NC Micro	39,303	887
Kinston, NC Micro	45,546	680	Sebring, FL Micro	43,160	784	Troy, AL Micro	39,034	888
Rexburg, ID Micro	45,513	681	Meridian, MS Micro	43,148	785	Clarksdale, MS Micro	38,999	889
Roseburg, OR Micro	45,499	682	Johnstown, PA Metro	43,140	786	Grenada, MS Micro	38,998	890
Dublin, GA Micro	45,474	683	Huntington-Ashland, WV-KY-OH Metro	43,131	787	Lumberton, NC Micro	38,887	891
New Iberia, LA Micro	45,458	684	Douglas, GA Micro	43,100	788	Yazoo City, MS Micro	38,881	892
Homosassa Springs, FL Micro	45,439	685	Glasgow, KY Micro	43,100	789	Dillon, SC Micro	38,726	893
Valdosta, GA Metro	45,435	686	Pittsburg, KS Micro	43,005	790	Tahlequah, OK Micro	38,566	894
Gaffney, SC Micro	45,428	687	Clovis, NM Micro	43,000	791	West Plains, MO Micro	38,552	895
Dickinson, ND Micro	45,422	688	Ardmore, OK Micro	42,965	792	Bastrop, LA Micro	38,521	896
De Ridder, LA Micro	45,414	689	Fairmont, WV Micro	42,950	793	Natchez, MS-LA Micro	38,433	897
Morristown, TN Metro	45,389	690	Alice, TX Micro	42,945	794	Indianola, MS Micro	38,428	898
Olean, NY Micro	45,341	691	DuBois, PA Micro	42,885	795	Greenwood, MS Micro	38,385	899
Statesboro, GA Micro	45,320	692	Taos, NM Micro	42,882	796	Bennettsville, SC Micro	38,375	900
Johnson City, TN Metro	45,289	693	Coffeyville, KS Micro	42,879	797	Miami, OK Micro	38,294	901
Grants Pass, OR Micro	45,239	694	Rolla, MO Micro	42,867	798	Forrest City, AR Micro	38,135	902
Cedartown, GA Micro	45,209	695	Cumberland, MD-WV Metro	42,841	799	Sweetwater, TX Micro	38,071	903
Klamath Falls, OR Micro	45,202	696	Berlin, NH-VT Micro	42,798	800	Selma, AL Micro	37,821	904
Danville, KY Micro	45,192	697	Forest City, NC Micro	42,759	801	Cleveland, MS Micro	37,729	905
Great Bend, KS Micro	45,189	698	Toccoa, GA Micro	42,651	802	Oak Hill, WV Micro	37,711	906
El Dorado, AR Micro	45,165	699	Palatka, FL Micro	42,650	803	Gallup, NM Micro	37,570	907
Hobbs, NM Micro	45,157	700	Crescent City North, CA Micro	42,646	804	Tuskegee, AL Micro	36,857	908
Mayfield, KY Micro	45,146	701	Chester, SC Micro	42,585	805	West Helena, AR Micro	36,390	909
Paris, TX Micro	45,097	702	Sunbury, PA Micro	42,553	806	Bogalusa, LA Micro	36,138	910
Washington, NC Micro	45,023	703	Lawrenceburg, TN Micro	42,515	807	Opelousas-Eunice, LA Micro	36,038	911
Corsicana, TX Micro	44,999	704	Roswell, NM Micro	42,515	808	Kennett, MO Micro	35,869	912
Madisonville, KY Micro	44,899	705	Crowley, LA Micro	42,470	809	Corbin, KY Micro	35,540	913
Lake Havasu City-Kingman, AZ Micro	44,890	706	Mountain Home, AR Micro	42,436	810	Newport, TN Micro	35,382	914
Marshall, MO Micro	44,884	707	Farmington, MO Micro	42,401	811	La Follette, TN Micro	35,360	915
Levelland, TX Micro	44,855	708	Greeneville, TN Micro	42,323	812	Pecos, TX Micro	34,348	916
Sault Ste. Marie, MI Micro	44,844	709	Union, SC Micro	42,318	813	Eagle Pass, TX Micro	34,061	917
Ontario, OR-ID Micro	44,833	710	Minden, LA Micro	42,283	814	Deming, NM Micro	32,831	918
Altus, OK Micro	44,804	711	Cambridge, OH Micro	42,275	815	Tallulah, LA Micro	32,074	919
Batesville, AR Micro	44,802	712	Lewistown, PA Micro	42,240	816	Raymondville, TX Micro	31,893	920
Danville, IL Metro	44,783	713	Moberly, MO Micro	42,175	817	Middlesborough, KY Micro	30,734	921
Malone, NY Micro	44,773	714	McAlester, OK Micro	42,169	818	Rio Grande City, TX Micro	27,764	922
Talladega-Sylacauga, AL Micro	44,736	715	Muskogee, OK Micro	42,152	819			
Mexico, MO Micro	44,715	716	Arcadia, FL Micro	42,151	820	CBSA Average	51,715	
Bay City, TX Micro	44,681	717	Starkville, MS Micro	42,142	821	United States Average	63,301	
Coos Bay, OR Micro	44,675	718	Bainbridge, GA Micro	42,137	822			
Russellville, AR Micro	44,667	719	Safford, AZ Micro	42,103	823			
Altoona, PA Metro	44,649	720	Martinsville, VA Micro	42,097	824			
Bradford, PA Micro	44,636	721	Indiana, PA Micro	42,072	825			
Pine Bluff, AR Metro	44,636	722	Mount Sterling, KY Micro	42,006	826			
Gadsden, AL Metro	44,589	723	Vermillion, SD Micro	41,997	827			
Richmond, KY Micro	44,584	724	Cookeville, TN Micro	41,995	828			
The Villages, FL Micro	44,529	725	Athens, OH Micro	41,982	829			

CBSA	SALES ($ MIL)	RANK
New York-Newark-Edison, NY-NJ-PA Metro	196,075	1
Los Angeles-Long Beach-Santa Ana, CA Metro	149,468	2
Chicago-Naperville-Joliet, IL-IN-WI Metro	114,708	3
Dallas-Fort Worth-Arlington, TX Metro	80,861	4
Miami-Fort Lauderdale-Miami Beach, FL Metro	76,054	5
Philadelphia-Camden-Wilmington, PA-NJ-DE-MD Metro	71,318	6
Washington-Arlington-Alexandria, DC-VA-MD-WV Metro	69,616	7
Atlanta-Sandy Springs-Marietta, GA Metro	66,855	8
Houston-Baytown-Sugar Land, TX Metro	64,859	9
Boston-Cambridge-Quincy, MA-NH Metro	62,501	10
San Francisco-Oakland-Fremont, CA Metro	54,895	11
Detroit-Warren-Livonia, MI Metro	54,196	12
Phoenix-Mesa-Scottsdale, AZ Metro	46,740	13
Seattle-Tacoma-Bellevue, WA Metro	45,819	14
Minneapolis-St. Paul-Bloomington, MN-WI Metro	45,156	15
San Diego-Carlsbad-San Marcos, CA Metro	38,485	16
St. Louis, MO-IL Metro	36,545	17
Tampa-St. Petersburg-Clearwater, FL Metro	36,175	18
Riverside-San Bernardino-Ontario, CA Metro	35,322	19
Baltimore-Towson, MD Metro	34,414	20
Denver-Aurora, CO Metro	32,188	21
Pittsburgh, PA Metro	30,742	22
Cleveland-Elyria-Mentor, OH Metro	29,515	23
Orlando, FL Metro	28,082	24
Cincinnati-Middletown, OH-KY-IN Metro	26,911	25
Kansas City, MO-KS Metro	26,672	26
Portland-Vancouver-Beaverton, OR-WA Metro	26,075	27
San Jose-Sunnyvale-Santa Clara, CA Metro	25,478	28
Columbus, OH Metro	25,389	29
Sacramento-Arden-Arcade-Roseville, CA Metro	25,199	30
San Antonio, TX Metro	23,941	31
Indianapolis, IN Metro	22,370	32
Las Vegas-Paradise, NV Metro	22,362	33
Milwaukee-Waukesha-West Allis, WI Metro	21,749	34
Austin-Round Rock, TX Metro	20,713	35
Charlotte-Gastonia-Concord, NC-SC Metro	20,133	36
Nashville-Davidson-Murfreesboro, TN Metro	18,084	37
Virginia Beach-Norfolk-Newport News, VA-NC Metro	17,841	38
Providence-New Bedford-Fall River, RI-MA Metro	17,387	39
Jacksonville, FL Metro	17,115	40
Richmond, VA Metro	16,122	41
New Orleans-Metairie-Kenner, LA Metro	15,868	42
Memphis, TN-MS-AR Metro	15,760	43
Oklahoma City, OK Metro	15,504	44
Louisville, KY-IN Metro	15,276	45
Hartford-West Hartford-East Hartford, CT Metro	15,177	46
Salt Lake City, UT Metro	14,940	47
Birmingham-Hoover, AL Metro	14,223	48
Rochester, NY Metro	14,125	49
Raleigh-Cary, NC Metro	12,963	50
Grand Rapids-Wyoming, MI Metro	12,806	51
Dayton, OH Metro	12,509	52
Buffalo-Cheektowaga-Tonawanda, NY Metro	12,405	53
Bridgeport-Stamford-Norwalk, CT Metro	12,319	54
Omaha-Council Bluffs, NE-IA Metro	11,209	55
Knoxville, TN Metro	10,896	56
Tucson, AZ Metro	10,749	57
Albany-Schenectady-Troy, NY Metro	10,659	58
Tulsa, OK Metro	10,404	59
Albuquerque, NM Metro	10,203	60
Greensboro-High Point, NC Metro	10,072	61
Honolulu, HI Metro	9,933	62
Oxnard-Thousand Oaks-Ventura, CA Metro	9,910	63
New Haven-Milford, CT Metro	9,648	64
Wichita, KS Metro	9,574	65
Sarasota-Bradenton-Venice, FL Metro	9,501	66
Toledo, OH Metro	9,366	67
Little Rock-North Little Rock, AR Metro	9,072	68
Baton Rouge, LA Metro	9,068	69
Worcester, MA Metro	9,044	70
Akron, OH Metro	8,964	71
Syracuse, NY Metro	8,818	72
Allentown-Bethlehem-Easton, PA-NJ Metro	8,767	73
Fresno, CA Metro	8,766	74
Columbia, SC Metro	8,655	75
Madison, WI Metro	8,342	76
Des Moines, IA Metro	8,204	77
Greenville, SC Metro	8,003	78
Scranton-Wilkes-Barre, PA Metro	7,865	79
Cape Coral-Fort Myers, FL Metro	7,816	80
El Paso, TX Metro	7,808	81
Charleston-North Charleston, SC Metro	7,641	82
Colorado Springs, CO Metro	7,584	83
Portland-South Portland, ME Metro	7,555	84
Poughkeepsie-Newburgh-Middletown, NY Metro	7,436	85
Springfield, MA Metro	7,362	86
Palm Bay-Melbourne-Titusville, FL Metro	7,213	87
Harrisburg-Carlisle, PA Metro	7,196	88
Youngstown-Warren-Boardman, OH-PA Metro	7,156	89
Boise City-Nampa, ID Metro	7,044	90
Lancaster, PA Metro	6,917	91
Bakersfield, CA Metro	6,895	92
Manchester-Nashua, NH Metro	6,872	93
Jackson, MS Metro	6,662	94
Lexington-Fayette, KY Metro	6,542	95
McAllen-Edinburg-Pharr, TX Metro	6,528	96
Stockton, CA Metro	6,209	97
Fayetteville-Springdale-Rogers, AR-MO Metro	6,182	98
Mobile, AL Metro	6,156	99
Deltona-Daytona Beach-Ormond Beach, FL Metro	6,118	100
Santa Rosa-Petaluma, CA Metro	6,018	101
Augusta-Richmond County, GA-SC Metro	5,967	102
Lakeland-Winter Haven, FL Metro	5,934	103
Spokane, WA Metro	5,914	104
Chattanooga, TN-GA Metro	5,837	105
Winston-Salem, NC Metro	5,821	106
Springfield, MO Metro	5,675	107
Canton-Massillon, OH Metro	5,657	108
Lansing-East Lansing, MI Metro	5,512	109
Boulder, CO Metro	5,392	110
Ogden-Clearfield, UT Metro	5,360	111
Pensacola-Ferry Pass-Brent, FL Metro	5,313	112
Flint, MI Metro	5,301	113
Santa Barbara-Santa Maria-Goleta, CA Metro	5,273	114
Roanoke, VA Metro	5,249	115
Provo-Orem, UT Metro	5,241	116
Davenport-Moline-Rock Island, IA-IL Metro	5,236	117
Asheville, NC Metro	5,231	118
Reno-Sparks, NV Metro	5,173	119
York-Hanover, PA Metro	5,107	120
Huntsville, AL Metro	5,011	121
Fort Wayne, IN Metro	4,972	122
Durham, NC Metro	4,970	123
Beaumont-Port Arthur, TX Metro	4,861	124
Modesto, CA Metro	4,842	125
Salinas, CA Metro	4,811	126
Peoria, IL Metro	4,783	127
Anchorage, AK Metro	4,763	128
Ann Arbor, MI Metro	4,736	129
Evansville, IN-KY Metro	4,707	130
Naples-Marco Island, FL Metro	4,694	131
Wilmington, NC Metro	4,692	132
Shreveport-Bossier City, LA Metro	4,636	133
Tallahassee, FL Metro	4,632	134
Savannah, GA Metro	4,521	135
Eugene-Springfield, OR Metro	4,478	136
Corpus Christi, TX Metro	4,461	137
Trenton-Ewing, NJ Metro	4,348	138
Rockford, IL Metro	4,327	139
Hickory-Morganton-Lenoir, NC Metro	4,302	140
Salem, OR Metro	4,273	141
Port St. Lucie-Fort Pierce, FL Metro	4,256	142
Vallejo-Fairfield, CA Metro	4,227	143
Green Bay, WI Metro	4,220	144
Montgomery, AL Metro	4,210	145
Myrtle Beach-Conway-North Myrtle Beach, SC Metro	4,194	146
Kalamazoo-Portage, MI Metro	4,112	147
Lincoln, NE Metro	4,091	148
Reading, PA Metro	4,078	149
South Bend-Mishawaka, IN-MI Metro	4,031	150
Charleston, WV Metro	4,002	151
Fayetteville, NC Metro	3,973	152
Barnstable Town, MA Metro	3,949	153
Fort Collins-Loveland, CO Metro	3,831	154
Lubbock, TX Metro	3,766	155
Erie, PA Metro	3,731	156
Hagerstown-Martinsburg, MD-WV Metro	3,725	157
Huntington-Ashland, WV-KY-OH Metro	3,714	158
Duluth, MN-WI Metro	3,657	159
Atlantic City, NJ Metro	3,641	160
Gulfport-Biloxi, MS Metro	3,608	161
Ocala, FL Metro	3,594	162
Brownsville-Harlingen, TX Metro	3,592	163
Lafayette, LA Metro	3,554	164
Amarillo, TX Metro	3,503	165
Sioux Falls, SD Metro	3,483	166
Eau Claire, WI Metro	3,481	167
Cedar Rapids, IA Metro	3,382	168
Killeen-Temple-Fort Hood, TX Metro	3,361	169
Visalia-Porterville, CA Metro	3,354	170
Utica-Rome, NY Metro	3,336	171
Spartanburg, SC Metro	3,296	172
San Luis Obispo-Paso Robles, CA Metro	3,281	173
Columbus, GA-AL Metro	3,242	174
Elkhart-Goshen, IN Metro	3,238	175
Norwich-New London, CT Metro	3,206	176
Appleton, WI Metro	3,201	177
Saginaw-Saginaw Township North, MI Metro	3,194	178
Gainesville, FL Metro	3,188	179
Tyler, TX Metro	3,169	180
Fargo, ND-MN Metro	3,127	181
Santa Cruz-Watsonville, CA Metro	3,055	182
Champaign-Urbana, IL Metro	2,997	183
Fort Walton Beach-Crestview-Destin, FL Metro	2,966	184
Waco, TX Metro	2,945	185
Burlington-South Burlington, VT Metro	2,936	186
St. Cloud, MN Metro	2,918	187
Springfield, IL Metro	2,894	188
Topeka, KS Metro	2,871	189
Medford, OR Metro	2,845	190
Fort Smith, AR-OK Metro	2,843	191
Holland-Grand Haven, MI Metro	2,796	192
Macon, GA Metro	2,723	193
Lebanon, NH-VT Micro	2,665	194
Billings, MT Metro	2,658	195
Seaford, DE Micro	2,654	196
Concord, NH Micro	2,652	197
Longview, TX Metro	2,647	198
Lynchburg, VA Metro	2,636	199
Hilton Head Island-Beaufort, SC Micro	2,624	200
Kingsport-Bristol, TN-VA Metro	2,596	201
Joplin, MO Metro	2,594	202
Olympia, WA Metro	2,548	203
Houma-Bayou Cane-Thibodaux, LA Metro	2,531	204
Binghamton, NY Metro	2,523	205
Torrington, CT Micro	2,518	206
Greeley, CO Metro	2,502	207
Florence, SC Metro	2,500	208
Johnson City, TN Metro	2,489	209
Lake Charles, LA Metro	2,488	210
Tuscaloosa, AL Metro	2,479	211
Traverse City, MI Micro	2,469	212
Racine, WI Metro	2,458	213
Panama City-Lynn Haven, FL Metro	2,449	214
Rochester, MN Metro	2,447	215
Lake Havasu City-Kingman, AZ Micro	2,437	216
Bremerton-Silverdale, WA Metro	2,428	217
Chico, CA Metro	2,421	218
Lafayette, IN Metro	2,407	219
Prescott, AZ Metro	2,404	220
Terre Haute, IN Metro	2,403	221
Bangor, ME Metro	2,356	222
Santa Fe, NM Metro	2,352	223
Charlottesville, VA Metro	2,350	224
Laredo, TX Metro	2,348	225
Yakima, WA Metro	2,345	226
Bellingham, WA Metro	2,344	227
Kennewick-Richland-Pasco, WA Metro	2,340	228
Daphne-Fairhope, AL Micro	2,336	229
Clarksville, TN-KY Metro	2,279	230
College Station-Bryan, TX Metro	2,265	231
La Crosse, WI-MN Metro	2,226	232
Ottawa-Streator, IL Micro	2,207	233
Statesville-Mooresville, NC Micro	2,204	234
Monroe, LA Metro	2,180	235
Dothan, AL Metro	2,147	236
Bloomington-Normal, IL Metro	2,140	237
Bend, OR Metro	2,125	238
Wheeling, WV-OH Metro	2,124	239
Columbia, MO Metro	2,122	240
Kahului-Wailuku, HI Micro	2,098	241
Anderson, SC Metro	2,098	242
Ocean City, NJ Metro	2,089	243
Albany, GA Metro	2,069	244
Bloomington, IN Metro	2,052	245
Wausau, WI Metro	2,040	246
Waterloo-Cedar Falls, IA Metro	2,027	247
Dalton, GA Metro	2,023	248
Oshkosh-Neenah, WI Metro	2,019	249
Dover, DE Metro	2,016	250
Pittsfield, MA Metro	2,015	251
Hilo, HI Micro	1,998	252
Sioux City, IA-NE-SD Metro	1,996	253
Greenville, NC Metro	1,980	254
Athens-Clarke County, GA Metro	1,974	255
Kingston, NY Metro	1,965	256
Muskegon-Norton Shores, MI Metro	1,958	257
Abilene, TX Metro	1,931	258
Altoona, PA Metro	1,923	259
Missoula, MT Metro	1,920	260
Battle Creek, MI Metro	1,919	261
Punta Gorda, FL Metro	1,918	262
Flagstaff, AZ Metro	1,902	263
Lima, OH Metro	1,882	264
Gainesville, GA Metro	1,880	265
Blacksburg-Christiansburg-Radford, VA Metro	1,875	266
Valdosta, GA Metro	1,867	267
Wichita Falls, TX Metro	1,861	268
Key West-Marathon, FL Micro	1,839	269
Vineland-Millville-Bridgeton, NJ Metro	1,839	270
Janesville, WI Metro	1,831	271
East Stroudsburg, PA Micro	1,827	272
Yuma, AZ Metro	1,821	273
Iowa City, IA Metro	1,817	274
Niles-Benton Harbor, MI Metro	1,817	275
Grand Junction, CO Metro	1,810	276
Augusta-Waterville, ME Micro	1,800	277
Rapid City, SD Metro	1,797	278
Parkersburg-Marietta, WV-OH Metro	1,787	279
Springfield, OH Metro	1,786	280
Merced, CA Metro	1,780	281
Mount Vernon-Anacortes, WA Metro	1,759	282
Texarkana, TX-Texarkana, AR Metro	1,758	283
Pueblo, CO Metro	1,756	284
Rocky Mount, NC Metro	1,749	285
Burlington, NC Metro	1,745	286
Hattiesburg, MS Metro	1,741	287
Tupelo, MS Micro	1,737	288
Harrisonburg, VA Metro	1,730	289
Mansfield, OH Metro	1,730	290
Jackson, TN Metro	1,721	291
Jefferson City, MO Metro	1,710	292
Vero Beach, FL Metro	1,706	293
Redding, CA Metro	1,698	294
Alexandria, LA Metro	1,690	295
Elizabethtown, KY Metro	1,674	296
Salisbury, MD Metro	1,664	297
Lewiston-Auburn, ME Metro	1,645	298
Florence, AL Metro	1,636	299
Sumter, SC Metro	1,633	300
Lexington-Thomasville, NC Micro	1,624	301
Kankakee-Bradley, IL Metro	1,618	302
Fond du Lac, WI Metro	1,612	303
Sheboygan, WI Metro	1,605	304
Dubuque, IA Metro	1,594	305
Jamestown-Dunkirk-Fredonia, NY Micro	1,590	306
St. George, UT Metro	1,588	307
Bowling Green, KY Metro	1,588	308

CBSA	SALES ($ MIL)	RANK	CBSA	SALES ($ MIL)	RANK	CBSA	SALES ($ MIL)	RANK
Idaho Falls, ID Metro	1,586	309	Logan, UT-ID Metro	1,107	413	Bemidji, MN Micro	750	517
Muncie, IN Metro	1,580	310	Sandusky, OH Metro	1,103	414	Easton, MD Micro	748	518
Jackson, MI Metro	1,580	311	Orangeburg, SC Micro	1,103	415	Talladega-Sylacauga, AL Micro	742	519
Watertown-Fort Drum, NY Micro	1,572	312	Casper, WY Metro	1,099	416	Seymour, IN Micro	741	520
Bismarck, ND Metro	1,569	313	Lufkin, TX Micro	1,096	417	Enid, OK Micro	740	521
Williamsport, PA Metro	1,562	314	Zanesville, OH Micro	1,093	418	Red Bluff, CA Micro	739	522
Chambersburg, PA Micro	1,559	315	Bristol, VA Metro	1,093	419	Tifton, GA Micro	732	523
Johnstown, PA Metro	1,553	316	Albertville, AL Micro	1,089	420	Lake City, FL Micro	730	524
Eureka-Arcata-Fortuna, CA Micro	1,551	317	Branson, MO Micro	1,089	421	Burlington, IA-IL Micro	728	525
Lawrence, KS Metro	1,546	318	Tullahoma, TN Micro	1,087	422	Bennington, VT Micro	727	526
Las Cruces, NM Metro	1,545	319	Weirton-Steubenville, WV-OH Metro	1,084	423	Aberdeen, SD Micro	725	527
Morgantown, WV Metro	1,534	320	Elmira, NY Metro	1,075	424	Batavia, NY Micro	724	528
Decatur, IL Metro	1,532	321	Grants Pass, OR Micro	1,075	425	Faribault-Northfield, MN Micro	719	529
Lawton, OK Metro	1,531	322	Martinsville, VA Micro	1,074	426	Oneonta, NY Micro	718	530
Midland, TX Metro	1,530	323	Southern Pines, NC Micro	1,074	427	Seneca, SC Micro	716	531
Sevierville, TN Micro	1,523	324	El Centro, CA Metro	1,067	428	Charleston-Mattoon, IL Micro	713	532
State College, PA Metro	1,519	325	Adrian, MI Micro	1,057	429	Roanoke Rapids, NC Micro	712	533
Mankato-North Mankato, MN Micro	1,513	326	Indiana, PA Micro	1,055	430	Oil City, PA Micro	706	534
Monroe, MI Metro	1,512	327	Midland, MI Micro	1,053	431	Palm Coast, FL Micro	703	535
Napa, CA Metro	1,511	328	Stevens Point, WI Micro	1,049	432	Aberdeen, WA Micro	699	536
Findlay, OH Micro	1,510	329	Plattsburgh, NY Micro	1,042	433	Gardnerville Ranchos, NV Micro	698	537
Cookeville, TN Micro	1,505	330	Mount Airy, NC Micro	1,017	434	Douglas, GA Micro	697	538
Sierra Vista-Douglas, AZ Micro	1,498	331	Mason City, IA Micro	1,016	435	Rockland, ME Micro	694	539
Winchester, VA-WV Metro	1,485	332	Madera, CA Micro	1,015	436	Klamath Falls, OR Micro	692	540
Odessa, TX Metro	1,484	333	Opelousas-Eunice, LA Micro	1,012	437	Ponca City, OK Micro	692	541
Decatur, AL Metro	1,482	334	Great Falls, MT Metro	985	438	Freeport, IL Micro	688	542
Anniston-Oxford, AL Metro	1,480	335	Edwards, CO Micro	984	439	Athens, TX Micro	687	543
Staunton-Waynesboro, VA Micro	1,464	336	Kill Devil Hills, NC Micro	984	440	Owosso, MI Micro	687	544
Homosassa Springs, FL Micro	1,463	337	Russellville, AR Micro	978	441	Roswell, NM Micro	687	545
St. Joseph, MO-KS Metro	1,457	338	Clarksburg, WV Micro	975	442	Albemarle, NC Micro	686	546
Victoria, TX Metro	1,457	339	Watertown-Fort Atkinson, WI Micro	969	443	Vicksburg, MS Micro	685	547
Yuba City-Marysville, CA Metro	1,452	340	Lexington Park, MD Micro	967	444	Sidney, OH Micro	685	548
New Bern, NC Metro	1,452	341	Cullman, AL Micro	965	445	Urbana, OH Micro	683	549
Lebanon, PA Metro	1,451	342	London, KY Micro	956	446	Sterling, IL Micro	682	550
Sherman-Denison, TX Metro	1,445	343	New Castle, PA Micro	954	447	Marion, IN Micro	680	551
Paducah, KY-IL Micro	1,434	344	Pocatello, ID Metro	945	448	Farmington, MO Micro	679	552
Brainerd, MN Micro	1,433	345	Somerset, NE Micro	944	449	Norfolk, NE Micro	676	553
Bay City, MI Metro	1,430	346	Sunbury, PA Micro	941	450	Thomasville, GA Micro	671	554
Bozeman, MT Micro	1,427	347	Gettysburg, PA Micro	938	451	Greeneville, TN Micro	670	555
Grand Forks, ND-MN Metro	1,419	348	Wilson, NC Micro	938	452	Dublin, GA Micro	669	556
Warner Robins, GA Metro	1,415	349	Corning, NY Micro	937	453	El Dorado, AR Micro	668	557
Jacksonville, NC Metro	1,397	350	Danville, IL Metro	934	454	Danville, KY Micro	663	558
Jonesboro, AR Metro	1,389	351	Kapaa, HI Micro	932	455	Gloversville, NY Micro	660	559
Farmington, NM Metro	1,383	352	Minot, ND Micro	929	456	Crossville, TN Micro	659	560
Hot Springs, AR Metro	1,375	353	Columbus, IN Metro	925	457	Winona, MN Micro	656	561
Owensboro, KY Metro	1,374	354	Rutland, VT Micro	925	458	Red Wing, MN Micro	656	562
Anderson, IN Metro	1,364	355	Pine Bluff, AR Metro	923	459	Greenville, MS Micro	654	563
Roseburg, OR Micro	1,356	356	Warsaw, IN Micro	921	460	Statesboro, GA Micro	653	564
Coeur d'Alene, ID Metro	1,354	357	Olean, NY Micro	920	461	Jackson, WY-ID Micro	650	565
Cheyenne, WY Metro	1,350	358	Hanford-Corcoran, CA Metro	918	462	Cadillac, MI Micro	650	566
Kokomo, IN Metro	1,344	359	Bloomsburg-Berwick, PA Micro	917	463	Auburn, NY Micro	650	567
Manhattan, KS Micro	1,341	360	Somerset, KY Micro	914	464	Granbury, TX Micro	648	568
Brunswick, GA Metro	1,338	361	Barre, VT Micro	907	465	Huntsville, TX Micro	647	569
Keene, NH Micro	1,334	362	Morehead City, NC Micro	907	466	Willmar, MN Micro	644	570
San Angelo, TX Metro	1,325	363	Salina, KS Micro	900	467	Elizabeth City, NC Micro	644	571
Pascagoula, MS Metro	1,323	364	Ardmore, OK Micro	898	468	Ruston, LA Micro	641	572
Cape Girardeau-Jackson, MO-IL Micro	1,313	365	Centralia, WA Micro	897	469	Hudson, NY Micro	639	573
Wooster, OH Micro	1,312	366	Columbus, MS Micro	894	470	Astoria, OR Micro	639	574
Shelby, NC Micro	1,309	367	Mount Pleasant, MI Micro	892	471	Hobbs, NM Micro	639	575
Meridian, MS Micro	1,303	368	Durango, CO Micro	890	472	Phoenix Lake-Cedar Ridge, CA Micro	638	576
Wenatchee, WA Metro	1,302	369	Enterprise-Ozark, AL Micro	886	473	Paragould, AR Micro	637	577
Auburn-Opelika, AL Metro	1,292	370	New Iberia, LA Micro	883	474	Clinton, IA Micro	637	578
Hammond, LA Micro	1,282	371	Beaver Dam, WI Micro	883	475	Palestine, TX Micro	636	579
Chillicothe, OH Micro	1,275	372	Marquette, MI Micro	881	476	Henderson, NC Micro	636	580
Morristown, TN Metro	1,274	373	Hutchinson, KS Micro	880	477	Natchez, MS-LA Micro	631	581
Ocean Pines, MD Micro	1,267	374	Greenwood, SC Micro	871	478	Portsmouth, OH Micro	631	582
Danville, VA Metro	1,262	375	Richmond, IN Micro	870	479	Fergus Falls, MN Micro	631	583
Bluefield, WV-VA Micro	1,260	376	Meadville, PA Micro	867	480	Moses Lake, WA Micro	631	584
Wisconsin Rapids-Marshfield, WI Micro	1,259	377	Carson City, NV Metro	864	481	Silverthorne, CO Micro	626	585
Kalispell, MT Micro	1,257	378	Dunn, NC Micro	863	482	Milledgeville, GA Micro	624	586
Michigan City-La Porte, IN Metro	1,236	379	Stillwater, OK Micro	857	483	McMinnville, TN Micro	622	587
DuBois, PA Micro	1,228	380	Nacogdoches, TX Micro	855	484	Selinsgrove, PA Micro	621	588
Richmond, KY Micro	1,228	381	Marion-Herrin, IL Micro	852	485	Washington, NC Micro	621	589
Pottsville, PA Micro	1,228	382	Frankfort, KY Micro	851	486	Platteville, WI Micro	620	590
Willimantic, CT Micro	1,223	383	Palatka, FL Micro	850	487	Muscatine, IA Micro	619	591
Goldsboro, NC Metro	1,220	384	Helena, MT Micro	849	488	McAlester, OK Micro	618	592
Ogdensburg-Massena, NY Micro	1,215	385	Gallup, NM Micro	847	489	Lancaster, SC Micro	618	593
Baraboo, WI Micro	1,207	386	Manitowoc, WI Micro	846	490	Rochelle, IL Micro	618	594
Cumberland, MD-WV Metro	1,206	387	Muskogee, OK Micro	845	491	Marshall, TX Micro	614	595
Lumberton, NC Micro	1,203	388	Pendleton-Hermiston, OR Micro	845	492	Norwalk, OH Micro	613	596
Ames, IA Metro	1,198	389	Poplar Bluff, MO Micro	842	493	Paris, TX Micro	612	597
East Liverpool-Salem, OH Micro	1,196	390	Galesburg, IL Micro	841	494	Marion, OH Micro	610	598
Ukiah, CA Micro	1,191	391	McComb, MS Micro	839	495	Oak Harbor, WA Micro	609	599
Rome, GA Metro	1,189	392	Boone, NC Micro	833	496	Scottsboro, AL Micro	609	600
Cleveland, TN Metro	1,181	393	Jasper, IN Micro	832	497	Walla Walla, WA Micro	609	601
Whitewater, WI Micro	1,177	394	Kearney, NE Micro	827	498	Ontario, OR-ID Micro	608	602
New Philadelphia-Dover, OH Micro	1,176	395	LaGrange, GA Micro	823	499	Lincolnton, NC Micro	607	603
Grand Island, NE Metro	1,165	396	Port Angeles, WA Micro	819	500	Clovis, NM Micro	604	604
Longview-Kelso, WA Metro	1,160	397	Nogales, AZ Micro	818	501	Rock Springs, WY Micro	603	605
Fairbanks, AK Metro	1,157	398	Sayre, PA Micro	799	502	Brigham City, UT Micro	603	606
Gadsden, AL Metro	1,154	399	Lewiston, ID-WA Metro	796	503	Kerrville, TX Micro	597	607
North Wilkesboro, NC Micro	1,151	400	Monroe, WI Micro	794	504	Menomonie, WI Micro	594	608
Sebring, FL Micro	1,149	401	Corvallis, OR Metro	782	505	Payson, AZ Micro	594	609
Ithaca, NY Micro	1,144	402	Searcy, AR Micro	779	506	Berlin, NH-VT Micro	591	610
Laconia, NH Micro	1,143	403	Laurel, MS Micro	778	507	Watertown, SD Micro	588	611
Albany-Lebanon, OR Micro	1,142	404	Sanford, NC Micro	777	508	Iron Mountain, MI-WI Micro	587	612
Allegan, MI Micro	1,138	405	Effingham, IL Micro	771	509	Fremont, OH Micro	585	613
Glens Falls, NY Tetro	1,138	406	Carbondale, IL Micro	768	510	Defiance, OH Micro	583	614
Twin Falls, ID Micro	1,134	407	Kinston, NC Micro	766	511	Waycross, GA Micro	583	615
Ashtabula, OH Micro	1,126	408	Forest City, NC Micro	766	512	Shawnee, OK Micro	583	616
Salisbury, NC Micro	1,124	409	Coos Bay, OR Micro	765	513	Duncan, OK Micro	582	617
Truckee-Grass Valley, CA Micro	1,122	410	Marinette, WI-MI Micro	763	514	Harrison, AR Micro	580	618
Quincy, IL-MO Micro	1,122	411	Columbia, TN Micro	761	515	Murray, KY Micro	579	619
Beckley, WV Micro	1,115	412	Georgetown, SC Micro	757	516	Fremont, NE Micro	578	620

CBSA	SALES ($ MIL)	RANK
Mount Vernon, IL Micro	577	621
Montrose, CO Micro	573	622
Calhoun, GA Micro	572	623
Columbus, NE Micro	568	624
Carlsbad-Artesia, NM Micro	563	625
Durant, OK Micro	561	626
Clearlake, CA Micro	559	627
St. Marys, GA Micro	559	628
Madisonville, KY Micro	558	629
Rockingham, NC Micro	552	630
Morgan City, LA Micro	552	631
Alexandria, MN Micro	545	632
Gillette, WY Micro	545	633
El Campo, TX Micro	544	634
Scottsbluff, NE Micro	543	635
Athens, TN Micro	541	636
Gaffney, SC Micro	540	637
Cortland, NY Micro	539	638
West Plains, MO Micro	537	639
Big Rapids, MI Micro	536	640
Burley, ID Micro	535	641
Jacksonville, TX Micro	535	642
Keokuk-Fort Madison, IA-MO Micro	534	643
Greenville, OH Micro	534	644
Bradford, PA Micro	531	645
Lock Haven, PA Micro	531	646
Mount Vernon, OH Micro	529	647
Athens, OH Micro	529	648
Escanaba, MI Micro	527	649
Bartlesville, OK Micro	527	650
Garden City, KS Micro	527	651
Corsicana, TX Micro	526	652
Plymouth, IN Micro	526	653
Austin, MN Micro	524	654
Union City, TN-KY Micro	523	655
Bedford, IN Micro	520	656
Owatonna, MN Micro	517	657
Tahlequah, OK Micro	515	658
Riverton, WY Micro	513	659
Ottumwa, IA Micro	512	660
Fort Dodge, IA Micro	508	661
Del Rio, TX Micro	507	662
Fort Leonard Wood, MO Micro	507	663
Ada, OK Micro	503	664
Alamogordo, NM Micro	503	665
Hastings, NE Micro	503	666
Marshalltown, IA Micro	502	667
Sedalia, MO Micro	499	668
Warren, PA Micro	499	669
Vincennes, IN Micro	498	670
Moultrie, GA Micro	497	671
Mountain Home, AR Micro	497	672
Cedar City, UT Micro	497	673
Glasgow, KY Micro	496	674
Crawfordsville, IN Micro	496	675
Elko, NV Micro	492	676
Point Pleasant, WV-OH Micro	492	677
Albert Lea, MN Micro	491	678
Auburn, IN Micro	491	679
North Platte, NE Micro	488	680
Rolla, MO Micro	486	681
Oxford, MS Micro	484	682
Houghton, MI Micro	484	683
Dodge City, KS Micro	482	684
Mount Pleasant, TX Micro	480	685
Sturgis, MI Micro	479	686
Taylorville, IL Micro	478	687
Abbeville, LA Micro	475	688
Lewistown, PA Micro	475	689
Cornelia, GA Micro	474	690
Hutchinson, MN Micro	471	691
Dyersburg, TN Micro	470	692
Gainesville, TX Micro	468	693
Wilmington, OH Micro	467	694
Walterboro, SC Micro	466	695
Malone, NY Micro	464	696
Eagle Pass, TX Micro	462	697
Blytheville, AR Micro	462	698
Dixon, IL Micro	460	699
Fairmont, WV Micro	460	700
Butte-Silver Bow, MT Micro	460	701
Marshall, MN Micro	459	702
Sault Ste. Marie, MI Micro	456	703
Newport, TN Micro	455	704
Crowley, LA Micro	454	705
Rexburg, ID Micro	452	706
Juneau, AK Micro	449	707
Alma, MI Micro	448	708
Tiffin-Fostoria, OH Micro	445	709
Picayune, MS Micro	443	710
Jacksonville, IL Micro	443	711
Wapakoneta, OH Micro	443	712
Pontiac, IL Micro	443	713
Sikeston, MO Micro	442	714
Batesville, AR Micro	441	715
Okeechobee, FL Micro	440	716
Corinth, MS Micro	438	717
Taos, NM Micro	438	718
Hinesville-Fort Stewart, GA Metro	437	719
Hays, KS Micro	435	720
New Ulm, MN Micro	434	721
Brownwood, TX Micro	433	722
Ellensburg, WA Micro	431	723
Lewisburg, PA Micro	430	724
Yankton, SD Micro	430	725
Harriman, TN Micro	429	726
Coffeyville, KS Micro	428	727
Amsterdam, NY Micro	427	728
Oak Hill, WV Micro	426	729
Sulphur Springs, TX Micro	424	730
Safford, AZ Micro	423	731
Brookhaven, MS Micro	423	732
Selma, AL Micro	422	733
Angola, IN Micro	420	734
Alpena, MI Micro	419	735
Kendallville, IN Micro	418	736
Pittsburg, KS Micro	417	737
Logansport, IN Micro	416	738
Kennett, MO Micro	416	739
Hannibal, MO Micro	415	740
New Castle, IN Micro	415	741
Minden, LA Micro	414	742
Ashland, OH Micro	413	743
Harrisburg, IL Micro	412	744
The Villages, FL Micro	410	745
Great Bend, KS Micro	408	746
Winfield, KS Micro	407	747
Bellefontaine, OH Micro	406	748
Fort Polk South, LA Micro	405	749
Altus, OK Micro	403	750
Washington, OH Micro	403	751
Greenwood, MS Micro	400	752
Lawrenceburg, TN Micro	400	753
Brenham, TX Micro	399	754
Moscow, ID Micro	398	755
Campbellsville, KY Micro	398	756
La Follette, TN Micro	398	757
Huntington, IN Micro	394	758
Maysville, KY Micro	394	759
Americus, GA Micro	393	760
Stephenville, TX Micro	393	761
Canon City, CO Micro	392	762
McPherson, KS Micro	390	763
Mount Sterling, KY Micro	390	764
Bogalusa, LA Micro	390	765
Plainview, TX Micro	389	766
Warrensburg, MO Micro	387	767
Lebanon, MO Micro	386	768
Alice, TX Micro	386	769
Sheridan, WY Micro	385	770
Middlesborough, KY Micro	383	771
Madison, IN Micro	382	772
Bay City, TX Micro	381	773
Merrill, WI Micro	379	774
Natchitoches, LA Micro	378	775
Laramie, WY Micro	376	776
Grenada, MS Micro	375	777
Paris, TN Micro	375	778
Mayfield, KY Micro	374	779
Kingsville, TX Micro	373	780
Troy, AL Micro	371	781
Macomb, IL Micro	371	782
Pierre, SD Micro	370	783
Shelton, WA Micro	369	784
Emporia, KS Micro	367	785
Mitchell, SD Micro	366	786
Cambridge, OH Micro	366	787
Cambridge, MD Micro	365	788
Fitzgerald, GA Micro	365	789
Coshocton, OH Micro	365	790
Starkville, MS Micro	364	791
Celina, OH Micro	361	792
Brevard, NC Micro	359	793
City of The Dalles, OR Micro	357	794
St. Marys, PA Micro	357	795
Rio Grande City, TX Micro	357	796
Brookings, SD Micro	356	797
Hood River, OR Micro	354	798
Worthington, MN Micro	352	799
Decatur, IN Micro	351	800
Bucyrus, OH Micro	351	801
Newton, IA Micro	350	802
Seneca Falls, NY Micro	350	803
Jesup, GA Micro	348	804
Fairmont, MN Micro	347	805
Centralia, IL Micro	346	806
Huntingdon, TN Micro	346	807
Greensburg, IN Micro	346	808
Shelbyville, TN Micro	344	809
Hope, AR Micro	343	810
Kirksville, MO Micro	341	811
Bainbridge, GA Micro	340	812
Valley, AL Micro	340	813
Canton, IL Micro	339	814
Dickinson, ND Micro	337	815
Thomaston, GA Micro	333	816
Clewiston, FL Micro	329	817
Peru, IN Micro	323	818
Toccoa, GA Micro	322	819
Newberry, SC Micro	321	820
Pecos, TX Micro	321	821
Brookings, OR Micro	321	822
La Grande, OR Micro	320	823
Coldwater, MI Micro	317	824
Pahrump, NV Micro	315	825
Indianola, MS Micro	315	826
Jennings, LA Micro	315	827
Liberal, KS Micro	314	828
Spencer, IA Micro	314	829
Williston, ND Micro	313	830
Camden, AR Micro	311	831
Washington, IN Micro	310	832
Deming, NM Micro	310	833
Cordele, GA Micro	307	834
Silver City, NM Micro	305	835
Boone, IA Micro	303	836
Fort Morgan, CO Micro	303	837
Wabash, IN Micro	302	838
Spirit Lake, IA Micro	298	839
Big Spring, TX Micro	297	840
Vernal, UT Micro	297	841
Price, UT Micro	296	842
Corbin, KY Micro	295	843
Laurinburg, NC Micro	293	844
Lexington, NE Micro	293	845
Miami, OK Micro	291	846
Bishop, CA Micro	291	847
Borger, TX Micro	289	848
Van Wert, OH Micro	285	849
Jamestown, ND Micro	284	850
Evanston, WY Micro	283	851
Lincoln, IL Micro	282	852
Prineville, OR Micro	277	853
Spearfish, SD Micro	277	854
Blackfoot, ID Micro	277	855
Cedartown, GA Micro	276	856
Magnolia, AR Micro	274	857
Guymon, OK Micro	272	858
Moberly, MO Micro	272	859
Chester, SC Micro	268	860
North Vernon, IN Micro	267	861
Mineral Wells, TX Micro	266	862
Storm Lake, IA Micro	266	863
De Ridder, LA Micro	264	864
Beatrice, NE Micro	263	865
Forrest City, AR Micro	262	866
Frankfort, IN Micro	262	867
Cleveland, MS Micro	261	868
Dillon, SC Micro	261	869
Las Vegas, NM Micro	259	870
Mountain Home, ID Micro	258	871
Fallon, NV Micro	258	872
Clarksdale, MS Micro	257	873
Maryville, MO Micro	255	874
Fort Valley, GA Micro	252	875
Espanola, NM Micro	252	876
Central City, KY Micro	252	877
Woodward, OK Micro	251	878
Uvalde, TX Micro	249	879
Parsons, KS Micro	249	880
Ketchikan, AK Micro	248	881
Pampa, TX Micro	247	882
Connersville, IN Micro	247	883
Mexico, MO Micro	246	884
Oskaloosa, IA Micro	243	885
Pullman, WA Micro	241	886
Summerville, GA Micro	241	887
Arcadia, FL Micro	240	888
Crescent City North, CA Micro	240	889
Bastrop, LA Micro	239	890
Arkadelphia, AR Micro	239	891
Sterling, CO Micro	235	892
Huron, SD Micro	229	893
Scottsburg, IN Micro	227	894
Wahpeton, ND-MN Micro	226	895
Bennettsville, SC Micro	221	896
Hereford, TX Micro	218	897
Grants, NM Micro	210	898
Havre, MT Micro	209	899
Union, SC Micro	194	900
Kodiak, AK Micro	192	901
Brownsville, TN Micro	190	902
Yazoo City, MS Micro	187	903
Dumas, TX Micro	185	904
Marshall, MO Micro	177	905
Portales, NM Micro	176	906
West Helena, AR Micro	175	907
Wauchula, FL Micro	173	908
Beeville, TX Micro	170	909
Lamesa, TX Micro	170	910
Levelland, TX Micro	148	911
Vernon, TX Micro	145	912
Atchison, KS Micro	137	913
Los Alamos, NM Micro	137	914
Sweetwater, TX Micro	132	915
Snyder, TX Micro	129	916
Pierre Part, LA Micro	118	917
Raymondville, TX Micro	117	918
Vermillion, SD Micro	113	919
Andrews, TX Micro	103	920
Tallulah, LA Micro	98	921
Tuskegee, AL Micro	86	922

CBSA Total	3,483,342
United States Total	3,682,710
CBSA (% of U.S. Total)	94.59

ZIP Code	3-Digit ZIP Code Areas	Total Households	Median Household Income	Average Household Income	Total Population	Population by Age: 0-4 years	Population by Age: 5-17 years	Population by Age: 18-34 years	Population by Age: 35-49 years	Population by Age: 50-64 years	Gray Markets 65 + years
000	Remainder Areas	6,367	40,162	57,501	25,342	1,220	4,063	8,889	5,875	3,522	1,773
001	Remainder Areas	2,043	44,815	69,304	4,966	272	820	1,001	1,314	1,075	484
010	Springfield, MA	178,273	48,677	60,500	461,201	23,168	75,580	111,716	107,408	78,571	64,758
011	Springfield, MA	62,888	34,395	48,987	167,469	11,691	33,573	41,482	34,756	24,631	21,336
012	Pittsfield, MA	55,142	42,615	56,865	131,232	5,969	21,251	25,791	29,573	24,946	23,702
013	Springfield, MA	34,509	43,417	53,269	83,610	3,966	14,176	17,212	20,399	15,671	12,186
014	Worcester, MA	78,920	54,921	69,004	210,436	13,538	39,629	43,342	54,964	33,874	25,089
015	Worcester, MA	137,262	62,981	77,364	364,369	22,586	67,297	72,592	95,361	61,533	45,000
016	Worcester, MA	70,953	39,390	52,162	182,117	10,823	29,739	52,626	38,344	25,560	25,025
017	Boston, MA	140,675	79,439	108,500	373,221	26,474	65,912	67,541	101,856	66,698	44,740
018	Middlesex-Essex, MA	252,670	64,270	82,423	695,681	49,079	128,629	146,568	173,420	113,670	84,315
019	Middlesex-Essex, MA	188,788	60,897	80,567	481,829	28,445	80,298	96,219	119,512	86,296	71,059
020	Brockton, MA	143,654	80,475	104,053	394,446	27,269	73,421	66,336	106,346	71,046	50,028
021	Boston, MA	507,167	50,066	68,028	1,240,404	69,187	166,404	388,256	275,793	183,321	157,443
022	Boston, MA	6,901	31,413	45,304	19,751	117	225	16,205	1,663	769	772
023	Brockton, MA	154,624	74,675	81,634	438,057	27,975	80,792	95,398	107,966	74,840	51,086
024	Brockton, MA	158,208	81,634	116,878	396,247	21,073	56,257	93,954	93,407	70,513	61,043
025	Buzzards Bay, MA	48,499	54,020	69,893	118,961	6,010	19,034	22,099	28,527	22,631	20,660
026	Buzzards Bay, MA	70,455	48,628	63,996	161,005	6,445	22,375	25,616	35,010	31,433	40,126
027	Providence, RI	205,847	47,446	59,462	527,032	30,409	89,918	118,613	122,728	88,910	76,454
028	Providence, RI	276,086	50,902	65,786	694,993	30,441	114,921	148,104	171,566	121,738	100,223
029	Providence, RI	148,834	38,287	52,480	387,248	21,942	61,514	108,577	83,532	56,615	55,068
030	Manchester, NH	137,838	67,921	82,718	379,013	24,485	77,307	73,935	105,286	64,006	33,994
031	Manchester, NH	58,266	50,702	65,424	146,492	9,248	24,610	35,938	35,234	23,207	17,955
032	Manchester, NH	72,564	50,960	63,948	185,920	9,302	33,665	37,590	46,714	34,173	24,476
033	Manchester, NH	22,987	52,336	64,742	59,960	3,192	10,809	13,026	15,564	9,844	7,525
034	Manchester, NH	32,131	47,760	59,640	83,100	4,096	14,579	18,476	19,314	14,960	11,675
035	White River Junction, VT	19,498	37,136	45,840	45,578	2,245	7,754	7,954	10,791	8,921	7,913
036	White River Junction, VT	5,232	46,490	57,467	12,865	688	2,356	2,187	3,164	2,551	1,919
037	White River Junction, VT	29,828	49,293	63,531	75,388	3,770	12,125	17,861	16,865	13,383	11,384
038	Portsmouth, NH	124,072	55,581	69,878	310,208	16,892	53,125	66,900	78,682	54,540	40,069
039	Portsmouth, NH	20,379	57,454	71,363	50,832	2,660	9,091	8,806	13,590	9,885	6,855
040	Portland, ME	132,050	48,408	61,057	333,330	17,903	58,217	67,126	85,062	60,985	44,037
041	Portland, ME	48,336	44,982	62,616	108,474	5,311	15,882	26,154	27,055	18,194	15,878
042	Portland, ME	71,613	39,137	48,860	174,936	8,909	29,935	36,242	43,208	31,315	25,327
043	Portland, ME	33,253	40,947	50,436	79,606	3,852	13,597	15,288	20,242	15,635	10,992
044	Bangor, ME	69,154	37,497	48,173	168,679	7,995	27,014	38,911	40,812	30,970	22,977
045	Bangor, ME	21,416	42,614	54,352	49,696	2,194	7,886	8,735	11,697	10,586	8,598
046	Bangor, ME	31,276	34,004	45,226	72,555	3,316	11,548	13,431	17,073	14,710	12,477
047	Bangor, ME	31,190	31,361	39,777	73,373	3,381	11,751	13,506	17,226	14,827	12,682
048	Portland, ME	18,065	42,276	54,553	42,357	2,069	6,608	7,789	10,087	8,590	7,214
049	Portland, ME	64,368	34,182	43,611	157,664	7,756	26,536	33,362	37,318	29,736	22,956
050	White River Junction, VT	25,302	46,070	59,696	61,727	2,811	11,085	11,230	15,320	12,469	8,812
051	White River Junction, VT	13,008	42,101	53,278	30,429	1,376	5,002	5,140	7,141	6,522	5,248
052	White River Junction, VT	13,648	43,631	58,168	33,614	1,613	5,738	6,319	7,689	6,520	5,735
053	White River Junction, VT	15,607	43,298	55,999	37,174	1,747	6,250	6,828	9,464	7,676	5,209
054	Burlington, VT	87,708	51,903	64,772	228,068	12,825	40,402	56,022	57,505	37,970	23,344
056	Burlington, VT	34,806	45,706	57,998	84,925	4,182	14,567	18,267	20,926	16,338	10,645
057	White River Junction, VT	33,522	41,452	52,787	83,725	3,855	13,881	17,615	19,817	16,257	12,300
058	White River Junction, VT	23,193	35,717	45,769	57,844	3,029	10,325	11,602	13,175	11,090	8,623
059	White River Junction, VT	1,515	32,648	39,473	3,734	177	707	663	898	736	553
060	Hartford, CT	259,942	61,366	78,504	656,546	39,013	120,511	125,521	163,507	115,153	92,841
061	Hartford, CT	113,819	42,607	59,716	292,646	19,563	55,352	66,019	61,918	46,202	43,592
062	Hartford, CT	56,923	56,344	68,105	157,291	8,912	27,992	40,500	37,164	25,265	17,458
063	New Haven, CT	102,165	53,798	67,089	260,330	15,520	47,716	56,340	62,992	43,143	34,619
064	New Haven, CT	273,888	67,689	84,361	708,737	43,789	130,925	125,856	179,887	127,901	100,379
065	New Haven, CT	108,716	42,646	58,073	279,772	17,512	49,952	75,534	58,352	40,981	37,441
066	New Haven, CT	85,105	48,201	67,745	233,667	17,199	47,188	49,187	50,940	36,075	33,078
067	Waterbury, CT	128,771	52,441	66,755	330,205	21,434	63,647	63,708	79,227	56,105	46,084
068	Stamford, CT	168,270	88,654	139,501	461,019	32,659	88,370	79,885	117,799	82,187	60,119
069	Stamford, CT	47,146	66,853	98,396	121,539	8,210	19,470	28,530	28,737	19,722	16,870
070	Newark, NJ	618,265	60,377	83,354	1,663,708	108,496	279,349	367,292	402,570	277,123	228,878
071	Newark, NJ	140,327	34,960	48,147	404,275	30,593	78,847	105,618	88,520	60,329	40,368
072	Newark, NJ	61,224	44,408	55,873	181,777	13,368	34,018	45,368	42,299	27,861	18,863
073	Newark, NJ	88,208	42,453	59,221	238,594	16,876	42,073	66,240	54,241	35,524	23,640
074	Paterson, NJ	165,550	84,642	113,061	461,099	30,343	87,352	77,268	121,403	85,761	58,972
075	Paterson, NJ	63,559	41,451	55,406	203,734	16,279	40,874	50,913	44,613	29,960	21,095
076	Hackensack, NJ	177,481	73,271	99,628	488,527	29,691	84,062	89,712	120,908	89,961	74,193
077	Monmouth, NJ	223,839	71,816	96,557	613,234	40,002	118,531	112,603	157,431	108,525	76,142

ZIP Code	3-Digit ZIP Code Areas	Total Households	Median Household Income	Average Household Income	Total Population	Population by Age: 0-4 years	Population by Age: 5-17 years	Population by Age: 18-34 years	Population by Age: 35-49 years	Population by Age: 50-64 years	Gray Markets 65 + years
078	West Jersey, NJ	129,471	77,462	96,841	358,782	23,671	70,217	64,997	97,237	66,082	36,578
079	West Jersey, NJ	93,172	104,523	146,962	252,895	17,507	44,485	41,913	65,631	48,454	34,905
080	South Jersey, NJ	425,569	60,967	75,323	1,134,876	67,595	213,220	224,677	278,851	198,067	152,466
081	South Jersey, NJ	55,095	38,247	49,544	160,790	11,804	35,791	37,089	34,982	22,878	18,246
082	South Jersey, NJ	95,155	49,307	64,316	246,028	14,300	45,455	45,939	58,913	43,093	38,328
083	South Jersey, NJ	76,955	46,759	57,565	226,770	13,736	43,141	50,747	54,700	36,425	28,021
084	South Jersey, NJ	25,501	33,430	50,337	62,012	3,882	10,098	13,278	13,309	10,472	10,973
085	Trenton, NJ	103,116	85,238	113,197	292,284	19,454	55,989	61,073	78,640	49,051	28,077
086	Trenton, NJ	95,490	54,582	68,203	270,023	17,089	46,477	67,383	62,486	41,806	34,782
087	Trenton, NJ	177,648	49,841	65,872	441,975	25,914	71,866	78,861	89,796	71,777	104,011
088	New Brunswick, NJ	319,042	72,877	91,420	882,443	59,169	156,858	182,126	226,643	148,393	109,254
089	New Brunswick, NJ	34,003	54,319	70,483	103,523	7,165	15,548	37,327	21,546	13,033	8,904
100	New York, NY	705,347	53,311	94,412	1,475,046	81,348	173,492	433,232	356,015	245,875	185,084
101	New York, NY	29,814	82,580	136,475	54,971	2,782	5,251	16,955	13,425	10,205	6,353
102	New York, NY	3,804	119,040	167,440	7,047	535	642	2,143	2,430	963	334
103	Staten Island, NY	164,800	59,893	73,895	465,729	29,812	84,126	106,265	110,030	80,767	54,729
104	Bronx, NY	476,168	29,316	41,569	1,374,264	109,099	286,823	357,484	291,809	188,814	140,235
105	Westchester, NY	228,881	83,759	124,439	643,997	43,345	120,676	117,168	164,923	115,840	82,045
106	Westchester, NY	31,087	68,401	98,948	80,701	4,836	12,351	17,871	19,128	14,445	12,070
107	Westchester, NY	87,304	53,004	76,269	229,022	15,161	40,077	51,233	50,148	37,956	34,447
108	Westchester, NY	28,609	64,964	100,628	79,640	5,231	14,085	17,132	17,990	13,332	11,870
109	Rockland, NY	167,160	69,125	87,173	514,358	37,122	104,597	108,071	119,502	88,241	56,825
110	Queens, NY	84,737	79,334	112,623	242,934	13,935	41,819	43,476	55,744	42,862	45,098
111	Long Island City, NY	86,533	39,149	51,025	220,328	13,105	28,676	69,765	51,403	31,894	25,485
112	Brooklyn, NY	890,305	34,329	50,359	2,496,933	182,932	462,103	641,450	536,290	382,209	291,949
113	Flushing, NY	410,429	46,805	61,034	1,148,615	71,132	164,596	291,626	273,194	189,483	158,584
114	Jamaica, NY	233,985	50,201	62,730	737,225	51,197	131,944	177,003	172,878	120,352	83,851
115	Western Nassau, NY	239,301	75,577	100,745	721,817	44,097	129,467	145,005	170,019	127,951	105,278
116	Far Rockaway, NY	37,049	36,178	51,580	107,218	8,527	21,154	22,824	22,524	16,682	15,507
117	Mid-Island, NY	514,794	77,052	96,255	1,568,632	104,721	293,158	316,343	390,231	273,788	190,391
118	Mid-Island, NY	25,072	86,007	106,235	74,641	4,394	12,652	13,007	18,689	13,490	12,409
119	Mid-Island, NY	90,241	58,922	75,141	244,356	14,640	43,189	46,733	59,609	42,381	37,804
120	Albany, NY	126,660	44,112	65,709	322,463	18,243	58,842	64,465	77,295	58,665	44,953
121	Plattsburgh, NY	109,504	47,368	59,593	271,333	14,882	47,019	60,244	62,986	48,025	38,167
122	Syracuse, NY	62,087	40,503	54,808	146,655	7,593	21,177	43,923	29,738	22,977	21,247
123	Syracuse, NY	63,750	46,684	60,533	157,716	9,218	28,257	31,058	36,513	27,139	25,531
124	Mid-Hudson, NY	62,253	42,762	55,685	154,795	7,809	26,708	28,843	37,040	30,488	23,907
125	Mid-Hudson, NY	157,423	57,379	70,600	441,602	25,718	83,419	94,872	109,571	75,143	52,879
126	Mid-Hudson, NY	31,696	50,262	64,429	87,768	5,109	15,366	23,677	18,838	13,611	11,167
127	Mid-Hudson, NY	36,887	41,020	52,957	97,269	5,437	18,203	19,029	22,849	18,135	13,616
128	Glen Falls, NY	86,451	44,112	65,103	219,730	11,288	38,667	47,660	51,882	39,660	30,573
129	Plattsburgh, NY	59,933	38,894	49,099	162,360	7,407	26,666	40,891	39,386	26,823	21,187
130	Syracuse, NY	149,430	47,770	59,947	383,709	23,179	72,056	79,332	92,590	66,871	49,681
131	Syracuse, NY	67,696	45,206	58,053	181,135	10,382	35,461	38,008	43,569	31,420	22,295
132	Syracuse, NY	93,162	32,943	45,799	228,375	14,538	40,179	59,186	46,779	33,336	34,357
133	Utica, NY	54,544	38,910	49,068	141,862	7,219	26,019	30,099	31,711	24,907	21,907
134	Utica, NY	72,302	41,603	52,313	189,747	9,769	33,868	39,595	43,631	33,540	29,524
135	Utica, NY	27,955	28,247	39,524	67,838	4,206	11,334	15,369	13,486	10,890	12,553
136	Watertown, NY	81,073	35,783	45,269	223,630	13,505	39,641	59,555	48,785	34,254	27,890
137	Binghamton, NY	56,451	39,574	50,469	138,611	7,450	24,594	27,752	31,673	25,022	22,120
138	Binghamton, NY	53,541	39,176	51,079	143,465	7,042	24,921	35,227	30,549	24,684	21,042
139	Binghamton, NY	32,160	34,047	47,070	75,427	4,112	12,118	17,503	16,247	12,662	12,785
140	Buffalo, NY	166,731	50,481	63,151	444,405	24,549	81,267	87,544	108,845	79,580	62,620
141	Buffalo, NY	77,184	47,402	58,612	196,966	10,390	35,487	37,441	46,618	35,263	31,767
142	Buffalo, NY	244,448	34,953	48,143	586,517	34,774	99,395	135,942	125,177	93,593	97,636
143	Buffalo, NY	29,295	30,861	40,943	68,427	3,925	11,782	14,337	15,088	10,993	12,302
144	Rochester, NY	111,044	51,727	63,798	305,806	17,027	56,195	68,857	74,419	52,982	36,326
145	Rochester, NY	115,141	56,101	70,464	307,187	18,158	60,193	55,500	76,204	56,998	40,134
146	Rochester, NY	193,511	40,600	52,894	482,203	30,450	86,277	117,597	104,563	76,330	66,986
147	Jamestown, NY	71,862	35,259	45,101	183,952	10,391	34,347	38,183	40,438	32,188	28,405
148	Elmira, NY	110,334	40,394	53,299	285,255	14,392	47,039	78,214	59,562	47,736	38,312
149	Elmira, NY	19,799	43,956	45,218	50,288	3,059	8,674	12,067	10,984	7,657	7,847
150	Pittsburgh, PA	187,177	42,662	56,496	459,442	24,691	76,211	80,892	109,571	82,798	85,279
151	Pittsburgh, PA	158,613	43,157	57,967	381,141	21,070	62,969	67,448	89,144	69,490	71,020
152	Pittsburgh, PA	307,679	39,662	56,618	716,116	37,769	108,998	164,773	158,825	121,180	124,571
153	Pittsburgh, PA	70,628	42,159	56,539	180,903	9,578	30,339	35,265	42,558	33,643	29,520
154	Pittsburgh, PA	61,639	30,832	41,809	152,151	7,798	24,311	31,744	33,246	27,533	27,519
155	Johnstown, PA	35,360	34,483	43,353	90,828	4,856	14,742	18,432	20,637	16,479	15,682
156	Greensburg, PA	124,908	41,853	54,399	308,737	15,016	50,206	56,434	73,387	59,088	54,606

ZIP Code	3-Digit ZIP Code Areas	Total Households	Median Household Income	Average Household Income	Total Population	Population by Age: 0-4 years	Population by Age: 5-17 years	Population by Age: 18-34 years	Population by Age: 35-49 years	Population by Age: 50-64 years	Gray Markets 65 + years
157	Johnstown, PA	44,144	32,113	41,763	113,248	5,271	17,273	29,429	23,774	19,601	17,900
158	DuBois, PA	37,883	37,449	46,438	93,431	4,934	16,149	17,493	21,335	16,576	16,944
159	Johnstown, PA	61,234	32,827	43,389	151,928	7,157	22,915	30,431	33,248	27,733	30,444
160	New Castle, PA	73,737	46,793	59,950	193,471	11,363	34,209	40,390	46,829	32,947	27,733
161	New Castle, PA	89,586	37,304	47,838	228,509	12,269	39,097	44,864	49,815	40,256	42,208
162	New Castle, PA	35,190	33,563	42,938	89,104	4,504	14,534	19,900	19,438	15,653	15,075
163	Oil City, PA	61,638	35,593	45,545	153,218	8,102	26,661	29,594	33,919	28,943	25,999
164	Erie, PA	46,350	41,629	51,077	130,802	7,393	24,999	30,273	29,729	22,300	16,108
165	Erie, PA	72,863	36,895	48,882	184,609	11,442	32,629	41,957	39,638	29,683	29,260
166	Altoona, PA	80,521	35,032	44,165	207,904	10,904	33,126	45,427	46,640	37,138	34,669
167	Bradford, PA	19,507	35,723	44,415	49,497	2,621	8,749	10,185	11,068	8,620	8,254
168	Altoona, PA	68,694	37,888	49,879	182,507	8,104	24,896	64,818	35,636	26,843	22,210
169	Williamsport, PA	25,513	36,056	45,608	66,266	3,460	11,842	13,681	14,172	12,267	10,844
170	Harrisburg, PA	228,537	47,364	59,667	579,957	32,219	98,510	120,153	134,517	104,398	90,160
171	Harrisburg, PA	64,518	43,595	56,380	156,906	10,004	27,552	33,275	37,322	27,144	21,609
172	Harrisburg, PA	72,448	42,738	51,554	187,622	11,118	31,919	42,643	40,338	32,533	29,071
173	Lancaster, PA	119,019	50,631	58,938	312,942	17,677	57,683	64,316	77,939	55,346	39,981
174	Lancaster, PA	61,581	43,779	55,825	154,960	8,731	25,709	33,855	34,664	26,798	25,203
175	Lancaster, PA	108,474	51,959	61,693	303,940	21,186	60,868	62,462	69,089	49,425	40,910
176	Lancaster, PA	59,439	44,883	53,019	151,600	9,747	26,306	34,296	32,855	24,705	23,691
177	Williamsport, PA	66,995	36,251	46,625	170,465	9,145	28,116	38,090	37,328	29,694	28,092
178	Harrisburg, PA	86,739	37,777	48,250	229,601	10,905	36,105	54,155	51,244	39,578	37,614
179	Reading, PA	49,581	36,044	46,169	125,015	5,714	18,883	25,646	28,620	21,906	24,246
180	Lehigh Valley, PA	191,883	52,079	53,718	497,900	26,501	86,632	100,825	120,248	87,610	76,084
181	Lehigh Valley, PA	59,685	39,754	51,684	153,471	9,650	26,463	34,379	33,365	24,441	25,173
182	Wilkes-Barre, PA	52,360	36,262	46,379	126,637	5,812	20,022	24,656	27,987	23,078	25,082
183	Lehigh Valley, PA	60,280	52,538	63,427	166,344	8,694	32,637	34,233	41,910	28,371	20,499
184	Scranton, PA	74,201	42,537	55,227	191,211	9,717	34,361	34,489	43,910	35,932	32,802
185	Scranton, PA	48,494	33,233	44,603	116,181	5,660	17,351	26,185	23,589	19,657	23,739
186	Wilkes-Barre, PA	67,860	37,559	48,083	167,354	8,032	27,519	32,868	37,342	31,346	30,247
187	Wilkes-Barre, PA	57,253	36,044	48,448	138,717	6,491	20,741	28,996	30,763	24,633	27,093
188	Scranton, PA	30,521	37,957	47,976	76,573	4,196	14,311	14,000	17,560	14,486	12,020
189	Southeastern, PA	129,711	72,118	92,312	356,044	22,300	67,202	63,780	91,858	65,030	45,874
190	Philadelphia, PA	428,673	60,089	81,535	1,125,915	64,716	200,670	228,862	266,444	191,170	174,053
191	Philadelphia, PA	575,707	32,768	45,101	1,477,224	97,807	266,006	373,511	310,105	225,197	204,598
193	Southeastern, PA	143,794	74,528	98,446	404,602	25,809	78,480	83,263	100,628	69,299	47,123
194	Reading, PA	183,820	65,866	84,167	479,562	31,201	82,789	101,577	120,463	80,355	63,177
195	Reading, PA	75,218	56,676	66,664	205,405	11,475	36,678	42,556	51,312	35,866	27,518
196	Reading, PA	77,196	42,281	55,640	198,103	12,637	35,722	43,454	42,210	31,814	32,266
197	Wilmington, DE	106,842	62,950	75,222	296,072	20,229	52,199	80,957	71,929	45,143	25,615
198	Wilmington, DE	89,876	54,889	74,286	221,562	13,236	36,016	46,922	52,019	38,335	35,034
199	Wilmington, DE	119,621	43,947	55,265	308,043	18,348	51,465	66,447	69,000	54,298	48,485
200	Washington, DC	246,343	44,928	71,949	560,178	32,835	73,853	170,410	122,479	92,559	68,042
201	Northern Virginia, VA	240,608	86,402	104,832	687,975	58,156	139,389	158,626	184,628	105,878	41,298
206	Southern, MD	106,949	67,842	77,963	305,255	20,448	63,916	66,084	78,945	48,986	26,876
207	Southern, MD	338,726	61,912	73,189	951,706	69,409	180,940	237,105	235,466	152,710	76,076
208	Suburban, MD	236,394	88,814	120,143	639,502	44,698	121,557	121,711	166,226	116,017	69,293
209	Suburban, MD	112,280	63,889	81,294	300,458	20,575	50,736	68,906	73,290	49,082	37,869
210	Baltimore, MD	260,275	69,297	86,887	688,718	44,523	133,843	138,382	176,515	121,898	73,557
211	Baltimore, MD	156,736	71,037	86,823	427,510	28,324	84,165	87,729	110,347	74,844	42,101
212	Baltimore, MD	476,874	40,336	54,012	1,191,538	76,656	206,357	282,355	266,956	189,379	169,835
214	Baltimore, MD	34,940	70,447	91,230	88,207	5,124	13,435	21,139	19,910	16,775	11,824
215	Cumberland, MD	39,813	33,596	44,033	102,851	5,341	16,069	24,263	21,598	17,921	17,659
216	Easton, MD	63,022	47,966	64,585	158,394	8,525	28,170	29,584	36,626	29,540	25,949
217	Frederick, MD	160,040	61,284	74,158	443,166	28,573	86,155	93,529	113,207	72,615	49,087
218	Salisbury, MD	63,980	41,821	54,245	164,508	9,449	26,844	38,208	36,531	28,333	25,143
219	Baltimore, MD	34,204	65,805	65,391	93,127	5,992	18,828	20,161	22,667	15,645	9,834
220	Northern Virginia, VA	158,118	84,683	108,218	443,453	30,771	79,425	99,880	112,214	82,989	38,174
221	Northern Virginia, VA	145,090	84,612	110,733	411,125	30,132	83,127	86,511	104,387	73,621	33,347
222	Northern Virginia, VA	89,139	70,901	95,334	195,811	11,783	21,032	62,153	49,805	32,585	18,453
223	Northern Virginia, VA	137,229	68,481	90,167	316,613	23,376	43,350	80,092	82,990	55,604	31,201
224	Richmond, VA	68,766	57,056	69,625	184,174	12,393	35,241	44,023	42,120	29,252	21,145
225	Richmond, VA	59,273	60,833	72,107	170,249	10,960	35,479	36,278	42,675	27,599	17,258
226	Winchester, VA	62,858	47,626	59,498	160,290	9,699	28,823	35,017	38,383	27,693	20,675
227	Culpeper, VA	25,324	49,890	62,434	69,989	4,106	13,206	15,608	17,163	11,840	8,066
228	Charlottesville, VA	55,444	39,979	51,003	150,503	8,181	23,087	45,270	30,312	23,746	19,907
229	Charlottesville, VA	90,011	46,511	61,748	228,566	13,532	36,921	60,316	50,337	38,017	29,443
230	Richmond, VA	74,509	53,614	67,117	194,211	12,327	35,820	40,501	48,641	33,811	23,111
231	Richmond, VA	114,941	64,064	80,189	314,721	17,876	59,950	64,969	78,176	56,838	36,912

ZIP Code	3-Digit ZIP Code Areas	Total Households	Median Household Income	Average Household Income	Total Population	Population by Age: 0-4 years	Population by Age: 5-17 years	Population by Age: 18-34 years	Population by Age: 35-49 years	Population by Age: 50-64 years	Gray Markets 65 + years
232	Richmond, VA	211,412	44,780	60,636	508,207	33,521	86,734	124,659	116,774	82,159	64,360
233	Norfolk, VA	86,871	53,153	63,881	242,089	16,481	49,239	51,579	61,596	38,228	24,966
234	Norfolk, VA	206,711	51,292	64,540	556,941	39,583	109,881	133,061	136,172	83,404	54,840
235	Norfolk, VA	91,006	34,375	47,318	242,602	18,989	40,726	79,598	48,294	29,588	25,407
236	Norfolk, VA	145,268	44,320	55,492	388,845	28,361	73,455	97,218	92,043	57,241	40,527
237	Norfolk, VA	37,200	36,378	45,671	98,240	7,319	17,712	24,472	20,948	14,457	13,332
238	Richmond, VA	114,231	46,278	57,917	316,616	19,009	56,849	73,509	76,511	53,697	37,041
239	Farmville, VA	37,895	32,979	43,153	102,402	5,151	16,176	24,320	22,754	17,504	16,497
240	Roanoke, VA	138,868	38,629	51,502	338,636	18,923	51,290	92,224	71,478	58,008	46,713
241	Roanoke, VA	91,979	38,077	48,957	224,100	11,518	34,923	49,387	49,350	43,606	35,316
242	Bristol, VA	80,088	30,212	40,693	191,759	9,785	29,562	42,283	42,692	36,849	30,588
243	Roanoke, VA	63,850	32,700	42,769	153,836	7,921	23,727	32,484	33,941	30,096	25,667
244	Charlottesville, VA	54,287	40,637	50,918	136,274	6,964	21,607	30,059	30,135	25,821	21,688
245	Lynchburg, VA	145,009	36,413	47,634	360,617	21,084	61,486	76,090	79,192	65,880	56,885
246	Bluefield, WV	28,247	28,111	37,549	69,451	3,176	10,852	14,917	16,213	14,208	10,085
247	Bluefield, WV	26,633	28,841	40,012	62,190	3,460	9,187	13,614	12,699	12,241	10,989
248	Bluefield, WV	17,611	21,493	30,777	42,317	2,212	7,038	8,128	9,927	8,617	6,395
249	Lewisburg, WV	21,863	30,601	41,913	53,334	2,504	8,150	10,713	12,003	10,917	9,047
250	Charleston, WV	29,598	31,754	41,755	70,956	4,003	11,231	14,947	15,714	14,131	10,930
251	Charleston, WV	33,347	33,252	43,274	81,350	4,549	12,634	17,532	18,107	15,864	12,664
252	Charleston, WV	22,670	32,131	42,099	56,582	3,214	9,652	11,418	12,885	11,027	8,386
253	Charleston, WV	51,535	38,697	57,336	116,687	6,406	17,771	23,447	26,973	22,674	19,416
254	Martinsburg, WV	59,419	44,310	54,253	150,884	9,089	27,259	33,880	35,587	27,458	17,611
255	Huntington, WV	56,373	34,227	46,373	140,990	8,236	23,700	30,311	31,753	27,356	19,634
256	Huntington, WV	21,118	24,645	35,900	52,083	2,845	8,649	11,307	11,986	9,988	7,308
257	Huntington, WV	32,274	28,112	41,723	73,377	3,717	9,737	20,257	14,146	12,872	12,648
258	Beckley, WV	35,034	31,479	44,242	85,981	4,421	13,292	19,125	19,017	16,490	13,636
259	Beckley, WV	20,107	26,435	35,328	48,662	2,506	7,638	9,907	10,689	10,496	8,266
260	Wheeling, WV	57,445	34,516	45,716	138,295	6,868	21,780	27,230	30,485	26,903	25,029
261	Parkersburg, WV	54,789	34,751	45,735	132,966	7,069	22,495	25,851	29,908	26,411	21,232
262	Clarksburg, WV	33,389	29,356	38,824	83,210	4,043	13,751	17,685	18,150	16,524	13,057
263	Clarksburg, WV	35,839	32,305	42,567	87,677	4,551	14,507	17,785	19,492	16,757	14,585
264	Clarksburg, WV	21,398	29,717	38,824	53,617	2,603	9,120	11,491	11,864	10,496	8,043
265	Clarksburg, WV	67,542	31,736	44,367	162,571	7,798	22,810	49,228	32,902	27,469	22,364
266	Gassaway, WV	13,313	29,777	41,350	33,138	1,607	5,560	6,802	7,544	6,647	4,978
267	Cumberland, MD	20,774	32,871	41,068	51,677	2,678	9,078	10,566	11,026	10,383	7,946
268	Petersburg, WV	13,989	34,814	43,279	33,962	1,850	5,622	6,644	7,678	6,781	5,387
270	Greensboro, NC	108,885	43,413	54,817	275,297	17,897	49,292	55,221	65,232	51,002	36,653
271	Greensboro, NC	92,657	41,540	58,015	227,511	15,968	38,277	57,334	48,952	36,318	30,662
272	Greensboro, NC	213,770	42,846	54,785	544,070	36,934	96,331	121,550	124,197	93,710	71,348
273	Greensboro, NC	132,686	45,277	53,486	342,926	23,439	61,184	73,460	79,821	60,029	44,993
274	Greensboro, NC	114,184	45,277	62,366	279,074	18,519	45,279	76,564	61,007	44,442	33,263
275	Raleigh, NC	330,880	50,334	66,252	878,126	63,638	161,353	222,688	213,392	133,682	83,373
276	Raleigh, NC	161,783	56,815	74,714	409,544	27,398	66,835	125,016	97,507	59,805	32,983
277	Raleigh, NC	91,995	46,262	61,247	231,516	17,649	36,847	70,691	51,426	33,058	21,845
278	Rocky Mount, NC	200,428	34,430	47,048	513,287	34,440	92,300	121,204	111,416	86,595	67,332
279	Rocky Mount, NC	71,863	37,108	49,107	182,370	10,625	32,613	36,736	42,129	33,287	26,980
280	Charlotte, NC	223,063	45,355	59,072	579,851	41,352	105,239	131,287	133,481	97,447	71,045
281	Charlotte, NC	190,699	47,339	59,907	511,813	35,795	96,074	114,966	119,993	84,720	60,265
282	Charlotte, NC	263,784	43,888	74,770	665,305	51,663	117,366	181,199	160,746	96,802	57,529
283	Fayetteville, NC	286,625	37,007	47,736	777,429	62,295	151,011	197,872	164,902	114,745	86,604
284	Fayetteville, NC	162,623	39,916	53,582	392,625	23,924	63,094	92,085	84,289	73,044	56,189
285	Kinston, NC	163,008	38,382	49,013	435,212	35,328	76,070	114,725	90,194	65,958	52,937
286	Hickory, NC	240,287	38,927	49,300	605,241	38,064	100,846	142,007	132,056	109,406	82,862
287	Asheville, NC	204,131	37,753	48,454	492,407	27,585	77,910	98,456	103,748	95,861	88,847
288	Asheville, NC	46,925	38,005	53,318	108,105	6,111	15,674	25,215	23,356	19,271	18,478
289	Asheville, NC	15,074	31,489	41,898	34,630	1,735	5,083	6,141	6,632	7,727	7,312
290	Columbia, SC	136,719	44,043	55,688	367,550	23,990	67,773	80,882	89,971	64,803	40,131
291	Columbia, SC	139,499	34,872	45,448	363,991	24,378	64,116	85,148	79,454	62,790	48,105
292	Columbia, SC	115,949	43,645	59,865	300,800	18,016	48,485	89,912	67,107	46,357	30,923
293	Greenville, SC	144,835	38,902	50,110	371,676	22,900	62,983	85,656	83,343	67,162	49,632
294	Charleston, SC	247,299	42,644	56,589	642,728	42,977	113,421	162,683	146,867	106,405	70,375
295	Florence, SC	226,039	36,494	48,865	567,342	35,794	94,149	129,379	124,368	105,422	78,230
296	Greenville, SC	348,945	41,722	54,633	885,054	56,062	146,339	215,662	198,419	155,367	113,205
297	Charlotte, NC	110,767	43,347	54,618	292,188	18,996	52,837	68,671	68,379	50,763	32,542
298	Augusta, GA	79,971	38,334	50,480	209,187	12,834	36,813	46,560	48,391	36,901	27,688
299	Savannah, GA	66,162	47,434	67,021	178,234	11,917	29,162	44,409	36,214	29,250	27,282
300	North Metro, GA	704,742	63,946	82,540	1,980,202	158,506	379,086	492,284	514,869	296,917	138,540
301	North Metro, GA	363,719	54,298	66,125	1,017,950	79,958	198,884	252,248	247,636	151,026	88,198

ZIP Code	3-Digit ZIP Code Areas	Total Households	Median Household Income	Average Household Income	Total Population	Population by Age: 0-4 years	Population by Age: 5-17 years	Population by Age: 18-34 years	Population by Age: 35-49 years	Population by Age: 50-64 years	Gray Markets 65 + years
302	North Metro, GA	305,611	51,885	63,946	869,228	65,309	179,491	207,279	206,917	133,467	76,765
303	Atlanta, GA	355,719	47,509	75,619	878,577	61,212	130,750	278,506	196,371	131,081	80,657
304	Swainsboro, GA	74,974	29,227	40,558	206,907	14,241	36,747	59,050	41,459	30,607	24,803
305	Athens, GA	196,571	44,406	57,180	535,881	38,837	94,327	132,744	117,828	88,091	64,054
306	Chattanooga, TN	129,362	37,881	51,923	340,485	21,525	56,990	104,586	68,407	51,102	37,875
307	Augusta, GA	123,931	39,473	49,825	334,963	24,573	61,465	81,277	73,769	55,034	38,845
308	Augusta, GA	55,795	43,797	55,188	157,631	11,665	34,255	33,015	38,073	25,696	14,927
309	Augusta, GA	75,631	37,825	52,887	200,764	14,604	37,355	50,960	43,110	31,414	23,321
310	Macon, GA	177,998	37,660	49,117	491,453	32,414	92,824	116,779	112,110	79,834	57,492
312	Macon, GA	65,173	37,543	53,057	167,992	12,847	31,888	38,957	36,757	26,617	20,926
313	Savannah, GA	59,949	42,986	53,932	172,854	15,787	37,027	45,504	39,098	22,806	12,632
314	Savannah, GA	85,452	40,025	58,905	219,439	15,799	39,078	55,585	45,958	34,749	28,270
315	Waycross, GA	112,202	35,164	47,294	300,908	21,645	58,459	70,788	65,984	48,728	35,304
316	Valdosta, GA	61,788	32,235	43,476	170,447	12,528	32,246	46,705	35,992	24,781	18,195
317	Albany, GA	136,279	33,363	46,053	371,236	28,041	73,077	88,975	77,749	58,606	44,788
318	Columbus, GA	28,256	40,554	54,099	74,242	4,653	14,445	14,950	17,303	13,525	9,366
319	Columbus, GA	69,450	37,714	51,396	191,567	15,787	36,507	50,743	40,339	26,554	21,637
320	Jacksonville, FL	186,217	45,975	61,468	503,367	30,183	91,791	105,495	116,731	93,617	65,550
321	Jacksonville, FL	216,571	37,307	50,406	499,093	22,684	70,097	86,513	94,537	100,293	124,969
322	Jacksonville, FL	334,135	44,977	59,149	856,471	65,011	165,136	200,460	202,772	134,383	88,709
323	Tallahassee, FL	152,080	37,791	52,150	391,535	23,547	61,375	121,819	82,408	62,728	39,658
324	Panama City, FL	121,221	35,938	47,431	312,369	18,531	53,580	67,347	71,693	56,482	44,736
325	Pensacola, FL	237,025	42,664	55,550	623,009	40,666	112,000	145,015	140,932	103,150	81,246
326	Gainesville, FL	132,557	33,692	48,900	332,823	18,755	50,645	106,623	64,847	52,873	39,080
327	Mid-Florida, FL	341,943	47,218	63,729	871,950	53,344	158,207	176,875	202,767	151,810	128,947
328	Orlando, FL	289,139	43,872	57,478	773,591	56,716	141,050	212,318	182,830	109,660	71,017
329	Orlando, FL	240,642	44,111	59,526	569,666	28,929	92,284	95,650	125,590	103,000	124,213
330	South Florida, FL	560,238	43,289	58,478	1,549,760	107,019	285,609	325,818	365,716	254,677	210,921
331	Miami, FL	643,085	39,517	60,002	1,817,042	116,049	314,152	404,708	422,555	303,959	255,619
333	Fort Lauderdale, FL	312,660	45,598	65,127	772,233	49,572	135,058	157,731	189,425	127,720	112,727
334	West Palm Beach, FL	562,334	48,521	72,876	1,337,029	75,857	211,660	238,616	285,252	222,714	302,930
335	Tampa, FL	217,694	48,369	62,516	574,613	38,948	108,110	113,621	130,150	97,144	86,640
336	Tampa, FL	276,305	41,338	58,292	680,961	47,929	122,947	171,751	158,036	106,649	73,649
337	Saint Petersburg, FL	338,620	39,551	54,732	743,636	38,714	105,898	132,415	164,724	140,860	161,025
338	Lakeland, FL	243,835	37,892	50,045	626,374	40,869	110,454	123,285	121,126	106,649	123,991
339	Fort Myers, FL	266,888	44,093	59,841	621,838	32,864	91,361	103,308	117,864	118,089	158,352
341	Fort Myers, FL	138,388	53,627	81,684	335,510	18,424	47,954	60,137	62,094	64,719	82,182
342	Manasota, FL	305,351	44,474	62,355	692,716	34,596	96,008	111,094	131,872	131,276	187,870
344	Gainesville, FL	157,901	34,479	45,910	369,899	17,545	55,745	58,065	66,887	70,054	101,603
346	Tampa, FL	256,231	40,143	54,518	590,485	28,980	89,741	119,115	119,702	109,988	150,959
347	Orlando, FL	165,241	43,320	55,906	448,278	29,610	81,622	96,767	99,736	73,064	67,479
349	West Palm Beach, FL	148,614	41,082	56,778	365,529	20,134	60,412	63,057	73,643	64,679	83,604
350	Birmingham, AL	158,939	39,202	49,684	408,260	26,851	71,511	91,537	91,113	71,549	55,699
351	Birmingham, AL	114,073	44,808	56,130	302,308	19,314	54,867	66,170	70,945	53,881	37,131
352	Birmingham, AL	201,342	41,838	63,597	493,959	33,445	86,678	118,859	112,279	78,944	63,754
354	Tuscaloosa, AL	80,679	34,129	47,821	202,896	13,269	34,025	58,380	41,196	31,291	24,735
355	Birmingham, AL	65,314	30,204	39,838	159,924	9,623	26,365	33,636	34,374	30,589	25,337
356	Huntsville, AL	142,091	36,726	48,794	354,012	21,913	61,708	77,814	79,609	63,426	49,542
357	Huntsville, AL	70,690	41,701	61,676	187,317	12,923	35,898	40,347	47,939	31,129	19,081
358	Birmingham, AL	76,007	44,524	59,560	180,452	10,680	30,462	43,177	40,700	30,926	24,507
359	Birmingham, AL	107,347	33,259	44,103	270,324	17,439	46,131	60,282	57,264	48,470	40,738
360	Montgomery, AL	101,855	34,666	47,181	274,512	17,634	51,399	65,071	60,362	45,442	34,604
361	Montgomery, AL	81,511	38,632	53,210	210,900	15,190	38,001	55,735	45,224	31,421	25,329
362	Anniston, AL	72,126	33,646	44,408	177,625	11,236	30,274	39,757	38,534	32,043	25,781
363	Dothan, AL	87,862	34,963	46,910	217,891	14,564	39,555	47,914	47,383	37,855	30,620
364	Evergreen, AL	43,798	29,221	40,161	106,960	6,706	19,349	21,739	22,647	19,405	17,114
365	Mobile, AL	120,966	41,346	53,234	320,043	20,696	59,602	68,991	71,076	56,492	42,973
366	Mobile, AL	108,388	34,396	48,883	280,814	20,696	53,333	65,989	60,086	44,513	36,197
367	Montgomery, AL	47,385	25,563	37,560	122,558	9,209	25,362	25,525	25,326	20,225	17,115
368	Montgomery, AL	89,335	31,758	43,299	222,558	13,633	37,194	67,991	44,592	33,757	25,391
369	Meridian, MS	8,543	24,186	36,269	21,312	1,367	4,217	4,263	4,408	3,915	3,142
370	Nashville, TN	291,859	48,830	64,089	767,082	54,302	144,136	179,156	186,960	126,465	76,063
371	Nashville, TN	192,361	45,677	55,976	508,616	34,688	91,825	126,621	120,075	81,644	53,763
372	Nashville, TN	169,117	42,135	61,135	407,430	28,102	61,979	112,491	93,858	62,806	48,194
373	Chattanooga, TN	207,152	38,943	51,585	528,612	32,553	90,714	116,699	118,243	99,309	71,094
374	Chattanooga, TN	79,196	35,417	49,963	186,785	11,252	29,384	44,772	39,753	32,515	29,109
376	Knoxville, TN	164,690	34,298	56,357	395,507	22,143	60,723	86,374	88,357	76,992	60,918
377	Knoxville, TN	132,810	44,224	44,907	325,190	18,529	52,749	69,711	72,219	63,974	48,008
378	Knoxville, TN	193,044	34,849	45,813	478,822	28,376	80,017	103,074	107,612	91,862	67,881

ZIP Code	3-Digit ZIP Code Areas	Total Households	Median Household Income	Average Household Income	Total Population	Population by Age: 0-4 years	Population by Age: 5-17 years	Population by Age: 18-34 years	Population by Age: 35-49 years	Population by Age: 50-64 years	Gray Markets 65 + years
379	Knoxville, TN	150,067	41,024	52,125	358,481	21,868	56,246	92,229	81,637	60,573	45,928
380	Memphis, TN	133,693	49,130	64,174	367,203	25,655	69,122	82,606	90,238	60,847	38,735
381	Memphis, TN	291,972	38,717	54,941	765,835	58,946	153,517	185,646	171,171	117,392	79,163
382	McKenzie, TN	46,741	33,040	42,433	114,885	6,760	18,362	25,857	23,908	21,396	18,602
383	Jackson, TN	111,606	34,881	46,407	280,012	17,326	48,738	61,694	60,123	49,940	42,191
384	Columbia, TN	66,369	36,603	47,445	173,279	10,843	31,092	37,725	39,290	30,761	23,568
385	Cookeville, TN	88,033	31,755	41,403	215,098	12,414	34,455	48,864	44,549	40,366	34,450
386	Memphis, TN	132,592	38,409	49,652	363,239	26,949	69,067	94,489	76,839	55,615	40,280
387	Greenville, MS	45,306	26,427	38,841	137,728	10,736	28,355	36,091	27,766	19,898	14,882
388	Tupelo, MS	99,056	33,903	44,556	252,460	17,539	46,079	56,837	54,328	43,294	34,383
389	Grenada, MS	43,724	27,286	37,879	117,103	8,335	22,910	26,711	23,763	19,014	16,370
390	Jackson, MS	96,453	37,972	50,467	267,891	19,222	52,820	63,129	58,087	43,043	31,590
391	Jackson, MS	101,754	36,441	52,423	277,587	19,546	53,462	63,899	62,189	44,273	34,218
392	Jackson, MS	84,954	34,025	48,677	232,549	17,926	44,291	61,510	50,170	33,825	24,827
393	Meridian, MS	80,043	30,449	41,662	210,289	15,173	39,734	47,967	43,206	33,991	30,218
394	Hattiesburg, MS	129,063	32,228	44,167	349,834	24,746	64,392	89,514	72,239	55,644	43,299
395	Gulfport, MS	143,538	39,888	50,935	381,409	26,639	71,247	90,674	85,648	62,795	44,406
396	McComb, MS	49,183	27,860	39,451	129,715	8,952	24,326	28,996	27,234	21,677	18,530
397	Columbus, MS	64,212	30,711	42,628	170,957	11,960	31,425	47,634	34,219	25,280	20,439
398	Albany, GA	41,589	29,067	40,938	111,662	7,961	21,853	23,932	23,508	18,382	16,026
400	Louisville, KY	78,373	50,508	66,192	217,465	13,142	39,263	47,931	55,445	39,275	22,409
401	Louisville, KY	51,436	41,741	49,997	138,939	9,195	26,232	34,161	33,822	22,592	12,937
402	Louisville, KY	290,636	43,061	58,619	697,218	44,887	113,387	159,835	164,947	120,101	94,061
403	Lexington, KY	119,343	39,245	50,754	309,697	19,006	52,596	75,345	72,336	54,014	36,400
404	Lexington, KY	69,047	32,569	43,510	175,650	10,132	27,528	48,637	38,654	29,718	20,981
405	Lexington, KY	112,069	43,019	60,110	267,484	16,331	37,006	82,279	62,429	41,919	27,520
406	Lexington, KY	20,856	44,093	55,422	49,617	2,860	7,563	11,741	11,888	9,442	6,123
407	London, KY	39,797	26,287	37,878	101,568	6,265	17,437	24,137	22,801	18,232	12,696
408	London, KY	15,828	20,381	30,153	39,242	2,179	6,629	8,489	9,123	7,556	5,266
409	London, KY	29,108	19,783	28,980	75,797	4,234	13,078	18,163	17,266	13,739	9,317
410	Cincinnati, OH	176,932	47,511	60,505	457,596	31,130	81,705	108,500	110,103	75,298	50,860
411	Ashland, KY	54,731	31,759	42,981	137,533	7,217	21,860	30,595	31,245	26,533	20,083
412	Ashland, KY	20,061	24,676	35,970	51,290	2,883	8,757	11,651	12,018	9,799	6,182
413	Campton, KY	14,597	21,173	30,701	37,521	1,904	6,436	8,611	8,795	6,854	4,921
414	Campton, KY	9,280	23,521	34,223	26,086	1,430	4,187	6,847	6,391	4,264	2,967
415	Pikeville, KY	29,280	26,287	38,197	71,351	3,688	11,575	16,104	17,104	13,778	9,102
416	Pikeville, KY	16,080	21,962	32,791	39,826	2,128	6,395	9,469	9,322	7,503	5,009
417	Hazard, KY	17,274	22,852	32,351	43,296	2,420	7,131	9,977	10,680	8,044	5,044
418	Hazard, KY	12,775	23,398	33,475	32,071	1,585	5,180	7,461	7,633	6,227	3,985
420	Paducah, KY	90,351	34,596	46,585	218,967	11,559	33,158	48,510	48,423	41,638	35,679
421	Bowling Green, KY	76,102	35,052	47,509	194,146	11,549	30,974	51,213	42,799	33,199	24,412
422	Bowling Green, KY	55,367	34,171	43,711	150,043	11,894	26,270	41,272	30,488	22,460	17,659
423	Owensboro, KY	65,649	36,816	48,018	166,474	10,357	27,873	36,425	37,584	30,465	23,770
424	Evansville, IN	54,902	35,262	46,716	136,031	7,797	22,395	29,735	31,158	25,325	19,621
425	Somerset, KY	29,594	28,893	39,276	72,349	3,864	11,587	15,539	16,230	13,887	11,242
426	Somerset, KY	25,995	23,319	32,700	63,362	3,579	10,725	14,069	13,873	12,265	8,851
427	Elizabethtown, KY	68,301	33,311	44,477	171,350	10,122	28,921	37,068	39,808	31,358	24,073
430	Columbus, OH	259,108	59,598	75,413	682,004	49,860	131,506	158,091	167,176	109,276	66,095
431	Columbus, OH	137,721	50,799	61,402	373,301	26,096	70,263	86,188	88,363	61,942	40,449
432	Columbus, OH	318,028	40,843	54,171	745,890	53,660	125,382	217,129	161,159	108,187	80,373
433	Columbus, OH	68,594	43,213	51,571	180,699	11,441	33,841	38,482	41,523	30,635	24,777
434	Toledo, OH	63,881	44,360	54,392	165,329	8,979	27,986	43,056	35,181	27,742	22,385
435	Toledo, OH	109,515	51,009	64,686	287,493	18,534	57,331	86,208	68,208	49,632	36,712
436	Toledo, OH	149,063	36,509	48,275	361,666	26,278	67,201	89,424	75,260	55,796	47,707
437	Zanesville, OH	73,630	34,690	44,445	192,473	12,129	35,905	41,861	41,985	32,560	28,033
438	Zanesville, OH	24,446	39,911	48,743	63,680	4,205	12,621	13,144	14,157	11,014	8,539
439	Steubenville, OH	74,799	32,623	42,418	183,197	9,753	29,584	36,447	40,202	34,121	33,090
440	Cleveland, OH	321,004	51,844	65,758	838,713	52,866	157,434	166,921	197,058	150,419	114,015
441	Cleveland, OH	536,903	41,436	57,233	1,301,278	86,899	237,502	268,854	293,205	211,864	202,954
442	Akron, OH	208,131	54,243	67,416	547,741	34,175	102,644	117,922	130,596	94,136	68,268
443	Akron, OH	116,867	38,384	51,777	283,528	18,920	50,260	65,969	62,017	45,655	40,707
444	Youngstown, OH	141,218	41,224	51,501	360,101	20,644	63,699	71,224	81,181	66,814	56,539
445	Youngstown, OH	71,056	34,514	46,197	174,954	10,383	29,495	35,790	37,145	29,606	32,535
446	Canton, OH	167,779	43,071	53,826	448,882	30,251	86,415	92,806	99,277	77,143	62,990
447	Canton, OH	79,777	41,649	55,584	196,021	12,710	34,728	40,232	43,480	34,186	30,685
448	Mansfield, OH	133,469	42,369	51,404	344,023	22,229	65,473	71,101	75,471	59,732	50,017
449	Mansfield, OH	37,259	39,268	50,624	96,238	5,794	16,303	21,053	21,847	17,058	14,183
450	Cincinnati, OH	196,680	56,179	69,186	537,283	38,166	101,998	130,260	127,467	83,225	56,167
451	Cincinnati, OH	120,083	49,636	63,275	322,952	22,968	64,410	69,681	77,347	52,944	35,602

ZIP Code	3-Digit ZIP Code Areas	Total Households	Median Household Income	Average Household Income	Total Population	Population by Age: 0-4 years	Population by Age: 5-17 years	Population by Age: 18-34 years	Population by Age: 35-49 years	Population by Age: 50-64 years	Gray Markets 65 + years
452	Cincinnati, OH	340,486	44,590	63,369	816,262	56,160	149,508	187,716	182,145	130,140	110,593
453	Dayton, OH	188,093	47,170	57,980	484,188	31,019	88,515	108,017	107,257	84,572	64,808
454	Dayton, OH	202,404	43,467	57,648	493,054	33,076	87,031	111,450	107,713	84,422	69,362
455	Dayton, OH	42,100	41,082	51,755	105,455	6,994	18,932	22,732	21,772	18,958	16,067
456	Chillicothe, OH	133,620	33,424	43,313	343,933	21,581	61,912	77,650	76,425	58,865	47,500
457	Athens, OH	60,417	32,920	44,180	156,289	8,232	24,105	46,441	31,584	25,827	20,100
458	Lima, OH	139,140	43,990	53,573	368,435	23,878	71,064	81,229	81,150	59,694	51,420
460	Indianapolis, IN	169,521	59,634	78,907	451,381	32,287	91,335	97,144	109,140	72,090	49,385
461	Indianapolis, IN	179,981	54,636	64,898	486,209	32,130	95,172	106,616	115,940	81,030	55,321
462	Indianapolis, IN	356,873	44,244	58,121	869,796	68,470	159,243	216,851	201,538	128,071	95,623
463	Gary, IN	236,489	51,108	62,243	628,359	41,118	117,601	136,839	145,063	108,085	79,653
464	Gary, IN	57,158	34,782	45,801	151,524	11,952	30,491	33,109	31,372	24,691	19,909
465	South Bend, IN	165,703	47,151	58,396	457,247	34,934	91,899	106,596	99,082	71,665	53,071
466	South Bend, IN	59,343	39,582	50,794	151,159	11,726	27,733	35,733	30,700	22,612	22,655
467	Fort Wayne, IN	120,203	47,290	55,844	325,829	23,156	66,739	70,453	72,730	52,703	40,048
468	Fort Wayne, IN	116,080	44,151	57,259	292,550	22,543	57,019	69,481	64,855	44,889	33,763
469	Kokomo, IN	124,963	42,418	51,822	318,534	20,367	58,586	68,065	68,707	56,050	46,759
470	Cincinnati, OH	42,390	49,150	58,353	114,430	7,857	22,858	23,798	26,726	19,143	14,048
471	Louisville, KY	107,938	44,213	54,741	273,937	17,839	50,017	60,888	64,073	47,810	33,310
472	Columbus, IN	77,548	43,914	53,439	200,016	13,777	37,901	43,571	44,948	34,450	25,369
473	Muncie, IN	130,801	38,454	48,943	325,748	20,068	56,139	76,910	67,097	56,712	48,822
474	Bloomington, IN	98,938	37,554	49,154	248,222	13,811	38,388	76,316	50,117	38,944	30,646
475	Washington, IN	61,112	40,719	49,941	158,748	10,016	29,552	34,376	35,380	26,681	22,743
476	Evansville, IN	47,289	48,219	58,688	123,401	7,322	23,947	24,259	29,549	22,249	16,075
477	Evansville, IN	71,712	40,424	53,906	174,950	11,136	28,878	42,305	38,278	27,946	26,407
478	Terre Haute, IN	70,684	37,012	47,583	184,645	11,077	31,331	45,655	39,819	30,269	26,494
479	Lafayette, IN	108,843	42,616	53,848	286,334	17,198	47,803	88,625	56,882	42,379	33,447
480	Royal Oak, MI	461,961	55,856	69,743	1,136,103	69,766	196,371	247,405	274,559	190,472	157,530
481	Detroit, MI	604,662	58,264	72,950	1,555,715	102,271	278,111	369,907	368,257	256,258	180,911
482	Detroit, MI	406,899	34,117	48,250	1,132,103	86,699	248,773	263,914	241,869	164,591	126,257
483	Royal Oak, MI	365,595	69,681	91,928	953,345	63,101	177,518	195,965	240,109	172,804	103,848
484	Flint, MI	174,718	53,394	64,991	462,525	28,764	90,190	93,037	113,305	82,242	54,987
485	Flint, MI	84,035	33,578	45,293	213,363	16,680	43,420	50,713	45,111	31,937	25,502
486	Saginaw, MI	165,682	39,423	52,580	421,471	25,410	78,015	85,839	92,390	76,254	63,563
487	Saginaw, MI	87,911	38,875	49,790	216,209	11,610	38,215	40,074	47,778	41,394	37,138
488	Lansing, MI	221,527	49,114	61,809	610,196	35,367	109,206	169,104	135,676	96,531	64,312
489	Lansing, MI	70,259	40,456	50,471	165,053	12,462	28,950	44,676	35,093	25,840	18,032
490	Kalamazoo, MI	288,777	43,492	54,910	748,883	48,028	139,382	175,189	165,788	125,546	94,950
491	Kalamazoo, MI	43,016	44,535	57,000	109,965	6,139	19,839	22,243	25,019	20,649	16,076
492	Jackson, MI	130,961	46,925	57,381	356,000	21,940	67,539	77,848	82,282	60,981	45,410
493	Grand Rapids, MI	108,756	53,481	66,208	303,319	21,326	63,888	65,761	72,512	48,846	30,986
494	Grand Rapids, MI	198,253	48,324	59,366	549,869	37,696	110,483	126,529	123,941	85,306	65,914
495	Grand Rapids, MI	156,284	45,344	57,924	411,035	32,047	78,222	110,494	89,369	56,072	44,831
496	Traverse City, MI	104,719	42,470	54,119	264,119	14,994	47,985	52,016	60,630	47,880	40,614
497	Gaylord, MI	94,059	39,372	50,147	235,090	12,379	40,943	46,611	53,339	43,171	38,647
498	Iron Mountain, MI	74,202	37,608	47,404	181,362	15,982	30,011	38,586	34,264	32,941	29,578
499	Iron Mountain, MI	34,096	31,837	41,366	83,704	3,796	12,933	19,699	16,787	14,820	15,669
500	Des Moines, IA	77,337	46,895	58,996	201,344	11,720	32,765	58,827	42,086	31,229	24,717
501	Des Moines, IA	62,319	45,063	57,305	161,833	9,783	29,228	34,071	36,218	27,505	25,028
502	Des Moines, IA	80,201	50,950	64,121	203,884	13,037	36,603	46,616	47,192	33,183	27,253
503	Des Moines, IA	107,421	46,030	59,003	267,357	19,137	45,471	66,450	60,684	43,497	32,118
504	Mason City, IA	43,982	39,975	49,252	107,216	5,889	18,835	19,885	23,726	18,864	20,017
505	Fort Dodge, IA	51,496	38,796	48,559	128,635	6,848	22,306	25,447	27,563	21,559	24,912
506	Waterloo, IA	64,336	42,803	52,936	166,839	8,837	28,645	38,586	34,264	28,987	27,520
507	Waterloo, IA	31,945	38,006	49,652	78,332	5,141	13,077	18,631	16,300	13,267	11,916
508	Creston, IA	14,226	34,711	43,231	34,057	1,751	5,714	6,038	7,077	6,188	7,289
510	Sioux City, IA	33,982	42,635	51,996	87,483	4,965	16,891	16,372	19,417	14,473	15,365
511	Sioux City, IA	32,796	41,532	54,155	87,257	6,437	15,998	21,554	18,396	13,461	11,411
512	Sheldon, IA	15,928	42,579	50,591	43,537	2,669	8,128	9,673	8,840	6,534	7,693
513	Spencer, IA	20,002	39,497	50,252	47,627	2,628	8,049	8,991	10,404	8,442	9,113
514	Carroll, IA	19,296	40,001	49,057	48,678	2,739	9,252	8,743	10,630	8,098	9,216
515	Omaha, NE	56,767	43,290	53,102	145,922	8,723	26,571	30,098	33,013	25,299	22,218
516	Omaha, NE	9,746	39,262	46,819	24,723	1,197	4,186	4,789	5,316	4,311	4,924
520	Dubuque, IA	53,318	42,323	53,530	138,366	8,447	25,429	28,263	30,942	23,601	21,684
521	Decorah, IA	23,504	40,064	48,974	61,000	3,047	10,769	13,207	13,252	10,054	10,671
522	Cedar Rapids, IA	63,921	43,680	57,014	159,658	9,045	23,834	53,479	33,403	23,118	16,779
523	Cedar Rapids, IA	53,638	49,824	60,650	139,077	8,779	25,970	29,267	33,069	23,145	18,847
524	Cedar Rapids, IA	53,922	47,803	60,108	131,506	8,955	21,849	33,278	29,187	21,092	17,145
525	Ottumwa, IA	45,594	35,568	45,457	111,512	6,086	19,188	22,412	24,029	20,166	19,631

ZIP Code	3-Digit ZIP Code Areas	Total Households	Median Household Income	Average Household Income	Total Population	Population by Age: 0-4 years	Population by Age: 5-17 years	Population by Age: 18-34 years	Population by Age: 35-49 years	Population by Age: 50-64 years	Gray Markets 65 + years
526	Burlington, IA	42,748	40,835	50,379	107,510	6,264	18,547	21,646	24,047	19,611	17,395
527	Rock Island, IL	64,737	48,735	59,629	165,472	10,294	31,084	32,837	39,029	30,216	22,012
528	Rock Island, IL	39,937	40,674	51,173	100,158	7,285	17,554	26,024	21,254	15,720	12,321
530	Milwaukee, WI	233,637	61,854	77,167	612,881	34,890	117,236	116,823	153,227	109,425	81,280
531	Milwaukee, WI	247,409	58,876	69,727	652,790	40,469	120,299	143,470	161,661	109,754	77,137
532	Milwaukee, WI	327,132	39,045	51,276	808,217	62,155	152,773	201,554	173,171	116,505	102,059
534	Milwaukee, WI	48,573	46,937	58,550	125,711	8,851	23,919	26,870	28,624	20,655	16,792
535	Madison, WI	195,375	54,979	66,094	504,752	32,471	97,514	102,692	125,614	84,726	61,735
537	Madison, WI	113,152	47,283	61,815	261,334	14,003	33,003	96,481	55,539	38,413	23,895
538	Madison, WI	22,031	39,431	48,525	58,454	2,877	10,251	14,460	12,201	9,581	9,084
539	Portage, WI	73,669	44,528	53,343	190,826	10,117	33,520	40,107	45,205	32,658	29,219
540	Saint Paul, MN	49,002	58,164	68,596	131,310	7,698	25,053	32,196	31,969	21,048	13,346
541	Green Bay, WI	92,730	48,665	58,450	241,218	14,621	46,239	49,635	57,762	40,059	32,902
542	Green Bay, WI	52,203	46,565	55,856	129,882	6,773	23,512	24,475	30,921	23,313	20,888
543	Green Bay, WI	69,539	47,780	58,437	176,010	11,662	31,724	44,348	42,061	26,860	19,355
544	Wausau, WI	149,168	45,472	55,522	384,247	22,140	72,101	81,494	88,703	64,269	55,540
545	Rhinelander, WI	39,978	38,490	48,955	94,160	4,062	15,663	15,530	21,067	18,580	19,258
546	La Crosse, WI	90,905	41,502	52,006	233,916	13,748	41,995	54,975	51,582	38,710	32,906
547	Eau Claire, WI	95,906	42,715	52,709	249,311	14,175	44,050	63,756	53,554	40,082	33,694
548	Spooner, WI	74,965	38,719	47,729	182,069	9,533	31,800	35,886	40,508	33,834	30,508
549	Oshkosh, WI	178,489	49,459	59,895	459,590	27,125	82,810	104,373	109,749	73,950	61,583
550	Saint Paul, MN	214,234	63,512	75,023	606,735	39,618	127,226	133,887	155,660	94,480	55,864
551	Saint Paul, MN	291,134	57,524	73,539	751,074	51,432	141,864	179,259	180,540	117,959	80,020
553	Minneapolis, MN	321,358	69,981	88,146	882,773	63,104	183,059	193,258	233,220	136,519	73,613
554	Minneapolis, MN	412,114	53,057	59,524	993,784	63,916	159,242	262,466	233,424	158,714	116,022
556	Duluth, MN	6,905	43,589	51,228	15,976	699	2,548	2,644	3,794	3,237	3,054
557	Duluth, MN	69,380	39,566	48,277	166,102	7,812	27,862	31,487	38,307	31,699	28,935
558	Duluth, MN	45,606	40,865	52,711	114,078	5,693	18,147	30,406	24,563	19,001	16,268
559	Rochester, MN	121,144	49,224	62,551	314,020	19,186	58,518	70,705	72,467	49,978	43,166
560	Mankato, MN	96,854	44,867	54,782	251,268	13,615	44,317	60,293	54,538	38,203	40,302
561	Windom, MN	37,166	38,300	46,674	92,462	4,972	17,141	16,032	19,690	15,893	18,734
562	Willmar, MN	57,631	40,888	50,566	147,324	8,122	27,049	30,080	32,027	24,089	25,957
563	Saint Cloud, MN	109,451	44,316	54,895	290,570	16,743	52,691	75,835	62,333	43,744	39,224
564	Brainerd, MN	55,710	39,576	50,020	137,276	7,077	24,492	26,044	29,155	25,791	24,717
565	Detroit Lakes, MN	64,540	39,271	49,584	165,149	8,524	30,072	35,043	35,373	28,041	28,096
566	Bemidji, MN	35,086	38,511	46,777	90,511	5,461	17,454	19,363	18,839	15,865	13,203
567	Thief River Falls, MN	27,176	40,054	48,553	68,809	3,813	12,958	13,907	15,634	11,435	11,062
570	Sioux Falls, SD	59,554	42,774	52,838	159,314	9,701	29,108	40,936	34,352	23,890	21,327
571	Sioux Falls, SD	55,874	46,039	58,537	140,132	9,980	24,516	37,467	32,306	20,662	15,201
572	Dakota Central, SD	28,114	36,508	46,116	71,029	4,518	13,741	12,962	15,163	11,890	12,755
573	Dakota Central, SD	32,181	33,591	43,891	81,282	4,871	15,817	14,655	16,930	13,487	15,522
574	Aberdeen, SD	24,339	36,112	46,239	59,491	3,389	10,324	11,318	12,676	10,387	11,397
575	Pierre, SD	20,159	33,963	45,425	54,890	4,089	12,300	9,913	11,788	8,910	7,890
576	Mobridge, SD	8,108	26,642	35,067	22,868	1,949	5,359	4,212	4,608	3,432	3,308
577	Rapid City, SD	67,771	38,462	49,879	177,848	12,290	34,692	40,780	39,077	28,721	22,288
580	Fargo, ND	27,671	43,897	52,615	70,610	3,997	13,135	15,442	16,415	11,638	9,983
581	Fargo, ND	41,964	46,039	54,365	96,297	5,608	13,627	34,257	19,941	13,153	9,711
582	Grand Forks, ND	38,487	39,208	49,203	96,553	5,539	15,954	27,070	20,115	14,750	13,125
583	Devils Lake, ND	19,829	33,594	43,340	51,152	3,414	10,352	8,929	10,874	8,633	8,950
584	Jamestown, ND	20,205	34,187	44,708	48,598	2,123	8,107	8,468	10,477	8,773	10,650
585	Bismarck, ND	49,781	43,423	53,825	125,166	7,003	22,511	27,383	28,915	21,533	17,821
586	Dickinson, ND	15,923	35,292	44,791	39,238	1,962	7,114	7,313	8,584	6,845	7,420
587	Minot, ND	32,392	35,838	46,054	80,938	5,200	14,359	18,899	16,963	12,954	12,563
588	Williston, ND	10,054	35,306	47,296	24,252	1,203	4,489	4,322	5,616	4,470	4,152
590	Billings, MT	31,678	36,442	46,653	81,185	4,991	16,653	14,582	18,960	15,718	10,837
591	Billings, MT	47,739	40,682	53,628	117,132	7,243	20,600	26,262	26,556	20,377	16,094
592	Wolf Point, MT	13,543	31,796	40,735	34,539	2,048	7,046	5,299	7,799	6,410	5,937
593	Miles City, MT	13,906	34,149	43,458	34,351	1,734	6,203	5,812	7,838	6,791	5,973
594	Great Falls, MT	50,762	34,161	44,532	127,855	7,684	24,743	24,948	28,837	22,650	18,993
595	Havre, MT	11,983	30,778	39,476	31,198	2,133	6,451	5,988	6,927	5,287	4,412
596	Helena, MT	28,600	41,869	51,530	70,074	3,862	12,979	13,093	17,323	14,324	8,493
597	Butte, MT	56,839	39,975	49,354	142,127	7,581	22,477	37,664	32,222	24,727	17,456
598	Missoula, MT	72,260	35,838	48,003	180,531	10,007	31,136	43,244	39,570	33,928	22,646
599	Kalispell, MT	41,653	35,883	47,846	102,951	5,603	18,848	18,523	24,464	21,122	14,391
600	Palatine, IL	579,485	71,587	99,219	1,630,866	115,038	320,906	335,340	400,569	273,248	185,765
601	Carol Stream, IL	479,617	66,890	82,528	1,377,540	103,543	264,008	334,874	330,845	213,362	130,908
602	Palatine, IL	30,826	62,558	91,605	77,315	4,619	11,334	24,065	16,695	11,913	8,689
603	Carol Stream, IL	26,645	69,943	104,097	62,486	4,292	10,940	13,783	16,277	10,663	6,531
604	South Suburban, IL	493,949	58,745	70,716	1,390,950	98,055	276,548	302,416	327,253	224,820	161,858

ZIP Code	3-Digit ZIP Code Areas	Total Households	Median Household Income	Average Household Income	Total Population	Population by Age: 0-4 years	Population by Age: 5-17 years	Population by Age: 18-34 years	Population by Age: 35-49 years	Population by Age: 50-64 years	Gray Markets 65 + years
605	Fox Valley, IL	329,635	71,909	93,406	923,459	71,795	183,496	203,717	226,797	146,306	91,348
606	Chicago, IL	1,045,958	42,422	60,193	2,853,710	217,631	522,112	808,677	603,981	404,830	296,479
607	Chicago, IL	40,047	54,646	68,343	105,743	5,306	15,635	19,691	23,167	19,201	22,743
608	Chicago, IL	48,755	43,130	52,391	159,120	15,659	36,408	41,042	32,766	18,886	14,359
609	Kankakee, IL	61,328	43,922	54,368	162,282	10,896	31,058	34,003	35,105	26,852	24,368
610	Rockford, IL	113,932	48,544	59,161	299,109	18,229	57,819	59,608	69,922	51,680	41,851
611	Rockford, IL	91,830	43,159	54,883	232,945	16,662	42,807	53,510	50,444	38,237	31,285
612	Rock Island, IL	86,125	43,687	54,270	214,545	12,970	37,443	45,514	46,937	38,840	32,841
613	La Salle, IL	60,443	43,538	53,363	150,376	8,991	27,044	28,908	33,218	25,988	26,227
614	Galesburg, IL	59,242	37,630	46,518	150,456	8,051	23,878	37,021	29,993	25,932	25,581
615	Peoria, IL	74,237	49,955	60,829	193,850	11,297	34,277	39,780	44,038	34,777	29,681
616	Peoria, IL	70,242	41,115	54,413	173,607	11,931	30,340	41,371	35,528	28,792	25,645
617	Bloomington, IL	83,941	50,420	63,213	221,516	13,951	38,385	63,907	47,654	32,647	24,972
618	Champaign, IL	110,361	40,735	53,037	275,815	16,845	43,535	87,318	54,833	40,414	32,870
619	Champaign, IL	42,532	38,622	48,682	107,602	6,331	17,263	29,137	21,705	16,850	16,316
620	Saint Louis, MO	119,843	42,607	53,347	305,521	17,932	54,360	67,800	67,947	50,938	46,544
622	Saint Louis, MO	168,646	45,833	56,963	447,296	28,807	84,879	99,830	103,694	69,849	60,237
623	Quincy, IL	43,916	38,044	47,889	112,965	6,481	19,680	23,656	24,126	19,169	19,853
624	Effingham, IL	57,991	38,175	47,520	148,719	8,442	26,994	31,143	32,957	24,728	24,455
625	Springfield, IL	73,741	42,121	53,027	183,627	11,047	32,865	37,492	40,543	32,923	28,757
626	Springfield, IL	61,342	44,358	53,893	161,217	9,220	28,980	34,479	36,829	27,518	24,191
627	Springfield, IL	61,197	44,012	59,321	140,911	9,258	23,812	31,076	31,720	24,476	20,569
628	Centralia, IL	86,060	34,693	44,169	214,960	12,178	36,765	44,550	46,319	37,856	37,292
629	Carbondale, IL	91,986	31,983	43,250	226,291	12,226	35,731	59,792	45,750	37,774	35,018
630	Saint Louis, MO	266,483	58,444	73,708	708,346	45,806	136,160	145,067	177,236	123,150	80,927
631	Saint Louis, MO	397,398	41,678	60,264	954,559	60,312	169,252	216,403	212,838	155,448	140,306
633	Saint Louis, MO	152,252	58,459	68,429	423,380	28,370	85,119	95,356	105,122	66,299	43,114
634	Quincy, IL	26,620	34,577	43,656	67,707	4,197	12,357	13,840	14,530	11,799	10,984
635	Quincy, IL	25,012	30,375	40,551	62,060	3,528	9,891	16,437	11,814	10,118	10,272
636	Cape Girardeau, MO	47,843	32,580	41,195	126,393	7,337	22,277	28,075	28,160	21,809	18,735
637	Cape Girardeau, MO	46,830	38,164	48,669	119,506	7,140	20,850	29,050	25,772	19,691	17,003
638	Cape Girardeau, MO	50,971	27,679	37,301	126,784	8,713	23,648	26,293	26,387	22,209	19,534
639	Cape Girardeau, MO	33,197	28,191	38,575	81,065	4,670	14,031	16,349	16,776	14,295	14,244
640	Kansas City, MO	215,769	52,096	63,412	565,959	39,245	108,196	124,812	133,983	94,428	65,295
641	Kansas City, MO	225,811	42,089	55,097	536,843	37,212	92,442	133,309	122,565	85,568	65,747
644	Saint Joseph, MO	38,008	37,701	47,386	99,928	5,193	16,837	23,197	21,988	16,498	16,215
645	Saint Joseph, MO	31,819	38,048	49,669	82,302	5,101	13,938	20,103	18,032	12,801	12,327
646	Chillicothe, MO	29,951	32,767	42,123	73,808	4,501	13,303	13,765	15,097	13,175	13,967
647	Harrisonville, MO	45,654	34,907	44,559	115,426	7,357	21,487	22,800	24,740	20,145	18,897
648	Springfield, MO	70,388	34,358	45,167	181,259	12,776	32,857	42,599	38,213	30,193	24,621
650	Mid-Missouri, MO	57,523	39,770	49,812	145,153	8,542	25,731	28,738	32,154	27,124	22,864
651	Mid-Missouri, MO	24,925	46,964	59,366	65,031	3,859	10,792	16,315	15,874	10,628	7,563
652	Mid-Missouri, MO	94,191	38,347	50,666	244,954	14,579	39,921	74,016	51,947	36,128	28,363
653	Mid-Missouri, MO	39,664	33,948	43,228	100,781	6,399	17,588	22,057	21,026	17,253	16,458
654	Springfield, MO	33,903	32,726	41,668	91,985	5,728	16,292	26,293	18,678	13,672	11,322
655	Springfield, MO	43,152	31,805	41,032	108,240	6,460	20,633	21,672	24,183	18,892	13,967
656	Springfield, MO	73,732	33,005	42,618	185,954	11,020	32,430	38,251	38,624	34,559	31,070
657	Springfield, MO	100,170	34,862	45,967	260,785	12,394	49,360	54,530	56,948	45,766	37,326
658	Springfield, MO	84,056	35,650	49,851	201,463	11,794	29,178	59,038	41,205	31,702	28,546
660	Kansas City, MO	159,968	52,047	64,105	437,502	30,212	81,339	121,206	99,696	63,802	41,247
661	Kansas City, MO	57,177	35,456	44,580	151,414	12,394	29,619	37,637	32,208	22,319	17,237
662	Kansas City, MO	141,371	67,698	91,125	350,144	22,740	64,382	74,992	86,698	60,220	41,112
664	Kansas City, MO	27,695	39,971	49,675	76,355	5,864	14,867	18,584	15,939	11,248	9,853
665	Topeka, KS	43,777	41,943	52,356	114,268	6,740	18,894	35,980	22,240	16,263	14,151
666	Topeka, KS	64,324	43,234	54,477	156,379	10,649	27,398	34,717	34,287	27,034	22,294
667	Fort Scott, KS	47,492	42,801	45,446	118,321	7,268	20,389	27,337	23,669	19,758	19,900
668	Topeka, KS	25,040	36,205	42,409	64,038	4,074	11,643	14,983	13,528	10,292	9,518
669	Salina, KS	11,256	33,154	42,409	26,694	1,255	4,401	4,111	5,390	4,805	6,732
670	Wichita, KS	64,483	46,974	57,090	174,043	11,049	36,228	33,598	40,044	27,924	25,200
671	Wichita, KS	41,774	46,318	55,215	110,787	7,012	22,437	21,422	25,368	17,909	16,639
672	Wichita, KS	154,607	43,887	56,299	387,670	30,866	72,903	95,772	85,508	57,484	45,137
673	Independence, KS	25,688	32,914	41,927	62,660	3,704	11,303	12,195	12,713	11,216	11,529
674	Salina, KS	54,303	40,258	49,074	136,053	8,009	24,810	27,129	29,842	23,032	23,231
675	Hutchinson, KS	48,598	37,303	47,376	122,452	7,282	21,459	24,556	26,630	20,699	21,826
676	Hays, KS	24,363	34,617	46,039	58,886	3,125	9,528	13,376	12,355	9,452	11,050
677	Colby, KS	13,477	35,466	45,988	32,841	1,831	5,894	5,940	6,877	5,589	6,710
678	Dodge City, KS	41,305	40,455	51,095	121,355	10,356	26,673	28,060	26,128	16,697	13,441
679	Liberal, KS	10,090	40,195	50,670	29,858	2,640	6,343	7,741	6,214	3,843	3,077
680	Omaha, NE	66,025	50,517	62,195	176,010	11,112	36,104	35,681	40,095	29,443	23,575

ZIP Code	3-Digit ZIP Code Areas	Total Households	Median Household Income	Average Household Income	Total Population	Population by Age: 0-4 years	Population by Age: 5-17 years	Population by Age: 18-34 years	Population by Age: 35-49 years	Population by Age: 50-64 years	Gray Markets 65 + years
681	Omaha, NE	211,582	49,086	63,959	543,449	42,050	101,887	139,795	122,710	81,536	55,471
683	Lincoln, NE	33,263	40,777	49,468	83,648	4,763	15,564	14,970	18,575	14,362	15,414
684	Lincoln, NE	27,033	43,102	52,000	69,786	4,003	12,941	14,140	15,153	11,871	11,678
685	Lincoln, NE	99,107	45,676	58,539	247,112	16,992	38,860	77,408	52,189	36,045	25,638
686	Norfolk, NE	28,225	39,846	48,427	73,446	4,679	15,215	13,146	16,424	11,796	12,186
687	Norfolk, NE	51,147	36,458	45,334	134,904	8,504	26,145	28,333	28,589	21,210	22,123
688	Grand Island, NE	59,789	39,003	48,630	157,461	10,484	30,031	35,979	33,060	25,092	22,815
689	Grand Island, NE	30,032	37,600	47,031	74,976	4,298	13,578	14,071	16,030	13,003	13,996
690	McCook, NE	10,874	33,891	43,103	26,438	1,485	4,726	4,696	5,546	4,654	5,331
691	North Platte, NE	32,522	37,117	47,104	78,564	4,596	14,541	14,641	16,934	14,055	13,797
692	Valentine, NE	4,030	42,541	42,419	9,546	559	1,867	1,530	1,981	1,727	1,882
693	Alliance, NE	28,733	34,687	45,516	71,462	4,273	13,158	14,974	14,755	12,149	12,153
700	New Orleans, LA	230,329	41,963	55,014	616,983	42,519	117,311	138,312	142,163	105,635	71,043
701	New Orleans, LA	200,148	31,184	48,922	507,239	35,782	92,722	126,744	110,006	80,705	61,280
703	Thibodaux, LA	95,248	38,285	49,616	266,666	19,056	53,198	62,170	60,131	42,809	29,302
704	Hammond, LA	139,692	41,569	57,744	379,778	25,938	75,465	85,455	87,095	64,021	41,804
705	Lafayette, LA	220,680	33,146	46,341	599,204	40,763	120,614	139,900	132,423	91,661	69,843
706	Lake Charles, LA	93,092	37,705	50,113	250,241	17,844	48,104	57,891	55,395	40,537	30,470
707	Baton Rouge, LA	118,923	44,067	53,534	345,181	24,679	68,738	83,011	82,531	54,111	32,111
708	Baton Rouge, LA	136,967	38,393	56,142	355,328	25,664	62,134	103,823	73,010	54,271	36,426
710	Shreveport, LA	67,772	33,464	45,245	177,692	11,637	34,580	36,538	38,346	31,168	25,423
711	Shreveport, LA	111,899	34,746	49,781	287,078	20,849	54,208	68,963	59,909	44,793	38,356
712	Monroe, LA	122,536	30,674	43,376	330,021	23,107	62,081	85,022	65,530	50,640	43,641
713	Alexandria, LA	76,891	29,352	41,885	206,202	14,582	39,276	45,435	44,125	34,071	28,713
714	Alexandria, LA	67,330	31,553	41,640	184,512	13,856	34,308	48,258	37,601	28,441	22,048
716	Pine Bluff, AR	66,683	31,495	42,939	179,099	12,231	33,187	41,093	37,730	30,245	24,613
717	Camden, AR	46,116	31,541	41,541	115,900	7,157	21,676	23,870	24,435	20,087	18,675
718	Texarkana, TX	49,199	31,848	42,582	127,059	8,959	23,873	21,676	26,285	21,746	18,060
719	Hot Springs National Park, AR	68,381	33,874	45,789	163,754	9,197	25,895	33,081	31,952	31,048	32,581
720	Little Rock, AR	129,278	40,038	49,955	338,827	22,433	63,373	81,627	74,992	55,612	40,790
721	Little Rock, AR	115,538	39,069	50,534	293,543	19,176	52,607	66,031	64,565	51,689	39,475
722	Little Rock, AR	86,455	41,697	60,970	205,694	14,850	35,615	50,373	46,609	33,963	24,284
723	Memphis, TN	67,056	29,094	39,659	184,500	14,492	38,661	41,462	38,712	29,049	22,124
724	Jonesboro, AR	82,220	31,978	42,610	206,178	13,331	35,578	49,634	42,288	35,920	29,427
725	Batesville, AR	41,782	31,049	41,656	101,500	5,397	16,718	19,026	20,827	20,001	19,531
726	Harrison, AR	56,690	30,867	41,239	134,512	7,284	21,762	24,156	27,039	27,284	26,987
727	Fayetteville, AR	136,163	41,469	54,063	358,575	25,778	65,097	95,758	74,801	54,004	43,137
728	Russellville, AR	44,601	32,757	43,371	116,575	7,470	21,077	26,968	24,670	19,755	16,635
729	Fort Smith, AR	82,678	35,886	47,807	213,773	15,519	40,468	47,040	46,704	36,442	27,600
730	Oklahoma City, OK	222,228	43,716	57,445	587,226	36,634	107,105	145,858	131,307	97,691	68,631
731	Oklahoma City, OK	249,733	37,252	49,842	610,545	45,761	106,196	157,130	131,097	96,597	73,764
734	Ardmore, OK	34,517	30,952	41,325	86,555	5,482	15,502	17,101	18,035	15,861	14,574
735	Lawton, OK	73,829	34,642	45,213	198,662	14,518	37,603	47,892	42,044	29,703	26,902
736	Clinton, OK	21,032	32,293	43,315	54,811	3,324	9,481	11,506	11,795	9,211	9,494
737	Enid, OK	40,017	35,770	46,967	103,487	6,156	17,722	22,301	22,633	17,388	17,287
738	Woodward, OK	12,199	35,748	45,808	30,063	1,731	5,242	5,665	6,647	5,531	5,247
739	Liberal, KS	10,214	38,141	47,657	28,285	2,159	5,480	6,825	5,964	4,391	3,466
740	Tulsa, OK	200,864	43,692	55,383	537,538	35,510	103,531	124,762	119,561	90,700	63,474
741	Tulsa, OK	173,722	38,549	55,717	413,743	30,024	70,264	104,030	88,909	67,234	53,282
743	Tulsa, OK	48,902	32,186	42,158	125,108	7,842	22,789	25,277	25,043	20,769	20,769
744	Muskogee, OK	83,432	31,113	41,693	215,246	14,059	39,312	48,023	43,115	38,317	32,420
745	McAlester, OK	34,129	28,958	39,263	88,814	4,808	15,583	18,364	18,521	16,439	15,099
746	Ponca City, OK	23,122	34,014	46,496	58,149	3,768	10,872	11,147	12,232	10,366	9,764
747	Durant, OK	32,974	28,353	37,890	83,649	5,703	15,518	18,718	16,585	14,533	12,592
748	Shawnee, OK	72,061	42,417	42,677	190,185	12,247	34,547	42,556	39,910	33,143	27,782
749	Poteau, OK	40,946	29,186	37,868	110,265	7,748	21,388	24,347	22,583	19,436	14,763
750	North Texas, TX	643,499	65,849	84,964	1,794,166	148,817	362,738	447,353	457,673	259,812	117,773
751	Dallas, TX	227,838	49,701	61,637	651,640	47,951	138,514	143,512	153,170	102,976	65,517
752	Dallas, TX	485,507	41,900	65,811	1,291,931	108,578	232,985	385,161	278,309	172,507	114,391
754	Greenville, TX	115,224	37,031	48,849	307,510	19,864	58,631	66,796	64,726	53,392	44,101
755	Texarkana, TX	47,136	33,866	46,756	125,329	7,610	22,323	27,638	27,031	22,090	18,637
756	Longview, TX	121,621	36,898	49,211	320,256	21,042	60,558	68,430	68,808	55,134	46,284
757	Tyler, TX	118,513	38,655	52,331	315,555	21,514	58,561	69,251	64,174	53,251	48,804
758	Palestine, TX	39,475	33,252	44,902	123,029	6,628	18,975	30,980	28,933	19,411	18,102
759	Lufkin, TX	91,992	32,623	44,202	248,236	16,879	45,468	59,659	48,668	40,636	36,926
760	Fort Worth, TX	384,375	55,373	71,491	1,043,770	75,733	209,709	249,075	253,971	165,474	89,808
761	Fort Worth, TX	300,148	44,350	57,922	824,103	67,098	161,937	211,454	183,309	118,986	81,319
762	Fort Worth, TX	118,381	51,581	68,990	322,823	22,724	61,828	85,179	73,577	49,412	30,103
763	Wichita Falls, TX	65,315	35,730	47,517	175,913	11,594	32,437	43,295	37,001	26,544	25,042

ZIP Code	3-Digit ZIP Code Areas	Total Households	Median Household Income	Average Household Income	Total Population	Population by Age: 0-4 years	Population by Age: 5-17 years	Population by Age: 18-34 years	Population by Age: 35-49 years	Population by Age: 50-64 years	Gray Markets 65 + years
764	Fort Worth, TX	51,658	34,446	46,028	135,415	7,990	24,310	29,683	27,083	23,650	22,699
765	Waco, TX	141,828	40,871	51,899	411,031	36,563	81,022	114,185	85,205	53,372	40,684
766	Waco, TX	57,200	39,628	51,035	157,202	9,997	30,924	32,008	33,493	26,948	23,832
767	Waco, TX	60,691	31,867	45,516	163,328	12,020	29,009	48,886	29,494	22,443	21,476
768	Abilene, TX	34,155	32,168	43,531	89,159	5,182	16,772	16,975	17,269	16,269	16,692
769	Midland, TX	47,501	35,939	48,799	123,896	8,788	23,572	28,747	25,683	19,645	17,461
770	Houston, TX	971,122	43,640	63,455	2,722,944	226,242	534,265	742,634	613,599	389,636	216,568
773	North Houston, TX	285,847	60,004	78,571	831,889	57,315	172,743	188,245	201,939	138,512	73,135
774	North Houston, TX	244,611	65,758	84,683	742,958	54,813	166,619	158,334	191,037	115,412	56,743
775	North Houston, TX	355,334	49,523	62,687	1,017,849	79,547	208,139	241,899	240,509	155,406	92,349
776	Beaumont, TX	102,939	38,858	49,997	271,088	17,697	53,327	55,871	59,313	46,431	38,449
777	Beaumont, TX	49,256	36,344	51,880	141,962	8,663	25,023	36,400	32,757	21,842	17,277
778	Bryan, TX	94,133	33,315	48,341	258,008	16,925	40,597	94,738	45,507	33,060	27,181
779	Victoria, TX	60,175	38,512	51,214	165,312	11,513	32,799	33,129	35,922	27,510	24,439
780	San Antonio, TX	143,968	36,680	51,936	464,135	40,457	103,924	106,760	92,566	67,303	53,125
781	San Antonio, TX	107,535	46,521	57,787	316,046	20,385	61,598	74,068	71,670	50,178	38,147
782	San Antonio, TX	491,127	41,901	56,617	1,391,209	109,689	280,032	350,711	300,041	203,913	146,823
783	Corpus Christi, TX	81,733	33,606	46,172	238,437	17,628	51,117	51,499	48,171	38,750	31,272
784	Corpus Christi, TX	100,793	40,172	53,580	282,202	22,119	55,735	65,819	62,223	43,879	32,427
785	McAllen, TX	305,814	27,341	39,206	1,086,506	110,892	261,831	275,237	196,071	132,080	110,395
786	Austin, TX	231,457	57,277	69,581	665,075	49,701	132,452	164,504	156,033	97,570	64,815
787	Austin, TX	328,868	50,484	71,673	820,559	61,651	129,029	273,883	189,712	108,519	57,765
788	San Antonio, TX	52,984	28,072	38,734	169,996	14,038	39,982	38,017	31,676	25,129	21,154
789	Austin, TX	26,056	42,820	51,820	68,314	3,998	12,810	13,147	14,295	11,762	12,302
790	Amarillo, TX	76,570	35,230	46,419	216,590	16,038	45,444	46,862	44,436	33,456	30,354
791	Amarillo, TX	78,190	38,412	51,532	208,992	15,878	39,773	49,815	46,038	31,834	25,654
792	Childress, TX	13,350	29,561	39,964	36,071	2,278	6,978	6,952	7,164	6,020	6,679
793	Lubbock, TX	47,532	32,195	43,693	138,387	10,054	29,360	29,327	29,103	21,389	19,154
794	Lubbock, TX	88,119	33,954	48,140	227,711	16,437	40,053	69,867	44,370	31,589	25,395
795	Abilene, TX	34,437	32,154	42,728	92,821	5,236	17,646	17,682	19,978	16,214	16,065
796	Abilene, TX	44,691	35,790	47,475	125,229	9,243	22,767	34,676	25,877	17,133	15,533
797	Midland, TX	123,944	36,680	50,640	347,880	25,738	73,785	77,037	76,064	52,507	42,749
798	El Paso, TX	20,483	24,799	33,273	69,654	6,254	17,648	16,651	13,463	9,251	6,387
799	El Paso, TX	208,848	34,119	47,364	663,818	58,499	148,030	158,484	137,505	91,640	69,660
800	Denver, CO	262,116	60,357	74,103	705,099	53,060	139,917	171,507	174,065	108,347	58,203
801	Denver, CO	214,675	80,643	103,258	585,103	42,207	124,596	114,629	158,990	100,306	44,375
802	Denver, CO	386,140	48,230	63,971	933,230	70,564	147,279	266,562	208,460	100,897	99,468
803	Denver, CO	48,290	54,091	77,258	114,948	4,695	13,431	44,519	24,312	18,238	9,753
804	Denver, CO	80,579	68,136	74,476	202,500	11,341	33,610	46,130	56,281	39,722	15,416
805	Longmont, CO	163,598	59,129	66,694	431,688	29,538	78,041	112,566	102,650	68,951	39,942
806	Brighton, CO	71,007	46,392	59,080	206,375	16,038	40,419	58,486	43,736	29,362	18,334
807	Brighton, CO	25,054	35,929	60,396	68,401	4,740	13,507	14,394	14,613	10,790	10,357
808	Colorado Springs, CO	34,835	49,560	65,066	99,052	6,634	20,346	21,667	25,432	16,597	8,376
809	Colorado Springs, CO	179,739	51,640	66,309	474,184	37,150	92,934	115,130	112,949	71,972	44,049
810	Pueblo, CO	85,425	34,566	46,309	223,872	14,047	41,561	48,933	47,542	37,503	34,286
811	Alamosa, CO	26,827	34,375	46,958	69,659	4,317	14,096	13,987	15,552	13,016	8,691
812	Salida, CO	29,608	39,417	51,280	83,216	3,860	12,127	20,790	20,213	14,824	11,402
813	Durango, CO	24,906	40,817	53,794	62,311	3,370	10,753	14,928	14,183	11,609	7,468
814	Grand Junction, CO	31,526	40,588	52,496	78,256	4,565	14,126	14,971	17,076	15,276	12,242
815	Grand Junction, CO	48,090	40,012	51,940	121,436	7,513	21,747	26,249	26,363	20,843	18,721
816	Glenwood Springs, CO	52,272	58,933	78,817	138,228	9,915	24,148	35,776	35,629	22,914	9,846
820	Cheyenne, WY	45,995	40,561	51,612	115,270	7,048	19,083	33,265	24,309	18,871	12,694
821	Billings, MT	287	53,592	60,540	541	26	69	124	199	109	14
822	Wheatland, WY	9,432	35,860	45,024	22,992	1,100	4,108	4,135	4,954	4,612	4,083
823	Rawlins, WY	6,335	41,385	51,196	15,891	871	2,761	3,063	3,930	3,296	1,970
824	Worland, WY	19,639	37,305	47,819	49,116	2,667	9,019	8,710	10,680	9,982	8,058
825	Riverton, WY	13,406	36,488	47,725	35,073	2,292	6,737	6,913	7,668	6,628	4,835
826	Casper, WY	33,259	41,995	52,761	82,446	5,036	15,490	17,874	19,001	14,601	10,444
827	Gillette, WY	19,085	52,227	60,404	50,843	3,219	10,636	11,143	13,017	8,595	4,233
828	Sheridan, WY	14,424	38,870	52,701	33,914	1,583	6,011	6,238	7,514	7,083	5,485
829	Rock Springs, WY	22,653	49,800	57,280	60,744	4,163	12,875	12,922	14,922	10,617	5,245
830	Rock Springs, WY	7,780	61,552	92,675	18,506	947	2,583	5,192	4,864	3,524	1,396
831	Rock Springs, WY	6,547	45,778	54,912	17,637	1,085	3,920	3,177	4,067	3,267	2,121
832	Pocatello, ID	56,943	39,425	49,450	164,311	13,397	36,070	38,694	32,494	24,964	18,692
833	Twin Falls, ID	61,362	38,802	52,667	168,906	12,670	35,069	35,957	35,397	27,655	22,158
834	Pocatello, ID	54,491	42,444	53,640	164,103	13,093	36,215	43,064	31,805	23,653	16,273
835	Lewiston, ID	26,609	36,344	45,718	66,025	3,502	11,615	12,436	14,224	12,928	11,320
836	Boise, ID	120,802	42,825	54,473	355,329	29,009	75,835	86,014	75,827	52,311	36,333
837	Boise, ID	95,571	48,005	62,418	240,273	16,388	43,689	62,784	55,901	37,531	23,980

ZIP Code	3-Digit ZIP Code Areas	Total Households	Median Household Income	Average Household Income	Total Population	Population by Age: 0-4 years	Population by Age: 5-17 years	Population by Age: 18-34 years	Population by Age: 35-49 years	Population by Age: 50-64 years	Gray Markets 65 + years
838	Spokane, WA	86,497	38,399	48,410	224,338	13,821	41,228	50,781	48,532	41,182	28,794
840	Salt Lake City, UT	296,817	61,263	74,422	1,014,854	102,091	241,357	278,751	200,728	123,824	68,103
841	Salt Lake City, UT	201,190	48,081	63,267	567,010	47,403	101,073	171,636	111,338	77,577	57,983
843	Salt Lake City, UT	46,010	46,563	56,921	151,379	14,448	32,259	49,002	25,688	17,056	12,926
844	Salt Lake City, UT	55,435	46,769	59,541	165,697	14,742	33,732	45,054	31,958	22,296	17,915
845	Provo, UT	18,009	35,970	45,172	52,293	3,898	11,813	11,877	10,449	8,066	6,190
846	Provo, UT	69,663	43,791	54,815	246,524	24,178	47,640	98,342	34,219	23,304	18,841
847	Provo, UT	59,100	40,301	50,697	178,050	15,587	36,434	47,991	27,997	23,494	26,547
850	Phoenix, AZ	453,526	42,776	58,674	1,291,952	114,133	260,077	361,640	277,915	171,080	107,107
852	Phoenix, AZ	591,566	54,877	72,932	1,574,074	117,566	289,243	394,539	338,991	239,796	193,939
853	Phoenix, AZ	354,446	48,085	61,063	976,121	73,512	187,848	207,358	194,112	150,855	162,436
855	Globe, AZ	33,192	34,058	44,692	91,842	6,172	18,682	17,508	17,488	16,627	15,365
856	Tucson, AZ	88,827	37,966	50,419	238,167	16,546	46,423	43,854	45,948	42,153	43,243
857	Tucson, AZ	336,487	40,592	55,277	855,971	59,528	152,511	209,296	181,417	138,761	114,458
859	Show Low, AZ	23,340	34,658	45,085	67,144	5,247	15,939	12,264	13,440	11,990	8,264
860	Flagstaff, AZ	55,606	38,269	50,271	169,746	14,614	40,113	45,339	35,163	22,797	11,720
863	Prescott, AZ	78,433	39,208	53,692	186,760	9,353	29,655	31,875	35,897	39,221	40,759
864	Kingman, AZ	70,056	33,987	44,831	168,792	9,285	28,330	27,194	32,705	35,589	35,689
865	Gallup, NM	17,323	21,711	31,179	63,165	6,412	18,892	13,588	11,410	7,675	5,188
870	Albuquerque, NM	64,750	40,789	54,272	187,305	12,847	40,684	36,860	45,060	32,646	19,208
871	Albuquerque, NM	249,264	43,614	57,808	628,598	43,864	113,023	151,805	142,601	102,335	74,970
873	Gallup, NM	20,593	37,295	37,817	70,922	6,401	19,405	16,002	14,544	9,244	5,326
874	Farmington, NM	42,209	37,440	47,999	125,928	10,327	29,035	29,383	27,270	18,139	11,774
875	Albuquerque, NM	92,202	43,303	60,477	225,959	13,743	40,330	45,309	53,199	46,721	26,657
877	Las Vegas, NM	16,493	30,428	40,829	42,139	2,360	8,143	8,494	8,980	7,891	6,271
878	Socorro, NM	7,169	25,776	37,388	18,394	1,122	3,493	4,188	3,681	3,473	2,437
879	Truth or Consequences, NM	7,453	26,007	36,156	18,245	1,032	3,464	2,918	3,224	3,437	4,170
880	Las Cruces, NM	85,544	30,602	41,479	241,844	17,772	49,818	59,512	47,146	36,653	30,943
881	Clovis, NM	24,689	31,074	41,990	65,760	5,441	13,626	16,722	12,969	8,842	8,160
882	Roswell, NM	61,394	33,187	44,587	167,070	11,890	35,019	35,361	34,875	26,608	23,317
883	Carrizozo, NM	30,558	34,476	44,112	77,628	5,062	15,190	15,461	16,582	13,725	11,608
884	Tucumcari, NM	6,948	38,486	37,467	17,343	882	3,197	2,979	3,741	3,315	3,229
890	Las Vegas, NV	170,152	54,977	68,734	475,863	36,421	95,664	107,674	105,041	79,265	51,798
891	Las Vegas, NV	446,646	45,915	60,132	1,188,752	88,855	214,105	296,251	262,932	193,552	133,057
893	Ely, NV	3,518	39,111	46,738	9,859	490	1,802	1,975	2,368	1,837	1,387
894	Reno, NV	95,361	51,871	65,881	258,336	17,791	52,289	51,390	60,248	46,529	30,089
895	Reno, NV	99,293	49,009	66,577	247,359	16,758	42,741	59,696	56,716	43,797	27,651
897	Reno, NV	25,849	48,417	60,986	67,618	4,098	11,892	13,119	15,605	13,009	9,895
898	Elko, NV	16,869	50,871	56,280	48,895	3,699	12,256	10,046	11,730	7,687	3,477
900	Los Angeles, CA	852,256	33,140	54,641	2,495,311	191,242	472,118	752,497	527,446	315,885	236,123
902	Inglewood, CA	414,906	52,180	82,136	1,287,043	102,589	264,564	338,863	282,131	181,922	116,974
903	Inglewood, CA	44,200	34,953	45,967	144,245	12,998	33,814	38,414	30,483	18,445	10,091
904	Inglewood, CA	47,889	57,685	93,981	90,251	3,469	9,771	22,515	25,385	16,004	13,107
905	Inglewood, CA	65,268	57,089	71,880	176,328	10,890	31,541	38,137	45,217	28,263	22,280
906	Long Beach, CA	217,191	54,096	66,775	742,625	56,982	156,788	183,678	159,433	104,216	81,528
907	Long Beach, CA	204,417	50,615	65,263	637,428	47,695	130,201	152,762	139,115	97,178	70,477
908	Long Beach, CA	170,788	40,002	57,382	490,089	39,482	100,477	134,146	107,352	63,659	44,973
910	Pasadena, CA	103,016	60,437	84,974	285,210	17,078	53,574	56,791	71,965	49,267	36,535
911	Pasadena, CA	66,258	54,016	85,507	173,750	11,113	28,671	44,606	40,447	27,115	21,798
912	Pasadena, CA	77,598	46,654	67,538	214,046	11,721	35,721	48,103	53,638	35,597	29,266
913	Van Nuys, CA	418,618	63,580	85,507	1,302,041	93,379	260,163	306,926	314,321	199,658	127,594
914	Van Nuys, CA	111,987	41,499	64,195	318,565	26,402	57,505	90,901	72,557	41,415	29,785
915	Van Nuys, CA	44,395	52,857	69,462	107,945	5,937	17,357	26,759	27,243	16,934	13,715
916	Van Nuys, CA	85,817	41,618	60,204	225,516	15,875	38,536	65,093	54,398	30,367	21,247
917	Alhambra, CA	557,968	53,963	68,156	1,965,466	146,502	423,520	504,057	441,162	276,418	173,807
918	Alhambra, CA	29,869	41,907	53,986	88,299	5,331	13,974	23,921	20,381	13,148	11,544
919	San Diego, CA	170,024	49,396	63,876	502,178	37,596	101,574	118,773	112,893	73,191	58,151
920	San Diego, CA	419,488	58,000	79,268	1,202,297	88,013	230,127	287,237	271,875	179,153	145,892
921	San Diego, CA	461,762	50,529	68,839	1,267,278	85,933	218,793	374,249	285,427	172,583	130,293
922	Palm Springs, CA	227,013	38,585	56,117	675,512	46,480	131,004	166,404	131,453	95,314	104,857
923	San Bernardino, CA	307,948	44,340	55,608	980,588	75,671	234,520	233,403	211,104	132,070	93,820
924	San Bernardino, CA	68,049	31,542	42,340	231,544	21,539	58,270	61,863	45,344	26,403	18,125
925	San Bernardino, CA	344,740	47,400	60,488	1,082,928	78,891	248,535	259,871	236,181	136,431	123,019
926	Santa Ana, CA	461,855	75,090	101,664	1,246,365	82,277	214,135	293,265	314,102	204,116	138,470
927	Santa Ana, CA	127,986	56,533	73,575	504,886	46,155	108,799	144,491	105,062	62,530	37,849
928	Santa Ana, CA	350,620	59,752	75,839	1,163,431	91,929	236,278	301,124	264,821	163,759	105,520
930	Oxnard, CA	209,909	62,208	78,225	664,919	48,620	137,678	157,536	151,813	99,641	69,631
931	Santa Barbara, CA	68,284	57,258	83,806	186,998	9,622	26,096	60,444	38,023	28,276	24,537
932	Bakersfield, CA	192,012	35,784	49,052	693,137	56,908	155,952	188,149	144,164	85,704	62,260

ZIP Code	3-Digit ZIP Code Areas	Total Households	Median Household Income	Average Household Income	Total Population	Population by Age: 0-4 years	Population by Age: 5-17 years	Population by Age: 18-34 years	Population by Age: 35-49 years	Population by Age: 50-64 years	Gray Markets 65 + years
933	Bakersfield, CA	141,260	40,072	53,758	433,228	36,179	100,876	107,127	92,092	57,161	39,793
934	Santa Barbara, CA	160,853	47,463	62,664	459,806	28,326	83,297	114,173	99,658	71,311	63,041
935	Mojave, CA	151,145	47,314	58,981	460,855	34,353	110,969	96,336	112,460	65,286	41,451
936	Fresno, CA	152,353	40,720	53,820	519,419	41,064	118,691	129,742	107,878	70,163	51,881
937	Fresno, CA	171,714	36,094	51,190	527,164	44,107	118,642	138,062	103,547	69,000	53,806
939	Salinas, CA	117,300	54,619	72,466	387,720	29,880	77,329	103,497	83,437	53,674	39,903
940	San Francisco, CA	290,986	85,236	117,675	787,743	52,797	121,836	178,587	197,524	137,797	99,202
941	San Francisco, CA	326,747	66,137	94,818	768,504	35,200	77,671	222,886	194,693	129,307	108,747
943	San Francisco, CA	35,112	82,810	126,577	102,013	6,721	17,447	29,010	22,069	15,150	11,616
944	San Francisco, CA	50,648	82,884	111,501	126,266	7,936	18,325	27,750	31,663	22,649	17,943
945	Oakland, CA	774,560	72,584	93,875	2,204,241	153,407	418,268	484,618	539,368	366,103	242,477
946	Oakland, CA	159,520	45,881	68,959	420,803	30,306	75,632	109,424	95,013	65,698	44,730
947	Oakland, CA	55,433	54,043	82,901	126,435	5,503	13,917	43,668	27,302	22,226	13,819
948	Oakland, CA	57,092	48,850	61,329	170,557	12,812	34,647	43,039	36,421	26,416	17,222
949	North Bay, CA	145,452	74,973	109,877	370,672	21,204	59,948	71,941	94,269	76,001	47,309
950	San Jose, CA	265,282	77,756	105,659	780,077	53,819	141,061	183,910	194,515	128,133	78,639
951	San Jose, CA	291,430	79,460	100,685	947,307	75,567	173,783	239,403	230,874	142,181	85,499
952	Stockton, CA	159,934	40,518	54,452	479,527	35,304	103,797	118,113	95,523	71,268	55,522
953	Stockton, CA	307,535	45,273	58,013	956,268	70,876	215,420	232,976	205,950	133,067	97,979
954	North Bay, CA	190,437	51,318	68,585	498,152	28,709	90,228	102,293	111,709	94,867	70,346
955	Eureka, CA	62,193	33,379	45,761	157,790	8,447	26,920	40,323	34,385	27,915	19,800
956	Sacramento, CA	402,463	56,038	70,873	1,102,938	66,593	210,270	261,426	251,994	180,382	132,273
957	Sacramento, CA	72,662	77,337	97,341	211,772	15,648	45,208	42,351	54,939	32,528	21,098
958	Sacramento, CA	297,618	53,384	56,086	797,668	57,403	161,135	209,562	170,601	112,009	86,958
959	Marysville, CA	182,222	37,929	51,598	486,108	29,008	92,817	114,267	98,115	81,283	70,618
960	Redding, CA	114,320	35,783	48,623	290,139	15,701	56,066	56,630	61,463	54,593	45,686
961	Reno, NV	44,309	46,992	61,706	117,827	5,994	20,674	29,765	29,129	20,341	11,924
967	Honolulu, HI	274,557	56,872	70,071	864,546	62,622	164,007	195,363	195,410	146,353	100,791
968	Honolulu, HI	151,315	47,322	67,056	404,653	21,678	55,028	93,942	90,343	72,630	71,032
970	Portland, OR	264,053	55,129	69,986	708,075	48,837	138,280	160,429	166,847	122,772	70,910
971	Portland, OR	106,364	51,377	63,499	293,722	21,268	56,303	71,141	65,135	47,195	32,680
972	Portland, OR	332,674	47,721	64,364	802,612	53,082	125,742	207,708	190,690	133,279	92,111
973	Salem, OR	209,478	43,326	54,925	557,568	35,445	100,935	135,285	118,203	95,150	72,550
974	Eugene, OR	215,975	38,310	50,064	528,641	28,317	87,575	116,590	112,032	101,771	82,356
975	Medford, OR	107,599	38,368	51,623	269,092	14,395	47,729	52,122	56,054	52,584	46,208
976	Klamath Falls, OR	27,719	33,571	44,923	69,560	4,353	13,326	13,393	14,448	13,290	10,750
977	Bend, OR	72,550	43,866	57,630	185,607	10,863	34,527	38,777	41,515	34,939	24,986
978	Pendleton, OR	53,076	37,931	47,844	141,764	8,932	27,408	29,129	30,306	25,633	20,356
979	Boise, ID	10,191	32,131	42,876	32,608	2,279	6,196	7,664	6,803	5,132	4,534
980	Seattle, WA	467,642	63,651	81,504	1,211,846	82,371	225,732	262,664	316,092	210,647	114,340
981	Seattle, WA	358,677	48,544	67,305	819,691	41,391	104,370	233,019	203,145	137,657	100,109
982	Everett, WA	301,063	51,134	63,306	803,894	52,527	153,672	188,704	190,699	129,956	88,336
983	Tacoma, WA	247,329	53,047	64,346	656,757	41,332	130,059	136,822	158,299	114,015	76,250
984	Tacoma, WA	153,888	42,138	54,524	401,218	29,042	73,416	108,256	87,508	58,461	44,535
985	Olympia, WA	166,527	45,666	56,654	425,814	24,561	78,490	91,986	96,270	77,539	56,968
986	Portland, OR	195,874	49,470	60,830	522,957	36,302	104,415	115,090	121,548	89,462	56,140
988	Wenatchee, WA	72,502	38,890	51,472	200,563	14,070	41,492	41,595	43,238	33,290	26,878
989	Yakima, WA	89,186	37,596	50,280	262,877	20,820	55,889	64,325	52,690	39,224	29,929
990	Spokane, WA	41,892	49,152	59,974	118,838	7,230	24,798	25,861	28,862	20,511	11,576
991	Spokane, WA	43,187	33,147	43,804	111,012	5,392	19,178	29,928	21,786	19,873	14,855
992	Spokane, WA	131,551	38,588	51,358	325,896	21,144	57,139	80,030	71,469	52,610	43,504
993	Pasco, WA	104,018	46,221	58,413	300,221	22,048	63,395	71,930	64,368	46,068	32,412
994	Lewiston, ID	8,419	36,482	48,836	20,613	1,276	3,708	4,035	4,422	3,739	3,433
995	Anchorage, AK	108,533	59,134	73,556	302,295	23,807	65,592	66,330	77,322	50,040	19,204
996	Anchorage, AK	53,585	52,557	64,102	156,843	10,778	37,596	29,357	41,713	26,939	10,460
997	Fairbanks, AK	41,736	52,291	64,069	119,748	10,221	27,572	28,370	28,440	18,496	6,649
998	Juneau, AK	18,811	59,671	72,022	49,247	3,052	10,173	9,167	13,227	9,854	3,774
999	Ketchikan, AK	8,140	49,225	60,338	21,015	1,473	4,514	3,444	5,530	4,244	1,810
TOTAL		109,949,228	46,475	63,301	292,936,668	19,696,271	53,752,430	68,747,982	66,620,117	47,563,878	36,555,990

Notes: Data is provided for residential areas only.
All figures are estimates. Because of rounding, the totals may not represent the sum of each individual item.
000 and 001 are not valid postal ZIPs. They represent collections of remainder areas throughout the country and are included for complete geographical coverage.

ZIP Code	3-Digit ZIP Code Areas	Black Markets	Hispanic Markets	Total Retail Sales ($Millions)	Retail Sales: Apparel & Accessories ($Millions)	Retail Sales: Automotive ($Millions)	Retail Sales: Drugs, First Aid & Health Care Products ($Millions)	Retail Sales: Food ($Millions)	Retail Sales: Furniture & Major Appliances ($Millions)	Retail Sales: General Merchandise ($Millions)	Retail Sales: Hardware, Lumber & Garden Supplies ($Millions)
000	Remainder Areas	2,578	3,298	191,818,779	4,724,773	38,145,311	7,780,771	34,704,754	7,743,276	25,507,505	12,627,098
010	Remainder Areas	42	385	79,587,850	2,823,100	16,452,022	2,955,200	12,636,214	2,952,358	10,947,991	5,996,809
010	Springfield, MA	8,708	37,461	5,647,565,940	231,632,044	1,111,481,877	303,221,690	929,452,346	220,610,344	660,769,835	375,030,469
011	Springfield, MA	34,104	47,385	2,127,763,481	94,635,311	448,923,371	107,422,664	326,790,095	84,064,505	298,007,466	136,366,876
012	Pittsfield, MA	2,853	2,695	1,984,359,727	104,811,184	380,025,451	108,526,637	345,117,467	68,942,725	191,786,424	119,566,688
013	Springfield, MA	848	1,862	829,330,370	19,951,517	177,112,253	38,813,181	152,078,360	30,758,991	73,633,965	60,875,768
014	Worcester, MA	5,642	15,399	2,731,727,333	129,227,609	712,148,766	147,907,900	407,033,235	123,314,589	325,282,815	132,187,531
015	Worcester, MA	5,007	12,361	4,768,247,130	196,788,459	1,305,360,732	254,732,610	713,087,258	209,578,113	589,962,885	236,633,533
016	Worcester, MA	15,081	30,919	2,386,433,544	98,834,216	647,213,404	128,457,514	360,142,562	103,094,519	294,847,611	118,378,716
017	Boston, MA	7,960	16,615	5,076,821,315	311,471,499	1,186,470,000	279,764,740	738,577,024	248,846,554	550,786,564	230,195,525
018	Middlesex-Essex, MA	14,741	85,890	8,788,160,050	528,340,580	1,973,854,340	501,526,752	1,293,002,368	402,868,885	948,185,155	440,001,249
019	Middlesex-Essex, MA	14,521	35,898	6,261,190,003	327,256,540	1,390,423,762	375,711,121	939,948,516	246,979,318	694,972,052	373,225,612
020	Brockton, MA	7,573	6,248	5,928,938,440	324,185,941	1,409,775,520	309,226,214	853,181,578	293,026,302	609,058,877	320,455,637
021	Boston, MA	191,272	140,975	17,285,486,474	1,209,964,935	3,122,883,087	1,036,383,266	2,441,318,173	807,936,224	1,595,485,872	616,998,098
022	Boston, MA	626	1,319	212,597,635	17,317,483	25,330,447	13,459,625	28,834,942	9,255,109	16,825,620	5,144,026
023	Brockton, MA	34,664	14,858	6,330,634,591	277,042,715	1,200,285,380	281,423,412	863,299,186	279,348,471	548,593,629	426,306,046
024	Brockton, MA	8,963	14,202	5,959,020,122	374,308,600	1,409,445,744	330,106,169	865,499,298	299,643,518	628,007,688	272,789,392
025	Buzzards Bay, MA	3,121	1,706	2,444,249,941	154,079,411	224,066,130	98,577,181	400,726,143	99,736,003	130,613,771	256,759,299
026	Buzzards Bay, MA	3,302	2,398	3,231,651,502	217,516,776	272,259,375	147,802,657	563,531,256	182,349,837	201,014,093	233,901,632
027	Providence, RI	12,824	22,801	7,449,237,327	458,103,938	1,247,803,845	405,498,960	1,180,758,466	283,624,744	1,162,411,972	468,583,848
028	Providence, RI	17,501	36,128	9,014,420,448	405,318,217	1,650,869,695	547,028,112	1,371,932,968	368,040,873	1,081,786,434	519,954,985
029	Providence, RI	33,840	68,365	3,767,688,777	149,668,254	598,780,906	301,981,745	663,784,931	133,420,880	324,014,761	129,090,571
030	Manchester, NH	3,899	10,279	6,653,810,711	322,925,935	1,361,582,244	247,820,640	998,572,456	381,996,723	1,203,399,405	469,285,655
031	Manchester, NH	3,166	6,546	2,533,691,542	117,687,938	561,664,450	102,482,521	368,589,560	128,333,656	440,527,050	193,864,582
032	Manchester, NH	559	1,430	3,158,092,151	125,493,791	833,374,566	125,568,030	543,846,180	111,959,551	320,691,102	220,565,869
034	Manchester, NH	543	745	874,211,622	26,798,682	295,863,156	45,004,708	138,964,089	26,306,017	86,039,686	55,350,758
035	White River Junction, VT	382	697	1,435,812,725	43,822,338	288,863,142	47,184,632	241,716,523	41,790,211	116,070,941	128,440,630
036	White River Junction, VT	86	293	758,485,351	17,993,342	161,162,132	30,281,396	136,735,571	21,193,775	71,198,668	50,003,174
037	White River Junction, VT	46	71	197,056,349	5,144,458	46,482,723	7,525,845	34,956,640	5,826,258	16,632,565	17,442,897
038	Portsmouth, NH	522	728	1,245,487,206	38,701,001	242,695,249	43,495,080	237,780,021	33,715,885	130,436,603	92,693,673
039	Portsmouth, NH	1,945	3,009	5,703,053,870	314,791,642	1,114,486,515	200,708,746	998,728,713	270,699,489	804,993,745	388,912,665
040	Portland, ME	312	458	595,815,251	47,811,682	108,053,263	22,927,461	103,284,491	26,930,306	27,745,975	36,188,067
041	Portland, ME	1,780	2,858	5,135,504,902	386,189,629	857,575,181	177,950,340	777,395,434	183,834,167	456,903,192	314,627,479
042	Portland, ME	2,221	1,705	2,459,010,898	191,697,238	380,541,981	75,611,970	328,935,368	74,642,593	278,868,454	148,668,875
043	Portland, ME	1,003	1,508	2,388,980,783	56,639,351	396,116,506	94,737,781	397,341,609	66,299,209	294,594,888	163,539,844
044	Bangor, ME	325	628	1,224,649,198	32,630,170	367,157,572	47,924,247	221,099,179	36,827,233	136,436,401	84,436,381
045	Portland, ME	765	1,056	2,648,862,450	89,619,279	592,180,227	104,465,252	432,079,662	78,662,956	223,765,252	223,765,252
046	Bangor, ME	209	398	648,893,520	14,260,311	111,966,252	25,910,160	137,396,804	16,120,189	35,655,192	60,325,130
047	Bangor, ME	261	542	1,120,360,755	29,573,974	205,566,332	42,123,865	262,941,816	23,160,671	80,473,440	129,065,152
048	Portland, ME	313	484	1,001,697,354	28,477,325	194,080,566	57,889,850	207,167,998	23,186,720	108,273,117	69,253,892
049	Portland, ME	104	273	591,790,238	28,767,391	94,322,795	23,684,250	128,686,123	13,620,939	50,091,935	75,336,556
050	White River Junction, VT	466	1,097	1,914,920,298	43,698,836	478,829,524	84,338,016	356,980,182	58,106,841	195,360,486	187,844,200
051	White River Junction, VT	276	505	671,865,755	8,402,853	164,996,353	21,803,798	111,937,509	11,903,403	27,325,991	86,129,972
052	White River Junction, VT	96	250	406,513,397	9,191,198	83,667,949	11,607,877	70,115,145	8,428,407	20,149,831	36,589,128
053	Burlington, VT	222	355	660,779,937	65,689,929	88,195,877	25,433,961	96,744,410	19,625,783	47,816,857	50,914,508
054	Burlington, VT	255	437	609,805,865	22,679,777	101,346,881	26,791,427	108,916,849	16,585,476	31,072,948	49,816,049
055	Burlington, VT	1,804	2,268	3,618,196,717	177,191,254	817,380,100	134,256,226	623,824,675	157,711,484	292,739,997	288,957,534
056	White River Junction, VT	402	950	1,282,246,747	35,077,149	325,711,726	54,556,647	248,718,627	32,516,203	80,532,352	124,337,099
057	White River Junction, VT	379	752	1,151,659,911	28,534,252	268,462,042	57,641,788	208,917,525	32,253,837	85,583,496	93,906,403
058	White River Junction, VT	238	494	738,659,576	18,210,163	147,745,518	37,810,058	151,542,775	10,909,277	67,352,286	79,121,809
059	White River Junction, VT	6	12	26,586,008	1,682,185	9,569,039	748,088	2,995,678	703,607	632,403	3,205,379
060	Hartford, CT	47,023	44,058	9,514,749,460	478,504,328	2,206,777,300	488,198,302	1,328,608,881	469,623,070	1,143,796,999	594,773,177
061	Hartford, CT	61,924	69,469	4,307,036,607	230,545,262	975,196,203	225,632,585	576,459,291	218,976,160	552,002,853	273,971,308
062	Hartford, CT	3,224	9,708	1,542,094,614	39,506,101	402,995,381	91,555,751	305,231,502	34,930,140	103,630,199	76,208,563
063	New Haven, CT	15,181	14,758	3,463,984,703	167,256,443	751,879,173	145,462,633	543,015,333	143,317,911	374,536,047	219,638,035
064	New Haven, CT	20,773	35,640	9,961,960,931	474,843,890	2,074,069,359	508,874,232	1,561,626,388	433,543,268	1,076,961,767	580,516,319
065	New Haven, CT	69,002	40,532	3,714,623,647	185,614,636	743,257,739	201,352,153	588,227,993	176,723,711	433,797,571	236,794,259
066	New Haven, CT	51,887	52,907	3,847,364,328	226,090,068	675,938,361	154,875,761	543,514,527	180,926,775	426,199,276	225,877,766
067	Waterbury, CT	22,860	32,839	4,140,233,730	164,810,640	927,389,555	222,358,894	714,982,344	160,847,579	386,602,330	293,372,405
068	Stamford, CT	21,279	23,607	8,094,716,791	495,064,555	1,421,300,802	308,448,811	1,120,218,891	389,233,845	886,588,182	468,680,988
069	Stamford, CT	17,815	23,607	2,208,013,586	132,086,130	387,038,619	85,571,492	308,164,282	105,374,714	243,341,620	128,820,203
070	Newark, NJ	247,225	385,606	21,558,465,902	1,457,687,741	4,936,035,034	1,152,834,071	3,328,301,495	1,437,741,640	1,999,765,243	920,523,011
071	Newark, NJ	198,709	107,210	3,817,216,443	275,969,877	562,212,064	255,079,496	663,411,281	210,543,759	363,389,204	152,470,726
072	Newark, NJ	48,996	79,288	2,055,199,127	79,145,562	659,761,798	120,185,036	334,962,692	164,015,433	79,130,636	81,327,301
073	Newark, NJ	66,527	71,488	2,410,383,059	240,659,741	431,910,913	151,374,844	377,901,844	178,683,007	189,559,138	57,530,872
074	Paterson, NJ	5,675	24,969	7,353,305,451	462,807,895	1,855,560,045	319,415,757	1,062,051,044	445,203,830	822,057,668	373,531,381
075	Paterson, NJ	51,215	89,523	2,629,927,555	154,167,114	520,082,747	114,108,640	316,090,621	219,104,968	382,803,561	147,906,588
076	Hackensack, NJ	42,147	68,062	8,443,832,656	662,310,319	2,114,374,102	392,064,924	1,241,717,575	452,235,830	880,670,757	370,426,896
077	Monmouth, NJ	50,284	44,723	9,160,884,650	587,500,615	2,240,678,054	399,977,463	1,506,433,400	529,486,381	1,088,623,591	417,238,754
078	West Jersey, NJ	8,643	31,100	5,373,035,994	196,526,287	1,737,485,387	208,083,034	886,889,759	230,968,251	448,881,528	349,170,663

ZIP Code	3-Digit ZIP Code Areas	Black Markets	Hispanic Markets	Total Retail Sales ($Millions)	Retail Sales: Apparel & Accessories ($Millions)	Retail Sales: Automotive ($Millions)	Retail Sales: Drugs, First Aid & Health Care Products ($Millions)	Retail Sales: Food ($Millions)	Retail Sales: Furniture & Major Appliances ($Millions)	Retail Sales: General Merchandise ($Millions)	Retail Sales: Hardware, Lumber & Garden Supplies ($Millions)
079	West Jersey, NJ	7,264	17,195	4,276,880,222	181,002,277	1,373,396,677	165,580,462	641,632,033	226,986,964	371,456,204	243,991,979
080	South Jersey, NJ	142,147	45,224	15,749,278,159	667,465,894	4,254,426,340	767,567,375	2,367,144,399	770,766,256	2,155,871,750	804,224,753
081	South Jersey, NJ	54,429	42,035	1,764,394,796	102,085,568	324,128,251	101,603,720	290,737,410	113,091,086	217,988,422	82,413,304
082	South Jersey, NJ	26,015	17,949	3,883,848,507	209,204,880	837,376,873	189,532,076	656,483,452	160,993,653	422,810,443	177,333,128
083	South Jersey, NJ	39,779	36,432	2,693,340,363	103,572,976	623,334,180	149,490,604	482,949,146	155,437,369	315,106,284	133,521,638
084	South Jersey, NJ	17,109	14,134	975,874,605	60,609,867	195,178,907	49,940,393	144,411,852	51,717,751	137,019,608	43,410,435
085	Trenton, NJ	15,666	17,983	4,045,365,551	198,560,642	1,010,265,543	187,235,345	637,943,343	243,098,840	471,994,617	222,194,942
086	Trenton, NJ	72,221	33,726	3,571,756,238	171,536,277	835,500,465	203,117,989	557,438,338	240,761,065	414,027,524	147,261,710
087	Trenton, NJ	14,753	26,556	5,946,132,711	227,578,234	1,568,560,122	298,091,353	1,095,826,655	274,550,523	581,468,542	471,432,843
088	New Brunswick, NJ	68,491	103,340	12,861,593,551	815,764,851	2,669,944,448	494,955,326	1,990,265,118	894,750,515	1,669,534,965	773,865,906
089	New Brunswick, NJ	17,684	29,920	1,334,453,146	92,209,481	251,492,820	52,999,632	204,737,214	102,986,890	200,033,075	81,072,361
100	New York, NY	251,993	419,236	28,961,663,505	3,738,013,007	1,212,929,373	1,464,896,227	2,412,670,215	2,383,484,413	3,054,395,557	415,053,667
101	New York, NY	2,795	4,909	1,277,795,022	168,818,453	53,457,577	63,295,249	104,764,191	106,609,067	133,783,827	18,123,059
102	New York, NY	221	413	168,911,754	22,911,433	7,026,301	8,141,576	13,652,723	14,439,201	17,661,551	2,374,068
103	Staten Island, NY	47,412	68,610	3,723,819,619	217,297,221	409,051,337	288,948,111	873,719,037	165,177,392	477,196,277	207,015,503
104	Bronx, NY	469,239	719,543	5,926,848,968	424,453,627	649,392,857	532,448,547	1,232,662,729	387,257,448	479,054,810	225,364,090
105	Westchester, NY	73,859	81,684	8,481,763,391	481,653,723	1,935,730,756	440,072,996	1,313,162,014	526,999,832	931,990,407	454,219,183
106	Westchester, NY	15,276	18,636	1,195,076,991	72,461,706	264,422,337	62,531,777	183,575,471	73,933,071	136,334,520	62,863,189
107	Westchester, NY	36,373	59,985	3,281,592,714	195,650,983	724,405,778	172,727,952	507,358,255	201,254,600	375,489,662	173,415,536
108	Westchester, NY	14,736	18,195	1,094,857,762	66,310,616	241,981,808	57,389,846	168,380,802	67,619,571	124,913,935	57,604,632
109	Rockland, NY	51,785	53,894	6,271,881,592	326,070,315	1,173,389,254	339,448,106	1,122,375,212	232,855,299	596,345,897	419,082,799
110	Queens, NY	25,661	23,753	4,194,927,330	255,653,068	856,881,660	226,204,070	532,281,308	273,991,780	369,578,569	214,629,648
111	Long Island City, NY	15,183	66,015	1,482,013,452	81,901,207	226,765,389	121,516,994	272,399,632	86,129,933	120,610,304	51,708,663
112	Brooklyn, NY	908,070	531,058	12,575,440,371	1,013,726,768	1,537,263,104	1,064,733,183	2,438,225,031	904,082,798	1,090,736,733	580,475,671
113	Flushing, NY	58,870	357,301	7,066,857,230	391,691,458	1,089,397,942	335,168,995	1,300,420,667	409,944,048	573,530,005	246,618,806
114	Jamaica, NY	321,888	145,222	4,040,596,563	224,660,775	624,105,900	666,580,968	743,443,947	235,273,673	328,214,192	140,919,548
115	Western Nassau, NY	120,240	109,499	12,688,194,491	772,302,951	2,613,945,951	666,580,968	1,584,071,666	835,011,773	1,125,248,246	658,190,422
116	Far Rockaway, NY	46,282	20,158	625,981,353	34,494,112	95,919,705	52,270,410	115,802,909	36,047,283	50,874,173	21,842,910
117	Mid-Island, NY	102,703	177,216	23,235,973,186	1,271,707,740	5,137,795,804	1,140,202,107	3,435,874,177	1,275,061,478	2,563,850,148	1,727,974,318
118	Mid-Island, NY	602	5,758	1,343,126,538	82,126,097	277,299,874	70,661,076	167,204,654	88,215,082	118,723,072	69,521,378
119	Mid-Island, NY	16,171	26,788	3,765,881,364	193,063,667	851,162,817	182,942,186	592,286,367	188,906,727	444,242,083	311,513,791
120	Albany, NY	7,430	11,203	3,993,905,541	149,686,463	992,440,380	220,254,432	693,168,805	160,695,534	439,737,605	277,338,975
121	Albany, NY	11,494	7,486	3,339,495,205	120,420,287	814,207,704	195,644,733	591,393,183	128,175,872	357,908,543	232,986,955
122	Albany, NY	31,632	7,759	2,713,213,755	173,426,259	780,032,664	127,524,691	330,462,928	138,301,903	410,510,187	102,647,286
123	Albany, NY	12,338	6,528	1,976,070,113	77,925,794	432,951,752	131,021,548	317,026,093	86,626,158	225,382,007	178,267,297
124	Mid-Hudson, NY	8,311	8,768	1,809,578,709	46,942,284	372,808,143	101,178,590	386,985,434	39,736,242	206,678,285	139,011,300
125	Mid-Hudson, NY	36,421	47,586	5,490,647,361	260,520,043	1,106,707,197	268,978,740	1,024,844,740	180,352,496	619,144,054	402,360,256
126	Mid-Hudson, NY	16,189	7,899	1,144,622,852	57,669,396	257,672,566	56,126,070	203,660,884	39,499,118	152,841,954	70,933,084
127	Mid-Hudson, NY	7,755	9,765	1,111,953,374	39,433,325	194,866,236	63,449,954	236,561,703	26,346,365	93,324,624	110,951,322
128	Glen Falls, NY	4,571	4,436	3,118,743,472	143,759,048	586,451,663	152,795,840	552,288,417	110,084,742	244,440,818	242,207,066
129	Plattsburgh, NY	8,066	5,411	2,075,687,511	120,420,287	474,681,502	110,294,357	366,682,263	31,363,646	249,697,511	198,817,766
130	Syracuse, NY	8,092	5,975	4,933,391,376	214,052,287	1,165,176,644	269,885,821	833,339,969	211,147,766	529,638,488	355,472,250
131	Syracuse, NY	2,684	3,441	2,053,037,155	63,864,829	513,609,783	119,561,361	351,672,102	78,223,652	214,041,933	157,357,216
132	Syracuse, NY	43,311	11,404	3,306,012,205	183,424,119	773,617,918	170,136,654	532,791,983	175,352,330	381,680,925	214,434,190
133	Utica, NY	1,460	1,855	1,503,336,948	41,314,839	342,678,756	113,925,051	245,512,548	59,992,146	156,794,042	114,002,687
134	Utica, NY	6,433	5,545	2,141,822,798	71,215,178	502,322,181	153,380,722	354,282,316	85,813,189	210,785,571	149,572,255
135	Utica, NY	8,187	4,439	840,632,276	32,935,609	191,906,712	61,704,435	136,262,950	35,219,192	79,886,098	58,442,568
136	Watertown, NY	14,012	10,730	2,785,280,820	123,410,098	599,535,132	182,953,687	450,898,421	44,939,386	276,640,673	242,207,066
137	Binghamton, NY	2,618	2,348	1,687,831,279	36,992,413	378,636,905	108,005,358	290,275,633	62,140,685	159,501,238	123,574,207
138	Binghamton, NY	2,838	3,218	1,595,528,782	36,069,089	377,809,683	99,609,302	264,119,739	47,156,011	152,038,541	138,278,022
139	Binghamton, NY	5,379	2,792	1,033,533,896	226,150,228	212,031,814	64,955,147	176,454,568	41,368,942	93,209,153	60,689,934
140	Buffalo, NY	11,583	10,789	5,299,762,745	107,506,786	1,206,725,677	308,543,037	894,160,512	267,186,872	616,140,006	300,097,010
141	Buffalo, NY	2,093	2,578	632,183,656	25,682,072	130,004,546	150,173,384	423,518,796	116,252,542	288,005,881	130,649,157
142	Buffalo, NY	123,310	30,280	7,953,203,070	348,799,237	1,836,329,008	438,571,550	1,298,265,927	454,243,722	1,009,853,408	422,872,108
143	Buffalo, NY	11,483	1,612	921,185,104	44,840,983	163,909,767	63,837,009	173,525,712	34,164,698	103,875,183	44,628,505
144	Rochester, NY	11,267	8,884	3,613,134,115	111,879,996	925,052,019	593,944,687	593,944,687	163,014,298	471,220,085	222,165,769
145	Rochester, NY	8,533	7,083	1,911,589,121	71,883,580	543,717,169	176,741,758	616,671,913	139,381,482	415,646,586	253,814,081
146	Rochester, NY	103,243	40,362	1,951,948,707	271,308,900	909,286,614	268,321,291	1,125,414,360	321,435,255	879,877,853	374,029,568
147	Jamestown, NY	3,242	4,508	919,046,701	50,558,866	222,739,517	117,432,923	321,240,953	63,442,568	203,906,961	149,556,807
148	Elmira, NY	7,606	6,424	1,890,190,268	86,855,608	455,612,667	198,911,228	566,143,284	93,274,988	336,018,943	242,441,831
149	Elmira, NY	4,878	1,403	3,125,657,859	25,682,072	710,521,212	315,199,028	866,027,609	21,755,578	110,705,111	39,012,089
150	Pittsburgh, PA	21,686	3,105	632,183,656	192,998,029	130,004,546	315,199,028	866,027,609	244,582,355	763,134,791	310,088,391
151	Pittsburgh, PA	35,406	2,547	5,366,831,103	259,775,906	1,209,026,693	316,536,770	753,002,870	273,641,759	727,781,070	233,286,787
152	Pittsburgh, PA	120,051	7,288	5,382,552,269	504,962,401	1,277,424,568	610,362,585	1,459,191,632	528,670,704	1,410,270,359	451,084,440
153	Pittsburgh, PA	6,144	1,110	10,437,815,603	47,754,476	2,467,780,903	110,532,518	341,461,620	70,343,802	173,951,774	134,342,800
154	Pittsburgh, PA	5,450	634	1,911,589,121	71,883,580	543,717,169	113,872,522	354,477,346	65,450,106	261,115,753	116,527,629
155	Johnstown, PA	1,533	651	1,951,948,707	71,948,707	447,246,008	43,950,900	134,489,615	31,184,684	69,347,378	51,760,696
156	Greensburg, PA	3,783	1,654	919,046,701	86,503,154	222,739,517	199,091,350	598,843,749	118,406,853	453,918,788	278,776,215
157	Johnstown, PA	1,497	560	1,248,130,840	31,284,024	905,444,509	64,800,007	221,978,164	32,492,130	155,969,180	75,945,929
158	DuBois, PA	229	431	1,012,831,615	33,513,663	229,796,648	62,111,283	193,978,994	27,987,255	96,373,356	69,629,418

ZIP Code	3-Digit ZIP Code Areas	Black Markets	Hispanic Markets	Total Retail Sales ($Millions)	Retail Sales: Apparel & Accessories ($Millions)	Retail Sales: Automotive ($Millions)	Retail Sales: Drugs, First Aid & Health Care Products ($Millions)	Retail Sales: Food ($Millions)	Retail Sales: Furniture & Major Appliances ($Millions)	Retail Sales: General Merchandise ($Millions)	Retail Sales: Hardware, Lumber & Garden Supplies ($Millions)
159	Johnstown, PA	4,278	1,323	1,673,078,685	44,848,648	370,657,981	98,588,405	305,833,365	55,992,200	229,795,776	98,202,514
160	New Castle, PA	1,681	1,025	2,331,411,924	51,215,242	555,220,818	115,299,437	318,605,258	130,984,204	334,222,928	200,280,027
161	New Castle, PA	9,674	1,443	2,518,463,021	75,990,871	487,385,006	148,745,846	409,103,024	93,040,413	337,318,153	184,852,292
162	New Castle, PA	686	420	888,041,474	23,108,548	196,508,798	53,977,787	171,474,215	22,826,257	90,973,068	69,742,557
163	Oil City, PA	1,945	882	2,497,512,966	39,546,197	344,102,518	92,035,234	278,845,694	41,424,763	222,294,421	114,925,383
164	Erie, PA	2,372	1,061	1,574,611,723	49,213,276	383,385,606	82,776,127	240,176,408	61,165,724	222,250,316	87,165,410
165	Erie, PA	15,477	5,450	2,514,286,927	89,370,752	638,760,601	139,875,245	398,366,687	110,209,427	370,209,393	124,747,633
166	Altoona, PA	4,996	1,456	2,594,956,403	72,899,932	479,062,697	156,123,679	406,977,486	112,813,131	336,775,221	173,151,437
167	Bradford, PA	703	483	489,253,455	8,176,522	97,550,406	33,806,971	110,891,323	12,513,972	40,479,000	25,403,504
168	Altoona, PA	3,868	2,375	2,333,458,923	95,580,666	542,582,059	98,223,582	342,882,753	90,702,534	314,977,815	167,771,613
169	Williamsport, PA	566	337	650,772,363	11,856,585	128,877,312	44,585,111	117,017,259	17,758,585	58,804,225	80,788,825
170	Harrisburg, PA	10,167	12,873	8,133,213,166	225,193,432	1,879,773,944	349,598,731	1,119,232,059	316,009,416	982,027,863	482,380,164
171	Harrisburg, PA	40,950	9,243	2,252,447,633	85,784,384	628,891,728	112,348,402	295,119,061	82,886,957	348,619,873	107,745,862
172	Harrisburg, PA	3,878	2,821	2,162,496,359	56,897,574	498,771,790	113,487,863	305,127,746	87,366,215	266,911,434	170,151,248
173	Lancaster, PA	2,666	6,165	4,003,499,682	94,198,859	882,064,567	151,985,882	546,746,142	122,367,429	494,608,402	236,706,158
174	Lancaster, PA	13,300	9,941	2,316,423,294	55,422,600	504,533,433	85,766,502	291,457,056	70,221,412	302,174,814	134,653,025
175	Lancaster, PA	3,034	6,080	3,838,085,929	185,926,534	916,236,528	166,924,811	590,825,167	233,687,293	374,946,581	307,829,793
176	Lancaster, PA	10,714	23,334	2,079,220,640	100,631,173	495,076,536	91,037,204	321,832,733	126,014,134	203,262,259	167,218,163
177	Williamsport, PA	5,219	1,008	2,160,835,593	85,970,617	529,880,241	108,115,078	341,234,155	64,466,171	216,417,751	135,520,734
178	Harrisburg, PA	5,854	3,787	2,606,276,115	59,059,011	455,286,132	136,337,188	391,258,151	67,809,701	308,058,574	189,865,600
179	Reading, PA	3,430	1,556	1,189,950,459	31,803,687	221,752,989	124,272,693	224,591,486	39,540,709	151,608,574	63,541,341
180	Lehigh Valley, PA	11,089	26,611	6,158,231,525	214,162,301	1,574,806,267	314,929,618	1,036,742,396	243,096,757	714,153,404	351,586,644
181	Lehigh Valley, PA	9,906	31,738	2,328,655,481	101,880,169	584,291,183	125,309,294	294,658,138	119,597,037	362,946,894	143,765,998
182	Wilkes-Barre, PA	1,402	3,062	1,369,590,189	33,188,996	318,573,615	94,931,524	232,670,148	56,980,514	158,575,731	116,004,721
183	Lehigh Valley, PA	11,027	10,820	2,177,864,461	85,266,468	390,523,008	100,499,919	376,683,457	93,469,706	260,481,856	181,037,497
184	Scranton, PA	5,431	5,163	2,399,827,874	85,777,317	458,091,217	148,555,827	415,120,914	68,110,143	213,091,776	202,743,790
185	Scranton, PA	2,614	2,559	1,520,767,867	73,050,819	322,697,631	111,970,784	244,957,033	42,728,811	305,514,792	100,688,587
186	Wilkes-Barre, PA	1,768	1,740	2,050,951,920	66,190,910	447,875,991	125,592,772	317,788,389	79,428,889	291,755,824	137,760,557
187	Wilkes-Barre, PA	4,119	1,733	1,779,780,730	59,339,280	395,452,631	111,241,044	264,620,160	69,344,311	69,687,804	114,996,575
188	Scranton, PA	425	506	807,074,852	14,441,782	153,298,268	50,304,192	133,822,237	—	—	60,053,211
189	Southeastern, PA	4,503	6,286	5,960,810,210	179,200,642	1,907,699,693	236,045,982	788,113,039	271,595,274	616,165,090	315,117,198
190	Philadelphia, PA	128,878	22,515	17,693,786,695	748,555,343	4,536,516,922	917,089,793	2,501,383,370	881,174,881	2,034,969,458	490,739,222
191	Philadelphia, PA	653,212	138,501	14,094,747,055	986,024,128	3,393,089,845	1,111,325,913	2,298,893,368	680,763,303	1,344,408,927	318,627,078
193	Southeastern, PA	27,216	15,350	6,495,627,238	159,575,764	941,350,841	229,312,262	778,969,073	189,116,968	294,801,741	139,418,130
194	Reading, PA	35,419	11,977	8,709,779,395	457,018,069	2,075,583,866	395,580,930	1,120,881,338	484,489,358	1,139,979,374	314,375,789
195	Reading, PA	2,296	3,360	12,464,796,507	196,041,630	688,313,050	120,792,659	370,522,417	132,472,328	386,429,443	565,225,059
196	Reading, PA	12,722	38,099	2,717,334,748	199,052,670	674,578,905	118,561,357	365,267,237	124,679,645	385,153,537	135,812,521
197	Wilmington, DE	51,691	15,701	4,597,620,797	163,104,737	1,020,890,935	216,869,447	638,166,436	295,602,110	735,209,957	236,999,552
198	Wilmington, DE	54,099	15,469	3,772,778,915	132,835,400	834,463,624	184,742,273	528,373,016	239,346,785	598,129,632	195,335,566
199	Wilmington, DE	51,402	13,021	5,180,498,932	215,425,651	1,105,321,052	224,831,942	706,005,424	231,871,598	729,853,966	528,242,011
200	Washington, DC	326,832	56,645	6,073,137,832	485,307,781	244,867,502	415,828,897	829,166,532	399,989,568	362,798,613	97,707,763
201	Northern Virginia, VA	52,288	76,219	9,800,427,771	495,519,905	1,888,091,917	340,067,991	1,545,981,095	575,514,771	1,258,047,848	650,293,171
206	Southern, MD	69,124	6,272	3,561,443,027	145,549,289	691,266,570	115,981,000	588,633,787	144,647,005	552,391,578	314,375,789
207	Southern, MD	558,360	75,388	12,464,796,507	572,633,973	2,883,428,046	497,161,850	1,966,381,929	673,195,520	1,760,305,824	565,225,059
208	Suburban, MD	55,739	65,458	9,933,867,381	622,394,797	2,805,838,910	369,898,995	1,462,677,845	833,691,562	950,172,410	422,011,452
209	Suburban, MD	73,050	60,629	4,568,548,812	279,423,134	1,285,701,277	174,239,883	675,917,342	371,714,032	439,056,612	195,380,386
210	Baltimore, MD	69,520	16,273	9,287,254,106	341,449,111	2,353,554,591	324,841,870	1,584,870,540	454,942,628	1,143,877,313	535,734,760
211	Baltimore, MD	66,178	8,490	6,436,697,109	272,678,680	1,579,444,106	234,160,495	978,351,892	343,639,246	955,677,217	396,123,498
212	Baltimore, MD	535,880	22,735	14,256,295,405	816,074,861	2,989,684,833	755,717,176	2,150,522,825	731,234,584	1,596,788,086	721,516,445
214	Baltimore, MD	13,916	3,907	1,460,374,236	57,888,583	364,274,209	47,352,951	216,657,919	73,766,399	229,131,864	96,232,738
215	Cumberland, MD	3,978	640	1,308,169,520	40,365,067	236,690,243	79,579,437	239,000,605	46,480,650	163,611,006	107,038,264
216	Easton, MD	23,044	2,885	1,856,474,989	91,358,600	335,262,229	82,103,817	341,125,850	70,024,278	126,746,331	135,443,033
217	Frederick, MD	26,560	9,127	5,818,574,720	140,119,521	1,386,741,046	233,083,999	891,077,046	258,005,133	811,349,580	426,646,432
218	Salisbury, MD	37,784	2,813	2,983,388,367	151,884,266	437,941,036	129,685,463	433,806,183	87,851,377	346,165,044	210,831,589
219	Baltimore, MD	3,242	1,393	1,129,081,121	52,378,957	235,962,185	31,927,460	152,202,909	17,733,869	59,958,013	82,072,414
220	Northern Virginia, VA	37,097	63,262	7,729,186,309	489,419,443	1,337,083,521	276,264,484	999,678,463	491,308,191	810,868,595	360,526,891
221	Northern Virginia, VA	55,719	49,531	5,571,000,268	401,954,695	1,256,944,320	174,198,205	804,275,291	447,112,140	658,095,237	313,847,347
222	Northern Virginia, VA	16,345	37,098	2,928,114,350	295,415,349	610,227,102	153,368,311	357,663,087	136,786,308	283,573,080	30,538,978
223	Northern Virginia, VA	55,665	50,866	5,446,288,314	322,140,844	1,053,673,489	196,706,445	712,785,929	544,496,468	715,868,927	208,245,996
224	Richmond, VA	31,771	6,628	2,564,813,195	76,058,308	477,918,860	121,874,138	399,043,556	98,083,211	340,447,536	210,619,307
225	Richmond, VA	34,764	6,138	1,861,615,801	39,604,005	432,798,896	84,434,540	314,893,114	123,235,912	175,875,130	96,299,213
226	Winchester, VA	7,890	5,071	2,268,615,371	60,281,600	479,200,642	103,375,631	361,871,462	35,188,048	262,015,934	183,639,007
227	Culpeper, VA	9,525	1,726	718,254,881	8,486,481	178,262,483	37,087,174	139,601,365	—	56,501,284	40,922,799
228	Charlottesville, VA	4,344	8,293	1,984,296,212	43,723,125	442,440,888	78,751,284	289,446,734	68,724,054	253,287,114	146,453,104
229	Charlottesville, VA	29,047	5,810	3,048,425,820	108,225,370	637,755,969	138,419,978	464,017,470	152,995,510	288,571,342	229,297,820
230	Richmond, VA	38,853	2,807	2,009,237,542	64,784,641	466,320,548	93,767,400	341,367,029	119,552,636	264,605,204	103,401,085
231	Richmond, VA	38,957	4,856	3,923,403,917	225,181,437	853,252,802	154,956,903	633,764,471	171,714,891	387,308,628	185,429,604
232	Richmond, VA	199,671	18,045	7,292,373,266	364,699,874	1,754,426,362	378,003,704	1,134,116,431	408,000,243	907,312,497	380,199,429
233	Norfolk, VA	71,292	6,227	3,040,286,420	136,663,500	803,737,115	165,058,446	398,474,072	123,642,144	498,723,343	233,175,965
234	Norfolk, VA	133,762	21,400	6,582,327,030	284,108,078	1,525,938,258	260,313,943	996,842,143	382,913,366	726,557,368	330,858,945

ZIP Code	3-Digit ZIP Code Areas	Black Markets	Hispanic Markets	Total Retail Sales ($Millions)	Retail Sales: Apparel & Accessories ($Millions)	Retail Sales: Automotive ($Millions)	Retail Sales: Drugs, First Aid & Health Care Products ($Millions)	Retail Sales: Food ($Millions)	Retail Sales: Furniture & Major Appliances ($Millions)	Retail Sales: General Merchandise ($Millions)	Retail Sales: Hardware, Lumber & Garden Supplies ($Millions)
235	Norfolk, VA	108,667	9,589	3,017,444,172	123,363,612	849,503,548	127,546,604	401,915,615	156,914,047	438,295,998	107,296,912
236	Norfolk, VA	151,158	13,279	4,889,955,564	184,463,912	1,189,238,127	176,415,370	576,872,214	207,636,766	717,128,519	265,817,452
237	Norfolk, VA	51,762	1,587	806,450,841	17,505,622	176,645,113	40,606,191	190,398,930	17,059,326	58,494,260	36,940,873
238	Richmond, VA	123,815	7,495	3,778,179,113	135,067,740	893,521,358	182,815,947	545,196,487	159,852,173	552,338,910	252,750,075
239	Farmville, VA	38,282	1,339	1,136,201,492	19,196,275	297,254,655	54,721,889	178,329,070	45,391,874	133,948,724	69,009,032
240	Roanoke, VA	40,924	6,400	4,942,397,403	143,347,682	995,998,218	205,468,533	651,570,465	272,414,893	722,691,337	332,454,716
241	Roanoke, VA	24,926	3,098	2,843,104,814	49,849,682	685,422,397	128,956,662	477,172,866	117,865,432	231,450,268	185,493,513
242	Bristol, VA	6,073	1,390	2,410,321,952	53,256,471	581,338,591	113,901,425	488,654,175	100,962,142	208,905,467	182,711,895
243	Roanoke, VA	4,691	2,441	1,911,209,978	47,343,263	496,219,018	86,463,944	310,016,328	77,516,299	103,398,537	155,761,656
244	Charlottesville, VA	8,899	1,357	1,668,112,426	32,531,365	440,229,722	60,430,168	214,099,560	66,878,431	185,657,734	121,955,539
245	Lynchburg, VA	94,202	4,229	4,672,778,482	111,297,635	1,024,732,831	144,489,624	633,812,073	234,614,890	580,434,112	287,938,913
246	Bluefield, WV	1,751	421	929,403,509	10,199,180	220,396,121	71,364,086	191,817,341	33,344,603	124,299,398	95,726,466
247	Bluefield, WV	4,040	259	882,802,005	30,706,750	160,423,352	51,727,313	123,530,547	19,023,251	161,346,011	59,157,448
248	Bluefield, WV	2,749	239	365,244,576	1,598,382	104,216,624	32,773,266	82,085,323	12,194,346	32,773,723	17,209,893
249	Lewisburg, WV	2,113	305	475,423,160	6,239,855	131,916,518	41,882,448	94,623,897	15,728,909	39,397,800	35,628,687
250	Charleston, WV	2,302	309	948,846,803	26,263,614	178,721,353	58,666,181	149,851,163	30,449,223	146,583,864	74,167,420
251	Charleston, WV	2,338	416	988,760,602	23,435,946	198,781,413	62,084,069	162,565,446	33,251,837	141,557,018	79,712,977
252	Charleston, WV	110	248	616,683,905	5,103,166	137,224,701	31,224,311	99,007,990	17,719,026	43,698,579	45,876,625
253	Charleston, WV	10,446	649	1,913,056,144	66,673,085	303,584,259	113,101,894	280,390,847	62,104,555	327,240,689	142,870,968
254	Martinsburg, WV	7,468	2,713	1,610,123,891	108,935,544	354,021,197	59,539,775	266,905,733	69,240,246	191,831,550	83,006,085
255	Huntington, WV	624	753	1,475,435,629	29,069,754	334,552,282	98,644,631	239,224,691	61,492,108	146,213,735	113,207,123
256	Huntington, WV	1,603	283	495,139,740	10,042,472	126,176,584	46,151,648	76,698,252	15,425,248	39,080,696	60,621,764
257	Huntington, WV	3,999	517	1,138,988,988	42,287,583	188,310,377	72,127,143	148,590,896	45,080,968	109,718,738	81,513,911
258	Beckley, WV	7,270	764	1,140,705,691	18,406,936	307,068,186	65,480,224	186,914,726	25,628,219	217,886,187	88,636,246
259	Beckley, WV	1,629	369	497,208,655	9,257,913	128,254,284	36,451,313	95,111,237	13,977,180	67,558,849	28,693,241
260	Wheeling, WV	2,971	799	1,495,967,686	32,075,717	335,074,353	95,111,237	254,792,843	75,394,386	193,758,822	95,044,037
261	Parkersburg, WV	1,131	625	1,785,732,962	58,688,970	413,019,441	98,311,149	258,266,433	56,712,248	304,533,157	118,203,775
262	Clarkburg, WV	544	434	830,760,210	10,503,994	200,962,593	48,795,549	159,895,998	23,846,049	102,778,327	85,423,892
263	Clarkburg, WV	1,326	717	1,087,947,131	32,358,839	271,311,520	73,248,921	167,658,646	25,959,249	183,318,483	84,481,362
264	Clarkburg, WV	270	361	531,918,357	10,042,472	143,182,181	34,406,403	96,240,066	15,337,676	68,237,501	31,932,061
265	Clarkburg, WV	4,973	1,340	2,026,667,744	42,436,937	413,032,517	116,115,818	317,747,549	49,519,930	356,578,302	176,643,256
266	Gassaway, WV	114	168	399,613,178	2,437,189	80,269,378	24,961,224	71,228,583	9,575,618	44,075,586	43,163,594
267	Cumberland, MD	999	291	413,852,035	4,560,277	123,323,440	26,162,583	62,641,908	20,026,789	47,911,052	26,459,310
268	Petersburg, WV	557	230	270,208,685	1,500,806	85,053,353	16,618,347	50,088,236	10,190,315	14,631,949	29,046,191
270	Greensboro, NC	17,013	12,798	3,235,943,295	106,890,046	798,094,247	173,544,440	473,366,196	149,919,526	379,923,720	234,299,241
271	Greensboro, NC	75,048	24,124	3,671,239,701	185,954,729	1,048,549,949	161,568,583	452,557,002	175,149,192	443,477,170	231,270,976
272	Greensboro, NC	89,326	40,067	6,866,412,555	282,215,593	1,526,758,874	329,261,279	976,622,719	405,698,607	746,389,958	473,032,540
273	Greensboro, NC	53,860	23,806	3,850,097,273	113,284,469	793,995,668	187,114,305	637,510,677	177,831,106	413,448,958	314,930,207
274	Greensboro, NC	95,582	14,645	4,781,006,681	197,223,605	1,110,120,135	230,825,340	535,972,122	430,497,815	571,081,745	302,644,864
275	Raleigh, NC	187,250	53,139	10,755,377,864	436,663,318	2,467,198,022	484,211,196	1,567,966,941	550,563,437	1,202,675,880	845,553,561
276	Raleigh, NC	100,758	20,135	6,521,449,413	315,515,644	1,631,755,527	290,801,768	830,614,113	368,817,217	875,520,253	535,232,504
277	Raleigh, NC	93,032	30,057	3,041,115,980	170,862,231	583,537,474	154,057,441	419,584,679	131,516,493	365,221,508	202,660,865
278	Rocky Mount, NC	214,331	15,878	6,474,278,701	239,215,161	1,458,705,108	280,643,707	1,004,315,219	249,239,559	747,694,330	647,347,642
279	Rocky Mount, NC	12,328	2,779	2,459,908,910	87,443,324	397,805,215	94,761,991	446,973,332	88,964,496	241,584,392	260,707,211
280	Charlotte, NC	56,578	29,497	1,710,900,171	241,866,866	1,827,718,670	286,077,119	1,078,669,005	304,972,100	869,674,827	574,999,411
281	Charlotte, NC	72,160	23,293	399,878,149	198,025,051	1,414,501,232	253,155,108	913,461,664	236,774,669	676,758,699	502,680,677
282	Charlotte, NC	77,594	60,527	11,527,704,578	559,333,776	3,439,344,545	468,532,226	1,314,758,397	618,143,325	1,401,919,695	764,864,070
283	Fayetteville, NC	216,486	47,551	8,923,651,082	300,427,515	2,153,204,488	356,704,486	658,359,792	325,687,431	1,152,178,803	759,758,694
284	Fayetteville, NC	246,509	14,507	5,725,110,404	199,854,702	985,836,589	282,209,057	854,106,129	202,085,835	791,591,808	455,873,820
285	Kinston, NC	79,129	20,135	5,528,114,906	188,268,936	1,287,811,960	235,397,497	810,513,245	280,599,688	715,893,504	477,706,691
286	Hickory, NC	100,210	25,537	7,735,418,599	250,978,417	1,686,343,002	373,764,581	1,213,780,525	464,180,490	910,500,485	730,238,115
287	Asheville, NC	41,642	18,068	6,405,345,247	190,458,398	1,519,366,725	309,356,114	1,053,370,590	227,921,009	704,505,599	605,090,275
288	Asheville, NC	13,080	5,013	6,984,118,442	85,445,816	286,077,119	94,355,526	245,738,537	85,189,616	241,584,392	120,821,326
289	Asheville, NC	497	362	198,025,051	9,445,498	81,409,257	19,000,291	84,414,730	12,434,231	25,367,233	32,544,621
290	Columbia, SC	115,262	6,769	4,139,112,580	125,844,531	921,434,062	174,482,407	673,730,576	178,148,653	451,944,338	386,695,273
291	Columbia, SC	160,801	9,448	3,909,795,223	125,454,126	809,880,424	151,834,579	658,359,792	150,683,870	413,669,958	390,242,327
292	Columbia, SC	137,493	9,074	4,455,165,615	219,183,990	1,073,429,961	176,762,136	491,068,009	248,809,773	696,700,889	333,151,701
293	Greenville, SC	86,475	10,794	4,163,646,226	160,762,037	946,915,468	218,976,105	1,198,860,577	180,402,025	511,532,307	305,547,268
294	Charleston, SC	211,862	15,799	8,428,937,961	348,301,351	2,100,079,879	353,413,018	1,424,339,191	415,147,282	998,755,137	596,665,807
295	Florence, SC	190,579	11,247	8,742,847,462	566,172,913	1,652,486,400	350,224,211	1,648,105,772	356,139,869	1,037,199,292	607,288,127
296	Greenville, SC	154,475	32,199	11,450,596,808	388,456,638	2,637,560,964	498,693,143	1,786,569,287	511,372,234	1,506,102,638	937,567,821
297	Charlotte, NC	69,285	6,712	3,061,458,183	88,570,423	677,664,006	159,396,466	584,457,032	124,989,254	322,624,770	204,537,302
298	Augusta, GA	69,608	4,427	2,083,988,700	78,681,414	357,209,753	107,789,911	398,118,235	57,775,242	297,667,467	152,762,379
299	Savannah, GA	56,829	13,055	2,806,880,335	221,204,172	809,880,424	78,754,098	388,839,085	114,260,573	257,083,848	170,289,794
300	North Metro, GA	537,589	191,129	27,923,632,016	1,233,742,778	6,710,657,582	1,058,009,673	3,651,767,620	1,673,457,044	4,069,686,046	1,758,849,235
301	North Metro, GA	139,409	54,078	11,776,198,872	347,597,319	2,852,905,722	492,406,902	1,752,855,348	505,634,419	1,772,139,248	720,875,550
302	North Metro, GA	293,748	43,474	10,720,315,050	342,569,086	2,664,410,728	425,607,106	1,424,339,191	388,915,625	1,506,896,545	579,068,859
303	Atlanta, GA	404,833	9,930	14,237,585,849	819,062,294	3,437,793,509	551,446,680	1,848,450,209	694,164,805	1,695,134,454	710,750,200
304	Swainsboro, GA	68,455	55,927	2,173,116,307	69,368,093	428,088,406	105,351,255	386,278,430	99,998,832	281,073,366	155,906,565
305	Athens, GA	26,722	55,927	6,432,070,057	245,346,852	1,500,768,942	312,366,419	915,965,155	312,111,209	748,077,182	532,529,921

ZIP Code	3-Digit ZIP Code Areas	Black Markets	Hispanic Markets	Total Retail Sales ($Millions)	Retail Sales: Apparel & Accessories ($Millions)	Retail Sales: Automotive ($Millions)	Retail Sales: Drugs, First Aid & Health Care Products ($Millions)	Retail Sales: Food ($Millions)	Retail Sales: Furniture & Major Appliances ($Millions)	Retail Sales: General Merchandise ($Millions)	Retail Sales: Hardware, Lumber & Garden Supplies ($Millions)
306	Chattanooga, TN	74,120	14,767	3,937,250,415	75,780,648	870,581,538	165,716,824	535,805,150	169,317,013	482,615,954	282,015,341
307	Augusta, GA	10,333	33,520	3,973,659,758	113,365,708	872,823,656	154,737,727	691,357,653	223,461,861	480,197,272	209,588,932
308	Augusta, GA	53,224	3,211	1,807,156,960	49,078,908	420,336,820	70,066,649	274,314,518	77,493,012	241,573,400	213,007,774
309	Augusta, GA	82,848	4,092	2,886,766,674	122,135,858	735,110,854	91,578,389	350,228,629	147,329,179	483,616,455	227,402,773
310	Macon, GA	173,263	10,057	5,761,671,374	163,763,350	1,866,722,773	253,385,313	804,102,728	220,685,967	622,293,926	421,956,335
312	Macon, GA	79,529	2,135	2,600,234,479	108,833,399	464,071,888	106,441,552	209,606,168	68,148,704	272,691,312	132,834,999
313	Savannah, GA	40,723	6,195	1,637,536,500	51,470,753	394,119,808	56,064,272	209,860,411	74,059,746	222,575,245	91,103,838
314	Savannah, GA	93,638	4,372	3,300,563,481	173,117,639	614,555,251	146,808,214	402,660,827	89,464,881	361,827,903	239,360,704
315	Waycross, GA	64,298	11,004	3,587,046,303	117,681,408	700,259,142	173,144,831	583,635,585	153,813,699	420,658,035	278,880,046
316	Valdosta, GA	50,447	6,372	2,168,566,096	118,479,816	440,635,492	81,782,162	384,555,492	128,620,543	273,973,338	149,789,449
317	Albany, GA	147,289	14,639	4,422,084,676	100,449,243	945,519,210	184,557,142	656,007,410	182,078,245	509,554,926	267,000,649
318	Columbus, GA	22,807	1,622	621,883,550	21,941,584	183,478,680	35,503,326	74,592,624	36,970,719	55,119,439	34,638,844
319	Columbus, GA	82,766	7,758	2,656,394,607	134,563,533	498,784,760	81,720,507	259,464,194	72,283,279	464,058,970	174,593,248
320	Jacksonville, FL	55,977	19,200	6,157,317,750	181,354,506	1,485,074,580	217,795,481	1,067,137,343	240,157,400	788,333,036	370,878,006
321	Jacksonville, FL	53,025	23,417	6,672,520,050	181,186,171	1,750,064,752	341,122,033	1,053,825,059	272,328,064	867,802,580	396,610,395
322	Jacksonville, FL	251,651	37,828	12,763,055,632	439,775,115	2,879,537,762	557,397,350	1,646,437,792	565,120,951	1,851,170,116	721,961,128
323	Tallahassee, FL	125,978	14,500	5,155,287,487	179,965,919	1,239,848,889	205,045,473	844,083,720	192,667,650	782,526,291	328,580,521
324	Panama City, FL	42,174	7,539	4,149,845,278	147,554,546	969,902,241	155,814,475	685,731,909	133,469,425	634,864,901	265,434,471
325	Pensacola, FL	94,504	17,127	8,455,476,753	243,613,524	2,469,803,069	354,004,544	1,058,511,856	363,814,362	1,124,691,723	453,096,780
326	Gainesville, FL	60,375	16,808	4,395,743,307	116,311,908	1,023,621,859	154,484,450	679,402,388	173,813,625	759,123,493	287,323,069
327	Mid-Florida, FL	91,570	104,411	12,999,792,840	511,694,661	3,750,849,611	525,899,212	1,778,944,467	679,441,745	1,771,740,241	769,646,860
328	Orlando, FL	170,138	184,503	13,398,414,593	678,636,128	3,883,564,710	481,400,311	1,580,930,228	576,465,693	1,634,709,971	662,469,578
329	Orlando, FL	48,774	33,848	9,130,344,032	235,881,315	3,544,203,640	418,105,896	1,160,773,639	362,772,916	1,092,787,114	422,367,840
330	South Florida, FL	314,980	624,767	24,715,445,625	1,316,816,000	9,060,221,443	1,298,359,837	2,909,604,984	1,340,444,191	2,466,291,154	1,135,762,528
331	Miami, FL	357,385	1,067,606	27,510,944,374	1,944,749,188	7,318,863,026	1,707,570,379	3,350,595,751	2,022,940,615	3,103,441,155	1,271,533,770
333	Fort Lauderdale, FL	200,177	136,480	14,167,212,084	969,965,578	6,150,085,843	669,950,633	1,584,085,220	676,244,507	1,357,637,868	607,837,706
334	West Palm Beach, FL	198,432	204,027	22,164,401,155	1,197,258,038	6,950,228,216	1,075,305,451	2,778,865,551	1,214,353,619	2,827,130,913	1,026,604,082
335	Tampa, FL	42,511	82,851	7,657,600,259	250,056,751	2,142,089,557	348,189,073	1,020,731,666	378,923,645	863,848,130	356,980,205
336	Tampa, FL	145,756	157,023	10,490,717,862	371,401,745	2,965,242,863	453,063,086	1,356,965,681	546,078,821	1,098,279,879	486,427,087
337	Saint Petersburg, FL	89,626	44,016	12,303,069,582	414,223,402	3,312,623,498	607,586,737	1,584,619,069	572,314,702	1,296,353,110	527,506,584
338	Lakeland, FL	84,684	78,688	8,075,532,904	219,599,290	2,389,617,548	369,072,556	1,191,508,250	519,600,696	1,069,695,560	534,774,054
339	Fort Myers, FL	45,167	67,468	9,589,798,849	377,018,882	2,500,393,171	458,348,247	1,371,758,107	569,129,836	1,290,509,696	728,867,025
341	Fort Myers, FL	15,970	80,090	6,285,128,284	377,112,953	1,301,014,746	309,446,860	927,048,100	583,940,905	709,348,656	458,561,194
342	Manasota, FL	46,040	60,717	10,177,208,663	473,220,430	2,848,642,565	556,859,804	1,482,657,099	612,107,002	1,169,567,351	597,413,670
344	Gainesville, FL	32,574	21,690	4,776,820,586	100,500,029	1,090,079,608	260,573,521	705,480,857	187,823,519	735,396,648	372,524,750
346	Tampa, FL	15,320	31,216	7,462,151,268	204,458,339	1,935,427,510	397,786,075	1,134,147,203	307,558,013	1,029,466,821	383,005,998
347	Orlando, FL	44,871	103,761	6,409,402,289	230,142,357	1,544,444,856	233,036,718	950,152,697	215,345,310	679,364,599	338,540,325
349	West Palm Beach, FL	44,177	39,196	5,189,430,112	175,520,663	1,436,940,565	300,583,188	848,118,884	227,599,173	634,617,398	363,879,732
350	Birmingham, AL	81,836	7,622	4,920,426,608	185,916,395	1,264,075,759	216,526,805	729,631,644	216,012,819	715,342,256	363,104,199
351	Birmingham, AL	33,508	6,555	3,309,818,005	102,298,717	803,680,764	148,671,731	481,998,705	158,796,628	520,527,937	253,146,391
352	Birmingham, AL	216,957	12,319	7,589,636,656	408,762,557	2,048,600,258	343,323,804	1,005,647,411	391,757,503	1,103,382,175	351,322,419
354	Tuscaloosa, AL	74,150	2,714	2,455,754,808	110,069,706	502,419,582	127,076,911	366,944,775	112,054,976	328,220,870	182,678,399
355	Birmingham, AL	8,792	2,150	1,680,281,776	40,766,582	462,043,823	95,302,718	318,740,461	58,578,076	217,340,658	130,077,884
356	Huntsville, AL	42,787	11,121	4,459,827,740	138,132,675	965,310,190	184,263,114	661,894,037	178,381,572	729,222,770	327,739,689
357	Huntsville, AL	17,936	3,297	2,297,333,029	108,735,051	491,724,128	71,189,439	310,232,851	87,328,421	302,907,442	171,836,443
358	Huntsville, AL	54,541	4,389	2,609,088,764	131,598,330	479,041,972	72,667,998	338,551,375	98,342,438	343,557,747	189,808,618
359	Birmingham, AL	19,465	14,194	3,236,066,786	164,613,120	848,393,497	133,492,917	493,296,896	129,024,309	430,360,948	178,863,255
360	Montgomery, AL	99,069	3,950	2,732,808,213	44,925,119	641,712,694	131,085,721	435,799,369	109,422,126	367,274,422	144,017,856
361	Montgomery, AL	109,645	2,937	3,245,440,221	176,795,623	508,360,586	132,744,119	378,361,841	103,959,082	367,461,646	128,114,691
362	Anniston, AL	31,848	2,856	1,963,574,226	51,899,520	525,984,742	85,071,556	286,128,871	80,922,319	298,253,813	240,117,101
363	Dothan, AL	49,054	4,674	2,984,164,082	99,935,735	548,580,120	63,287,357	408,439,059	99,298,416	328,766,977	91,839,677
364	Evergreen, AL	29,501	959	1,182,166,128	40,796,123	274,768,311	66,124,229	181,374,248	39,037,570	139,067,671	277,237,787
365	Mobile, AL	46,539	5,103	4,070,591,341	179,769,147	886,118,853	205,909,842	674,789,128	151,526,547	494,920,824	253,231,473
366	Mobile, AL	125,098	4,024	3,675,978,593	138,690,066	841,771,375	188,506,408	527,127,983	154,054,340	574,152,140	189,554,729
367	Montgomery, AL	73,903	1,123	1,204,487,710	34,493,759	295,395,956	63,287,357	238,104,074	42,218,160	149,202,325	351,859,731
368	Montgomery, AL	68,947	3,517	2,448,280,995	68,426,921	666,779,983	80,326,399	416,391,201	97,578,937	341,764,479	232,876,423
369	Meridian, MS	11,743	185	187,212,292	2,427,514	53,152,649	9,741,226	37,919,810	7,557,088	13,252,165	8,064,708
370	Nashville, TN	79,260	22,981	10,005,793,600	303,258,486	2,718,605,383	380,152,558	1,413,476,375	449,710,055	1,394,182,109	661,218,564
371	Nashville, TN	40,573	20,403	6,176,195,829	178,192,386	1,691,699,632	245,199,665	909,725,493	266,240,485	754,257,625	435,973,259
372	Nashville, TN	100,043	25,120	7,858,431,014	346,983,013	2,203,702,995	283,448,688	856,885,660	482,813,705	1,176,984,111	374,130,779
373	Chattanooga, TN	18,834	9,418	6,630,090,958	182,997,669	1,513,667,907	283,418,683	1,069,522,767	256,505,403	903,261,602	480,910,045
374	Chattanooga, TN	59,728	4,274	3,022,882,163	137,179,891	624,805,084	123,669,385	381,657,043	114,656,215	480,305,434	189,554,729
376	Knoxville, TN	8,920	4,498	5,412,965,399	156,623,454	1,595,871,499	218,374,924	694,494,978	226,493,170	924,863,336	351,859,731
377	Knoxville, TN	5,999	3,951	3,922,059,163	111,369,724	928,994,747	164,490,809	619,961,984	142,722,268	475,958,761	232,876,423
378	Knoxville, TN	10,506	9,807	6,646,749,227	285,245,805	1,510,191,512	263,568,164	976,021,888	226,499,151	738,796,968	421,542,929
379	Knoxville, TN	32,935	5,544	6,660,010,362	254,798,261	1,198,393,576	276,777,014	786,835,469	322,834,786	923,175,486	579,047,600
380	Memphis, TN	77,607	6,985	4,166,186,760	142,438,836	1,179,544,508	198,092,405	561,072,488	178,065,915	567,799,231	223,580,425
381	Memphis, TN	446,096	24,388	10,900,146,445	515,632,681	3,185,496,619	277,561,733	1,290,650,268	431,924,117	1,604,782,829	444,473,536
382	McKenzie, TN	9,613	1,852	1,230,852,132	40,656,234	292,922,614	60,465,309	188,194,218	43,104,420	138,480,554	121,677,776
383	Jackson, TN	49,972	3,821	3,246,918,213	101,505,406	761,238,287	154,228,112	459,981,944	150,047,651	446,092,641	242,370,744

ZIP Code	3-Digit ZIP Code Areas	Black Markets	Hispanic Markets	Total Retail Sales ($Millions)	Retail Sales: Apparel & Accessories ($Millions)	Retail Sales: Automotive ($Millions)	Retail Sales: Drugs, First Aid & Health Care Products ($Millions)	Retail Sales: Food ($Millions)	Retail Sales: Furniture & Major Appliances ($Millions)	Retail Sales: General Merchandise ($Millions)	Retail Sales: Hardware, Lumber & Garden Supplies ($Millions)
384	Columbia, TN	15,086	3,686	1,886,294,250	58,114,169	426,969,371	88,064,963	329,846,262	64,440,708	235,871,765	154,170,987
385	Cookeville, TN	2,450	4,101	2,534,791,948	101,852,245	597,416,385	99,539,234	457,115,371	93,019,959	265,531,947	237,989,117
386	Memphis, TN	117,728	7,245	3,417,447,968	81,412,269	666,621,887	176,967,230	677,509,313	118,206,386	475,414,775	164,558,610
387	Greenville, MS	93,465	1,526	1,259,742,443	55,095,964	257,770,401	50,047,525	255,939,720	52,184,449	205,136,447	56,392,257
388	Tupelo, MS	46,424	3,988	2,919,218,313	121,949,657	467,525,931	117,158,084	463,410,121	111,779,593	534,274,120	242,673,885
389	Grenada, MS	59,312	1,466	1,116,162,106	38,007,428	202,593,123	47,301,837	196,576,241	38,370,096	114,708,934	64,457,608
390	Jackson, MS	111,674	4,280	2,618,442,484	68,476,336	601,384,597	120,695,017	442,690,434	92,168,244	390,390,866	191,762,475
391	Jackson, MS	116,276	4,684	3,117,005,590	125,386,674	565,047,839	136,282,143	488,035,198	95,061,508	611,856,123	162,199,863
392	Jackson, MS	146,675	2,378	3,198,240,203	94,321,406	1,044,690,838	135,173,383	433,951,440	111,825,699	456,524,593	192,597,471
393	Meridian, MS	82,283	2,352	2,136,142,530	51,254,166	374,205,097	99,619,897	371,524,797	70,967,348	352,922,564	168,833,057
394	Hattiesburg, MS	89,808	5,543	3,278,586,603	111,151,135	744,328,060	160,500,298	566,350,723	115,235,163	542,899,232	241,123,126
395	Gulfport, MS	78,997	8,741	4,161,894,868	84,214,256	965,195,461	161,289,447	661,746,063	123,877,565	787,717,142	243,634,790
396	McComb, MS	55,831	1,079	1,200,723,515	47,124,486	228,501,746	66,876,498	190,539,486	43,305,031	162,607,779	81,073,695
397	Columbus, MS	72,624	1,972	1,638,307,118	76,951,715	302,045,760	62,180,441	281,507,173	69,619,251	250,547,876	105,217,142
398	Albany, GA	48,910	3,626	1,016,962,933	19,994,220	236,672,258	108,079,034	192,635,798	54,618,336	109,799,305	67,619,407
400	Louisville, KY	10,907	4,985	1,940,960,790	24,870,347	495,366,641	53,473,911	317,049,012	77,655,964	229,450,234	110,598,296
401	Louisville, KY	10,565	3,796	1,451,390,739	38,101,495	394,321,787	47,366,252	176,872,055	56,814,444	206,636,084	124,746,956
402	Louisville, KY	137,221	15,759	10,426,280,237	360,791,198	1,721,572,697	520,145,696	1,418,466,568	478,504,234	1,540,194,002	566,625,908
403	Lexington, KY	10,280	4,798	3,389,500,053	61,214,761	733,253,149	169,900,483	583,941,756	113,272,572	379,051,802	201,632,339
404	Lexington, KY	6,832	2,038	1,957,526,164	55,533,830	421,455,998	82,162,103	326,790,400	63,853,254	246,066,993	180,121,920
405	Lexington, KY	36,714	11,707	4,957,821,002	272,471,944	1,153,845,396	189,312,324	586,797,670	281,023,073	871,165,318	223,254,807
406	Lexington, KY	4,450	860	637,839,416	20,564,171	133,401,254	34,907,390	111,612,089	18,946,362	86,057,501	42,031,213
407	London, KY	562	736	1,288,753,019	35,120,724	249,434,968	49,304,463	195,727,284	34,406,177	165,663,007	127,227,940
408	London, KY	880	261	379,026,337	4,757,663	97,371,060	20,099,368	63,179,149	13,347,446	68,149,859	22,355,732
409	London, KY	2,074	829	835,648,147	18,882,722	179,420,631	47,397,983	150,657,803	24,537,915	143,824,337	71,414,111
410	Cincinnati, OH	12,585	6,854	6,681,864,570	168,364,664	1,070,588,439	348,751,218	867,707,097	166,060,045	951,450,572	439,507,359
411	Ashland, KY	1,599	1,174	1,666,614,913	53,757,213	321,232,503	92,435,097	260,881,894	51,930,058	268,998,485	114,205,752
412	Ashland, KY	142	348	645,467,614	7,841,376	124,856,880	30,652,199	126,047,020	17,236,425	102,774,685	63,871,739
413	Campton, KY	385	223	332,203,346	2,729,473	90,119,255	28,326,317	54,971,465	12,356,409	33,669,984	16,713,650
414	Campton, KY	638	133	190,622,735	1,497,950	57,749,940	14,933,425	21,961,061	7,945,420	13,890,409	8,582,056
415	Pikeville, KY	320	448	952,355,067	32,420,600	196,228,748	52,047,056	178,493,365	25,289,156	159,752,868	62,108,796
416	Pikeville, KY	548	253	416,241,843	6,645,379	99,501,725	26,414,053	70,843,190	13,679,555	52,181,924	37,357,307
417	Hazard, KY	623	235	522,041,433	18,766,117	107,156,764	21,706,930	93,359,129	14,748,149	92,652,908	35,418,870
418	Hazard, KY	179	211	289,700,352	4,246,569	79,250,660	17,690,369	45,418,519	10,924,037	35,119,889	18,900,667
420	Paducah, KY	13,269	3,301	2,963,705,810	114,626,971	680,105,260	142,764,302	394,147,156	115,862,003	424,053,286	322,305,158
421	Bowling Green, KY	12,228	4,779	2,692,176,220	89,897,480	484,403,403	110,268,945	387,812,673	87,708,642	321,372,064	233,244,000
422	Bowling Green, KY	23,239	4,715	1,366,607,535	33,765,729	339,600,651	67,272,132	221,914,580	52,497,995	133,927,678	109,916,438
423	Owensboro, KY	5,789	1,603	1,931,331,691	40,426,341	398,652,773	108,283,383	335,430,638	77,452,142	326,480,901	121,268,541
424	Evansville, IN	9,458	1,928	1,593,570,205	41,770,759	338,695,115	82,333,671	238,957,710	50,321,773	213,740,626	88,717,408
425	Somerset, KY	673	825	878,564,801	33,669,205	196,811,188	30,087,249	145,080,744	38,973,646	147,702,208	94,987,530
426	Somerset, KY	515	884	600,022,219	5,035,190	161,398,947	39,693,547	126,870,163	22,139,910	52,348,957	51,827,043
427	Elizabethtown, KY	6,955	1,911	1,990,899,882	66,357,687	531,268,215	85,424,735	282,667,240	68,647,480	211,988,210	182,933,084
430	Columbus, OH	25,292	9,054	8,607,091,755	233,661,278	2,132,327,456	310,682,909	1,074,289,975	392,192,597	1,154,758,901	492,683,737
431	Columbus, OH	18,047	4,454	4,505,418,548	120,900,428	1,074,686,671	104,565,819	664,884,457	179,665,341	545,548,964	284,684,440
432	Columbus, OH	183,557	22,383	13,373,880,884	471,762,409	3,283,322,266	436,861,938	1,574,670,886	627,247,034	2,082,523,474	570,994,904
433	Columbus, OH	4,986	1,787	1,897,534,419	41,127,194	432,938,223	87,686,308	261,581,038	72,155,362	327,773,947	116,441,488
434	Toledo, OH	2,855	8,274	1,887,701,238	40,411,993	410,474,311	77,542,954	307,816,312	71,518,043	211,345,500	102,065,775
435	Toledo, OH	4,022	11,467	3,473,237,883	158,057,768	796,028,591	173,496,118	541,542,350	144,133,401	456,330,946	222,729,830
436	Toledo, OH	74,860	20,551	5,391,690,756	104,289,975	1,284,835,774	282,273,899	746,304,798	242,028,612	961,518,734	269,296,865
437	Zanesville, OH	5,696	1,068	2,040,018,706	62,636,502	452,190,178	104,289,975	309,209,557	101,073,621	149,768,786	149,768,786
438	Zanesville, OH	683	381	657,893,611	19,886,180	152,958,901	28,756,995	114,133,902	30,633,299	62,659,564	53,322,808
439	Steubenville, OH	7,558	951	2,102,464,168	66,357,687	461,721,583	147,742,487	381,531,501	75,274,417	320,405,683	105,358,038
440	Cleveland, OH	38,787	30,551	3,831,169,718	100,998,533	844,148,086	237,434,866	567,936,595	150,176,586	486,911,381	267,179,789
441	Cleveland, OH	383,496	50,163	10,780,396,637	297,587,525	3,018,191,356	685,503,298	1,574,670,886	449,836,052	1,921,296,005	751,718,825
442	Akron, OH	11,260	4,575	16,213,941,636	819,262,521	3,550,523,081	1,306,063,081	2,258,027,997	956,203,153	2,258,027,997	750,303,724
443	Akron, OH	64,689	3,242	6,963,420,162	165,510,546	2,068,073,910	354,075,637	1,015,723,795	243,291,418	687,115,442	541,476,003
444	Youngstown, OH	19,722	4,827	3,858,052,075	145,691,464	1,001,377,293	216,814,887	625,979,716	136,858,476	396,668,197	312,032,353
445	Youngstown, OH	38,465	5,859	4,229,492,362	139,068,302	1,162,940,096	237,869,888	764,499,837	211,031,576	622,496,524	231,439,009
446	Canton, OH	9,683	6,663	2,348,830,500	92,241,861	589,826,117	166,772,290	315,757,539	137,015,514	333,910,867	116,787,772
447	Canton, OH	20,253	1,946	5,218,050,796	128,216,357	1,538,201,367	260,285,276	820,063,283	201,269,303	537,157,996	438,925,219
448	Mansfield, OH	9,303	7,663	2,713,682,685	71,417,832	530,211,300	140,239,446	426,005,604	93,697,830	270,190,091	142,687,370
449	Mansfield, OH	11,769	894	1,300,026,832	35,478,834	262,200,100	61,249,153	164,332,658	43,391,957	237,838,211	75,453,009
450	Cincinnati, OH	24,229	7,627	5,287,227,537	114,798,774	1,236,919,317	237,175,371	867,613,805	189,291,424	687,115,442	382,665,617
451	Cincinnati, OH	3,800	2,503	3,645,292,790	80,296,319	816,442,528	145,806,595	584,484,288	140,512,705	443,387,255	344,249,544
452	Cincinnati, OH	198,045	9,817	12,673,026,357	582,162,532	3,097,321,159	615,142,394	1,859,309,331	404,663,097	1,732,308,162	739,494,887
453	Dayton, OH	14,027	4,902	5,396,565,523	130,880,962	1,397,096,982	215,866,252	681,819,854	249,315,162	844,489,002	287,275,705
454	Dayton, OH	109,063	6,663	6,671,832,540	220,657,092	1,538,201,367	276,987,052	764,499,837	354,968,546	1,395,391,311	333,187,840
455	Dayton, OH	11,988	1,131	1,187,823,111	24,848,886	279,322,066	64,103,862	147,778,499	50,096,280	237,667,875	74,770,514
456	Chillicothe, OH	9,016	2,140	3,623,152,428	60,600,066	809,841,781	199,100,387	599,820,877	141,019,399	610,153,063	272,132,491
457	Athens, OH	2,349	1,124	1,580,682,683	31,701,776	388,529,410	81,430,344	298,049,838	65,371,196	145,170,960	99,144,152

ZIP Code	3-Digit ZIP Code Areas	Black Markets	Hispanic Markets	Total Retail Sales ($Millions)	Retail Sales: Apparel & Accessories ($Millions)	Retail Sales: Automotive ($Millions)	Retail Sales: Drugs, First Aid & Health Care Products ($Millions)	Retail Sales: Food ($Millions)	Retail Sales: Furniture & Major Appliances ($Millions)	Retail Sales: General Merchandise ($Millions)	Retail Sales: Hardware, Lumber & Garden Supplies ($Millions)
458	Lima, OH	14,676	7,289	4,693,565,975	94,982,972	1,039,340,663	210,071,927	612,588,091	192,431,735	801,324,336	343,485,859
460	Indianapolis, IN	16,153	11,058	5,566,044,202	80,757,541	1,438,171,846	326,378,178	649,266,789	208,567,455	838,963,634	404,952,337
461	Indianapolis, IN	5,749	6,655	5,827,366,444	142,303,128	1,386,750,120	284,707,300	707,680,402	274,186,730	859,918,638	331,113,661
462	Indianapolis, IN	218,682	42,902	14,752,216,171	536,132,178	3,461,887,967	731,019,010	1,640,316,351	805,702,352	1,995,477,818	837,135,131
463	Gary, IN	41,282	64,571	7,834,675,918	324,062,664	1,717,871,754	500,772,638	1,097,800,183	319,675,782	970,508,718	514,614,872
464	Gary, IN	94,466	11,861	1,953,048,123	79,593,472	406,741,315	132,395,143	272,110,191	89,556,676	266,908,561	510,788,155
465	South Bend, IN	12,634	31,620	5,698,486,582	136,668,067	1,521,069,202	296,374,076	738,912,710	206,038,275	814,169,676	510,389,105
466	South Bend, IN	27,578	11,451	2,085,433,326	69,529,981	533,881,781	131,634,380	284,907,579	106,336,142	351,529,912	124,378,090
467	Fort Wayne, IN	1,014	9,380	3,826,002,611	80,171,573	925,682,640	180,560,031	545,094,218	147,625,963	517,329,508	227,713,169
468	Fort Wayne, IN	38,261	16,335	4,372,756,741	156,692,566	1,109,829,940	234,057,481	520,232,769	240,316,969	732,963,803	341,285,652
469	Kokomo, IN	12,665	9,047	3,675,964,979	79,193,284	823,244,337	204,807,537	518,091,060	134,737,152	527,470,604	275,425,244
470	Cincinnati, OH	427	863	1,107,865,165	19,733,705	298,760,573	68,806,067	171,990,249	43,491,277	155,650,852	77,247,642
471	Louisville, KY	9,943	4,188	3,599,546,805	62,766,743	982,767,327	171,353,078	477,440,063	125,028,208	626,963,028	273,696,300
472	Columbus, IN	2,267	4,041	2,504,399,224	103,903,999	470,344,372	115,001,134	350,362,930	73,794,154	391,306,408	185,922,846
473	Muncie, IN	12,272	3,812	3,792,958,813	68,427,722	848,552,770	209,957,915	550,685,596	138,998,361	581,722,365	226,840,973
474	Bloomington, IN	3,609	3,514	2,828,509,098	84,125,090	626,614,054	139,112,130	436,289,942	122,410,674	440,922,045	176,403,850
475	Washington, IN	1,487	2,920	1,999,552,708	61,206,225	366,415,009	91,111,646	258,189,929	62,605,559	293,610,551	181,942,795
476	Evansville, IN	1,757	1,007	1,207,734,996	11,180,517	346,853,745	57,059,677	172,283,890	50,981,586	205,703,369	45,765,135
477	Evansville, IN	13,667	1,823	2,896,360,078	142,549,244	672,034,544	125,727,843	331,953,019	86,302,441	349,296,139	220,066,609
478	Terre Haute, IN	7,475	1,771	3,571,847,947	37,420,060	532,667,073	109,784,627	290,618,094	78,671,844	322,619,414	149,921,952
479	Lafayette, IN	4,361	13,081	3,636,024,718	84,157,611	773,619,859	173,500,727	463,150,864	113,545,544	457,064,732	235,496,680
480	Royal Oak, MI	88,418	20,763	19,930,279,972	856,387,560	5,848,266,808	1,108,347,551	2,098,859,685	1,142,249,101	3,276,212,827	1,120,747,098
481	Detroit, MI	114,830	45,769	19,801,916,491	790,514,578	5,512,395,766	1,084,052,363	2,167,900,972	911,950,935	3,103,800,022	1,110,995,625
482	Detroit, MI	806,191	58,472	11,666,218,971	503,594,908	2,876,957,233	735,928,743	1,468,044,918	530,250,378	1,751,251,379	593,817,553
483	Royal Oak, MI	62,390	28,903	17,273,413,860	922,822,352	5,243,065,118	888,281,222	1,673,648,172	1,090,168,611	2,798,695,434	884,277,489
484	Flint, MI	11,500	10,567	6,164,491,324	204,024,613	1,531,590,475	320,316,469	750,034,372	260,736,718	993,406,564	468,411,552
485	Flint, MI	79,109	6,349	3,098,523,032	100,563,946	778,849,811	164,269,667	318,774,342	135,395,445	614,611,875	218,766,732
486	Saginaw, MI	41,515	17,252	5,756,113,100	261,971,336	1,027,513,306	276,532,164	750,474,681	262,729,575	919,574,819	420,036,998
487	Saginaw, MI	2,639	6,252	2,719,578,546	77,305,037	714,406,169	122,019,427	385,479,690	78,162,401	405,480,797	209,921,233
488	Lansing, MI	14,634	15,935	7,377,897,238	168,695,658	1,888,985,263	246,332,658	866,489,756	287,211,784	1,463,961,442	600,726,034
489	Lansing, MI	31,053	15,293	2,623,718,200	90,166,769	640,345,380	76,751,054	257,545,558	151,807,021	560,483,824	164,229,045
490	Kalamazoo, MI	66,264	26,992	9,214,784,371	274,131,650	2,242,545,642	360,741,970	1,081,880,149	375,859,101	1,805,691,112	663,145,434
491	Kalamazoo, MI	4,898	3,778	1,182,258,554	23,709,696	309,587,127	59,360,681	161,782,050	35,797,687	154,340,430	89,137,049
492	Jackson, MI	17,918	13,021	4,076,203,420	79,622,075	962,878,265	220,500,728	457,031,690	131,887,177	928,392,055	285,587,507
493	Grand Rapids, MI	4,927	7,901	3,888,723,610	112,453,891	1,060,359,430	131,683,705	458,195,671	196,000,041	655,689,528	282,889,372
494	Grand Rapids, MI	28,442	35,518	6,315,294,714	198,669,688	1,553,523,671	205,075,933	722,272,611	266,467,762	1,267,154,148	555,301,407
495	Grand Rapids, MI	52,472	44,311	6,344,560,405	263,358,199	1,741,495,311	184,732,573	610,978,465	393,539,646	1,287,516,312	440,229,295
496	Traverse City, MI	2,281	4,173	4,333,575,422	163,903,069	1,035,160,723	170,299,544	577,505,550	173,948,611	594,115,172	395,068,168
497	Gaylord, MI	3,137	2,471	3,792,408,689	138,047,835	720,442,460	131,113,164	615,738,992	77,562,079	293,900,683	412,693,102
498	Iron Mountain, MI	2,574	1,429	2,334,501,391	72,712,664	567,448,363	64,642,211	385,583,953	61,124,155	263,354,266	194,555,763
499	Iron Mountain, MI	2,104	732	993,394,246	29,648,484	256,588,623	38,206,594	163,486,486	27,400,859	103,182,950	74,025,735
500	Des Moines, IA	2,144	2,969	2,543,386,089	85,752,158	599,461,520	96,417,670	390,007,208	98,567,256	354,571,112	178,098,047
501	Des Moines, IA	1,217	5,551	1,826,533,956	43,870,114	455,230,777	80,498,200	292,892,248	69,743,393	240,063,723	125,806,928
502	Des Moines, IA	1,726	6,007	2,544,732,400	70,691,583	637,541,543	96,377,333	384,126,181	102,079,839	341,549,685	189,480,272
503	Des Moines, IA	16,869	17,610	4,555,205,489	167,265,806	1,037,135,226	162,688,585	666,837,832	158,624,941	731,148,187	379,912,602
504	Mason City, IA	492	3,012	1,267,112,263	29,639,455	341,198,294	46,589,366	177,873,114	41,516,155	208,500,238	92,483,260
505	Fort Dodge, IA	1,594	5,037	1,453,333,298	38,373,362	342,226,387	61,009,535	254,149,989	48,342,548	212,712,024	106,021,774
506	Waterloo, IA	1,068	1,809	1,806,811,284	36,507,480	507,805,257	68,212,105	266,716,806	71,037,855	221,089,528	158,674,858
507	Waterloo, IA	9,777	2,226	1,239,822,932	29,154,284	345,412,037	46,454,029	163,263,332	47,026,874	197,206,762	112,562,582
508	Creston, IA	45	465	377,747,593	6,621,765	93,586,194	13,453,784	75,336,318	13,208,047	33,659,041	17,730,714
510	Sioux City, IA	292	1,621	982,503,417	24,376,923	238,688,791	45,716,177	159,504,712	35,668,127	104,625,317	66,617,898
511	Sioux City, IA	1,920	9,836	1,215,748,361	28,300,615	268,670,896	40,403,343	170,725,585	47,163,283	116,040,375	81,392,248
512	Sheldon, IA	89	1,071	383,546,973	9,262,016	106,848,386	21,055,492	56,595,109	15,110,765	35,062,995	30,985,995
513	Spencer, IA	145	958	640,051,907	24,991,881	133,808,264	26,320,166	99,391,926	18,900,304	62,008,705	52,323,552
514	Carroll, IA	213	2,341	572,442,543	21,184,252	128,487,236	24,616,560	92,598,440	18,160,921	80,389,598	41,543,350
515	Omaha, NE	863	3,889	1,929,943,062	53,254,550	620,968,469	102,474,382	253,796,969	71,278,739	160,064,610	81,547,982
516	Omaha, NE	355	459	264,019,344	6,720,854	64,476,906	15,121,412	39,091,874	9,107,741	42,394,286	18,963,570
520	Dubuque, IA	1,050	1,322	1,778,299,316	43,278,470	411,307,577	88,759,794	263,792,097	83,128,581	271,005,025	151,216,612
521	Decorah, IA	269	1,357	584,019,695	15,724,842	156,966,895	19,185,820	99,336,157	22,183,208	47,694,450	48,750,095
522	Cedar Rapids, IA	3,977	3,862	2,100,293,051	58,097,733	494,535,954	89,255,108	316,700,802	91,452,325	297,985,816	170,977,908
523	Cedar Rapids, IA	696	2,227	1,705,753,448	65,355,232	419,159,214	67,923,594	244,098,035	76,533,527	219,332,424	140,668,595
524	Cedar Rapids, IA	4,941	2,394	2,146,585,649	59,831,911	499,991,206	98,190,618	285,363,735	112,897,886	372,765,545	194,270,212
525	Ottumwa, IA	877	2,823	1,287,207,122	39,526,419	302,106,546	44,853,051	225,268,536	42,680,727	161,114,088	85,342,391
526	Burlington, IA	2,692	2,246	1,338,822,099	32,392,699	286,672,139	61,582,396	217,716,807	40,530,360	230,892,155	75,865,057
527	Rock Island, IL	2,141	8,299	2,194,331,791	64,060,377	522,616,973	101,586,790	316,336,080	104,911,864	346,106,032	104,036,144
528	Rock Island, IL	9,291	5,329	1,646,796,066	54,336,827	397,195,639	70,418,440	193,275,685	95,469,858	301,682,709	92,849,455
530	Milwaukee, WI	4,622	12,320	8,425,315,718	177,752,659	2,338,736,800	326,505,198	1,271,652,220	391,948,637	1,119,349,666	732,489,195
531	Milwaukee, WI	15,426	35,413	9,024,104,722	341,707,044	2,405,358,735	370,292,504	1,263,608,932	450,901,922	1,134,196,437	636,157,145
532	Milwaukee, WI	238,394	88,662	10,339,661,872	436,689,954	2,474,771,908	612,875,917	1,440,586,026	674,811,987	1,317,695,103	588,207,868
534	Milwaukee, WI	18,690	14,705	1,580,658,234	44,114,608	379,990,081	87,174,271	248,174,148	70,442,586	231,031,693	143,335,010

ZIP Code	3-Digit ZIP Code Areas	Black Markets	Hispanic Markets	Total Retail Sales ($Millions)	Retail Sales: Apparel & Accessories ($Millions)	Retail Sales: Automotive ($Millions)	Retail Sales: Drugs, First Aid & Health Care Products ($Millions)	Retail Sales: Food ($Millions)	Retail Sales: Furniture & Major Appliances ($Millions)	Retail Sales: General Merchandise ($Millions)	Retail Sales: Hardware, Lumber & Garden Supplies ($Millions)
535	Madison, WI	10,108	13,121	8,756,516,915	175,430,001	1,804,632,061	241,204,531	937,662,983	334,834,054	932,441,366	608,357,498
537	Madison, WI	15,417	14,280	4,542,303,091	169,156,139	1,188,283,589	144,975,549	538,559,338	340,557,699	538,325,732	395,553,738
538	Madison, WI	619	349	635,768,155	10,663,118	162,173,524	19,448,709	97,466,794	15,715,865	84,898,769	49,396,299
539	Portage, WI	3,847	4,157	2,259,539,621	42,037,609	578,268,760	74,984,221	308,772,425	53,728,210	257,564,231	180,643,491
540	Saint Paul, MN	514	1,136	1,439,105,536	12,116,039	387,733,490	41,145,208	194,992,877	65,244,957	165,292,142	105,391,631
541	Green Bay, WI	677	2,684	3,030,908,176	85,483,603	841,313,888	78,252,555	365,425,626	153,383,524	467,852,251	307,835,368
542	Green Bay, WI	550	1,740	1,553,516,705	32,972,409	371,289,900	39,038,879	241,298,613	43,750,928	256,651,952	103,597,398
543	Green Bay, WI	2,914	9,908	2,803,550,802	87,497,068	780,924,839	52,265,793	323,622,836	141,962,453	568,498,083	273,270,697
544	Wausau, WI	1,225	3,717	5,168,435,257	126,322,477	1,326,287,035	98,276,010	708,339,023	194,554,864	853,314,901	406,914,922
545	Rhinelander, WI	402	793	1,393,732,913	29,623,264	372,979,083	34,899,805	216,193,789	38,491,756	126,833,648	124,723,665
546	La Crosse, WI	1,949	2,509	3,224,833,935	68,913,957	688,210,772	74,108,234	434,309,379	96,357,833	328,983,438	251,359,728
547	Eau Claire, WI	1,013	2,018	3,362,056,370	98,136,493	732,145,504	125,630,073	393,121,110	114,785,540	493,900,384	292,818,314
548	Spooner, WI	772	1,614	2,355,019,107	37,676,867	556,336,097	69,601,239	350,941,704	67,889,120	264,669,738	239,430,491
549	Oshkosh, WI	4,052	11,082	6,402,984,317	200,209,873	1,596,889,971	187,185,924	849,631,799	294,257,022	885,969,337	547,799,344
550	Saint Paul, MN	8,038	16,565	7,211,075,504	218,987,781	1,702,535,751	239,192,782	1,066,229,847	288,238,856	976,549,809	681,592,446
551	Saint Paul, MN	49,837	38,126	10,819,505,789	413,012,836	2,620,209,298	387,325,739	1,361,025,256	567,613,886	1,720,779,641	764,092,591
553	Minneapolis, MN	11,971	19,807	11,457,136,407	381,606,181	2,911,042,107	366,437,065	1,406,595,951	615,642,192	1,458,704,566	897,581,800
554	Minneapolis, MN	104,412	56,249	16,834,230,613	769,893,892	4,215,874,566	529,623,309	1,948,614,736	1,006,552,502	2,316,174,196	1,079,812,662
556	Duluth, MN	31	110	279,931,363	1,613,194	43,218,923	7,420,328	33,705,911	5,912,666	14,741,672	19,067,014
557	Duluth, MN	729	1,113	2,164,893,761	57,566,646	500,890,319	90,970,597	333,525,316	75,596,509	312,284,421	168,125,014
558	Duluth, MN	1,553	1,023	1,528,306,385	54,333,054	354,888,168	62,412,143	210,289,668	54,186,185	287,576,847	98,678,953
559	Rochester, MN	4,401	7,608	4,124,569,720	146,084,614	1,014,505,432	120,374,446	515,971,604	206,717,181	618,404,529	428,539,236
560	Mankato, MN	1,976	8,365	2,873,835,185	107,188,087	612,896,418	109,404,392	404,011,488	102,177,181	403,528,253	273,595,277
561	Windom, MN	348	3,525	934,736,421	32,622,811	226,885,922	44,044,487	136,905,596	30,610,396	111,082,319	95,127,060
562	Willmar, MN	963	5,863	1,622,714,255	38,670,946	355,709,411	71,361,901	233,825,880	48,333,958	226,434,837	166,543,247
563	Saint Cloud, MN	3,012	4,250	5,080,718,306	68,362,345	817,082,406	121,457,315	519,579,415	127,397,355	361,099,197	474,209,619
564	Brainerd, MN	497	1,055	1,867,819,480	31,700,148	343,426,406	65,048,422	269,681,895	54,186,151	259,612,011	212,119,547
565	Detroit Lakes, MN	683	3,257	1,789,862,099	42,444,259	458,628,335	67,095,173	253,182,654	65,068,900	232,749,185	135,882,334
566	Bemidji, MN	272	727	1,127,464,076	36,743,067	217,084,416	35,097,225	179,718,686	29,444,056	139,891,336	90,615,899
567	Thief River Falls, MN	200	1,859	698,765,351	15,906,326	184,373,502	37,222,450	112,504,773	26,840,376	54,669,674	51,774,094
570	Sioux Falls, SD	958	1,433	1,969,509,330	58,969,871	483,094,452	73,041,308	237,393,912	75,391,652	249,624,459	113,147,031
571	Sioux Falls, SD	2,822	3,640	2,610,415,166	53,640,886	485,054,133	123,471,480	273,576,077	89,729,074	224,875,213	136,471,041
572	Dakota Central, SD	92	591	877,597,445	38,414,575	219,416,630	26,286,554	114,202,189	31,104,173	144,019,812	81,314,973
573	Dakota Central, SD	308	780	1,027,628,722	34,312,092	248,860,782	48,159,339	142,994,088	35,100,948	91,018,406	76,847,422
574	Aberdeen, SD	153	373	829,913,374	31,700,148	189,625,209	19,781,774	99,723,985	20,038,380	136,236,915	60,095,545
575	Pierre, SD	83	652	659,279,520	21,597,331	157,134,624	18,307,276	84,617,102	22,245,357	86,354,417	37,381,871
576	Mobridge, SD	22	242	213,049,153	5,542,817	138,161,569	6,471,745	29,523,116	8,602,614	26,910,911	13,124,173
577	Rapid City, SD	1,719	4,184	2,613,727,014	72,878,784	725,330,886	85,818,091	323,704,552	117,089,451	400,379,831	79,562,631
580	Fargo, ND	292	864	953,107,275	24,012,894	245,538,259	30,567,343	117,913,459	33,095,802	150,662,192	192,670,328
581	Fargo, ND	1,306	1,419	1,837,366,554	60,092,422	372,100,183	47,114,727	200,674,004	58,694,212	371,243,647	108,567,857
582	Grand Forks, ND	1,160	2,508	1,501,468,880	48,290,927	339,516,943	39,210,726	165,387,515	48,456,317	293,106,089	38,838,303
583	Devils Lake, ND	91	365	573,016,938	13,226,172	171,090,057	22,409,006	69,209,033	19,616,442	55,556,514	35,079,975
584	Jamestown, ND	119	433	565,938,869	14,396,920	173,943,085	24,005,745	80,088,474	20,038,380	70,994,308	107,798,580
585	Bismarck, ND	357	934	1,795,446,287	53,882,568	439,927,548	76,345,948	221,345,838	65,101,122	190,411,212	22,924,757
586	Dickinson, ND	79	349	523,620,535	11,613,071	138,161,569	19,252,625	64,199,721	16,143,608	77,943,131	64,242,049
587	Minot, ND	1,665	1,368	1,148,002,868	36,073,445	348,547,393	43,761,966	126,791,090	32,764,125	217,129,598	18,890,371
588	Williston, ND	49	277	305,427,000	10,762,470	87,656,705	32,306,380	37,945,369	10,090,259	28,475,675	65,762,797
590	Billings, MT	160	1,889	899,355,899	18,549,874	205,101,174	30,306,388	125,065,914	36,628,734	72,608,957	162,256,811
591	Billings, MT	632	4,862	2,091,265,224	64,531,295	593,674,988	52,116,903	259,258,286	95,661,804	357,373,636	32,058,186
592	Wolf Point, MT	45	543	339,352,909	11,384,450	65,883,014	12,334,832	61,878,681	12,348,638	15,207,959	59,477,925
593	Miles City, MT	78	442	363,681,448	11,862,368	68,286,193	17,553,576	66,459,810	12,863,930	12,986,043	191,828,125
594	Great Falls, MT	1,176	2,535	1,703,493,619	53,882,568	429,153,918	60,110,092	251,373,966	43,144,778	234,898,854	211,398,344
595	Havre, MT	45	359	330,541,658	11,292,269	198,040,317	12,403,575	68,383,987	10,989,668	30,802,266	177,516,326
596	Helena, MT	158	1,066	889,570,710	17,536,205	254,426,549	29,644,198	153,952,213	44,569,111	107,246,126	
597	Butte, MT	468	2,991	1,989,657,009	69,353,871	421,639,068	85,605,950	275,691,725	110,270,453	152,711,586	
598	Missoula, MT	466	3,528	2,524,902,771	62,726,914	669,395,957	60,110,092	390,906,286	123,303,230	345,755,853	
599	Kalispell, MT	288	1,748	1,499,477,367	35,713,128	335,588,074	43,508,181	250,412,634	79,179,682	176,245,445	
600	Palatine, IL	62,896	218,223	23,284,527,712	1,164,992,222	6,641,981,347	1,388,558,041	2,991,964,680	1,383,028,223	2,391,484,898	1,348,925,569
601	Carol Stream, IL	98,541	236,097	19,736,694,948	1,068,821,611	5,030,787,090	1,146,147,650	2,432,599,733	1,240,878,999	2,400,123,124	1,195,852,684
602	Palatine, IL	16,500	5,708	1,057,482,418	61,666,292	226,533,493	72,827,517	139,530,882	64,087,663	101,780,343	46,567,650
603	Carol Stream, IL	12,493	3,196	923,447,037	54,438,661	198,040,317	94,587,435	121,330,492	56,418,728	101,857,789	40,447,311
604	South Suburban, IL	275,954	158,532	16,031,101,611	720,645,251	3,766,993,832	1,064,267,688	2,088,699,303	869,664,176	1,870,544,535	833,953,718
605	Fox Valley, IL	42,121	160,620	13,700,180,171	719,970,394	3,672,464,499	769,990,811	1,612,070,245	858,254,212	1,719,084,120	857,011,108
606	Chicago, IL	1,028,506	814,989	34,790,199,245	1,984,436,511	7,451,222,802	2,399,203,015	4,660,005,343	2,076,804,551	3,952,771,367	1,555,757,739
607	Chicago, IL	3,792	13,516	1,335,620,972	74,686,133	290,251,612	94,587,435	178,878,746	79,491,970	148,449,912	59,580,204
608	Chicago, IL	34,068	75,404	1,616,781,871	91,771,444	346,977,325	97,301,459	216,834,384	94,278,727	183,074,977	726,994,252
609	Kankakee, IL	16,768	8,492	1,935,658,866	53,980,137	468,184,729	175,109,339	252,928,496	94,314,675	274,861,279	126,994,252
610	Rockford, IL	7,940	20,400	3,202,502,730	60,768,646	851,896,265	170,515,463	450,507,287	116,700,818	415,524,306	221,957,823
611	Rockford, IL	30,167	23,279	3,160,037,887	98,915,348	629,636,395	147,928,441	437,814,065	115,102,056	364,054,990	258,160,727
612	Rock Island, IL	12,011	15,745	2,691,747,606	87,887,181	684,575,625		393,912,385	112,185,978	355,072,944	150,855,560

ZIP Code	3-Digit ZIP Code Areas	Black Markets	Hispanic Markets	Total Retail Sales ($Millions)	Retail Sales: Apparel & Accessories ($Millions)	Retail Sales: Automotive ($Millions)	Retail Sales: Drugs, First Aid & Health Care Products ($Millions)	Retail Sales: Food ($Millions)	Retail Sales: Furniture & Major Appliances ($Millions)	Retail Sales: General Merchandise ($Millions)	Retail Sales: Hardware, Lumber & Garden Supplies ($Millions)
613	La Salle, IL	1,108	8,572	1,825,194,148	52,035,957	522,509,640	84,713,598	254,207,855	66,261,117	269,663,509	112,979,792
614	Galesburg, IL	5,670	4,637	1,676,550,874	37,698,679	427,113,606	76,232,350	240,333,178	72,536,736	289,824,588	80,257,385
615	Peoria, IL	3,035	2,400	2,450,287,613	48,661,723	799,634,795	109,204,595	323,861,475	97,496,439	281,929,059	124,597,232
616	Peoria, IL	30,253	4,501	2,557,480,994	88,673,868	630,258,679	142,215,997	299,490,946	129,255,849	278,613,061	146,986,231
617	Bloomington, IL	11,690	6,371	3,121,701,847	139,869,660	737,516,432	160,271,682	364,334,894	158,283,217	374,471,322	176,081,460
618	Champaign, IL	29,343	8,916	3,476,527,637	126,537,475	781,214,486	65,290,565	452,677,813	164,054,955	592,168,724	202,051,099
619	Champaign, IL	1,847	2,033	1,181,496,343	31,684,669	302,973,722	139,727,936	144,285,099	32,944,068	145,986,180	71,200,238
620	Saint Louis, MO	19,404	4,444	3,351,105,408	51,064,938	883,612,640	215,112,711	554,075,690	135,173,131	429,747,642	225,675,456
622	Saint Louis, MO	83,582	10,545	5,222,907,620	155,652,881	1,333,910,308	51,453,723	643,602,879	239,740,185	936,422,324	317,734,413
623	Quincy, IL	3,711	1,293	1,237,821,987	41,334,036	311,284,914	65,184,007	175,299,594	58,199,063	230,736,361	77,733,447
624	Effingham, IL	2,544	1,486	1,773,311,014	36,196,553	411,761,452	121,479,542	217,306,800	44,378,472	246,570,390	146,878,467
625	Springfield, IL	16,800	1,949	2,474,485,132	77,156,736	726,734,459	91,559,799	304,206,242	87,880,999	364,530,403	126,453,440
626	Springfield, IL	4,704	3,564	1,729,593,250	41,784,186	455,988,819	110,800,775	229,852,209	63,761,925	224,959,380	91,024,101
627	Springfield, IL	19,233	2,034	2,240,785,998	50,444,435	497,438,111	106,305,476	246,742,167	119,325,401	243,093,414	113,349,181
628	Centralia, IL	6,765	2,131	2,280,705,573	50,531,384	604,985,064	113,569,497	322,373,599	65,738,058	360,273,198	144,943,964
629	Carbondale, IL	19,408	4,648	2,656,682,339	67,329,025	612,734,007	389,166,918	341,348,034	69,867,573	581,456,264	216,543,763
630	Saint Louis, MO	52,420	9,985	9,846,515,385	358,407,746	2,656,666,471	651,721,102	1,298,675,441	480,378,133	1,615,417,380	503,956,995
631	Saint Louis, MO	334,055	17,250	14,061,749,257	643,499,968	3,673,304,056	176,100,735	1,849,726,625	761,555,834	1,988,486,219	598,398,276
633	Saint Louis, MO	14,003	6,436	5,050,843,809	141,934,900	1,196,630,999	21,729,210	713,000,828	228,600,406	721,869,353	504,029,422
634	Quincy, IL	2,316	463	743,454,323	9,180,276	178,634,907	23,987,636	93,202,112	23,851,014	143,724,225	50,215,778
635	Quincy, IL	799	1,441	664,837,830	16,379,057	165,952,831	50,077,481	101,046,351	22,134,118	102,424,898	40,600,042
636	Cape Girardeau, MO	2,214	949	1,247,811,208	23,189,871	319,849,291	52,643,865	194,416,184	42,655,374	193,587,838	66,267,663
637	Cape Girardeau, MO	4,480	941	1,736,504,928	50,609,713	404,593,638	66,328,364	212,780,397	42,521,360	377,714,055	141,956,728
638	Cape Girardeau, MO	18,909	2,081	1,376,303,611	23,554,619	335,941,672	29,245,599	191,959,767	44,845,819	201,275,627	76,958,326
639	Cape Girardeau, MO	2,363	870	957,667,288	21,012,411	218,710,981	260,588,943	120,939,911	29,167,130	132,331,221	67,541,426
640	Kansas City, MO	24,108	15,522	7,095,489,995	201,239,083	1,908,093,737	282,163,133	905,407,422	301,943,007	1,157,123,191	371,152,309
641	Kansas City, MO	146,477	37,934	7,963,998,898	243,341,416	2,173,406,201	24,894,673	1,030,917,983	342,397,640	1,206,748,910	420,583,111
644	Saint Joseph, MO	1,836	911	1,074,351,553	13,064,848	260,435,652	24,656,997	142,600,182	34,976,796	178,315,462	58,937,303
645	Saint Joseph, MO	3,826	1,922	1,050,941,143	22,589,214	221,915,480	18,466,114	168,779,108	34,294,228	152,588,125	39,172,217
646	Chillicothe, MO	761	732	738,080,373	11,661,883	199,095,615	35,506,392	118,140,803	26,573,127	135,473,565	51,743,510
647	Harrisonville, MO	1,058	1,323	1,209,995,733	16,602,090	308,760,578	54,578,161	170,056,722	41,039,750	211,853,503	78,023,292
648	Springfield, MO	2,358	7,846	2,442,133,960	70,235,756	485,458,193	31,242,076	340,463,363	63,422,848	302,487,283	164,034,562
650	Mid-Missouri, MO	1,186	1,577	1,834,845,209	73,794,153	416,221,363	23,808,122	246,179,300	74,899,679	274,197,316	152,645,517
651	Mid-Missouri, MO	6,943	1,019	974,045,813	27,854,313	244,793,064	84,263,155	120,962,377	37,907,990	247,506,747	76,784,892
652	Mid-Missouri, MO	19,742	3,757	3,317,882,593	93,610,021	888,818,032	41,327,924	400,091,392	137,838,200	591,536,910	280,651,537
653	Mid-Missouri, MO	3,161	3,592	1,133,592,771	21,040,069	266,548,850	18,179,426	161,539,224	37,433,792	183,134,195	93,381,100
654	Springfield, MO	3,814	2,735	981,693,447	39,140,821	229,124,009	21,164,382	110,274,152	30,420,690	144,530,048	84,260,342
655	Springfield, MO	3,233	1,681	1,220,747,241	63,704,359	289,299,261	50,470,776	153,661,698	39,918,656	192,363,550	102,768,984
656	Springfield, MO	1,038	3,158	2,263,244,772	54,413,010	511,578,905	78,341,161	328,329,306	65,706,861	330,498,469	152,550,116
657	Springfield, MO	1,092	5,117	2,975,611,827	122,428,451	688,935,479	85,100,162	430,101,240	93,019,047	448,848,071	209,951,009
658	Springfield, MO	5,478	4,184	4,047,579,929	163,282,748	585,556,197	161,147,805	438,220,326	76,667,178	405,425,615	318,623,195
660	Kansas City, MO	19,492	17,756	5,135,887,692	19,465,137	1,340,401,396	58,645,583	714,286,078	327,627,888	810,657,466	264,512,063
661	Kansas City, MO	43,828	30,680	1,268,011,331	194,335,852	282,892,422	210,572,651	219,160,345	28,829,343	173,913,913	72,782,802
662	Kansas City, MO	11,127	14,805	6,367,307,089	9,418,349	1,816,059,025	25,954,447	726,234,919	485,881,495	1,096,212,464	268,758,816
664	Kansas City, MO	6,444	3,471	681,269,149	53,522,369	171,753,042	33,702,998	96,753,571	24,947,674	118,747,967	42,479,031
665	Topeka, KS	3,130	3,220	1,214,299,117	65,260,302	334,648,258	103,704,630	172,037,632	39,678,773	186,761,296	63,031,247
666	Topeka, KS	15,337	13,552	2,308,839,358	21,213,894	532,868,716	42,653,051	260,840,813	124,848,610	460,040,338	146,764,057
667	Fort Scott, KS	1,887	2,606	1,134,425,438	17,499,168	271,194,985	25,133,806	173,879,955	37,200,485	170,557,155	81,003,229
668	Topeka, KS	929	7,338	643,595,035	4,762,878	144,760,080	11,551,330	97,670,553	20,071,758	82,164,130	34,509,415
669	Salina, KS	92	229	251,126,456	45,725,331	63,337,898	36,518,769	37,995,279	8,649,789	33,744,927	17,194,568
670	Wichita, KS	2,322	5,440	903,950,483	210,775,377	288,829,120	140,749,486	194,506,373	48,999,766	258,709,666	75,320,589
671	Wichita, KS	1,370	6,193	5,910,454,013	14,283,045	1,594,317,898	26,519,786	817,258,894	233,580,530	691,685,598	409,154,827
672	Wichita, KS	42,688	42,199	654,759,090	41,936,315	145,964,582	42,744,824	115,925,677	19,990,399	111,236,175	35,181,034
673	Independence, KS	3,194	1,707	1,652,013,818	41,143,888	315,059,927	50,167,621	232,845,988	60,695,114	262,920,452	121,112,439
674	Salina, KS	2,465	5,356	1,406,884,535	25,740,721	363,233,459	13,670,536	214,369,255	43,572,007	241,146,708	83,908,572
675	Hutchinson, KS	2,490	8,531	785,615,098	17,488,842	139,546,961	33,621,985	122,851,671	19,134,583	135,233,259	44,080,977
676	Hays, KS	695	1,224	421,860,838	53,029,408	77,227,513	10,436,029	56,319,933	10,566,705	50,906,484	25,981,536
677	Colby, KS	160	1,055	1,364,958,441	20,034,529	242,764,566	70,594,793	174,067,241	33,512,624	233,212,280	91,275,812
678	Dodge City, KS	1,089	41,078	413,558,611	41,195,505	59,204,069	308,909,860	59,572,719	8,178,062	37,465,312	15,237,171
679	Liberal, KS	822	12,734	1,873,205,203	311,305,349	448,521,157	42,043,824	261,492,783	78,603,939	178,236,638	90,182,903
680	Omaha, NE	2,503	5,260	7,993,698,750	18,959,927	1,950,921,616	34,196,827	1,103,031,570	689,736,595	1,093,258,116	331,376,599
681	Omaha, NE	57,981	40,823	852,662,932	23,968,936	219,913,118	149,906,507	119,408,270	26,696,514	94,333,418	53,812,954
683	Lincoln, NE	310	2,461	732,884,860	147,879,181	180,020,970	21,680,019	103,445,231	22,764,192	83,350,959	48,935,710
684	Lincoln, NE	307	1,475	3,440,833,062	18,062,273	760,486,821	52,869,641	446,619,282	174,234,805	393,080,510	224,965,973
685	Lincoln, NE	7,540	10,292	773,419,373	23,208,822	184,699,153	68,441,566	117,419,649	19,528,078	111,212,796	75,565,894
686	Norfolk, NE	207	6,127	1,404,727,446	79,323,639	330,033,767	35,814,580	228,078,570	37,865,811	226,533,089	94,053,305
687	Norfolk, NE	1,091	11,237	2,188,047,813	16,388,284	440,215,463	12,397,043	266,752,130	65,488,024	411,513,117	169,395,961
688	Grand Island, NE	685	18,015	790,485,294	8,504,845	195,652,522		128,958,625	20,658,812	122,043,614	55,197,983
689	Grand Island, NE	298	2,458								
690	McCook, NE	43	697	326,975,213		69,974,853		48,830,745	7,374,092	53,776,397	17,847,112

ZIP Code	3-Digit ZIP Code Areas	Black Markets	Hispanic Markets	Total Retail Sales ($Millions)	Retail Sales: Apparel & Accessories ($Millions)	Retail Sales: Automotive ($Millions)	Retail Sales: Drugs, First Aid & Health Care Products ($Millions)	Retail Sales: Food ($Millions)	Retail Sales: Furniture & Major Appliances ($Millions)	Retail Sales: General Merchandise ($Millions)	Retail Sales: Hardware, Lumber & Garden Supplies ($Millions)
691	North Platte, NE	302	3,420	1,390,473,744	22,508,237	211,909,953	40,149,255	146,695,403	22,369,006	153,466,808	71,718,105
692	Valentine, NE	10	90	116,701,055	3,391,086	25,884,999	2,830,935	18,914,526	2,729,473	16,086,176	9,921,592
693	Alliance, NE	359	7,885	869,819,172	25,635,022	186,614,836	27,477,425	128,496,905	19,694,628	153,388,102	51,938,072
700	New Orleans, LA	165,843	41,312	9,076,846,547	304,388,379	2,330,104,641	408,564,461	1,418,654,595	493,639,033	1,459,637,449	413,876,970
701	New Orleans, LA	318,021	16,315	5,580,675,272	337,797,762	903,050,042	388,148,225	844,440,163	242,094,613	584,835,333	223,911,556
703	Thibodaux, LA	52,411	4,918	2,964,786,877	69,968,102	649,376,652	149,054,149	566,464,787	92,707,083	483,512,005	217,800,059
704	Hammond, LA	73,521	8,783	4,612,675,235	135,686,491	1,019,932,675	227,990,800	781,460,355	135,075,760	694,519,080	244,820,937
705	Lafayette, LA	167,892	8,462	6,989,482,907	233,820,224	1,387,963,994	363,908,774	1,121,119,309	276,518,543	1,032,236,115	447,517,551
706	Lake Charles, LA	54,700	3,705	3,026,976,812	97,239,672	808,115,560	116,183,102	491,739,153	94,514,775	484,875,333	216,021,303
707	Baton Rouge, LA	82,816	5,742	3,557,507,951	58,036,163	811,389,295	146,694,781	629,269,467	117,614,870	581,993,178	197,632,283
708	Baton Rouge, LA	154,795	7,916	5,278,575,421	202,665,714	1,345,259,401	208,169,541	765,044,765	150,696,528	780,172,779	308,081,350
710	Shreveport, LA	55,838	2,626	1,768,935,850	55,498,891	411,876,429	70,200,270	290,924,990	65,306,652	286,751,751	87,668,096
711	Shreveport, LA	123,897	6,344	3,706,318,300	130,393,489	656,657,233	171,128,697	495,935,063	171,815,240	654,381,958	202,833,928
712	Monroe, LA	120,927	4,534	3,848,878,903	122,908,527	973,009,825	182,405,626	569,527,239	135,427,439	666,281,580	197,849,622
713	Alexandria, LA	68,371	2,589	2,185,704,762	59,293,531	465,265,103	105,762,496	377,863,661	70,344,558	427,723,795	126,642,841
714	Alexandria, LA	42,746	6,414	1,599,895,168	33,470,290	427,517,963	67,221,156	281,784,254	44,631,357	239,032,989	83,841,582
716	Pine Bluff, AR	75,484	4,068	1,797,878,617	59,370,683	474,861,253	61,818,649	297,830,838	52,164,464	257,388,945	110,518,111
717	Camden, AR	41,837	1,727	1,241,125,624	47,571,348	254,945,502	61,468,712	220,355,126	31,004,967	170,506,069	77,972,607
718	Texarkana, AR	31,124	8,029	1,313,659,607	18,300,196	304,518,315	45,323,958	226,508,902	37,473,509	204,925,138	60,388,639
719	Hot Springs National Park, AR	12,182	4,988	2,096,211,500	46,106,857	538,806,046	73,195,934	305,174,449	46,782,995	348,820,652	178,705,590
720	Little Rock, AR	34,978	6,609	3,880,507,970	107,362,421	1,048,170,737	128,852,233	530,095,297	135,592,647	703,703,893	273,597,898
721	Little Rock, AR	50,021	5,252	3,826,528,242	130,647,140	1,106,649,904	117,029,268	489,586,336	154,438,125	664,858,677	227,825,931
722	Little Rock, AR	84,013	5,486	3,699,788,976	151,539,477	1,181,044,932	99,031,062	383,995,490	178,066,170	694,360,153	199,858,487
723	Memphis, TN	85,639	3,768	1,987,169,889	44,427,454	407,758,411	79,495,919	288,444,192	49,892,623	283,456,657	80,433,481
724	Jonesboro, AR	9,341	3,481	2,414,725,019	88,112,598	454,781,749	78,057,082	302,413,343	86,708,370	519,760,760	217,494,732
725	Batesville, AR	1,253	1,277	1,021,897,797	19,062,969	230,747,618	35,863,735	164,677,629	37,841,964	152,817,101	94,199,943
726	Harrison, AR	318	4,071	1,534,556,015	27,391,403	312,837,682	43,768,775	246,037,484	37,713,879	198,576,324	151,321,405
727	Fayetteville, AR	5,542	36,467	4,886,369,804	118,418,519	1,471,548,338	91,265,639	567,192,967	192,441,808	775,053,248	391,709,077
728	Russellville, AR	2,613	6,435	1,293,515,744	31,789,459	247,092,960	41,363,900	203,085,967	30,232,709	204,784,701	92,705,588
729	Fort Smith, AR	8,603	12,883	2,851,643,292	66,128,323	605,014,065	93,148,644	372,308,367	75,473,261	649,059,726	223,496,289
730	Oklahoma City, OK	26,440	22,457	6,665,710,003	207,094,558	2,097,370,391	234,723,260	915,956,999	246,756,881	1,005,125,798	269,943,297
731	Oklahoma City, OK	97,752	67,427	9,288,247,356	376,935,960	2,818,517,171	321,554,775	1,129,187,121	500,798,281	1,397,543,387	428,533,479
734	Ardmore, OK	4,237	3,702	930,546,043	35,441,188	178,809,897	36,984,290	161,428,149	14,714,668	146,727,343	49,823,986
735	Lawton, OK	26,879	16,751	2,038,284,417	61,957,565	467,506,882	72,374,349	291,163,720	63,056,870	402,096,462	103,543,083
736	Clinton, OK	1,940	3,843	587,088,701	19,854,583	108,783,703	20,707,247	98,800,866	8,989,864	88,167,938	28,604,452
737	Enid, OK	3,129	5,377	1,186,285,794	29,809,163	313,746,587	46,295,382	178,759,793	32,794,042	224,010,608	51,749,582
738	Woodward, OK	235	1,589	335,536,554	10,828,657	63,385,925	11,290,878	58,403,669	5,280,599	45,930,494	23,057,855
739	Liberal, KS	176	7,784	237,875,521	6,287,582	53,174,548	9,226,141	38,711,191	4,529,035	38,951,607	15,446,945
740	Tulsa, OK	12,898	14,678	6,271,382,997	207,278,429	1,747,553,479	200,377,708	823,710,707	231,393,240	913,972,761	287,428,573
741	Tulsa, OK	64,855	34,490	7,007,857,769	273,365,845	1,745,241,561	224,891,661	860,340,176	331,039,660	828,841,834	345,666,685
743	Tulsa, OK	910	2,935	1,145,271,270	17,892,346	254,543,725	50,333,566	206,862,554	20,970,913	182,953,338	61,802,679
744	Muskogee, OK	16,020	6,054	2,095,817,781	53,226,791	491,008,126	68,643,454	377,577,964	64,609,609	365,235,131	102,245,313
745	McAlester, OK	2,760	1,731	744,895,043	20,232,253	176,615,210	23,680,101	131,218,207	14,406,520	102,200,820	37,760,291
746	Ponca City, OK	919	2,463	660,909,563	19,672,084	133,197,996	27,818,839	92,562,806	10,930,830	123,138,329	30,540,736
747	Durant, OK	5,398	2,264	730,463,808	16,516,508	170,605,903	28,869,560	135,902,779	13,976,742	122,626,639	207,904,346
748	Shawnee, OK	6,380	4,569	1,912,510,553	48,324,919	510,850,275	75,122,522	260,009,580	40,964,879	295,007,633	87,094,936
749	Poteau, OK	1,868	3,911	987,818,564	13,017,836	211,023,893	60,017,219	193,876,349	21,794,071	167,669,854	36,826,726
750	North Texas, TX	145,602	369,126	23,948,707,872	981,592,238	6,801,601,101	812,446,172	3,167,406,969	1,270,979,947	3,751,236,594	1,118,739,688
751	Dallas, TX	123,405	109,376	8,223,071,617	295,556,106	2,275,658,879	306,608,428	1,095,513,122	643,534,400	1,145,310,175	367,229,593
752	Dallas, TX	302,613	522,472	20,007,375,904	923,980,430	5,867,434,652	596,102,143	2,366,235,205	582,711,488	2,737,613,106	841,317,825
754	Greenville, TX	26,379	31,692	3,437,708,537	121,494,294	803,188,731	148,734,333	543,683,816	97,024,962	465,442,981	195,725,996
755	Texarkana, TX	27,257	5,541	1,556,222,085	72,813,588	394,520,976	46,717,597	219,947,398	44,313,115	198,618,369	83,374,055
756	Longview, TX	61,275	27,033	3,932,978,771	111,626,463	1,000,177,480	285,268,408	565,101,399	113,039,650	499,413,626	207,904,346
757	Tyler, TX	47,339	38,017	3,816,814,975	123,524,988	893,802,159	147,815,820	541,991,308	113,972,608	724,134,658	269,933,406
758	Palestine, TX	25,859	13,820	1,015,849,998	21,041,995	211,023,893	60,017,219	197,350,313	25,411,976	113,134,919	55,409,551
759	Lufkin, TX	43,767	29,242	2,586,163,391	108,291,482	491,683,687	120,483,037	484,203,443	59,345,499	318,818,792	160,873,735
760	Fort Worth, TX	76,743	158,270	1,429,150,257	32,664,389	414,490,370	482,152,962	1,944,979,962	643,534,400	1,911,937,080	715,156,086
761	Fort Worth, TX	129,072	109,376	10,996,277,234	375,140,154	2,946,717,450	368,534,515	1,445,347,243	582,711,488	1,522,061,082	575,338,295
762	Fort Worth, TX	13,002	40,909	3,528,776,011	102,774,394	773,797,361	115,511,496	284,751,351	105,384,374	537,366,261	166,267,162
763	Wichita Falls, TX	14,098	23,869	2,118,744,060	58,101,619	571,852,856	63,722,158	262,962,444	83,161,463	405,079,795	121,464,517
764	Fort Worth, TX	2,054	18,975	1,429,150,257	32,664,389	410,075,441	64,180,780	237,789,614	34,245,809	132,938,542	62,312,475
765	Waco, TX	68,417	75,970	4,065,938,808	95,886,128	1,303,708,700	93,643,111	603,247,126	147,084,138	670,763,338	200,564,443
766	Waco, TX	16,274	19,967	1,596,036,271	81,705,853	351,538,042	60,108,721	284,751,351	49,770,430	193,911,617	85,515,741
767	Waco, TX	29,680	38,344	1,958,877,592	57,404,650	449,565,316	62,878,718	331,515,388	78,121,219	357,900,645	120,005,162
768	Abilene, TX	2,329	18,966	878,213,303	24,338,268	183,318,006	39,507,633	162,062,103	22,033,030	75,612,806	59,824,965
769	Midland, TX	3,973	44,277	1,525,434,446	49,688,909	410,075,441	251,620,599	251,620,599	67,403,412	242,518,026	
770	Houston, TX	603,996	1,093,871	37,991,551,899	1,725,810,686	10,300,692,891	1,500,356,120	5,664,481,307	2,239,992,240	5,437,891,106	1,631,210,617
773	North Houston, TX	58,737	117,039	9,242,296,719	366,748,339	2,732,812,475	325,007,650	1,459,699,421	355,307,194	1,187,441,561	460,611,820
774	North Houston, TX	104,306	155,252	8,378,407,279	234,878,683	2,352,163,037	269,953,066	1,261,058,485	341,526,654	1,189,958,803	442,547,004
775	North Houston, TX	101,819	300,877	12,173,779,484	494,406,448	3,240,045,511	471,134,654	2,051,384,850	513,086,916	1,766,720,361	533,304,205

ZIP Code	3-Digit ZIP Code Areas	Black Markets	Hispanic Markets	Total Retail Sales ($Millions)	Retail Sales: Apparel & Accessories ($Millions)	Retail Sales: Automotive ($Millions)	Retail Sales: Drugs, First Aid & Health Care Products ($Millions)	Retail Sales: Food ($Millions)	Retail Sales: Furniture & Major Appliances ($Millions)	Retail Sales: General Merchandise ($Millions)	Retail Sales: Hardware, Lumber & Garden Supplies ($Millions)
776	Beaumont, TX	37,309	20,420	3,470,560,993	96,437,955	968,027,965	132,720,349	524,912,135	106,369,712	492,290,908	180,524,790
777	Beaumont, TX	61,322	14,934	1,863,922,400	77,991,050	493,009,775	72,253,327	243,134,840	53,182,884	249,085,866	102,800,752
778	Bryan, TX	34,173	46,795	2,869,104,447	92,621,982	643,448,237	76,169,083	485,334,029	87,076,053	490,771,131	146,511,925
779	Victoria, TX	10,610	58,991	1,920,901,764	59,625,699	460,775,834	68,638,737	352,463,539	52,530,870	230,064,700	115,327,481
780	San Antonio, TX	3,919	310,532	6,757,105,937	444,224,683	832,229,720	153,800,147	1,108,813,074	500,113,568	1,281,936,166	339,584,990
781	San Antonio, TX	17,867	109,271	3,352,707,413	111,973,195	979,714,791	84,121,541	509,139,585	118,671,915	506,945,573	160,034,978
782	San Antonio, TX	91,101	815,690	17,028,103,126	873,931,076	4,365,428,380	516,750,131	2,634,501,771	714,022,224	2,483,923,336	607,495,965
783	Corpus Christi, TX	4,129	146,829	2,445,024,904	60,104,607	583,927,739	72,359,256	528,965,778	70,547,691	255,099,185	110,620,478
784	Corpus Christi, TX	11,225	163,627	3,823,373,399	152,268,841	982,401,789	103,322,744	652,299,104	109,125,494	624,145,912	182,203,208
785	McAllen, TX	4,872	964,386	11,999,926,012	807,961,754	2,014,209,674	244,989,755	1,998,655,060	516,149,564	2,609,991,499	678,598,848
786	Austin, TX	38,024	167,108	7,262,446,505	255,909,833	2,130,164,875	190,770,744	1,090,622,411	285,935,756	960,306,833	317,624,723
787	Austin, TX	66,223	255,784	13,113,618,381	514,610,741	3,076,340,568	382,987,112	1,851,870,731	763,643,390	1,674,693,636	784,918,680
788	San Antonio, TX	1,789	133,345	1,647,573,809	102,954,745	282,719,720	39,393,144	352,619,200	33,690,022	236,792,587	91,143,982
789	Austin, TX	6,112	11,358	676,690,773	12,835,344	158,275,453	22,555,243	139,538,667	18,861,156	77,864,192	36,210,276
790	Amarillo, TX	6,500	72,783	1,990,107,146	67,472,341	439,918,359	82,823,274	357,845,374	55,431,712	215,998,054	104,681,716
791	Amarillo, TX	12,944	47,795	3,136,699,036	122,104,332	761,241,400	64,389,907	385,731,973	155,757,890	394,750,584	152,318,207
792	Childress, TX	2,540	9,703	276,245,260	4,137,839	70,615,115	12,151,478	58,949,176	8,369,112	32,559,705	10,980,909
793	Lubbock, TX	5,762	57,363	1,214,528,871	30,318,390	300,186,157	52,366,039	256,626,699	39,958,443	142,205,649	58,186,951
794	Lubbock, TX	18,197	67,733	3,463,903,656	147,252,609	946,833,777	85,105,675	473,533,108	155,901,604	611,099,320	153,636,287
795	Abilene, TX	3,937	20,653	851,952,907	26,731,110	195,005,832	41,727,400	159,728,112	23,696,591	101,048,118	29,216,731
796	Abilene, TX	9,658	26,345	1,612,861,031	49,559,505	357,753,376	63,654,921	230,068,002	47,491,808	332,821,703	91,525,725
797	Midland, TX	16,674	147,097	4,110,199,956	135,825,899	988,124,807	172,934,164	718,489,827	118,483,579	655,765,565	177,193,697
798	El Paso, TX	513	59,385	674,893,279	25,253,543	127,878,136	21,236,620	104,792,905	30,112,073	104,691,196	31,559,394
799	El Paso, TX	16,686	539,643	8,127,481,044	422,620,378	1,489,736,909	209,624,272	1,233,373,484	445,351,981	1,603,608,562	412,322,272
800	Denver, CO	50,498	137,375	10,909,053,462	305,038,461	3,491,746,347	224,577,638	1,583,059,993	535,323,400	1,518,559,969	652,743,011
801	Denver, CO	7,813	43,850	8,252,750,768	209,361,171	2,671,373,743	156,314,500	1,267,722,341	453,997,244	1,139,734,436	476,196,246
802	Denver, CO	70,000	286,162	12,502,373,642	531,102,097	2,477,342,967	316,280,458	1,916,977,340	832,920,652	1,354,134,818	700,386,899
803	Denver, CO	1,312	9,608	1,878,468,092	58,406,906	490,571,432	36,004,445	263,510,697	103,066,018	208,255,659	128,692,417
804	Denver, CO	1,115	15,052	3,499,602,840	226,003,628	588,706,347	67,735,011	565,697,459	143,395,460	371,699,151	216,548,389
805	Longmont, CO	2,929	55,446	5,879,120,057	175,706,227	1,459,865,780	132,907,510	802,059,369	900,704,826	932,815,409	485,192,047
806	Brighton, CO	1,688	68,520	1,990,732,842	35,115,725	533,215,074	30,797,299	315,616,437	90,258,483	266,060,924	122,356,731
807	Brighton, CO	621	13,530	736,517,125	16,004,501	133,058,671	20,858,771	124,320,204	32,289,546	82,454,388	40,315,966
808	Colorado Springs, CO	2,959	8,536	1,201,526,633	21,302,559	250,002,686	30,346,011	158,603,606	58,196,495	151,416,390	95,840,813
809	Colorado Springs, CO	34,954	60,168	6,598,709,105	174,591,022	1,597,259,485	155,268,419	795,206,358	351,976,726	968,325,728	391,686,360
810	Pueblo, CO	4,127	84,737	2,504,506,642	45,279,920	488,766,936	72,087,579	426,775,436	115,655,978	408,933,494	123,216,413
811	Alamosa, CO	364	24,930	882,287,063	17,604,802	141,647,724	26,449,571	164,010,922	36,922,403	78,663,273	79,185,423
812	Salida, CO	2,847	7,321	888,830,012	18,127,742	156,873,290	24,268,004	138,423,351	38,854,081	104,247,967	69,617,002
813	Durango, CO	225	5,651	980,571,319	35,209,265	132,451,577	27,235,111	170,110,680	41,051,798	70,224,409	107,183,897
814	Grand Junction, CO	322	10,066	1,080,125,676	22,039,261	166,763,585	26,661,098	180,160,767	41,346,075	136,584,057	148,990,647
815	Grand Junction, CO	623	12,766	1,673,815,465	37,275,522	305,880,700	29,281,396	274,627,175	76,636,040	322,014,510	108,663,343
816	Glenwood Springs, CO	669	27,157	3,070,602,947	217,920,249	283,798,405	78,522,122	394,030,346	120,646,683	223,133,668	242,782,697
820	Cheyenne, WY	2,835	12,297	1,685,695,963	41,295,930	388,949,343	29,432,611	188,221,912	52,912,732	239,874,326	63,061,442
821	Billings, MT	0	4	17,590,142	1,110,638	2,223,950	229,852	2,094,956	279,076	2,299,382	1,417,093
822	Wheatland, WY	57	1,600	254,455,403	2,793,251	68,557,200	6,568,515	36,654,698	8,270,630	29,737,440	12,784,899
823	Rawlins, WY	136	2,258	239,279,419	2,607,718	46,884,903	6,756,352	34,410,235	5,710,998	13,574,428	12,534,428
824	Worland, WY	71	2,763	617,783,693	13,270,853	143,877,417	18,307,570	94,807,251	17,418,242	91,256,648	33,550,063
825	Riverton, WY	96	1,733	419,064,199	9,997,255	98,332,172	11,586,395	60,076,259	11,897,108	65,155,821	25,638,195
826	Casper, WY	633	4,170	1,115,929,335	32,128,190	297,477,918	20,805,932	162,539,825	41,754,793	146,743,981	49,275,746
827	Gillette, WY	122	1,982	632,820,898	13,723,180	145,287,421	14,095,004	96,610,992	18,041,226	77,383,620	30,388,524
828	Sheridan, WY	88	818	486,474,719	13,196,891	106,105,179	10,726,764	63,217,427	12,909,287	76,216,505	25,638,560
829	Rock Springs, WY	369	4,866	860,381,486	25,347,105	171,595,174	12,158,410	150,981,294	21,178,759	101,911,503	45,972,593
830	Rock Springs, WY	33	1,706	658,712,531	57,463,575	60,045,469	5,446,938	76,482,264	7,649,098	67,940,986	61,662,328
831	Rock Springs, WY	32	385	1,713,675,280	2,702,559	49,029,989	7,078,173	33,043,286	6,009,638	22,893,298	14,627,145
832	Pocatello, ID	643	13,167	1,713,305,157	31,933,093	469,851,129	65,433,279	296,115,226	74,524,698	174,887,557	130,329,511
833	Twin Falls, ID	496	28,021	2,347,529,134	92,130,940	669,688,405	52,857,131	380,275,237	85,668,295	185,446,016	198,395,971
834	Pocatello, ID	735	13,222	2,086,010,093	58,091,036	535,124,382	69,375,598	304,008,897	99,509,945	315,491,268	199,400,920
835	Lewiston, ID	180	1,239	930,398,267	21,499,825	161,484,962	31,665,468	141,408,548	24,669,146	128,683,206	60,100,351
836	Boise, ID	2,377	48,734	4,019,202,329	88,895,909	1,219,141,285	111,373,091	597,479,474	183,578,176	447,179,559	353,491,659
837	Boise, ID	1,838	13,650	3,912,399,453	130,153,371	933,934,488	107,583,790	519,850,618	244,683,650	601,655,755	299,263,274
838	Spokane, WA	625	5,494	3,076,618,458	107,317,645	818,876,829	84,928,194	543,327,589	112,129,164	284,330,529	308,918,802
840	Salt Lake City, UT	7,666	74,118	11,136,564,045	413,854,739	2,907,245,451	217,327,360	1,838,715,559	635,449,937	1,455,889,029	698,191,730
841	Salt Lake City, UT	8,295	97,055	8,202,992,957	377,380,960	1,994,017,753	169,079,043	1,313,433,952	527,660,050	1,074,606,330	525,600,638
843	Salt Lake City, UT	552	10,747	1,302,297,923	40,946,265	282,328,631	35,291,899	242,943,652	53,975,867	181,090,303	106,857,988
844	Salt Lake City, UT	2,487	25,683	2,134,406,717	69,287,315	570,908,526	37,604,308	341,058,239	96,937,130	400,203,922	123,625,486
845	Provo, UT	143	3,192	546,547,230	3,817,160	102,608,519	15,557,535	113,001,422	19,281,080	51,979,218	23,280,146
846	Provo, UT	878	20,749	2,361,546,831	63,015,340	538,940,259	63,180,549	377,174,908	138,848,493	374,089,243	165,180,586
847	Provo, UT	603	8,861	2,392,794,565	72,178,131	604,886,240	42,597,417	374,612,084	64,186,917	269,047,258	231,344,145
850	Phoenix, AZ	67,510	544,444	16,359,094,110	537,731,868	4,463,481,822	725,889,478	2,480,671,172	814,587,982	2,169,298,564	829,167,063
852	Phoenix, AZ	42,197	310,371	21,219,887,286	705,093,059	5,572,242,344	921,876,643	3,297,757,605	1,087,067,930	2,851,854,335	1,022,795,304
853	Phoenix, AZ	30,791	291,399	12,841,564,080	396,271,305	3,370,970,709	562,562,629	2,007,846,196	619,708,644	1,666,709,489	680,728,629

ZIP Code	3-Digit ZIP Code Areas	Black Markets	Hispanic Markets	Total Retail Sales ($Millions)	Retail Sales: Apparel & Accessories ($Millions)	Retail Sales: Automotive ($Millions)	Retail Sales: Drugs, First Aid & Health Care Products ($Millions)	Retail Sales: Food ($Millions)	Retail Sales: Furniture & Major Appliances ($Millions)	Retail Sales: General Merchandise ($Millions)	Retail Sales: Hardware, Lumber & Garden Supplies ($Millions)
855	Globe, AZ	728	20,393	950,192,797	16,269,035	130,261,630	33,472,870	203,040,114	28,464,521	122,525,500	58,162,738
856	Tucson, AZ	5,065	89,503	2,960,057,598	222,425,382	434,645,018	103,105,137	535,942,215	90,381,180	461,545,581	144,831,714
857	Tucson, AZ	25,751	287,244	11,126,625,651	398,061,874	2,520,284,762	558,000,500	1,614,092,440	508,054,821	1,772,430,688	645,555,901
859	Show Low, AZ	348	6,509	702,402,708	12,282,666	91,959,002	14,371,840	146,679,868	18,678,474	102,251,772	35,882,481
860	Flagstaff, AZ	1,778	17,860	2,521,132,053	67,772,929	339,929,379	62,743,190	429,328,398	49,549,096	332,491,485	190,484,523
863	Prescott, AZ	722	19,782	2,494,516,914	64,160,316	487,809,118	83,393,943	496,394,311	68,363,758	257,474,603	244,111,084
864	Kingman, AZ	915	19,181	2,801,178,000	54,537,326	637,314,416	113,973,737	443,181,734	116,836,620	314,730,548	192,744,285
865	Gallup, NM	19	555	374,875,134	3,141,091	67,702,074	10,484,202	89,598,200	14,202,351	30,114,153	11,768,198
870	Albuquerque, NM	1,793	75,203	1,965,992,529	32,585,282	453,097,890	78,190,671	299,157,796	101,714,380	236,280,404	115,632,523
871	Albuquerque, NM	18,278	272,548	9,457,396,982	290,940,170	1,518,845,040	455,627,704	1,159,773,437	434,503,602	1,479,181,436	482,126,302
873	Gallup, NM	296	9,196	988,561,384	33,942,886	196,500,807	15,230,929	150,274,956	21,399,171	136,644,546	47,327,790
874	Farmington, NM	598	19,556	1,629,299,411	44,174,387	418,450,564	45,117,105	276,066,616	67,467,044	241,052,130	141,792,868
875	Albuquerque, NM	1,404	122,508	3,685,439,759	160,762,335	675,276,667	116,597,194	500,969,536	141,137,383	287,021,164	265,845,253
877	Las Vegas, NM	250	28,714	562,441,977	8,834,065	156,928,096	21,448,262	75,581,158	17,079,941	44,152,781	40,676,603
878	Socorro, NM	118	7,717	185,309,483	2,005,399	67,926,834	4,686,434	28,809,248	7,355,638	8,393,749	2,705,239
879	Truth or Consequences, NM	82	8,382	196,630,156	2,339,504	63,127,302	5,819,027	32,624,592	8,416,961	13,275,873	15,926,786
880	Las Cruces, NM	3,402	150,947	2,498,841,545	71,311,102	576,630,870	70,320,570	377,664,405	126,727,268	312,394,238	152,990,638
881	Clovis, NM	3,503	22,357	779,440,242	29,144,929	236,897,344	25,641,488	104,352,366	25,982,120	114,308,868	63,837,894
882	Roswell, NM	4,682	73,193	2,029,395,256	70,950,454	586,151,475	86,287,473	324,456,201	64,448,259	219,700,120	89,407,155
883	Carrizozo, NM	2,422	22,869	991,881,642	31,625,645	292,086,723	20,063,163	146,839,091	32,141,111	106,510,488	66,458,571
884	Tucumcari, NM	157	7,855	456,177,363	1,669,592	65,426,952	5,789,644	30,113,153	7,020,812	18,244,718	5,656,318
890	Las Vegas, NV	34,596	96,748	6,457,177,363	254,727,660	1,511,914,353	233,926,874	956,085,576	316,906,269	696,472,769	357,624,993
891	Las Vegas, NV	105,763	311,530	17,132,097,372	660,727,352	3,903,353,024	613,087,729	2,516,006,192	817,329,659	1,967,896,199	871,398,269
893	Ely, NV	400	1,083	228,228,867	2,796,120	25,158,757	4,666,180	21,275,535	3,900,778	18,462,268	4,051,981
894	Reno, NV	3,457	39,499	3,556,044,612	108,931,660	775,649,964	127,198,971	562,562,639	157,910,559	567,797,346	274,530,045
895	Reno, NV	4,312	45,331	4,054,091,486	135,693,952	890,988,524	143,813,704	590,155,819	212,634,201	660,510,526	341,628,433
897	Reno, NV	932	9,771	1,300,105,957	14,307,175	188,632,998	44,712,536	238,019,654	31,317,394	210,030,534	122,098,035
898	Elko, NV	204	9,689	673,685,686	29,460,364	121,668,737	22,391,934	113,010,856	19,622,184	91,509,718	47,827,014
900	Los Angeles, CA	378,471	1,367,032	29,049,233,018	1,444,684,576	6,580,225,614	1,395,997,673	4,350,590,858	1,873,577,460	3,729,291,276	1,410,914,961
902	Inglewood, CA	129,650	685,354	14,552,863,947	747,494,376	3,326,550,546	688,512,484	2,135,138,711	962,794,415	1,860,495,509	687,458,018
903	Inglewood, CA	53,706	82,403	1,506,477,211	74,740,969	341,319,971	72,310,540	225,342,568	96,968,486	192,669,579	72,929,489
904	Inglewood, CA	3,187	12,070	1,689,070,410	87,432,885	386,255,792	79,819,211	246,975,473	112,436,350	216,031,626	79,487,742
905	Inglewood, CA	7,720	40,141	2,285,517,424	117,056,050	523,142,657	108,981,627	335,950,152	150,737,607	291,172,279	107,866,006
906	Long Beach, CA	18,323	438,841	7,989,272,017	408,923,675	1,864,423,162	372,096,305	1,146,177,214	529,845,955	1,051,283,181	395,365,311
907	Long Beach, CA	69,615	272,259	7,216,156,075	366,551,841	1,658,241,251	343,733,235	1,058,381,688	473,367,010	929,652,807	348,709,798
908	Long Beach, CA	72,986	200,056	5,884,146,610	295,544,444	1,337,705,951	279,627,623	873,911,562	382,937,680	754,965,597	282,950,650
910	Pasadena, CA	21,210	69,339	3,623,150,426	187,219,323	829,574,775	173,352,018	531,350,443	239,928,396	460,797,353	170,170,125
911	Pasadena, CA	19,212	57,098	2,322,760,271	119,448,933	530,815,427	110,364,780	341,258,559	153,702,233	297,133,338	109,869,898
912	Pasadena, CA	2,720	41,707	2,681,502,984	135,774,318	610,873,403	129,549,907	398,110,358	174,897,185	341,645,334	128,075,399
913	Van Nuys, CA	47,865	485,038	15,000,219,717	732,082,855	3,587,952,207	714,044,089	2,186,086,772	961,512,857	1,921,717,888	731,892,921
914	Van Nuys, CA	15,937	162,299	3,876,519,168	195,418,175	882,425,706	183,521,377	573,780,590	150,737,607	497,413,443	185,823,730
915	Van Nuys, CA	2,430	28,535	1,548,383,308	78,690,263	353,665,273	73,612,743	228,167,384	101,770,846	197,881,249	73,586,833
916	Van Nuys, CA	11,570	104,655	2,968,674,966	149,249,519	675,590,321	140,266,771	439,355,970	87,947,422	380,839,957	142,371,777
917	Alhambra, CA	86,747	978,129	19,059,848,874	879,081,065	4,348,651,657	877,310,752	2,862,219,208	1,114,025,572	2,624,569,714	981,098,645
918	Alhambra, CA	1,401	32,066	1,024,877,860	51,111,094	232,973,893	49,239,888	152,766,738	66,327,142	130,997,499	49,414,697
919	San Diego, CA	30,655	211,192	5,819,340,658	291,125,621	1,286,582,315	265,364,409	837,992,740	366,766,432	792,336,008	325,311,405
920	San Diego, CA	35,092	309,508	14,518,666,585	737,286,212	3,220,199,777	658,754,497	2,075,507,007	925,006,013	1,976,860,840	803,669,285
921	San Diego, CA	96,027	359,361	15,913,215,657	802,026,491	3,520,700,370	714,809,958	2,277,961,451	1,009,812,026	2,176,120,453	886,186,290
922	Palm Springs, CA	22,704	341,984	7,525,667,193	310,414,680	1,437,318,629	362,842,705	1,344,349,956	269,352,790	1,146,142,382	434,214,480
923	San Bernardino, CA	90,581	405,199	9,894,399,764	337,815,451	2,225,560,445	425,417,404	1,562,736,221	410,211,249	1,579,022,353	608,530,633
924	San Bernardino, CA	35,357	122,521	2,167,525,098	120,257,909	481,598,279	92,860,549	343,896,269	87,947,422	345,955,975	134,757,485
925	San Bernardino, CA	82,011	391,258	11,201,796,182	483,743,728	2,391,897,542	548,463,771	1,867,359,860	454,592,494	1,539,503,077	667,203,416
926	Santa Ana, CA	14,191	201,527	19,348,532,420	1,045,202,614	4,694,516,515	838,934,900	2,578,092,234	1,347,228,965	2,679,068,129	992,430,616
927	Santa Ana, CA	7,836	311,280	5,273,491,913	277,374,790	1,274,600,960	229,506,058	711,624,948	360,993,493	731,957,144	275,648,496
928	Santa Ana, CA	13,877	449,646	13,925,002,856	717,321,495	3,312,856,812	616,653,400	1,937,712,475	897,814,488	1,928,830,578	739,165,787
930	Oxnard, CA	2,597	274,118	8,031,257,759	243,133,466	2,354,474,062	408,392,022	1,179,671,903	387,880,389	1,050,193,776	497,377,093
931	Santa Barbara, CA	28,259	53,811	2,346,661,907	133,633,684	376,833,582	142,167,750	397,855,876	130,933,256	279,303,536	138,837,854
932	Bakersfield, CA	28,349	373,887	5,778,468,500	291,125,621	1,038,357,673	361,152,201	1,089,405,862	222,213,899	866,357,075	367,841,957
933	Bakersfield, CA	11,379	170,298	4,454,127,308	120,257,909	844,685,258	264,313,084	751,502,872	199,096,670	661,241,913	258,815,160
934	Santa Barbara, CA	14,100	134,012	5,387,764,564	198,807,968	1,129,897,069	287,614,495	880,687,528	247,484,538	480,947,496	340,543,286
935	Mojave, CA	57,221	136,439	5,203,093,347	231,640,699	1,080,926,275	257,568,708	807,158,923	293,459,761	663,402,595	282,472,956
936	Fresno, CA	10,125	277,833	4,939,841,913	277,374,790	1,151,262,408	277,867,029	886,176,096	225,974,509	621,989,010	316,679,801
937	Fresno, CA	39,963	226,698	5,878,352,482	717,321,495	1,367,734,310	352,538,966	989,037,912	264,792,220	796,963,178	356,489,573
939	Salinas, CA	14,453	192,428	4,274,387,769	229,316,231	788,296,771	241,241,765	652,707,952	194,080,214	620,595,944	216,679,801
940	San Francisco, CA	16,763	153,315	12,497,949,874	590,071,613	2,865,267,726	683,882,365	1,623,436,792	1,017,323,334	1,835,990,510	667,852,574
941	San Francisco, CA	56,652	108,756	11,726,011,314	1,298,781,742	935,877,968	587,833,123	1,523,389,069	891,275,976	994,729,380	335,489,573
943	San Francisco, CA	7,558	24,542	2,189,065,123	127,031,551	347,031,920	78,862,795	196,013,924	127,228,463	202,547,578	77,561,678
944	San Francisco, CA	2,651	21,804	4,189,065,123	198,128,547	492,600,177	122,755,438	281,992,849	169,961,023	337,889,856	119,609,068
945	Oakland, CA	163,836	436,035	26,650,604,732	1,181,995,248	5,567,039,347	1,419,046,623	4,185,039,189	1,648,057,398	3,896,644,018	1,625,626,163
946	Oakland, CA	131,385	103,593	5,179,454,229	223,043,857	1,072,175,332	312,144,556	799,571,984	376,495,112	621,762,671	302,767,497

ZIP Code	3-Digit ZIP Code Areas	Black Markets	Hispanic Markets	Total Retail Sales ($Millions)	Retail Sales: Apparel & Accessories ($Millions)	Retail Sales: Automotive ($Millions)	Retail Sales: Drugs, First Aid & Health Care Products ($Millions)	Retail Sales: Food ($Millions)	Retail Sales: Furniture & Major Appliances ($Millions)	Retail Sales: General Merchandise ($Millions)	Retail Sales: Hardware, Lumber & Garden Supplies ($Millions)
947	Oakland, CA	12,820	12,472	1,822,282,427	79,830,490	377,542,050	107,242,968	280,016,667	132,774,481	224,855,642	105,842,440
948	Oakland, CA	43,423	59,600	1,951,016,777	88,407,736	371,898,490	102,332,519	316,698,053	111,678,527	351,174,751	114,371,165
949	North Bay, CA	8,465	48,907	5,873,419,195	303,655,268	1,084,846,973	339,335,748	901,082,813	396,221,742	723,959,054	400,591,745
950	San Jose, CA	10,804	202,716	10,330,298,929	461,035,161	2,577,349,878	570,586,987	1,550,868,608	708,606,645	1,160,642,408	572,462,518
951	San Jose, CA	28,840	303,504	12,223,777,844	626,549,168	2,901,599,541	636,814,844	1,624,405,009	1,077,146,049	1,613,217,092	629,817,530
952	Stockton, CA	37,890	161,269	4,766,490,595	117,625,281	1,004,857,300	316,227,504	854,275,132	190,760,963	620,077,242	343,005,216
953	Stockton, CA	32,236	339,591	10,178,109,933	276,004,706	2,121,781,316	657,440,128	1,716,650,899	468,943,053	1,484,318,757	681,361,985
954	North Bay, CA	7,135	100,672	6,531,826,051	159,317,672	1,146,626,369	420,757,154	1,225,908,216	320,520,106	837,604,219	636,576,954
955	Eureka, CA	2,372	13,991	1,905,912,319	58,816,518	287,752,321	162,596,209	412,761,412	55,882,649	166,788,425	183,734,445
956	Sacramento, CA	40,485	169,274	14,537,294,233	464,712,202	2,818,210,373	660,020,262	2,331,830,375	671,481,398	1,602,688,106	1,015,357,268
957	Sacramento, CA	8,780	27,207	2,857,613,149	85,155,744	579,406,114	128,133,711	459,900,381	116,143,003	302,886,695	218,822,621
958	Sacramento, CA	107,702	173,663	10,028,224,067	418,204,151	1,956,669,069	436,377,703	1,543,021,036	674,666,846	1,230,093,944	663,926,821
959	Marysville, CA	7,492	80,264	5,429,798,706	140,483,249	1,022,499,249	330,354,824	969,021,217	259,425,778	806,543,473	428,918,788
960	Redding, CA	2,451	26,804	3,615,407,675	77,792,416	563,119,029	174,454,402	670,622,102	150,375,616	519,857,449	312,026,691
961	Reno, NV	2,421	19,508	1,455,448,367	38,666,538	265,772,897	73,302,928	270,737,415	46,707,828	168,147,654	126,282,458
967	Honolulu, HI	18,719	75,929	13,948,954,083	919,151,539	2,011,093,641	939,520,372	2,163,537,394	575,890,636	2,028,059,510	529,802,988
968	Honolulu, HI	10,654	17,744	7,426,554,454	531,150,149	1,121,411,616	489,112,751	897,910,076	306,657,737	1,548,736,347	213,200,148
970	Portland, OR	7,678	79,352	10,435,395,832	379,915,855	2,640,839,782	266,010,714	1,251,918,432	551,479,275	2,012,293,770	668,955,756
971	Portland, OR	1,887	42,237	4,137,454,151	115,779,689	965,461,151	121,681,270	548,141,245	214,965,612	702,293,762	333,015,021
972	Portland, OR	39,591	70,309	12,773,545,824	665,291,114	2,825,030,680	237,735,412	1,412,140,375	751,136,501	2,357,746,216	749,049,006
973	Salem, OR	4,499	61,057	6,827,230,784	216,234,920	1,721,900,230	256,133,991	989,190,826	261,851,812	1,044,059,723	514,293,133
974	Eugene, OR	3,055	24,251	7,226,120,960	208,955,635	1,909,602,149	245,055,002	1,078,913,121	271,183,780	1,134,644,846	521,772,729
975	Medford, OR	1,118	17,472	4,048,707,940	84,006,979	898,377,479	125,923,925	520,717,996	153,177,645	714,564,597	291,957,285
976	Klamath Falls, OR	473	6,121	924,669,360	21,296,493	181,764,960	31,120,904	135,571,563	33,358,322	185,875,203	61,015,062
977	Bend, OR	543	10,997	2,987,334,858	90,783,190	644,421,164	130,779,851	492,689,396	142,097,741	411,457,730	333,451,779
978	Pendleton, OR	849	17,514	1,568,056,060	42,479,292	354,290,127	90,811,778	295,101,537	54,122,708	146,287,430	103,696,965
979	Boise, ID	415	8,718	384,543,020	15,467,529	67,145,356	19,058,138	71,863,574	8,048,627	53,684,636	28,419,104
980	Seattle, WA	40,401	71,718	17,738,932,449	920,521,769	3,664,231,493	789,185,720	2,453,612,282	1,127,024,920	2,308,467,275	973,344,640
981	Seattle, WA	64,087	58,926	13,568,179,789	715,033,357	2,879,079,260	591,342,527	1,869,885,233	863,998,396	1,783,428,636	736,588,768
982	Everett, WA	11,564	53,257	11,753,064,732	432,216,392	2,223,578,050	493,470,980	1,736,319,593	551,586,475	1,541,902,143	947,174,731
983	Tacoma, WA	14,904	28,575	8,166,604,787	244,252,821	1,966,896,851	348,592,987	1,176,261,596	407,139,705	1,179,416,547	748,290,515
984	Tacoma, WA	45,265	33,552	5,135,111,259	171,673,923	1,357,211,123	164,472,394	683,667,443	269,901,864	756,581,887	412,321,456
985	Olympia, WA	6,911	22,326	5,359,316,897	143,321,952	1,082,277,624	239,952,230	907,730,876	247,737,123	813,260,726	456,289,496
986	Portland, OR	8,213	29,634	5,594,584,216	140,988,325	1,236,277,284	290,463,575	998,236,672	187,420,356	799,831,757	460,416,595
988	Wenatchee, WA	1,253	43,481	2,427,527,439	65,303,153	510,430,927	128,341,622	490,423,418	93,411,618	157,068,588	254,201,443
989	Yakima, WA	2,543	89,605	3,064,421,813	100,683,223	595,090,584	124,304,191	550,001,548	97,991,835	470,320,391	263,957,382
990	Spokane, WA	1,189	3,281	1,506,946,442	62,066,628	374,901,863	48,039,782	222,705,432	78,376,349	216,468,727	113,650,415
991	Spokane, WA	785	2,958	1,045,119,320	13,812,205	258,986,921	53,913,273	218,857,992	48,322,643	68,863,553	58,449,326
992	Spokane, WA	5,900	11,176	4,880,224,833	204,452,274	1,209,518,833	148,749,486	702,670,025	247,581,927	733,721,565	373,602,620
993	Pasco, WA	4,050	76,078	3,766,187,376	94,261,158	660,553,367	174,263,378	560,892,784	169,744,324	671,338,771	281,277,992
994	Lewiston, ID	54	434	234,030,974	712,171	51,028,746	17,711,801	49,926,790	9,484,788	18,605,455	29,351,649
995	Anchorage, AK	16,398	18,119	5,120,471,579	258,532,366	986,946,050	188,587,408	746,005,308	188,479,467	927,862,696	308,846,923
996	Anchorage, AK	1,328	4,863	1,836,011,892	45,020,725	303,904,299	60,270,752	447,213,048	60,403,409	91,085,235	171,459,701
997	Fairbanks, AK	5,613	4,655	1,631,491,937	34,542,811	237,286,481	56,272,552	256,526,946	45,072,558	245,794,336	94,605,093
998	Juneau, AK	299	1,633	795,600,716	26,786,431	107,791,208	28,286,097	149,212,899	20,555,590	78,886,799	45,726,119
999	Ketchikan, AK	97	477	326,535,126	16,113,283	45,660,548	10,860,935	81,236,209	8,617,017	19,448,189	30,598,401
TOTAL		36,299,387	41,143,351	3,816,891,207,628	158,322,316,730	895,766,727,035	172,091,537,339	551,369,021,155	186,169,818,001	503,718,109,119	230,034,909,638

Notes: Data is provided for residential areas only.
All figures are estimates. Because of rounding, the totals may not represent the sum of each individual item.
000 and 001 are not valid postal ZIPs. They represent collections of remainder areas throughout the country and are included for complete geographical coverage.

U.S. Air and Highway Mileage Chart — a triangular distance matrix. The top figure in each cell is highway mileage and the bottom figure is air mileage. Cities are listed along the left (top to bottom) and along the bottom (left to right). The leftmost data column gives mileage to ALBUQUERQUE, NM.

City (row)	to ALBUQUERQUE, NM
WASHINGTON, DC	1844
TORONTO, ON	1787
SEATTLE, WA	1468
SAN FRANCISCO, CA	1109
SAN DIEGO, CA	811
SAN ANTONIO, TX	730
SALT LAKE CITY, UT	608
ST. LOUIS, MO	1041
PORTLAND, OR	1372
PITTSBURGH, PA	1629
PHOENIX, AZ	456
PHILADELPHIA, PA	1933
OKLAHOMA CITY, OK	542
NEW YORK, NY	1999
NEW ORLEANS, LA	1147
NASHVILLE, TN	1257
MONTREAL, PQ	2121
MINNEAPOLIS, MN	1233
MILWAUKEE, WI	1375
MIAMI, FL	1970
MEMPHIS, TN	1030
LOS ANGELES, CA	811
LAS VEGAS, NV	586
KANSAS CITY, MO	777
JACKSONVILLE, FL	1641
INDIANAPOLIS, IN	1270
HOUSTON, TX	841
DETROIT, MI	1550
DENVER, CO	430
DALLAS, TX	642
COLUMBUS, OH	1456
CLEVELAND, OH	1583
CINCINNATI, OH	1378
CHICAGO, IL	1301
BUFFALO, NY	1770
BOSTON, MA	2197
BIRMINGHAM, AL	1260
BALTIMORE, MD	1890
ATLANTA, GA	1400

Bottom axis cities (left to right): ALBUQUERQUE, NM · ATLANTA, GA · BALTIMORE, MD · BIRMINGHAM, AL · BOSTON, MA · BUFFALO, NY · CHICAGO, IL · CINCINNATI, OH · CLEVELAND, OH · COLUMBUS, OH · DALLAS, TX · DENVER, CO · DETROIT, MI · HOUSTON, TX · INDIANAPOLIS, IN · JACKSONVILLE, FL · KANSAS CITY, MO · LAS VEGAS, NV · LOS ANGELES, CA · MEMPHIS, TN · MIAMI, FL · MILWAUKEE, WI · MINNEAPOLIS, MN · MONTREAL, PQ · NASHVILLE, TN · NEW ORLEANS, LA · NEW YORK, NY · OKLAHOMA CITY, OK · PHILADELPHIA, PA · PHOENIX, AZ · PITTSBURGH, PA · PORTLAND, OR · ST. LOUIS, MO · SALT LAKE CITY, UT · SAN ANTONIO, TX · SAN DIEGO, CA · SAN FRANCISCO, CA · SEATTLE, WA · TORONTO, ON · WASHINGTON, DC